HISTORY BOOK

Zhan Toshchenko

Translated by prof. Romanovskiy N.V.
and Southwell (Romanovskiy) I.N.

Saint-Petersburg   ALETHEIA   2010

UDK 316
BBK 60.5
T77

Toshchenko Zh.

T77   Paradox Man in Contemporary Russia / Zh. Toshchenko. —
St. Petersburg: Aletheia, 2010. — 428 p.

ISBN 978-5-91419-412-0

The purpose of this manuscript is to raise an unusual social problem —
paradoxes of social consciousness and behavior. It is a result of a longer work
dealing with paradoxes of consciousness and behavior as they have been
massively displayed in USSR/Russia transition. Paradoxes always exist in
the life of humankind. For the first time attention to them had been paid in the
Ancient Greece, than in the Middle Ages and New History. Hence paradoxes
of social consciousness are inherent not only to previous stages of historical
development — science and social practice have been facing them in modern
time. Paradoxes tend to increase and to affect most spheres of social life.

Sociological approach to paradoxes permits to reveal their manifestations
in real life, in process of realizing these or other kinds of activity, for paradoxicality is inherent not only to process of cognition, but also to reality itself.
But especially evident, sharp and outspoken this paradoxicality becomes for
societies with an unstable development, those in a state of instability, amorphy,
uncertainty with regard to vector of historical process. In these conditions
paradoxes of consciousness and behavior become massive, universal, give
rise to freakish combinations of good and evil, honor and intent, fidelity and
treachery, reckless innovation and obstinate traditionalism.

For the researchers of social and political life, social consciousness and
behavior, for the students and for all people, studying contemporary Russia

UDK 316
BBK 60.5

ISBN 978-5-91419-412-0

Introduction

I would like to start our analysis of paradox with a quote from a prominent French mathematician, physicist, philosopher and writer B. Pascal (1623–1662): «What sort of a chimera is this man? What an innovation, what a monster, what chaos, what a tangled knot of contradictions, what a wonder is he? The judge of all things, a feeble-minded worm, bearer of truth, cesspool of unreliability and mistakes; glory and scum of the Universe... Discover, oh proud one, what a paradox you are to yourself! Resign, powerless mind, keep quiet, you stupid nature; realize that a human is endlessly superior to a human!»

This evocative statement of the great thinker reflects yet another attempt to cognize the essence of man, his contradictory nature, as well as his place and role in resolution of burning social issues. The New Age brought about a principally new style of thinking, where not just God, not just State or Society, they all became an object of careful scientific examination. The best minds of all mankind have turned to the individual as a measure of all phenomena, and all things.

The very first steps towards the cognition of the essence of human nature have already uncovered previously unknown difficulties and anomalies: the rift between man and himself, as well as social institutions, in whose activities he is involved, with social organizations, within the frames of which he operates, with official groups, which he belongs to, i.e., with the whole micro, mezzo and macro-world. This discord can be characterized by a variety of indicators from quite logical contradictions in cognition and development, to extreme forms of contradiction that find expression in the paradoxical.

A role of an individual, a person, cannot be reduced only to the subjective factor, as commonly done by postmodernists when revealing his essence, his nature and peculiarities. This phenomenon is endlessly extensive and expansive, it is very versatile in its manifestations, thus necessitating considering not only subjective, but also objective aspects of social life.

Among new challenges that modern scientific thought is facing, a phenomenon of paradoxes of consciousness (particularly characteristic of currently functioning pubic life) is of special interest for philosophical comprehension and sociological interpretation. In this context following questions arise: 1) What are the paradoxes of consciousness? 2) What is their relation to «contradictions», «metamorphoses» and «manipulation»? 3) Do they constitute a new class of problems or are they a special form of expression of social consciousness? 4) What are the specific manifestations of paradoxes?

5) How and by what means is it possible to explain the reasons for such a broad and massive emergence and presence of paradoxes? 6) What are they indicative of, and are there any possible ways of solving them?

Many thinkers have written about paradoxes as a phenomenon of social consciousness and behavior. A special chapter of this book covers this topic. Our task is to reflect the position of the author, to demonstrate how sociological trail led us to understanding of this phenomenon. As a matter of fact, during implementation of an academic project: «Social consciousness as an object of sociological research» (1985–1992), under the guidance of present author, while studying conditions, trends and problems of economic, political and moral consciousness, existence of such situations, along with other findings, where consciousness and behavior were clearly and distinctly defined as paradoxical have been recorded.

Analyzing this material and other empirical data at my disposal, the author discovered a specific class of contradictions, already existing or emerging in social consciousness. Analysis of contradictions revealed during the course of our studies, has shown that we encountered a special group that might be classified as paradoxes, since they reflected a specific situation in public consciousness under dramatically changing circumstances.

The very first attempts to purposefully analyze this phenomenon have shown, that paradoxicality is not a reflection of some random or rarely emerging combination of barely explainable situations, but a sufficiently stable tendency of occurrence and existence of a special type of contradictions, volume and weight of which were on the increase in the course of incessant changes in already existing economic and political relations, of breaking down the old ways and lifestyles, of destabilizing previous stereotypes and national mentality, as the case in recent Russia was.

Such material has been accumulating, which gradually led to the need of evaluating and formulating author's own opinion on this phenomenon. The first more or less systemic analysis of the given phenomenon was done by the author in his article «O paradoksakh obshchestvennogo soznania (About the paradoxes of social consciousness)» (Journal «Sotsiologhicheskie Issledovaniya — Sociological Studies», 1995, No. 11). Later, these ideas were developed primarily applicable to different spheres of public life — economic, political, and in connection with analysis of national and historical consciousness issues, as well as their interrelation with such phenomena as frustration, stereotypes, mythological consciousness, centaur-problem etc.

Starting this monographic account of the given materials accumulated in the course of recent Russian turmoil, the author set several objectives.

First, to investigate the theoretical and methodological bases of paradoxicality in social consciousness and behavior of the people. For this purpose it was required to describe the sociological vision of social consciousness, which has its differences from philosophical and psychological knowledge.

Second, an attempt to build a historical retrospection is realized in the monograph in order to trace the genesis of these ideas, emergence of knowledge about this phenomenon and its enrichment in the course of constant renewal of human ideas about the world and its current state of being.

Third, while analyzing paradoxicality of individual's consciousness and behavior a necessity arose to correlate it with such phenomena of social practice and social knowledge as mythological consciousness, the centaur-problem, stereotype, frustration etc., in order to more precisely present their qualitative (possibly quantitative) characteristics, their essence, their nature and peculiarities in comparison with other manifestations of public consciousness, including the process of its manipulation.

Fourth, paradox of consciousness and behavior is not manifested generally, but in connection with a specific public practice. Therefore, the book deals with specific forms of paradoxes that manifest themselves in mainstream human activities — economic, political, spiritual, and in such particularly significant forms as historical and national consciousness displayed in Russia in its recent history.

And at last, the final part contains analyses of both special cases of paradoxicality and situational forms of paradoxes, thus making it possible to enrich our understanding of social, group and individual consciousness, people's activities in various spheres of public life. A special feature of this part is a journalistic interpretation of theoretical material, which had received its approbation through articles in Russian nation-wide periodicals — newspapers and magazines in 1990's.

The author expresses his gratitude to the academy members of the Russian academy of sciences A.A.Gusseynow, V.A.Lektorsky, L.N.Mitrokhin, G.V.Osipov, V.S.Stepin, to correspondent-members of the Russian Academy of Sciences Ju.V.Arutyunyan, A.V.Dmitriev, M.N.Rutkevitch, B.G.Yudin, to professor N.V. Romanovsky, to candidates of philosophical sciences V.V. Platkovsky and M.B. Sapunov, who had taken part in reviewing and editing of several sections and chapters of this monograph.

The author's thanks also go to doctor of philosophy A.E. Krukhmalev, candidate of sociological sciences L.A. Orlova, to Yu.Z. Toshchenko, who actively participated in preparation of this work.

Part I. Theoretical and methodological bases for studying paradoxes

Chapter 1. Social consciousness: sociological vision

> Revolution is not made on barricades —
> it occurs in the minds and souls of the
> people.
>
> *T. Carlyle* (1795–1881),
> English historian and philosopher

Logic of historical development demonstrates that social consciousness is acquiring an increasingly more significant role in addressing social problems, that the scale of its influence is impacting the processes underway in the world in general, as well as every society or state, in economic, social, political and other organizations, as well as vital activities of all social groups, strata and communities. This process corresponds with the general tendency of the increasing role of subjective factor (subjectivity); relevance and impact of such characteristics of social consciousness as dignity, self-assertion, self-esteem, which serve to elevate the individual under the conditions of incessant attempts to enslave his mind and intellect whether with political, economic or technical innovations, all of which by themselves cannot (and should not) be the self-sufficing factors.

Modern scientific research has assessed the importance and identified the role not only of such components of social consciousness as knowledge, interests and needs, but also value orientations, attitudes and — especially — the phenomenon of understanding. *In studies of social consciousness a new methodological approach is gradually taking hold. In essence — for all its apparent obviousness — it amounts to the following: people don't live for the sake of theories or concepts, nor for the sake of state doctrines or programs of political parties — they primarily pursue their own goals that fancifully commix a variety of orientations, values, attitudes,* and, it happens in such a way that individual and group interests and needs take priority. People judge their own position not based on the loudly prophesied promises and declarations, but the real situation, which they face in their daily lives.

Whatever might be currently said about various trends and changes in social consciousness, a high rating and self-rating of the «I» factor is an undeniable consideration, with all the resulting consequences, which ultimately lead to the necessity to take into account every person's self-realization of their own value and self-worth. Finally, it should be taken into account that significant changes do take place in consciousness and behavior of people with regard to structure of the incentives to live and act: external stimuli weaken, but internal ones, on the contrary, keep growing, attesting to increasing role of the subjective factor, as well as spiritual origin in the development and functioning of the modern world. Thus, once again it is worth emphasizing that consciousness develops autonomously, independently and not always in accordance with socio-economic trends. There is no automatic correlation between consciousness and being. And this relative autonomy of social consciousness, its growing importance as an independent social force requires special analysis.

1.1. *From the history of philosophical and sociological thought*

Social consciousness has long been studied basically within the framework of philosophical thought. Later on, ideas took shape, which became a focal point for psychology, exploring phenomenon of individual consciousness, or that of small groups, as well as psychology of crowds, extreme situations, disasters, and psychology of interaction with the second «nature» — machinery, technology, and information. In spite of the fact that sociological vision of social consciousness began to take shape on the verge of the 19th and 20th centuries, gradually accumulating fragmented information, it has so far been unable to develop a complete, widely accepted concept.

With regard to philosophical thought, it treats consciousness as a specific human form of ideal reflection and spiritual exploration of reality. It emerges, functions and develops as a component of practical activities of a social person. It is included in these activities and represents a point of interaction between an object (a subject) and a person, which is clearly manifested in social practice. Active consciousness is reflected in selectivity, in consistency of its goal, in specific characteristics of this consciousness as a process (acts of consciousness, their content, cognitive tools, purpose etc.). Activity of highly organized nervous system — of the brain — is a precondition for emergence and development of human consciousness. It should be especially emphasized that cognition, mastering the subject, revealing the essence of being — is the meaning of consciousness. Furthermore, consciousness includes not only reflection of the objective world, but also awareness of an individual of his own mental activities (self-consciousness). Man makes consciousness itself the subject of consciousness and assessment, comprehends its forms, as well as his own self as its carrier. At the same time, consciousness can be reduced neither to intellection, nor to acts of self-awareness, for it covers both abstracting activity of thinking and productive imagination. In addition, consciousness includes intuition, human emotions, will, conscience, etc. All this suggests that consciousness is the totality, the focus of mental functions of a human being. Along with consciousness, the subconscious and unconscious processes are singled out in human psyche. Consciousness is also closely connected to language. It materializes through it. Materializing through language, products of consciousness can be passed down to succeeding generations. Language is only one of the forms of materialization (communication) of the consciousness. In addition, it is embodied both in objects of labor as well as works of art, etc. And finally, consciousness also includes values of a person, his orientations, characteristics of his state of well-being and mood (*Obschestvennoe soznanie i ego formy.* 1986; *Vvedenie v filosofiyu.* 1979; *Novaya filosofskaya...* 2001).

Exploring consciousness in all its diversity, philosophical thought has also carefully and thoroughly analyzed the phenomenon of the subjects of this consciousness, which led to the conclusion that it can also be considered (assessed) in social aspect: as public, as group (class) and as individual (personal) one. All these types of consciousness have both general and specific characteristics. Undoubtedly these findings have greatly enriched scientific knowledge of social consciousness (Alexeev. 1984; Arefyeva. 1988; Barulin. 1994; Demichev. 1970; Ilyenkov. 1984; Kelle, Koval'zon. 1973; Lektorskiy. 1988; Oyzerman. 1999; Spirkin. 1972; Stepin. 1992; Frolov. 1989; Tchinakova. 1985; Shevchenko. 1984; etc).

Thus, individual consciousness characterizes the consciousness of a specific person, belonging to a particular community, class, a certain social group, and commonality. Social being is reflected and realized through a prism of personal identity of a particular person. Individual consciousness is a single system of knowledge of a person, which makes up the core, a way of comprehending reality and experiences, of conscious existence and shaping individual's attitudes toward various aspects of objective world, as well as other people and their relations. On this basis, subjective experience of an individual is being formed as a kind of generalized reflection of external world, through knowledge and relations, as well as potential ability to regulate activities, behavior and socialization. Specific content of individual consciousness existing in the form of beliefs, opinions, concepts, empirical knowledge of a person, is conditioned by the influence and interaction between general and specific factors of spiritual, social and material life of that individual. Every historical period in societal development, with its specific economic structure and political system determines the existence of corresponding types of individual consciousness (*Entsiklopeditsheskiy sotsiologhicheskiy slovar'.* 1995).

It should be emphasized that in its essence, individual consciousness is a combination of socio-typical and individualized consciousness. Correlation between these two sides reflects its place and role in the life of society. But it is incapable of achieving complete comprehension of complexity of social being. The next phase of achieving this purpose is group consciousness, which represents a set of ideas, opinions, feelings, moods, and expression inherent to a particular social community. This is one of the levels of social consciousness, wherefrom an individual «scoops» meaningful ideas, opinions and notions, and correlates them with personal interests and values.

Phenomenon of group consciousness had been studied in late 19th century by French sociologist E. Durkheim (1858–1917), who had identified its integrative role and its distinctions from individual consciousness. «Group thinks, feels and acts in an absolutely different way, than any of its individual members, if they were separated. If, therefore, we were to start out based on these latter, they would not understand anything of what is happening in the «group»» (Durkheim E. Russ. Ed. 1995).

Group consciousness varies from one group to another, acquiring its own specific characteristics (class, ethnic, professional, etc.). During the process of group self-organization, members of the group become aware of their own interests, their position in society and their relations with other groups. The main element of group identity is a sense of «we», as a perception of their group «sameness», as opposed to «them» — other social communities (Antipina G.S. 1995).

In this chain of reasoning public consciousness acts as a supreme form and covers all aspects of perception of social being, the totality of public problems (Spirkin. 1972; Mikhailov. 1990; *Obshchestvo i soznaniye.* 1980; Rubinstein. 1973; Toyber. 1999). At the same time social consciousness exists in individual and group dimensions; interaction between them is ambiguous and full of contradictions, since not all that passes through them is ultimately included in the public consciousness. The fact that the process of assimilation of the contents of social consciousness by an individual is determined by a number of objective and subjective reasons is very important for sociology. The objective causes are: the conditions of social and personal life, as well as spiritual atmosphere created in each particular society, which is expressed in prevailing morality, traditions, national customs and other manifestations of spirituality. Subjective determinants of a person's familiarization with the content of social consciousness are influenced by his socio-psychological characteristics, as well as such social characteristics as his worldview, convictions, needs, interests, etc.

In the 20th century attention of the scholars began to more and more be focused on the issues of social consciousness, which led to a number of important discoveries and findings. Gradually accumulated knowledge of nature, characteristics and specificity of social consciousness resulted in a number of important theoretical and methodological conclusions regarding the processes of its development and functioning.

First of all, the statements that alleged that «social being determines social consciousness» and «social consciousness lags behind social being» were questioned and critically analyzed. In fact, analysis of sociological data demonstrates that the above conclusions are not the absolute truth, but only one of possible aspects of the interaction between social consciousness and social being. It is true that social consciousness, in many vital situations, might lag behind social being, and sometimes requires a considerable amount of time to overcome (if at all possible) this lag. But the situation (for example, under the conditions of revolutionary, radical social changes), when ideas far surpass social being, influencing it and forcing it to change (perhaps partially) in accordance with the objective needs of society, is no less real and no less common.

This particular situation allows us to conclude that social consciousness (social ideas) might serve as the decisive force, which, under special circumstances, determines the course of history. In this regard it is worth recalling the well-known Marxist thesis, according to which consciousness reflects the material world, is its product and depends on the processes that take place in it. While accepting this fact, another Marxist idea is underrated: consciousness creates the world, and only in the course of practice does a person prove «the truth, i.e. reality and might, the this-sidedness of his thinking» (Marx K., Engels F. *Works.*Vol. 3).

Moreover, history is replete with examples where social consciousness is as important as social being, and both sides in equal measure define their interaction.

Finally, in the history of mankind, social consciousness often becomes a decisive force predetermining development of society. And there is not a grain of subjectivity, idealism, lack of understanding of scientific truth about the role of material relations and economic basis in this statement. Recognition of the primacy of existence does not exclude the possibility that under specific historic conditions, influence and impact of consciousness on social processes can and do assume paramount, critical importance.

Consequently, *social consciousness, while reflecting the diversity of connections and relations of the objective world, can be an active, neutral or passive social force.* During the period of revolutionary upheaval and drastic changes in social life it becomes more active, starts to influence the course of social development to a greater degree. The leading role of social consciousness increases during the periods of radical changes, since the processes taking place in objective reality are stronger than ever being reflected in ideas, theories and even in everyday consciousness. The key to effectiveness of social consciousness in that case is the degree of depth of cognition of the objective course of social development and its utilization in historical activity of classes, social groups and strata and their political and social associations. Mutual interaction and synergy of social being and social consciousness are the basis for transforming the latter into an objective material force.

Understanding, dissecting the mechanism of symbiotic relationship between material and ideal, between objective and subjective can, if not completely resolve, explain many problems of social development, provide science-based interpretation of their contradictory nature, complexities, and anomalies.

Analysis of the state and trends of development of social consciousness in recent Russia poses quite a reasonable question: could social consciousness have turned into a real physical force under the current conditions? The conclusion is unambiguous: it could have and has been transforming, but unfortunately, often with a «minus sign». The fact is, social consciousness, at various stages of existence of society, has not always embodied only advancement and progress. Its state of existence was not always reflected in scientifically grounded theories, concepts, opinions and ideas.

By formulating the question in this way, we necessitate not only the determination of the relationship between theoretical and everyday (ordinary) consciousness, but also of the role of the first (theoretical consciousness) in impacting destinies of social development. If ordinary consciousness emerges in the course of everyday life as a product of spontaneous reflection of external side of reality, theoretical consciousness represents the knowledge of substantive relations, reflecting underlying processes that require scientific comprehension and insight into the essence of things. Theoretical consciousness finds its embodiment in theories, concepts, and ideas that tend to come closer to a more adequate level of cognition and reflection of reality, opening up new layers of knowledge, new insight into previously unknown aspects of societal life.

Thus, analysis of the problems of social development has allowed modern philosophical thought to substantiate the conclusion that «the most important — indeed epochal, world-wide historical change associated with transition from traditional society to industrial society, is the emergence of a new value system... The values of technological culture set a fundamentally different vector for human activity. Transforming activities here are considered to be the main purpose of a human being. Active, activity-oriented ideal of man's interaction with nature extends to social relations, which are also starting to be regarded as special social objects that can be purposefully transformed by humans» (Stepin V.S. 2000).

However, scientific validity and vitality of the theories and concepts that were supposed to be actualized and realized did not always correlate with the needs of social development. Quite often these theories and concepts had only partially or incompletely reflected objective laws of social development, as well as the state and problems of functioning of real social consciousness. Moreover, they often distorted the true picture, since claiming the absoluteness of their own «truth» they would not allow other approaches and explanations of current social processes. This was a fertile ground for blossoming dogmatism, project mongering and blind imitation of outside experience, as well as just self-concocted gag. Sometimes they (theories, concepts) were not matched to objective reality, detached from real life, reflecting their own conjectures or phantom ideas, while their theoretical and methodological theses were in fact sterile, barren blooms. But if only their role had ended there! Alongside with other far-fetched ideas, the authors demanded their implementation and active role, disputed any findings that even partly questioned their dogmas. Carriers and developers of these ideas acted like oracles, militant preachers — everyone who expressed a differing point of view was subjected to ostracism, ridiculed, labeled with an «appropriate» tag, permanently forced to justify one's position. Only those points of view, espoused by the biased groups and associations of people that have monopolized influence in society and politics, was accepted and advocated.

Analysis of functioning of theoretical consciousness leads to the conclusion that, first, it cannot transform into a material force by itself; second, many theoretical perspectives that laid claim to this role were not implemented, since they were basically flawed, unscientific, dogmatic and far removed from reality; third, truly innovative ideas and views, spontaneously making headway, were often torpedoed, ignored, restricted if any attempts to put them into practice were made.

This situation has not changed during the emergence of the new Russia, when foundations of former political and economic system, as well as its ideological support were broken. All efforts and vain attempts of the «creators» of Russia's reorganization have resulted in immeasurable misery for the majority of population. These theories built on the basis of abstract theorizing, blind borrowing and copying, never tested under experimental conditions, have only confirmed the conclusion — that the ultimate criterion of viability of any concepts or programs are real life and practice, rather than speculative schemes, however attractive they might appear at first glance.

Therefore, it would be appropriate to briefly describe the status and trends of social consciousness at the present stage of functioning and development of modern Russia.

1.2. *Main features of modern social consciousness in Russia: experience of constructing*

Cardinal changes that took place in Russian society in 1990-2000, led to emergence and consolidation of new characteristics of the state of social consciousness dissimilar from prior stages of its development and functioning.

First of all, the process of *universalization* of social consciousness, which erases boundaries of national, national-ethnic character and professional perception, should be noted. When real thinking acquires certain features of global consciousness, this becomes (sort of) an ultimate form of its revolutionary and evolutionary transformation. Presently, the theory of globalization of social processes that also encompasses the sphere of social consciousness is very popular. The world, its economic, social and spiritual life are acquiring common features, possessing increasingly converging characteristics. It is worth mentioning, however, that a number of scholars are questioning the substantiality of such interpretation of ongoing global processes, describing them as a disguised form of Westernization or even Americanization (Pokrovskiy. 2000).

Simultaneously, a process of *diversification* of social consciousness is underway, with increased variability of value orientations and attitudes among certain social groups that substantially differ on fundamental issues, which govern individuals (people) in their decision-making pertaining to both the present and the future.

Furthermore, social consciousness began to reflect a process of comprehension and implementation of new economic, social and political realities. All of the new and emerging problems that were discussed in society contributed to the **expansion** of the scope of social consciousness, to its *deepening and increased activity*. The media, especially print, acting as a testing ground for expressing ideas, views and concerns of the public, has accelerated the formation of ideological pluralism. However, this pluralism turned out to be quite peculiar, since by the end of 1990's all media were divided among oligarchic groups, with their pluralism acquiring very specific orientation.

But real life in all its contradictory development, offers more and more food for thought, elaboration of various approaches to understanding of occurring changes. Even such an achievement of *perestroika* as *glasnost* (or openness), later legislated in the «Law on the Press» stipulating freedom of expression, has traveled a difficult and dangerous pass of evolution, resulting in a significant change in perception of the role, purpose and functions of the media. And along this road, social consciousness became a real participant in search for the truth in this difficult and complex reconstruction of democracy, human rights and freedoms, accompanied by incessant discussions of the ways of implementing market reforms and methods of their realization.

Under the conditions of transforming society, *dynamism,* yet another feature of real social consciousness became clearly evident. People's perceptions of political and economic structure of society kept changing constantly, and quite often dramatically. Rejecting the Soviet form of so-called mature socialism, social consciousness was inspired by ideals of society modeled after the ones implemented by industrialized countries. But reality quickly dampened these dreams. Fueled by failed hopes, one group's attention was concentrated on certain Eastern models of society, second — on searching for truly Russian, genuine willed roots and comprehension of Russia's historical experience of transformations, third — on controversial Eurasian concepts, fourth group's — on return to an updated Soviet model. And, there were freakish combinations of all of these models popping up, which once again signified vagueness, uncertainty and instability of social orientations and public mood.

The actual processes occurring in social consciousness reveal yet another one of its important features: it became *acute*, keenly interested in and responsive to occurring processes. Back under the conditions of perestroika a situation arose, when for the first time in many years, public interest in domestic problems far exceeded their interest in international affairs. People became much more interested in learning what was happening around them, interpreting events both statewide, or on the scale of a republic, city, district, village, or industrial organization.

People started responding faster and more pointedly to the issues that undermined their social status, their material and spiritual needs. That resulted in emergence of many grass-roots associations and political parties, leaving practically no free corner in public consciousness.

Such characteristic as *critical nature* (criticality) is also inherent in modern social consciousness. People do not want to put up with poverty, failures, corruption, theft and crime, existence of which many politicians keep trying to justify citing objective reasons. Assessment of economic and social life is highly critical. Under the conditions, when credibility of quasi-market forms of management, triumph of corruption schemes and methods of work, a number of unfavorable assessments of socio-economic situation, of its consequences for public and private life does not decrease, since processes and developments in the system of state governance and management, reflected in social consciousness, are evaluated very negatively, with a high degree of frustration with occurring changes.

Sharp decline in credibility of main political institutions of the country during the second half of 1990's was reflected in negative evaluation of the President, the State Duma and the Government, which by far exceeded the percentage of positive ratings. The leaders have not been forgiven for a single miscalculation — slump in production, impoverishment of general population, crime or ethnic conflicts.

However, such a feature of social consciousness as an acquired quality of *realistic thinking*, possessing to a great extent *the foresight and maturity* has to be noted.

There is an assertion in politics that states: «People cannot be deceived. When it happens, it's not for long». Empty promises of the early 1990's were initially met with approval and enthusiasm (majority of population recognized that they «could not live like that any longer»). But people quickly realized their perversion and disastrous consequences, leading to political deaths of many «architects» of *perestroika* and «creators» of these reforms.

Finally, we need to point out characteristics, which cannot be ignored when assessing the state and trends of social consciousness: *growth of individualism, increase of the impact of chauvinism and nationalism and decrease in the influence of humanism and tolerance.*

* * *

Regarding sociological knowledge of the essence, contents, structure and functions of social consciousness, its evolution and enrichment developed in several directions.

One of them is *the study of social consciousness through cognition of activities,* which in turn has enabled us to formulate and ascertain a qualitative determination of such forms of social consciousness as political, moral, legal, aesthetic, etc. (Leontyev. 1975; *Obshchestvennoe soznanie i ego vidy.* 1983).

This key to analysis of social consciousness — *through activity* — marked a new approach, which expanded and enriched our understanding of social consciousness, gradually laying a foundation for its sociological comprehension. The need for a new, deeper interpretation was also dictated by the fact that philosophical approach to social consciousness as theoretical and everyday consciousness «does not work» in sociological research, since those phenomena of consciousness, which had been analyzed and indeed existed, represent various combinations of both science and daily life that are difficult (and in most cases impossible) to separate from each other. However, they can be understood and interpreted only from the viewpoint of inseverable connection between these components. In other words, in real life (as opposed to the theory of knowledge) *we deal with the real (really functioning, practical) consciousness,* where, in various proportions and combinations, both scientific views and ordinary ideas, mythologized opinions and errors, politicized attitudes and primitive orientations are intertwined in most creative ways. They are significantly varied among different social groups and strata. One can only assume that in the process of social development ordinary (routine, everyday) will more and more be replaced by scientific, theoretical knowledge, but a complete replacement of the ordinary will never happen.

Significant results in the study of real-consciousness, which have greatly enriched our understanding of social consciousness, were achieved researching *public opinion* as a special, specific form of its manifestation. This was a very important step toward sociological comprehension of social reality, its classes, social groups and individuals. Research of phenomenon of public opinion has revealed peoples' assessment, their attitude toward urgent, burning, vital economic, social and political problems; helped understand their motives, interests and needs (Uledov. 1964; Grushin. 1967; Andriushchenko. 1988; Gorshkov. 1988; Korobeynikov. 1989; etc).

But public opinion studies mainly concentrate on people's reactions to the current, burning issues. They identify people's attitudes and their evaluations, which often have a short-term, quickly passing nature. And it is not so much the process of public opinion research itself that is dangerous, as the overestimation of its importance. «... It is almost monstrous, — wrote the famous Russian philosopher N.A. Berdyaev (1874–1948) in «Fenomen Neravenstva (The Phenomenon of Inequality)», — how people could reach such a state of consciousness where the source, the criterion of the true (trueness) and the truth was based on the opinion and will of the majority (Berdyaev. 1990). Therefore, informational value of public opinion has its limitations, and by no means can substitute the research of phenomenon of social consciousness in general.

The next significant step towards a more in-depth perception of social consciousness was the introduction of the concept of *«mass consciousness»* into scientific practice, sociology. This term appeared in Soviet literature in 1960–1970 (Grushin. 1987. Diligenskiy. 1969; Uledov. 1968; Levada. 2006).

Thus, Russian sociologist, B.A. Grushin (1930–2005) employed concepts of «mass individuals», « masses of individuals», «and mass communities». But the use of these concepts not only expanded our ideas about social consciousness, which for 1970's was a serious scientific and ideological achievement, but it also had both serious scientific and ideological drawbacks. Despite relevance of the research of mass consciousness, its profound differentiation, an open question still remained: how should we classify non-mass consciousness, reflecting positions of separate, special and specific groups and sectors, of individuals? Vulnerability of the phenomenon of mass consciousness is mainly due to the fact that new developments in the behavior of certain social groups, which do not practice and do not adhere to the positions of the majority, remain beyond its grasp, unexplored, and often unnoticed. These social groups do not profess and do not follow positions of the majority, but their consciousness senses and/or anticipates future changes, only barely emerging in society; changes that might become crucial and even decisive for future development. For example, consciousness of an innovative artist, writer or composer never fits the concept of «mass consciousness», although, according to a number of daily indicators, it differs only slightly from vital attitudes of the majority of people. Collective consciousness does not coincide with the views, opinions of those groups of people that due to historical and ethnic reasons have not come into full contact with world civilization and remain true to their own, quite often — insular way of life.

Exaggerating the role of mass consciousness in recent past has also served as a basis for ignoring and even prosecution of those, who did not fit into its framework, «stood out» from the usual, sanctioned, officially approved norms. It is exactly for this reason that this contradiction was easily «resolved» — it was thought that all those who did not share the positions of mass consciousness (the majority), professed controversial, and, most often, say, erroneous ideas.

Life persistently amended the perception of mass consciousness that the majority («mass consciousness») was always right. We are already well aware of the sad fact of ignoring (including in political life) the consciousness of the «generation of the Sixties» and, later, dissidents, which did not really reflect the views of the masses, but was capable — albeit in a very specific form — to anticipate and prejudge processes and changes in social life. Is the life of academician and Soviet dissident A.D. Sakharov (1921–1989), whose civic positions for a long time were not shared by the officials and misunderstood by the mass consciousness, not a testament to that fact?

Studies conducted in 1980–1990 made a significant contribution to sociological interpretation of public consciousness. This research of political, economic, moral, ecological and other forms of consciousness examined: the state of each form of social consciousness, its differences from the other forms of consciousness according to a variety of indicators; information regarding the knowledge, assessment of attitude toward specific processes in their particular sphere of activity; possible ways and methods of utilizing obtained information in the practice of governance and management (Boykov, Ivanov, Toshchenko. 1990; *Gorizonty ekologicheskogo znania.* 1986; Ryvkina. 1994; Sokolov. 1986; Semashko. 2006; Sysoeva. 1989; Kharchenko. 1999).

During the same years, domestic sociology began to investigate such components of social consciousness as values, attitudes, needs and interests allowing to glance at the functioning mind in all its complexity, inconsistency, without excluding the information about «zigzags» of consciousness not only of separate social communities, but individuals as well (Anisimov. 1988; Babosov. 1983; *Dinamika zennostey naseleniya reformiruemoy Rossii.* 1996; Zdravomyslov. 1986; etc).

This research helped identify a specific phenomenon — *«social mood»*, which proved to be a rather steady characteristic, dominant of the public consciousness. It embodied a sensation of life and wellbeing, reflected level, duration and degree of emotional and rational perception of reality by individuals and social groups (Toshchenko, Kharchenko. 1998; Ol'shanskiy. 1995).

All of this research led to the discovery of the fact that sociological interpretation of social consciousness utilizes several variants of its examination. The basis for all of them is recognition of the fact that it *(social consciousness) represents a real, almost functioning consciousness, which in various most bizarre combinations organically combines interwoven theoretical (scientific) and ordinary (everyday) consciousness.* Variants of this combination are rather diverse. Sociologists, in most cases try to identify a level and a degree of presence of one or the other, as well as their possible interconnection in the practical, objectively functioning consciousness.

In other words, we are not dealing with social consciousness in general, impersonal and amorphous, with no beginning or end, not just some logical constructs, but with real functioning social consciousness, which should be approached from very specific theoretical and methodological positions.

1.3. Real consciousness as a subject of sociological research

An individual develops as an ancestral, social being primarily with the help of consciousness and its realization in all the spheres of his social life and types of activities. It was noted by A.A. Bogdanov (1873–1928), Russian revolutionary and scholar. When revealing the essence of teachings of K. Marx (1818–1883) on the subject of nature and society, he wrote that in their struggle for existence, people can not unite «in any another way, except by means of consciousness» (Bogdanov. 1906).

The content of real consciousness represents, on the one hand, synthesis of theoretical and everyday consciousness, on the other – a combination of rational and emotional, interweaving of philosophical elements, of established traditional ties and customs. And if emotional component of real consciousness is based more on immediate impression, on momentary influence, its rational component might also integrate past experience and lessons not only of the personal, but also group and collective life, capturing the social vibe of many ongoing events. And this is exactly what connects separate elements of practical perception of reality with scientific, theoretical consciousness. Prevalence of spontaneous and emotional in real consciousness and behavior in no way diminishes the importance of the rational, or the possibility that it will ultimately determine the directionality and maturity of public consciousness and social activity.

Real consciousness is characteristic of not only an individual, a group or community. It is *a product of collective creativity* that is characteristic of the whole society, as well as social groups, strata and communities. Emerging as a reaction to direct perception of reality, as a representation of prevailing conditions of existence, real consciousness gains an independent role, reflected in public opinion and people's mindset.

Real consciousness includes common sense, which does not reject a possibility of deep understanding of essential underlying processes – it even presumes its constant enrichment and use in human practice. Real consciousness is not a result of some specialized activities (unlike its concrete forms – political, aesthetic, moral, etc.) and is reproduced in all kinds of human activities. Since every activity includes principal, intrinsic elements of social functioning, we can say that consciousness generated by this activity is capable of securing the general line of development. The fact that this consciousness deals with «primary cogitative forms» in no way means that the scope of real, practical consciousness is limited only to «minor» existential issues. It is this very contradiction, a reflection of the obviousness of surrounding reality and a possibility of deep, rather than superficial perception of that reality that characterizes the actual state of real consciousness and corresponding behavior of the people.

The products of consciousness and the results of human activities, «including their errors, have an opposite effect on all social development, even on economic» (K. Marx). Although real consciousness is formed under the influence of direct experience, in its social incarnation it forms a peculiar phenomenon, created by a class, a nation, social group or a social stratum, and ultimately every single individual. Real consciousness is not a collection or mechanical compilation of ideas and opinions — it forms a new specific entity, which tends to objectively reflect both its own actual state, as well as the depth of perception of social existence.

Real consciousness, growing out of direct practical activities *is not separated from social existence.* Moreover, it reflects (and we think, justifiably so), not only random, spontaneous connections and relations, but also some stable patterns and trends of societal developments (albeit in an imperfect form) as well. «Consciousness emerges as a reflected and meaningful existence, replication of a certain way of life of individual and society» (A.G. Spirkin, Russian philosopher — 1918–2002). Consciousness cannot be explained without taking into consideration the real context of human life, as part of a specific structure of socio-economic, political and socio-cultural relations. In this case we are referring to the real, existing people as bearers of social and individual consciousness, the synthesis of both. Real consciousness is sometimes characterized as practical, i.e. the one which reflects the knowledge of communal activities, individuals own activities and social status.

Real consciousness reflects social contradictions, a wide range of everyday illusions, often very close in nature to ordinary consciousness. «...Taken... as a collection of everyday experiences, that is, all the sorrows and joys, hopes and disappointments that make up daily life, this ordinary consciousness appears to be continuous anxiety, compared to which the scientific and philosophical consciousness seems something like ataraxia of the Hellenistic period thinkers» (Oyzerman. 1967).

In examining the actual functioning of social consciousness it is necessary to pay attention to the possibility of a very high degree of its operationalization, although we still come across the assertion that studying public, group and individual consciousness is the prerogative of philosophy, psychology and natural sciences only. Despite the apparent difficulty (where to start?), methodology of its study is tested in sociology. Social consciousness consists of such components as knowledge, attitude (evaluation) (when a sociologist finds out what people do know, how well they are informed; how «scientific» their understanding of various processes and phenomena really is); value orientations (aspirations, desires are considered as an important condition for the existence and regulation of behavior); motives (realization, implementation of the needs and interests that people's efforts are directed at); guidelines, i.e. value attitudes to a social object, as represented by their psychological preparedness for positive or negative reaction to it. Interests and needs as steps in transformation of social, public consciousness into real social behavior are often analyzed as well.

Phenomenon of social attitudes deserves special attention. According to the results of sociological studies, this phenomenon is a dominant, relatively stable characteristic of social consciousness, with potentially extremely volatile indicators of popular attitudes toward specific economic and social realities. Social mood is an «urgent», actualized real consciousness, which governs person's life during a particular period of time. It is also a background that «colors» life, demonstrates, with a high degree of probability, the likelihood and orientation of peoples behavior and helps predict the possibility of strengthening positive and mitigating negative aspects of social consciousness. Social mood, simultaneously, is also a probabilistic form of expression of consciousness in the process of its transformation into a social force (Toshchenko. 1998; Levada. 1998).

Analysis of practice of sociological studies in 1980–2000 demonstrates that information regarding the status and trends of the changes in social consciousness, in most cases was extracted within the framework of studying specific social groups, sectors, organizations and institutions. A pattern of economic and political orientations and preferences of various groups of population was ascertained on that basis. Other groups, other layers and communities were often left out of the picture. Therefore, drawing generalized reliable conclusions based on the studies of local communities was difficult, and in most cases impossible. These findings and data were usually of limited value and, as a rule, could be applied just to the object of research, nothing else. Attempts to apply these conclusions to the whole society were vulnerable on most counts.

Limited character of research of local communities and social associations was demonstrated by nation-wide (all-Union) studies of social consciousness, including public opinion. These studies revealed sufficiently significant distinctions between the parameters of separate groups and society as a whole. Sociological findings regarding the population of the entire country, in many ways did not coincide with similar indicators where single social groups were the subjects of this research. Moreover, it was the research, studying social consciousness as a whole that revealed its latent characteristics that were more relevant than those measured in the course of studying specific social groups. No less frequent were the situations, when indicators of various changes in public consciousness within a single social community were assessed as minor or insignificant, but compared to the similar parameters in other social groups and communities they acquired serious, sometimes opposite significance.

At the same time it is clear that study of social reality cannot be confined to the analysis of the state of social consciousness. Its components (knowledge, ideas, motivations, values, attitudes) become a real force only when they are embodied in activities and actions of the people. It is no secret that public intentions, desires, orientations for various reasons are not always realized in acts, actions or real deeds. Understanding of what prevents their implementation is one of most important tasks of any sociological research.

Therefore, it is important for sociology to cognize the process of «transformation of public consciousness into a social force» (K. Marx). The process of implementation of the predictive function of sociology, living consciousness and behavior are very rich (in their content) specific states of existence of public life, which intertwine both science-based knowledge, judgments and inferences, as well as spontaneous, dictated by practical experience, direct perception of reality and corresponding action. In other words, living, practical consciousness and behavior — is an objectively functioning social life in the whole complex interplay of both natural connections and relations, as well as random, isolated ideas, and sometimes, views opposing social progress. This particular approach to real consciousness and behavior — as living social phenomenon, full of contradictions and drama, functioning at the empirical level, under the conditions of direct practical experience, capable of anticipating (or including) some elements of theoretical consciousness, helps explain many processes in sociological language; identify commonalities, inherent not only in all spheres of social life, but also under the conditions of various social and economic systems.

Notions of social consciousness are being expanded and enriched. Therefore, in modern Russian sociological literature attempts were made to determine its leading components: interests (A.G. Zdravomyslov, V.N. Lavrinenko, N. Stefanov, A.T. Khanipov), values (N.I. Lapin, A.M. Makarevich, A.M. Yakovlev), social mood (Yu.A. Levada, B.D. Parygin, Zh.T. Toshchenko, S.V. Kharchenko). Short of analyzing the whole variety of this research, it is worth noting that each of these new approaches has enriched our notions of social consciousness.

Summarizing these available empirical research findings and suggestions, we can say that *sociological interpretation of social consciousness is based on the indicators of its following components: knowledge, attitude to knowledge, value orientations and motivations, attitudes, interests and needs.* As an indispensable element of social consciousness, public opinion is identified as its specific form, which reflects people's attitude relevant to current, burning issues of both public and private life. We also have some research experience of such operationalized components of real consciousness as social mood and social health (well-being). In general, this approach enables us to fully and comprehensively analyze the phenomenon of social consciousness and obtain relevant results.

The majority of domestic sociological studies analyze social consciousness in connection with people's activities and human behavior. In this particular case, we do not dwell on refinement and special consideration of the relationship between the concepts of «work» and «behavior» — for us it is important to emphasize the fact that consciousness, becoming an active transformative force, is realized in practice.

We should stipulate that not all acts of consciousness become acts of behavior or activity. There is a wide range of conditions and factors that either facilitate or hinder this process. But one thing is certain: a sociologist cannot confine himself/herself to the analysis of social consciousness as a whole or its individual manifestations as such — it is very important to test it in «action».

In this connection we should recall a characterization of sociology by the prominent Russian and American scholar P.A. Sorokin (1889–1968) as «a science that studies the behavior of people living amongst their own kind» (Sorokin. 1992).

As long as we agree with this statement, *the second basic concept of sociology is behavior,* which acts as a step in realization of the whole entirety or individual components of functioning social consciousness. Since consciousness and behavior are inextricably linked, interdependent, interacting, enriching each other, and conflicting with each other, they should be analyzed in inseparable unity, interrelation and interdependence.

In other words, the real, living consciousness and behavior are the «richest» social processes in their manifestation. In fact, they reflect, on empirical level, the state of social relations and interactions in all their diversity, inconsistency, accidental nature and necessity. It is they that act as a sensitive indicator of the state, development and functioning of social processes, of entire social life. Therefore, their research represents an important tool for making scientifically sound decisions, without exception, in all spheres of public life — from economic to spiritual.

However, in order not to fall into subjectivism, it is necessary, in our opinion, to analyze not just consciousness and behavior, but their functioning under specific socio-economic, socio-political and socio-cultural conditions, representing an impact of all kinds of social macro-, mezzo — and microenvironment. A sociologist is called upon to take into account «special vital circumstances», defining consciousness and behavior of the people, «each of whom wants that, which he is attracted to by his physical constitution and by external, in the final analysis, economic circumstances (either his own, personal, or general social ones) ... « (Marx K, Engels F. *Works.* Vol. 37). In other words, live, practically functioning consciousness — is indeed the consciousness of an active individual.

Thus, social consciousness and behavior in a specific socio-historical context, explaining the development and functioning of various socio-demographic, ethnic, socio-professional structures, are the subject of sociology. The study of consciousness and behavior of the people converts sociology from the plane of simply recording science into an active social force, participating in solving all, without exception, pressing issues of the development of mankind.

This expansion and enrichment of theoretical and methodological approaches and opportunities for cognition of social consciousness have contributed to a deep and detailed analysis of spiritual life of modern society, helped create a more colorful, substantive vision of the state of contemporary Russian society, revealing a new class of problems.

In this connection it is worth recalling that social consciousness and behavior become a subject of research only under the conditions of civil society — one born at a certain stage of historical process, as a result of a new era of modern history, which started its countdown during the period of great bourgeois revolutions, those times when society had separated itself from the state. No one doubts why under the conditions of totalitarian dictatorships, or monopoly of power there is no necessity to study people's moods, opinions, their destinies and life prospects (as sociology itself becomes unnecessary either). Only under the conditions of civil society can a person demonstrate fundamentally new features of behavior and lifestyle, when he has an opportunity to act as an autonomous social force, whose influence is largely dependant on the level and degree of consciousness and creativity of the participants of real historical process. The fact that the creator and driving force behind the development of this society are consciousness and behavior of the people is confirmed by historical experience — until people understand and accept what suits them, what brings them together, and undertake efforts in order to achieve this goal, there will be no peace, no harmony or stability.

In sum, we can say that sociology is the science about the driving forces of consciousness and behavior of people as members of civil society. The subject of sociology as a science includes: real social consciousness in all its contradictory development; activity, the actual behavior of the people, acting as an objective embodiment (form and contents) of knowledge, attitudes, value orientations, needs and interests recorded in the living consciousness; conditions under which real consciousness and activity, actual behavior of the people are being developed and implemented. All this allows us to refer to the totality of above ideas as sociology of life, since it deals with indicators of interactions and attitudes of people toward real problems, situations, everything that happens in a society in which they live and work (Toshchenko. 2005; Reznik. 1995; Dyl'nov, Klimov. 2003).

References

Alexeev V.P. *Stanovlenie tshelovetshestva (Formation of Mankind)*. Moscow, 1984.

Andriushchenko E.G. *Obshchestvennoe mnenie i glasnost v sisteme upravleniya oshchestvom (Public Opinion and Glasnost in the System of Governing Society)*. Moscow, 1988.

Anisimov S.F. *Dukhovnye tsennosti: proizvodstvo i potreblenie (Spiritual Values: Production and Consumption)*. Moscow, 1988.

Antipina G.S. *Soznanie gruppovoe (Group Consciousness)* // Entsiklopeditshesky sotsiologhichesky slovar' (Encyclopaedic Sociological Dictionary). Moscow, 1995. P. 68.

Arefyeva G.S. *Obshchestvo, poznaniye, praktika (Society, Cognition, Practice)*. Moscow, 1988.

Babosov E.M. *Duchovnyi mir sovetskogo tsheloveka (Spiritual World of Soviet Man)*. Minsk, 1983.

Barulin V.S. *Sotsial'no-filosofskaya antropologhia (Social and Philosophical Anthropology)*. Moscow, 1994.

Berdyaev N.A. *Filosofiya neravenstva (Philosophy of Inequality)*. Moscow, 1990. P. 41.

Bogdanov A. *Iz psichologhii obshchestva (From Psychology of Society)*. St. Petersburg, 1906. P. 57.

Boykov V.E., Ivanov V.N., Toshchenko Zh.T. *Obshchestvennoe soznanie i perestroyka (Public Consciousness and Perestrojka)*. Moscow, 1990.

Demichev V.A. *Obshchestvennoe bytie i obshchestvennoe soznanie (Social Being and Social Consciousness)*. Kishinev, 1970.

Diligenskiy G.G. *Rabotshiy na kapitalistitsheskom predpriatii (Worker at Capitalist Enterprise)*. Moscow, 1969.

Dinamika zennostey naseleniya reformiruemoy Rossii (Dynamics of Values of the Population in Reforming Russia). Pod Red. N.I. Lapin, L.A. Belyaeva, Moscow, 1996.

Durkheim E. *Sotsiologhia. Eye predmet, metod, primeneniye (Sociology. Its Subject, Method, Applicability)*. Moscow, 1995.

Dyl'nov G.V., Klimov V.A. *O ponyatii «sotsiologiya zhizni» (About Concept «Sociology of Life»)* // Sotsiologhicheskie issledovaniya. 2003. No 4.

Entsiklopeditsheskiy sotsiologhicheskiy slovar' (Encyclopaedic Sociological Dictionary). Moscow, 1995. P. 682–683.

Frolov I.T. *O tsheloveke i gumanisme (On Human and Humanism)*. Moscow, 1989.

Gorizonty ekologicheskogo znania (sotsial'no-filosofskie problemy) (Horizons of Ecological Knowledge (Social and Philosophical Problems). Moscow, 1986.

Gorshkov M.K. *Obshchestvennoe mnenie (Public Opinion)*. Moscow, 1988.

Grushin B.A. *Massovoye soznanie (Mass Consciousness)*. Moscow, 1987.

Grushin B.A. *Mneniye o mire i mir mneniy (Opinion about the World and the World of Opinions)*. Moscow, 1967.

Ilyenkov E.V. *Dialektitsheskaya logika. Ocherki istorii i teorii (Dialectical Logic. Outline of History and Theory)*. Moscow, 1984.

Kharchenko S.V. *Povedenie: ot real'nogo k ideal'nomu (Behavior: from Real to Ideal)*. Belgorod, 1999.

Kelle V.Zh., Koval'zon M.Ya. *Obshchestvennoe soznanie i obshchestvennye nauki (Social Consciousness and Social Sciences)*. Moscow, 1973.

Korobeynikov V.S. *Avtoritet obshchestvennogo mnenia (Authority of Public Opinion)*. Moscow, 1989.

Kutyrev V.A. *Sovremennoe sotsial'noe poznanie (Modern Social Cognition)*. Moscow, 1988.

Lektorskiy V.A. *Sub'ekt, ob'ekt, poznanie (Subject, Object, Cognition)*. Moscow, 1980.

Leontyev A.N. *Deyatelnost' – soznanie – lichnost (Activity – Consciousness – Personality)*. Moscow, 1975.

Levada Yu.A. *Indeksy sotsialnykh nastroyeniy v «norme» i v krizise (Indices of the Social Mood in «Norm» and in a Crisis) // Monitoring obshchestvennogo mnenija: ekonomicheskiye i sotsial'nye peremeny (Monitoring of Public Opinion: Economic and Social Changes)*. Moscow, 1998. No. 6.

Levada Yu.A. *Ishchem cheloveka (Seeking a Man)*. Moscow, 2006 .

Marx K., Engels F. *Works* (In Russian). Vol. 3. P. 1.

Marx K, Engels F. Works (In Russian). vol. 37. P. 395, 396.

Mikhailov F.G. *Obshchestvennoe soznanie i samosoznanie individa (Social Consciousness and Self-Consciousness of an Individual)*. Moscow, 1990.

Novaya filosofskaya enziklopedia (New Philosophic Encyclopedia). Moscow, 2001. Vol.3. P. 589–591.

Obshchestvennoe soznanie i ego vidy (Social Consciousness and Its Kinds). Moscow, 1983.

Obshchestvennoe soznanie i ego formy (Public Consciousness and Its Forms). Moscow, 1986.

Obshchestvo i soznaniye (Society and Consciousness). Moscow, 1980.

Ol'shanskiy D.V. *Massovoe nastroenie v politike (Mass Mood in Politics)*. Moscow, 1995.

Oyzerman T.I. *Filosofiya kak istoria filosofiyi (Philosophy as a History of Philosophy)*. St. Petersburg, 1999.

Oyzerman T.I. *Filosofiya i obydennoye soznanie (Philosophy and Everyday Consciousness) //* Voprosy filosofii, 1967. No. 4. P.127.

Paryghin B.D. *Obshchestvennoe nastroenie (Social Mood)*. Moscow, 1966.

Pokrovskiy N.E. Rossiyskoe obshschestvo v kontekste amerikanisatsii (osnovnaya skhema). (Russian Society in a Context of the Americanization (Basic Schema) // Sotsiologhicheskiye issledovania. 2000. No. 6.

Reznik Yu.M. *Sotsial'noye izmereniye zhiznennogo mira (vvedenije v soziologhiyu zhizni)*. *(Social Dimension of the Vital World (Introduction into a Sociology of Life)*. Moscow, 1995.

Rubinstein E.P. *Problemy obshchey psihologhiy (Problems of General Psychology)*. Moscow, 1973.

Ryvkina R.V. *Mezhdu sotsialismom i rynkom: sud'ba ekonomicheskoi kul'tury v Rossii (Between Socialism and Market: Destiny of Economic Culture in Russia)*. Moscow, 1994.

Semashko A.N. *Sociologiya iskusstva (Sociology of Art)*. Kiev. 2006.

Shevchenko V.N. *Sotsialno-filosofski analiz razvitia obshchestva (Social Philosophical Analysis of the Development of Society)*. Moscow, 1984.

Sokolov V.M. *Soziologhia nravstvennogo rasvitia litshnosti (Sociology of the Moral Development of Personality)*. Moscow, 1986.

Sorokin P.A. *Tshelovek. Tsivilisatsia. Obshchestvo (Person. Civilization. Society)*. Moscow, 1992. P. 534.

Spirkin A.G. *Soznanie i samosoznanie (Consciousness and Self-Consciousness)*. Moscow, 1972.

Stepin V.S. *Filosofskaya antropologhia i istoria nauki (Philosophical Anthropology and History of Science)*. Moscow, 1992.

Stepin V.S. *Teoretitsheskoe znanie (Theoretical Knowledge)*. Moscow, 2000. P. 20.

Sysoeva L.S. *Esteticheskaia deyatel'nost' i esteticheskoe vospitanie (Aesthetic Activity and Aesthetic Education)*. Tomsk, 1989.

Tchinakova L.I. *Sotsialnyi determinism (Social Determinism)*. Moscow, 1985.

Toyber A.Kh. *Istoriya soznaniya (History of Consciousness)*. Moscow, 1999.

Toshchenko Zh.T., Kharchenko S.V. *Sozialnoye nastroyenie (Social Mood)*. Moscow, 1996.

Toshchenko Zh.T. *Sotsiologhia. Obshchiy kurs (Sociology: a General Course)*. Moscow, 2005;

Toshchenko Zh.T. *Teoretiko-metodologhicheskoye osmyslenie sotsial'nogo nastroyenia kak fenomena sovremennoy obshchestvennoy praktiki / Sotsiologhia na poroge XXI veka. Novye napravleniya issledovaniya (Theoretical and Methodological Comprehension of Social Mood as Phenomenon of Modern Public Practice / Sociology on the Threshold of the 21st century. New Lines of Research)*. Moscow, 1998.

Uledov A.K. *Obshchestvennoe mnenie (Public Opinion)*. Moscow, 1964.

Uledov A.K. *Struktura obshchestvennogo soznania (Structure of the Public Consciousness)*. Moscow, 1968.

Vvedenie v filocofiyu (Introduction into Philosophy). Part 2. Moscow, 1979. P. 445–455.

Zdravomyslov A.G. *Potrebnosti, interesy, tsennosti (Needs. Interests. Values)*. Moscow, 1986.

Chapter 2. **Metamorphoses of modern social consciousness: methodological bases for sociological analysis**

> Slaves dream of a market where they can buy their own masters.
>
> *Stanislaw Erzy Lets* (1909–1966),
> Polish author

Applying the concept of metamorphosis to the analysis of social consciousness problems, we recognize that, just as in animal and plant world, where a living organism as a whole, as well as its major (individual) organs, is undergoing profound transformations, in a society as well, implementation of various combinations of its transformation into a qualitatively different state is underway, or conditions are created for emergence of separate stable formations, indicating a dramatic change in economic, socio-political and spiritual life. Metamorphoses are also inherent in social consciousness, especially during the periods of transformation processes. In his times, French philosopher and mathematician R. Descartes (1596–1650) spoke of anti-consciousness, trying to explain a phenomenon, evading logic of social development. Metamorphoses can occur in social consciousness as a whole and its specific forms, kinds and mechanisms of its functioning.

Moreover, these metamorphoses may reflect both single shifts and changes occurring in consciousness, and their most bizarre combinations. They are a peculiar result of deformations in social consciousness, marking an appearance of its transformed forms at all levels of social organization of society — macro-, mezzo- and microenvironments. But one other fact is beyond any doubt — contemporary metamorphoses do not appear and emerge by themselves, but under certain traumatic conditions, develop long before they morph into a complete entity, which becomes a noticeable phenomenon of public life (Sztompka, 2001).

2.1. Conditions for the emergence of metamorphoses

Usually, when characterizing trend and problems of development of social consciousness, real conditions, in which people live, work and exercise their right to personal and public life are being analyzed. However, in spite of the legitimacy of this approach, *study of metamorphoses of social consciousness should begin with analysis of preconditions for their emergence.* In this case we draw attention to the fact, that shifts and changes in social consciousness start to ripen at the previous stages of social system, manifested, for example, in the form of discrepancies in interests, needs, value orientations and popular attitudes with actually existing public (economic, social, political, spiritual etc.) relations.

Changes indicating degeneration or deep deformation of modern social consciousness in contemporary Russia have been accumulating gradually. On the one hand, they reflected a reaction to those objective circumstances that developed in society primarily in economics and politics; on the other hand, they marked the shifts, which signified an emergence of new, or transformation of previously existing and functioning stereotypes and operative standards. As a result, all of us witnessed metamorphoses in all spheres of societal life, especially in social consciousness and human activities.

These underlying preconditions of shifts and changes in social consciousness have very clearly displayed themselves during the period of Gorbachev's perestroika. With regard to the objective conditions, false economic priorities, initial disorientation of economic life, coupled with such measures as establishment of coops at enterprises, financial and economic activities of the Party, Komsomol and other public organizations became a powerful foundation for creation of a shadow economy, the basis for destruction of possibly over-organized, but unitary national economic complex. Before the eyes of millions of people, processes have emerged that were difficult to explain and even more difficult to understand, which year after year kept deteriorating their social status, and made them witnesses strange, impulsive actions of the country's leadership.

At the same time, public consciousness has favorably and gratefully received a declared policy of openness (*glasnost*) and the first steps toward democratization (elected leaders, elimination of uncontested elections, access to previously classified information, etc.). This reaction was caused by the fact that by that time, people were tired of increasing dominance of lies, doublethink, aspirations «to appear, instead of to be» (Kozma Prutkov — the Russian literary person, ridiculing shallowness, banality, small-mindedness, etc. — *Zh.T.*) and moral corrosion, since degeneration and perversity of the former official monolithic world outlook with socialist overtones has become apparent. The atmosphere of deceit, lies, absurdity and fatigue from continuous campaigns of pomp and pageantry, misuse of sacred symbols such as, for example, World War II (the Great Patriotic war), was felt by many, the fact that could not have left social consciousness unaffected. Grounds for rejection of imposed standards of behavior established and promoted by authorities began to ripen, drifting further and further away from the real interests and needs of the people. Domination of primitive forms of ideological indoctrination (anniversaries, «Lenin's lessons and tests», «show off» all around, artificially fabricated masks) — all this has resulted in a multiplication of metamorphoses — that is, transformed forms of social consciousness.

But, having taken a swing at eliminating these obstacles on the way to objectively developing public consciousness, perestroika has not only failed to resolve, but on the contrary, exacerbated pre-existing problems. Moreover, it has caused and promoted the emergence and consolidation of new deformed kinds of consciousness.

Even the so-called market reforms that came to replace *perestroika,* have not resolved these problems of social consciousness. Feelings of betrayal, mood of pessimism and skepticism was reinforced in the 1990's, in post-soviet Russia, when the change in economic and political order was declared. It could not have happened any other way.

Russia's entry into market economy in the 1990's has aggravated the processes of deformation of public life, creating new metamorphoses of social consciousness with even more profound and drastic social consequences. These transformed forms of social consciousness began to particularly vigorously emerge in connection with implementation of economic reform policies and, especially, privatization of state property, which, during its first stage, was voucher privatization (1992–1994) and the second stage (since 1994 and on) — monetary privatization continues until now. The fact that informal privatization began prior to the years of *perestroika* should not be ignored. As soon as official state and party structures have been sanctioned to engage in commerce, Soviet officials began to appropriate property of their organizations and «reorganize» them into private enterprises. They used the same suppliers, the same buildings and the same personnel. Only the signboards changed. Assets of pre-existing organizations became property of the new owners.

Voucher privatization, launched in October 1992, followed the «savage» privatization of perestroika times. Shares offered some help for the population of Russia, although only few were able to receive dividends and have voting rights in dealing with issues of governance, even if these vouchers were invested in factories or enterprises that employed these investors. However, vouchers have been rather useful for those who had an opportunity to buy them in large quantities. Criminal and commercial structures tried to get them as soon as possible. Vouchers were bought up on the streets, sometimes for a bottle of vodka from alcoholics. In other cases, these structures set up voucher funds that were advertised on TV with promises of high dividends. Then they either did not pay dividends at all, or simply disappeared. This way, criminal and commercial structures accumulated huge blocks of vouchers, which were used to purchase most attractive enterprises, often at bargain prices. And, at the same time, inefficient and unprofitable industries remained in the hands of the state, heavily weighing on the suddenly impoverished state budget (in contrast to the economic policy in Poland — shock therapy, where unnecessary and inefficient enterprises have been sold off first).

Hyperinflation, accompanied by deliberate deception of the people, contributed to deformation of social consciousness. How was the social consciousness supposed to react to the assertions of President B. Yeltsin and the Head of the Government E. Gaidar in 1992, and again in 1993, that prices will go up no more than three to five times, and then will start falling? However, within just ten months of 1992 prices rose three to four hundred times, which led to massive impoverishment of the population. During three months of 1992, 99% of the savings deposits kept by Russian citizens at the banks have vanished — the money that had been saved for decades for an apartment, a car, for a wedding or a decent funeral was gone. When Gaidar was reminded that in autumn of 1991, the Supreme Council voted for indexation of citizens' savings in the event of price liberalization he replied, as if nothing happened, that the imbalance in the economy is the fault of the former regime, not the newly formed government.

Simultaneously there was widespread squandering and plundering of national property, which severely affected social consciousness. Prices, at which many enterprises were sold off, have stunned Russian society. 324 factories were sold at an average price of less than 4 million dollars each. «Uralmash», a giant machine-building manufacturer in Yekaterinburg, was sold for 3.73 million dollars. Chelyabinsk Metallurgical plant — for the same price. Kovrov Mechanical factory, which supplied the army, Ministry of Internal Affairs and State Security with firearms was sold for 2.7 million dollars. Telephone companies were sold for 116.62 dollars per line, while in North America, their value was 637.00 and in Hungary — 2083.00 dollars per line (*Nezavisimaya gazeta.* 1999. № 1).

Another glaring fact: during «privatization», a Russian oligarch Roman Abramovich bought «Sibneft» — a huge oil company for 130 million dollars, and sold it back to the government in early 2000's for $13 billion.

As a result, Russia with its world's richest natural resources found itself on the verge of economic collapse. Within a decade, gross domestic product fell by half, which has not happened even during the Great Patriotic war (1941–1945). Russia basically turned into a third world country, selling its raw materials — oil, gas, precious metals — in exchange for imported consumer goods.

At the same time in the 1990's the volume of investment into Russia's economy had fallen by 80%. Due to lack of investment, many sectors of Russian industry, including aircraft manufacturing, mechanical engineering, food processing, textiles and microelectronics were practically on the brink of extinction. Capital was being smuggled out of the country in huge quantities. According to the Interior Ministry, nearly 350 billion dollars was illegally exported from Russia over those years. They were transported in suitcases through customs offices of «Sheremetyevo-2» airport («black market»), or transferred as payments to the front companies, ostensibly, for the services that have never actually been provided («gray market»). That became a powerful foundation for the formation of a shadow and criminal economy, which, according to experts, since mid 1990's, included between 45% and 55% of the GNP in its sphere of influence.

Economic difficulties were accompanied by a demographic catastrophe. The average male life expectancy fell by more than six years compared to 1985. In late 1990's it was 57 years, which is the lowest in the industrialized world. Out of one hundred Russian boys that in 1999 reached the age of sixteen, only 54 will, according to statistics, celebrate their diamond jubilee. For comparison: a hundred years ago, 56 of every hundred of sixteen− year-olds from Russia's provinces had a chance to reach the age of sixty.

The destructive character of economic and social policy has seriously undermined the health of the nation. Over 2 million people in Russia suffer from TB. The official number of registered cases of open stage tuberculosis had doubled − from 50 thousand in 1991 to 118 thousand in 2005. The number of patients diagnosed with syphilis increased 50-fold − from 8 thousand in 1990 to 545 thousand in 2005. Other serious diseases like polio, cholera and even plague attest to an alarming state of the health of society and the entire system of public hygiene.

All this has brought about a situation, where many people live under constant stress. Delays in wage payments from three to eight months were the result of speculation at all levels of the economy. Private land plots, where people grew up to 40% of the total amount of food, helped the situation.

This desperation caused by the economic situation, resulted in an increased suicide rate (from 38,9 thousands to 61,9 in 1995 and 46,1 in 2005) and violence (9,4 thousand killings in 1970 and 35,8 thousands in 2005) in Russian society.

Information about economic lawlessness, financial scams, crude and brazen looting of the people, when made public, left some to wonder in amazement, others in shock or with a sense of confusion. Many were indignant, protesting and simply losing direction, resulting in apathy and indifference. In other words, *economic shock therapy led to a shock in Russian society.* In this situation, similar to the period of initial accumulation of capital, with its bloody showdowns and ruthless struggle for property, in social consciousness, a new metamorphosis inevitably formed and developed. How could the social consciousness not be deformed when, in opinion of a US sovietologist, professor Steven Cohen, «modern Russia − a country where 75% of the population is impoverished or close to poverty, where there are more orphans than after the Second World War ... This impoverished state, threatened by starvation, cold and ruin ... an unprecedented result: the literal de-modernization of the country» (Cohen. 1998).

The conditions for emergence of metamorphoses were also created by deeply contradictory processes in the political life of society: when people were openly suspended from participation in governance; or when an appearance of popular involvement in the election process was staged during electoral campaigns (which were manipulated to a high degree).

Confidence in all government structures has fallen to a level that in developed countries would automatically lead to an immediate resignation of the government, new elections, and dismissal of many politicians. In Russia, even having lost their official posts, they continued, as if nothing was wrong, to participate in political decisions and blab about destinies of the nation. However, people intuitively crave protection and trust in those who are supposed to defend them, take care of them, and offer assurances for at least foreseeable future. These sentiments have led to a surge of confidence in the new president of Russia, which was not so much due to his actual deeds, but, mainly, to hopes for serious adjustments in internal and foreign policies of the country. However, when these expectations are in question, a decline in confidence and rejection of the political establishment follow shortly.

A proclaimed, but falsely understood, and even more falsely applied freedom played a destructive role as well, which to a considerable degree, facilitated metamorphoses in social consciousness. Paradoxes of its interpretation and application generated new contradictions — freedom began transforming into permissiveness with complete atrophy of responsibility and denial of rights to the very same freedoms for «people next door» (Shabanova, 2000; Kudryavtsev, 2006). Not surprisingly, the concept of «democracy» has undergone astonishing metamorphoses — from revered, highly valued, it turned into something almost objectionable, obscene, abusive and unacceptable. And this happened within a few brief years since its grand entry into Russian social life! Metamorphoses that this concept, as well as other similar notions included into the 1990's lexicon (freedom, sovereignty, market etc.) underwent (according to the data collected by psychologists and sociologists in their research of semantic differentials) were possible not only due to the changes in objective reality, but subjective activities of those, who attempted to implement the ideas of market society (Levashov, 2008).

These contradictions altered the search for effective mechanisms of functioning of social life in general and real consciousness in particular. Consequently, a huge number of «oracles» (individuals, groups and even political parties and movements) have appeared in contemporary Russian society, who categorically claimed a monopoly to knowing the absolute truth and capability of its implementation. Just like during Soviet times, in post-Soviet Russia, this attitude generates baseless claims, and, because of that spawns, on the one hand, adventurers of all sorts, and, on the other — conformists, uncritically thinking people, thick-headed and unscrupulous aids to the «creators» of market reforms.

With regard to metamorphoses of theoretical knowledge we should note the fact that in 1960–1980's theoretical level of social consciousness in the Soviet Union came more and more into conflict with reality and did not adequately reflect its dialectical development. Ideas, concepts, both imperfect, one-sided and limited in their essence, not only failed to positively influence social processes, but also hindered them, torpedoed many progressive initiatives and gave incorrect, flawed (in their orientation) guidelines to social practice. Subjects of theoretical knowledge turned out to be incapable of comprehending the course of historical process and therefore could not focus and mobilize creative forces of the country. And it is quite natural that the court of history was severe and unrelenting: theoretically erroneous concepts were denied the right to existence; they were rejected as having inflicted almost irreparable harm to the development of society (Osipov, 2006).

Theoretical concoctions of ideologues of the new transformation of Russia failed to become a real force, they only exacerbated existing contradictions in the social consciousness. Moreover, they were developed, deliberated and proven, on the basis not of scientific analysis of real life, but some pre-postulated doctrines and attitudes related to political convictions of their authors, having none, or at best a very approximate relation not only to science, but common sense as well. Furthermore, the impact of persistently spread and uncritically borrowed concepts should not be underestimated or disregarded as well. Under those circumstances, official or semi-official theoretical thinking kept persistently trying to introduce two ideas into the public consciousness. First, the idea that the entire past (mainly, the Soviet past) should be rejected without any regrets, ostensibly, because it is flawed from beginning to end. Presently, under the influence of objective realities such nihilistic attitude is being partially disputed, although, on many counts the momentum was irreversibly lost. Second, the market idea was depicted as the only way out of crisis. Time has also shown that idealization of the market backfired at a very high cost, taking its toll especially on the social sphere of public life. For theorists, market apologists, the opinion of many influential figures of Western world did not serve as a warning. In particular, the former head of the French government Lionel Jospin, who at the end of 1990, stated that modern world should implement a principle: «Yes — to market economy, no — to market society» (Abalkin, 2000). We have to agree with the famous Russian writer A. Solzhenitsyn, that «as a result of Yeltsin's era, all basic segments of state, national economic, cultural and moral life have been crushed» (Solzhenitsin, 1998).

In sum, we can assert that deformations in social practice and scientific thought created conditions that brought about metamorphoses of social consciousness, resulting in emergence of various forms of transformed consciousness, affecting all aspects of public life, as well as its individual segments. Based on the principles of typology of social phenomena, we shall examine a variety of situations reflecting different manifestations of these metamorphoses. In first approximation, we shall analyze two dimensions of these manifestations: global metamorphosis and their singular expressions (cases).

2.2. Global metamorphoses of social consciousness

Under the conditions of transitive and destructive development, various forms of deformed or distorted perceptions of reality emerge and take shape, followed by their subsequent transformation into similar types of inadequate, contradictory and deviant behavior. They emerge under the impact of global macro-economic and geopolitical processes, as well as the influence of mezzo— and microenvironment, i.e. processes that occur where people live and work, where their daily lives unfold.

Scientific and socio-political thought offers a fairly detailed description and analysis of contemporary reality. Therefore, it makes no sense to reiterate the facts that are already common knowledge. In our opinion, it is necessary to pay attention to the fact that existing theoretical and methodological, as well as applied research, made numerous attempts to comprehend the phenomena and processes typical of the period of collapse of outdated social relations, and chaotic formation of the new economic and political order. Particular attention is drawn to the fact that social consciousness, in a state of stress and constant overload, created (and still creates) an extremely confusing interweaving of paradoxical views, opinions and assessments of current events. History of Russian (Soviet) society, has more then once demonstrated that social consciousness can significantly strengthen or weaken progressive development and processes of functioning of economic, social, political and spiritual relations. It is this active nature of social consciousness that is capable of exerting powerful and not necessarily positive influence on political and ideological decisions. In Russia, this relates both to the period of revolution and the new economic policy, to the first five-year plans and the time of the Great Patriotic War. Stagnation of the 1970's was not just a time of economic and political failures and losses, it was also the time when people opposed officially proclaimed values, with their actions rejecting whatever was being imposed on them. However, in the vast majority of cases, this protest assumed a passive and latent character. It is due to the latency of these processes occurring in the minds of the people, in their real consciousness, that their destructive force was becoming more impressing in its scope and impact.

Evolutionary process in contemporary Russia is characterized by virtually the same toll on the social consciousness. The changes occurring here attest to a burdensome path, ranging from inspiring hopes to complete disillusionment in real results, from faith in the possibility of reaching a new level of human self-affirmation, to loneliness and vulnerability in the face of the new social forces, unleashed by the so-called market relations.

In other words, a thorough analysis of the processes occurring in social consciousness at various stages of development of national history reveals the problematic character of this development, serious flaws and weaknesses in the social organism, which can be characterized not only by means of economic analysis, but also with the help of sociological research methods of spiritual life. In this regard, it should be noted that it is not stating the suitable (of what's due), but identifying the state and the problems of evolution of real social consciousness that marks the essence of scientific research, for however paradoxical such acknowledgement may be, preaching the norms, appeals, proclamations and slogans, does not help us an inch with overcoming existing contradictions in society.

In an effort to identify the causes of contradictory and transformed state of social consciousness, many sociologists pay attention to both general and individual forms of its manifestation, analyzing those processes that are relevant, and issues that determine the content, background and characteristics of the present stage of societal development. Let us start with extremely common global metamorphoses of social consciousness, which became or may later become a subject of thorough scientific analysis.

First of all, I would like to point out a characteristic of the state of modern social consciousness that is described through the concept of «*split*» or «*broken up*». In our opinion, researchers who use this terminology are dissatisfied with such definitions as diversity, differentiation and discrepancy of social consciousness. Using the term «split social consciousness» they emphasize such features (or attributes) as existence of not just competing, but also mutually exclusive attitudes and orientations within it, as well as unwillingness to find common ground and reconcile their differences, renunciation or waiver of compromises and even readiness to promote extreme forms of hostility toward dissenters. With the split in consciousness and its realization, processes of opposition, inconsistency and contradiction might even be discovered in related concepts, such as personal and social, legal and moral, professional and universal (Gorshkov. 2006; Levada, 2000; Lisovsky, 1998; Popova, 2000). Split consciousness in its essence means the breakdown of the integrity of social consciousness and, as a consequence, a precondition for collapse of economic and political system of the country.

The aspiration to grasp the new tendencies in social consciousness connected to changing economic realities led to an emergence of such a derivation as «*market consciousness*» (Bushchik, 2002; Rutchkin, 2004; *Rossia na rubezhe vekov*. 2006). Proponents of this notion believe that the market fundamentally changes the structure of thinking, knowledge and attitude toward values and information. But this conviction more likely reflects the desired or, at best, certain regulatory requirements. In reality, however, it turns out that the components of consciousness, which could be characterized as market components, have basically failed to emerge, and even if they became a reality, then only for a small group of people, mainly businessmen. As for the majority of working people, in their minds, these innovations are negligible, unnoticeable, and barely influential. In any case, studies conducted within the framework of a joint Russo-Canadian project «Russia on the way to market» in 1990th, have shown that the comparison of workers' consciousness in private, joint-stock and public enterprises failed to reveal any significant differences between them (Toshchenko, 1999).

The ongoing metamorphoses of social consciousness, its problems and condition are often described by the term *«marginal consciousness»* (Balabanova, 1999; Popova, 1996; *Marginal'nost v sovremennoy Rossii.* 2001). This viewpoint is based on the assumption that the collapse of the USSR and complex processes that accompanied the formation of post-Soviet Russia, have resulted in a radical change of all previous forms and types of public consciousness, forcing all individuals, without exception, to comprehend (immediately or with some lag) their new social status, which in most cases proved to be volatile. This led to substantial changes in prior characteristics of the consciousness (some have disappeared altogether), with new ones not yet established in real social practice. And, in addition, there is no certainty that these new or enhanced formations are something that will satisfy society and as well as the people. This instability, uncertainty, ambiguity of social status has led to marginality of social consciousness, when in strangest ways, it combines the old and the new political ideas, cosmopolitan and nationalistic orientations, republican and monarchist beliefs, religious and atheistic convictions, labor and consumerist guidelines.

Supporters of this viewpoint may rightfully suggest that the leading (according to some claims, the principal) characteristic of social consciousness is its marginality, when all of its manifestations reveal the borderline nature (imbalance) between the traditional and the new entities.

Social consciousness is hugely overloaded. Changing political and economic reference points inevitably disrupt the value system, generating various perceptions of current changes. Moreover, this process not only continues unabated, on the contrary, it is gaining momentum, amplifying, growing, manifested in various forms, most often in the form *of false consciousness,* when the objective picture of the world is reflected in a distorted, prejudiced, biased way. Not just objective, but also subjective conditions contributed to the birth and expanding boundaries of false consciousness. The ideas and ideals were not always tested for strength and durability by worthy methods; they were corrupted and discredited by those who were supposed to guard their purity and sanctity (Pokrovskiy, 2000; Krivosheev, 2000; *Neterpimost' v Rossii*. 2005; Ryvkina, 2000).

False consciousness is a direct consequence of those conditions, when the so-called «masters of life» used to say one thing and, in actuality, do the complete opposite. In such situation, a person is forced to adapt to this as well. In turn, this imposed process of adaptation pushed people to social mimicry: one's consciousness simply could not (and even now is still often unable to) be other than false, or distorted.

False consciousness is manifested mainly in two forms: myths and stereotypes. They ambiguously influence people's lives, often suppressing everything new that is not a cliché, generating enduring defects in people's consciousness and behavior. False consciousness also contributes to the spread of the «little man» ideology: «nothing depends on me», «let the bosses decide, let the authorities think», «I would like to, but ...» etc. This position is one step away from social indifference, feelings of hopelessness, violation of human rights, denial of selflessness and disrespect for professionalism. False consciousness, to a large degree, is associated with circulating ideas, most of which reflect a desired, not the real picture of a particular social process or phenomenon.

Political and economic authorities developed a lot of clichés, designed to conceal a lack of thought, unwillingness to deal with reality, dogmatic style of thinking. There is a concept of «*glittering uncertainty*» in the theory of propaganda. It is fully applicable to the statements, which have been repeatedly made without any intention of understanding basic essence of the phenomenon in question. For example, «the market and democracy are inseparable». Ostensibly, a market without democracy is not a market in the true sense of the word. And democracy cannot demonstrate its full advantages without a market.

In this regard, I would like to mention the analysis carried out in 1994 at the 13th International Sociological Congress in Bielefeld (Federal Republic of Germany). During deliberations of one of the sections of the Congress, different concepts of market development were demonstrated, supported by research of a number of scholars: from Western European to totalitarian, from socially oriented to one based on unrestrained freedom of entrepreneurial intentions. Many of these versions were productive and effective in their own way, especially when implemented with due consideration to national culture and mentality. And since this «glittering uncertainty» — the market — was not «tied» to real problems in Russia, false promises and hopes of Russia's westernization proponents collapsed, undermining public confidence in power of the market.

False consciousness leads to distorted conclusions and, respectively, deformed practical actions. Its danger lies in the fact that it traumatizes not only lives of individual groups and social strata — it distorts the real functioning consciousness in general. When the extent of false consciousness is significant, it turns the whole society into a crowd of sorts; manipulation becomes a matter of technique, «black» PR, capable of drastically changing people's behavior in a desired direction.

2.3. Cases of metamorphoses of social consciousness

Analysis of sociological data shows that metamorphoses of social consciousness affect not only its overall condition, development and functioning, but also its various manifestations, flares, giving rise to phantoms, capturing its separate segments and forms. First, *catastrophic consciousness* that develops according to three possible scenarios: «bad», «very bad», «unbearable» should be attributed to this category. At the same time it does not mean that all people, the entire society, is affected by catastrophic thinking — it is most likely due to the fact that people (and this is manifested in their assessment of the country's leaders) do not understand and fail to see the strategy of development — their attention is focused only on short-term problems and immediate needs and goals. However, effective and rational implementation even of the short-term strategic plans is only attainable through long-term development programs, an essential component of which is trust and confidence of people in the productive nature of the changes (Mitev, Ivanova, Shubkin, Yadov, 2004).

The collapse of hopes for rapid reconstruction of public and private life has accelerated an emergence of various forms of catastrophic consciousness, when a considerable number of people were convinced that Russia has ceased to be a great power, that Russian society has lost many of its achievements, that the country was facing difficult trials. These catastrophic judgments became particularly apparent while evaluating the situation in the country in its entirety, to a lesser degree, people's personal situations. This in turn revealed a paradoxical and highly specific feature of contemporary public consciousness: people were more worried about the prospects of development of society than their own place, future and social status in this society. According to VTsIOM (All-Russian Center for public opinion studies) data, during a number of years, this gap became considerable (*Monitoring obshchestvennogo mnenija. Ekonomicheskiye i sotsialnye peremeny.* 2007).

Comprehending realities of the transitional period in Russia, and recognizing the existence of a number of extraordinary phenomena in social consciousness, such definitions as *sick, pathological consciousness* (not in the medical, but social sense) appeared and were utilized not only in journalistic, but scientific literature as well. It is obvious, that such definitions reflect those parts of the phenomena of social consciousness that cause concern, fear for the fate of the people, nation and state. These definitions are similar to catastrophic consciousness, although they are not expressed in hopelessness terms, rather in the form of a diagnosis, with hope that such an approach will allow us to understand the current dangerous situation in society, to evaluate the extent and nature of possible complications and shocks, and, based on their analysis, contribute to the development of such measures that would relieve social tensions, facilitate prompt recovery and return of Russian society to the bosom of world civilization.

While characterizing specific manifestations of the transformed and deformed social consciousness, sometimes the term *«demagogic consciousness»* is used to interpret such manifestations, when its subjects deliberately, for the sake of personal gain, abuse normative attitudes and moral values (Balabanova, 1999). Conscious distortion of these values has many faces and usually pursues the achievement of either personal, or a narrow group's interests in all spheres of public life. Moreover, this distortion varies in form, not in essence, since demagoguery tends to most successfully and parasitically exploit the complexities of societal developments. Consciousness of demagogues clearly grasps social priorities and moods and uses them to cover up their self-interests. Thus, in the sphere of economic activity, demagogic consciousness is manifested in a form of constant attacks and rejections of all, without exception, guidelines, laws, regulations that limit maximization of their profits and revenue. Carriers of this type of consciousness regard everything that is aimed at regulating cash flow as an infringement on rights and freedoms of market economy. In comparison with the Soviet era, when similar practice was in most cases limited to the aspirations of obtaining an additional salary or a bonus, appetites of present benefactors of economic gains are limitless, aimed at huge profits and a complete rejection of the appeal that was voiced by the former Finance Minister of Russia A. Livshits: «We must share» (meaning, newly rich have to share their wealth). According to the renowned economist S.Yu. Glaz'ev, this has resulted in 50 to 60 billion dollar annual loss from the sale of Russia's raw materials being appropriated by those who «saddled» privatization and seized big chunks of state-owned property. This, in turn, has caused envy of those who failed to get their share, and led to attempts, including criminal ones, to redistribute this property (Glaz'ev, 2000). These attempts resulted in such phenomenon as raiding, i.e. forceful seizure of property under the guise of the gaps in existing legislation.

In the political sphere demagogical consciousness is manifested in pursuit of power at any cost, in order to retain the ability to influence crucial decisions at all levels of societal political organization. In general, there is nothing impossible or unacceptable in these aspirations — what matters are the motives and the methods of exerting such influence. And these methods have been recurrently demonstrated by the participants of modern Russian political life: «destroy» all standing in the way to the position of power, willingness to step over corpses, building one's own political well-being through all available, including criminal, means. All of this is accompanied by proclamations that all such actions are carried out in the name of the people, for the benefit of the people and their wellbeing. The extent and the consequences of this consciousness led Russian writer V. Rasputin to assert that demagoguery was no less of a dire a threat to Russia than alcoholism.

The attempts to define such phenomenon as *twilight consciousness* are of some interest (Orlova, 2006; Vavilina, 2000; Bogoyavlenskiy, 2008). It might have appeared, first, due to the loss of past orientations and guidelines in public and private lives of many individuals. Second, this loss was accompanied by a conviction that return to former ideals and guidelines is, and will be impossible, a fact regarded by many as a loss of value and meaning of their former life. Third, these people strongly reject new social goals, new economic and political realities. Moreover, they do not see any possibility of accepting them, or coming to terms with them. All this gave rise to a phenomenon of social consciousness, where the future of personal and public life is practically rejected and the consciousness of individuals is oppressed; they lose sight of ways and means of escape from the circumstances of their lives. An indicator of twilight consciousness is growing neuroses, psychoses, and especially such form of existential discord as suicide. According to the World Health Organization, a level of over 20 suicides per 100 thousand of population is considered high. In Russia, by the mid 1990–2000, this level had more than doubled: it went up from 16,4 in 1990 to 34, 3 cases in 2004.

Such a state of social consciousness is very dangerous, for it engenders, on the one hand, a sense of hopelessness, skepticism, disbelief in the possibility of a fulfilling life, on the other, hardly explainable and sudden outbursts of rage, recklessness, and desire to resort to violent means in order to change the existing situation.

Sociological research data permits us to discuss some other metamorphoses of social consciousness. Thus, consciousness and behavior, which might be tentatively termed *nonconformist, protest* became very important. It is not inherent to specific groups or communities, rather it is «scattered» among all social strata and groups, when a fraction of their members does not wish to reconcile with the ongoing changes and initially rejects them as encroaching on their vital principles. The forms of nonconformist behavior are diverse: from passive dissent to participation in protests and expressions of discontent, as well as incessant and continuous struggle against ideas and phenomena that carriers of this consciousness reject both for themselves and for other people. From the standpoint of social psychology people living with attitude to always say «no», form a fairly stable social layer, which is persistent and consistent in its intentions and actions. This layer practically does not decrease in volume; it can only grow due to those joining in during the periods of acute social tension (Afanasiev, 2001; Golovakha, Panina, 2003; Kinsburskiy, 1998).

Utopian consciousness can be attributed to the specific forms of transformed consciousness and its metamorphoses. It (utopian consciousness) constitutes a specific synthesis of convictions, orientations and attitudes, poorly, if at all, correlated with real life. Utopian consciousness in a transforming society is usually represented in two ways: one idealizing the past, another idealizing certain proclaimed standards, which are yet to be tested and approved. And it is not the matter of incorrectness of these orientations — it is the «outrunning», the desire to justify and support whatever has not yet been determined by life itself. Despite them being direct opposites, both orientations have one common characteristic: their bias, which is expressed in an unquestioning aspiration to justify or impose their cherished idea, concept, or theory. Sometimes utopian consciousness takes shape of something fantastic, which in fact does not change its content, only increases the diversity of the forms of its manifestation (Butenko, 1999; Nazarov, 1999).

While analyzing metamorphoses of public consciousness, we should mention *illusory consciousness*, which embodies, however paradoxically, the process of birth and collapse of fantasies, myths, and self-deceptions. It is human nature to dream, make plans and to hope. But, what was cherished in dreams, passively expected, or, set as a goal (which, allegedly, was to unite many, if not all), was almost never realized or achieved. However, the result was always different from what was intended or anticipated. The doom of illusory consciousness undermines unfounded hopes, since the achievement of stability and prosperity cannot be realized by way of good intentions, questionable promises and fairy tales (Belen'kiy, 2001).

Accumulation and an increase of contradictions in real consciousness are clearly evident in the form of a peculiar *manipulated consciousness*. Its essence lies in a fact that an individual apparently possesses two (and sometimes three or more) forms of consciousness: for formal, official settings and for family and friends. How else can we explain the proliferation of embezzlement of public funds, bribery, theft of property, or a decreased sense of responsibility of ordinary workers and double life of their bosses, whose values and ideology are not that different from the criminals? Under these conditions, real consciousness, to a large extent, could not help losing out on its stability, perseverance and implacability. While generally boldly denouncing such negative phenomena as corruption, bureaucracy, bribery etc., people are often unable to deal with them in a specific situation — at their industrial enterprise, or in the immediate environment. All of these behaviors breed perverse forms of relationships between the subjects of historical process, which in its turn reduces the creative force of social consciousness, simultaneously increasing the degree of conformity.

This form of consciousness became evident, spread among the population, and has become the ideology of political and social organizations. How was this possible? First, because at the official level, plutocratic tendencies in exercise of political authority were maintained and supported, meeting approval of those in possession of wealth and usurping the right to manage national property. Secondly, the majority of mass media became channels for distorting, twisting information, serving the interests of their respective owners. In these circumstances, freedom of speech became «freedom of words», freedom of speech of certain corporations (political and economic) defending their privileges, property and capital by all means possible. Third, political leadership, oligarchs, as their primary means, have chosen Jesuit methods of influencing people, which were originally aimed at deception, misrepresentation, search for potential and imaginary enemies (Ermakov, 1995; Kara-Murza, 2000).

In an attempt to comprehend the real role of public consciousness, a well known French historian Marc Bloch in his work «Apologia pour l'histoire» has suggested studying its dominant — *daily,* or *ordinary consciousness,* which, in his opinion, allows maximum, true understanding of why these specific, and not any other events are taking place in this particular country, at this particular time. He correctly asserted that it is not necessary to study lives of tsars and kings, or events themselves, but the consciousness of the majority, since the course of history is determined precisely by none other than this specific form of social consciousness (Bloch, 1986; Bauman, 2005). In Soviet social science, for a long time, this consciousness was interpreted as *mass* consciousness (B. Grushin, G. Dilighensky, A. Uledov). Subsequently, the author of this work suggested its interpretation as *really functioning consciousness* (Toshchenko, 2003; 2005).

Comprehension of the phenomenon of metamorphoses of social consciousness in modern domestic sociological literature is carried out fairly intensely. Reflecting a trend of shifting focus from analysis of objective social realities to the study of subjectivity and subjectiveness (*Butenko I.A.* 2000), in the description of various deviations (fluctuations) in social consciousness sociologists offer such terms as *arch* (Yu.A.Levada), *situational* (L.A. Gordon), *ambivalent* (Z.M. Grishchenko), *elite* (G.K.Ashin, E.V. Okhotsky), *leveling* (N.M. Rimashevskaya) *consciousness,* etc.

Thus, the metamorphoses of social consciousness are multi-faceted and diverse, their role and impact on public life are significant. Many of them are an expression of «social diseases», a barometer of society, and an indicator of the disruptive and destructive impact of many official actions. It is the deformed kinds of social consciousness, its metamorphoses, which reflect not so much progressive, but rather a zigzag development that need to be studied and comprehended in order to assess their prevalence and influence, and to identify the conditions that prevent (or promote) their spread and reinforcement.

All these metamorphoses have laid a foundation, created a framework, which has led to the emergence of one of the most striking phenomena of the transition period — paradoxicality of social consciousness. It is the result and direct expression of instability and inconsistency of changes occurring in Russia, the consequence of disrupted rhythm and specificity of the life style, which has clearly registered in popular consciousness. Both the theoretical and applied analysis of real social consciousness make it possible to reveal metamorphoses that reflect its contradictions, which become a reality during the turmoil of the transformation of Russian society, and help discover causes and ways of abating destructive processes and deformations in social and private life. This phenomenon — still ingrained in people's consciousness — might explain the unusual and specific situation that has arisen in contemporary Russia, enrich theoretical and applied interpretation of the essence of social consciousness and, moreover, contribute to the development of social science.

References

Abalkin L.I. *Smena tysyatsheletyi i sotsial'nye alternativy (Change of Millenia and Social Alternatives)* // Voprosy Ekonomiki. 2000. No.12. P. 29.

Afanasiev Yu.N. *Opasnaya Rossiya (Dangerous Russia).* Moscow: RGGU. 2001.

Balabanova E.S. *Andeklass: ponyatie i mesto v obshchestve (Underclass: a Concept and Place in Society)* // Sotsiologhicheskiye issledovaniya. 1999. No. 12

Balabanova E.S. *Sotsial'no-ekonomicheskaya zavisimost' i sotsialniy parasitism: strateghii negativnoy orientatstii (Social Economic Dependence and Social Parasitism: Strategies of Negative Orientation)* // Sotsiologhicheskiye issledovaniya. 1999. No. 4.

Belen'kiy V.Kh. *Sotsial'nye illyuzii: opyt analiza (Social Illusions: an Analysis)* // Sotsiologhicheskiye issledovaniya. 2001. No. 5 .

Bloch M. *Apologiya istoriyi, ili remeslo istorika (An Apologia of History, or Craft of Historian).* Moscow, 1986.

Bauman Z. *Individualizing society.* Moscow, 2005.

Bogoyavlenskiy D.D. *Rossiyskie samoubiystva I rossiyskie reformi (Russian Suicide and Russian Reforms).* Moscow: Kanon+. 2006.

Bushchik V.V. *Sotsial'naya baza podderzhki sotsialnykh preobrazovaniyi (Social Base for Supporting Social Transformations).* Moscow: Mir. 2002.

Butenko I.A. *Postmodernism kak real'nost', dannaya nam v oshchushcheniyakh (Postmodernism as Reality Given to Us in Feelings)* // Sotsiologhicheskiye issledovaniya. 2000. No. 4.

Butenko A.P. *Istoricheskoye zabeganiye kak novatsiya XX veka (Historical Running Forward as an Innovation of XX Century)* // Sotsiologhicheskiye issledovaniya. 1999. No. 6;

Cohen S. *Issledovanie Rossii — bez Rossii (Studying Russia — without Russia) //* Swobodnaya mysl. 1998. No 9–12. P. 24.

Ermakov Ju.A. *Manipulyatsiya lichnost'ju: smysl, priemy, posledstviya. (Manipulating a Person: Reasons, Methods, Consequences).* Ekaterinburg, 1995.

Glaz'ev S. Yu. *Vstupaja v XXI vek (Entering the XXI century) //* Zavtra. 2000. October 31.

Golovakha E.I., Panina N.V. *Potentsial protesta ukrainskogo obshchestva (Protest Potential in Ukrainian Society) //* Sotsiologhicheskiye issledovaniya. 2003. No. 10

Gorshkov M.K (ed.). *Russkoie obshchestvo v usloviyakh transformatsii (sotsiologhicheskij analiz) (Russian Society in Conditions of a Transformation (a Sociological Analysis).* Moscow: Nauka. 2006.

Kara-Murza S.G. *Manipulyatsiya soznaniyem (Manipulating the Consciousness).* Moscow, 2000.

Kinsburskiy A.V. *Sotsial'noye nedovol'stvo i potentsial protesta (Social Discontent and Protest Potential) //* Sotsiologhicheskiye issledovaniya. 1998. No. 10.

Kudryavtsev V.N. *Svoboda slova (Freedom of Speech).* Moscow: Nauka. 2006.

Krivosheev V.V. *Kriminalisatsiya obshchestva: sushchnost' prozessa, rossiyskaya spetsifika (Criminalization of Society: Essence of Process, Russian Specifics).* Kaliningrad: KGU. 2005.

Levada Yu. *Ot mneniy k ponimaniyu. Sotsiologhicheskiye ocherki (From Opinions to Understanding. Sociological Sketches) 1993–2000.* Moscow: VCIOM. 2000.

Levashov V.K. *Sotsiopoliticheskie strateghii razvitia Rossii (Sociopolitical Strategies of Russia's Development) //* Sotsiologhicheskiye issledovaniya. 2008. No. 7

Lisovskiy V.T. *Dinamika sotsialnykh izmeneniy (opyt sravnitelnykh sotsiologhicheskih izmeneniyi rossiiskoy molodezhi) (Dynamics of Social Changes (a Study of Comparative Sociological Changes of Russian Youth) //* Sotsiologhicheskiye issledovaniya. 1998. No. 5.

Marginal'nost v sovremennoy Rossii (Marginality in Contemporary Russia). Moscow, 2001.

Mitev P.E., Ivanova V.A., Shubkin V.V. Yadov V.A. *Katastrofitsheskoye soznanie v Bolgarii i Rossii (Catastrophic Consciousness in Bulgaria and Russia).* Moscow: Nauka. 2005.

Monitoring obshchestvennogo mnenija. Ekonomicheskiye i sotsialnye peremeny (Monitoring of Public Opinion. Economic and Social Changes). 2007. No. 3.

Nazarov M.M. *Sotsial'naya spravedlivost': sovremenyi rossiyskiy kontekst (Social Justice: a Modern Russian Context) //* Sotsiologhicheskyie issledovaniya. 1999. No. 11.

Neterpimost' v Rossii. Starye i novye fobii (Intolerance in Russia. Old and New phobias). Moscow, 1999.

Orlova I.B. *Samoubiystvo — yavleniye sotsial'noye (Suicide — a Social Phenomenon).* Moscow: Mir. 2006.

Osipov G.V. *Sotsiologiya i sotsialnie mifi (Sociology and social myths).* Moscow: Norma. 2006.

Petrenko V.F., Mitina O.V. *Psikhosemantichesky' analiz dinamiki obshchestvennogo soznaniya (A Psycho-Semantic Analysis of the Dynamics of Social Consciousness).* Moscow: MGU. 1997.

Pokrovskiy N.E. *Rossiyskoye obshchestvo v kontekste amerikanizatsii (printsipial'naja skhema) (Russian Society in Context of Americanization (a Basic Outline)* // Sotsiologhicheskiye issledovaniya. 2000. No. 6.

Popova I.M. *Povsednevnye ideologhii. Kak oni zhivut, meniayutsya i iztshezayut (The Daily Ideologies. How do They Live, Vary and Disappear).* Kiev: Unipress. 2000.

Popova I.P. *Marginal'nost. Sotsiologhicheskiy analiz (Marginality. A Sociological Analysis).* Moscow: MGSU. 1996.

Rossia na rubezhe vekov (Russia on the Boundary of the Centuries). Moscow, 2006.

Rutchkin B.A. *Molodezh i stanovleniye nowoy Rossii (Youth and Formation of New Russia).* Moscow: MosGU. 2004.

Ryvkina R.V. *Tenevizatsiya rossiyskogo obshchestva: prichiny i sledstviya (Shadowing of Russian Society: Causes and Effects).* Moscow: Kanon+. 2005.

Shabanova M. *Sotsiologhia svobody: Transformiruyushcheesya obshchestvo (Sociology of Freedom: A Transforming Society).* Moscow: Nauka. 2000.

Sikevich Z.V. «*Obraz*» *proshlogo i nastoyashchego v simvolitsheskom soznanii Rossian. («Image» of Past and Present in the Symbolical Consciousness of Russians)* // Sotsiologhicheskie issledovaniya. 2007. No. 9.

Sotsial'naya mifologhiya i problemy sovremennogo sotsial'nogo myshleniya (Social Mythology and Problems of Modern Social Thinking). Moscow, 1999.

Solzhenitsin A.I. *Krakh Rossii (Russia in collapse).* Moscow, 1998.

Sztompka P. *Sotsial'nye izmenenia kak travma (Social Changes as a Trauma)* // Sotsiologhicheskiye issledovaniya. 2001. No. 1.

Toshchenko Zh.T. *Sotsiologhiya zhizni kak kontseptsiya issledovaniya sotsial'noy real'nosti (Sociology of Life as a Concept of the Research of Social Reality)* // Sotsiologhicheskaya Encyclopediya. Vol. 2. Moscow: Mysl. 2003.

Toshchenko Zh.T. *Sotsiologhiya (Sociology).* Moscow: UNITY-DANA. 2005.

Toshchenko Zh.T. *Vzaimodeistviye rabotshikh i upravlentsheskogo personala (Interaction of Workers and Administrative Personnel)* // Nauka, politika, predprinimatel'stvo (Science, Politics, Business). 1999. No. 1-2.

Vavilina N.D. *Bednost' v Rossii kak sotsial'noye yavleniye i sotsial'naya problema (Poverty in Russia as Social Phenomenon and Social Problem).* Novosibirsk: Nauka. 2000.

Chapter 3. Paradoxes of social consciousness: question of essence

> They say, the truth in the end will triumph, but that's a lie.
>
> *A.P. Chekhov* (1860–1904),
> Russian writer

Full-scale analysis of contemporary social consciousness is impossible to carry out without considering a special group of contradictions — paradoxes, a number of which grows immeasurably under the conditions of drastic changes in society that comes to experience a critical stage in its functioning and development. History repeatedly demonstrates that during social upheavals, revolutions and critical events paradoxicality of consciousness and behavior becomes intensified beyond all expectations, above any usual measure. And it is not surprising. Social and individual consciousness cannot be changed right away, by pushing a reset button, immediately following unfolding events. Mankind is not capable of escaping from itself, from past experiences, prior knowledge, from what it professed, what it was guided by, what it wanted to achieve and to avoid.

Under these conditions social consciousness is exposed to a powerful influence of new public needs, changing social, economic and political priorities. This change/ replacement of public purposes causes confusion in popular moods and orientations, as well as reassessment of previously professed ideals or, at least, their radical modification.

At the same time, due to substantial inertia of social consciousness, it continues to retain old dogmas, established orientations and preferences, its previous, although deformed value system. Therefore, it is quite logical that social consciousness under the impact of external and internal factors experiences fundamental changes, a product of which is the paradoxicality of thinking, cognition and evaluations of phenomena and processes that surround an individual. Hence, paradoxes of social consciousness are not inherent only to the present stage of historical development — science and practice had encountered them already at the previous stages of their existence.

3.1. Genesis of ideas: a brief historical overview

Before proceeding to the sociological interpretation of the essence of paradoxes, to revealing the causes for their emergence and prevalence, forms of their manifestation, let us review some conclusions and results gained by philosophical thought at the previous stages of development of scientific knowledge.

Paradoxes always existed in the life of humanity. They personified a certain class of contradictions, assuming special forms, kinds and features of their manifestation at various stages of historical development.

For the first time attention to paradoxes had been drawn in Ancient Greece when they were used to indicate contradictions in arguments that defied formal logical correctness. Their interpretation is similar to the concept of *«aporia»* (*Greek* aporia — difficulty, bewilderment). It essentially denotes intractable contradictions arising from breach of logic during arguments. An aporia quite often characterizes a contradiction between the observation (experience, research) data and its mental analysis. Classical examples of aporia are paradoxes of Zeno of Elea (about 490–430 BC) in his reasoning about Achilles and a turtle. Their essence is as follows: Achilles pursuing a turtle, moving ten times faster than that turtle never catches up to it, for at the moment, when he reaches the spot where the turtle was, it would have moved ahead 1/10th of that distance, and when Achilles passes this 1/10th, the turtle is already ahead by 1/100th, etc.

The specificity of this paradox lies in the fact that the two processes are identified and considered coincident — physical movement and logical sequence of its components. Identification of what took place with what did not take place breeds an obvious contradiction, and while logically impeccable, its flaw lies in the illegitimacy of applying mathematics to natural phenomena (1).

Phenomenon of paradoxes drew a lot of attention in the eastern social thought. Elaborating on Confucianism ideas, his followers in the sixth century B.C. formulated the problems of paradoxes in a document, known as *Ten Discourses of a Paradoxical Man*. It analyzed problems of the relationship between Good and Evil, between Heaven and Earth, contradictions that arise in person's daily life.

A significant contribution to understanding the nature of paradoxes was made by the studies of the phenomenon of *ataraxia* (from *Greek* ataraxia — absence of excitement, or equanimity). This term, introduced by Epicurus (341–270 BC), means an ideal emotional state that a person should aspire to. Epicurus interpreted ataraxia as deliverance from fear of the Gods, death and the next world, as self-withdrawal from public and civil affairs. This state can be achieved by restricting consumption, by moderating pleasures, regularity of life and activities. But this very appeal to rejecting excitement, equanimity in regard to misfortunes and difficulties in life was in constant contrast with the real situation of an individual in society, resulting in various conflicts, including those that were very hard to resolve. Only in exceptional cases, individuals managed to observe this principle of consciousness and behavior. And for the majority of those practicing ataraxia, this state often resulted in a situation when reality forced them to violate the proclaimed principle, act in a way dictated by circumstances, or enter into inextricable conflict with these circumstances.

History of mankind always attested to the tragic dilemma of a person's opposition to involvement in public life and attempts to disengage from it. Virtually no one managed to achieve the state of ataraxia, but that aspiration caused many conflicts manifested both in real and imaginary paradoxes.

Medieval philosophical thought began to comprehend *antinomy* (from *Greek* antinomia — a law contradicting itself, contradiction within a law), designating a connection between two opposite statements in the course of argumentation, when each of them can be equally justified. It should be noted that the concept of «antinomy» originally had a legal meaning, reflecting a contradiction between two laws, or within a single law. The Code of Justinien (535) provides for a case where a law contradicts itself, and this contradiction is termed antinomy. The first mention of this term is found in the 1613 «Philosophical dictionary» by R.Goclenius.

However, *the notion of antinomy assumed philosophical meaning only starting with I. Kant* (1724–1804). According to Kant, contradictions inevitably emerge in our minds because a concept of the absolute, infinite is applicable only to the world of things in themselves (thesis), it is used to describe the world of experience, where only transitory, finite and conditional (antithesis) is present. He had formulated four antinomies: 1. The world has a beginning in time and is limited in space. — The world has no beginning in time and is infinite in space. 2. Any complex substance (thing) consists of simple parts. — Not a single thing consists of simple parts. 3. The laws of nature are not enough to explain all phenomena. — Everything in the world can be explained only by natural laws. 4. An undoubtedly necessary essence, as its cause, is inherent to the world. — Neither in this world, nor outside of this world is there an absolutely necessary essence as its cause.

All these statements are demonstrable and indemonstrable to the same extent. These contradictions, according to Kant, appeared only because human mind had the courage to embark on a study of things existing in themselves («Ding in sich»). But since each of these provisions is equally substantiated, Kant concluded that capabilities of a human mind are limited and it is incapable of penetrating into the essence of things.

Kant's antinomies had a considerable impact on the development of science, since they helped refine logical foundations of mathematics in the 19th century, on one hand, and led to emergence of Hegelian dialectic, on the other. G. Cantor (1845-1918), on the basis of set theory, has attempted to overcome well-known difficulties in the foundations of mathematics after the discovery of differential and integral calculus by I. Newton (1643–1727) and G. Leibniz (1646–1716).

By that time the great crises in the foundations of mathematics were unraveling, caused by the discoveries of irrational numbers and infinitesimal. Cantor himself, however, found a number of paradoxes in his own theory, which led him to mathematical logic (2). Later, the paradox of set of all normal sets, discovered in 1902 by Bertrand Russell (1872–1970), has shown that both positive and negative answers are equally demonstrable. It was the discovery by G.Cantor in 1893 and by B.Russell in 1902 of a series of paradoxes, related to actualization of infinite sets that caused the third great crisis of mathematics, which continues to this day (Arnold. 1999. P. 556).

The whole galaxy of outstanding mathematicians and philosophers (Gilber, Brouwer and others) have devoted their research and their entire lives to solving *paradoxes of set theory.* However, if we delve into the essence of the problem, as professor A.A. Zenkin writes, the paradox of actualization of infinite sets is nothing but an attempt of interpreting the famous paradox of a «liar», authored by the Greek sage Eubulides (IV century BC): «I affirm that I am a liar. Am I a liar? If I am a liar, I lie when I say that I am, therefore I am not a liar. But if I am not a liar, I am telling the truth when I say that I am a liar, therefore, I am a liar».

As evidenced by historical science, cumulative intelligence of humanity, including, naturally, science, for more than 2600 years has failed to find an answer to this «childish» question: «What am I after all, a liar or not a liar?». Briefly and symbolically this argument can be mathematically depicted as (here L=LIAR): IF «L», THEN «not − L», but IF «not − L», THEN «L» (Zenkin, 2000b, p. 448).

Considering this class of contradictions, we need to point out the fact that these paradoxes, analyzed by scientific thought, describe contradictions in reasoning and logical conclusions. Clarification and substantiation of the accuracy of opinions, remarks and suggestions, along with the ways of eliminating these contradictions is required as well. These set-theoretical paradoxes can no longer be refuted by simple referencing to the facts of reality or by attributing them to the category of scholastic philosophical constructs unrelated to science.

In 1926 English mathematician and logician F. Ramsay proposed the first (and the most widespread) classification of paradoxes, dividing them into two groups: *logical paradoxes* (Russell's paradox, paradox of Cantor) and *semantic paradoxes.*

Semantic paradoxes formed a special group of paradoxes only at the beginning of the 20th century, when theory of cognition was confronted with the necessity to explain and interpret a new class of contradictions. A semantic paradox in modern language sounds something like this: «A regimental barber shaves those, and only those soldiers and officers of his regiment, which do not shave themselves. Should he shave himself?» This statement is true if we assume its falsity, but this, in turn, implies that it is false. I.e., this statement, if formulated with appropriate clarifications, cannot be considered a statement at all (each statement, by definition, is either true, or false). In other words, an answer to this question turns out to be both true and false at the same time.

Semantic paradoxes are also based on the fact that many words have different meanings, and in each separate case, only the analysis of semantic relations makes it possible to reject irrelevant ones. In everyday speech we frequently ignore some of the relevant accuracy requirements, which can lead to a paradox. For example, the following statements are considered to be true: «Every person is mortal» (i.e. can die) and «every person can only die once». But the word «person» can mean both living and dead, leading to a paradox: it is recognized as true that (a person) Napoleon is dead. Hence, he cannot die, so he is immortal, which contradicts the first of the above statements. Solution to this paradox is achieved by clarifying the meaning of the word «person» in first of these statements: every person, who is not already dead, is mortal. Therefore, the subject of tracing semantic links and «incidental» meanings of words should be included into development issues within the foundations of mathematics, for both this one, as well as the rest of the paradoxes discussed above are related to the basis of set theory.

The distinction between logical and semantic paradoxes is rather arbitrary, since many paradoxes can be formulated both with the use of semantic terms («true», «false», «designates» etc.) and without them.

Non-stereotypical, unusual, «un-cliché-like» statements, which eventually turn into popular «winged» expressions, can be categorized as a special type of paradoxes. For example, everyone knows the definition of traditional philosophy as «no man's land between science and religion», defined by B. Russell in his «History of Western Philosophy». In his 1922 Conway memorial lecture «Free Thought and Official Propaganda» he clarifies the definition of philosophy as a reflection of such things, precise knowledge and understanding of which is so far impossible (Russell, Russian ed. 1999). Consistent application of the conclusions of his philosophy of logical analysis led logical positivism to the denial of traditional philosophy, although Russell himself did not go as far as his followers, for he had a much clearer sense of reality, as well as aversion to all kinds of dogmatic philosophy. In this respect he was alone among his followers and colleagues, remaining a strongly pronounced non-conformist.

Problems of paradoxicality have gradually become a subject of analysis of other sciences. We shall not enumerate paradoxes found in other areas of scientific knowledge, we shall consider, however, how the discovery of paradox phenomenon and opportunity to prevent and resolve paradoxes in modern scientific knowledge contribute to the theory of cognition.

With regard to clarification of theoretical knowledge, here (with the help of the phenomenon of paradoxicality), a concept *of substantiation* is elucidated. The paradox of a «pile»: one grain cannot make a pile — is also attributed too

Eubulides. If *x* amount of grains cannot make a pile, then it cannot be formed by *x + 1* neither. However, empirical evidence proves that such situation is feasible, and, under certain stipulated conditions, a pile nevertheless appears. It is the requirement of accuracy (which in daily life is quite often ignored) that strengthens the arguments if favor of substantiation of this definition. Justification of this evidence helps overcome an apparent contradiction (paradox), but only subject to observance of certain logic and methods of verification of the facts.

Experience of eliminating and resolving paradoxes shows that a universal method of overcoming them does not exist. There are some achievements in mathematics and logic (theory of types, distinction between languages of differing levels). There is also some historical experience of resolving such contradictions connected with the fate of certain nations, practice of solving legal, moral and religious problems, which indicates an ability of in-depth (including latent) knowledge to uncover the essence of a phenomenon or a process and formulate ways of addressing emerging paradoxes. However, none of the ways of resolving these contradictions, including mathematical methods, can claim complete relevance, comparability and consistency with the real process. Moreover, none of these formalized methods of analysis and resolution of uncovered contradictions can claim general acceptance or uniqueness. Because of that, the role of qualitative methods, which are gaining increasing importance in resolving paradoxicality problems, is becoming more essential.

In other words, paradoxes — or rather, knowledge of them — were and are, basically, a reflection of contradictions in the process of cognition, for they are practically not correlated with the world of experience, had not been studied and analyzed in relation to reality, social life, process of human activity at all stages of historical development.

3.2. *Essence and content of paradoxes*

Establishment of non-contradictory, consistent concepts and theories is the most important task of science. In order to achieve this requirement, it is necessary to find an answer to the question of essence and content of paradoxes, reasons for their emergence and ways of their existence in the process of cognitive and transformative human activities. In this interpretation of the problem, we face, on the one hand, the need to use the knowledge about paradoxes accumulated by philosophical science, on the other — to recognize limitations of existing knowledge, complexity (and sometimes even impossibility) of its application in social reality. Therefore, in our opinion, in addition to F. Ramsey's classification, which is mainly confined to theory of cognition, it is necessary to define yet another class of paradoxes, namely, paradoxes of life — paradoxes of vital circumstances, paradoxes of consciousness and behavior of social groups and individuals (3).

However, it is obvious that this classification does not reflect the richness of manifestations of paradoxes in real life. The fact is this classification focuses: first, on difficulties and contradictions that surface in epistemology, in theory and logic of cognition; second, on those situations arising in interrelations between man and society, between man and social groups and between people. This classification virtually does not address the group of paradoxes inherent in a human being as an individual.

It is therefore appropriate to consider paradoxes both according to their levels and spheres of social organization. They can characterize a situation in society as a whole, in its certain regions, industrial and other entities, in life of separate social groups and individual people. Analysis of paradoxes that characterize basic and non-basic human activities — economic, political, social, cultural, spiritual, etc. is of equal importance. Paradoxes arise in the course of interaction between man and nature, man and economy, man and politics as well.

If we were to analyze not all paradoxes in general, but only those related to consciousness and behavior, we would have to point out the following: specificity of sociological approach to this phenomenon lies in the fact that this approach corresponds not so much with theory and logic of cognition, not with conclusions, but with real life, with process of functioning of social structures, as well as human activity. Analysis of the real situation in Russia shows that paradoxicality became an integral part of modern life.

Paradoxicality of consciousness and behavior is constantly demonstrated by the fact that both public institutions, as well as many individuals proclaim or declare certain goals and orientations, when in reality, implementing other, sometimes directly opposite guidelines. Paradoxicality of behavior is particularly evident in specific life situations, when practical actions contradict publicly and verbally proclaimed opinions.

Presently, we more and more often encounter a new class of paradoxes, when people not maliciously, subconsciously, personify the most surprising phenomenon — one and the same person, at the very same time internalizes, incorporates opposite, sometimes mutually exclusive evaluations, attitudes, guidelines and intentions. It is as though a person is running away from himself and from society at the same time in opposite directions. Our disoriented contemporary, frequently, unwittingly, professes opposing truths, and surprisingly, tends to trust mutually exclusive opinions and judgments, sincerely relying on them, quite often unaware of this blatant discrepancy.

At the same time, such conflicts, where various strategies of behavior might be appropriate, are possible as well, although contradicting each other, but able to claim autonomous, independent existence in real life. Like Kant's antinomies, real patterns of behavior can at the same time be both demonstrable and not demonstrable.

Latent forms of paradoxes can also be observed in such specific form of manifestation of consciousness and behavior as *anomie*. Anomie is a state of an individual, when the significance of all social norms and regulations is lost. Moreover, this loss could signify a tragedy leading to abnormal, wrongful conduct, including acts against oneself (suicide). State of anomie also indicates the lack of norms, standards of behavior for comparing individual's own conduct with the actions of others, which leads to the state of uncertainty and de-socialization, reducing the sense of solidarity with a particular social group. And finally, anomie means a discrepancy between universal goals and expectations formally proclaimed by a given society and socially acceptable, sanctioned means of their application. Unattainability of these goals, results in a state of extreme contradiction, paradox, inability of individual consciousness to internalize, comprehend and accept such situation in society, prompting people to resort to illegal ways of achieving them.

It is this very state of anomie that results in such paradoxical situations, when in society that proclaimed the creation of prerequisites and conditions for rational development and functioning of individuals and social relations, simultaneously, a sense of helplessness, isolation, emptiness, futility of life, apathy is born, that, in turn may result in deviant or extremist behavior.

Under such circumstances, various forms of paradoxes are possible, when a person mistakes his sense of entitlement for reality, confuses necessary with accidental, desirable with mandatory etc. etc. E. Durkheim, who introduced the term «anomie» in sociology to explain such contradictions that constantly arise in society, emphasized its characterization as a phase of preparation for changes in society, since an individual cannot endlessly suffer and tolerate unsatisfactory conditions, without devising plans (often spontaneous) to change this existing situation.

At present there are many approaches to the interpretation of «paradox» phenomenon. Due to their diversity, paradoxes feature various depth and scale of their manifestation, and consequently can be systematized (classified) on different basis. First, we should mention *the classification of paradoxes associated with certain types of activities*: economic (Zaslavskaya. 2003; Makarov. 2003), political (Beck. 2003; Eisenstadt. 1999, Elbert. 1991; Gorshkov 2004; Khalipov. 2004); social (Alexander. 1997; Kudryavtzev. 2004; Urry. 2000), spiritual (Alexander. 2003; Men'. 2003; Schluchter. 1996) (according to the spheres of social life). Some paradoxes in various spheres of Russian society are evaluated by *V.Barulin, Yu.Levada, V. Tomalinzev, Zh. Toshchenko* and others (4).

Further, paradoxes can be analyzed *within the framework of* the spheres *of scientific knowledge* that are subject to analysis: in mathematics, physics, history, logic, philosophy etc. (Alexander. 1997; Dutton. 1997; Goryunov. 1997, Luhmann. 1981; Owen. 2000; Polanyi. 1966).

Analysis of the subjects of paradoxicality acquires great importance for social science – studying society in general, *classes* (Maximov. 2005), *social groups* (Smith and Berg. 1997), *communities* (Mnatzakanian. 2004)*; and individuals* (Bauman. 2001; Nicolson. 1959); as well as social institutes (family, religion) (Mchedlov. 2004; Solodovnikov. 2003) and social organizations (production associations, political parties, voluntary communities) (Boykov. 2004; Inglehart. 2003) etc. We need to emphasize manifestations of paradoxicality related to the activities of regional or local autarchy, where interests of a certain territory or settlement are opposed to the interests of the country and other similar territorially-spatial structures (Robertson. 1995, Tzvetkova. 2002).

Furthermore, paradoxes can be classified *in accordance with the most pressing, burning issues* (affecting the entire society) and, consequently, analyzed in connection with the existence of such controversial phenomena, as elite, centrism, place and role of intellectuals in modern society, etc. (Ritzer. 2004; Smith., Johnston. 2002; Sokolov. 2005; Krishtanovskaya. 2000). At the same time, paradoxes of consciousness and behavior of people are diverse, affecting various aspects of their lives, and manifested in a number of different ways, depending on specific circumstances, or in reference to certain problems.

There are some studies of paradoxes in management and organizations done by C.Button and P.Dourish (1996); R.Farson (1997), S.Lewis (1995), C.Veney and S.Adamson (1997). And at last, there are some random *cases (incidents) of paradoxicality,* which often are derivatives and/or elements of more significant social paradoxes (R.Braungart, M.Braungart. 1997; Kozlova. 2005; Lapaeva. 1998; Popova. 2000).

From viewpoint of the role of paradoxes in regulating social life, it is possible to classify them as *creative, constructive* and *destructive;* information that enables us to devise means of resolving emerging social problems. With this approach, it is important to determine whether this paradoxicality is supported consciously and deliberately, promising considerable benefits and significant dividends to its proponents, or if it develops spontaneously. The so-called *hidden (latent) paradoxes,* are of certain interest; their formation can be foretold, if the consequences of the decisions are thoroughly and carefully analyzed, as, for example, in the case of deliberations over destinies, ways and methods of implementing policies and practices of land tenure and property ownership in Russia.

However, it is worth noting the difficulty of classifying the «hybrids» of theoretical extravagances and social practice, that gave birth to such phrases as «people's capitalism», «ethnic socialism» or «ethnic capitalism», «oligarchic democracy», «sovereign» or «managed» democracy, etc.

Sociological approach to paradoxes reveals their manifestations in real life, in the process of implementation of various types of activity, for paradox is inherent not only in the process of cognition, but also in reality itself. In fact, careful analysis of history will inevitably lead us to the conclusion that paradoxicality of consciousness and behavior had been inherent in the human beings at all stages of social development. But this paradoxicality becomes especially vivid, sharp and dimensional in societies with unsustainable development, those in a state of instability, amorphy, and uncertainty of (over) the direction of historical process. Under these circumstances, paradoxes of consciousness and behavior become massive, all-encompassing, generating bizarre combinations of good and evil, honor and malice, loyalty and betrayal, reckless innovation and stubborn traditionalism.

Summing up the above, we can say that the term «paradox» means:

a) *a strange opinion, deviating from generally accepted ones or a statement, contradicting (sometimes only at first glance) common sense.* Such situation is widespread, covering a considerable range of phenomena — from delusions to new, pioneering ideas that quite often are met with hostility;

b) *a phenomenon that seems improbable* (or an improbable, extraordinary case). A sufficiently wide range of real processes and phenomena falls under this interpretation — from unidentified flying objects to situations where a manufacturer considers it unprofitable to plant cotton, buckwheat or to cultivate gardens (or pay taxes) under seemingly benevolent official economic and social policies;

c) a *process*, where its implementation (or the achievement of its goals), leads to a result, *directly opposite to previously stated objectives, or, at least is significantly qualitatively different from the original plans or intentions.*

Thus, analysis of actual functioning consciousness and behavior uncovers a special class of phenomena — paradoxes, which should be regarded as a specific form of contradictions, requiring a thorough identification of the cause-and-effect relations between mutually exclusive attitudes and popular orientations. The fact that paradoxes are characteristic not only of society, state, social groups or organizations, is of particular importance; it is significant not just for understanding of the relationship between material and ideal, but for the consciousness of the very individual, where mutually exclusive motives and values coexist. This could be simply disregarded, had these phenomena not gained such a massive scale. Moreover, paradoxicality of consciousness tends to increase. How can this be explained?

3.3. Causes of paradoxical consciousness

There are obvious and latent causes for the broad spread of paradoxes.

The initial fundamental cause of paradoxical consciousness and behavior is the fact that Russian society is not monolithic and uniform — it includes a lot of the former, soviet, as well as some new, market characteristics. This potent combination of old rooted, accumulated and persistent combined with new attitudes creates (must create) extremely strange combinations, metamorphoses, contradictions and paradoxes. Ignoring these major phenomena of public consciousness and behavior, which are of strategic importance for understanding the developments in Russian society, has and will result in those failures, costs, zigzags, miscalculations and inconsistencies that are so characteristic of social sciences, as well as social practice, resulting in the collapse of many projects and programs offered to contemporary Russian society. And the prospect of building the future based on questionable assumptions and illusions is no less disastrous than attempting to persistently and stubbornly adhere to old dogmas, outdated theories and doubtful concepts. Both case scenarios lead to social crisis, resulting in changing lifestyle and way of life, radical alteration of pre-existing value system, loss of former ideals, obscurity or absence of the new ones. As a result, emergence and existence of paradoxes is accompanied by revival of the processes that were previously latent and undeveloped, and which, in modern conditions, designate a new level of contradictions in social consciousness.

Emergence of paradoxes is influenced by *frustration* − the situation of inability to satisfy a significant human need, to implement a motivation or reach a desired goal, which result in stress, tension, feeling of hopelessness and despair. This inability, in its essence, is a break between motivations for activity and its results, which is accompanied by appearance of paradoxes, emerging on the verge between former values and recognition of impossibility of their former existence, on the brink of confrontation between former cultural foundations and re-emerging ones, due to the destruction and loss of pre-existing, not only political, but also civic ideals and a lack of new ones. To no lesser degree, violation of continuity in the development, reckless and premature experiments, little or no consideration or even complete disregard of the influence of mentality, customs and traditions, affects the emergence of paradoxes in consciousness and behavior.

It should be especially emphasized that the overarching crisis of social consciousness in today's society is multifaceted, diverse, as indicated by a rapid increase in its paradoxicality: social consciousness in the conditions of social upheaval cannot be changed at once, immediately, following the events. Mankind is incapable of escaping from itself, from its prior experiences, from what it had known and professed what it had been guided by and wanted to achieve, and what it would not want to repeat.

An important precondition and cause of paradoxicality are those objective contradictions that emerge during the process of cognizing and implementation of its findings and conclusions, regardless of the will and consciousness of an individual or groups of people. This is what the researchers, involved in the studies of logic of cognition, pay attention to in the first place. Thus, A.A. Zenkin gives following example: «One great scientist discovers a completely abstract formula

$E=m2c$, another great scientist discovers a new chemical element, U-238, the third, a talented engineer, invents the technology for enriching uranium and makes a nuclear bomb, the fourth, a politician, makes a decision to use this nuclear bomb the for «the highest and most humane» purposes, fifth, a pilot, delivers this «baby» to the destination and does what he was ordered to do. The consequences of such «humanitarian gift» are to this day felt and not forgotten. Who is to blame? This is a question to which there is no answer. So, one of the greatest factors of industrial progress — the principle of division of labor for the sake of increased efficiency «for the benefit of ...» as its consequence, initially has an effect of division of responsibility, and then — split of conscience and morality»(Zenkin A., 2000a, p.45-48). Is this global historical situation not a fertile ground for emergence of paradoxes, where every single act by itself is legitimate and competent, but the result of their joint consecutive actions leads to unforeseen and unacceptable consequences for humanity?

The situations, which T. Kuhn calls *anomalies and crises of knowledge* (Kuhn T., 1975), can cause such emergence of paradoxes, where new phenomena, whose presence tends to gradually undermine the validity of existing picture of the world and its individual components, are quietly drawn into the sphere of research. As a result of this situation, the system of knowledge accumulates inexplicable data, often assuming a form of paradoxes.

A significant cause of formation of the paradoxical is also the fact, that the process of cognition as a whole and even within specific sciences has generated, first, a huge amount of various research «logics», and, second, such semantic diversity of expression of the very same essence that it resulted in difficulty of mutual understanding not only between various sciences, but also within the same science. And this process, objectively reflecting differentiation and deepening of learning experience, resulted in a situation where the creators of various branches of knowledge no longer understand each other, having their own, rather unique and specific opinions regarding particular situations. Moreover, the debate is not so much about different methods of cognition of the same essence, but exclusive correctness of the chosen approach. This kind of scientific intolerance toward the other's logic has resulted in a phenomenon alien to science, when the whole field of knowledge is declared a sphere of exclusive professional interests of a single science without the right of interference in its jurisdiction, primarily insulating and separating from philosophy, let alone related sciences. This peculiar taboo is regularly surfacing in academic life, becoming a hindrance to scholarly development, and slowing down the resolution not only of theoretical but, as it turns out, practical problems as well. In an article by the academy member V.I. Arnold it is clearly illustrated, based on the example of attitude toward G. Cantor's theory, when its absolutization led to «left-hemispheric crime» and «left-hemispheric abstractionism». In his opinion, in the middle of the twentieth century, the influential mafia of left-brained mathematicians has managed to exclude geometry from mathematical education (first in France, then in other countries), replacing the whole substance of this discipline with training in formal manipulations of abstract concepts. This «abstract» description of mathematics is not suitable for either training, or for any practical applications, and moreover, breeds «modern abhorrence of society and government towards mathematics» (Arnold, 2000, P. 555–558). This is characteristic of not only mathematics. Based on the material regarding the development of relativity theory (analyses of its history is still the subject of numerous discussions) V.S. Stepin ascertains the mechanism of emergence and resolution of paradoxes in this field of knowledge (Alexander, 1997; Stepin, 2000).

Such situations to some extent are common to all sciences. This is quite a natural process of development of scientific knowledge, which helps comprehend and resolve many abnormal paradoxical situations. The key question is not if paradoxes exist, but how to approach their solution.

The contradiction between theory and facts is contributing, in no small measure, to the emergence of paradoxes. According to M.Polanyi, there is no «logical bridge» between them, since «in every act of consciousness there is a passionate contribution of a cognizing person, and this addition is not an evidence of imperfection, but an essential element of knowledge» (Polanyi. 1966, P.19). The theory of implicit knowledge formulated by M. Polanyi, largely explains the emergence of paradoxes and contradictions between two types of knowledge: fundamental or obvious, explicit and peripheral, latent, implicit (Lektorskiy. 1998, p.41).

Main obstacle to overcoming these contradictions is the fact that in explicating paradoxes, one of the concepts becomes dominant, claiming exclusivity, the absolute knowledge of truth, rejecting all other possible versions. Something similar happened with Marxism in the Soviet Union, which led to numerous paradoxical situations both in theory and practice.

As previously stated, probability of emergence of paradoxicality increases immeasurably during revolutionary, transformational changes in society, which are typically accompanies by crisis processes. Under these conditions, pre-existing paradoxes are modified, transformed and give rise to a new form (guise) of this social phenomenon. In a transforming society, we witness the development of such processes as violation of clear, well-defined correlation of values and orientations to the social structure of society, growing influence of «pressure groups» on functioning of social consciousness, inadequate response of society and power structures to the ongoing changes; we face the necessity to redefine, clarify interpretations of the false, catastrophic, protest, mythologized and «sick» consciousness, role and place of myths, stereotypes and archetypes in social life.

When analyzing paradoxes, we should emphasize not only the fact that their common characteristic is divergent and/or contradictory and conflicting views, opinions, statements, attitudes and orientations, but also the fact that they coexist, combine and function in the consciousness of one and the same person. This paradoxicality is also amplified because the modern «world demands an involvement of a person in a constantly growing variety of social structures, which results in tremendous psychological overloads, as well as stresses, destroying his health. Volume of information, stress loads, carcinogens, contaminated environment, accumulation of harmful mutations — all these are the problems of modern reality, its daily realities» (Stepin, p. 32). Sociological studies have revealed paradoxes primarily in those spheres of public life that have undergone significant deformations and changes and that influence daily lives of people, their mood and well-being. Currently, the search for answers to the question — who is responsible, who is to blame for such disappointing (for the majority of population) social changes, is particularly relevant for the Russian people.

Analysis of the essence, content and features of paradoxes and their place in social consciousness and behavior leads us to the following conclusion. Sociological study of paradoxes is one of the most productive sources of knowledge of real contradictions in consciousness and behavior, effective means of obtaining more complete and extensive information on the processes occurring in society. Study of paradoxes helps avoid one-sidedness, exaggeration of the significance of some phenomena while ignoring others, warns against unconditional (absolute) reliance on limited data. Refusal to oppose, match one information against the other, based on the principle «true — false», «right — wrong», «necessary — incidental» acquires particular importance in the study of paradoxes. Only a comprehensive, integrated, systematic study of a phenomenon or a process can lead to scientifically validated conclusions and recommendations, as far as practical solution to social problems concerned.

Such methodological requirement, where the assessment of a person's knowledge about his environment is compared to the forecast of his probable behavior in the ongoing processes, becomes extremely relevant in the study of paradoxes. Taking into account just one of these components yields incomplete, unbalanced conclusions and possible errors, leads to inadequate reflection of reality, wrong orientation and even misinformation of social consciousness.

Research of paradoxes of consciousness and behavior is inevitably associated with the study of the measure of person's readiness to take risks, endure a possibility of discomfort in his life, his attitude to the anticipated costs and sacrifices. And if the degree of this readiness is insignificant, then, at a critical stage of development of the country, popular desire to avoid social cataclysms, sacrifices by any means possible, is clearly manifested. Under these circumstances, the most «ferocious» verbal statements and declarations are meaningless, since they might reflect short-term, fleeting and situational human sentiments, quickly fading under the pressure of possible serious social consequences.

In my opinion, an important point in understanding the nature of paradoxes is individual's self-evaluation, especially in a situation when a choice has to be made. «Experiments show — writes M.A. Rozov — that this choice presumes self-assessment, not an assessment of activities of other people, but precisely the assessment of oneself, one's own behavior. This might seem odd: a man is surrounded by a huge number of behavior patterns, a huge quantity of «scenarios», he must choose the best one, and, therefore, only these «scenarios» need to be analyzed, and not the others... Evaluation of the others does not change the behavior of the one evaluating: his behavior is only changed by self-evaluation» (*Teoriya poznanija.* Moscow, 1995. P.16)

At turning-points in history, the increase in numbers of formally logical paradoxes is possible, when external inconsistency of mutually excluding motives, attitudes and goals conceals deep contradictions that often belong to another sphere of human activity and are mediated by another group of interests, which sometimes, for whatever reasons, move into the forefront.

It is these paradoxical phenomena that have to be analyzed, since, in our opinion, ultimately, the root cause of all tensions, conflicts, misunderstandings and struggles is often concealed in consciousness and behavior of a man himself. And the more a man can influence other people, destinies of society or a particular social organization, the more significant are the social consequences of his actions and the greater is his responsibility. «The man shall heal thyself « — this biblical wisdom, in our opinion, is as relevant as ever for solving not only personal but social problems that originate deep inside individual's consciousness and behavior.

In sum, we can conclude that as a real manifestation of contradictions in social consciousness and behavior, paradox has following characteristics.

First, paradox is reflected in contradictory process of cognition, when existing arguments regarding a particular process or phenomenon prove in equal measure both truth or falsity of certain assumption. In other words, when available knowledge (information) does not permit to draw unequivocal conclusions and to obtain indisputable findings. This possibility of obtaining not simply different, but mutually exclusive results is the basis (base) for continued existence of already present, as well as emerging paradoxes. Another variant of paradoxes, emerging in the process of cognition, is ambiguity (variance) of interpretation of a specific concept, which can be overcome through reconciliation (harmonization) of meanings of certain definitions.

Second, paradoxes of consciousness and behavior are generated by contradictions of life experience, when real practice demonstrates not only the possibility of existence of mutually exclusive values and attitudes of individual people and separate social groups, but cultivation of this contradiction, resulting in conflicting statements, actions and deeds.

Third, paradox is manifested in a situation where the actual process and the perception (knowledge) of that process are identified, equated, which most commonly occurs in the course of transforming social activities. This identification of reality with knowledge (of this reality) often leads to intractable contradictions, when the process of cognition can generally (approximately) reflect reality, and sometimes only one-sidedly, thus failing to correspond to practice, which on this basis, rejects not only this particular information, but all scientific knowledge as well.

Fourth, absolutization of prior knowledge leads to emergence, appearance of paradoxical situations, when changed life circumstances dictate different logic and program of social behavior. It is especially clearly manifested in socio-political activity, when the achievement of political party's objectives, partially or entirely rejected by prior experience, becomes a paradox.

Fifth, paradoxes are generated by the situational nature of activities of the subjects of economic, political, social or spiritual process, when decision-making and actions of their «creators» is guided by limited information sources, does not account for all the data in its entire entirety, disregarding contradictory knowledge.

And *finally,* paradoxes are manifested in the case where most diverse actions that by themselves (alone) are rational, but brought together in a system, display not just simple inconsistency, but absolute contrasting incompatibility with each other.

Thus, in most cases, paradoxes are the divergent, contradictory, and even conflicting views, opinions, statements, attitudes, orientations, actions, which simultaneously exist, merge and function in consciousness and behavior of the same person.

Notes

1. For more details, cf.: *Filosofskaya entsiklopediya (Philosophical encyclopedia).* Vol. 4, Moscow, 1967. P. 207–208;

2. Speaking about role and value of sets theory by G. Cantor and the paradoxes formulated by him, it is necessary to point out, that in scientific literature some critical voices appeared (academician V.I. Arnol'd, prof. A.A. Zenkin), questioning his discovery, naming it «a flagrantly naive argumentation», where in «10 lines of the proof there are 7 (seven!) very significant logical mistakes», which are «bound in an inconceivable tangle of almost plausible arguments». In our opinion, such severe criticisms of one of the foundations of modern mathematics

might be explained by the nature of thorny roads to knowledge, complexity of methods of solving arising issues, and also by attempts to absolutize and even to idolize some of the possible methods of cognizing the world around us. (For more detail: Arnol'd V.I. *Antinauchnaja revoliutsiya i matematika (Anti-scientific revolution and mathematics)* // Vestnik RAN, 1999 No. 6; Zenkin A.A. *Oshibka Georga Kantora (A mistake of Georg Cantor)* // Voprosy filosofii, 2000. No. 2.

3. Scholars, especially psychologists, turned their attention to this phenomenon rather recently, but they also analyze this problem in the context of solving other research problems. Cf.: Vasiljuk F.E. *Psihologiya perezhivaniya (Psychology of the excitement).* Moscow, 1984; Abolin L.M. *Psihologicheskie mekhanizmy emotsional'noy ustoychivosti cheloveka (Psychological mechanisms of emotional stability of a person).* Kazan, 1987; Ageev V.S. *Mezhgruppovoe vzaimodeystvie (Intergroup interaction).* Moscow, 1990; Kitaev-Smyk L.A. *Psikhologiya stressa (Psychology of stress).* Moscow, 1983; Grimak L.P. *Obshchenie s soboy (Communicating with oneself).* Moscow, 1991.

4. About paradoxes of public life and public consciousness, see: Barulin V.S. *Rossiysky tshelovek v XX veke. Poteri i obreteniya (Russian individual in XX century. Losses and findings).*, 2000; Castels M. *Informatsionnya epokha: ekonomika, obshchestvo i kul'tura (Information era: economy, society and culture)* / Transl. from English, O.I. Shkaratan ed. Moscow, 2000; Levada Yu. *Ot mneniy k ponimaniyu: sotsiologicheskiye ocherki (From opinions to understanding: sociological sketches).* 1993-2000. Moscow; Tomalinzev V.I. *Tshelovek na rubezhe tysiatsheletiy. Paradoksy dukhovnogo pazvitiya (A person on the boundary of millennia. Paradoxes of spiritual development).* St. Petersburg, 1999 etc. Also: http://www.google.com «Paradoxalniy chelovek» (Paradoxical Man)»

References

Alexander J.C. *The Paradoxes of Civil Society* // *International Sociology.* 1997. Vol.12. No. 2. P. 115–133.

Alexander J. *The Meaning of Social Life: a Cultural Sociology.* Oxford — New York: Oxford University press. 2003.

Arnol'd V.I. *Antinauchnaja revoliutsiya i matematika (Anti-scientific revolution and mathematics)* // Vestnik RAN (Bulletin of Russian Academy of Sciences). 1999. No. 6.

Bauman Z. *Community: Seeking Safety in an Unsure World.* Cambridge: Policy Press, 2001.

Beck U. *Power in the Global Age.* Cambridge: Policy Press, 2005.

Boikov V.E. *Sotziologiya vlasti (Sociology of power).* Moscow: Academy of Administration, 2004.

Bortolini M. *Necessary Immunity: Talkott Parson and Sociology of Modernity.* Rome, 2005 (in Italian).

Braungart R. G., Braungart M. M. *At century's end: Globalization, paradoxes and a new political agenda // Journal of Political and Military Sociology.* 1997.

Button C. and Dourish P. *Technomethodology: Paradoxes and Possibilities,* In: *Proc. CHI '96.* ACM Press, New York, NY, 19-26.

Crow G. *Sociology's Paradoxes* www. Sociology.ed.ac.uk/seminars 2004–05_1.html.

Dutton W. H. ed. *Information and communication technologies: visions and realities.* Oxford, 1996. Oxford University Press.

Eisenstadt S.N. *Paradoxes of Democracy: Fragility, Continuity and Change.* The Jones Hopkins University Press, 1999.

Elbert M.M. *Man of the Crowd //* Modern Language Studies. Vol. 21. No 4. Autumn 1991. P. 16–30.

Farson R. *Management of the Absurd: Paradoxes in Leadership.* NY: Free Press. 1997.

Filosofskaya entsiklopediya (Philosophical encyclopedia). 1976 Vol. 4. P. 211.

Gannon M.J. Paradoxes of Culture and Globalization. California State University, 2007.

Gorshkov M.K. *Russia in Transition.* M.: Nauka. 2004.

Goryunov V.P. *Philosofiya nauki I techniki (Philosophy of Science and technology).* Moscow: Mir. 1997.

The Idea of Autonomous Sociology: Reflections on the State of the Discipline // Current Sociology. 2006. Vol. 54. No1. *Special issue.*

Inglehart R. *Human Values and Social change. Findings from the Values Surveys.* Leiden, 2003.

Khalipov V.F. *Entsiklopediya vlasti (Encyclopedia of Power).* Moscow: Academia. 2004.

Kozlova N.N. *Sovetskie lyudiy (Soviet people).* Moscow: Europe. 2005.

Krishtanovskaya O.V. *Rossiyskaya elita (Russian elite).* Moscow: Institute of Sociology. 2000.

Kuhn T. *Struktura nauchnykh revoliutsiy (Structure of scientific revolutions).* Moscow. 1975.

Kudryavtzev V.N. *Nravi obshchestva perechodnogo perioda (Moral in transformational society).* Moscow: Nauka. 2003.

Lapaeva V.V. *Rossiyskaya soziologiya prava (Russian sociology of law).* Moscow. Academia. 2005.

Lektorskiy V.A. *Theory of Cognition.* Moscow: Nauka. 1998.

Lewis St. *Paradox, Process and Persention: the Role of Organizations in Clinical practice guidelines development. //* Canadian Medical Association Journal, 1995. No 153. P. 1073–1077.

Luhmann N. *Observation on Modernity.* Stanford, California: Stanford University Press. 1998.

Luhmann N. *The Paradox of Decision Making.* Ed. by D.Seidl and K.Y.Decker // Niklas Luhmann and Organization Studies. Copenhagen and Malmo: CBS Press and Li. 2005.

Makarov D. W*hat the Market Does to People: Privatization, Globalization and Pov*erty. London: Zed Book. 2003.

Maximov B.I. *Rabochie v reformiruemoy Rossiye 1990–2000 (Workers in modern Russia).* St. Petersburg: Nauka. 2005.

Mchedlov M.P. *Religovedcheskiye ocherki (Essays of religion).* Moscow: Encyclopedia. 2004.

Men A. *Mirovaya duchovnaya kultura (World spiritual culture).* Moscow: Svoboda. 2001.

Mnatzakanyan D.M. *Kultura. Ekonomika. Naziyi (Culture. Economy. Nations).* Moscow: MGIMO University. 2004.

Nicolson M.H. *Mountain Gloom and Mountain Glory: The Development of the Aesthetics of the Infinitive.* London: Victoria Web. *1959*

Owen T. *Genetic-Social Science and the Study of Human Biotechnology* // Current Sociology. 2006. Vol. 54 No 6. P. 827–850.

Polanyi M. *The Tacit Demention.* Carden City. New York: Doubleday & Co. 1966.

Polanyi M. *Knowing and Being.* Chicago: The University of Chicago Press. 1989.

Popova I.M. *Povsednevnie ideologii (Everyday ideologies).* Kiev, 2000.

Ritzer G. *The Globalization of Nothing.* London — New York — New Delhi: Sage. 2004.

Robertson R. *Clocalization: Nime-Space and Homogeneity-Heterogeneity* // Global Modernities. Ed by M. Featherstone, S. Lash, R. Robertson. London. Sage. 1995.

Russell B. *The Art of Philosophizing and Other Essays.* New York. 1968.

Schluchter W. *Paradoxes of Modernity: Culture and Conduct in the Theory of Max Weber.* 1998.

Smith J., Johnston H. *Globalization and Resistance: Transnational Dimensions of Social Movements.* Lanham, MD: Rowman and Littlefield. 2002.

Smith K., Berg D. *Paradoxes of Group Life: Understanding Conflict, Paralysis and Movement in Group Dynamics.* Jorsey-Bass. 1997.

Sokolov V.B. *Intelligenziya and intellectuali (Intellgentsia and intellectuals).* St.Petersburg. 2005.

Solodnikov V.V. *Aktualnie problemi sotziologiye semyi (Actual problems of sociology of family).* Moscow University. 2003.

Stepin V.S. *Teoretitsheskoe znanie (Theoretical knowledge).* Moscow. 2000.

Teoriya poznanija (Theory of knowledge). In 4 volumes. Vol. 4. *Poznanie sotsial'noy real'nosty (Knowledge of a social reality)* / Pod red. V.A. Lektorskij and T.I. Ojzerman. Moscow, 1995.

Ten Discourses by a Paradoxical Man. Yannshoufu: Catholic Press, 1930, Vol. II.

Toshchenko Zh. *Paradoxical man.* Moscow. Gardariki. 2001.

Tzvetkova G.A. *Mestnoye samoupravlenie (Local Democracy).* Orel. University Press. 2002.

Urry J. *Sociology beyond Society: Mobilities for the Twenty-first Century.* London. Routedge. 2000.

Viney C., Adamson S. *Paradoxes of fast-track career management* // *Personnel Review.* 1997. Vol. 26. No 3. P. 174–186.

Wheen F. *Karl Marx.* New York: W.W. Norton & Company. 2000.

Zaslavskaya T.I. *Sovremennoe rossiyskoe obschestvo (Contemorary Russian Society).* Moscow, 2004.

Zenkin A.A.(a) *Oshibka Georga Kantora (A mistake of George Cantor)* // Voprosy filosofii, 2000. No 2.

Zenkin A. (b) *Nauchnaya kontrrevoliutsiya v matematike (Scientific counterrevolution in mathematics)* // Nezavisimaya gazeta. No.7 July 19, 2000.

Part II. Paradoxes in context of social knowledge and social practice

Chapter 4. Mythological consciousness as a form of paradox manifestation

> Past generations left us with more questions, than answers to those questions.
>
> *Seneca Jr.* (circa 4 century BC–65 AC)
> Roman philosopher

4.1. Multifaceted essence of myths

Myth is one of the phases in human cognition of the world around us. And, perhaps, one of the first, where humans were still incapable of differentiating themselves from Nature and did not have any comprehension of being anything other than Nature itself. During the infancy of our civilization, people could not explain various phenomena, processes, and forces of nature that completely dominated their lives. However, constantly striving and attempting to comprehend the essence of forces at work, humans started utilizing a very specific form of exploration of this surrounding world – creative mythology that personified, without exception, every aspect of their lives. Mythology embodied a distinctive idea about surrounding world ruled by higher forces – gods, spirits, incomprehensible and powerful entities.

In accordance with a famous idea of Karl Marx, regarding activities essential to the development and exploration of the world – practical, practical-spiritual and spiritual, in the process of human evolution, – we can distinguish three stages of cognition – emotional-practical, emotional-reflexive and rational-reflexive. Ancient mythological consciousness emerged at the stage of emotional-reflexive exploration and comprehension of social experience based on irrational feelings. Its essence is self-determination and life-affirmation of a value system of social community (primitive society) in a symbolic form, based on a need for «illusions» and positive emotional reflection (self-evaluation).

Myths reaffirmed adopted value system, helped sanction and support certain norms of behavior, economic and social order. Mythological world perception was expressed not only in narrative (folk tales), but also in activities (rituals, dances), as well as the lifestyle.

It should be noted that contemporary understanding of the myth is different from people's attitude toward it during various other stages of social development. In this regard, the study, conducted by researchers in an attempt to explain the essence and content of primitive myth is very telling. Stages of this research reflect successive steps of the cognition of the myth.

Myth as fiction. Myth is an arbitrary fabrication that appeared as result of ignorance and fear, lack of understanding of laws of nature. Myths dissipate, vanish under the influence of genuine knowledge. Certain Ancient Greek philosophers and writers of 17th century Renaissance period were of this opinion about the myth. Some Marxist philosophers, to some extent, shared this viewpoint as well (Bogdanov. 1923).

Epistemological explanation. Myth could have and did emerge only during the period of undivided knowledge, when there was no definite interpretation of object and subject, object and symbol, object and word, space and time, etc. It should be emphasized that knowledge was not separated from emotion, during the time when pre-logical thinking fully dominated the process of cognition. During this particular period, dominated by figurative perception of the outside world, specificity of mythological and religious consciousness remained unrecognized, mixed with fantastic interpretation of reality (Sorokin. 1997; Pivoev. 1991).

Semantic (linguistic) approach. Myth is a «disease of the tongue (language)». It emerges based on metaphors and images of ancient poetry. At first, a person is aware of figurative nature of his comparisons (e.g., «stars — eyes of heaven»), but then, for some reason, forgets about their non-literal character and gives literal meaning to rhetorical expression, resulting in turning the sky into a being, a creature with multiple eyes. This theory was introduced by the 19th century English philologist *M. Muller.* In Russia A.N. Afanasiev and A.A. Potebnia offered a similar theory with certain amendments (Deleuze. 1995. P. 11; Barth. 1996. P. 76).

Evolutionary approach. In the opinion of E. Tylor, the 19th century British ethnographer, myth is a form of social consciousness during various stages of its existence, a product of early, infant stage of individual and social development. Attempting to explain forces of nature, a savage uses available techniques, animating the world around and utilizing all aspects of his personal life to describe it. Myth, on the one hand, is identification of reality with fairy tale, on the other, with rudimentary prehistoric philosophy and religion, which is expressed in animism (Avtonomova N.S. 1988. P. 178).

Structure-Functional approach. Myth is a language of images, clearly structured and capable of reflecting knowledge about the world, no less than abstract logic (French ethnologist C. Levi-Strauss). Myth explains social reality and extends that explanation on to nature. According to Durkheim, mythological «collective notions» convey the structure of primitive society. Functionalism is a variation of this approach, rating the importance of the myth for stability of primitive communities (British-Polish ethnographer B. Malinovski) (Aberkromby, Hill, Turner. 1997. P. 172–173).

Symbolic approach. Myth is one of symbolic functions (along with science, art, religion and language), inherent in humans, when the mind is searching for complexity. Myth offers simplicity of being immediately granted. This theory is offered by a German philosopher E. Cassirer. Another theory close to that, describes the myth as «vitally experienced and created material reality» in the works of Russian philosopher *A.F. Losev.* In this approach, fantasies are interpreted as myth-like symbols, leading to creation (appearance) of archetypes (Losev. 1995. P. 33).

Ritualistic approach. Myth is a verbal script (explanation, scenario) of a ritual (British ethnographer George Frazer). This viewpoint is shared by a considerable number of contemporary researchers.

Psychoanalytic explanation. Myth is the most complete expressions of individual (Z. Freud) or collective (K. Jung) unconscious.

Post-structural approach has emerged as a reaction to the spread of structuralism. What is known as mythology emerged as a result of recording, criticism and possession of oral tradition at the dawn of written language, and then was expanded, edited and interpreted by philosophers, philologists, historians, ethnographers and folklorists. Strictly speaking, «primary myth» is inaccessible to us due to multidirectional nature of written and oral means of communication. So, we are forced to settle for the «secondary product» (Shkuratov. 1997).

Cosmological, synergistic explanation operates with notions of transforming chaos into a logically constructed order, where myth holds a specific place in the cognition of a complete picture of surrounding world, where it contributes to comprehending the origins of animal and plant world and the role of mankind in its transformation, and even anticipation of possible future changes (Popova. 1999).

There are other explanations of the concept of essence, origin and evolution of the myth. This is a question of how its perceptions have changed in the course of human development, what characteristics of its explanation became primary defining.

Analyzing the essence and the content of the myth, one should bear in mind that primitive consciousness thought of it as quite real, non-fictional, and perceived it as possible reality. In the value system of primitive man myth equates with culture, as means of preserving peace (mainly through ritual). Furthermore, mythological consciousness in primitive society is the main way of explanation and understanding of the world.

Primitive mythology, as a form of primitive worldview, included rudimentary, pre-scientific ideas of the world, humanity and various art forms, mainly verbal. That is why the task of separating mythology from the other folk art, close to it by genre and time period: fairy tales, heroic epics, fables and historical legends, – is extremely difficult. Its relationship with religion is even more complicated. At the very early stages of its development mythology was an inseparable component of religious ceremonies and an integral part of religious beliefs. Mythological representations are often a mandatory subject of religious beliefs, turning into religious dogmas. Religious ceremonies (rites), inherited from mythology became the most stable part of religion. In the words of A.F. Losev, mythology does not constitute religion, while religion is a «mythical creation», «mythology of life». If we interpret religion as self-affirmation of «an individual in the scope of eternity», Kant's question of «what can I hope for?» becomes the main question of mythology.

First rational attempts of comprehending mythology date back to ancient times. Aristotle, Olimpiodorus Jr., Evtemerus attempted to, in varying degrees, analyze the role of myth in societal and individual lives. However, these interpretations were quite peculiar and were aimed at understanding its place and influence on processes taking place in the world around them. Plato, for instance, viewed the myth as a kind of a «bridle» used by the ruling class to keep people in obedience. This pejorative interpretation survived until Middle Ages, when a myth about the second coming of Christ became widespread. This was the first attempt to revise established doctrines of Christian religion and inspire new hope for deliverance from the burdens of «this world». This myth was particularly insistently developed by dissident, schismatic and heretic movements, whose strength was largely dependent on «inbuilt» perception and its (this myth's) integration into the existing notions about Jesus Christ.

Social movements such as Renaissance, Reformation and Enlightenment were based on mythological perceptions of the world that inspired people to reassess their values and be proactive in light of these renewed ideals. Myths about the Man, Divine Intellect, who had rationally and reasonably created the universe, helped overcome countless obstacles on the way to forging a new capitalist (bourgeois) society. However, even during this period such well-known thinkers as Voltaire (1694–1776), Diderot (1713–1784), Montesquieu (1689-1755), thought (to some extent continuing the line of Plato's reasoning) that myths were meant to openly support authority of rulers, clergy, etc., and considered them to be a product of ignorance and deception.

Redefining myths and mythological consciousness began with the «New Science» by G. Vico (1668–1744), continued in R. Emerson's (1803–1882) and Friedrich Nietzsche's (1844–1990) research, and then, was subjected to scientific analysis in the works of F. Schelling (1775–1854), J. Grimm (1785–1863), E. Tylor (1832–1917), H. Spencer (1820–1903), W. Wundt (1832–1920), etc.

In Russia the subject of myth was intensively studied by ethnographers and folklorists A.N. Afanasyev (1826–1871), O.F. Miller (1833–1889), F.I. Buslaev (1818–1897) and others. Generally, thinkers of the 18th – early 20th century formed two separate branches of the elaboration of mythology theme: irrational-subjective absolute and scientific rationality (especially clearly manifested in positivism). These two dueling trends still exist in various guises and under different names.

According to A.F. Losev, «myth is a generalized reflection of reality in a form of sensory perception, or, to be more precise, in a fantastic form of various animate beings».

Myth should be distinguished from Utopia, which, according to Jean Sorel, is interpreted by theorists as an ideal model of society, as an example, a benchmark for comparison and criticism of the state of modern society. However, there is no insurmountable barrier between the two – Utopia that has become the only «true» picture of the world, turns into mythology.

Myth is extremely difficult to destroy, since it is based on hope and illusions. In primitive societies it was basically indisputable. As an example we can refer to the phenomenon of the «Voodoo Death», well-known to ethnographers. Among African slaves in Haiti, an unfortunate Taboo breaker, for which the rules called for punishment by the Spirits, would lay down on the ground and die. Cause of death here was not so much fear, but hopelessness, anticipation of inevitable retribution; similar to hypnotic stare of a snake, paralyzing his victim.

There is a different attitude towards myth in modern society. Its violation does not carry the same punishment, as was imposed in the past. However, consequences of the destruction of a myth can be truly devastating for both private and social lives of an individual. It is especially typical of *social mythology*, when social myth becomes an illusion, a dream, an ideal that has nothing (or very little) in common with real life. When fantasies capture the imagination of large social groups, not just single individuals, the consequences of rupture between real and imaginary are much more bitter and tragic. Achieving harmony within the myth often directs a person to achieve unattainable and generally questionable goals, which, nevertheless, are emotionally extremely appealing. History convinces us that attempts to achieve harmony, when based of mythology, are usually just illusions that are crushed at first contact with reality. This leads to disappointment, frustration, feeling of deception and desire to withdraw into one's own suffering and emotions, or, rarely – to actively fight against them.

In this regard mythological dream is not to be confused with an ideal, ideal goal that are based in reality and are grounded in actual practice, which implies utilizing real means of achieving this goal, and helps foresee possibilities of negative consequences. Myth, on the other hand, is based on public gullibility and illusions that has positive connotation. This once again emphasizes the fact that irrationality is a defining component of the myth.

Analyzing modern interpretations of mythology and corresponding mythological consciousness, we immediately notice very significant differences from even recent concepts, which reduced the myth to «fabrication», «false illusion», or considered it to be a phenomenon exclusive to the 20th century, a particular kind of spiritual activity aimed at creation, dissemination and support of political illusions intentionally fabricated by ruling elite in order to manipulate the masses (Osipov. 2002; Gurevich. 1983).

Mythological consciousness is a specific form of social consciousness. It dominated social consciousness of primitive society. But it still exists at the present stage of human development. For modern men, myth is a story, a compilation of ideas surreally depicting reality. However it is not a literary genre, but definite representation of the world that often appears as means of narration or acquires characteristics of specific notions.

Indeed, if ancient mythology and mythological consciousness are characterized by naive humanizing of forces of nature, assigning human qualities, ascribing human feelings to natural objects, in modern mythology, generally, explanation of the essence of an object and the world is narrowed down to specific forms of the search for answers about their origins and existence. Therefore, ancient man's intellect appears to be emotional-irrational and affective. G. Vico compared this underdeveloped form of mentality to juvenile physiology. Modern phenomenon of the myth is much more complex and contradictory since the scope of themes, plots and topics covered by myths, — questions of origin of the universe, human race, cultural achievements, social structure, mysteries of birth and death, etc. — affects a wide, «global» range of fundamental, universal questions. That is why, presently, myth is more of a specific form of ideological vision that calls for certain type of activity, rather than a sum or system of «naïve» tales of ancient people.

Analysis of essential aspects of modern mythological consciousness suggests that it includes: encoded attribute of core societal values; symbolic, metaphysical expression of eternal social and socio-physiological conditions; expression of universal structures of human intellect through the logic of myth (*Bolshoi tolkovyi sotsiologhicheskiy slovar (Collins).* 1999. Vol. 1. P. 427). Accordingly, the functions of myths are: justifying, glorifying, reassuring, and, in some cases — manipulating ideas, notions of the forms and methods of cognition and functioning of social reality.

4.2. Fundamental characteristics of mythological consciousness

There are following principal characteristics of mythological consciousness:

First, mythological consciousness paints an illusory-hopeful picture of the world, which has the status of true-life reality. In this case, the faith in possibility of achieving proclaimed goals is of vital importance, while the means of achieving these goals are too often ignored, or replaced with schemes that have very little to do with reality. This particular manifestation of mythology presently forced upon society: «market economy is a necessary condition for prosperity», — is very indicative for that. Practical significance of the market in contemporary Russian society was utterly exaggerated, absolutized, even canonized, and leading to the creation of a special type of a myth: «market can do it all». Actual reality has dashed these hopes, dispelled unwarranted illusions, and has demonstrated not only capabilities, but also serious limitations of its use in the life of contemporary society.

Second, principle characteristics of mythological consciousness should include simplification, polarization and division of the world picture based on the principle of «ours» and «theirs». It is equally applicable to both ancient and contemporary mythology. This very opposition constantly feeds and supports the myth, clearly outlining boundaries of its application. Additionally, Levi-Strauss's structuralist approach to myth reveals recurring universal «binary opposites» between nature and culture, male and female, friendship and enmity.

Third, mythological consciousness has such characteristic as symbolic way of expressing ideas (ideals), objectives and certain aspirations. In this regard, V. Khodasevich's (who happens to be one of ideologists of symbolism) opinion on the subject of the role and importance of this literary and social movements, is of particular interest. «Symbolism persistently sought a genius in its midst, capable of merging life with creativity. We now know that this genius was never found, the formula — never discovered. The history of symbolists ended up turning into the history of broken lives, their creativity was never realized: part of their creative energy and inner experiences were expressed through literary works, the other part dissipated, like electricity without proper insulation» (*Filosovskaya entsiklopediya.* 1964. Vol. 3. P. 458). The myth that »the introduction of religious worship in school and in the army consolidates a nation around «universal values», forcefully implanted in Russian society since the mid 1990's, should receive a similar evaluation.

Fourth, positive self-evaluation of ongoing processes, rejection, even prohibition of critical reflection is typical for mythological consciousness. The law of mythological axiology states (reminder) that: myth does not permit critical reflection. Being within a myth (i.e., sharing directives and value orientations of mythological consciousness) one can only positively reflect, commend its postulates and dogmas. Critical reflection is only possible outside the myth, beyond its boundaries.

And, finally, mythological consciousness has powerful motivational and organizational potential, capable of mobilizing the existing social reserves (social groups, individuals) for achieving declared goals. Dreams of socialism, at one time, hopes for democracy in 1990's inspired creative, constructive forces of the nation. These ideas sustained, helped mobilize and unite the efforts of many population groups, made people's lives more meaningful. This situation, however, existed until reality undermined these hopes, destroying or diminishing motivational aspirations (Zobov, Kelasyev. 1995. P. 22; Shenkao, Maleeva, Shenkao. 2006).

The irrational component deserves special attention, since it represents one of the most significant characteristics of mythology and the basis for emerging paradoxes, when «myth-making» is compared with reality. Moreover, in our opinion, the very paradox that exists between real life and myth contributes to deeper understanding not only of mythology, but creation in general. But it is especially important to grasp this point, to fully comprehend how a contradiction is conceived in human consciousness and behavior when a person is professing a myth.

Ethnographers and ethnologists have long discovered that as far as the primitive man was concerned, he was incapable of distinguishing contradictions in his consciousness and behavior, which gave rise to multiple paradoxes. But, if in ancient times this inability was due to the primitive level of thinking and superficial knowledge of the essence of things, how can we explain the fact that the modern man does not notice (does not see) the paradoxical nature of his own mythological consciousness and behavior?

Modern mythological consciousness (impressions, images, and feelings) and its expression through specific symbol systems — the myths, undoubtedly have its own particular characteristics. Among them, we need to note their rational components that provide stability, viability, and make them difficult to oppose form the standpoint of scientific knowledge. We should point out that in modern world abstract concepts are sometimes replaced with specific images or characters (including symbolic); that social mythology (in its own way) continues the efforts to systematize historical reality without reaching conceptual level; that modern mythology, loosing some functions, retains others and even gains new ones, which, like the past ones, act as a regulator of consciousness and behavior.

4.3. *Types of paradoxes of mythological consciousness*

When analyzing the essence of mythological consciousness as the base for paradoxical consciousness, we need to emphasize the fact that this consciousness is not metaphysical, it is real, vital, but unscientific; although scientific aspects are present in modern myths in one form or another.

Analyzing paradoxes we have to wonder if mythological consciousness can be attributed to each and every person. In our opinion, the answer is «yes», but the degree and the depth of it varies considerably in individuals, as well as from one social group to another.

So, *what types of paradoxes are created by mythological consciousness?*

First, mythological consciousness breeds illusions, helping provide refuge from complex collisions of modern world. It has a clear tendency to not «untangle» delusions, «scatter» hopes, but, on the contrary, to complicate them, multiply and strengthen, often turning them (according to Plato) into a «bridle» that helps ruling class keep people in check. And the more people believe in these illusions, the bitterer their disappointment can be. When the illusion of «we are the masters of our destiny» became a thing of the past, it was substituted by another — that «new capitalism» is capable of providing a normal life and desirable lifestyle. Eroded by reality, suffering constant blows from fate (in the form of loosing one's old ideals, lack of social protection, a number of thefts — seizing their personal assets, etc.), illusions either increased, or pulled back, but the same faith (we need something to believe in!) always returned. Perhaps, humans cannot do without illusions, since reality becomes far too bleak, somber and hopeless. People need faith, sometimes fairy tales, in order not to be left alone facing dark and mysterious destructive forces. They, despite boorish behavior of the government, at times loosing faith in it, cursing it, in the final analysis, ultimately, paradoxically, hand over their savings, once again believing in its promises, still hoping for the best.

Second, mythological consciousness often appears as a surrogate of the truth that emerges due to lack of availability or complete absence of information, implementation of purposeful manipulation of public opinion. A significant role in this process is played by substitution of information, perpetrated, «produced and narrated» to serve the interests of one or the other political or economic group. In Russian society the notion that Russia continues to play a leading role in world politics, that it retains its influence, and, therefore, claims the position of power to be reckoned with is vigorously promoted. It is obvious that this approach is a deferred solution, which will become apparent when a chain of defeats and concessions reduce Russia to a regional power at best.

Third, mythological consciousness can generate mass psychosis, based on collective experiences and «cross-contamination». Irony of this situation lies in the fact that not just single individuals, but hundreds and thousands of people are «infected». They start believing in «miracles», opportunities to get rich, change their destinies, possibility of «luck» in the form of most unexpected «gifts» of fate. Psychosis related to financial pyramids scheme (MMM, «Vlastilina», etc.), which ruthlessly exploited the «freebies» mentality and the «greed effect» inherent in many people, is especially revealing. The paradox of this situation lies in the fact that despite the obviousness of deception, expert evidence, tens of thousands of people continue to believe in get-rich-quick schemes, possibility of striking it rich, «winning» without any effort, hoping for a magic carpet ride.

Evidently, the reason for this is, on the one hand, the «you-owe-me» type of attitude toward the government, embedded in people's psyche during the past 70 years; backlash against the same government for robbing people blind: «if authorities can, why can't I?» on the other. This explains staying power of schemers that lure people into gambling, speculating on their desire to get something for nothing. This happens despite regular warnings, information and explanations of the nature of this deception.

Fourth, paradox of mythological consciousness is manifested in its coexistence, interweaving with and use of such phenomenon as mysticism and its means such as fortune-telling, astrological predictions and occultism. Since mythology is, to a large degree, based on irrational parts of people's consciousness, this irrationality is manifested through different versions of mysticism, belief in ability to foresee future changes by means of occult, not scientific knowledge. So far 15% of the population still believe in possibility of existence of supernatural forces that affect theirs lives, the lives of other people and society as a whole. This fact is confirmed by the flourishing of various forms of non-scientific knowledge that openly oppose all rational methods of cognition, offering very questionable, but effective forms and methods of manipulating mass consciousness.

Fifth, paradoxical nature of mythological consciousness occasionally produces a fairy tale, «pink» or sweet dreams, weakening constructive and creative force of men, replacing them with a hope for a miracle, for some good luck. These hopes for a possible self-resolution (especially under grave or unforeseen circumstances) make people passive, inert participants in ongoing developments, disarm them in the face of potential negative processes, even when active resistance is feasible.

Sixth, mythological consciousness is sometimes a product of the «scarecrow» effect. Paradoxical nature of this situation lies in inadequacy of people's reaction (often a result of irrational fear, expectations of invisible social dangers and enemies, fear of loosing one's savings and stability) to the reality that indeed exists or is expected. Paradoxically, for a lot of people, their consciousness is still effected by scare tactics like GULAG, 1937, Beria, *«Judicial Troikas»* and the possibility of their resurrection. This «bogeyman of fear» is alive and well, still influencing and exploiting people's consciousness and behavior. As a rule, during reelection campaigns, politicians are constantly searching for new pseudo-myths, new means of influencing social consciousness and preserving existing ochlocratic-oligarchic system.

And, finally, mythological consciousness can manifest itself in one other paradoxical variation — tragedy of the myth that collapses, burying all values and orientations that people regard as support and foundation of their prosperity and stability in the modern world. The myth of the free market, which will rescue, bring wealth and prosperity, provide everything necessary for human well-being, in reality, for many, turned into a tragedy, into ruin they could not foresee. This mythological consciousness that rejects critical reflection, recognizing only positive aspects of free market, from a multitude of information selected exclusively only those facts that supported such hopes and illusions while ignoring everything that questioned its promise of salvation. Bitter disappointment in market expectations that were never fulfilled led to the collapse of many aspirations. During the early years of free market relations up to 30-35% of people polled by the ALL-Union, and then ALL-Russian surveys have stated that they would have liked to start their own business. Only 8–10% managed to accomplish that. During the second half of 1990's, this number fell to 14-16%, while only 4-6% actually attempted to start a business, and a lot of those who tried, admitted their failure (Mramornov. 1999; Chepurenko. 2004).

Table 4.1.

Degree of readiness to engage in business

(% of interviewed. N = 1870)

Level	1992	1996	2001	2006
Already engaged	12,6	7,5	5,7	5,9
Willing and able	12,1	3,0	3,0	2,8
Willing, but no start-up capital	38,3	19,7	21,3	17,1
Want to, but cannot due to specifics of character or education	4,8	11,1	14,5	23,2
Want to, but unable due to health and age	–	16,4	17,1	12,3
Do not want to — it contradicts their beliefs	32,2	27,2	34,2	36,1
Do not want to, but are forced to due to threat of unemployment	–	4,1	4,4	2,6

Source: Data from Institute of Sociology, Russian Academy of Sciences

Disillusionment in the myth — «the market is all-powerful», «it can fix everything» leads to loss of faith in own abilities, to rejection of intense constructive, creative work, turns people into «enemies» of market economy, at times pushes them to extremes, even suicide.

4.4. Correlation between mythology and ideology.

History knows many examples when mythology was used for ideological purposes by certain political forces. German fascism, for example, sought not only to revive and utilize ancient German pagan mythology, but created its own original myths — the racial myth, merged with the cult of Fuhrer, rituals of mass gatherings, etc.

Analysis of contemporary problems of social development indicates that ideology often replaces myth in today's society. As a reminder, the term «ideology» was introduced by a French philosopher and economist Al.K. Destutt de Tracy in 1801 to denote the doctrine of ideas, allowing to establish a solid foundation for politics, ethics, etc. According to Marx, ideology is a phenomenon of social consciousness that follows general laws of its development. It constitutes distorted or inadequate reflection of social reality, expressing specific interests of a particular social group or identifying itself with interests of the entire society.

As far as scientific interpretation of this phenomenon is concerned, in the 20th century, Jean Sorel, K. Jung, V. Pareto, in their theories, viewed ideology as social mythology, practically equating these two phenomena as invariants of social fiction. Analysis of real historical process demonstrates that ideological illusions are not just a random error: ideology fulfills specific social functions, reflecting interests of a specific social group, which is manifested in ways of thinking and types of behavior, as well as programs of social action. In other words, ideology is very close to mythology in its intended purpose. But it is this very different qualitative definiteness of mythology and ideology, their varying interpretations that generate paradoxical situations.

In this connection, we have to point out, that ideology is always based on some sort of true, «higher» knowledge, which its carriers allegedly possess. The same applies to myth that is typically built on a legend of some great, brave and holy hero, or a sacred totem ancestor. But if «higher» knowledge constantly rediscovers its own relativity, myths demonstrate remarkable lasting stability of constructs (perceptions) and relevance in the organization of people's lives.

In the 20th century the very theoretical conceptions of ideology became an arena of intense ideological struggle. Opinions on the matter are polarized. Some ideologues proclaim irrational, mythological character of any ideology, along with fundamental denial of its scientific nature, which, understandably, makes it absolutely identical to mythology based on its qualitative characteristics. But paradox lies in the fact that ideology often contains contemptuous assessments of other ideological views, while myths rather tolerantly coexist with similar and even opposing ideas and stereotypes.

Others view the purpose of ideology as truly rational, aimed at maintaining an existing order and declared system of values. The same goal is inherent in mythology, which, through myth and ritual, preserves and supports certain order and rules of conduct as traditions within its community.

Thus, we are witnessing the transformation of mythology into ideology, especially at the present stage of historical development, as well as the loss of significance of the myth in its original form and its preservation only in literature and art in a form of a specific genre. In modern social systems, social and political functions of mythology, namely: establishment and preservation of certain systems of values and maintenance of public order, — are increasingly adopted by ideology. However, this situation does not exclude the fact that, while in essence denying mythology, ideology (therein lies a colossal paradox) assumes and successfully exploits modern myths: «Slavic unity», «community», «Russia — the chosen one», which can only distort the consciousness, complicate its functioning and erect new obstacles on the road to social development.

This is why every era is characterized by its own unique approach to the interpretation of myths. But these interpretations are always based on man's definitively organized perceptions of the world, moral values and norms of behavior in that world. In other words, we are talking about the emergence of unlimited number of interpretations of myths, in accordance with the rules of their derivation from a limited amount of basic mythological layouts, as well as rethinking of already existing mythological plots in accordance with modern realities. N.I. Soboleva has convincingly demonstrated that in her analysis of the pattern of changes, occurring at the turn of the century is the mythological layer of social consciousness in all of the post-soviet states, in her case — the Ukraine.

Followed by the collapse of Soviet ideology, accompanying mythology was destroyed as well, although the latter, due to its archetypal nature, is far more tenacious than theoretical dogmas. Thus, the myth of «bright communist future» became an anachronism; «His Majesty the working class» was toppled from its pedestal.

At the same time, a number of myths have demonstrated their vitality, transforming in accordance with changing socio-economic, political and cultural realities. Flag-waving myths still have certain attractiveness for a considerable group of the population, to a lesser extent, however, than during Soviet times. The myths about the sacredness of state authority, the myth of «leaderism», a group of «uniformity» myths, based on simple sentiments such as — «everyone is capable of everything» and «how am I worth than others?» sustained serious damage, but are still functional.

Such myths (as well as realities), as the one about bureaucratic omnipotence of officialdom that made people fear every, even minor, government employee; blind faith in the power of official papers and regulations; myth of «inferiority of common people», according to which we are condemned to historical «defectiveness,» doomed to the backyard of civilization; struggle with the difficulties of our own creation («wanted to do better, turned out as usual»); the myth of «universal harmony», originating from a vulgar notion of the social harmony ideal, — have undergone practically no correction.

Simultaneously, the modern mythology is emerging. Among the new myths are: free market is necessary for our well-being; selling land into private hands will solve the problem of food shortage; initial equality is provided by voucher issuance to the population; introduction of religious practices in educational institutions and the army consolidates our nation around «common values», etc. (Paramonova. 1997; Volkov, 2004; Kozhinov. 2006).

However, anchored in social consciousness, paradoxically, these myths tend to slow down social change, not permitting the echoes of ongoing transformations to crystallize into new myths. On top of that, the absence of universally accepted constructive goals that help consolidate society adversely effects the situation. These days there is a number of promising national, statehood ideas that might potentially produce some positive myths and help them mature. However, none of these ideas are capable of fully assuming the function of the nucleus, the core of the new social ideology and mythology in the foreseeable future.

All this suggests that modern post-Soviet social consciousness is actively re-mythologizing. At the heart of this process lies practical functioning consciousness. This consciousness can never be completely rid of formations, mythological in their origin, yet, it is capable of providing them with a fertile ground. If at times mythology surrendered its leadership role to a number of specialized forms of social consciousness, it is experiencing a renaissance at the turn of the third millennium — however, not as a system of world explanation, but as a mosaic method of thinking (Zaslavskaya. 2004; *Rossiyskoe obshchestvo I radikal'nie..*, 2001).

References

Aberkromby, N., Hill S., Turner B.S. *Sotsiologhicheskiy slovar' (Sociological Dictionary)*. Tr. from English. Kazan', 1997. P. 172–173.

Avtonomova N.S. *Rasuudok. Razum. Ratsional'nost' (Mind. Intellect. Rationality)*. Moscow, 1988. P. 178.

Bart R. *Mifologhii (Mythologies)*. Tr. from French. Moscow, 1996. P.76.

Bogdanov A.A. *Nauka ob obshestvennom soznanii. Kratkiy kurs ideologhichesckoi nauki I (Science of Social Consciousness. A Short Course of Ideological Science)*. Moscow, 1923.

Bolshoi tolkovyi sotsiologhicheskiy slovar (Collins) (Sociological Dictionary). Moscow, 1999. Vol. 1. P. 427.

Chepurenko A.Yu. *Osobennosti economicheskogo soznaniya rossiyan (Specfics of Ecomomic Consciousness of Russians)* // *Ismenyaushchausya Rossia v zerkale sotsiologhii.* Moscow, 2004.

Deleuze J. *Loghika smysla (Logic of Meaning).* Moscow, 1995. P. 11.

Filosovskaya entsiklopediya v 5 tomah (Encyclopedia of Philosophy). Moscow, 1964. Vol. 3. P. 458.

Gurevich P.S. *Sotsialnaya mifologhiya (Social Mythology).* Moscow, 1983.

Kozhinov V. *Grekh I svyatost' russkoy istorii (Sin and Sanctity of Russian History).* Moscow, 2006.

Losev A.F. *Problema simvola i realisticheskoe iskusstvo (Problem of Symvol and Realistic Art).* Moscow, 1995.

Mifologhiya:Bolshoi entsiklopedicheskiy slovar' (Mythology: Grand Encyclopedic dictionary) // Pod red. E.M. Meletinskiy. Moscow, 1998; Mifologhicheskiy slovar'. Minsk, 1989.

Mifologhiya (Mythology) // Saratov, 1994. Vol. 2.

Mramornov O. *Rastoptannaya lira, obernuvshayasya gorodom myortvikh (Crushed Lyre, Turned into a City of Dead)* // Nezavisimaya gazeta. 1999. February 11.

Osipov G.V. *Sotsiologhiya i sotsial'noe mifotvorchestvo (Sociology and Production of Myths).* Moscow, 2002.

Paramonova S.P. *Dialektika moralnogo soznaniya (Dialectics of Moral Consciousness).* Perm, 1997.

Pivoev V.M. *Mifologhichesckoe soznanie kak sposob osvoeniya mira (Mythological Consciousness as a Way to Mastering World).* Petrozavodsck, 1991.

Popova I.M. *Predstavleniya o nastoyashchem, proshedshem i budushchem kak perezhivanie sotsialnogo vremeni (Images of Past, Present and Future as Experience of Social Time)* // Sotsiologhicheskiye issledovaniya. 1999. No 10.

Rossiyskoe obshchestvo I radikal'nie reformi (Russian Society and Radical Reforms). Pod red.V.K.Levashova. Moscow, 2001.

Shenkao G.H., Maleeva M.A., Shenkao M.F. *Mif kak fenomen sotsial'noy zhizni I kul'tury (Myth as Phenomenon of Social Life and Culture).* Cherkesk, 2006.

Shkuratov A.A. *Istoricheskaya psikhologhiya (Historical Psychology).* Moscow, 1997.

Sorokin P.A. *Relighia kak sotsialniy fenomen (Religion as a Social phenomenon)* // Sistema sotsiolghii. Vol.2. Moscow, 1997.

Stepnova I.A. *Sotsialnaya mifologhiya i problemi sovremennovo sotsialnogo myshleniya (Social Mythology and Problems of Modern Social Thinking).* Moscow, 1999. P. 81-83.

Volkov Yu.G., Malitskiy V.S. *Idiologiya I gumanism (Ideology and Humanism).* Moscow, 2004.

Zaslavskaya T.I. *Sovremennoe rossiyskoe obshchestvo: Sotsial'niy mechanism transformatsii (Contemporary Russian Society: Social Mechanism of Transformation).* Moscow, 2004.

Zobov S.A. Kelasyev V.N. *Mifi rossiysckogo soznaniya i puti dostizheniya obshchestvennogo soglasiya (Myths of Russian Consciousness and Ways to Social Consensus).* St Petersburg, 1995. P. 22.

Chapter 5. **Manipulation as mechanism of creating paradoxes**

> We don't believe in progress any more — is this not progress?
>
> *Jorge Luis Borges* (1899–1986)
> Argentinean author

Manipulation of social consciousness is essentially common practice in modern history, when the new era, times of great bourgeois revolution have created a fundamentally new phenomenon: each and every person now had a chance to actively participate in historical process, in changing social relations, and could become an independent subject of the socio-economic process. And if this person was capable of affecting these developments, it became possible to influence his social consciousness and behavior, to motivate him to take part in realizing certain goals, often quite distant from social needs, reflecting corporate, group and egotistic personal interests.

During transitional periods in the development of society, in the process of its destruction and revolutionary transformation, process of manipulation escalates and becomes more objective than during relative calm of its regular functioning, generating various forms of transformed consciousness. This phenomenon (namely, violation of natural process of development of social consciousness through manipulation) reflects the disruption of existing logic and essence of the entire social organism. It is during this very period that political leaders, active and advanced groups' desire to interfere with historical processes, to channel their development, to adapt them to their own purposes and «dissect» them in a way that suits their interests, grows stronger. This is the essence of the process of manipulating social consciousness and behavior. This process is characterized by deliberate influence on social consciousness, by modification, distortion of its natural logic of development, as well as disruption of social behavior.

Currently, problems of manipulating social consciousness and behavior are subject to careful analysis of many social sciences – philosophy, psychology, political science, law and sociology (Vlasov. 1982; Kara-Murza. 2000; Gadzhiev. 1992; Ermakov. 1995; Zamoshkin. 1980; Kopalov. 1985; Landemann, Sogomonov. 1971; Feofanov. 1987; Sherkovin. 1973; Hayek. 1992; Fromm. 1990; Shiller. 1980; Shostrom. 1992). Without addressing the details of research on this phenomenon by each of these sciences, we shall only discuss the sociological approach. This approach demands clear definition of indicators, which can help us evaluate occurring manipulations.

5.1. Forms and methods of manipulation

Utilizing sociological analysis in the theory of propaganda, developed by P. Lazarsfeld, we shall attempt to answer following questions: *who is the subject of manipulation, what the methods of manipulation are, who is the target*, which problems became its real *object* and what *results* are achieved by this process.

As far as the first question is concerned, *social forces,* such as political parties, pressure groups and various forms of lobbies, which manipulate people's consciousness and behavior and set the tone of political debates, are therefore the subject of manipulation. Many of them are, in essence, mouthpieces of the oligarchy, plutocratic and nationalistic circles that seized political and economic power in the country. The main methods (tools) employed by them are the media, especially television, advertising, PR-techniques, oral and printed propaganda, and rumors. In other words, manipulation is generated by corporate, group interests, which generally do not coincide not only with the state and public interests, but with the interests of «parallel», competing groups and, most importantly, with the sentiments and intentions of the people. The degree of difference between popular opinion and policies of the lobbyist groups was convincingly demonstrated by M.K. Gorshkov (Gorshkov M. 2000). According to a study conducted by the Russian Independent Institute of Social and National Problems in July 2000 (a survey of 1750 individuals in 58 cities, villages and towns, representing 11 different social groups), media turned into a instrument of political struggle. They are highly politicized, imposing their own or «ordered and paid for» points of view. In autumn 1999 and winter 2000, for example, the idea that the country is under a threat of dictatorship was actively forced upon the public. This concern, however, was shared by about 2% of the population. And how many video and print materials were aimed at convincing society of the existence of a fascist threat? Yet studies have showed that a mere 1% was concerned about it (*Izvestiya.* 2000. December 5).

In other words, we are constantly witnessing media attempts to impose viewpoints best suited to certain groups without taking into consideration an opinion of the country's citizens. Utilizing the power of mass manipulation, they try to impress an idea of »righteousness» of certain position upon their audience, instead of taking an interest in the processes, reflecting the state and trends of development of social consciousness in the country.

With regard to *forms of manipulation*, several techniques are utilized, such as informational assault, but, mainly propaganda. Let us name a few of them.

First, it is worth mentioning the «*white propaganda*», based on the principle — the one who speaks first, not the one who speaks the truth — is always right. Accordingly, manipulators are attempting to get ahead of their rivals without distorting the sources of information in principle, observing main parameters, their authorship. At the same time, this propaganda often omits large parts of available information without mentioning by whom and for what purpose it was fabricated. In this case silencing or sharing only parts of the truth, not the whole truth, and not just the truth allows for an entirely different perception of reality, very dissimilar to the one that would emerge from complete, unadulterated, non-castrated and unabridged data. Namely, pre-emptive delivery, lead in applying information and its conscious, deliberate compression allows for considerable changes, aimed at achieving desired impact on public opinion.

Recently, one of such graphic examples was information about Chechnya, or rather, about the ongoing war in the region. Many European officials and media were extremely critical of the policies of Russian authorities and of Russia's public opinion. This criticism, in general, was based on the information from real sources and reporting real facts (but not ALL the facts), assessing only limited segments, which seemed to be quite convincing, logical enough to condemn Russia's official position and public opinion.

Another form, which in relevant literature is termed «*gray propaganda*», represents one of the versions of real propaganda, when the source, the issues, the authorship, or the purpose of manipulation are deliberately distorted. In our opinion, proportion of this type of propaganda in the media is quite substantial and its application allows its authors to achieve their specified, desired goals relatively successfully, since real social consciousness in its mass manifestation is virtually incapable of sorting through the kaleidoscope of information and isolating the truth, separating it from fiction.

In late 1980's through early 2000's many ambitious politicized fractions, clans, cliques and groups, under the guise of «kitchen», «neighborhood» or «fellowship» and «Compatriot» parties tried to sell themselves to public opinion as the only saviors of the Motherland, its economy, its future. And under the slogan of searching for ways of ending the crisis (especially since the crisis became quite apparent to most people), multiple attempts have been made to convince carriers of social consciousness through all possible means and channels of information of absolute truthfulness, correctness of a new zigzag (often unpredictable) in policies of the authorities, or the next «true» way of saving Russia. We cannot state with certainty that these numerous oracles have only told lies or used deliberately distorted information. Paradox lies in the fact that social consciousness could not distinguish which information was distorted or cooked, whose interests were being represented and how reliable and realistic were the development plans proposed to society by one or the other political force. Social consciousness, unable to sort through the stream of information in order to identify these distortions, responded with gradual increase and reinforcement of mistrust, suspicion and rejection of all those who perused narrow sectional, rather than public interests.

And, finally, we have to mention one other way of manipulating social consciousness known as *«black propaganda»,* when everything without exception is distorted: the source, the content, its true masters, and their goals. This method is becoming prevalent during drastic transitions, when the information market is literally flooded by 'black» fakes. During this period practically everybody is using them — central government structures, economic monopolies and oligarchs, as well as regional authorities, etc, etc. Political parties, groups and numerous individuals with political ambitions are especially successfully utilizing these methods. Unfortunately, in this situation many scientists participate in this manipulation as well, creating made-to-order fabrications proving, in scientific terms, anything the customer wishes to prove.

Our daily life is filled with vivid examples of black propaganda. Starting with commercials trying to promote not the items that would support consumer, or benefit his health, make life more comfortable and convenient, but what is profitable for the advertiser. Nationalistic and ultra patriotic parties and movements that are furious over growing inter-racial tensions, blaming all the problems on «dark-skinned people», «Jews, masons», etc. etc. (Lyubomudrov. 2000). Federal and regional authorities, as well as multiple political parties do not shy away from black propaganda themselves. Furthermore, 'blackness» of this propaganda is increasing, first, growing proportionately to the desire of political forces to express their ambitions and aspirations, second, proportionately to their uselessness (an attempt to cover emptiness of their promises), third, as they are facing their own futility and possible collapse (in most cases they instinctively feel that they are politically or socially bankrupt), in an attempt to prevent the demise, they make most over inflated, colorful promises or intimidating predictions.

All of these methods of propaganda (there lies their essential similarity), *despite certain differences, utilize the same methods of exerting pressure on social consciousness and behavior.* Here, for example, are some methods of propaganda that were tested in many countries around the world in times of political struggles, which allow to actively pursuing policy of manipulation.

First, none of these forms of propaganda and information rejected the method of *«finding an enemy»,* «pinning» the responsibility for all calamities (past and present) on this enemy, «forewarning» about the possible future catastrophes, if the «enemy» is elected to the position of authority. The flaw of these techniques is that the opposing sides define their positions not as opponents, expressing their own ideas, their side of the objective reality, but as forces that question the very existence of the opposition. Under these circumstances, the opponent is perceived as the enemy that needs to be crushed and eliminated from the political or public arena, and, possibly, physically or emotionally destroyed. This is the way that the political struggle in Russia in 1990th can be characterized. It repeated the sad experience of a similar situation in the Soviet Union, when any original, albeit incomplete, inaccurate or unique interpretation of reality by the opposition was not recognized or accepted — dominated by a single point of view, denying and rejecting all other possible concepts and interpretations, their 'creators' were completely removed from historical arena, and, sometimes, from existence.

Second, a «tactic of «glittering uncertainty» was widely utilized by all these forms of propaganda. It is based on the premise of accompanying any sort of texts and information by phrases that are vague, but generally cause a positive reaction (Petrenko, Mitina. 1997).

Third, such method as «reference to an indisputable authority» is utilized in the presentation of all of these forms of information. Public consciousness is very easily affected by the opinions of individuals who received general recognition in sciences, arts, literature or sports and prominent celebrities. This is generally a positive phenomenon, when people really deserving of acknowledgement become arbitrators of various events. Their opinion becomes an important consideration in controversial issues, in determining the ways and means of resolving vital (especially conflict) situations. But, in this case as well, we are clearly encountering manipulations, since the celebrity of these people is often misused. Even those, who ignored or prosecuted academician A.D. Sakharov in the past are now referring to his works and quoting his opinions. An outstanding contemporary academician D.S. Likhachev was quoted left and right, whether it was appropriate or not. As far as many movie and theatrical actors and filmmakers are concerned, their opinions became less influential due to their inconsistency, frequent shifts in their personal and social positions, and swings across the entire spectrum of political likes and dislikes. But, despite this inconsistency, arbitrary use of thoughts and ideas expressed by prominent or famous contemporary figures, «joining in» with people that were previously considered unacceptable, this method is still alive and well, widely utilized in manipulating social consciousness.

The «our guy», «our pal» method of manipulating social consciousness is widely used as well. In essence, it is an attempt to convince everyone that the subject of this propaganda is just one of people, and if this person stands out in some way, it is in a way that embodies the best traditions of such historically prominent groups as nobility, Cossacks, merchants, etc., which, supposedly, always aspired to serve popular interests through their best representatives. An attempt to merge with the environment, to prove that they are similar to or identical with their audience leads to such frequently encountered phenomenon in modern politics, where the candidate (for president, governor, mayor, deputy, etc.) tells the audience what they want to hear, what reflects their needs and interests, at the same time trying to convince them that those are «his» needs, desires, wishes, interests and aspirations as well.

The growing influence of television and its specific methods of impacting the consciousness of the listeners and viewers of its «video clips» are being much wider utilized these days *the method of «convincing primitivism»* (also known as «brainwashing») is quite simple. «Just show the viewer a few similar plots (negative for instance), a catastrophe, fire, or a strike at the beginning of the program. It is all factual and true; but, subconsciously, for the viewer the mood is already set. The clip is followed by the report from the session of the congress or a meeting with Putin. In this situation, no more thinking is required; people are already pre-programmed to make the «appropriate conclusions». These days, this method of manipulation is much more widely used and applied by certain political and economic groups. It is quite effective; in fact, not a single political campaign in Russia was conducted without it. These days, when various TV channels belong to different owners, especially the ones representing opposing interests, the viewer is receiving contradictory information, which leaves him in a trance-like state, since it is impossible to sort through this twisted stream of rumors, insinuations, conjunctures and mutual allegations. As a result, the situation creates either non-critical processing, thoughtless perception of the information, or (more often) social apathy, a paradoxical state, total rejection of all and any information including truthful and objective.

The researchers of the problems of manipulating social consciousness isolated such *method as «labeling»*, which is based on the principle of contrast and association that amplifies the impact of widespread stereotypes («red-brown», «democrats-embezzlers», «voucherization of the entire country», etc.). No less effective is *the method of «bandwagon»* that encourages conformity in an individual, his desire to «be like everybody else» adopting the views, opinions and assessments without critical evaluation (Ermakov. 1995. P. 157–164).

The preponderance, pressure of propaganda and information, coupled with the use of the previously discussed, as well as other known methods have created an unforeseen effect: after several years of deceit and frustration all the data was now scrutinized or regarded as false. Furthermore, the authors and the sources of this information and propaganda, as well as the rest of their products were rejected by the public opinion.

5.2. Gambling with trust

Sociological data clearly demonstrates that the level of trust in authorities (trust not only in promises, but deeds) is dropping catastrophically. Under these circumstances, at this level of confidence in the government, in any Western European country political leaders immediately resign, giving way to other political forces. Yet in Russia, just like under the Soviet rule, authorities blame everyone else, but themselves for all the failures and misfortunes. It turns out, the whole thing is the people's fault, since they fail to understand what a wonderful future awaits them; they (the people) have to be convinced to overcome eventual difficulties, brace themselves and have more patience. Sometimes, during hard times in order to lessen the pain of the masses, authorities promise to restore order, get rid of corruption, punish corrupt bribe-taking officials, which once again «helps» cool down, sooth public opinion and hope for a possibility of a favorable outcome.

In reality, the fact that the general population mistrusts authorities does not particularly bother the authorities themselves: people ultimately want to believe in something, rely on somebody, and trust someone. In their aspiration to find some kind of support, people, paradoxically, are willing to believe the information, most outrageous, blatant, shameless and full of promises, just to realize that they once again «have been had».

This was the case with the «Democratic choice of Russia»: at first, many people trusted them, but soon became disillusioned and withdrew their trust. The same way the influence of the LDPR (Zhirinovsky's party) began declining over time, after the initial landslide victory in the first parliamentary election of 2003. Similar faith, due to different reasons, befell some other social movements like «Women of Russia», Russian Union of Industrialists and Entrepreneurs, not to mention such far-fetched political organizations as the Party of «Unity and Accord» (Shakhrai), «Socialist Party of Russia« (Rybkin), Party of Economic Freedom (Borovoi), etc.

So what is the goal (purpose) of manipulation? (Shmelev. 2000)

First of all, it is an attempt to convince people of Russia that the path chosen by its leaders in the early 1990's was not so bad. The spectrum of this manipulation is wide. Radical-democrats, for example, tried to convince people that the situation worsened due to the fact that they were prevented from completing the proposed reforms, that the full implementation of suggested measures would have done the country a lot of good. At the same time the Nobel laureate L. Klein, objecting to radical views of Gaidar's team, claims that «Russia does not need a liberal, but rather a social market transformation». He sharply criticized the methods of systemic transformation that included «shock therapy», which the «boys in short pink pants» started implementing in early 1990's.

We can list many examples of the modern day social and political movements and parties' participation in such manipulations. They all developed their own «recipes» for ending the crisis, in essence representing attempts to coerce the public opinion into compliance with the corporate and group interests, attempting to achieve the rise to power in order to partake in dividing the remains of the national pie.

5.3. Results and implications of manipulation

Long years of political manipulation of the social consciousness resulted in (and later revived) such deformed forms of its existence as disappointment, disbelief, frustration, apathy, rejection of universal values, and, in general – alienation of the people from their ideals, as well as their own selves. Extremely widespread was the most destructive expression of distortion of the principle of telling people the truth (thank goodness we had a lot of experience): it was replaced by half-truth, partial truth, truth served in a certain way, truth mixed with political demagoguery and abuse of popular trust. This is a situation different from everyday practice of deciding, when and in what case truth might be told or not. That is why comparisons with dialogue of physician with his seriously ill patient are out of place here: government cannot claim the role of doctor, and the role of seriously ill person suits people but poorly. Moreover so that with the passage of time, however desirable this is for sponsors of manipulative actions, truth all the same works its way thanks to obvious cleavage between false promises covered with bluff and those realities people are living in. Results of manipulative politics are manifestly obvious from the public opinion surveys on occasion of *Bielpovezhye* agreements of 1991 breaking down the USSR (Table 5.1.)

Table 5.1

Question: Do you approve of the agreement by Russia, Ukraine, and Belarus' dated December 8, 1991 on cessation of the Soviet Union existence

(% of the respondents)

Republic	Approval		Disapproval	
	1991	*2006*	*1991*	*2006*
Russia	67	17,6	12	71,8
Ukraine	62	48,5	19	33,5
Belarus'	69	17,6	10	63,4
Georgia	–	76,3	–	17,8
Armenia	–	31,9	–	40,2
Kazakhstan	–	43,4	–	44,6
Moldova	–	31,5	–	56,7
Kyrgyzstan	–	28,5	–	57,5

Source: International Sociological Consortium (ECCSR) data // Sotsiologhicheskiye issledovaniya. 2007. No. 4.

The data are an acute evidence for tue attitudes of people to USSR dissolution owing to the practically experienced results. Should we wonder that practically all so called democratic forces lost popular confidence?

We have to point out a similar reaction of the population to the defects, produced by the zigzags of market reforms, which was manifested at the level of practical consciousness. The process of deformation intensifies, manifested in new forms, reflecting the unhappiness and serious flaws in the consciousness of the majority of people. The consequences of manipulating social consciousness and public opinion became especially fateful and devastating, disrupting spirituality and inhibiting creative expression of the people. It is a clear case of manipulation, not just errors or misconceptions that are understandable and explainable. This is a conscious, systematically implemented policy that consistently and strictly directed, and still guides the spiritual development of society according to a specific mapped-out blueprint.

On the surface, it all looks decent and noble: the goal is to make us and our world unique, rich and multidimensional. And the trouble usually is not in this noble intention; the trouble is that the goals are achieved without any regard for the actual situation and objective requirements of social development. Influenced by PR technologies, people are being convinced that the interests of government, political parties, or various owner-investors (especially oligarchs) are their interests as well, and that their support will solve many social and personal problems. Everything was directing, pointing the social consciousness toward a pre-formulated goal, toward primitive perception of reality, encouraging people to once again «suck it up» in the name of achieving the goal of satisfying narrow selfish wants and, at the same time justifying thievish seizures of property, contempt to human beings, and immeasurable desire to retain the stolen and appropriated assets. This tendency is stimulated in a not inconsiderable degree by chatter about social responsibility of business that — in the best case — started allocating few crumbs from the fabulous earnings for specific social projects.

Under these circumstances, people's views and perceptions undergo severe transformation, and, essentially represent a colossal paradox, unnatural compromise between official directives and individual thoughts, reflections, discussions among friends and family members. In this situation «dual accounting» is flourishing: officially, an individual represents one thing, but in his private life — something entirely different (Zen'kovich. 2005; Livshits. 2005).

Manipulating social consciousness is extremely widespread. The brightest, most cherished ideals are being traded on the open market. It is manifested in a constant obsessive desire to prove that we are the best, most progressive, and that our difficulties and shortcomings are temporary and short-lived.

In conclusion, it is worth noting that *the policy of manipulation is carried out less and less spontaneously — it has increasingly been turned into a weapon of social and especially political struggle.* Furthermore, it (this policy) tends to expand the size and the scope of its influence, especially since the transformation period for Russia is not over and has not yet been clearly defined. The policy of manipulation, in essence, is aimed at concealing, reducing or sometimes embellishing the rift between the social consciousness and social being. This ability to manipulate social consciousness is increasing, due to enormous gain in the scale of information access. The latest PR technologies, use of internet is multiplying these opportunities of influencing the world outlook, changing or correlating this outlook, utilizing global information space in the interests of certain political and social forces. This, in turn, significantly increases paradoxicality of consciousness and behavior of individuals. We shall examine these paradoxes in the next chapter.

References

Ermakov Yu.A. *Manipulyatsii lichnostyu: smisl, priyomi, posledsviya (Manipulating personalities: reasons, methods, implications).* P. 157–164.

Ermakov Yu.A. *Manipulyatsii lichnostyu: smysl, priyomi, posledsviya (Manipulating Personalities: Reason, Methods, Implications).* Ekaterinburg, 1995.

Feofanov O.A. *Agressiya lzhi (Aggression of Lies).* Moscow, 1987.

Fromm E. *Begstvo ot svobodi (Escape from Freedom).* Moscow, 1990.

Gadzhiev K.S. *Totalitarism kak fenomen XX veka (Totalitarianism as a XX century Phenomenon)* // Voprosy filosofii. 1992. No 2.

Gorshkov M. *Ambitsii SMI i mnenie rossiyan (Media Ambitions and Opinion of Russians)* // Nezavisimaya gazeta. 2000. July 13.

Hayek F.A. *Pagubnaya samonadeyannost' (The Fateful Conceit).* Moscow, 1992.

Izvestiya. 2000. December 5.

Kara-Murza S. *Manipulyatsiya soznaniem (seriya: Istoriya Rossii. Sovremenniy vzglyad) (Manipulating Consciousness).* Moscow, 2000.

Kopalov V.I. *Obshestvennoe soznanie: Kriticheskii analiz fetishistskikh form (Social Consciousness: a Critical Analysis of Fetishist Forms).* Tomsk, 1985.

Landemann R.A., Sogomonov Yu.V. *Spor s pessimizmom: Zlokliutsheniya massovogo burzhuaznogo soznaniya (Polemics with Pessimism: Misadventures of Mass Bourgeoisie Consciousness).* Moscow, 1971.

Livshits R. *Provintsial'naya demshiza (Provincial Scizo-democrats).* Moscow, 2005.

Lyubomudrov M. *Udavka na shee naroda (A Slip-knot on People's Neck)* // Molodaya gvardiya. 2000. No 5–6.

Petrenko V.F., Mitina O.V. *Psikhosemantitsheskiy analiz dinamiki obshchestvennogo soznaniya. Na materiale polititsheskogo mentaliteta (Psycho semantic Analysis of Social Consciousness Dynamics).* Moscow, 1997.

Sherkovin Yu.A. *Psihologhitsheskiye problemy massovykh informatsionnykh protsessov (Psychological Problems of Mass Information Processes).* Moscow, 1973.

Shiller G. *Manipulirovaniye soznaniem (Manipulating Consciousness).* Moscow, 1980.

Shmelev G.P. *Intervyu (Interview)* // Nezavisimaya gazeta. 2000. November 21.

Shostrom E. *Anti-Karneghi, ili chelovek — manipulyator (Anti-Carnegie, or Manipulating Person).* Minsk, 1992.

Vlasov A.N. *Politicheskiye manipuliatsii: (istoriya i praktika sredstv massovoi informatsii SSHA) (Political Manipulations: History and Practices of USA Mass-media).* Moscow, 1982.

Zamoshkin Yu.A. *Litshnost' v sovremennoy Amerike (Personality in Contemporary US).* Moscow, 1980.

Zen'kovich N. *Mal'chiki v rozovikh shtanishkakh (Boys in Pink Trousers).* Moscow, 2005.

Chapter 6. Stereotypes and paradoxes: generalities and specifics

> believers in all sorts of «isms» should be hung on a rope, no matter how contradictory their panacea.
>
> *Bertrand Russell* (1872–1970),
> English philosopher and historian

The most important characteristic of modern social consciousness is its internal inconsistency, rupture, susceptibility to sudden fears and illusionary hopes, unexplainable jerking, displays of infantilism and zigzag development. Under these circumstances, an in-depth study of the elements of social consciousness that indicate its relative stability, its continuity and resistance to change and looming conflict is of considerable interest. These traits, to a substantial degree, are characteristic of a specific expression of social consciousness — *stereotypes.* However their manifestations are quite peculiar. On one hand, influence and significance of certain «schematics» in social life is increasing. They are accepted automatically, outside rational practice, and often become semantic essence of both individual, as well as group and social consciousness. On the other hand, new distorted forms of social consciousness are emerging, new irrational manifestations that oddly combine positive, as well as negative values, real and appropriate in people's behavior, contradictory moods and motives of group and individual consciousness. The very interaction of these two tendencies produces multifaceted paradoxical situations, and a necessity to understand the role and significance of stereotypes, the process of their emergence and functioning.

6.1. Stereotypes as realm of paradox

The concept of «stereotype» was introduced by W. Lippmann in 1922 during his research of racial problems. This phenomenon was discovered while studying mechanisms regulating social behavior of individuals. In his opinion, stereotype significantly impacts human activities, quality of thinking, acting as a schematic, regulated, cultural measure of individual, group and social consciousness. He maintained that the system of stereotypes is a more or less orderly depiction of the world of an individual who does not recognize the difference between the real world and the world of stereotypes... and thus living in a world of his own imagination, detached from the real world (Lippmann. P.66). However, further research showed that this assumption does not fully and accurately depict the essence of this phenomenon, placing an extremely obvious barrier between real and imaginary worlds. Analysis of social consciousness and behavior shows that this line, this transition between reality and the world of stereotypes is highly flexible, mobile, volatile and transient.

For a long time stereotype was interpreted only as a negative phenomenon, which significantly hampered its objective scientific examination as a contradictory process that characterizes mind's pursuit of absolute truth, discovering along the way unexplored aspects of psyche, human activity and consciousness. But, stereotype and its manifestations are undoubtedly multifaceted and cannot be measured from the «positive-negative» point of view. Their role is especially important for the process of socialization; as a result of that, stereotypes, as they are assimilating, recurring in people's activities, are no longer recognized, acquiring the character of mechanical action and automatic functioning.

Exploring *the essence of stereotypes,* we need to point out that their internal inconsistency, conflict with the outside world, commonly occurring opposition to the rational components of social consciousness creates paradoxes, allowing to reveal generalities, as well as the specifics of their content and their interaction. All this is clearly evident when we get down to defining (describing, analyzing) the characteristics of stereotypes.

First, the stereotype is associated with the formation of a simplified notion of a social object, subject, process or phenomenon. Its essence lies in formation of a schematic concept of imaginary social reality that can be modeled, standardized and simplified. In this, rational, in principle, approach, perusing the goal of organizing the knowledge of the outside world, its interpretation is simplified, adapted to the interests and needs of corresponding groups, commonly attached to the habitual and, therefore, comprehensible and acceptable. Stereotype excludes and does not allow the variety of approaches and nuances in the cognition of the outside world, focusing its attention on the mechanisms of achieving its goals. However, such attitude toward utilizing existing knowledge does not mean that it is immanently flawed and unusable. This very situation to a large degree contributes to the emergence of paradoxes, especially when the line between general and specific is shifting, subject to situational changes depending on varying conditions. If we take a look at such concepts as «believer» and «atheist», we can create some generalized image of these subjects of freedom of conscience that will be much different from the multiple manifestations, defining either a specific individual, or a certain social group. Thus, the emergence of such paradoxical characteristics of people and social groups is underway, where they appear to be both believers and non-believers, positively evaluating some religious norms and rejecting others, interpreting actions of the hierarchy of the church with mixed emotions.

Second, stereotype commonly represents a deformed reflection of various realities. It often happens when certain characteristics of a person's actions are considered more important than others, especially regarding the perceptions of models of behavior and structuring of daily life. This is the very reason for the negative attitude toward the subjects of market economy — entrepreneurs, bankers, brokers that are associated with the stereotype of a «new Russian», which, according to the popular opinion, are leading lifestyles that are unacceptable for the majority of people. This stereotype creates paradoxical attitude toward people that, in essence, should embody an example of desired changes, but, in reality, presents a rejected type of both consciousness, as well as behavior.

Third, stereotypes are often characterized by a distorted perception of various processes. This distortion differs from the alteration that is caused by personal experiences and personal impressions, which occurs primarily due to external influences — mass media, official propaganda, statements and declarations of political and social forces that are attempting to impose opinions other than the ones reflecting objective reality. A striking example of that, for instance, is the process of changing perceptions of democracy, which lately became unpopular under the influence of experiences resulting from social and economic changes in Russia.

One of the specific characteristics of stereotypes is the notion that a particular process or phenomenon does not corresponds with an actual object, but with available information (often false), or in some way, a certain image or meaning. References to the statements of authorities (often falsely attributed to them), books, reflecting opinions and vital conclusions similar to the general outlook are very common in public consciousness; as well as vivid (for a particular consumer) ideas that occasionally produce a special clan of fighters, attempting, at any cost, to convince their opponents not by ways of analyzing daily situations, but based on references to the information tailored to their goals. And, since these arguments are not viable, dictated by momentary selfish considerations and assumptions, this category of people can be classified as «roving forwards» easily switching political parties, movements, their own preferences and attachments.

We have to emphasize another feature characteristic of stereotypes that in turn breeds paradoxes — a high level of bias, little or poorly substantiated conviction in the truthfulness of the knowledge that a person or a specific social group adheres to. Stereotypes become particularly stable when it takes a long time for them to emerge under the influence of archetypes, or when they acquire features of traditions. As far as archetypes, they are clearly manifested in the form of «ethnic enemy», which goes against the widely accepted norms of ethnic tolerance or general perceptions of civilized society. As for traditions, many of the stereotypes that emerged during the Soviet rule are still a powerful social force, since they had touched upon the deepest layers, foundations of human thought and, to some extent, were justified by practice, but, later on, came into conflict with the reality of the situation and the necessity to correlate their perception of reality with the official policy and ideology.

A particularly important characteristic of stereotypes is their increased resistance to external influences, their «closed-ness» and their opposition to new knowledge and information, which can destroy them.

Comparing these traits (characteristics), we can conclude that *the essence of the stereotype represents a set of simplified, schematic perceptions*, which allow to classify people's behavior or social events (phenomenon) according to the above mentioned criteria, and to interpret them stereotypically, in accordance with orientations and expectations. Stereotypes may represent all, without exception, popular perceptions — in economics, politics, social and spiritual life, not to mention everyday life. All of them, to a certain extent, possess schematized, deformed, distorted and simplistic knowledge of the processes that affect their vital guidelines. But this is not false knowledge. This is more of a special type of knowledge, often in the form of an image, certain form of manifestation of a social guideline, directive. We have to emphasize that stereotypes sometimes appear as a result of the so-called «economy of thought» (people do not tend to react to events and phenomena in a new way every time, using already established ways and methods instead). In addition, stereotypes perform the function of protecting group values through establishing their specificity, their «self», creating the foundation for emergence, appearance of paradoxes.

Describing stereotype, we need to point out that it often develops on the subconscious level and is a fairly widespread, but specific manifestation of functioning consciousness. It is inherent not only to the ordinary (according to some researchers), but also theoretical consciousness. However, in real life these levels of consciousness do exist not in pure form, but in different combinations, constituting the essence of real consciousness, they, in various proportions, produce assorted stereotypes in the form of certain reinforced conscious notions.

A substantial number of stereotypes are relatively stable. They may remain unchanged for prolonged periods of time; they are not considerably affected by new experiences, since stereotypes are formed as images in the process of assigning similar characteristics without sufficient foundation or understanding of possible differences between them. But these very contradictions with new experience, renewed reality leads to paradoxes, casting doubt and sometimes even destroying the stereotype itself.

Stereotype can also function as a *special type of social guideline*. This trait is related to its openness, as well as closeness. Thus, stereotypes function at the level of subjective moods that individuals, as well as society prefer to keep hidden (Vasil'eva. 1988. P. 4). Or, as noted by several researchers, «stereotypes are often impossible to describe, they exist at the level of taboo: people respect these statements, but usually do not talk, or do not like talking about them. Individuals and whole communities may not recognize, for example, stereotypes of their own culture, since they have never studied it as a structured object» (*Upravlenchesckoye konsultirovanie.* 1992. P. 105).

6.2. *Structure and functions of stereotypes*

A majority of researchers tend to think that *the stereotype has a three-tier structure:*

• *affective level* that includes feelings of sympathy or antipathy toward a real or symbolic object;

• *cognitive level*, represented in judgment, opinion or knowledge of that object;

• *behavioral level* that characterizes a plan of action regarding the object (Vanina. 1998; Merenkov. 2001).

A special place in characterizing stereotypes belongs to its affective component, which sometimes allows researchers to narrow down their study to this component alone, at the level of «sympathy-antipathy». However, this is not enough. A statement attributed to M. Rokich: «A man might be aware of dangers of smoking, and, nonetheless, might be addicted, just because he simply likes to smoke», indicates that affective and cognitive level of stereotype (or guideline, or rule) does not necessarily coincide, which in turn leads to a paradox. Thus, *a priori* assumption about the coincidence of cognitive and affective levels is incorrect and such identification can lead to unreliable conclusions, misconceptions about the phenomenon in question, or, to the creation of an artifact.

With regard to the behavioral component of the stereotype, it is, despite the difficulty of measuring it, a very important characteristic. Moreover, it often registers the gap between verbal and actual behavior of a person. These components of the stereotype's structure should not be compared to one another or set against each other, if only because various stereotypes in different situations display cognitive, affective or behavioral levels. In this case, it is necessary to point out that various methods of combining, inconsistency (discord) of the elements of this structure lead to paradoxes.

Discordance of cognitive and behavioral levels sometimes leads to astonishing paradoxes. Thus, when a group of businessmen was surveyed regarding the hard currency purchases, most of them defined their position this way:»It is profitable. It makes sense; it is forward looking and visionary. But it is undermining Russian economy» (Vanina. 1998).

As far as *functions* of stereotypes are concerned, they are primarily aimed at *maintaining individual identity.* Sociological studies of 1970-1980 consistently demonstrated the fact of identification with the social («I am a Soviet citizen», «I am a worker», I am an internationalist») or professional values («I am a miner», «I am an officer», «I am a scientist»). During the 1990, self-identification underwent radical changes. Resulting from the collapse of the social structure and serious shift in the position of employees at work, a number of stereotypical notions disappeared or drastically changed. Sociological studies of the 1990's indicated that the stereotypes of ethnic affiliation have gained importance ('I am Russian», «I am Tartar», etc.), followed by personal characteristics «I am a Father (Mother, Grandmother, Grandfather)», «I am a Daughter (Son)». Moreover, these characteristics often formed some rather paradoxical combinations: «I am Soviet» as well as «I am a Democrat», «I am a free market supporter», and, simultaneously, «a supporter of strong government», «I am a monarchist» and «I am a liberal» at the same time, etc.

During this transitional period, stereotypical notions related to global or gender issues gained a lot of importance. For example, the survey conducted among the students of the Russian Humanitarian University in 1998 showed that a significant proportion of them tended to identify themselves in anthropomorphic terms: «I am a person», «I am a young woman», «I am a daughter», «I am loved». During this period of time students, especially freshmen, did not often identify themselves with a profession, or, far less, with political or national origin (Levicheva, Toshchenko, 1998). But the paradox is that these personal reference points, private life and private characteristics started to be contrasted, set against social orientations and social attitudes (Levicheva.2001).

Among the functions of stereotypes we have to highlight their likely *focus on justification of possible negative attitudes* toward other social groups (individuals), as well as ongoing social processes. For example, studies of ethnic orientations in 1990's demonstrated that due to the escalation of the inter-ethnic tensions, a significant number of people (up to 1/3) started assigning extreme significance to defending interests of their nation by any means including the use of violence (V.N. Ivanov, 1987). The stereotype of the «persons of Caucasian descent» is a prime example, when a firm belief that these individuals are carriers of negative traits and actions, preventing efficient and rational organization of normal societal life was imbedded into social consciousness (Ivanov. 1998; Drobizheva. 2003).

This function — justification of these negative attitudes — is compounded by people's attempts to not only proclaim, but also prove their correctness, which does not exclude *bias and prejudice* from the perception of reality. Evidence of that are materials, regularly appearing in the pages of press and on television, trying to prove the «fairness» of actions of various social forces, as well as their undeserved praise or equally undeserved disdain (Kazenkov, Kumatshev. 1999).

And, finally, we have to emphasize that in modern society total identity crisis is associated with *the spread of zones of local identity,* when comfort and stability of private habitat is perceived only in the context of professional and social communities, despite the fact that their communicative value and meaning are practically lost. Such conventional concepts as engineering and technical intelligentsia, peasants, working class, etc. are become increasingly symbolic.

6.3. How stereotypes breed paradoxes

Stereotypical thinking generates different types (forms) of paradoxes.

There is primarily the *«halo» effect* arising from the notion of wisdom of the supreme ruler (the tsars, khan, king, Secretary General, President). Analysis of actions of such individuals shows that the majority of them started out as fairly ordinary people and became leaders as a result of a right combination of objective and subjective circumstances. Many of them had no sufficient training or formal education, were often inarticulate and, at times, primitive in their reasoning. But gradually, in the eyes of their countrymen, the halo of the position (title, rank) acquired a right to independent existence. The leader now is being judged not by what he personally represents (as a specific person), but as a result of merits like courage, intelligence and other notable features attributed to his position. This metamorphosis — transposition of reality by what's expected — in a distorted way, to some extent might be observed in attitudes toward people occupying such posts as chief, director, president of the company, etc. As a result of this, a paradoxical situation emerges — a real person gives way to the imaginary, and the halo of his significance determines his fate for years to come. It is extremely hard to resist all these types of halo stereotype, they have a life of their own until it is changed by an onset of the crisis that a halo bearer cannot always handle.

This conclusion to a certain degree correlates with observations by M. Weber about a charismatic leader who, in his opinion, is assigned characteristics desirable to his subjects.

We should also point out a type (form) of paradoxical stereotype, which can be termed — an *effect of lost souls, rejection.* Stereotypes quite often harshly divide people into certain groups, ascribing certain qualities to them. Any person in a borderline situation, when some of his qualities correspond to one group, and other features — to another, ultimately finds himself in paradoxical situation: either both groups accept him as their own, or they both simultaneously reject him.

In the first case — affiliation with different groups of stereotypes forces a person to go along with the attitudes and orientations that are expected of him. This is how some electoral candidates behave, proclaiming in front of different groups and audiences whatever they think people want to hear, thereby creating an appearance of involvement with (belonging to) each of these groups. This applies not only to political aspirations: mimicry as a way of behavior and marginality as self-recognition are becoming the way of conduct and intellection for many people.

In the second case, the carrier of the borderline views is often rejected by both groups, unable to fully, without reservations, represent their interests, ideology and social positions. This situation is especially vividly depicted in the saying «friend among strangers, stranger amongst friends». A while back the wide spread opinion about the last chairman of the Supreme Soviet of Russia, R. Khasbulatov was: «Democrat among Communists, Communist among Democrats». But in either case, after a while, these people have to accept the rules of just one group, or be rejected turning into a marginal, whose position, as a rule, does not suit any of the groups or, for that matter, society as well.

Further, we have to mention such a paradox, created by a realm of stereotypes, as *effect of «hypertrophyication»,* when ideas, perceptions, characteristics of individual entities, organizations and processes are exaggerated, while others — understated (disparaged) and ignored (as «their problems»). Thus, stereotype of a «trader», market participant is characterized (or at least was until mid-

1990) by only positive traits, such as energy, resourcefulness, ability to make money, and, most importantly, — embody progress, future development of the country. Consequently, the fact that the very same entrepreneur, «trader» due to the specifics of Russian reality, was brazen, arrogant and greedy was deliberately downplayed.

Equally important is the paradox of *group egotism*, when only the positive qualities are attributed to a particular group (organization), or social community, in spite of explicit (or implicit) obvious facts. Such attribution only distorts the real picture, unduly exalting, glorifying features and characteristics of this group. Ultimately, this leads to group favoritism, which is a peculiar embodiment and cover-up of the actions aimed at achieving selfish goals, often to the detriment (or at the expense) of other social groups.

Moreover, paradoxes created by stereotypes may assume *the form* of «*Manilovism*» (after the character of Manilov — dream-man), a dream transformed into verbiage that no one ever intended to fulfill. But the proclamation often brought its proponent certain dividends, since he was now regarded as an innovator, a hero, a man of noble deed. Assessing similar situation count Rostopchin had said: «I can understand a peasant's desire to become a count, count's desire to become a peasant eludes me». In this instance, we have a typical case where the stereotype of a peasant (hard working, selfless, uncomplicated, close to nature, etc.) becomes very appealing, positive figure in society, whereas the stereotype of a «landowner»/nobleman (greedy exploiter, with no understanding of plain folk's needs, etc.) has all the negative traits. Under these circumstances the movement of «going to the people» might have been born, along with the emergence of county teachers and doctors, the belief of Russian and Soviet rural intelligentsia in being «eternally indebted to the people». But in this case these aspirations were in fact «Manilovism», which was capable of acquiring more or less intelligible features only on a verbal level.

And finally, we need to mention such type of paradox, emerging due to stereotypes, as *changeling effect*, when under the weight of changing circumstances, for fear of losing one's resources and reserves, a reassessment of stereotypes is underway, re-evaluation of their own attitudes, as well as the attempts to convince the others, even the entire society. In late 1980, when perestroika lost its steam, and, later in the early 1990's during the first years of new Russia, a stereotype of the state as a phenomenon that has brought only hardships to the people was created by the «first wave» of the Democrats. According to this notion, the state interfered in everything, regulated every detail of peoples' activities, hindered the initiative, drove people to poverty and would not allow any room for thought or actions. And then in 1999, in an article published in the «Kommersant» newspaper, a different approach toward the state was proclaimed: it turns out, it is necessary. The liberal radicals' tactics of taming the state and putting it to work for liberal reforms replaced their struggle against the government. So, what is the essence of this paradoxical situation? Why did the attitude toward the state change? Mostly because the government was now forced to change it's functions and start protecting the interests of the new owners, to prevent the redistribution of property (and vice versa, to secure it).

In conclusion, it should be noted that stereotypes are often not recognized by their carriers and are perceived as the only possible, natural worldview and behavior. Initial stereotypes, originating in the course of family upbringing through the mechanism of persuasion and imitation, ultimately, are the result of institutional impact of establishing a «world view». Evaluation of the variety of characteristics of real stereotypes suggests that as a social phenomenon, they possess a number of properties: in static terms — integrity, assessment, presence of misinformation; dynamically — stability, rigidity, conservatism, low flexibility with regard to new information. But the final conclusion is equally important: within stereotypes, during the transformation of society, under the conditions of the «crisis» of social consciousness, certain irrational components begin to emerge as means of defense from social upheavals or as methods of realizing self-interests in the process of deliberate manipulation of social consciousness. This, once more, begs the conclusion that ignorance, week knowledge of the process of emergence and functioning of stereotypes (and archetypes) becomes a serious obstacle on the road to positive changes in any society.

References

Drobizheva L.M. *Sotsial'nie problemi mezhnatsional'nikh otnosheniy v postsovetskoy Rossii (Social Problems of International Relations in Post-Soviet Russia)*. Moscow, 2003.

Ivanov V.N. *Rossiya: Obretenie budushchego (razmyshleniya sotsiologa) (Russia: Acquiring the Future — a Sociologist's Deliberations)*. Moscow, 1998.

Kazenkov S., Kumatshev V. *Evangelie ot Petra: prozrenie ili prizyv k liberalnoi diktature? (St.Peter's Gospel: Insight or a Call for Liberal Dictatorship)* // Nezavisimaya gazeta. 1999, February 12.

Levicheva V.F. *Gumanitarnaya intellighentsiya: osnova korporativnoi identitshnosti (Humanitarian Intelligentsia: Bases for Corporate Identity)* // Sotsiologhicheskiye issledovaniya. 2001. No. 2.

Lippmann W. *Public opinion*. New York, 1966. P.66.

Merenkov A.V. *Sotsiologiya stereotipov (Sociology of Stereotypes)*. Ekaterinburg, 2001.

Upravlenchesckoye konsultirovanie (Managerial Consulting). T. 1. Moscow: Interexpert, 1992. P. 105.

Vanina O.N. *Stereotipy eckonomitsheskogo soznaniya rossiyan (Stereotypes of Russians' Economic Consciousness)* // Sotsiologhitsheskiye issledovaniya. 1998. No. 5.

Vasil'eva T.E. *Stereotipy v obshestvennom soznaniyi (sotsialno-filosovskiye aspecty) (Stereotypes of Social Consciousness (Social and Philosophical Aspects)*. Moscow: INION AN SSSR. 1988. P. 4.

Chapter 7. **Frustration and paradox**

What we know, we don't want

J.W. Goethe, (1749–1832)
Great German writer

7.1. What is frustration?

A significant amount of sociological research on social consciousness has gathered an enormous amount of empirical material, which made it possible to clarify, specify and enrich our perceptions, making our knowledge of its condition, trends and problems more accurate. This material provided access to elucidation of a new class of phenomena that were not previously recorded or overlooked.

Of great interest, among these new phenomena, is *frustration*, which can generally be characterized as an *extremely critical condition, manifested in oppressive tension, anxiety, feelings of hopelessness.* This state of social consciousness and behavior is possible in any society, but it is especially noticeable in times of critical transformations, when society in engulfed in disillusionment, created by impossibility of accomplishing the tasks, caused by frustration, a sense of inevitable disaster, uncertainty about the future. Placing a person in an extreme situation in life creates frustration — a consequence of inability (impossibility) to satisfy relevant requirements, essential need of human life, provide for realization of the motives of action. This inability essentially represents a gap between the motive of action and its result, which is accompanied by the appearance of paradoxes, surfacing on the brink between professing former values and realization of the impossibility of their previous existence, on the edge of a confrontation between established and emerging vital guidelines, due to loss or destruction of the old, not only political but also civic ideals and lack of the new ones.

Frustration is a relatively new subject of scientific research. Separate aspects of this phenomenon were previously covered in studies of human aggression (Z. Freud, W. MacDougall, D. Dollard, D. Miller, A. Bandura, A. Bertkovitz, K. Lorenz, etc.); stress (J. Selye, R. Lazarus, N. Brown, S. Silsbegerd, L. Levi, etc.). A special place in the study of frustration belongs to the work of Emile Durkheim «Suicide. Sociological Studies». This particular study and writings of Durkheim's followers revealed the main social and socio-physiological causes of suicide — loss of social connections, depression, loss of social status, family problems, disillusionment in future perspectives, i.e. much of what results from frustration. In addition, references to the term «frustration» or concepts in essence depicting it, is commonly found in theories, concepts, hypotheses related to problems of motivation, emotion, behavior, and activities of the individual. However, a complete, coherent theory that studies this phenomenon has not yet been created. Social and socio-psychological aspects of frustration remain the least studied. Perhaps, this is due to the limited capacity of experiments and difficulty of obtaining accurate scientific results of such studies.

In recent years, in Russian literature the concept of «frustration» and the individual aspects of this issue were investigated not only in the context of study of just this particular phenomenon, but addressing other research problems (Abolin. 1987; Ageev. 1990; Antsiferova. 1997; Bespartochniy. 1999; Vasilev. 1998; Vasiliuk. 1984; Grimack. 1991; Kitaev-Smyk. 1983; Puzanova. 1998; Toshchenko, Kharchenko. 1996). First detailed studies of this subject started appearing in print (Ermolaeva. 1993; *Tsennostnoye soznanie litshnosti...* 1997; Galliulina. 1995).

If we sum up all the available approaches, we can identify important characteristics of frustration in general and social frustration in particular. Sometimes the term frustration is understood as a fact of obstruction, an obstacle on the road to the implementation of a motive, or a response, reaction to a traumatic factor. But since frustration emerges as a result of the transition of a person (group of people) from a balanced, stable, «normal» state into disorganized and uncomfortable, it has to be viewed as a phenomenon that unites (in its objective content) interdependent, interrelated and interactive elements of the outside world (environmental conditions, «frustrators») and the condition of the subject (internal socio-psychological, registered in one's conscious and subconscious feeling of discomfort and distress), and externally observable — emotional reactions, actions and behavior.

Which conditions and what factors (frustrators) block the satisfaction of essential, fundamental needs in Russian society?

With regard to the conditions, they are manifested in rapid deterioration of the socio-economic status of the people due to the loss of social status, diminishing prestige of many professions, mass «liberation from labor», resulting in the growth of all forms of open and disguised unemployment, declining living standards of the overwhelming majority of Russian population. Considerable impact on the development of frustration can be explained by the lack of clarity in ideological orientations — uncertainty about the country in which we live, loss of the national idea that would be associated with ennobling ideology, mistrust in the governing authority, as well as those seeking power.

All this creates a rather unfavorable background for the well being of the people, for their confidence in tomorrow and the future, for guaranteeing their sense of safety and security. We can add *factors (frustrators)* that actively influence mood, self-esteem and opportunity to satisfy key interests and needs to that list. This is manifested in a person's inability to guarantee a comfortable life-style for themselves or loved ones; when the profession is devalued and reduced to an official status, which does not always match personal and professional needs; when opportunities for leisure, recreation, cultural, educational, sports and other activities decline. In these conditions primitivization of popular needs often occurs, when people become capable of focusing only on the utmost important, without which the very survival of a normal human lifestyle is impossible.

7.2. Paradoxes in context of frustration

Analysis of social frustration as a critical life situation requires clarification of essence and content, identification of signs of its development, as well as studies of specific forms of its existence, often expressed in paradoxical nature of consciousness and behavior. The scientific research shows that as a result of frustration people (social groups) start to behave in such a manner that various aspects of manifestation of this behavior are not only contradictory, but also mutually exclusive (See: table 7.1).

Table 7.1.

What feelings emerged, strengthened among the people around you in the past year?

(% of respondents. N = 1600)

Feeling	1998	2001	2004	2006
Hope	13	33	24	35
Fatigue, Indifference	45	39	39	38
Fear	24	14	21	7
Sense of human dignity	4	8	7	10
Bewilderment	24	12	17	12
Feeling of freedom/ liberation from falsehood	3	2	1	5
Animosity, aggression	35	17	21	15
National pride	3	4	3	6
Hard to say	7	6	8	8

Source: Public Opinion — 2006. Moscow, Levada-Center. 2007. P. 10.

In order for frustration to emerge and manifest quite distinctively, its evolution requires far more compelling conditions than blocking of all the needs and necessities. In order to adequately understand the frustration mechanism, we need to identify *the potential frustrator* (traumatic factor capable, under certain circumstances, of causing frustration) and examine conditions of its transformation into an active factor. Such conditions for social frustration are: the significance of denied (blocked) necessity; sufficiently lengthy period of exposure to the blocking factor; the intensity of exposure; prevalence of coverage and the extent of traumatic influence on the totality of subjective components; predisposing characteristics of the subject (personal, group, social). It is during this very process of development of frustration, under these conditions, we turn our attention to the evolution of paradoxes, whose extremes coexist in most fantastic of ways.

Let us take a closer look at the forms of paradox created by critical life situation — frustration.

The first group includes socio-economic and socio-political frustration reactions. Sociological studies of the second half of 1990 have documented a negative evaluation of the government and the economic situation. According to the Russian Independent Institute for Social and National Problems, in December of 1999, 61% of the subjects evaluated the situation in Russia as critical, 29% as catastrophic and 5% as normal (Gorshkov. 2000. P. 327). This evaluation is very similar to the ones of mid-1990. But if the level of aggression manifested in loss of hopes and patience («reduction of the degree of conditionality of consciousness *via* adequate motivation») as a consequence of discord between motive and result during the first half of 1990 was fairly high, at the turn of the millennia social and especially political activity has decreased significantly. Slightly less negative assessment of all branches of government, as well as declining numbers of people eager to participate in open forms of protests — strikes, rallies, demonstrations, pickets, not to mention those, willing to defend their convictions by force of arms, indicate a lower level of aggression. According to VTsIOM (All Russian Institute for Public Opinion Studies), aggressiveness, at least verbal, tends to decline — from 32,6% in September 1998 to just 25% in September of 2006 among respondents that expressed their potential willingness to personally participate in rallies and protests against declining living standards and in support of civil rights (while 47,8% and 65,9% accordingly were not prepared to take such actions and 19,6% and 16,4% refrained from defining their position) (Monitoring obshchestvennogo mneniya. 1998. No 6; 2000. No 6. P. 67. Russian Public Opinion Herald. 2006 No 6. p.70). The abstainers, in our opinion, were closer to the group willing to be patient and wait, rather than to active protesters (*Monitoring obshchestvennogo mneniya*. 1998. No 6. P. 76; Public Opinion, 2007. P. 51).

So, how can we explain the decline in aggressiveness? People hope that the current situation is a temporary state, worth waiting out, until their luck changes and life takes a positive turn. Apart from hope, fear holds people back from participating in protests, fear that resistance might cause an explosive situation resulting in bloodshed, serious cataclysms, or will turn against both society and the individual.

Paradoxical situation associated with a really low estimate of short-term expectations can be attributed to the socio-political group of frustrations. In September 2000, for example, every second person (51,7% of interviewed) was convinced that the following year will bring no improvements to their living conditions. Given that approximately one in four respondents (24%) refrained from answering, we can conclude that pessimism became all-encompassing, defining the state of people's lives. At the same time 51,4% of respondents positively answered the question, if they were satisfied with their lifestyle («fairly», »mostly», «and partly«). However, the situation, when the majority of population (64%) is at a crossroad (answers «partially» or «not entirely satisfied»), clearly indicates the actuality of a gap between people's motives and the social status (*Russian Public Opinion Herald.* 2006. No 6. P. 66).

Judging by the popular evaluations, the prospects for future development of Russia is extremely dismal — 77,4% are convinced that «the events are leading us to a dead end» (Ibidem. P. 73). At the same time, despite all the pessimism, hope is still alive — 34,9% are convinced that their families have adapted or are successfully adapting to the changes occurring in the country during the past ten years. Moreover, 67,2% with 13,9% abstentions are confident that they will not starve and will be able to find reserves to successfully survive the crisis. In other words, a paradoxical situation is emerging: on one hand — potential for considerable discontent, since the majority of people are in a critical situation; on the other — the outlook is generally optimistic. (See: table 7.2.)

Table 7.2

What will the next year be like for you compared to the previous one?
(in % of respondents. N = 1800)

	1993	1997	2000	2004	2007
Certainly better	4	5	6	7	8
Hopefully better	35	28	46	47	41
Hopefully the same	12	12	17	21	17
No change	21	30	18	19	25
Probably Worse	23	19	6	3	5
Hard to say	5	6	7	3	4

Source: Public Opinion — 2007. Moscow. Levada-Center. 2007. P.8.

The second group of problems is ideological frustrations, which in turn, can be a basis or a source link of paradoxical consciousness and behavior. Ideological frustrators are the factors that block satisfaction of spiritual needs and hinder the development of the ideological sphere of individual and social consciousness. This means that the need for ideals and ideology as well as the opportunity of its gratification are destroyed.

Analysis of sociological data shows that modern man is deeply convinced that every society has to have binding ideals, and these ideals have to be shared by many (most) people. During Soviet times, such ideals were embodied in the official socialist ideology. But the collapse of the Soviet Union and pejorative criticism of the socialist ideals, as well as its ideology, for a lot of people led to rejection of ideology in general, as well as the values reflected in its socialist variant. This rejection of the old ideas, and, consequently — ideals, in conjunction with the absence of the new ones, led to a total lack of spirituality and disregard for national interests. End of the socialist ideology in Russia led to the loss of ideological orientations and prospects for future development of the country. Ideology was replaces by worries, concerns about everyday, immediate needs and interests. This situation became a basis for concluding that the ideals and national ideas were completely lost, and Russian people were left without idealistic aspirations. This in no small measure contributed to the fact that in the second half of 1990 an attempt was made to reformulate or revive the national idea.

Strikingly, despite the criticism of lack of ideology, ideals and national ideas, «the Russian soul» continuously preserved centuries-old principles of national mentality: high standard of moral values, search for meaning and purpose in life. For the Russian national «I» the ideals of justice, community, self-sacrifice and devotion to common cause have always been extremely important. Socialist ideology was widely accepted due to the fact that it was based on these values and skillfully utilized them. Therefore, the discreditation of socialist ideals in the absence of new ones led to an ideological vacuum of sort, especially among young people just entering the social arena. Centuries-old treasures of national identity were hidden, buried deep and barely manifesting themselves. A paradoxical situation was created: a lack of ideals on the official level and on the surface of social consciousness (officials and intelligentsia) does not mean that these ideals are dead and the national idea is lacking, that society is devoid of ideology and guidelines. Rather, these ideals, values and ideas live in the deep layers of social consciousness of the people. We have to take extreme care not to destroy these spiritual principles that make people a nation, worthy of having their own state, their own country.

No less revealing is the paradoxical situation that tends to mislead various social and sometimes opposing forces in their assessment of an important ideological factor – the evaluation of 1991 events leading to the disintegration of the Soviet Union. Sociological studies reflect that the majority (60 to 70%) of people in Russia and former Soviet republics, now independent countries, still regret the disintegration of the great country. (See table 7.3).

Table 7.3

Do you approve of the agreement between the leaders of Russia, Ukraine and Byelorussia of December 8, 1991 regarding the cessation of existence of the USSR?

Republics (states)	Approve	Approve	Disapprove	Disapprove
	1991	*2006*	*1991*	*2006*
Russia	67	17,6	12	71,8
Ukraine	62	48,5	19	33,5
Byelorussia	69	17,6	10	63,4
Georgia	–	76,3	–	17,8
Armenia	–	31,9	–	40,2
Kazakhstan	–	43,4	–	44,8
Moldova	–	31,5	–	56,7
Kirghizstan	–	28,5	–	57,5

Source: Sotsiologicheskiye isslodovaniya. 2007. No 4.

Nostalgia for the «Soviet» times is still very strong, especially among the poor and underprivileged. People highly value social guarantees they enjoyed in the Soviet Union: social protection and confidence in the future that were crucial for people generally modest and quiet, but relatively secure existence.

But does this regret and nostalgia for the days gone by indicate a desire to return to the USSR? Most people realize that «a broken pot can not be glued back together» and history cannot be reversed, and even if some sort of integration of the former republics into a union is possible, this will not be a rebirth of the Soviet Union. Nostalgia for Soviet guaranties of a quiet life is more of a wish that the new State would borrow the best of the old one and implement it in its socio-economic policies.

The third group of frustration reactions that provide a foundation for paradoxical consciousness and behavior is represented by the communication factors.

It is particularly evident in the phenomenon of public opinion, which is primarily shaped by the media, exerting enormous influence on the consciousness and psyche of individuals. In modern Russia, this serious and diversified pressure achieves only moderate results, at times opposite to those intended.

In our opinion, despite all the efforts of official propaganda and the majority of mass media to present liberal values as dominant and defining the face of society, we can state that Russian public opinion is either demoralized (45,2% do not sympathize with any political party), or is still leaning more toward patriotic and leftist views and orientation (Levashov. 2006. P. 460). There is one other indicator of the activities of mass media that creates serious frustration reactions. We are referring to information warfare campaigns that periodically flare up and each time become increasingly more vicious. The downside of these wars is that the opponent is trampled; his character destroyed and nothing constructive comes out of it. Information warfare campaign during the Chechen conflict, which was won by the militants and not Russia's official propaganda, is a clear example that attempts to manipulate public opinion can fail.

The fourth group of paradoxical behavior and consciousness emerges based on frustrations of social identity, as one of the basic needs that people seek to realize consciously or subconsciously throughout their entire lives. They are determined, on one hand by objective affiliation of an individual with a social group or type of society; on the other — by subjective attitude toward this affiliation, the nature of realization of group and role identity, and emerging difficulties of these interconnections.

The paradox of this situation is that social identification with a professional group, field of expertise, with colleagues (organization, company), with the country has considerably weakened. At the same time the number of frustrating situations has increased — unemployment, emigration and immigration, employment outside the field of expertise in order to survive. The loss of Soviet identity pushed people to turn to their national identity, to false patriotism or rabid nationalism, when ethnicity becomes number one priority, along with faith in its people, in ability to protect and shelter their countrymen under adverse conditions.

Sociological information at the same time demonstrates that, despite the «killing» of the official «Soviet Man», disregard of his professional affiliation and sharp rise in the importance of ethnic factor these attributes are alive and well, resisting policies of destruction and remaining an important motive in the behavior of Russian people, who, in overwhelming majority, have been brought up on these principles. Studies conducted by the Institute of Sociology in 1992 and 2005 demonstrated that 47,1% of the respondents still regard themselves as «Soviet people», 48,8 and 46,5% respectively, identify themselves as «citizens of Russian Federation», 75,1 and 87,5 — with their nationality, 71,0 and 74,3% — as Russians (in our opinion, this figure is affected not only by the institutional affiliation, but ethnic factor as well), 34,2 and 37,1% expressed a sense of community with entire humanity (*Rossiya na rubezhe vekov.* 2000. P. 195; *Russian Public Opinion Herald.* 2006. No 6. P.54). Incidentally, the identification of a «Soviet person» with «Russian» was fairly wide spread during Soviet times as well. Therefore, a formal rejection of «everything Soviet» does not mean the rejection at the level of social consciousness — rather then a loss of the first (Soviet), it meant its substitution by the latter (Russian).

And, finally, socio-psychological factors form a special group of frustrations. According to the nationwide study, conducted in March 2000, over 40% of Russians lived with feelings of adverse psychological state, experiencing fear and desperation (opinion of 15%), depression (opinion of 19,5%) and anger (opinion of 17%). If to this we add the 68%, who felt that injustice is prevailing, 54% that are ashamed of the current state of the country, 49% convinced of impossibility to go on living the old way and 49% consumed by loneliness and uselessness, we can grasp the scope and the magnitude of disorganizing frustration factors, which are also extremely difficult to overcome in the foreseeable future (Gorshkov. 2000. P. 340–341).

7.3. Marginality — social field of frustration

The first steps in the study of marginality are usually associated with the name of American sociologist R. Park (1864–1944), who was the first to use this term in his work «Migration and the marginal man». After 1937 publication of E. Stonequist's monograph «Marginal Man», the term «marginality» firmly became a part of scientific and literary lexicon. Since then numerous works devoted to the problems of marginality were published in the United States, Western European and Russian scientific communities (Popova. 1996).

If we generalize the existing different points of view, it is possible, in our opinion, to single out the one that focuses on the *marginality of the social role*, which emerged as a result of its borderline position (location) between different social groups. This borderline (marginal) quality is clearly evident as a result of a social shift, when certain groups of people have (are forced or intend) to accept an alternate lifestyle, different from the one they led up to a certain point. The resultant discord does not just have a temporary character — then and now — it is a conflict of mentality, identity, which is impossible to renounce or simply refuse by instantly accepting different rules of the game.

No less significant is the original form (referring to the studies of Park and Stonequist) — *cultural marginality*, which is based on the conflict of values within different cultures that govern individuals. This situation creates uncertainty of the social status, ambiguity of personal position, which, on one hand can create nostalgia, embodying the desirability of the motives and goals and, simultaneously, the impossibility of their realization. And, on the other hand

— unfounded, exaggerated expectations that contradict (or may contradict) the real capabilities of individuals and the real political situation.

A significant amount of studies analyze *structural marginality* that characterizes political and/ or economic situation of individuals and social groups, deprived of basic rights with limited (and/or lacking) civil rights and liberties, which puts them in a position of inadequacy and disadvantage compared to other individuals, social groups and communities.

We find different approaches to defining and characterization of marginality in Russian literature. Thus, E. Starikov characterized the entire Russian society as a marginal, while emphasizing primarily the destruction of work ethic, loss of professionalism, obliteration of time tested norms and rules of conduct (Starikov. 1989). A.I Atoyan is trying to utilize the possibilities of the interdisciplinary approach to explain this unique phenomenon (Atoyan. 1993; Makhmutov. 2003). Z.T. Golenkova focuses on the place and role of marginalized groups in the social structure of Russian society (Golenkova, Ighithanyan. 1999). Also of interest are studies of individual social groups characterized as marginal — informal associations (Rashkovskiy. 1989), unemployed (Polyakov. 1993; Rutkevich. 1998; Sigareva, Khasaev. 1997), the «new poor» (Vavilina. 2000), refugees and migrants (*Vynuzhdennyie migranty i gosudarstvo. 1998; Migratsiya i rynki truda v postsovetskoi Rossii.* 1998), etc.

Without attempting a comprehensive analysis of all aspects and manifestations of marginality, we need to point out that this characteristic does not apply to entire society, all social processes and relations without exception: if we start with a notion of the ideal as an absolute perfection, we can conclude that not a single process or phenomenon fully fit the description of the optimum, norm or model. In reality, all of them feature certain degree of deviation. We can judge the significance of this deviation, variation or departure from the norm or ideal based on a number of parameters, which comprise the concept of marginality.

To determine these parameters, indices and indicators of marginality, the concept of frustration as socio-physiological phenomenon that occurs as a result of a real or imagined obstacle on the way to reaching a goal, is of particular interest. The first frustrational characteristic of marginality is associated with the role of goals. It is the contradictions between the goals of an individual or a group and the target orientations of the wider social groups and communities that may be described, for instance, by experiences of those representatives of farming community that decided to become city dwellers. They are facing challenges of professional self-determination, settling into an unfamiliar household arrangement, entering a different cultural environment, familiarization with new rules of interrelations, which greatly vary from the old ones, not to mention the fact that now a farmer loses his old established perception of social protection, only possible in the familiar setting.

This situation with the target goals leads to paradoxes of consciousness and behavior, when a person is determined to achieve certain social status under changing conditions, and, at the same time, is incapable of reconciling with the loss of the old one. This is especially vividly illustrated by the behavior of the refugees. When individuals make a conscious decision to accept a new lifestyle, and, nevertheless, are unable to part with the memories of the past, which simultaneously remains irretrievably lost, but still desirable, overshadowed by the harsh and merciless present. In this situation, goals of the past and future life are canceled out by the present, marking the border that the person in pushed toward by the circumstances, the border he instinctively is unwilling to cross. This contradiction is almost never resolved in favor of the past, even when a person attempts to return to it, since he is unable to reconcile with the loss of all good (in his opinion), especially when the present suggests a hopeless future.

The second frustrational characteristic of marginality is linked to the importance and significance of blocking factors that are generated by the macro-, mezzo— and microenvironment of a person. Under the new or changing conditions, people cannot always comprehend why the environment rejects their claims, or at least casts doubt upon them. And the stronger the drive to identify with the new environment, the stronger the resistance of the environment becomes — whether professional, social environment or contact groups in the process of interpersonal communication. These situations create paradoxes — when an individual is only capable of recognizing obstacles in the immediate environment (microenvironment), unaware that the current situation is being affected by more powerful factors — socio-economic and socio-political relations predominant in the society. At times this rejection, resistance and opposition, bordering hostility, is deliberately cultivated by the ruling (and often political) forces, that benefit from directing discontent of the marginalized groups, channeling this protest (conscious or spontaneous) onto a different path, so that it affects them (or attracts attention) to a much lesser extent. Thus, the interests of refugees and immigrants are often artificially contrasted against the people residing next to them (this is particularly evident in small towns, or rural areas), despite the fact that their marginalization is not the migrants' fault, rather a result of the official migration policies.

Signs and symptoms of marginality are their third frustrational characteristic: feelings of oppressive tension, anxiety, desperation and anger that are fairly clearly documented in opinion polls on burning issues of human activity. Marginalized groups, in this situation, are behaving so paradoxically that it is virtually impossible to predict directional changes of their social mood — from depression, reconciliation with their existing situation to possible aggression. Rigidity, i.e. difficulty, unwillingness to change the scheduled plan of action, when the adjustment is absolutely imperative, can also be attributed to this group. So, for instance, the farmers who chose to move to the city, on one hand, realizing that they need to make an effort to fit into the new environment, develop a plan of action. But on the other hand, they are incapable (or are experiencing serious difficulties) of implementing their specific plans, since they do not always have the capacity to change the perception of their environment, mimicking stereotypes, patterns from the old environment, based on a different worldview.

The fourth frustrational characteristic of marginality is associated with the measurement of such indicators of vital functions as determination of the extent and scale of feelings of discomfort and distress, presence of at least a slight hope for achieving acceptable objectives and ideals, degree of loss of orientation toward realization of the goal to stabilize their social status, as well as individual ability to find some means of escape from existing situation. We have take into consideration the fact that when the circumstances are backing people into a corner, a dead end, they can either submit, accepting the rules of behavior dictated by society, or pursue some illegal actions in order to cut the Gordian knot of irreconcilable motives and results.

The fifth frustrational characteristic of marginality lies in its ability to retreat and conserve, i.e., when the subjects of this activity, having lost all hope (or questioning the possibility) of overcoming blocking influences, retreat into a circle of individuals of their own kind, forming a community with its specific subculture. This temporary solution, seemingly constructive, only aggravates the situation of the marginalized, since, under the circumstances, it symbolizes a very real paradox: on one hand, the feeling of a more favorable position and social protection; and the loss (or decrease) of prospects of integration into the environment, equal members of which they want to become — on the other.

In conclusion, examining marginality as social field of frustration, we have to note that high level of neuroticism among the marginal is extremely common — a condition characterized by emotional instability, resentment, anxiety, low self-esteem, which go back and correlate with the actual neuroses — a disruption of adaptive capabilities, failures of individual in his social relations. In this case we are not analyzing clinical aspects of neurosis (this is a subject of medical science), we are exploring their social significance, although they are difficult to separate from each other in the process of systemic analysis. All three major forms of neurosis — neurasthenia, hysteria and obsessive-compulsive disorder (*Kratkiy psikhologhitsheskiy slovar'*. 1985. P. 203) — affect marginalized to a greater extend than people with relatively stable social situation. Neurasthenia in its social aspect tends to turn into depression — affective state, characterized by negative emotional background, changes in motivation, cognitive (knowledge-related) states and general passivity of consciousness and behavior. This type of clinical and social deviation is especially widespread among displaced persons and refugees. Hysterical forms of social neurosis are manifested as inadequate response to external stimuli, expressed in various forms of aggression or acts of public protest. As far as obsessive-compulsive disorder is concerned, it is most clearly manifested in various types of phobias, reflected in hard— to-overcome emotional experiences of specific content. In this case, an individual finds himself in a paradoxical situation: on one hand, he is aware that his fears and emotions are unfounded; on the other hand, he cannot get rid of oppressive discomfort, inability to reconcile motives and outcomes, to implement plans that are important to him. These fears, in the case of refugees, for example, are supported by both real as well as imaginary difficulties, while the importance of false (imaginary) problems is seriously over-exaggerated, and sometimes becomes dominant (*Neterpimost' v Rossii.* 1999). In general, all three major groups of neurosis characterize, according to V.N. Myasishchev, a «mental illness based on unfortunate, irrational and counterproductive personality permitted conflict between itself (personality) and significant (for that personality) aspects of reality» (*Lichnost i nevrozi.* 1960. P. 241).

All this suggests that cognition of the nature, meaning, problems and ways of overcoming marginality lies in realization and utilization, application of knowledge accumulated while studying, understanding, as well as explaining frustration processes and phenomena of paradox.

References

Abolin L.M. *Psikhologhitsheskiye mekhanismy emotsionalnoy ustoitshivsti tsheloveka (Psychological Mechanisms of Human Emotional Stability).* Kazan', 1987.

Ageev V.S. *Mezhgruppovoe vzaimodeystviye. Sotsialno-psikhologhitsheskiye problemy (Intergroup Interaction. Socio-Psychological Issues).* Moscow, 1990.

Antsiferova L.I. *Chelovek pered litsom zhisni i smerti (Individual Facing Life and Death)* // Rossiyskiy mentalitet. Moscow, 1997.

Atoyan A.I. *Sotsial'naya marginalistika. O predposylkakh novogo mezhditsiplinarnogo i kulturno-istoritsheskogo sinteza (Social Marginalistics. On Preconditions for a New Interdisciplinary and Cultural Historical Synthesis)* // Polititsheskiye issledovaniya. 1993. No 6.

Bespartochniy B.D. *Obshchestvennoe mnenie kak factor reguliuatsiy (Public Opinion as a Regulatory Factor).* Moscow, 1999.

Ermolaeva L.I. *Frustratsiya kak sotsial'no-psikhologhitsheskiy fenomen (Frustration as a Social and Psychological Phenomenon),* Aftoref. diss. ... cand. psikhol. nauk. Moscow, 1993.

Galliulina Z.K. *Marghinaly: ponyatie i empiritsheskaya real'nost (Marginal Persons: Notion and Empirical Reality)*. Avtoref. diss. ... cand. sotsiol. nauk. Kazan', 1995.

Grimack L.P. *Obshchenie s soboi. Nachala psikhologhii activnosti (Communicating with Self. Bases of Psychology of Activity)*. Moscow, 1991.

Golenkova Z.T., Ighithanyan E.D. *Protsessy intergratsii i dezintegratsii v sotsialnoi strukture rossiyskogo obshchestva (Processes of Integration and Disintegration in Social Structure of Russian Society)* // Sotsiologhicheskiye issledovaniya. 1999. No. 9.

Gorshkov M.K. *Rossiyskoye obshchestvo v usloviyakh transformatsii (sotsiologhitsheskiy analiz) (Russian Society under Transformation. A Sociological study)*. Moscow, 2000. P. 327.

Kratkiy psikhologhitsheskiy slovar' (A Concise Psychological Dictionary). Moscow, 1985. P. 203.

Kitaev-Smyk L.A. *Psikhologhiya stressa (Psychology of Stress)*. Moscow, 1983.

Levashov V.K. *Sotsiopoliticheskaya diynamika rossiysgogo obshchestva. 2000–2006. (Sociopolitical Dynamics of Russian Society)*. Moscow, 2006. P. 460.

Lichnost i nevrozi (Personality and Neuroses). Moscow, 1960. P. 241.

Makhmutov T.A. *Marghinal'nost v obshchestvennikh transformatsiyakh (Marginality in Social Transformations)*. Moscow, 2003.

Migratsiya i rynki truda v postsovetskoi Rossii (Migration and Labor Markets in Post-Soviet Russia) / Pod red. G. Vitkovskaya. Moscow, 1998.

Monitoring obshchestvennogo mneniya. Ekonomitsheskiye i sotsialniye peremeny. 1998. No 6; 2000. No 6. P.67.

Monitoring obshchestvennogo mneniya. Ekonomitsheskiye i sotsialniye peremeny. 1998. No 6. P. 76.

Neterpimost' v Rossii: staryie i novyie fobii (Intolerance in Russia: Old and New Phobias) / Pod red. Vitkovskaya, A. Malashenko. Moscow, 1999.

Polyakov V.I. *Problema marghinalizatsii v kontekste bezrabotitsy. Sotsial'no-psikhologhitsheskiy aspect (Problem of Marginalization in the Context of Unemployment)* // Bezrabotitsa v Rossii. Moscow, 1993.

Popova I.P. *Marghinal'nost. Sotsiologhicheskiy analiz (Marginality. A Sociological Analysis)*. Moscow, 1996.

Public Opinion – 2007. Moscow. Levada-Center. 2007. P. 51.

Puzanova Zh.V. *Odinotshestvo. Opyt filosofsko-sotsiologhitsheskogo analiza (Solitude. A Study in Philosophical and Sociological Analysis)*. Moscow, 1998.

Rashkovskiy E. *Marghinaly (Marginal Persons)* // 50/50. Opyt slovarya novogo myshleniya / Pod red. Yu. Afanass'ev, M. Ferro. Moscow, 1989.

Rossiya na rubezhe vekov (Russia on the Boundary of Centuries). Moscow, 2000. P. 195.

Russian Public Opinion Herald. Data. Analysis. Discussions. 2006. No 6. P.54.

Rutkevich M.N. *Protsessy sotsialnoy degradatsii v rossiyskom obshchestve (Social Degradation Processes in Russian Society)* // Sotsiologhicheskiye issledovaniya. 1998. No 6.

Sigareva E.P., Khasaev G.R. *Regional'naya bezrabotitsa: opyt sotsiologhicheskogo issledovaniya (Regional Unemployment. A Sociological Study)*. Moscow, 1997.

Starikov E. *Marghinaly i marghinal'nost' v sovetskom obshchestve (Marginal People and Marginality in Soviet Society)* // Rabochiy class i sovremenniy mir. 1989. No 4.

Toshchenko Zh.T., Kharchenko S.V. *Sotsialnoe nastroenie (Social Mood)*. Moscow, 1996.

Tsennostnoye soznanie litshnosti v period preobrazovaniya obshchestva (Individual Value-Oriented Consciousness in the Period of Society Transformation). Moscow, 1997.

Vasilev G.N. e.a. *Problemy individualnogo i kollektivnogo razuma (Problems of Individual and Collective Reason)*. St. Petersburg, 1998.

Vasiliuk F.E. *Psikhologhiya perezhivanya. Analiz preodoleniya krititsheskikh situatsiy (Psychology of Experienced Feelings. Analysis of Overcoming Critical Situations)*. Moscow, 1984.

Vavilina N.D. *Bednost' v Rossii kak sotsial'noie iavlenie i sotsialnaya problema (Poverty in Russia as Social Phenomenon and Social Issue)*. Novosibirsk, 2000.

Vynuzhdennyie migranty i gosudarstvo (Involuntary Migrants and the State). Moscow, 1998.

Chapter 8. Centaur-problems as a special form of paradox

> During socialist years conditional capitalism was heaven,
> Now, it seems, quite the contrary —
> conditional socialism.
>
> *Yu. Bogomolov,*
> Russian publicist, 2001

8.1. Is combining non-combinable possible?

This problem was brought to light while researching paradoxes, which, as I already mentioned, have become typical characteristic of modern social consciousness. The essence of this phenomenon is that under the conditions of market experiments a unique occurrence became widespread, when the very same person, the very same groups of people simultaneously follow mutually exclusive social and political orientations, profess opposite, conflicting attitudes. In other words, the same person can at the same time be both liberal, internationalist, chauvinist, monarchist and republican. This suggests that the majority of people appear to be centaurs, combining mutually exclusive viewpoints and beliefs.

Is this an accidental phenomenon, is it localized in space and time, and is it generated by deeper causes than it seems at first glance? And is our use of a term «centaur-problem» justified in this case?

In our opinion we have encountered a special category of phenomena of social consciousness and behavior. An attempt to reveal the essence and specificity of each phenomenon requires understanding certain points, just like the reality of human spirituality was comprehended or interpreted from different positions at the previous stages of human development, compared with the tenets of the modern theory of knowledge. *Researching centaur-problems permits us to: study less-known, controversial issues of the nature of cognition and reformatory activities*, their interactions; as well as identify a number of particularities in correlation between knowledge and reality, conditions of reliability and validity of this knowledge.

Let us journey back into history. I would like to start by recalling an ancient Greek myth: in the towns of Thessaly, lived a tribe of men who never dismounted from their horses. This image created a myth of centaur, embodying the possibility of combining two mutually exclusive beginnings — human and animal. The myth of a man-horse representing unity, wholeness, was depicted in literature («Battle with Centaurs»), in symbols (Sagittarius), in myths and fairy tales (*Mify narodov mira.* 1987. Vol. 2. P. 638-639).

In the process of discussing this phenomenon, it is important not to forget one fundamental principle: centaur never really existed. It was a product of people's imagination, representing mental images, processes and phenomena. The image of a centaur reflects a paradoxical state of consciousness that generates the phenomenon, which does not exist in a real world. A peculiar realization (representation) of an imaginary world was embodied in the image, symbolizing the possibility of combining the non-combinable. In other words, the Centaur is an embodied incompatibility of different origins, the way of overcoming, reconciling this incompatibility. It is also a metaphor for combining the incompatible.

What causes the emergence of this image? Just a phantasmagoric interpretation of the real world? Or limited cognitive ability of human race? Or a compromise? Illogical explanation of an exceptional, unexplored phenomena?

If we limit ourselves only to this particular example, this product of human intellect can be classified as temporary prominence of human consciousness. But this perception of the world is not an exception. We can recall the Egyptian

Sphinx, which we also encounter in Ancient Greek mythology in a form of a winged half-woman, half-lion, residing in a mountain cave near ancient Thebes. In ancient mythology, we also come across such a unique creature as chimera that was far more whimsical than centaurs or sphinxes: lion's head, a second head on its back — one of a goat, and the tail of either a snake or a dragon.

These creations of human imagination exist in practically every culture. Slavic people have mermaids — half-fish, half-women that are broadly depicted in fairytales, legends and epics. Their image is also circulating in daily life.

We can continue the list of similar examples. We encounter angels in religious mythology — human-like creatures with wings that bring goodness to people, deliver blessed news, comfort and support during hard times. Analyzing these expressions of the human mind, one could argue that these examples of combining the incompatible existed in mythology, human imagination, or fairy tales back in the days when humans were still incapable of separating themselves from nature, when everything around them merged into a unified image of indivisible universe. From the perspective of scientific knowledge, this is undoubtedly nonsense. Any biologist will tell you that a human and a horse are dissimilar, that they have different sets of chromosomes, and are, in fact, genetically incompatible. Does this mean that centaurs exist only in fantasy world and have no place in reality? But why, for what reason did the human mind create such images? Was it only because of the limited cognitive abilities of the humans?

More detailed analysis demonstrates that human exploration of the universe at all stages of development, gradually led to discovering the processes that *an individual could only envision in the form of centaur-phenomena, centaur-processes, and centaur-metaphors — first in nature, and later — in society.* Here is an example of atomic sub-particles, which we can call micro-centaurs — electrons, positrons. In fact, how else can we explain, or envision that these micro-particles are simultaneously particles, but also waves, which are contrary not only to classical physics, but also common sense, which rejects such duplicity as physical nonsense.

The road to this conclusion was surrounded by much drama, since the minds of scientists, alongside with the experiments they were conducting rejected the possibility of existence of such paradoxes. Many great thinkers as Max Born, Albert Einstein, and Ernest Rutherford for a long time could not grasp the contradictions of their discoveries. It was first Louis de Broglie, and, later Niels Bohr that attempted to connect the unconnected — and the atom became a centaur of our consciousness. Louis De Broglie has proven that the electron is capable of behaving as both a particle and a wave. This was a revolution that marked the beginning of the new era in physics (Trofimov. 2000). In order to explain this phenomenon N. Bohr substantiated the principle of subsidiarity that explained «centaur» nature of the atom based on two mutually exclusive approaches, which complement each other, creating a complete picture of the phenomenon at hand. However, as demonstrated by many foreign as well as domestic scientists, this principle cannot be applied to all natural phenomena, especially social processes.

If we continue listing manifestations of centaur-problems, we can offer an example of a seemingly absurd assertion, an assessment, later proven by W. Heisenberg: A, multiplied by B, can and cannot equal B, multiplied by A.

D. Danin in his book-reflection, «The inevitability of a Strange World» argues that if a man was able to journey (only forward) through the Universe, after an unspecified period of time he would return to the starting point of his journey. Absurd? Nonsense? No, we have encountered a special case (albeit hypothetical) of paradox that characterizes our inability of imagining this combination of non-combinable within our perception of the universe (Danin. 1964).

Studying the principle of uncertainty and its consequences allowed L. Landau to assert that an individual in the process of cognizing nature is capable of breaking loose from his imagination, of discovering and realizing even substances that he is not capable of envisioning.

Summarizing, we can say that new phenomena were uncovered (primarily in the micro-world, later in society) that were reflected in social, group and individual consciousness as centaur-problems, making adjustments to understanding and interpretation of many situations of social life.

8.2. Centaur-problems in social life

Situations, when scientific knowledge focuses on issues of social life, which appear before us as an unusual kind of social centaurs, are especially difficult to explain.

Analyzing paradoxes of consciousness we notice that artistic thought had long utilized the method of combining the non-combinable. Artistic theory allows creating such combinations, if it helps reveal flukes of history or oddities of human life. In Hellenic poetry a stylistic method was applied, known as oxymoron, which literally means «witty-dumb», symbolizing combining the incompatible. For example, we find «living corpse» in Leo Tolstoy's work, Turgenev's «living relics», A. Block's «cold number's heat» and «Oh, look! She is happy to be sad, so overdressed and naked!» by Anna Akhmatova.

You have to agree that we do not object to these word combinations, we do not call these images nonsense or absurdity, and we do not feel puzzled by them. On the contrary, we admire imaginative comparisons and such unusual verbal skills.

What if we turn our attention back to reality? Do these problems-centaurs, phenomena-centaurs and images-centaurs really exist? In my opinion, we encounter them daily. They emerge, function and surround us in everyday life. But with one amendment. They emerge in our consciousness, manifest themselves in our perception of incomprehensible, unexplained processes and phenomena. The very object of research focus is not always aware of its own «centaur-likeness».

Take the example of a factory owner-industrialist Savva Morozoff, a prominent representative of Russia's society of the late 19th and early 20th centuries. The fact that alongside with successful business ventures, he was also an enthusiastic patron of arts and serious supporter of cultural figures is hardly surprising. His friendship and financial support of Bolsheviks is much harder to explain. There were several attempts to clarify this outstanding man's strange behavior. Some considered it a whim that he could easily afford. Others though it was a form of public protest against the social circle he belonged to, lifestyle and values of which he did not share. The third group blamed the Bolsheviks for misleading Morozoff, lying to him. But perhaps this individual was a centaur, whose consciousness and beliefs are a vivid example of combining the non-combinable, but from the standpoint of comprehending reality that was prevalent then and still continues to dominate. Up until now, many cannot comprehend how various styles of thinking, contradictory values and orientations, paradoxical actions can co-exist in a single individual. Similar examples, when individuals exist in one dimension, but profess ideas rejecting that dimension, their origins, lifestyle and environment are significant enough to warrant special consideration.

Paradoxically, such «centaur-like» consciousness and behavior is typical of many historical figures. For example, T.More, one of the brightest minds of utopian socialism, in 1529–1532 was a British Chancellor and occupied various other important government posts, preaching ideas incompatible with his social status and official rank. Similarly, John of Damascus was one of such centaurs, 8th century Christian devotee, an author of the majority of Orthodox Chants. He was also a minister to the Caliph, naturally, a Muslim, who valued John a great deal and missed him every time he left on a desert monastic retreat. «John, beloved by the Caliph...» − the opening words of A.K. Tolstoy's poem about John of Damascus.

This centaur-like consciousness and behavior can explain the phenomenon, when many members of nobility and bourgeois culture became active supporters of the proletarian dictatorship and the Soviet state. Many have not renounced the value systems that they professed, but thought they could serve the new ideals, despite the fact that they often contradicted or ruled out the old ones. They would not betray the old values; they did not renounce or criticize, and even tried to follow them (lifestyle, indentured servants, concepts of honor and dignity, rejecting the «vulgarity of the bourgeoisie», etc.). Perhaps it was the very combination of the incompatible, their centaur-like nature that led many of them to a tragic end in 1930's, when primitive intellect of the group that rose to power was unable to comprehend this phenomenon. According to their pursuers, it could have only been explained by duplicity, deliberate concealment of their true intentions and reluctance to contribute to the progress of socialism, to be «like everyone else».

We came across centaurs in modern life as well. How else can we explain a phenomenon of entrepreneur-communist? If «normal» way of thinking rejects the possibility of combining un-combinable, carriers of this mentality are suspected of all mortal sins: faking (one or the other position), or conscious falsification, fulfilling the task of »preserving the Party funds», even in attempting to secure their future in case of return to communism, etc., etc. Perhaps, we are dealing with a centaur-problem, created my modern day reality?

As far as social phenomena are concerned, we have to point out the fact that a number of unique economic structures (former collective and state farms, enterprises, organizations) have sprouted in modern day Russia, phantasmagorical combining socialist and capitalist beginnings, methods of providing social protection and social guarantees or achieving productivity, new managerial methods. Often times, such centaur-enterprises are more stable, viable than their counterparts that merely follow rules of liberal or socialist economics only (Kalughina. 2000; Vishnevskiy, Shapko.2006).

Individuals can be centaurs as well. Academician B. Raushenbach believes, that «any normal human being is born with the makings of a centaur» (Raushenbakh. 1996: See also: Baranov. 2006). Analysis of socio-political views of individuals demonstrates that they can share liberal with socialist views, republican with monarchist, or chauvinist with internationalist. Studies show, this is not a fluke, not an exception, but rather a norm, very characteristic of *homo sapiens et sensis.*

We have to question dubious attempts on behalf of politicians and their think tanks to divide the population (people) into supporters of socialism or liberalism, monarchists or republicans, patriots or nationalists. Real people are, in essence, centaurs, combining mutually exclusive views and ideological orientations in their consciousness and behavior.

8.3.   Centaur-problem as a special form of manifestation of paradoxes of consciousness and behavior

So, why do centaurs emerge in people's consciousness and behavior? How can centaur-problems be resolved? If we analyze symbiosis of mutually exclusive orientations in the consciousness of individuals and groups of people, we can explain the «centaur-ism» in a variety of different ways. First, I would like to once again point out that a *centaur is a special form of contradiction, specific manifestation of paradoxes.* This is not just multiplicity, contradiction that is inherent in social or group consciousness. It is a state of consciousness (and knowledge as well) that reflects combining the un-combinable, — that is, when the mind cannot explain concurrent existence of two (or more) mutually exclusive beginnings. Consequently, we are encountering a different class of processes and phenomena that possess outstanding characteristics in cognizing the world.

Summarizing, I would like to say that, *firstly, centaur-problem is a special, specific, but not exclusive form of paradox of human consciousness and behavior* that existed at all stages of human development. The modern state of social consciousness and activities does not exempt us from various expressions of centaur-ism. *Secondly, centaur-problems reflect a special case of search for answers to unexplored objective processes,* where our cognitive capabilities are limited due to various circumstances. *Thirdly, centaur-problems have a pronounced tendency to grow in their manifestations during periods of change in social relations,* disruptions in social connections and instability. To a certain degree, it becomes a norm. *And finally, ignorance and neglect of centaur-problematic situations in society leads politicians and their research teams to false assumptions, conclusions, and creates conditions for the failure of their actions,* especially when they continue to think along the lines of the principle of linearity of societal development, not noticing contradictions or paradoxes of many situations.

Centaur-problem can manifest itself in different ways. It may exist on a subconscious level, when people do not even suspect that they are «carriers» of such a paradox. The fact that they possesses centaur-like consciousness is apparent to a researcher, but not to the individuals incapable of recognizing their contradictory position, demonstrating irrational potential of real functioning consciousness.

With regard to the study of newly discovered contradictions in objective reality, it is appropriate to say that their identification and validation substantially enriches the theory of cognition. In particular, it needs to be clarified how centaur-problems relate to the law of unity and struggle of the opposites, with universal formula of dialectics, which permits, requires, and sometimes demands predominance of one of the opposing forces over the other.

In order to ascertain the essence and content of this category of phenomena a number of methods can be applied. First of all, the principle of subsidiarity (complementarity) (Bohr. 1967; Danin. 1978). It is in the form of a centaur, that a man and a horse complete each other. This combination creates a fundamentally different image, not reducible to its two constituent parts. It has independent significance and a life its own. As mentioned above, this principle was applied by

N. Bohr to explain paradoxes of the microcosm. It can, with certain stipulations, be used to explain social phenomena.

Here, the principle of subsidiarity suggests that social phenomenon, process or image can be explained and interpreted from different, or even mutually exclusive positions, generally forming a single phenomenon. Thus, a person can be an internationalist and a chauvinist simultaneously. In one case, his attitude toward one or two issues is revealed and recorded, for example, his attraction to internationalist beliefs. On the other occasion he demonstrates nationalist, chauvinistic attitude toward a different problem. He considers them both to be true, sincerely convinced of their authenticity. Despite these conflicting positions, human consciousness and social consciousness are integrated, merged together and act as a unified entity, which can be split in the process of cognition, but not by the carrier of this consciousness. Thus, the principle of complementarity, recognizing the existence of mutually exclusive perceptions of social reality, nevertheless suggests that within the framework of common approach these opposing positions need to be investigated permitting to achieve a more complete, and comprehensive description of the other process, phenomenon, image or personality that is being studied, since it now possesses new characteristics, different form its constituent elements.

In order to explain and resolve centaur-problems, the concept of convergence may be utilized. This concept is widely used in natural sciences. In social sciences and public life this notion appeared relatively recently. Comparing the development of two social systems — capitalism and socialism — many scientists concluded that we need to analyze their interpenetration, mutual enrichment and rapprochement rather than each system separately. In the USSR, academician A.D. Sakharov raised this problem, its socio-political aspect in all its global importance.

However, there are a few different interpretations of the concept of convergence.

With regard to social consciousness, the essence of particularities of applying the concept of convergence lies in the fact that when explicating this phenomenon as a centauric (incongruous merger of socialist and liberal views) this paradox should be resolved as follows. We can assume that human consciousness is specifically focused on those points that are common to all operating philosophies, for both socialism and liberalism, their acknowledgement of the quest, initiative, their own particular interpretation of social protection, belief in technological progress and several other common characteristics. In this situation, a person sees certain something, unifying these two mutually exclusive positions and completes this union with what he considers rational, meaningful and important from these two different approaches. Based on this, a centaur emerges, though in this case we can explain its existence, its prevalence, and not just exclusiveness and paradoxicality.

Consequently, centaur-ism in human consciousness and behavior can be overcome through search for certain common (and important) characteristics that can be evaluated from the viewpoint of the convergence theory, as starting point for accomplishing combination of non-combinable.

Solving a centaur-problem in the consciousness and behavior of individuals is possible based on the principal of *dualism, the antinomies,* when both mutually exclusive opinions and concepts are recognized as true. Moreover, both of them can be proven with fairly convincing argumentation. But they can successfully coexist only when their existence does not imply the elimination of one of them. On the contrary, their simultaneous functioning is possible and likely. Thus, two mutually exclusive statements are vividly manifested in social consciousness: discovery and use of nuclear power as a blessing and a tragedy, the source of possible catastrophe, complete and total annihilation of all humankind. In other words, scientific knowledge, often in spite its greatness and pride for the human mind, has caused and still can cause incalculable harm. This conclusion to a certain degree correlates with the passage from the Old Testament, the book of Ecclesiastes«...in much wisdom, there is much grief: and he that increaseth knowledge increaseth sorrow.»

The method of consensus in solving the centaur-problems is of extreme importance. Centaur — is a metaphor for compromise, but a special kind of compromise, when all (we emphasize — ALL — *Zh.T.*) the participants arrive at a unanimous decision. This is not a principle of majority rule, or a principle of «people are always right», far less a suppression or rejection of one view point by another, replacement by the prevailing one (especially if it comes from power or wealth), rather a principle of consent (harmonization of interests) of all the participants of the process without exceptions.

This is a very complex and labor-intensive process, since it is much easier to achieve subordination of «minority» to «majority» than to reach *a consensus.* Modern world has already developed certain principles of consensus that do not allow one position to dominate over the other, even under the majority banner. A vivid example of it is the work of the UN Security Council. Undoubtedly, these principles are cumbersome and complex, sometimes unpredictable, at times confusing and absurd, but as history demonstrates, in most cases, following them have insured humanity from many mistakes. It should be emphasized that the results of consensus become clear from a distance, not at the time of reaching a joint decision.

This model is being followed not only by international associations. This style gradually becomes a norm for economic and political organizations, attempting to introduce this principle into other spheres of social activities. Although, the implementation of this principle is extremely complex, contradictory and often paradoxical, but, as experience demonstrates, it is extremely productive.

The other method of solving the centaur-problems — *compromise* — is no less important. Its primary purpose is reaching an agreement through mutual concessions. This concept is close to the notion of consensus, but has independent significance, since it is not always possible to reach an acceptable agreement on all issues. But the compromise is aimed precisely at reaching such an agreement. Firstly, compromise presumes that some problems can be left out, remain «behind the scenes», removed from the agenda, postponed, but not at the expense of fundamental issues, for the sake of which the participants come to this agreement in the first place. Secondly, all parties are compromising to some extent, resulting in positions, which now have different essence from the ones initially stated. It is obvious, that the Russian-Ukrainian treaty, governing relations between the two countries, despite harsh criticism from both extreme right and left-wing fractions in both states, in essence represents such rational balanced compromise that addresses the fundamental issues of relations between the two countries. However, it is leaving out multiple problems that presently exist (Black Sea Fleet, Crimea, question of language, some territorial disputes). The art of compromise lies in balance between the interests of the parties, so that they do not feel slighted or limited in their rights.

It is no less important for the mutual compromise not to emasculate the essence of the principal issue; otherwise it would not take long to figure out that it «does not work». An example of such compromise are the decisions regarding the functioning of the Commonwealth of Independent States — during 15 years of its existence there were about 2500 documents adopted. Most of them were just empty declarations, in actuality incapable of solving a single issue, since they were devoid of all rational meaning and common sense. Those sorts of agreements cannot be defined as compromise — it is conciliation, which is extremely counterproductive. Furthermore, it always fraught with unforeseen consequences, concealing incompetence, mistrust and other evils.

And in conclusion. Perhaps D.A. Danin was right, when working on his book «The Inevitability of a Strange World» he wrote: «You can prophesy, even joke that some day, a whole science — centauristics — will emerge. Its subject will be the delicate structure of paradoxes (and more)» (Danin. 1996. P. 19).

References

Baranov Y.U. *Paradox Taneeva (Taneev' Paradox)* // Literaturnaya gazeta. 2006. No 51.

Bohr N. *Zhizn i tvorchestvo (Life and Creations)* (Trnsl. from Danish.). Moscow, 1967.

Danin D. *Neizbezhnost' strannogo mira (Strange World is Inavoidable).* Moscow, 1964.

Danin D. *Start kentavristiki (Starting Centauristics)* // Vestnik RGGU. Vyp. 1. 1996.

Danin D.S. *Nils Bohr.* Moscow, 1978.

Kalughina Z.I. *Paradoksy agrarnoi reformy v Rossii: sotsiologhitsheskiy analiz transformatsionnikh protsessov (Paradoxes of Agrarian Reform in Russia: an Analysis of Transformation Processes).* Novosibirsk, 2000.

Kentavrisitka: opyt sotshetaniya nesotstetaemogo / Pod red. D Danin, D. Khubova. Moscow, 1996. P. 19.

Kentavrisitka: opyt sotshetaniya nesotshetaemogo... P. 73.

Mify narodov mira (Myths of Nations of the World). Moscow, 1987. Vol. 2. P. 638–639.

Raushenbakh B. *Kentavr i ne kentavr (Centaur and Non-centaur)* // Vestnik RGGU. Vyp. 1. Moscow. 1996.

Trofimov D. *Vek Nobilya: ludi i proekty (The Age of Noble. Persons and Projects)* // Nezavisimaya gazeta. 2000. No 11. December 20.

Vishnevskiy Yu.R., Shapko V.T. *Paradoxal'niy molodoy chelovek (Paradoxical Young Man)* // Sociologhicheskie issledovaniya. 2006. No 6.

Chapter 9. **Phantoms of social consciousness and behavior**

> Enlightenment should to be introduced in moderation, avoiding bloodshed if possible (from a statute of Mayor Benevolenski).
>
> *M.E. Saltykov-Shchedrin* (1826–1889),
> Russian writer

In the process of analyzing paradoxes of social conscious one other specific phenomenon was identified – the phantoms. The term «phantom» describes occurrences that embody unique, sometimes abnormal, extravagant forms of social (public) activity, capable of unexpected influence on political, economic and social processes. Carriers of these forms of activity possess certain hypertrophied social characteristics (excessive thirst for power, boundless desire for wealth and unhealthy aspiration for celebrity and fame). In conjunction with certain personal socio-psychological characteristics, they personify a very specific group of political and public figures, representatives of financial-oligarchic circles, whose emergence became possible in modern day Russia due to drastic political and economic transformations. It is important to point out that the phantom phenomena, which latently existed throughout the entire history, during every historical period, and in every country in a state of collapse of social and moral foundations, tend to manifest themselves as a profound social occurrence, significantly impacting ongoing social processes. Moreover, their influence is essentially destructive, manifested at all the levels of social structure, including basic level of our lives — our personal and work environment.

During the 1990's, in particular, phantoms of varying scale and caliber have reemerged based on new specific forms of social consciousness and behavior. A well-known writer Yuri Bogomolov noted the fairytale-like emergence of the «supernatural» with the collapse of the Soviet system (referring to the tale of disappearing demonic creatures with the first rooster sounding off at the crack of dawn). «At first we had Mr. Kashpirovsky with his s ances and healing powers pop up out of nowhere. Than we were slammed by Mr. Zhirinovsy with his political clowning, followed by Mr. Mavrodi with his financial trickery and Mr. Nevzorov and Dorenko with their informational meditations. Then our social sc ne was hit by a truly paranormal occurrence — oligarch Boris Berezovsky» (*Izvestiya*. September 10, 2001). These peculiar splashes did not go unnoticed: in sociopolitical journalism and political rhetoric the definition of «phantom» was applied to certain extravagant figures of modern social scene and eccentric political stage players. This class of phenomena is comparable to solar flares disrupting social and political space. Who else's rooster did not crow across the political, economic and even cultural sc ne from 1990-2000, and then vanished, leaving behind a baffling impression, momentary or mystical imprint in people's memories? Many of them, however, fascinated the minds of Russian people and occupied top spots of social surveys. For instance, according to the A.V.Kinsburski's data, comparing 100 upper echelon politicians in 1993 and 2000, only 13 of them remained on the list after 10 years (Kinsburski. 2003).

In the process of detailed analysis of paradoxes of consciousness and behavior, certain phenomena came to light that could not be explained by available data, including sociological. This analysis suggested to the author of this book that non of the available theoretical and applied research contains answers regarding the emergence of such phenomena, within the constraints of their paradoxical nature, which stand out from the balanced and relatively stable state of social consciousness, personifying certain exceptional, phantom individuals, whose influence on the social life of our country is unprecedented (Toshchenko. 2005). Alongside with that a purely epistemological question emerges: how appropriate and justified is the use of the word — phantoms — while analyzing social consciousness and social practice?

In order to establish that, let's first concentrate on the utilization of that term in scientific lexicon, political and literary vocabulary.

9.1. What is a phantom?

The term «phantom» in V.I. Dal's classic Russian-language dictionary is described as paintings, phantasmagoric occurrences or a dummy for practice of midwife craft, obstetrics. C.I. Ozhegov concentrates in his dictionary on its first meaning, interpreting it as «bizarre, surreal occurrence, ghost» (Dal' . 1994; Ozhegov. 1991. P. 846). The Academic dictionary of the Russian language defines «phantom» as an apparition, a ghost, fantasy and a figment of imagination; or as an anatomically correct life-size model of a body or a body part used as a visual aid (*Slovar russkogo yazyka.* 1984. Vol. 4. P. 513. Also see: *Novi Slovar russkogo yazyka.* Vol. 2. Moscow, 2000. P. 892). In «Psychological Dictionary» the concept of phantom is associated with «phantom pains» in post-op patients in different stages of recovery from contusion, injuries or amputation. In such cases amputees feel actual pain in limbs that no longer exist (*Psychologichesky slovar.* 1993. P. 388-389. See also: *Universalny slovar inostrannykh slov russkogo yazyka.* 2000. P. 603). Although the latter definition applies to a highly specialized lexicon (medical in this instance), we do encounter a particular phenomenon, when the physical reality is absent, but, at the same time, its imaginary existence represents objective reality, invoking very real feelings and emotions. It carries similarity to phantom memories of certain painful events in people's past that are re-lived with the same unbearable intensity as the actual event.

Occasionally, emergence, existence and functioning of various mystical, secret societies and organizations, whose inner workings remain a mystery not just to their contemporaries, but the subsequent generations as well, is also classified as phantom. And, if their secret life is accidentally disclosed, it is usually just enough to fuel conjunction and speculation that only deepen their mystique (Nikitin. 2000).

This list of definitions is by no means a complete and exhaustive depiction of the diversity of these specific processes and phenomena of our surrounding environment. Especially if we set out to explain social events.

Currently, in real scientific and political vocabulary the term «phantom» is increasingly used to describe and interpret processes and phenomena that do not fit the commonly accepted, normal flow of economic, political social and cultural life. Current use of this concept far exceeded previously recognized limits of its meaning. *First, a number of researchers assign this term to the emergence of such states* as the Taliban regime in Afghanistan, which has undoubtedly been a phantom, a special phenomenon, non-standard, not fitting our typical notion of a state. Some political analysts consider the existence of such countries as

Nicaragua and Cambodia, at certain stages of their historical development to be phantoms that personified very specific, and widely unaccepted by the international community, forms of political rule and the consequent social structures that emerged as a result (*Izvestiya.* September 22, 2001). Regardless of not being officially recognized by the International Community, certain political formations that are still functioning as independent political entities can be classified as phantoms. Nagorni Karabakh, appears to be a unique form of phantom, which exists on one hand, as a sovereign republic, with all the attributes of an independent state (such as president, government, army, etc.), and, at the same time, as a peculiar symbiosis with Armenia (that completely supports it). Clearly, this situation cannot continue indefinitely. Even the participants of the conflict — Armenia and Azerbaijan are eager to admit it.

Second, the «existence» of multiple political parties can be classified as a phantom. For example, during the first half of the 1990's a lot of «informational» noise, as well as primitive, «kitchen racket» (nothing more substantial) was made by the political parties of Konstantin Borovoi, Valeria Novodvorskaya, Lev Ubozhko and a few other mythical characters, followed by the emergence of a series of «democratic parties», organized by various liberal front political figures. In the 1990's every contender had «his or her» party: Mr. Nemtsov, Mr. Kiriyenko, Ms. Hakamada, Mr. Yushenkov, etc. In addition, there were many (up to 180) parties, whose purpose was not always clear even to their creators. In reality, these phantom-parties did not represent anything or anybody. At best they reflected the mood and the sentiment of the «capital gang» — a bunch of painfully ambitious people. They were cluttering the political landscape of the country, discrediting the very purpose of political parties as social institutions, misleading public opinion. The leaders of these so-called «parties» were desperately trying to attract public attention. Considering the uncivilized state of our political culture, as well as barbaric journalistic ethics, any rampantly wild statement guarantied you a spot on television and newspaper pages (Kiva. 2001).

Events of the early 21-century confirmed the diagnosis regarding the phantom nature of such parties. They were long forgotten by the public as well as the very «leaders» of these entities. Many of them disappeared without a trace, with no pomp or circumstance, not unlike those demonic creatures disappearing with the rooster crowing at the crack of dawn. Some turned into insignificant, but occasionally noisy players of political circus.

Third, the phantom manifestations began especially distinctly appearing during political debate and election campaigns, when the «twins», the contenders with the same last name started popping up on the gubernatorial and mayoral candidate lists. That allowed these «candidates» to not only steal the legitimate candidate's votes but also occasionally win a third or fourth place in the race. These methods of cheating voters are achieved through deliberate conscious creation of phantom figures that help deliver real results and have real impact on the election campaign (*Izvestiya.* November 9, 2001).

According to the experts, the ban on discrimination in Russian law in its current interpretation can be safely classified as fictional or phantom rights, since, in Mrs. M. Levin's opinion, «they are practically devoid of substance, are not interpreted in the legislation and are not used in legal practice». Ultimately, this is one of the reasons for the emergence of the «hierarchy of the citizens with different levels of legal status» in Russia (Quoted from: *Obshestvennye nauki i sovremennost.* 2003. No.5. P. 40).

Fifth, the phantom phenomenon is used in ideological struggle. According to V.Senderov, terminology is extremely important in ideological brainwash: phantom notions emerge and gain actual strength via linguistics. This is particularly evident in the development of totalitarian ideology: successfully chosen terms, words — are half the victory. However, these are not simple choices: the «chosen» words must possess a number of non-trivial qualities: for instance, they have to be virtually invulnerable to criticism. In order to achieve that, the phantom terminology has to, first, «almost adequately» depict reality. So that the mere possibility of labeling them as nonsense is nonexistent, and criticism would not require any meaningful or strategic explanations — rendering it absolutely ineffective as weapon in the fight for hearts and minds. Furthermore, all-conquering words have to be picked out so that any potential criticism would appear immoral, thus preemptively preventing any anticipated revisions, even ineffective ones (Senderov. 2003).

Thus, during Soviet times the entire population of the country was thoroughly convinced that the whole world was divided into socialist and capitalist society. Moreover, the socialist society, regardless of what was occurring within it, was undoubtedly better than the capitalist, since there was no exploitation of people by other people. These global phantoms were supplemented by no less important ones: such clichés as «building Communist (developed Socialist) society», «social equality», «progressive mankind» that were in essence ideological phantoms, have been widely utilized in the ideological work of the CPSU. These slogans that captured the imaginations of millions of people, turned out to be phantoms, failing to withstand the test of time and historical reality.

Phantoms in ideology of the new Russian State can be clearly traced. As poet and journalist I. Golubnichiy noted: «the principal tragedy of the modern Russian society (in its entirety, all social circles included) is that our daily, real life, on our free will or by someone else's design, always ends up being dominated by various imaginary constructs, which, more often than not, turn out to be groundless. Deliberating (often irresponsibly and incompetently) over what needs to be, we often forget that real life does not necessarily correspond to our fabrications and usually follows its own rules» (Golubnichiy. 2003).

Contradictions between realities of life and the very «best» among the concepts produce ideological phantoms. For instance, since the 1990's the necessity and inevitability of «free speech» or «market democracy» for any kind of «progress» were persistently forced onto the mass consciousness. This resulted in the media being overrun by uneducated, embittered and often unbalanced individuals. Consequently, the public opinion that they shaped matches our acrimonious and demoralized consciousness.

The most baffling aspect of this was the fact that a sizable portion of writers and journalists were advocating «freedom of speech», the very people that should understand better than anyone that the power of the word can become a potent weapon of creation or destruction, depending on the persons that yield it. This would be comparable to professional military advocating for free use of weaponry. This situation, when the famed level of trust in printed word plummeted and became almost nonexistent, and literary and journalistic professions were demoted from creative to service sphere, catering to special interests and manipulating social consciousness, resulted in well deserved and unwavering contempt among common people. Over time, many advocates of the «freedom of speech» experienced that freedom on their own skins: they were fired (or their services were no longer required), when their position on the subject matter did not match the sentiment of their masters. On top of that, this «freedom of speech» became the freedom for a chosen few, since any attempt to speak out by anyone «uninvited to the party» was brutally suppressed. Finally this freedom became a potent tool of manipulation. Is this not an example of a phantom that has disappeared leaving the «phantom» pain behind?

Sixth, the phantom phenomenon did not spare science, expressed in numerous attempts to: 1) return to various types of para – and pseudo-scientific knowledge; 2) revise social and humanitarian knowledge. As far as para-scientific phantoms are concerned, they were revived in the form of numerous fabrications about UFOs, eternal energy sources, new *Perpetum mobile*, etc., etc., which can not be substantiated by logic, scientific thought or, far less, by experimental elaboration. With regard to the second, phantom thinking manifested in ambitious efforts of tracing particular national origins and cultural heritage all the way back to Paleolithic period, or attempts to prove superiority of one nation over another. Here, for example, is a phantom statement concocted by Mr. Fomenko and his disciples describing historians: »...they have been doing God knows what for a few hundred years. How many books, dissertations all in vain. How much effort wasted studying «phantom» ...events»? «Traditional historiography is dominated by strictly defined, pre-programmed, subjective approach to the analysis of past events» (Bocharov, Efimov, Chachukh, Chernyshev. 1998. P. 11, 222). But, in turn, they created phantoms of their own that do not withstand any side-by-side comparison not only to the works of historians of the past century, but the entire known history of mankind. Incidentally, it should be noted that real social consciousness rates these historical «compositions» quite sensibly: not as real history, but a kind of historical fantasy and adventure.

And, lastly, the concept of «phantom» is used to describe both real, as well as purely hypothetical problems in the field of culture. So, S. Zemlyanoi, analyzing the works of George Lukacs and Bertolt Brecht, concluded that in the 1930s they inadvertently contributed to the birth of another phantom — Soviet literature. This was reflected in the letter of B. Pasternak to N. Aseev: «The difference between modern Soviet literature from its predecessors, it appears, is mostly that it is established on a solid foundation, regardless of whether anyone is reading it or not. It is a proud, self-dominating phenomenon, resting within itself and sharing sanctity and infallibility with other government establishments. Literature that is independent from uncertainties of reading. This is powerful, however incomprehensible: present-day exists foreshadowed by death of the author and dictatorship of the reader». In S. Zemlyanoi's opinion, this state matches the definition of a phantom, or a centaur of socialist realism, which combines both ideological as well as aesthetic requirements. It is their very deficiencies that lead to the disappearance of this particular phenomenon that could not withstand the test of time, regardless of its fairly lengthy existence (Zemlyanoi. 2002).

Occasionally the concept of phantoms is used in the analysis of the problems of art culture, methods and techniques of explaining various literary works. Thus, A. Khomutov while examining the «Queen of Spades» from the perspective of comparative analysis of the A.S. Pushkin's and P.I. Chaikovsky's approaches, talks about the ghosts and phantoms of this opera, expressing his deeply personal view of the whole range of issues: content, interpretations, and even publishing efforts (Khomutov. 2003).

So, this overview of various interpretations and perceptions of phantoms in social life allows us to define them as: 1) an unusual phenomenon that manifests itself in an extremely specific form; 2) an anomaly that does not conform to the commonly accepted forms of social organization; 3) extremely destructive processes that inhibit or discredit existing rules of operation; 4) not just divergent, but confrontational and deliberately provocative actions that clash with the surrounding reality; 5) contradictions between the desired and real life, when subjective aspirations oppose objective trends of social development.

9.2. The essence and content of the phantoms of social consciousness and behavior

Analysis of the various existing view points that reflect deliberations over distinctive peculiarities of various economic and political realities, seldom, if ever refers to such specific phenomenon as phantoms of social consciousness and behavior, characteristic of a sizable group of political and social figures, representatives of financial and economic cliques, functionaries of the mass media that embody certain splashes, bursts, anomalies, characteristic of the 1990's. In other words, the notion of «phantom» has presently undergone significant changes and includes a fairly diverse class of processes and phenomena of social consciousness and behavior.

First, mystics, serial killers with philosophical mindset, vampire-rapists, killers-for-hire started appearing. Their numbers have increased significantly, although their emergence is difficult to explain. In this regard, certain researchers believe that «revealing the depth of human soul is their ultimate creative task» (*Versia.* 2001. No. 19). *Second, phantoms appeared in political and social arenas.* For the past 15 years, just about everybody in politics and economics, who was guilty of audacious behavior, has then vanished without leaving as much as a memory or a trace. And some of them used to be at the top of public opinion surveys, gripping the minds and imaginations of Russian people. Not surprisingly, the 2001 survey of the students of the Russian State University for the Humanities demonstrated that 17 and 20 year-olds did not respond to such names as Burbulis, Shakhrai and Shumeiko, etc., the very people that decided the fate of the country in recent past. This is completely understandable: in early 1990's today's students were children that did not care about the «grownup» civic problems. What caused this sudden appearance and rapid disappearance of these politicians from the pages of current history of our society and state has to be examined. We should give it some thought and try to ascertain the essence and the latent causes that lead to emergence of these phantoms in Russian reality in general, and politics in particular.

Objective trends of development of Russian society contributed to the *reasons* for emergence of phantoms of social consciousness and behavior. The collapse of the Soviet Union led to disintegration of established way of life, revision of the old value system and orientations of tens of millions of people. It was not just the country that disappeared; it was the very foundation of the philosophical platform that people used to rely upon in their interaction with society, national and professional organizations, colleagues, friends, next-door neighbors and the rest of the world. This led to changes in people's consciousness, open or latent rejection of many of the old values, aims and goals. But the world outlook as a key link of consciousness is fairly conservative: it continues to accumulate attachment to the past, approval and criticism of the present and uncertainty about the future, or, to be precise, the means of achieving the goals, intentions and interests.

On the other hand, the changes that entered into our lives with the arrival of market economy led to the appearance of such people who, in this new environment, due to their personal socio-psychological characteristics, recognized not only the possibility changing their lives, but improving their social standing, official status and gaining recognition. Often these individuals were incapable of making an adequate assessment of their own abilities and potential, which only escalated the situation in the form of ambitious rhetoric and actions, extravagant claims of greatness, genius and exclusivity. Frequently this attitude and behavior was dictated by desire to compensate for their former lack of recognition (as they believed) in Soviet society. So, they did not just demand rehabilitation, but often times — recognition and admiration of their former «heroism», as compensation for what they considered to be, their past humiliations and abuses.

With regard to the *substance* of this phenomenon, in the environment of unstable social processes, during crisis situations or due to circumstances phantom personalities are characterized by the following features: a) particular attitude toward major or particular, but crucial political issues; b) ambition, aspiration to «make it», to possess (or have) capital (financial resources); c) desire to impose their vision of social problems and even attempt to carry it out; d) «claim to fame» — real or imaginary, virtual or accidental.

Let us not discount such features as *ambitious goals,* exhibited in particular characteristics of their carriers. In other words, this category of people represents a particular social phantom, a solar flare, exploding onto a fairly even, balanced scene of social consciousness in the form of an exceptional and unique phenomena, disrupting social life with their behavior, their actions, while, at the same time, imposing their vision and interpretation of the occurring changes. Their activity influences (to a great deal, in some cases) principal and fundamental questions of the political structure and social life.

Among all the categories of political, economic and other figures, only the ones that possess very specific characteristics are of great scientific interest: first, their behavior fully (or substantially) contradicts the interests and concerns of the rest of the population; second, they suggest (or even implement) certain actions that can be called outlandish (to say the least); third, they possess very specific personal qualities.

9.3. Main characteristics of phantom personality types

Analyzing phantoms of social consciousness and behavior, we need to point out personality traits of this type of people, which made them «light up» political, economic or socio-cultural scene. Moreover, we need to draw a clear distinction between phantom type and classical type political or a social figure. The latter are extensively described in scientific and, particularly, psychological literature (Rakityansky. 2001). But, from the sociological perspective, we need to uncover particular type — phantom and, therefore, his main character traits, rather then describe specific persons.

So, what should be the basis of our approach? *First,* even preliminary research of these personality types revealed that *many of them are characterized by insatiable, limitless and even pathological thirst for power.* Power for these people becomes an end in itself. In their quest for power they are prepared to jump ideological barriers, step over corpses, turn friends into enemies and visa versa. This category of people is inherently immoral, with no ethics or principles, prepared to lie and cheat in order to possess it. Many among these phantoms, filled with lust for power, were deprived of it during the Soviet days for some objective and subjective reasons. So, their «arrival» symbolized certain revenge, a measure of achievement of desired goal. They crave revenge on those, who, in their opinion, kept them out of the positions of power. Often, among these people, we find a few that during Soviet times were allowed to participate in the leadership of political and social processes, but still felt disadvantaged, since they have not attained a higher position or social status than they used to occupy. Feeling underappreciated, «undervalued», they sought more tangible power then they used to have during the previous political system.

Second, phantom types are characterized by explicit or implicit (undeclared) desire for fame, celebrity and publicity. This category of people needs to be in public eye, have a say in political and social issues, and claims that they express public opinion. They react very painfully to any lack of notice or failure to mention their actions, which leads to defiant outlandish behavior in an attempt to provoke a public outcry. These personality types are prepared to take any kind of actions in order to stay in the limelight, behaving in a way that would keep them the center of public attention.

This painful quest for fame prompts their participation in all kinds of functions and events that attract an audience, and the bigger — the better. This partially explains their «love affair» with the media, particularly television, since it can bring their ideas, fantasies and, often, ravings to millions of people, especially since television encourages this type of outlandish behavior (it showcased more that a few of these insane characters), as a way to broaden their audience. Lust for fame for these people becomes an all-consuming pursuit, invading their thoughts, desires, taking up all their time and effort.

The third indicator of phantom type personality is a pathological thirst for wealth. In order to possess it they engage in various machinations, wheeling-and-dealing, unseemly, improper and, sometimes, criminal activities, utilizing loopholes and gaps in legislation, personal and social connections. In the rest of the world, typically, wealth creation takes years of hard work and dedication, while in post-Soviet Russia various other methods were employed: financial pyramid schemes, voucher and deposit auctions, widely spread threats and violence, including physical elimination of competition or just anyone who got in the way, false bankruptcies were perpetrated and unjustified privileges were granted.

Not surprising, therefore, was such phenomena as portfolio investors (bankers) that achieved their wealth and power in financial markets due to highly speculative activities, accumulating mind-boggling fortunes, without investing a single ruble in creation of material wealth or spiritual values.

And, finally, let us not discount personal characteristics that are manifested as lust for power, vanity and unbridled ambition. These characters easily changed their political beliefs, actively utilizing the method of «wearing political masks».

In addition, we need to analyze:

a) Ambitions as a specific form of value orientations. In contrast to the traditional values, these aspirations are manifested as a quest for: wealth, resulting in profit-seeking and enrichment at any cost; authority, which fosters extreme lust for power; fame, that is manifested as hypertrophied vanity;

b) Means of their achievement, which can be classified as: first, legitimate, illegitimate or a combination of the above; second, as open or latent, and, third, as a quest for financial, economic or material gains, privileges over the rest of the contenders (ownership of banks, properties, mutual funds, stocks, etc.); state (political) appointments with the government or associated with the government; attempts at becoming a leader of public opinion (claiming the embodiment of needs of the people, or specific groups of people) by forming political parties, social movements or lobbying groups. All of them, to some degree, demanded the support of the media, especially television;

c) Search for answers to the question: *what role* do these phantoms want to assume — defenders of the public interests, corporate representatives; or clearly personal (individualistic) interests.

d) The methods employed by these phantoms: audacious, arrogant statements and declarations; manipulation, and, often, lies and slander. Financial resources, political connections, the degree of identification with religion, ethnic or corporate interests might serve as regulators of phantoms' activities as well.

While analyzing these characteristics, we need to take into account the environment, against the background of which these ambitions, means and methods of their implementation are realized.

9.4. Classification of phantom type personalities

With regard to the classification of phantom personality types, we will only focus on the ones that characterize very specific manifestations of their consciousness and behavior. This is the first preliminary provision. The second restriction is that we do not analyze a wide cross-section of characters of the contemporary historical process, but only representatives of money and power, since this environment produced practically all forms and types of phantom activity. Thus, political leaders, active players of market economy, representatives of the media that are characterized by very specific, non-trivial and anomalous (in the modern sense of this word) forms of consciousness and behavior are the main subject of our sociological study. If we narrow our focus even further, from the sociological standpoint, socially significant features of both official, as well as personal activities that have destructive influence on the progress of social and political life in Russia, are of great interest to our research. Since they are extremely diverse, we need to classify the phantoms of social consciousness and behavior based on the analysis of orientations, directions and socially significant features of their bearers, and determine their role in the changes taking place in the social life of Russia.

Information at hand suggests that phantoms are an unavoidable attribute of transitional period. It cannot be ignored or dismissed. It needs to be researched, and the knowledge has to be utilized to help answer urgent questions of development of Russia. We have to emphasize that phantom characteristics of consciousness and behavior are diverse and multifaceted. Phantoms as phenomenon of our era appear before us in all their contradictory guises, since the causes of their emergence are far from straightforward or simple. Nevertheless, we are confident that it is the phantoms along with the paradoxical man that define the modern day era in our country. They are a powerful destabilizing factor. The danger of this phenomenon also lies in the fact that they are active and extremely destructive participants in manipulation of public opinion.

In our opinion, for the purpose of classifying the phantoms of social consciousness and behavior, research of such basic features (characteristics), as power, fame and wealth, which in various combinations contribute to the formation of corresponding phantom personality types, is the most promising kind of analysis. This approach, i.e. analysis of the role and place of power, fame and fortune in the consciousness and behavior of these personality types, allows following classification of the phantoms:

For the first type all three major pretensions — wealth, power and fame are very important. This group corresponds to such distinctive type of phantom consciousness and behavior, as «mutants» or «demons», whose numbers are significant. The following behavioral algorithm is characteristic of this group. For most of their lives they professed a certain ideology, and then, during the period of change, declared themselves to be supporters of directly opposite ideas and beliefs. And this denunciation usually took shape of fiercest criticism, not just a rejection. At the same time, they often lay claim to possession of authority and power, regardless of the direction it is heading. Their «oracle-like' discoveries often go against simple morality, since the rejection of old ideology turns into a «garage sale» of this denunciation, trafficking of new beliefs and criticism of old ideas. They do not abide by Christian morality, which demands that during life-altering transitions, a human being should spend time alone with God and his conscience, pondering over these life changes. Otherwise, this transition signifies a complete mutation, not just changes in consciousness and behavior.

«Imitators», «Equilibrists» and «Pharisees» can be classified as the fist type. (This particular terminology should be utilized in this instance and for future references as a method of attributing conditional meaning — a term that has certain ring, sense and significance to the public, most accurately describing basic social characteristics of the phantoms).

The second type pursues wealth and power. It is particularly vividly embodied in the personality type that can be described as «predator» or «adventurer». This is the ideology of modern day oligarchs, swindlers and petty scammers, whose objective is to ensure that embezzlement and misappropriation of the national treasures is justified as «concern» for the future of the people and the nation. These are the people that are making statements that palaces built and fortunes amassed, regardless of who they belong to, still constitute a national treasure (heritage), since they can trade hands, and, it is the society that ultimately benefits from it. Often times predators use the following argument: yes, the first generation of the wealthy (just like in America) — is a generation of thieves and looters, but their children and grandchildren (the next generation) are respected members of a democratic society. The danger of this type is has to do with the fact that having gained the economic power they start pursuing political ambitions. The «power-wealth» combination also attracts such types as «hypocrites» and «the mummers» (carnival performers).

The third type focuses on power and fame. It corresponds with the «roving forwards» (jumpers). We witness many examples of such «migrations» across party lines (or social movement lines), from one to another, and another, and the third, fourth, infinitely. Moreover, it is almost always accompanied by fundamental changes in the previously proclaimed principals, rejection of the old adherences, praising of the new preferences or advantageous (to themselves) «discoveries». All of this is hiding behind excuses that the new orientations are the embodiment of the «voice of the people», reflection of their desires and aspirations. In reality this is nothing but a struggle for power, capital and thirst to satisfy their ambitions at the expense of the nation. This category is characterized by conscious support of paradoxical behavior and consciousness of the general population, since it promises considerable benefits and significant personal gains. These features are also characteristic of the «malingerers», «information killers» and «weathervanes».

The fourth type, also focused on fame and fortune, is epitomized by the term *«poser»*. Theirs is a typical behavior of a character, tirelessly professing «preoccupation» with social well-being, which is rather descriptively manifested, on one hand, as rhetoric, irresponsible chatter (that is attracting maximum attention), and, on the other hand, hoarding and looting of former national treasures (these activities are thoroughly concealed). This is accompanied by putting on a show, like helping an orphanage or a nursing home, a hospital or a sports team. According to the election results, such «care» is quite effective, yielding tangible dividends in the form of top administrative positions or parliamentary seats. Moreover this personality type extremely painfully reacts to any signs of fading attention to their persons: they are willing to go to any length to keep public attention focused on them. It corresponds to the terms «remora» (sucker fish), «snob» and «lackey».

However, there are special types of phantom personalities, whose consciousness and behavior are dominated by just one of these orientations. *So, the fifth type only craves power.* This phenomenon is multifaceted, diverse and treacherous. For example, let us describe the behavior of political nationalists. They are the ones responsible for various types of «independences», «sovereignties» or, simply, concealed, «undercover» seizure of power. On one hand, they often declare universal values – respect for other nations, recognition of their rights to their own language and culture. But, on the other hand, in specific circumstances, they implement the policies of infringement on rights and freedoms of other nations, fuel xenophobia, and, often times, instigate assassinations and humiliation of people of other races and nationalities, just because they have different political views and «stand in the way» of «their» nation. They are the ones that instigate mental violence. They resurrect social myths, reshuffle history and «scientifically» prove their claims against other countries and nationalities. This is the basis for emergence and sustenance of domestic chauvinism. Similar or corresponding features, taking into account certain peculiarities, can be attributed to the «chauvinists», «quasi–dictators», «muscleman» or «hired guns» and some other characters of political theater, consumed by relentless pursuit for power.

The sixth type is obsessed with being the center of public attention, achieving maximum fame. This feature is mostly characteristic of the widely spread personality type that can be called «herostrats». This phantom personality type is ready to risk life and limb to be famous, even commit a murder, just to gain recognition or make an everlasting impression. They are prepared to destroy a country or break up an organization, burn down a house, even kill anyone who stands in the way, or simply in order to validate their actions. This phantom behavior develops in hypochondriacs, painfully ambitious, convinced of their self-importance and originality. They do not like to admit defeat – for them their life is filled with victories and successes, imaginary at times. This pursuit of fame is characteristic of the «marginals», «weathervanes», «twits», «infantiles», «oracles» and «imitators».

And, finally, *the seventh type* is solely focused on *accumulating wealth.* «Pillagers» (or looters) are characteristic of that type. This personality type is trying to profit from the wreck of the past, regardless of whether it has any present value or not. The situation after the collapse of the Soviet Union was reminiscent of a battlefield, where it is not quite clear who won and who lost, or what awaits the participants tomorrow. But there is a brief cease-fire, when there is no clear outcome of the battle. Under these conditions (of economic and political uncertainty), convinced of their total impunity, the urge to plunder emerges. The looting is widespread, as long as there is a way to profit from it — in the political jungle, in economic, ethno-confessional, and even cultural spheres. Within this personality type we find such characters as «comrades = comrades + nouveau riche» and «thugs».

Therefore, our analysis of the modern state of social consciousness and behavior helps us understand the diversity of phantom type personalities. The transitional period in history uncovered this contradiction and painted a clearer picture of what we, as people, currently represent. This very openness and comprehension of the situation at hand inspires hope that a correct diagnosis offers possibilities of overcoming social malaises of modern day Russia. Furthermore, such research enriches our perceptions, our knowledge of social consciousness and behavior, identifies untouched and unanalyzed aspects of the spiritual development of our society. In our opinion, this opens up new horizons of theoretical ideas about the nature and the content of social consciousness, enriches our knowledge of the mechanisms of its transformation into a real social force, and opens new possibilities of explaining the contradictions of social development, especially during a transitional period.

References:

Bocharov L.I., Efimov N.N., Chachukh I.M., Chernyshev I.Yu. *Zagovor protiv russkoi istorii (fakty, zagadki, versii)* (*Conspiracy against Russian history (facts, riddles, versions)*. Moscow, 1998. P. 11, 222.

Dal' V. *Tolkovy slovar zhivogo velikorusskogo yazyka (Dictionary of the Live Great Russian Language)*. Vol. 4. Moscow, 1994.

Golubnichiy I. *Fantom ideologii (Phantom of ideology)* // Predprenimatelstvo. 2003. No. 3.

Portretologiya vlasti. Teoriya i metodologiya psikhologocheskogo portretirovaniya lichnosti v politike (Portretology of power. Theory and methodology of a political portrait of a personality in politics). Moscow, 2004.

Khomutov A. *Sravnitelny analiz (Comparative analysis)*. St. Petersburg, 2003.

Kinsburski A.V. *Transformatsiya strukturi rossyiskoi elity v otsenkakh ekspertov (Transformation of the structure of Russia's elite in the estimates of experts)* // Sotsiologicheskiye Issledovaniya. 2003. No. 9. P. 91.

Toshchenko Zh. T. *Fantomy obshestvennogo soznaniya I povedeniya (Phantoms of the social consciousness and behavior)* // Sotsiologicheskiye Issledovaniya. 2005. No. 12.

Kiva A. *Blizitsya konets «partyi mertvykh dush» i «partyi-fantomov» (The end is coming for the «party of the dead souls» and «phantom-party»)* // Nezavisimaya Gazeta. February 9, 2001.

Nikitin A.L. *Mistiki, rozenkreitsy i tampliery v Sovetskoi Rossii: issledovaniya i materially (Mystics and Templars in the Soviet Russia: materials and research).* Moscow, 2000.

Ozhegov S.I. *Slovar russkogo yazyka (Dictionary of the Russian Language).* Moscow, 1991. P. 846.

Petukhov V.V., Pahomov E.I., Sedova N.N. *Prava cheloveka diskriminatsionnye praktiki v sovremennoi Rossii (Human rights, discrimination practices in modern Russia)* // Obshestvennye nauki i sovremennost. 2003. No.5. P. 40.

Psychologichesky slovar (Psychological Dictionary) / Pod red. A.A. Davidova. Moscow, 1993. P. 388–389. See also: *Universalny slovar inostrannykh slov russkogo yazyka (Universal dictionary of the foreign words in the Russian language).* Moscow, 2000. P. 603.

Rakityansky N.M. *Semnadtsat mgnovenyi demokratii, Lidery Rossii glazami politicheskogo psichologa (Seventeen moments of democracy, Russian leaders through the eyes of a political psychologist).* Moscow, 2001.

Senderov V. *Fantomy yazika i politiki (Phantoms of language and politics)* // Vestnik Evropy. 2003. No. VII–VIII. P. 210.

Slovar russkogo yazyka (Russian language dictionary) / Pod red. A.P. Evgenyevoi. Moscow, 1984. Vol. 4. P. 513. Also see: *Novi Slovar russkogo yazyka (New Russian language dictionary). Tolkovo-slovoobrazovatelny.* Vol. 2. Moscow, 2000. P. 892.

Versia. 2001. No. 19.

Zemlyanoi S. *Lukacs i Brecht kak sovetskie pisateli (Lukacs and Brecht as Soviet authors)* // Nezavisimaya Gazeta. November 14, 2002.

Part III. Types of paradoxes

Chapter 10. Paradoxes and contradictions of economic consciousness and behavior

It is a pity that, when market decisively wins, we will be decisively gone

M. Zhvanetsky (b. 1934)
Russian satirist

Analyzing economic paradoxes, it is appropriate to start with recalling characteristics of economic consciousness and its basic components that are reflected in studies of economists, philosophers, and sociologists (Dratshev. 1977; Kolesov. 1986; Popov. 1981; Fofanov. 1979; Zaslavskaya, Ryvkina. 1991; Verkhovin. 1998; Boykov , Ivanov, Toshchenko. 1990; Sokolova. 2005; etc).

Economic consciousness, throughout the history of mankind, has always reflected, and still reflects, developing situation in the sphere of social production; it has always reacted (although not always adequately) to the changes in socio-economic situation of the population. This consciousness has always represented, and still represents, one of the main forms of comprehending existing social relations, and at the same time, level of knowledge, awareness and evaluation of the ongoing changes in the economy.

Economic consciousness includes cumulative body of knowledge, assessments, motivation, values, attitudes and moods that capture the minds of people and guide them in real life. It is a reflection of property, distribution, exchange and consumption relations. But these, just like all social relations, do not transform by themselves. Any change, especially a drastic one, however paradoxical it may seem, starts with alteration and reorganization of the consciousness. In other words, objective requirements, once they are «ripe», should be mentally perceived, experienced and accepted by the social consciousness. Without this process, these changes can not take root, if they do not resonate in the hearts and minds of the people's.

Analyzing conditions and trends of functioning economic consciousness, specific factors that determine the style of thinking, beliefs and attitudes of people are of great academic and practical importance. They assume particular forms in different social groups, depending on their position in the structure of economic relations and historical situation. These conceptions are refracted in the consciousness through a prism of socio-professional, demographic and other factors. Multidimensional, mosaic, multi-vector and contradictory character of economic consciousness, its links to specific life circumstances are manifested in various forms of people's activity, interests and creativity.

The fact, that consciousness develops, depends upon and specifically reflects (and affects) the relationships of ownership, distribution, exchange and consumption, does not necessarily mean that all of them without exception should be taken into account and analyzed, although this is precisely the essence of theoretical scientific approach. However, theory is only strong when combined with practice. But practice — i.e. real life — poses questions and raises issues that are relevant for a particular society, certain social groups and for a specific historical period. This requires finding the factor, which determines the overall situation in economic consciousness and helps identify problems that majority of population wants solved. True, practice varies as well.

10.1. State and trends of economic consciousness as product of «trophy» economy

State and trends of economic consciousness in modern Russia are determined by attitudes to the idea and realities of the market, which, as events demonstrate, experiences difficulties, complications and contradictions in its development.

Up until mid-1980's market ideas were present in social consciousness as something not related to reality, people's lives, or their families. However, during *perestroika* these ideas gradually captured the minds and hearts of the people, pointing them toward market as their new future. The State commission on economic reforms at the Council of Ministers of the USSR, established July 5, 1989, headed by Academy member L.I. Abalkin, by October 1989, prepared a program, which was the first formally articulated rejection of socialist dogma, recognizing market priority over planning, and admitting the necessity of free prices, competition, stock exchanges and convertible currency for an efficient economy. In early 1990's, sociological studies already reflected that the majority of people accepted market ideas (completely or partially). But did they really? Or was this another myth? This statistical fact (70-80% interviewed declared themselves market-orientated) lacks sound scientific interpretation: what were people guided by in their decision, and was one truth substituted by another?

In our opinion, *this shift of orientation involves, first of all, an intuitive sense of necessity for radical, substantive change.* Gorbachev's reforms failed to persuade people that his vision of the changes was preferential. Actually, since late 1987 party and state leaders were not masterminding or directing these changes, but trailing in their wake, trying to keep up with their logic, lagging behind them more and more.

Second, market ideas proved to be the most attractive of all offered for popular consideration. It appeared that these ideas could help overcome numerous discrepancies and failures in the economy. The fact that a single agency — Gosplan (the State Planning Commission) was in charge of centralized planning of production and distribution of goods (according to some data, up to 25 million articles, leaving national economy unexpectedly facing shortages of one or the other type of products) became increasingly absurd. «The market will fix everything» — this slogan gradually captures minds, although only a few were able to foresee consequences of this experiment.

Third, comparison with industrially developed countries of the West was a powerful factor: «look how they are thriving thanks to the free market!» However, mass consciousness did not pay any attention to the fact that most countries in the world — in Asia, Africa, or Latin America — do not always flourish in market economy.

And finally, historical memory was «working», where economic order of the 1920's, which incorporated various forms of property ownership («NEP effect»), had demonstrated fairly efficient functioning of national market economy.

All these factors contributed to the fact that people have adopted market-oriented system, resulting in a radical change in economic consciousness. Now, however, it is in a state of confusion and collapse. People did not get what they were expecting. Millions of unemployed (some experts estimate that this number, together with latent form of unemployment, is close to 28 million), drastic social differentiation: income of the upper class 10% (of total population) surpasses the earnings of 10% of people living below official poverty level, according to official figures, 15–16 times and according to experts — 30–40 times, which if typical for the least developed countries: i.e. former colonies. This gap is sticking, even when comparing similar data in former «People's democracies» — Czech republic, Slovakia, Poland, Hungary, and Slovenia, where average per capita incomes of the 10% richest people exceed respective incomes of the poorest no more than 4,5 to 5,5 times.

In Russia there are few rich and super-rich people — according to both official and unofficial data — they make up 1 to 3% of the population. There is an adjacent thin layer — approximately 12–15% of people (sometimes in scientific literature referred to as middle class), which is occasionally benefiting from these new realities (however, after August 1998 default crisis, their number decreased almost by half). And what about the rest? The rest are still living below the levels of the stagnation (Brezhnev period), as well as the beginning of *perestroika.* This number has not significantly changed: according to the studies done by the Institute of Sociology, in 1999, 57,6% Russians (34% in 2005) were low income or living below official poverty line. Those spending over a third of their wages on food (82% of Russia's population in 1999, 70-75% in 2007), are classified as poor. It is therefore not surprising that many people live under constant stress, always expecting further deterioration of the economic situation (table 10.1).

Table 10.1.

**What awaits Russia in the coming months
in the sphere of economics?**
(% to the number of interviewed)

Possible answers	IX.1994 N=2959	VII.1996 N=2392	IX. 1998 N=2408	IX. 2000 N=2405	XI.2005 N=2100	V.2007 N=2007
Considerable improvement	1,6	1,7	0,5	1,8	1,0	2,0
Some improvement	16,1	23,3	16,0	30,8	25,0	31
Some deterioration	28,0	25,6	21,8	22,6	26,0	19
Considerable deterioration	25,0	18,2	36,9	7,3	8,0	4
Hard to say	29,1	31,0	24,9	37,5	40,0	44

Source: Monitoring obshchestvennogo mneniya. Ekonomitsheskiye i sotsialniye peremeny (Russian Public Opinion Monitor). 1996. No 5; 2000. No 4; 2007 No 3; Obshchestvennoye mneniye, 2005 (Public Opinion, 2005). Moscow 2005. P. 27.

In these circumstances, under the impact of market forces, loss of former standards of living and lower threshold of social expectations have become clearly apparent, which quickly affected people's consciousness and behavior. Some came to terms with the overall collapse of living standards; others view it as a temporary sacrifice. In actuality, there is an ongoing process of primitivization of life, its degradation, when it is reduced to the necessity to survive. If we utilize a well-known idea of the American sociologist A. Maslow regarding hierarchy of needs, in order to explain this process, we can conclude that many people, to a certain degree, abandoned their social and spiritual needs (creative, cultural and recreational) reducing them to purely physiological level, the level of survival, to satisfying the most pressing needs, essential to person's existence. There has been an involuntary «retreat» from the «higher» needs for the sake of assuring most essential, primitive forms of survival. Popular surveys prove it: people spend 70 to 90% of their income on food and other essentials, putting off purchase of durable goods (large ticket items) using what has been acquired earlier. This is a kind of retreat to the final (or temporary, emergency) limit; surrendering which would hardly be tolerated.

Under these circumstances such problems as phases of the public owned production operations were of little concern to individuals. Social consciousness identified several issues that reflect their real anxieties, expectations, and true state of social mood.

So, what is the economic consciousness preoccupied with?

First of all, a persistent idea that the economic situation in Russia, in a city, region, where people reside, is extremely alarming, complex and, moreover, tends to deteriorate has developed in social consciousness. According to VTsIOM data, if in July 1997 70% of respondents evaluated economic situation in Russia as bad or very bad, in July 1999 this assessment was shared by 83,4% of people (in 2005 — 45,8%). The number of those who view «present state of affairs as intolerable» has increased. Furthermore, 35% (2005) of the respondents expected the situation to deteriorate (38% — hard to say) (Table 10.2).

Table 10.2.

Generally speaking, how satisfied are you with the life that you lead?
(% to respondents)

Possible answers	1997	2000	2005	2007
Completely satisfied	3,7	5,2	8	10
Mostly satisfied	12,1	10,8	16	21
Partly satisfied, partly not	34,0	33,9	40	41
For the most part not satisfied	26,5	25,7	23	19
Not satisfied at all	21,7	21,8	11	7
Hard to say		2,1	2,6	2

Source: Monitoring obshchestvennogo mneniya. Ekonomitsheskiye i sotsialniye peremeny (Russian Public Opinion Monitor) 2000. No 4. P. 48; 2007, No 3. P. 69; Vestnik obshchestvenogo mneniya (Russian Public Opinion Herald). Moscow, 2005. P. 73.

These and similar evaluations indicate that people's attitude toward the results of economic reforms, despite dome positive changes, continues to be negative or uncertain. People no longer value promises or assurances, they evaluate the accomplished results. People's economic consciousness clearly captures reality of the situation and main characteristics of functioning of the national economic mechanism that affect their well being.

Social consciousness quite clearly expresses understanding of reality, following centuries-old popular observation that there can be no wealth arising out of nothing. In such situation, a person begins to compare his/her situation with not only what happened in the past, but with what he sees around him. And he often finds that his former neighbor, who does not substantially differ from him, suddenly and inexplicably begins to enjoy the benefits that do not adequately reflect his real contribution to social production.

In this situation, the income gap, which is hard to explain by business qualifications of the suddenly rich functionaries, most destructively affects people's consciousness and behavior. But, it becomes abundantly clear that the «new Russians» utilized the power that was in their hands to begin with, or they somehow managed to «join in» later (it concerns both old *Nomenklatura* and newly arrived «democratic wave» figures).

Second, the shadow capital, which was illegally of semi-legally accumulated even during Soviet times, and especially during *perestroika*, received an opportunity to realize its claims. Third, the implementation of hastily adopted legislation on privatization, provided space and opportunity for adventurers and «businessmen» to convert former state property into a private for next to nothing, thus accumulating enormous fortunes. How else can we explain the fact that within a short period of time, certain people accumulated billions on their personal accounts?

Economic reforms led to the emergence of a new phenomenon that is inherent in current situation — the «new poor». Previously, the «poor» category was defined clearly enough: low wages in certain professions, life in rural areas, large families, etc. Now the «new poor» cover a significant portion of the population, including practically all occupations and social strata. Moreover, this category now includes such groups, which have never been in dire poverty — scientists, artists and educators, much of the scientific-technical and humanitarian intelligentsia, many skilled workers.

A phrase, humiliating their professional dignity: «If you are so clever, why are you so poor? » is now applied to them — cynicism, which is even difficult to characterize. And the reality is that the proportion of the poor remains high. According to the official Goskomstat data in late 1998 income of 42 million Russians, or 12,86% of the country's population, was below minimal standard («poverty level»). Compared to autumn 2003, when the number of those living below poverty line grew by over 16 million people, or nearly 12%. In 2000's their number reached 45-48 million, reflecting continuing social differentiation. Impoverishment of the population leads to a growing gap opening between rich and poor. It should be noted that such situation is not unique to Russia, but all of the Eastern European countries that embarked on market reforms experienced it. According to the UN data, 147 million people in these countries, including Russia, currently have an income less than $4 a day, whereas in late 1980's only 14 million people fell into this category (*Desyat' let ...* 2000. P. 6).

And this is reflected in social consciousness. Sociological data confirm that 74% of respondents felt that in 1999 their life was worse (34% in 2005), than they had expected, and mere 6% felt their life was better (13% — in 2005) (*Russian Public Opinion Monitor.* 1999. No 3. P. 17; 2006. No 4. P. 67). This primarily justified the assumption of those scholars who had argued that significant polarization of incomes not only fails to stimulate economic growth (as proposed by the liberals), but begins to hinder it. And that, to a certain extent was confirmed by the fact of emergence and existence of a second — parallel to the official one — shadow, clan, including criminal — economy, through which, according to experts, no less than 50 to 55% of total monetary turnover, cash flow and goods were circulating at a time. Its functioning creates a special climate in the relationships between subjects of economic life, which is expressed in massive tax evasion, in refusal to officially register results (including revenues) of various business activities, in domination of different forms of barter and net exchanges, in the cult of «fast» money, in widespread withdrawal of investments in manufacturing and in preference to invest in trade, services and short-term projects or programs. In other words, in the real economy, a paradoxical situation is emerging: whatever is officially declared, affirmed and analyzed has an indirect, but not a principal relation to the true state of affairs. Real life was dominated by «black cash»; barter is practiced beyond any registered account. In Russia, as some experts put it figuratively, not a market but a bazaar has formed.

New realities affecting interests of millions of people were most clearly reflected in social differentiation processes, resulting in consequent emergence of a small group of rich and superrich and impoverishment of large segments of the rest of the population. However, not everybody sees it. Short-sighted analysts reduce their personal understanding of ongoing social stratification to a trivial analysis of paradoxical, at first glance, phenomena. For example, on the one hand, how can one explain a sharp increase in numbers of private cars, construction of expensive houses and purchase of expensive apartments, growth of consumption of durable goods? Indeed, according to official statistics, it could not have occurred due to scarcity of financial resources among the population. These facts were interpreted by some politicians and even scholars as proof for successful market reforms, while ignoring how and under which circumstances these changes in aggregate consumption have occurred. If we want to understand its true causes, we must recognize that a parallel economy emerged in our society, which ensures functioning of many of its branches. It has generated the wildest, most predatory and destructive forms of management. This process completely evades state control, but not popular economic consciousness that reflects unregulated development of shadow and criminal economy, where prosperity is ensured by means unrelated to the officially proclaimed economic policy.

Mass consciousness is steadily internalizing (confirmed by life) a perception that people live in some parallel universe of exchange and distribution, which exist without manufacturing or state participation, and this can bring a certain degree of prosperity, regardless of labor input. But it does not suit the majority of population. It intuitively and spontaneously protests against such state of affaires (Rutkevich 1997). It is these sentiments that might explain Putin's support during his presidential elections.

We have to point out the fact, that in Russian mentality, for a number of centuries, a stereotype of behavior had emerged that produced a special kind of morality, condemning prosperity and wealth. In this model of behavior, hard working way of life that assured a very modest existence was the standard of moral conduct. This attitude was supported and actively implanted not only by the Church, but also by the Soviet government in the minds of millions of people. Any attempts of financial gain outside of the state-owned production sphere were condemned by both moral and legal norms. In contemporary Russia these moral guidelines are not only subject for debate, but are also constantly eroded by real practice, which is consistently parading fortunes that are built with disregard to, and at the expense of the rights and interests of others, thus justifying most brutal and inhumane forms of wealth accumulation.

Under the influence of these sentiments, in social consciousness there is a growing conviction that we must review the results of privatization and looting of state property that occurred in early 1990's. According to a nationwide survey (conducted by V.E. Boykov, March, 1999, interviews with 2109 citizens and 475 government officials from 21 subjects of Russian Federation), 51,2% of all surveyed and 79,6% of civil servants consider it appropriate to revise privatization results. Ordinary citizens were especially determined: 33% of them demand complete nullification of the results of privatization (*Sociologhia vlasti.* 1999. No 2–3). According to other studies undertaken with 5-year intervals by Russian Independent Institute for Social and National Studies (RIISNS), in 1995 38,6% of all Russians and more than 2/3 of them (70%) in 2000 (in 2005 − 75%) considered the revision of privatization and restoration of a leading role of state sector a necessary measure for improvement of their situation.

Social consciousness of the new Russia is at a crossroads. It is continuously deformed by the practice of functioning of the economy, which stubbornly, persistently is trying to implant the principle that it is better to trade (speculate), than to produce in everyday life. Current economic situation is such that more and more people − workers, peasants and professionals − are convinced that nowadays neither mind nor talent, nor skilful hands can guarantee success. Moreover, prestige of labor, participation in creating material wealth and spiritual values are barely, if at all, encouraged or supported by the government.

Unfortunately today, this opinion is shared by millions of people since neither a good job, nor flawless and creative execution of duties determines people's well being and confidence. The results of this study serve as indirect indicator of decline of the significance of labor is (table 10.3).

Table 10.3.

Did people like you get an opportunity to earn more?
(% to respondents)

Possible answers	1994	1997	2005
Yes	17	15	38
No	70	73	59
Hard to say	13	12	4

Source: Monitoring obshchestvennogo mneniya. Ekonomitsheskiye i sotsialniye peremeny (Russian Public Opinion Monitor). 1999. No 3. P. 18; Obshchestvennoye mneniye — 2005 (Russian Public Opinion). Moscow, 2005. P. 31.

In people's opinion, other things are valued much higher these days: attaining varying degrees of access to the commodities flow or financial transactions, ranging from resale of state goods to manipulating prices, from speculation on the difference in relative value of national currencies to primitive forms of petty street sale and resale. This speculative nature of modern lifestyle is especially clearly manifested among the small group of people who make astronomical profits by means of financial and commercial games and scams. Most people who were hoping for arrival of market relations, thinking that in market economy their labor, skills and desire to work effectively would finally be appreciated, at first were disappointed, then demoralized, sunk into apathy and indifference. In fact, social consciousness refuses to recognize the righteousness of those acquisitions that have enriched a handful of people, and not as result of industrial achievements, but questionable transactions. In this regard, an opinion of our compatriot, world-renowned American scholar V. Leontiev is quite revealing. Shortly before his death, in an interview with *Komsomolskaya Pravda* newspaper, he said that he did not know an entrepreneur by the name of Berezovsky, since he had no idea what this person did for the development of production enterprises in Russia.

Economic consciousness often responds to privatization process, establishment of private property *in a unique way.* If during the Soviet period, property ownership was declared and ideologically justified to the population by means of propaganda, in post-Soviet Russia a program was announced, aimed at creating a stratum of small, medium-size and large property owners, who, they claimed, would be true owners, not camouflaged or fake, as in socialist form of economy. By the way, we might add that, basically, only large property owners stood to gain from this concern for creating conditions for «effectively functioning economy».

In order to achieve that, such measure of economic policy as privatization was carried out and implemented in a form of vouchers for the entire population. Voucher, according to its architect A. Chubais, for its owner was a sum equal to the price of one or two statistically average cars. However, soon it became clear that attempts to make people into property owners by means of vaucherization had failed, only enriching a small group of people involved in government, a number of potential and real-life adventurers, figures of shadow economy and criminal world, who were allowed to seize (for ownership or administering) huge chunks of «nobody's» (state) property. There have been cases of privatization of state property in exchange for interest payments or even a fraction of a percent of its real value. According to V. Polevanov, who headed the State Property Committee after A. Chubais, Russia's 500 largest enterprises worse more than 200 billion dollars worth were sold for mere 7,2 billion. Thus, one of largest enterprises in the country – the Likhachev automobile works with its fixed assets valued at no less than 1 billion dollars was sold for only 4 million. The implemented model of privatization has brought just a trillion rubles to the country's budget for 1992–1994, which is just half of the proceeds from privatization of state propriety in Hungary alone. By and large, this behavior of the looters whose battlefield-like mentality spared no one, dishonoring the memory of the fallen, paying no attention to the cries of the wounded, realizing only one goal – cash in on the aftermath of personal and national tragedy.

The above situation was further exacerbated by huge miscalculations in implementation of economic strategy. And this was not just due to the fact of selecting radical means of utilization of unregulated market, propounded by F. Hayek, instead of more deliberate and incremental measures, substantiating the role of the state, advocated by other well-known economists, Nobel prize-winners L. Klein, K. Arrow, J. Tobin and partly A. Åslund. «The most important thing, apparently, is that liberal-democratic reforms were initially pursued based on Western models, without taking into account historical uniqueness and originality of Russia. The idea of the primacy of a person (individual), his rights and interests is at the heart of modern Western (European) culture, while the communitarian idea lies at the basis of Eastern-European and Asian mentality. And mechanical replacement of one by the other, quickly, under pressure from the state, is impossible without serious consequences. Thus, it is understandable why attempts to transplant Western individualism onto the Russian soil to replace previously prevailing collectivism and collegiality have failed, causing wide-spread hostility» (Steilmann. 1998. Vol. 1. P. 199).

This policy has left an imprint on economic consciousness and behavior creating a situation, which, figuratively speaking can be termed as crisis within the crisis. This is not just a financial or industrial crisis — it is also a structural, social, political, moral and cultural one. Actually, this is exactly what such activists as a German scholar and businessman, member of the Roman club, Dr. Klaus Steilmann is tirelessly reminding us about: «I oppose economic philosophy that professes a principle: «First, strong economy, then — culture and morals» (Ibid).

Overcoming structural crisis means, first of all, establishing rational proportions between state and economy, branches of production and between national and global economy. It is especially important to determine the role of the state. From the viewpoint of radical liberals, state should withdraw from the sphere of economy and abandon its direct guidance and management, letting the market develop according to its own laws. The outcome of this «experiment» in Russia is now obvious to all. According to scholars from the Institute for World Economics and International Relations, Russian Academy of sciences, «widespread assumption that there is a steady cause-and-effect link between reduction of state participation in redistribution of national income and increased economic growth, was false. And this is easy to detect, by comparing the proportion of public expenditure in GDP of the countries with positive (Poland, Hungary, Slovenia) and negative (Bulgaria, Romania) economic dynamics. In the first group of countries this rate is now within the range of 45–50%, and in the second — 25–35%. In Russia relative size of public expenditure in GNP in mid-1999 declined to an unprecedented low — 24,4%, a fact, which, incidentally, is alarming even to the IMF and growing number of foreign experts, including those of neo-liberal orientation. They are rightfully pointing to the growing threat posed by inability of Russian government to provide the public with minimal necessary amount of basic social services» (*Desyat let transformatsionnogo protsesa.* P. 6).

A powerful movement, supported by social consciousness has emerged, which was a reaction to the devastating effects of government withdrawal from economy, convinced that the state should not completely abandon its regulatory role, progress made in planning and managing production, provided it is not in the forms used by the old State Planning Commission, but those tested and approved in industrialized countries. In this connection it is worth recalling, that one of the first mentions of theory and practice of social planning was made in the 1933 «New Deal» by F.D. Roosevelt — in which he formulated the ways out of prolonged crisis in the United States.

With regard to overcoming social crisis, it is necessary to resolve unemployment problems, raising the level and quality of life, ratio of social policy and state budget (which does not mean cutting social spending, but raising general revenues). In Russia, during the years of reform, unemployment quickly emerged and was increasing rapidly, reaching, at the end of 1990, 12 to 14% of the working population, (8–9% – in 2005) (in the USSR in 1989 it was 1,5–2%). Devaluation of intense creative and rationally organized work, rejection of universal values for the sake of «hard cash» resulted in *a moral crisis,* where ethics were no longer acting as internal discipline.

Cultural crisis is manifested not so much as disarray in creative search of writers and artists, but in declining business culture, lifestyle culture and culture of interrelations between individuals and the state. For example, this manifests itself in the culture of paying (or unwillingness to pay) taxes or returning credits.

However, the main task is to overcome the *political crisis* that stems from the loss of political will of the state, whose position is to primarily stay out of what is happening in the economic sphere; state's failure to set priorities, to define radical (not just some) measures toward resolving issues that negatively affect people, such as combating crime and flight of capital abroad. This was why former deputy prime minister of Poland Grzegorz Kolodko stated that Russia «had the worst case of post-communist neo-liberalism in the world» (*Izvestia.* December 9, 1998). As a result, Russia carried out a parody on shock therapy, which was effectively applied in several European countries. It was a shock without therapy.

Thus, socio-economic situation and the state of economic consciousness are characterized by contradictory trends, which became the basis for emergence of numerous paradoxes. Let us examine them in detail.

10.2. Key economic paradoxes of consciousness and behavior

Current situation in economic life resembles an artist's rendering (in a form of stylized drawing): a Knight, like in a wise old legend, is at the crossroads, where he sees a stone that has an inscription: «If you go left – you'll get smacked in the head, right – you'll get a black eye, straight – you'll get a kick in the...». Our knight, deep in thought, suddenly hears a voice from above: «Well, how long do you intend to stand here and think? We can beat you up right here». It is the same in economic sphere – no matter where you go and which way you choose, or if you stay at the same spot, all the same, you'll get a kick in the head or a beating. Whichever road is chosen, it might cost you everything you own. Under these circumstances, paradoxes of economic consciousness and behavior are so substantial and complicated that it is preferable to have them at least partially classified and organized, in order to identify most significant characteristics of their emergence and functioning.

A global phenomenon, which emerged as a result of years of competition between capitalist (western) and socialist (Soviet) models of development, in our view, should be classified as a basic paradox of economic consciousness and behavior. In the Soviet Union according to the ideological guidelines a program of implementation of social equality, social justice and protection was proclaimed.

Some of its provisions were implemented. Furthermore, novelty and innovative spirit of these provisions, as well as fear of revolutionary changes, forced Western leaders to take into account these developments and implement many similar measures in order to provide their population with a wide range of social services. As a result, by 1970–1980's, a paradoxical phenomenon had become increasingly apparent: many ideas and declarations of the socialist initiators of social programs remained empty phrases, while their opponents actually implemented theirs. Moreover, this contradiction was worsening, growing, spreading, and increasingly impacting people's consciousness and behavior. And no matter what official propaganda declared, which words it used trying to convince people of the advantages of socialist way of life, there was a growing conviction in the consciousness of Soviet people that people in the West live much better, are more prosperous and have an opportunity to enjoy many benefits and services that Russian people could only hope for in far-off future, or not at all. All this led to the fact that the two opposing aspirations — a formal, declarative, and personal, individual could not coexist in people's consciousness any longer, which ultimately resulted in complete indifference to the fate of socialism in early 1990's.

However, paradox remained: while some people wasted words, others let their actions speak for them. And as history, as well as the Marxist doctrine has repeatedly reaffirmed, actions do speak louder than words. At the same time, against the background of this all-embracing paradox, existing contradictions developed, grew and escalated, generating new specific paradoxes that were inherent in both Soviet and in post-Soviet period. As far as the Soviet period was concerned, in the Soviet Union the subject of property was extremely depersonalized: it became amorphous and all-encompassing — the state and society left no *niche* for any special interest. And, no matter how much was said about the sense of ownership, that every Soviet citizen was the owner and the manager of national wealth, it remained nothing but an empty declaration. During the period of growing disillusionment with socialist property concept, which, paradoxically, increased parallel to meddlesome official propaganda about the progress of developed socialism, in 1970–1980-ies, a bitter joke became widespread: *«the sense of ownership is present, but the owner is missing»*.

Soviet economy was never able to implement Lenin's idea that socialism can only win as a result of superiority of its labor productivity growth. This productivity, during «developed socialism», even began to deteriorate in virtually all sectors of national economy. At the final stage of development of socialist economy (with all the shortcomings and distortions of official statistics) lag in productivity became a factor — in the industry — 2 times below the level of industrialized countries, and almost 5 times in agriculture. Unfortunately, in modern Russia this gap only increased: industrial labor productivity is 20–25% of the world top indices, and approximately 15% in agriculture. This paradoxical situation was clearly and ironically captured in a couplet: «we do not sow, we do not plough, and we do not build — we take pride in our social system». And this «pride» without a solid material base could not lead to anything but growing disappointment, bitterness, frustration and mistrust in the social consciousness and such contradictory mindset among Soviet people, best reflected in a saying «our system is better, yet they live better».

In market economy some emerging paradoxes have acquired mass character. *One of these paradoxes is related to market economy and to its principal, basic subjects* — bankers, entrepreneurs, large property owners, etc. But first a little history. When market ideas began to penetrate social consciousness, many people did not need a lot of convincing, since life had already done it for them. Initially, during the perestroika years, the majority of people hoped for a possibility of a sharp spurt in the growth of national economy. But by late 1980's people's concerns were elsewhere: having realized the futility of economic restructuring attempted by the authors of *perestroika*, people turned their attention to other possible measures, especially those utilized in the countries with high levels of development and standard of living.

In retrospect, looking back at the dynamics of changes in public attitudes toward the market, introduction of land ownership and some other market related issues, at first, in 1988, these ideas were only shared by a few. By the end of 1989 — beginning of 1990 there was a serious shift in social consciousness. All-Russia study in May 1990, under the guidance of the present author showed that 43% of people shared positive attitude toward introduction of market economy (completely or partially). In March 1991 57% supported the market; in 2005 — this number was up to 70-80% of the working population. However, growing hardships in connection with Gaidar's shock therapy led most people to negatively evaluate market reforms (See table 10.4.).

Table 10.4.

Should economic reforms be continued or discontinued?
(% of respondents)

Possible answers	1994	1997	1999	2006	2007
Continued	32,4	33,6	31,7	40	40
Discontinued	27,5	28,7	27,8	20	21
Hard to say	39,8	37,7	40,5	40	39

Source: Monitoring obshchestvennogo mneniya. Ekonomitsheskiye i sotsialniye peremeny (Russian Public Opinion Monitor) 1996. No 3. P.43; 1999. No 5. P. 53; Vestnik obshchestvenogo mneniya (Russian Public Opinion Herald). 2006. No 6. P.75; 2007. No 3. P.70.

Thus, market orientation, as primary means of transforming economy and lifestyle, has not yet become a leading theme in public and private life of the Russian people. They compare not only bumps and miscalculations of Russia's experience, but also experience of most countries, sustainably and productively functioning under market conditions. A split in popular understanding of market related opportunities continues to exist, despite some increase in positive evaluations of forms and methods of its realization. Today all political forces, from liberals to communists, from agrarians to national-patriots are market orientated. Controversy and very heated debate revolve around the kind of price people must pay for the transition to new economic and organizational forms of production operation, for what period of time and at what costs. Unfortunately, this dispute continues to be dominated by old habits — if you don't absolutely agree with me, you are against me, my program, my ideas and concepts. But people do not live by the rules of political struggle (often far-fetched and absurd), or preferences and sermons of political parties and movements, not in accordance with socio-economic concepts and theories, but based on real life environment that affects them most of all. And by that virtue a person finds himself in an extremely contradictory, paradoxical situation that prevents him from making correct decisions, evaluating contradictions, correctly assessing situation, ultimately pushing him toward mutually exclusive actions.

Social consciousness of individuals is not dominated by categories of political economy — monetary, fiscal or socio-orientated. In their daily life people ask a very simple question: who is to blame for their plight, for lack of social and legal protection and support? People often blame those in position of power for their troubles: President, Government, State Duma, and entire bureaucracy. This, however, is abstract criticism, since in higher echelons of power situation often changes, which makes it harder to pinpoint accusations against a specific person — change and reshuffle of favorites at the top is too rapid. It is an unusual situation, since, while not rejecting ideas of market economy, people start searching for those who drove them into this social impasse, trying to find a way out, take actions in order to change their humiliating position in society. People have a desire to work, a clear head and hard-working hands, which they can use to seek a decent life. But what or who stands in their way?

Therefore, it is not surprising that people's discontent begins to focus on those individuals who actually represent market relations, namely: businessmen, bankers, entrepreneurs and others related «actors» in the new economic theater that are frequently referred to as «new Russians». In essence, these people are paving the way for new economic relations, representing triumph of these new realities. But, since their evolution into full-fledged participants in market relations is often accompanied by most reckless and criminal forms of profiteering and illegal privatization of property, or international speculation and money laundering, in social consciousness these people are associated with criminals, which, incidentally, is not always far from truth. According to experts, only 25% of interviewed managers and entrepreneurs conduct their business activities in a civilized manner (Dushatskiy. 1999).

Social consciousness does not accept it and refuses to put up with it. People are outraged by arrogance of wealth, excessiveness, overindulgence and immodesty of newly rich people often combined with complete lack of taste and ethical concepts. Regardless of how we chose to explain these facts, the result is indisputable: public consciousness developed an extremely negative assessment of the carriers of market relations: 40 to 60% of the population, when asked about their activities, responded very unfavorably. In 1999 and 2005, According to Institute of Sociology and VTsIOM data, wealthy bankers and businessmen (ones that acquired their wealth in 1990's), evoked negative feeling in 55% of respondents. And since, according to popular opinion, these figures are responsible for economic collapse, countrywide poverty, they do not deserve respect or support, or even right to exist, and a number of people advocate for use of repressive measures against them. Very often during written surveys sociologists came across the following inscriptions in questionnaires: «they should be hanged», «jailed», «exiled to Siberia», etc.

In other words, *paradox lies in the fact that social consciousness, while supporting market transformations, is flatly and categorically set against the subjects of these transformations, against those, who really and actually personifies the changes in economic life in Russian.* And how could it be any different, if, in K. Steilmann's words, nobody associates a Russian businessman with «self-realization of the national principle, national goals or national calling. Some see a combination of the worst, universally condemned human sins: bribery and swindling, greed, vulgarity, mafia-like behavior» (Steilmann. Op.cit., Vol. 1, p. 216).

Further, *a paradox of consciousness and behavior emerged in connection with official policy, aimed toward «capitalization» of consciousness — turning private interests into main, leading ones.* Life, however, has shown that such orientation failed to produce desired results. On one hand, the old slogan «working for the common good, for the benefit of society» is practically forgotten, or faded in social consciousness, although communal, collectivist beginnings, albeit deformed, continue to exist. As a matter of fact, this factor is often ignored by those researchers, who consider following changing trends of industrialized Western countries as the only possible path for Russia. On the other hand, according to the «Public opinion» foundation, such indicators of «capitalization» motives as acquisition of property (13%), purchasing equity (5%) and investment are pretty low.

In connection with a problem of «capitalization» of consciousness, we should point out prevalence of such paradoxical phenomenon as comparison of role and value of private property with other forms of property — *paradoxes of attitude toward private property.* A simplistic, complimentary approach to private property is widely spread in public and private lives of people, press and sometimes scientific literature. Sociological information, in particular the data of Russo-Canadian study «Russia's path to market» (1992–1997) (J. De Bardeleben, Zh.T. Toshchenko, V.E.Boykov, A.A. Kasakov) did not reveal any significant differences in popular attitudes toward labor processes, labor efficiency, increase of productivity related to the form of ownership. And it is especially evident in assessment of joint stock companies, where the majority of employees continue to build their work relations in the same way as they used to during state property ownership, including Soviet period. Doesn't the fact that acts of protest at some companies are often directed against the State and not against the administrators responsible for managing these businesses with their specific form of ownership confirm it?

Analyzing this paradox, some researchers argue that under conditions of uncertainty, ambiguity, unpredictability of economic development the majority of shareholders are ready to hand over the reigns of power to those capable of providing stable high wages and resolution of social problems of the enterprise. In practice, however, this means that people are willing to give up ownership, which they consider useless (Tumanov. 2000).

Paradox linked to contradistinction between social qualities of a person as a worker and as a consumer in consciousness and behavior is no less revealing. Currently, these qualities are aimed in opposite directions, although it is well known that only when they concord, it is possible to achieve rational functioning of economy, as well as economic behavior and lifestyle. But realities of life in Russia are such that these vectors of effort in these two manifestations are mutually exclusive. As a consumer, a person seeks to maximize efficiency and quality of satisfaction of their material and spiritual needs, to have an opportunity for their fuller enriching and renewal. However, as a manufacturer or an employee a person faces a different situation. He is not always paid for his labor, and if he is, his compensation is inadequate due to constantly changing socio-economic situation (inflation). Often, goods in production of which a person is involved, are not in demand. Results of his work are often redundant, devalued. No less 'effective' tool of maintaining this paradoxical contradiction is the tax burden stifling any industrial initiative. Selling and reselling goods became more profitable than engaging in production. Using «scissors» in prices between public and private sector, as well as between regions, it has become much easier, more accessible and less cumbersome to purchase and resell goods at a profit. And reselling goods from other countries is even better, including infamous back-and-forth «shuttle» trips, supplying homeland with everything that delivers a profit — even defective, damaged and stale products, past their expiration date. This massive turn to trade in all what is conceivable, even in criminal forms is not a vicious intent — it simply become more profitable compared to manufacturing. This is a situation leading to the fact that the sphere of exchange became excessively hypertrophied at the expense of production.

A special group of paradoxes in «manufacturer — consumer» interaction leads to a widespread contradictory behavior between patriotically oriented desire to support domestic manufacturers through purchasing Russian goods and products and actual behavior of the same people, when addressing specific needs — mostly personal and family. Its essence lies in the fact that imported goods are superior in quality and more attractive. Hence, declared statements and intentions are at odds with actual behavior in dealing with specific life situation. And such behavior is typical not just for a single person or small population groups — this is actual behavior of many Russian consumers, when desires and intentions do not coincide with the actual activity. True, in recent years there has been a certain increase in confidence in domestic products, especially food and consumer goods. However, in general, Russian-made products in many cases are in short supply, unavailable or fail to reach the consumer, or are inferior to Western and Eastern-made goods in many aspects.

No less significant paradox exists between appeals to conform to market democracy and everyday orientation — primitive requirements related to a single need — to survive. Moreover, this paradox is aggravated by the environment where making money by any means possible is a highly praised skill, ability to snatch, if situation is «favorable» or to simply snooker other people with the help from banks and funds, or dilettantes looking to profiteer by all available means, including illegal ones. Another robbery — default, which once again undermined the credibility of the state, as well as market relations, occurred in August 1998. Therefore, naturally, after years of impoverishment, there is a popular growing desire to revise privatization results, where enormous wealth, for next to nothing, fell into the hands of individuals that were able to snatch from public pie much of what belonged to the entire society. And when you consider the ongoing wide-spread land speculation (before introduction of legal regulations), plundering of rare and unique raw materials and remnants of state property, it all makes people think about lawlessness and chaos in country's economic life.

Another paradox is that many people (70–80%) opt for enduring, adapting to progressively worsening situation, despite the fact that they are dissatisfied with their economic situation, assessing it as poor and very poor (70%). In this case, just like with paradoxes in theory, there is a contradiction between the world of conceptualized and real-life experience, which often differs or confront each other. How else can we explain the fact that tremendous dissatisfaction with prevailing socio-economic situation in society continues to co-exist with positive or neutral evaluation of people's own personal situation? Certainly, we might need to take into consideration the process of primitivization of popular demands, displacement of higher forms of satisfying the needs by lower ones, desire to survive in an extreme situation. But this does not negate the fact: people hope that these problems can be resolved peacefully, but under specific conditions with regard to political forces. In fact, to this day they retain extremely adverse historical memory, which persistently reminds of the enormous costs to each and everyone, if contradiction between actual and desired is resolved in a forcible way.

Special attention should to be paid to a paradox that arises in social consciousness when assessing current personal economic situation and that of the entire country. If in Soviet times people used to say, «We live modestly, but our country gets richer every day», currently, people tend to assess the state of the country as being worse than their own. This trend was reflected in the polls practically throughout all the 1990–2000 (see Table 10.4).

Table 10.4.

How do you assess the economic situation?
(% of respondents) N=1600

Possible answers	Country-wide			In their family		
	VII.1997	V.2005	V.2007	VII.1997	V.2005	V.2007
Very good	0	0	0	0,2	1	1
Good	0,7	5	8	3,6	7	10
Average	19,5	38,0	47	44,4	54	57
Bad	50,2	39	27	36,4	31	26
Very bad	19,2	6	4	14,5	5	5
Hard to say	10	11	13	0,8	2	1

Source: Monitoring obshchestvennogo mneniya. Ekonomitsheskiye i sotsialniye peremeny. (Russian Public Opinion Monitor) 2000. No 4. P. 48; 2005, No 3. P. 73–74; Vestnik obshchestvennogo mneniya (Russian Public Opinion Herald). 2008. No 3. P. 69–70.

Real, rather than exalted idea of the market began to develop in social consciousness. An increasing number of people begin to realize that Russian-style free market does not provide social protection, does not eliminate unemployment and poverty, does not prevent, but instead, exacerbates social stratification. As far as the experts involved in economic transformation are concerned, many of them travelled from ecstatic eulogizing to critical and even negative views, since it became apparent that market itself cannot implement rational structural shifts long-term, can not be socially efficient (to provide social services, meet social needs), does not prevent monopolization of production and price formation. Social consciousness has to respond to these processes, it can not remain on the sidelines. This results in a «cure», i.e. getting rid of failed expectations and hopes for and return to reality.

10.3. Paradoxes in labor sphere

A special group of paradoxes emerged due to contradictions in labor sphere, i.e., in the part of economy, where people's consciousness and behavior is most clearly manifested in connection with objectively existing interests and needs. Regarding general situation in labor sphere: *we have witnessed the destruction of traditional labor motivations;* there is a maturing conviction in mass consciousness that conscientious attitude toward work does not guarantee or offer any assurance that work efforts will be adequately rewarded. Rise of initiative, which was witnesses in late 1980's in connection with attempts to establish new production relations, quickly faded away, since manufacturing and quality improvement became unprofitable. Such motive, when work was valued for its creative content, for satisfaction it brought to individuals, has also gradually faded away. At the same time, long-term decline in production, which led to unemployment, growing poverty and hopelessness began to increasingly impact social consciousness. After the shock of the transformation years, by the end of 1990's and the beginning of 2000's it became apparent that in current situation people were actively searching for ways to survive, and, in some cases, even start manufacturing enterprises. But what about today's real picture? In our opinion, we have to take a look at real life developments and question what is happening in people's consciousness, in their behavior, how do they define their attitude to ongoing changes and what is their view of the future.

In all-Russia monitoring survey of public opinion, conducted since 1989 by VTsIOM, respondents were asked to choose one out of four options, best describing their basic vital attitude. Two of them reflect a trend, which is easily and unquestionably observed in real life. First, number of those who believed that work is a main source of livelihood has increased from 25% in 1989 to 61% in 1997 (in 2005 — 71%). Or, in other words, material incentive, primary focus on receiving wages and income, became determining motives in people's lives. Second, a number of people focused not only on importance of labor, but also on values that lie outside its scope has sharply decreased from 54% in 1989 to 17% in 1997 (in 2005 — 10%). However, the same study has also revealed a paradoxical fact that requires careful evaluation. Namely, from 1989 to 2005 the number of people, whose position was «my work is interesting and important, regardless of my wages», remained the same. Their number fluctuated between

10-12% and remained stable in spite of the cataclysms occurring in the country during that decade. Neither change of social order, nor reforms or crises, including political ones, affected their position. This raises a question — why does the number of people in this category, who can be called workaholics and who retain their orientation despite any adversity, remain stable?

No less notable is the fact that the number of people that regard their work as unpleasant duty remained virtually the same — 6% in 1989 and 5% in 1997 (3% — in 2005). It turns out that this category of people, as well as the previous category, is barely influenced by any, including radical, changes in the country or economy. But, at the same time, it is not replenished by those in difficult life situations, those who lost their jobs or any sort of orientations in life (*Russian Public Opinion Monitor.* 1999. No 6. P. 40; 2005. No 3. P.63).

Answers to the questions about work motivations help complete this picture. As expected, the primary reason for labor mobility is wages (salary). From 1993 to 1998 its importance remained practically unchanged: 64 to 56% of respondents considered this motive crucial. With regard to work content and eventual career opportunities, value assessment of this factor decreased from 20 to 14%, while the number of those who considered «conditions and organization of work» as important factor declined from 34 to 22%. On the other hand, growing fears that their company (organization) might be closed was mentioned by 10% of the interviewed (4% in 1993) in 1998. However, over these years, evaluation of relations between the employees and between management and employees has not changed or even slightly improved. There was a decline in importance of such factor as housing problems (from 12% in 1993 to 10% in 1998), but not due to improvement of housing situation, but because enterprises (organizations) no longer participate in their resolution (Ibidem. 1998. No 4. P. 16). In other words, these data add little to (they only elaborate on) what was known from previous research: significance of the role of material factor and meaningful reduction of the role of content and creative motives of work.

These conclusions are also confirmed by regional survey data. Thus, a survey of 2107 workers from 18 enterprises in Vladimir, Nizhni Novgorod and Ryazan' region confirmed that for them three values are of paramount importance: work as means of existence (61,8%), stability and confidence in the future (31,1%), communication with colleagues (25,6%). With regard to such values as the value of life and opportunities for creative growth, they are important to, respectively, 12,6 and 8,3% of respondents (*Konsul'tant direktora.* 2000. No 12. P. 13).

In this regard, we should take another look at the always-pertinent issue of value of work, its place in social consciousness and magnitude of this phenomenon. Unquestionably, work-oriented attitude is firmly rooted in social consciousness. It reflects eternal high valuation of labor in thousand-year experience of Russia and other nations, and practice of Soviet society steering people toward realization of the slogan «work is a matter of honor, valor and heroism». But, at the same time, we have been, are and, perhaps for a long time, will be, affected by inefficiency of labor in Russia.

What is the matter? It turns out that work-oriented attitude as such is not enough. We need to focus more on the quality of this work. But what does that mean? First, regardless of the fact that personal well-being is a leading motivation; it is not accompanied by noticeable intensification of labor activity. There is a clear contradiction between declared motive for possible activization and real behavior. According to the data of studies, conducted by the author in 1980's — early 1990's the proportion of those, who recognized that improving effectiveness and efficiency of their work will result in salary (wage) increase, was declining. At the end of 1990's the number of people convinced that there was a direct correlation between work and compensation has rapidly decreased. This fact may explain a paradoxical phenomenon — huge number of people (80-85%) believe they have the capacity to increase productivity and efficiency, while at the same time, only a very small fraction (about 15%) thinks that their diligence will be noticed and rewarded.

No less *paradoxical and contradictory is the fact that popular desire to earn good money does not correlate with the aspiration to improve existing knowledge and skills.* And although an average of 38% are focused on training, improving their professional skills, mere 15% of them, or 5% of the total working population, have actually realized this intention («Public opinion» foundation data). Main characteristic of labor consciousness is that it is not geared toward self-transformation: a person would like to earn more, while only relying on knowledge and skills, which he already possesses. Therefore only one out of ten (10%) cares about possible career opportunities when choosing a job. This motive is significant for 31% of managers, 14% of specialists (partly) and 11% of civil servants. Lack of motivation for improving professional skills or career advancement is largely due to the fact that there are no incentives for acquiring new knowledge and skills. This phenomenon is largely explained by the fact that for a long time professional development was not really in demand due to low rates of modernization of labor process and outdated technological equipment. And modern realities with constant necessity for professional improvement are at odds with these deep-rooted socio-psychological attitudes. In the meantime, we have what we have: a desire to earn good money combined with lack of incentives to improve existing professional knowledge and skills.

Analysis of labor market situation demonstrates that a significant number of people become more active only if they are threatened by unemployment or if satisfaction of their primary needs is endangered. It appears that these variables happen to be most effective incentives; since almost half of the interviewed acknowledged that they are facing a real danger of losing their job or that they actually lost it. In other words, people's reaction and their quest for a way out of the situation are rather primitive — they do not take any steps to find more meaningful and long-term solutions, like, for example, improving professional qualifications. Of course, people's reaction to the threat of unemployment and loss of financial well-being is justifiable: these dangers are particularly significant for the population, but attempts to address them often do not involve utilizing untapped potential — Russian mentality prefers to solve emerging problems quickly, urgently without any special effort, without «wasting» any energy or mental capacity.

In this regard it is worth recalling the words of a philosopher A. Vogt from his book about the history of utopian thought: «When will economic freedom arrive? My answer will be absolutely the same: human freedom, as well as justice, does not depend on economic system, it depends on the people. It's not the economic system, but the man himself, who can and must be absolutely free» (Zabelin. 1993). K. Steilmann, a contemporary German scientist and successful businessman, made a similar statement: «Since Russia is unique as «a spiritual nation», economic morality, economic spirituality should be primary in material and economic relations (may K. Marx, F. Engels, V. Lenin and other materialists forgive me for such «economic idealism»)» (Steilmann. Op.cit).

There is another very significant contradiction bordering on paradox. The fact of the matter is, labor is highly valued as a process — high rating of such human trait as diligence proves it. But, at the same time, evaluation of the results of economic activity, as well as responsibility for them, is still rated very low. Even representatives of the private sector have a very restrained attitude toward labor efficiency. Such quality as entrepreneurial spirit was positively evaluated by 48% of businessmen, and anywhere from 9 to 35% of respondents among other population groups. Supremacy of process over result is, to a certain extent, a residual phenomenon (sequel) of psychology of a natural or a small-scale manufacturer, working «for himself», when the main efforts were focused more on the process of achieving the result, rather than the result itself. Achieving results becomes a leading component in the context of modern production, although, economists and sociologists interpret it in different ways. If for economists the basic principle is to «achieve result while minimizing costs», for sociologists results are correlated to maximization of social indicators. In Soviet times, results were achieved due to enthusiasm, mobilization of efforts in the fight against external enemies in the process of realization of socialist ideals. This concept failed, since the result was unable to merge the socially significant with personal and group goals. In all fairness it should be noted that based on certain lessons from failures of Russian economy, even neo-liberal economists

(H. Gref, for example) suggested taking social aspects of economic development into consideration.

The fact that popular comprehension of surrounding realities has hardly changed is confirmed by VTsIOM data (similar data was obtained by sociological laboratory of Samara university), when answering the question: «How should, in your opinion, each of these conditions influence wages and salaries? And what is the real situation like?» (Table 10. 5).

Table 10.5.

Conditions that effect people's wages
(% of respondents)

Condition	1991 N=2200		1996 N=1930		2006 N= 2240		Real situation
	Should be	*Actual situation*	*Should be*	*Actual situation*	*Should be*	*Actual situation*	
Education	60	14	62	17	65	18	17
Difficult working conditions	71	17	70	12	73	15	12
Hard work	76	11	67	12	70	13	12
Family size	28	5	27	5	29	5	5
Importance of work	59	15	60	18	65	18	18
Experience	38	17	39	12	45	14	12

Source: Center of Sociological research. Samara University.

Thus, it is possible to say that external conditions, coupled with internal motives did not create a real basis for updating the situation, improving attitude toward work and, consequently, made no significant changes in the structure of social labor relations in the workplace. Furthermore, they generated numerous contradictions and paradoxes.

10.4. Paradox of economic consciousness and behavior of Russian peasantry

Among paradoxes of economic consciousness and behavior those related to former collective and state farm workers, present farmers and workers of agricultural joint-stock companies, occupy a special place. What is it really like? Let us consider the data obtained by the Institute of Economic and Industrial Engineering organization of the Siberian Branch, Russian Academy of Science (Table 10.6).

Table 10.6.

Responses to the question: «In your opinion, how did your opportunities change during the years of reforms?»

(% of respondents)

Opportunity	Improved	Deteriorated	Did not change	Hard to Say
To have full-time work	2,4	60,0	33,3	4,3
To work in my profession, specialty	3,9	57,6	32,4	6,1
To work in full force	7,8	49,0	35,4	7,8
To demonstrate my skills, knowledge, initiative	10,9	40,1	35,0	14,0
To earn good money	6,8	70,5	15,7	7,0
To do what I like	24,6	24,8	25,1	25,2
To influence work results of my enterprise	9,8	29,2	35,3	25,7
Not to depend on managers in solving production issues	10,1	28,5	40,7	20,7
Participate in management	9,2	27,0	37,7	26,1
Defend my labor rights and interests	14,7	42,0	23,9	19,4
To become independent business owner, proprietor	29,1	22,4	26,4	22,1

Source: Kalugina Z.I. Paradoxes of Agrarian Reform in Russia: sociological analysis of transformation processes (In Russian). Novosibirsk, 2006. P. 43. The study was conducted in 1996 and 2007. Sample size of 341 and 736 persons, respectively, representing population of the region (oblast') according to sex, age and educational level.

Even based on this local, but representative data we can conclude that a paradoxical situation has emerged: almost every third farmer acknowledges an opportunity to become an independent owner, while, at the same time, 70,5% note deteriorating earning capacity, 49% — lack of opportunity to operate at full capacity, 60% inability to find full-time employment. In other words, the right to independence, autonomy and initiative is not realized in real life. Moreover, it is accompanied by serious negative repercussions, declining social mood and social well-being.

So how can we explain such seemingly paradoxical phenomenon, when land privatization is least likely to be supported by the peasantry? Why are so many more people among urban dwellers and so-called democratic intelligentsia support land ownership? And peasants do not. According to Z.I. Kalugina's data, in 1999 only 19,2% of all interviewed farmers agreed that land should be traded (bought and sold), with 8,3% partly agreeing and 58,5% rejecting such possibility (14% were unsure) (Kalugina. 2000. P. 94). Why? Due to a number of objective, as well as subjective reasons. Objective reasons include: economic conditions (cost of equipment, agrochemicals, fertilizers etc.), lack of state support for agricultural production, high taxes, vulnerability and lack of protection of property rights, monopoly in processing, procurement and service enterprises, which makes any attempts at farming unprofitable, inefficient and even senseless. This situation is further aggravated by subjective factors: farming is hard, intense, ceaseless work, whereas in collective or state farms workers were guaranteed a small, but regular income, structured and regulated work, permitting a poor but quiet life, without any stresses or conflicts. And if we add social infrastructure that had been established during Soviet era, such as child care and educational institutions, cultural centers, libraries, health services etc., nowadays, farmers have no idea how their social needs can be met under the system of individual farming. These results in a *paradox: collective farms are the past, farmers are the future, and people must be fed today,* without delay. Attempts to postpone it «for later' lead to the fact that consumer market is filled with foreign goods and services, exacerbating the plight of Russian agricultural producers.

This paradox has disastrous consequences. Since mid-1990 number of those who dared to become farmer has been declining. We are talking about real farmers, not «contingency plan», or «in case of emergency» ones. Experience proves that thousands of peasants, unable to bear the yoke of artificial barriers, exposed to barbaric morals of the market are forced to abandon their land and return to the city or former state and collective farms, back to their old bleak, but hassle-free existence. And if we take into account that significant percentage of farmers has transformed their land into primitive subsistence economy units, not even remotely related to the idea of profitability, a picture of agrarian desolation becomes even more dramatic. Another paradoxical fact should be noted: after 1997 number of farms ceasing their operation began to exceed the number of newly established ones. In 1997 their numbers decreased by a thousand over the previous year: in 1998 by 4,3 thousand, and in 2003 by 9,4 thousand (*Rossiyskiy statisticheskiy ezhegodnik.* 1999. P. 283).

Consequently, we have a disappointing result. If in 1991 the share of unprofitable agricultural enterprises was 5%, in 1995 it was 57 %, in 2000 — 51%, and in 2005 — 40%. This negative trend continues (table 10.7).

Table 10.7.

Unprofitable agricultural enterprises in Russia in 1970–2005

Year	Number of unprofitable enterprises, thousand	Share of unprofitable enterprises, % from total number
1970	2,9	13
1980	16,8	71
1990	0,7	3
1991	1,3	5
1992	1,3	5
1993	2,6	10
1994	15,9	59
1995	15,4	57
1997	21,3	79
2000	14,1	51
2003	10,8	49
2005	7,6	40

Source: Rossiyskiy statisticheskiy ezhegodnik 2006. Stat.sb. (The Russian Statistical Yearbook. 2006. A statistical collection). Moscow, 2006. P. 442.

In addition, if we consider the fact that in 1998 in overall structure of agricultural production, 41% of goods (in current prices) were produced by agricultural enterprises, 57% — by individual part-time private land owners and only 2% — by full-time farmers, it becomes clear that agriculture faces a dire situation, which, in turn, leads to paradoxes and deformities in economic consciousness and behavior of the peasantry (*Rossiyskiy statisticheskiy ezhegodnik.* 1999. P. 203).

From historical perspective, the foundation for contradictory behavior of the peasantry had been laid by the 1929 decision to launch an all-out mass incorporation of farmers into cooperatives, which was the beginning of introduction of collective farm system in Soviet agriculture. This decision ignored an emerging and sufficiently effective trend of collective land utilization. Analysis of real-life situation in 1920's demonstrated that in many counties and townships 14 to 16 different forms of cooperatives were successfully implemented: from seed-growing and supply to associations for joint land cultivation, from marketing associations to communes where everything, including household services, was socialized. And all these forms of management existed and functioned, competing among themselves in efficiency and social development (Bolshakov. 1929). We can only guess that if this diversity was preserved, maintained and supported, the path of development chosen by Soviet authorities would not be quite so tragic and historically pointless.

Peasants' consciousness and behavior reacted to the launch of collective farm system as follows: private property was regarded as a derivative of the public one. But then, without creating rational and effective forms of combining individual and collective interests, comprehensible to the peasants, aggravated by never-ending blunders in agrarian policies, consciousness of the peasantry had gradually transmuted leading to radical changes in basic attitudes toward correlation between the personal and the public. In 1950–1960 new ideology was already beginning to take shape – now collective farming was becoming part of personal property. But it is this ideology that led to wide-spread theft and pilfering of public goods, to neglect and abandonment of collective and communal values (Vinogradskiy. 1996).

Simultaneously, *we were witnessing a profanation of ideas of land ownership,* for the sake of dubious, but very «modern» concepts, just like attempting to «run ahead of a locomotive». On the one hand, division of land belonging to collective and state farms into parcels did not deliver desired results – it did not bring peasants any closer to understanding of their historical mission. Instead, this process had most devastating consequences – desolation of land, sharp drop in marketability of agriculture, catastrophic decline of livestock, falling crop yields and mass transition among individual farms to growing crops strictly for their own personal consumption. Suffice it to say that during the years of agrarian reforms sown areas shrank by 40 million hectares or by 1/4 (from 1985 to 2003), number of productive livestock fell by over 50% (from 54,7 million in 1991 to 24,9 million in 2003), while the fleet of main types of agricultural machinery – by 40–60 %. During this same period capital investment into agribusiness (in comparable prices) decreased 20 times, volume of land-reclamation – 30 times (Gourde. 2000). On the oth er hand, half-baked tactics in land sales led to a surprising phenomenon, when, as in Saratov *oblast'* (region), agricultural lands were sold for amounts that did not even cover the cost of tendering. Here are some examples. In Volsk district 160 hectares were sold for 4000 (!) rubles. And in Saratov region 27,3 hectare lot was offered for sale to 490 rubles (!) (Velikiy, Eliutina., et al., 2000. P. 32–33). Sale for the sake of sale? Was it a desire to be in the front ranks, to report on time? Or was it just an arbitrary decision of a particular governor?

Situation in agriculture was further complicated by the absence of consistent, logical national agricultural policy, which would take into account not only interests of the new owners, but interests of the peasants as well. Under these circumstances, a colossal paradox has emerged: ongoing agrarian reforms did not just fail to promote market consciousness and behavior among working people, but practically destroyed labor motivation. Wages ceased to be the main source of income for peasants. Links between salaries and results of labor are also broken. There are absolutely no moral incentives to work (and they are not supported); opportunities to solve social problems of rural life were drastically reduced. As a result, there was a steep decline in motivation for professional, high quality and efficient work, as well as a tremendous reduction in prestige of agricultural labor, especially among rural youth (Kuz'min. 2007. P. 5).

In this situation, the rural retirees' lack of rights is rather indicative. What kind of protection or enforcement of their rights can we possibly be talking about, when after dissolution of collective and state farms, followed by transformation of farmers into farmland owners, 28% of pensioners do not have documents for their allocated land plots, 14% are not sure and 3,5% do not even know whether they have their land shares or not (Velikiy, Eljutina, Shteynberg, Bakhturina. Op.cit. P. 28). By the way, in my opinion, the situation of a rural retiree is the most vivid representation of paradoxical social position: long-term self-sacrifice, working for the sake of society, forbearance and limitation of daily social needs, on the one hand, and complete neglect, lack of basic care and security, on the other have become a real tragedy for contemporary elderly inhabitants of the Russian villages.

It is obvious that until society starts encouraging and supporting those, who grow and produce, in farmers' consciousness there will be no conviction that farm work can be as gratifying and profitable as any other kind of work (and in some cases even more profitable). In such situation, nothing and no one can guarantee the success of rural market transformations.

Two other paradoxical situations, depicted by Z.I. Kalugina in her book, arose as a result of agrarian reforms. *First, instead of inefficient public sector, the society now has an inefficient private sector in rural economy.* To the negative results of erroneous, formal implementation of agrarian reforms we should be also adding the fact that the majority of peasants felt that they lost many past advantages, unattainable in their current (imposed) situation. *Second, instead of the planed prosperous future for farms and joint-stock farms there was an expansion of small-scale production,* with small-scale private farming now determining the character of Russia's agriculture (they produced 55,8% of the bulk agricultural product in 2003). It is this category of farmers that managed to double the volume of agricultural production and its marketability during 1990's. These indicators could have been a positive sign, if the explosion of small-scale farm production was not accompanied by the process of switching back to growing crops strictly for their own personal consumption, by return to barter exchange, decrease of technical equipment, failure to comply with requirements of agricultural technologies and intensifying social problems (Fadeeva. 2007).

All this allows concluding that despite all the promises and intentions, agrarian reforms created a lot of obstacles and caused many problems for the farmers. The tragedy of peasant consciousness, however, lies in the fact that rural workers do not see a way out of this situation, because they are unable to overcome all the barriers erected in their path. In the meantime, only a few of them regard what is happening in village life as positive changes.

* * *

Market relations cannot make their way by virtue of their proclaimed advantages alone. If they are not socially oriented, people (or rather, a significant part of the population) will be faced with poverty, deprivation and despair. And this, in turn, might lead to social cataclysms, whether we like it or not. Thus, Russian society does not have a lot of choices — a road of primary (bloody, nasty and very long) accumulation of capital with a hope for brighter future after unknown period of time; or regulation of market relations, revision of forms and methods of economic policy. And if the first road is fairly «hands-free» (history will lead us to prosperity), the second one requires a lot of effort, in order to reach the path worthy of a 21th century man.

Thus, enormous changes that have occurred in society in general, and in the life of every person lie at the basis of economic paradoxes. In present conditions of contemporary Russian society the situation, based on property relations and its derivatives: relations of ownership use and disposal underwent a radical, fundamental change. We are witnessing a change of essential features of economic consciousness and behavior, which, during the years of Soviet regime were not just regulatory requirements, but also became a tradition, a pattern of thought and activity of many millions of people.

This gap between the imaginary and the existent, between official policy and socio-economic realities, between orientations and results of real changes is at the heart of paradoxicality, which we observe in life today.

It should be noted that chaotic, contradictory concepts of scientists that represent various ideas — dogmatic, populist, or ones blindly copying someone else's experience, made a significant contribution to this paradoxical confusion. Management experience in Russia in the 1990's has convincingly demonstrated that, first, it is impossible, even guided by noblest of aspirations, to accelerate the pace of transformation, to ignore lessons of global experience, to break away from life. Second, scientific or political extremism, based on absolutization of monetarist methods while ignoring the whole spectrum of contemporary ideology, cannot lead to success. Hence, paradoxicality of current and future socio-economic situation and, respectively, economic consciousness and behavior, lies in the fact that objective and subjective forces of historical process act in different, and sometimes opposite directions, which does not offer stability and certainty in rapid resolution of pressing problems of Russian society.

References

Bolshakov A.M. *Derevn'ya 1917–1927 (Village 1917–1927)*. 1929.

Boykov V.E., Ivanov V.N., Toshchenko Zh.T. *Obshchestennoe soznanie i perestroyka (Social Consciousness and Perestroika)*. Moscow, 1990.

Desyat' let transformatsionnikh protsessov v stranakh TZVE i Rossii: resultaty i uroki (Ten Years of Transformational Processes in the Countries CEE and Russia: Results and Lessons) // Mirovaya ekonomika i mezhdunarodnye otnosheniya. 2000. No 5. P. 6.

Dratshev V.K. *Ekonomicheskoe soznanie kak factor razvitiya obshchestvennogo proizvodstva pri socializme (Economic Consciousness as Factor for Developing Social Production in Socialism)*. Minsk, 1977.

Dushatskiy L.E. *Tsennostno-motivatsionnie dominanty Rossiyskikh predprinimateley (Dominant Values and Motivations of Russian Business People)* // Sotsiologhicheskiye issledovaniya. 1999. No 7.

Fadeeva O.P. *Khozyaistvennie ukladi v sovremennom rossiyskom sele (Economical Production in Contemporary Russian Countryside)* // Sotsiologhicheskiye issledovania. 2007. No 11.

Fofanov V.P. *Ekonomitsheskiye otnosheniya i ekonomicheskoe soznanie (Economic Relations and Consciousness)*. Novosibirsk, 1979.

Gordeyev A. *Kursom stabilizatsii i razvitiya (Following the Course of Stabilization and Developments)* // APK: ekonomika i upravlenie. 2000. No 3–4.

APK: ekonomika i upravlenie. 1998. No 4. P. 16.

Izvestia. December 9, 1998.

Kalugina Z.I. *Paradoxy agrarnoy reformy v Rossii: sotsiologhicheskiy analiz transformatsionnikh processov (Paradoxes of Agrarian Reforms in Russia: Sociological Analysis of Transformation Processes)*. Novosibirsk, 2000. P. 94.

Kolesov N.D. *Ekonomitsheskoe myshlenie trudyashchikhsa i razvitie narodnogo khozaystva (Economic Thinking of Workers and Development of National Economy)*. Moscow, 1986.

Konsul'tant direktora (Director's Consultant). 2000. No 12. P. 13.

Kuz'min S.A. *O transformatsii derevenskogo uklada I sud'bakh sel'skokhozyastvennogo proisvodstva v Possii (Transformation of Economy and Future of Production in the Countryside in Russia)* // Mir Rossii. 2007. No 1 . P. 5.

Popov V.D. *Ekonomitsheskoe soznanie: suzchnost, formirovanie i rol' v sotsialisticheskom obshchestve (Economic Consciousness: Essence, Formation and Role in Socialist Society)*. 1981.

Rossiyskiy statisticheskiy ezhegodnik (Russia's Statistical Yearbook). Goskomstat of Russia. Moscow. 1999. P. 203.

Russian Public Opinion Monitor (Monitoring obshchestvennogo mneniya. Ekonomitsheskiye i sotsialniye peremeny). 1999. No 3. P. 17; 2006. No 4. P. 67.

Russian Public Opinion Monitor. 1999. No 6. P. 40; 2005. No 3. P.63.

Rutkevich M.N. *Transformatsia sotsial'noy strukturi rossiyskogo obshchestva (Transformation of Social Structure in Russian Society)* // Sotsiologhicheskiye issledovaniya. 1997. No 7.

Sotsiologhia vlasti (Sociology of Political Power) // 1999. No 2–3.

Sokolova G.N. *Ekonomitsheskaya sotsiologhia (Economic Sociology).* Minsk. 2005.

Steilmann K. *Novaya filosofia biznesa (New Philosophy of Business).* 3 vols. Berlin, 1998. Vol. 1.

Tumanov S.V. *Sovremennaya Rossiya: massovoe soznanie i massovoe povedenie (Contemporary Russia: Mass Consciousness and Mass Behavior).* 2000.

Velikiy P.P., Eliutina M.E., Shteynberg I.E., Bakhturina L.V. *Stariki rossiyskoy derevni (Elders of Russian Village).* Saratov, 2000. P. 32–33.

Verkhovin V.I. *Ekonomitsheskaya sotsiologhia (Economic Sociology).* 1998.

Vinogradskiy V.G. *Krestyanskie soobshchestva segodn'ya (yuzhnorossiyskiy variant) (Peasants' Communities Today. South-Russian Version)* // Sotsiologhicheskiye issledovaniya. 1996. No 6.

Zabelin A. *Razdum'e vslukh (Thinking aloud)* // Rossia. 1993. No 15.

Zaslavskaya T.I., Ryvkina R.V. *Sotsiologhia ekonomicheskoy zhizni. Otsherki teorii (Sociology of Economic Life. Sketches of Theory).* Novosibirsk, 1991.

Chapter 11. **Polarity of political consciousness: differences and commonalities**

> The main task of Russian authorities is to sustain a feeling of deep amazement in its people.
>
> *M.E. Saltykov-Shchedrin* (1826–1889), Russian writer

Up until mid-1980's, prior to Gorbachev's *perestroika*, political consciousness and behavior of Soviet people were seemingly monolithic, free of any doubt that socialist was the «sole true» ideology, constantly reaffirming the CPSU's right to absolute domination over people's minds and hearts. As it turned out later, the few dissidents, in their majority, were intersystem opponents: they hoped to improve socialist system, believing in possibility of socialism with a «human face». They criticized Soviet system for inertia, conservatism, decrepitude and detachment from real processes taking place in the world. In this sense, especially significant is the contribution of A.A. Zinoviev, who created a series of brilliant scientific and journalistic works analyzing ills and vices of the Soviet system.

At the same time, since 1970's Russian public began to tire of dominance of gerontocracy, its inability to solve problems of scientific, technological and information revolution. It was also dissatisfied with the growth of party-state bureaucracy, with inability of authorities to respond to new challenges. The society lived in expectation of changes. Although, during this period, some ideas of economic transformations, Soviet government and party reforms have emerged and were being discussed, most of them were aimed at improving and enhancing their functioning, search for reserves, limiting negative aspects of political life.

Hopes for major changes and corrections in social and public life had surfaced after L.I. Brezhnev's death, when Yu.V. Andropov came to power in 1983 giving rise to a premonition of forthcoming changes in political consciousness. However, these hopes remained unrealized due to the restoration of conservatism and rejection of innovation under the next general secretary – Konstantin Chernenko. But awareness of the necessity and inevitability of reforms got its internal momentum, allowing them to sprout with renewed force the beginning of *perestroika* in mid-1980s.

Political consciousness has made powerful strides toward changing its content, methods of implementation, and forms of manifestation in public life during the years of *perestroika*, which began with Mikhail Gorbachev coming to power in 1985. In other words, it has undergone serious and profound transformation, modification and modernization.

11.1. Magnitude, directions and characteristics of changes in political consciousness

Sociological analysis of political consciousness and behavior in 1980–1990's allows us to outline these changes.

First, political consciousness has become more open. The range of issues, subject to free discussion has tremendously expanded and, at the same time, spectrum of opinions has been immeasurably enriched. There practically remained not a single sphere of political life that was not subject to public opinion, with multitude of political and public organizations and associations that have not yet defined their position. The restrictions on expressing opinions regarding lives and actions of political leaders, parties and movements, current and crucial socially significant issues were lifted.

Second, political consciousness has become pluralistic. It has come to reflect the diversity of opinions — from liberal to socialist, from religious to monarchist, from nationalist to internationalist or cosmopolitan. Radical views of both right and left wing, although their share was insignificant, were also represented. A number of attempts were made to transplant some extravagant conceptions onto Russian soil, to reanimate old views and ideas. In other words, political consciousness reflects a huge range of orientations and preferences, anything imaginable, including certain ideas of individuals with deviant, schizophrenic imagination.

Third, political consciousness has become sharply critical. It is especially evident in evaluating activities of state and official organizations. And if at the initial stages of ongoing changes this criticism was respectful, over time it acquired traits of intolerance. Paradoxicality of the situation lies in the fact that the more changes are implemented, the tougher and more relentless this criticism becomes. In this situation, many politicians do not want to be «left behind»: many of them turned an opportunity for public criticism into offensive behavior towards their opponents, bordering on rudeness and lack of basic culture.

Fourth, a braking mechanism of the second order, which emerged due to the imperfection of occurring changes, *has already developed in political consciousness.* The gap between the words and the deeds has affected the new generation of Russian leaders as well, which is manifested in inadequate understanding of ongoing processes and, consequently, in activities inconsistent with new realities. And this in turn, is reflected in growing tension, loss of credibility of all official structures (Levashov. 2007. P. 476).

Fifth, analysis of political consciousness makes *it extremely difficult to find «supporters» or «opponents» of market reforms.* At a time when virtually everyone operates under the banner of necessity of economic transformation, opinions, positions of various social and political forces regarding a particular issue can be inconsistent or even highly contradictory: people acting in support of left or right-wing forces with regard to one group of issues, might use wait-and-see tactics with regard to others, or be centrists toward the third group of problems, etc.

Thus, political consciousness came to reflect only the first shifts in political life, which were related to utilization of surface reserves, i.e. access to more exhaustive information, ability to discuss it and to express one's opinions openly, without reservations. However, deep reserves of democratization and openness, such as real participation in governance, remain virtually untapped, and, according to a number of indicators, the situation is degrading.

And, at last, political consciousness came to be characterized by anxiety, instability, and uncertainty with regard to the future. It cannot be any other way, since it has not yet been decided at the highest political level what kind Russia we are building. This lack of clear vision, uncertainty generates instability and political apathy inherent in the majority of population.

However, the very political consciousness, reflecting the ongoing search, has experiences some ups and downs during the 1980–1990's, which resembled more of a zigzag rather than forward development. Since the middle and during the second half of 1990's some new trends emerged in political consciousness. A shift to the left was becoming clearly detectable, which was manifested not only in growing *left* (socialist) orientations, but also in nostalgia for the past (most likely for serious social safeguards that existed in the USSR) (Gorshkov. 2000).

People were disillusioned with the ruling regime, hoping that market reforms would help renew and improve their living conditions. As a result, social consciousness still retains values and attitudes linked to the Soviet way of life, a fact affecting electorate of radical-democrats, who suffered a crushing defeat in 1993 parliamentary elections taking a mere third place after LDPR and CPRF (communists). In 1995, 2003 and 2007 elections they lost voters' confidence and failed to gain even 5% and 7% of the votes necessary for winning parliamentary seats. Some of their success during 1999 elections is largely attributable to support from official structures and inclusion of previously rejected provisions, associated with patriotism and Russian national identity in their programs. Similar processes are occurring in former People's democracies: according to the data of Prague Institute for Public Opinion Studies, in 1999 40% of Hungarians, 32% of Czechs and 22% of Poles agreed with assertion regarding the decline of socialism (*Nezavisimaya gazeta.* 1999, November 19).

To illustrate the split between various political and social institutions, on one hand, and people, on the other, I would like to offer a very revealing example. In 1998 the newspaper «Argoumenty i Facty» printed a list of political orientations of officials and journalists, members of the media. According to that list there were a lot of supporters of «communist ideas» and «communist revenge» both in the presidential circle, the government, ministries and State Duma, while 95% of journalists were committed to «democratic ideas». At first glance, everything seems to be correct, there is nothing to argue about. However, this chart is missing a link, and an important one — the people. The fact is, with this link added, we have a completely different picture: according to sociological data, up to 30-35% of the population support (or share) socialist ideas.

In the 1990's and 2000's there was *a shift towards national and even nationalist orientations* in political consciousness of the population. And their range is quite diverse — from Russian (not necessarily ethnic) patriotism to unbridled chauvinism and racism. But the fact remains: at the end of 1990's patriotic sentiment gained importance and now plays a significant role in public life. It is the exploitation of these very ideas that played a leading role in V. Zhirinovsky's phenomenon. These orientations are also present in CPRF (Communist Party) program and the entire people's patriotic forces block. Pro-fascist, nationalist groups in their propaganda proclaiming Russian and Slavic superiority also exploit the spirit of patriotism in its extreme forms. Right wing forces turned toward ideas of patriotism as well convinced that it is imperative to their success in political struggles.

Moreover, ways of using patriotism diversify more and more. Extreme nationalistic forces, led by Barkashov, the leader of «Russian national unity», a pro-fascist organization, took part in 1999 election battles (the State Duma elections). Yavlinsky's «Apple» was suddenly patriotism-smitten as well, although it was never even suspected of such predilection prior to the Presidential elections; numerous ads were flashing on TV with G. Yavlinsky against the background of all significant events in the life of our country: labor feats of five-year plans, Great Patriotic war, space exploration, etc. Liberals, realizing hopelessness and futility of advocating western ideas and concepts alone, no longer shun actions in support of patriotism.

This correlates with the search for national idea, identity and ideology, which Russian government and its supporters initially rejected, but then returned to it, because spiritual vacuum in people's consciousness is harmful for both people themselves, as well as the newly established state. However, this search proved unsuccessful, despite numerous discussions and regular attempts at displaying ambitious projects.

Another phenomenon of political consciousness should be noted: less and less people share extreme radical positions, both right and left wings. The fact that the majority of population does not support extremists was demonstrated by the outcome of State Duma elections (2003, 2007) — all radicals failed. Results of many regional election campaigns also indicate rejection of extreme political views — very few representatives of the extremist forces got access to legislative assemblies of the regions, territories, and republics.

This bias toward extremes is rather firmly and persistently maintained in real consciousness and, in our opinion, there is no reason to assume that this situation will change in favor of radical orientations. Basically, people follow both liberal and socialist ideologies, patriotic and religious and even monarchist values, provided that there is a possibility of their coexistence and comparability, in contrast to intolerance emanating from the leaders of many political parties and social movements.

At the same time, while stating these characteristics of political consciousness, we should consider the depth of their penetration into all segments of population. In our opinion, in Russian society, political forces or leaders, capable of renouncing past legacy have not yet emerged. Almost all contemporary politicians are inherently lacking commitment to a policy of compromise; they wish to impose their will and program of action at any cost. Meanwhile society craves reasonable, balanced, long-term future prospect based on common sense. But having lost faith in the possibility of effectively influencing the government, people began to complicate, diversify forms and methods, and change techniques of pressuring power structures in order to achieve desired results.

In this regard, very indicative of that was the process of changing methods of political struggle and social confrontations that took place in the 1990's. Indeed, immediately following (the) proclamation of the slogans of creating a genuinely democratic society in Russia, which would observe rights and freedoms of the citizens, respect individual honor and dignity in public life (and especially at work), after they failed to materialize, a method of harming oneself in order to attract authorities' attention to socially significant issues became widespread. In early 1990's opposition would use such methods as hunger strikes, or chaining (handcuffing) themselves to fences, heavy equipment or buildings. Sometimes people even resorted to such methods as self-immolation and suicide. These were attempts to draw attention of businessmen and politicians who mocked individual rights and freedoms of the citizens. However these methods quickly ceased to affect both the authorities, as well as employers. Therefore, it was not surprising that in mid-1990 another form of opposition emerged: harming their organizations, its production, its staff, which manifested in seizure of enterprises, suspending their activities, conflicts with management. This form, however, was ineffective and very quickly exhausted itself, with little or no results for its participants.

As the next stage, such means of struggle as actions detrimental to the state were being utilized: blocking transportation routes (railways, highways), blackouts — switching-off electric power, refusal to deliver raw materials and necessary goods to other consumers, disorganizing, paralyzing many sectors of national economy and life in the regions. And, in late 1990's, these methods of struggle were already embodied in slogans to radically rethink economic decisions made at the beginning of market reforms, expressed in demands for nationalization, transfer of control functions to labor collectives and their return under the wing of state regulation. These actions resulted in a number of cases of seizure of enterprises, establishment of self-management and even use of violence while implementing these actions (Maximov. 2005).

The beginning of 2000 marked revival of traditional method of struggle — increasing use of strikes. Tables 11.1 and 11.2. show its real development and popular opinion about strikes.

Table 11.1.

Number of strikes in Russia

	2000	2002	2005
Number of organizations, which had strikes	817	30,980	2575
Number of workers involved in strikes (thousands)	284,4	3,9	84,6
Number of persons per organization	33	48	32,8
Amount of losses in men/days (thousands)	236,4	29,1	85,9

Source: Rossiiskii statisticheskii ezhegodnik — 2006. Stat.sb. (The Russian Statistical Yearbook. 2006. A statistical collection). Moscow, 2006. P. 162.

Table 11.2

Popular opinion regarding strikes
(in % of respondents N = 1800)

Possible answers	1998	2001	2004	2007
Strike is the only method of achieving one's goals	17	13	14	14
Strike is normal means for solving social problems	12	13	19	21
Strike is an extreme measure, but unavoidable due to present circumstances	44	30	29	33
It is impossible to solve any problem by striking	5	33	29	17
In our country strikes are impossible	14	5	4	6
Hard to say	8	6	6	9

Source: Public Opinion — 2007. Moscow. Levada-Center. 2007. P. 51.

11.2. Paradoxes of political development of the country

Under the conditions of great social renewal, when huge masses of people re-enter the arena of history making, some truly astonishing contradictions of this process can acquire the character of paradoxes. They presently reflect at unexpected, unfamiliar course of development, which is far more difficult to explain than to discover, let alone eliminate or mitigate.

During the period of transformational processes, these paradoxes are created jointly by the state, political parties and movements, people themselves as well as their activities. Emergence of these paradoxes is often illogical; it also partially or completely excludes common sense, traditions and experience of previous eras, which still teaches us anything.

Finding causes for emergence of political paradoxes mainly involves answering the question of to what degree are people involved in political life, how are the basic, vital issues that affect the population reflected in political being, why after several years of euphoria, dreams and hopes for democratic development, did political apathy and growing frustration with social reforms and current changes become so wide-spread? How did people develop such sharply negative attitude towards existing power structures? Why did the number of abstaining voters increase so dramatically, when even meager 25% required in order to legitimize the elections, often cannot be reached? Where did the enthusiasm and the passion, typical of the rallies raging during the last weeks of *perestroika* and the first months after the August 1991 events, disappear to?

And the main question is — did the majority of people really participate in political changes in the country? In our opinion, however paradoxical it may sound, people by and large were not involved in demolition of the Soviet system and implementation of reforms.

Most researchers, politicians, journalistic deemed it necessary to uncover the reasons why the majority of people after the first few years of hope for democratic reforms became disillusioned and started to withdraw from participation in state and public affairs. Political analysts listed all sorts of possible and partly plausible reasons such as the fact that people were allegedly disappointed in their expectations; that they do not trust anyone — neither the State, nor political parties, not the army, nor religion; that Russia is being run by non-professional amateurs and even criminals who nearly «wrecked» the great country, etc.

In our opinion, all these arguments are one-sided and even primitive, since they are based on a false assumption that people rose, they say, to accomplish great economic, political and social achievements. Actually people did not rise, or participate in any of these «great» changes and had no intention to. The history of the twentieth century knew only two cases when people became the creators of the historical process — the events of 1917–1920 (Civil war) and The Great Patriotic War. These the two events were characterized by mass, not partial, not superficial, but deep popular involvement in implementation of historic changes.

All other events were characterized by outbursts of activity not so much of specific social groups, but rather separate fractions or political actors. If we take into account the events after 1985, without analyzing the whole Russian and Soviet history, we can assert that in general people kept silent. Prior to 1988 sociologists had consistently recorded the fact that the majority of people, answering questions about societal changes, acknowledged them as occurring «somewhere at the top», but not where they lived and worked. «The trees sway at the top, the forest is always quiet at the bottom».

Since 1988, and especially since 1989 when impassioned rallies started spreading across the country (mainly large and partially mid-size cities), a *«popular presence effect»* has emerged, when in fact an insignificant number of ambitious power addicts, as well as persons offended and humiliated by the former regime, and, lastly, adventurers of all kinds were setting the tone of the evens. According to all-Union surveys of 1989 to 1991, no more than 3-4% of the people considered themselves as participants in such political and social events as rallies, marches, demonstrations, strikes, etc. However, militant and aggressive minority presented itself in front of the entire world as the voice of the majority of Russian population, even attempting to convince the people.

Something similar happened in August 1991. There was no revolutionary upsurge, no action in support of either side. Few people went to defend seized buildings of district, city and regional committees of the CPSU, few people followed Yeltsin and his team's appeal to strikes against the State Committee for Extraordinary situations. Provinces were working, and kept working as usual, and kept silent as usual, paying no attention to the events in Moscow. And in Moscow itself barely one percent of the population was involved in actively supporting Yeltsin: the majority of Muscovites were working, shopping, and viewing all the events surrounding the «White House» as something unrelated to their immediate concerns and anxieties.

Similar events took place in October, 1993, when even fewer people were involved in the actions surrounding the same «White House» — where tank units and police forces were making their «statement». Even gunfire, followed by shelling of the Supreme Soviet attracted no special attention of the majority of Muscovites, except, as noticed by A. Gamov (Komsomol'skaya pravda. 1994. September 30), for a few onlookers, who viewed this tragic event as a spectacle of sorts. Moreover, in contrast with August 1991, all the action took place in Moscow alone, leaving other cities absolutely unaffected.

So what was it? From the historic viewpoint, it was not such a rare case, when an active, aggressive and politicized minority managed to impose its will on the people by misrepresenting their actions as popular goals and intentions. Thus, active participation of the public in transformations occurring in society is out of the question.

Analysis of actual events suggests that behind the apparent universal politicization of popular consciousness and activity, reaching new frontiers of rethinking current events, with tens and hundreds parties and movements emerging — shallow, superficial and momentary politicized judgments and passions were predominant. Political arena was and still is dominated by emotions, poorly motivated attitudes and rapidly changing orientations, giving rise to towering ambitions, unfulfilled aspirations and even hatred. Danger lies in the fact that these unstable phenomena and events are quite often falsely presented as natural processes and basis for long-term forecasts. Meanwhile, leapfrogging, emotions, feelings in motivations and actions are very fluid and changeable, making it an impossible basis for judging the depth of ongoing transformation. However, the situation is such that virtually all political forces that swear by the name of the people, don't have a clue about true aspirations and genuine interests of those on whose behalf they claim to act. This equally applies to right and left-wing, conservatives and radicals. This total disregard for the people, their desires and intentions has become apparent during the all-Union referendum on preservation of the USSR, on March 17, 1991 (73% people voted for it).

In our opinion, the fact that the majority of participants voted for the preservation of the USSR does not mean they support ideas of renewed federation, socialist choice, or union of sovereign republics. Rather, it was survival instinct. Well aware of all negative and perverse aspects that characterized our lives, people still chose to support a situation, which was not entirely satisfactory, but familiar to them, instead of voting for something novel and unknown. *Collapse of the Soviet Union led to a paradox: people in their majority* (up to 70%, and not only in Russia, but also in other former republics that are now independent states) *still regret its disintegration. But, it does not mean that they would welcome it back.*

A contradictory, difficult and very complex process of rethinking the past is underway. After years of frantic rejection of all things Soviet, social consciousness returned to more sober assessment of past events, evaluating a variety of phenomena and achievements, thus enabling people to see the life of the country not only through rose colored (as in the past) or black tinted glass (as in 1990's), but in much better balanced, dimensional, multi-color light. Moreover, the West has also changed its attitude toward the «Soviet Empire». According to some experts, *Russia's image abroad, in late 1990's and especially in the beginning of 2000's, become worse than under Soviet rule.* This paradox, if closely examined, has a rational and realistic basis.

11.3. Paradoxes of mass political consciousness and behavior

The main paradox lies in the fact that, *on the one hand, there is a decline of confidence in the state and its political institutions, and, on the other — eternal hope for help and its participation in solving vital problems.* People still rely on its paternalistic role. According to VTsIOM and other sociological centers, in late 1990's, the credibility of the President, Government, State Duma and Federation Council fluctuated between 4–12% (in 2005 — 13–17%), marking a level of not just mistrust, but complete rejection of these state institutions, or rather, those embodying the authority over the country. In this connection, we should point out that, among all structures of power hierarchy, local authorities enjoyed relatively high popular confidence, a fact never registered by sociologists throughout 1980's and early 1990's. We can assume that regardless of all the deficiencies in functioning of regional authorities and their limited power, people recognize optimistic changes, positively affecting their lives (See: Table 11.3).

Table 11.3

Trust/distrust of the socio-political institutions
(% of respondents. N = 2400)

Socio-Political Institutions	1995	1999	2001	2004	2006
The President	9/74	4/88	49/35	49/33	51/34
Government	8/69	18/60	23/53	17/59	18/57
State Duma (Parliament)	10/61	14/62	12/63	6/69	10/68
Police, Courts, Office Of Public Prosecutor	16/59	12/70	12/70	9/72	11/76
Army	35/40	38/44	39/39	27/48	30/49
Trade Unions	18/52	15/61	17/56	16/56	15/54
Church	—	26/48	33/38	35/37	37/36
Political parties	6/63	7/64	12/58	5/68	8/68
Regional leaders	11/59	23/51	17/55	15/60	18/54
Media	21/53	12/66	12/66	19/57	23/56
Business and banking circles	6/65	5/78	10/68	12/62	10/59
Do not trust anyone	25	32	19	21	18

Note: Numerators are the index of *trust*, denominators — *distrust*.
Source: Institute for Socio-Political Research, Russian Academy of Sciences.

This rejection of state authority, lack of faith in its structures are inexplicably combined with hope and reliance on the state as a sort of authorized and responsible social institution. The state is blamed for unemployment and, at the same time, people rely on its help. The state is blamed for the collapse of economy, but at the same time, the majority believes in its ability to cope with economic ruin. The state, in many people's opinion, is responsible for rampant embezzlement and corruption, but at the same time, people hope for its capability to get rid of these ugly phenomena. The state is blamed for the results of privatization, but at the same time people associate it with hope for cancellation or significant correction of these results.

Personification of power plays a special role in evolution of political consciousness. Early in the 1990's all hopes for improvement of the conditions in the Russia, family situation or individual well-being was directly associated with the name of President Yeltsin. As his authority was declining, so was the trust in all other government structures. However, the degree of confidence in Duma and the government was not quite as low as the President. Thus, in 1999, 71 to 75% «did not trust President at all», with 37% mistrusting the Parliament and 28–35% the government. When the new President came to power in 2000, public opinion regained traits of optimism and hope: 77–78% of respondents expressed their commitment to fully or partially support the new president. Credibility of the new Duma and new government also increased slightly — from 53 up to 63%. Reflection of V.V. Putin's popularity had a positive impact on the assessment of activities of other government bodies. But how long can it last? Analysis of mood fluctuations when evaluating authorities suggests that people are not yet got rid of idealizing the government, faith in its power. Eventually, they hope, it will «see the light», come to its senses and become an advocate for popular interests.

This situation is very conducive to paradoxical occurrences. This was demonstrated, for example, by the events on *Gorbatiy Bridge* near the «White House» in 2000, when coal miners were banging their helmets, demanding that the state impose order in their mines. They refused to recognize the fact that the mines had long since been operated as joint-stock companies, and miners' claims should have been addressed to their managers. But this group consciousness is difficult to refocus, first, because previously miners lives had always been dependent on state policy, and, second, it was difficult for them to get rid (and in this they are right) of the conviction that this disgraceful situation, their dire poverty, months of delayed wages, ultimately, depend on the state, which created such economic relations where larcenous institutions and organizations are living in clover, completely ignoring the interests of those, at whose expense they operate (*Krutoy plast.* 1999). (See: Table 11.4.)

Table 11.4

In your opinion, whose interests does the state represent and defend today?
(% of respondents. N = 2400)

Monitor' time	Reach ones	Bureaucracy	All Russian citizens	Middle strata	Poor strata	Hard to say
2000, December	46	44	9	8	1	9
2001, December	40	38	9	8	0	21
2002, December	61	54	6	7	1	10
2003, October	53	54	6	7	1	13
2004, June	50	52	9	8	1	15
2005, September	54	52	8	8	1	15

Source: Department of social policy and socio-political research, Institute for Socio-Political Research, Russian Academy of Sciences

A *paradoxical gap between desire for further development of democracy and aspiration for authoritarian rule, which is getting more distinct,* is no less remarkable. Political consciousness had long been satisfied with achievement of freedom of speech, freedom of public and political associations, absence of persecution of dissidents, access to information previously unavailable to the population, etc. But political rights and freedoms were gradually monopolized by certain clans, cliques, groups that cultivated bribery, manipulation of public opinion, and contributed to penetration of criminal elements into positions of authority. And if we add corruption, along with widespread venality of officials (and not just them), blatant forms of political lobbying, voter fraud, rapid succession of politicians, it becomes clear why there was a popular desire to counter these negative phenomena. So a solution was found in supporting a leader who was willing to establish «iron discipline» in the country, but only using «positive» aspects of democracy. In VTsIOM studies respondents were asked: «Are there situations in life when people need a strong and authoritative leader?» In 1989 41,9% of respondents shared the positions of «always» and «sometimes», while in 1996 that number was 68,4%. At the same time, during this period, the number of those opposing the possibility of such leader's rise to power fell from 45,1 to 18,2% (*Monitoring obshchestvennogo mneniya.* 1997. No 1. P. 10; 2006. No 4. P. 71). However, in 2000 75% (82% in 2005) of respondents believed that order was more important for their country then restriction of democratic principles and personal freedoms, which would have been necessary for its achievement. Paradox lies in the fact is that regardless of popular conviction that democracy as an ideal government structure (66% believe that Russia needs democracy), in reality, people tend to support the establishment of authoritarian regime. Disappointed with anarchy, 60% of respondents (VTsIOM poll, June 2000) voted in favor of concentrating power in the hands of a single person.

Popular attitude toward political power and assessment of possible means of influencing it appears to be paradoxical as well. On the one hand, according to VTsIOM data in September 2000 60% (in 2005 — 52%) of respondents (N = 2408 in All-Russia sample) considered political situation in Russia tense. And taking into account that 10% (in 2005 — 9%) agreed that the situation was critical and explosive, while 12,2% (in 2005 — 14%) were unable to make up their mind, we can conclude that the overall assessment was quite pessimistic. On the other hand, while two thirds of the population demanded resignation of president Boris Yeltsin in 1998-1999, in 2000 this measure was supported only by 9%. Therefore, growing refusal to support protests demanding government resignation (down from 40,6% to 14,3%) or dissolution of the State Duma (from 31,1 to 23,8%) is quite understandable. But we should pay closer attention to assessment of possibility of mass protests against declining living standards, 47,9% of people (i.e. almost one out two) acknowledged their likelihood, while, at the same time, only 32,6% expressed their willingness to become personally involved. In other words, many have placed the burden of responsibility on others, adopting more humble attitude — being a critically minded bystander.

Attitude of «letting other people do the dirty work», i.e. protest, refraining from personal involvement in specific actions, creates another paradox — «revolutionary» intransigence (verbal only!), and, at the same time, refusal to participate in real actions aimed at improving their unsatisfactory situation. Example: in 1998 65,6% of people (i.e. two out of three) did not want Yeltsin to become president of the country, yet only 32,6% were willing to engage in concrete protest actions, and only 7 to 12% were inclined to take decisive steps such as civil disobedience, or were ready to defend their convictions by force. Why and how did such contradiction between verbal and real willingness to protest emerge in political consciousness? In our view, tolerance, patience reserves, which in Russian people are historically fairly substantial, did not yet run out. The same historical experience demonstrates that people fear escalation of political situations, since it often leads to bloodshed, which, naturally, is not just undesirable, but unacceptable. In other words, despite extremely negative attitude to the government, to politicians, people are still willing to tolerate these institutions and their leaders, among other reasons, because of the negative attitude toward other contenders for political power. However, even after electing a new president, the leitmotif of popular value attitude to the quality of governance remains unchanged (table 11.5).

Table 11.5

In your opinion, what prevails in current political leadership of the country ?

(% of respondents. N = 1800)

Response options	1998	1999	2000	2005
Democracy	2,2	2,3	8,8	8,9
Bureaucratic arbitrariness	13,5	12,3	22,8	29,9
A one-man rule of top leaders	18,9	19,8	18,5	21,7
Total mess	54,6	52,8	38,6	20,5
Hard to say	10,8	12,8	11,3	19,0

Source: Boikov V.E. Narod i vlast'(People and powers). Moscow, 2006. P. 165.

In other words, the power structure, from peoples' viewpoint, still represents a symbiosis of disorder, lawlessness and administrative dictate. Under these circumstances, general population, still hopeful, supported the new president of Russia, since he embodies their desire to restore order in the country. In general, attitude toward Putin can be classified as cautiously-friendly, which is predominantly expressed in evaluations such as «credible, but not in all aspects». Against the background of high evaluation of the president, a rather low score of the government and Duma (opposite of what was under Yeltsin) is rather paradoxical.

But why do people, despite their indignation over the government policies and their financial situation, choose to avoid decisive action? In our opinion, concerned about possibility of violence, people are hoping that an authoritarian (possibly dictatorial) government can save people from deprivations, fulfill their desire and need for a «strong hand», achieve social justice and avoid bloodshed.

In this context, we should mention positions of analysts representing various political forces. Some of them, taking under consideration only one side of social mood — harsh criticism and practically unanimous rejection of existing political bodies and political leaders, argue that people are on the verge of universal indignation bordering on revolt, revolutionary actions, or desire to overthrow existing political system. However, they pay no attention to the other side of the very same negativistic attitude — basically, people still tolerate (and are willing to further tolerate) current political system. The majority of people see the real way out of this situation in disregard of all political parties, retreat into their private lives, which is especially evident in prevalence of civic apathy.

11.4. Multy-party system: myth or reality?

The essence of this paradox: we have a multi-party system, but we don't have any parties (almost any — except for the Communist Party). How many hopes and expectations were linked to the emergence of multi-party system! This idea was cherished, admired; it was associated with dreams of genuine competition in the field of ideology and political actions. But illusion quickly dispelled.

First, many parties do not represent anything or anybody. In most cases they are small groups of people created according to «kitchen» principle — often within the Garden or Boulevard ring of Moscow, or with a few schizoid representatives in individual provinces. Many of them have chosen membership in those parties not so much because they share their proclaimed principles, but mainly because they want to be «visible» or in power (or anywhere near positions of authority, even provincial). It is indicative that when in November 2000, leaders of all 186 public and political associations legally registered with the Ministry of Justice and entitled to participate in elections were invited to parliamentary hearings in connection with preparation of a new draft bill «On political parties», paradoxically, 41 invitations returned back to Duma offices — the recipients could not be found at specified address.

Second, many parties' programs are so close and so similar to each other that even political analysts can hardly tell them apart. That is why, in public (political) consciousness they merge into a kind of a mass, seeking power and preoccupied with their own problems, rather than actual concerns of the people. It should be added that there were been numerous attempts to create parties, which fully imitate the spectrum and even nuances of similar parties in the West, attempts poorly (if at all) correlated with the actual political situation in the country. Significantly, people responded quite adequately to all this hustle and bustle of political parties trying to get into the Duma in 1995: out of 43 political parties and movements only four — Communist Party of the Russian Federation, LDPR, «Apple» and «Our Home — Russia» made it into the parliament. In 1999 six parties had been represented in the third State Duma: besides those parties mentioned above, the right-wing — Union of the Right Forces — made a comeback, «Fatherland» gained some support, while «Unity», successor of «Our home — Russia», took over its place. In 2003 four parties made it: the majority — «United Russia» (promptly concocted by the officials to edge out CPRF), Communist party, Liberal party (Zhirinovsky) and nationalist party «Homeland» (in 2007 instead of it — left-wing party «Just Russia»).

An indicator of lack of real multi-party system is the fact that in 1998 only 0,8% of the population (in 1999 — 1,0%) participated in activities of political parties, and only 6,7% (in 1999 — 8,1% and in 2006 — 3,1%) came to the meetings with politicians and MP candidates. It should be added that only 13,7% of respondents in an All-Russian study felt that political parties' activities should be further developed, while 22,2% thought it was best to abandon multi-party system altogether and 45% voted for limiting activities of all or some parties (*Sotsiologhiya vlasti.* 1999. P.49).

So, here is *an intriguing paradox — lots of parties, a lot more fuss around them, immeasurable and incalculable claims and ambitions, political turmoil, mutual insults and accusations — impossible to count, and as result — their complete rejection and reluctance of social consciousness to recognize and deal with these power-hungry characters.*

The only amendment to this argument can be made in connection with the fact that specific public figures, which have a certain degree of recognition are of greater importance for a regular voter. They remain a primary focus for parts of the electorate. This fact, however, should not be made an absolute, since often a political leader and his party do not represent the same thing for ordinary voters. It is for these very reasons that sociologists have failed forecasting results of the first Duma elections in 1993. Applying the principal that equates political party leader's image to that of a party, some sociological centers concluded that if 37% of residents of large cities are sympathetic to Gaidar and nearly 30% — Yavlinsky, their political parties would respectively receive this (or close to it) number of votes. However, Russian reality demonstrated validity of yet another paradox, refuting these predictions with a bang. These forecasts may very well work effectively under different conditions: real rating of these parties turned out to be 2,5 to 3 times lower than expected.

A side effect of paradoxical consciousness was the fact that lack of confidence in existing political institutions has merged with mistrust in real ability of political forces to change existing situation, loss of hope for possible emergence (at that given stage of development) of sensible organizations, capable of implementing popular wishes and desires. This resulted in widespread apathy, trusting only those people who became part of one's personal and everyday life. According to a nationwide survey (2004, 1628 people, headed by V.E. Boykov), 87% of people rely on relatives and friends in emergency situations, 24,4% — on help from their co-workers (organization) and only 5,9% — on authorities.

Paradox associated with a complex process of resocialization of people's consciousness and behavior, which was occurring in 1990's, is very illustrative and revealing. E.B. Shestopal pointed out that: «this process varies from drastic revisions of former political values to aspirations of preserving their views unchanged despite pressure from political environment» (Shestopal. 1996. P. 46). This paradoxical combination of old attitudes and new realities was incredibly prevalent. That is why the process of resocialization encounters so many obstacles in its path. If for younger generation this process is less painful, for older people, even those seeking to adopt new political values, it is agonizing, since reconciliation of former convictions and new beliefs leads to alteration of consciousness as a result of dysfunctional political system. With all political uncertainty, people with life experience return to basic ideas acquired during the stage of primary socialization. This explains considerable stability of social consciousness among older generations toward values that were shaped during previous stages of their life. But this mismatch of former and present ideas, on one hand, obviously creates peculiar centaurs combining incompatible reference points and indicators. On the other hand, this leads to tragedies, when people become aware of impossibility of realizing themselves in the new life, which generates feelings of helplessness, worthlessness and uselessness. Lack of social protection and social services exacerbates this already painful break from reality and generates nostalgia for the past.

In addition, *there are paradoxes characterizing specificity of Russia's political life.* Thus, the loudest claims of serving public interests, acting as guardians of the people come from the leaders of liberal forces that were once fairly cohesively opposed the CPSU's dominance in political life, calling for renewal of economic and political system. But it was their policy that delivered a huge blow to the welfare of the people: reforms like price liberalization, privatization, and robbing people of everything that was accumulated during Soviet times. The result of their activity is well known – universal rejection of their policies, social discontent, irritation with real conditions of life, dissatisfaction with concentration of power in the hands of few individuals and hatred toward those who made millions of people destitute (Perestroika glazami rossiyan).

These people were also discredited by the fact that many individuals from the first democratic wave turned out to be dishonest, used their power for personal (quite successfully) gain, did not defend Russia's national interests and actively participated in plundering state (public) property. Simultaneously with emergence of new bourgeoisie former nomenclature members were replenishing its ranks. A potent fusion of power and capital was taking place. By means of presidential decrees many large established commercial structures have been transferred to certain officials, and their share (charter) capital was paid for with state funds (Rabotyazhev, Isaev. 2000; Shubin. 2005).

These paradoxes are not an exceptional phenomenon. In real social life there are many conflicts that are shocking, due to lack of logic in actions and deeds of people involved in these processes.

References

Gorshkov M.K. *Rossiyskoe obshchestvo v usloviyakh transformatsii – sotsiologhicheskiy analiz (Russian Society under Transformation –Sociological Analysis).* 2000.

Komsomol'skaya pravda. 1994. September 30.

Krutoy plast. Shakhterskaya zhizn' na fone restrukturizatsii otrasli i obshchestvennykh peremen *(Sloping Layer. Miners' Life against Background of Restructuring the Branch and All-Russian Changes)* / Pod red. L. Gordon, E. Klopov, I. Kozhukhovskiy. 1999.

Levashov V.K. *Sotsiopoliticheskaya dynamika rossiyskogo obshchestva (Sociopolitical Dynamics of Russian Society).* 2000–2006. Moscow, 2007. P. 476.

Maximov B.I. *Klassovie konflikti: nablyudeniya i analiz (Class Conflicts: Observations and Analysis).* St. Petersburg. 2005.

Monitoring obshchestvennogo mneniya. Ekonomitsheskiye i sotsialniye peremeny. (The Russian Public Opinion Monitor). 1997. No 1. P. 10; 2006. No 4. P. 71.

Nezavisimaya gazeta. 1999, November 19.

Perestroika glazami rossiyan (Perestroika – Public Opinion) // Nezavisimaya gazeta. 1996, January 24.

Rabotyazhev N., Isaev V. *Glubokoe obosnovanie deyatelnosti gosudarstva — uslovie ozdorovlenia rossiyskogo obshchestva (Profound Grounding of State Activity — a Condition for Russian Society Recovery)* // Obshchestvo i ekonomika. 2000. No 7.

Shestopal E.B. *Perspektivy demokratii v soznanii Rossiyan (Prospects for Democracy in Consciousness of Russians)* // Obshchestvennie nauki i sovremennost. 1996. No 2. P. 46.

Shubin A.V. *Paradoxi perestroyki (Paradoxes of Perestroika).* Moscow, 2005.

Sotsiologhiya vlasti. Informatsionno-analititcheskiy bulleten' (Sociology of Political Power. Information and analytic newsletter) . No 2–3. Moscow, 1999. P. 49.

Chapter 12. **Paradox of legal consciousness**

> Revolutions have always been conceived
> by idealists and carried out by
> romantics. But only marauders enjoyed
> their results.
>
> *T. Carlyle* (1795–1881),
> English historian and philosopher.

The idea of rule of law along with the idea of civil society has always been appealing in modern history. For the sake of their substantiation, development and strengthening, numerous studies and experiments have been were conducted, tens and hundreds of versions of law application were tested and approved, practice of law enforcement was summarized in accordance with specific historical context, taking into account national features and particularities of different countries.

The idea of a lawful state was received with approval, even enthusiasm in New Russia. Practices of lawless regulation of social development were condemned. Experience of lawmaking and law enforcement in Imperial Russia and in Western democracies was being reexamined (incidentally, often uncritically). Almost all provisions of the Constitution of the USSR and RSFSR, legislative acts of the Soviet Union were subjected to severe criticism. Many of them were cancelled peremptorily, without sufficient reasons, creating a huge hole in legal regulation of state and public life of the country. *At the same time, attempts to establish the rule of law were accompanied by contradictory and paradoxical phenomena, the meaning and content of which defied logic.* These paradoxes were equally characteristic of legal theories, concepts, norms, as well as the newly formed State. These contradictions, inconsistencies, incompleteness and limitations of legal foundations of the State have increased uncertainty and complexity of legal space many times over, which severely impacted legal consciousness and legal behavior, reinforcing old and generating new paradoxes.

12.1. Paradoxes of the legal status of people

A well-known truth: rights and freedoms of citizens must be guaranteed by the Constitution of the country. However, it is Russia's Constitution, its status, legitimacy and legality that are questioned by many experts, researchers and politicians for a variety of reasons. And there is still no definitive answer to such questions as: was the Constitution really approved by a majority of voters? Can Constitution be adopted by popular vote, when an overwhelming majority of the population did not know, does not know and is unlikely to be aware of its main provisions in the foreseeable future? But most surprising was another issue: proclaiming democratic rights and freedoms, the Constitution practically gave absolute power to one person — to the president, who was above all the other braches of authority: legislative, executive and judiciary (*Eltsinshchina.* 1993; *Konets Eltsinshchiny.* 1999; Tomash. 2000). Isn't this a *paradox: claiming democratic system and establishment of credible governance, «the best» democratic Constitution laid a basis for authoritarian and, possibly, totalitarian rule with nothing in the legal system to balance or counter it?*

And that is not to mention the fact that the very Constitution of Russia submitted to referendum (plebiscite), was presented to the public less than one month prior to vote, which allows to reasonably suggest that the majority of people are not familiar with it (did not read it), and still have not read it to this day. In other words, it was a grand political spectacle which legalized the existence of this power structure, legislating interests of specific political forces.

The groups that seized power were extremely interested in this and similar performances, including those dressed up in legitimate legal form. Moreover, they created an environment where none of the social strata was interested in establishing and strengthening the rule of law: greedy «oligarchs» and «new Russians» deemed it unnecessary, since it restricted their predation. Middle class was too small to support balanced functioning of State legal mechanism. Low-income groups were too preoccupied with their own survival, in this situation, perceiving the state system only as a culprit of their plight. The paradox lies in the fact that despite differing, sometimes opposing attitudes all these social groups had little or no interest in whether that authority, which has so complicated their life, was legal or illegal, although such attitude was dictated by different reasons.

Selective, not uniform application of law, deliberately maintained by political authority, has detrimental effect on legal life of Russia. The main thing that public consciousness cannot ignore is the fact that the law is more lenient and flexible toward people who have power, as well as capital (money) than a »universal man» or just ordinary working people.

And an alliance between three forces — thieving business, violent («bloody») *crime and corrupt officials has the most devastating effect on legal consciousness as* *well.* Earlier, in the beginning of 1990's they often operated separately. In the process of market reforms, people who possessed questionably obtained (from a legal standpoint) capital and, at the same time, did not shun ties to the organized crime began to occupy positions of power including gubernatorial and cabinet ones. As a result criminal elements attempt to undertake (?!) law enforcement. According to press reports, in several cities of the Far East criminal groups have opened offices (reception-rooms), where people affected by injustice could turn to and have their problems solved more effectively (compared to official law enforcement). But, if criminals begin to undertake law enforcement even in a single region, what does that say about the level of compliance with legal norms and legal order in the country? It is obvious that both, the alliance with criminals, as well as granting them opportunities to act as defenders of popular interests presents an enormous paradox, which not in words, but in deeds undermines the foundations of both rule of law and civil society.

Situation that emerged after declaration of establishment of the rule of law, was *no less paradoxical, when in society the «war of laws» and «parade of sovereignties»* *were unleashed with enormous energy,* completely sweeping away not only remnants of orderliness in organization of both public and political life but also giving rise to legal nihilism that led to realization of Hobbesian idea of «war of all against all». This phenomenon contributed to emergence of symptoms of «political cannibalism», when proof of your point of view and position is based on complete rejection of not only opposite, but every other point of view. In these conditions law enforcement agencies are put in especially difficult position, since ambiguity of laws and regulations only disrupt their activity, makes it inefficient in the eyes of public opinion.

In this connection, it is worth recalling transformations in public attitudes toward law enforcement and state security that occurred during the years of market reforms. When the process of dividing state property was underway, these agencies stood in the way of (or could interfere with) implementation of takeovers, seizures and criminal privatization of public property. Therefore, criticism of them was boundless, scathing, contemptuous and simply indecent. Now, when this division is largely accomplished, attention of wealthy and powerful is again focused on law enforcement structures, which are now no longer seen as a possible obstacle, but as necessary instrument of consolidating results of seizures and redistribution of property and preventing possible encroachments.

In this case there is a formal logical contradiction in these paradoxes. Analysis of its logic or its truth is not obvious, it is hidden deep in the processes of social life, and hence, firm knowledge of actual processes is required to eliminate apparent inconsistency of this phenomenon.

In our opinion, *we are dealing with the phenomenon of legal nihilism.* What else can we expect, if society keeps hearing and reading about the necessity to strengthen the legal system, in particular the fight against *Mafia* and organized crime? However, in reality nothing is being done in order to influence these negative phenomena, at least, adopting relevant laws. On this basis, an old Russian proverb comparing the law to a shaft used to steer horses — it can be directed and lead any way you want — gained new popularity. This proverb is a real reflection of age-old practice of legal nihilism, which for centuries flourished in Russia, and in Russian Empire. Little has changed during Soviet times either. Initially, rather than legal norms, «revolutionary expediency» was predominant, then Stalin's «troikas» were setting the tone, which excessively amplified role of the prosecutor, while in 1960–1980-s opinions of party officials often determined the outcome of many criminal and civil cases. Especially if leaders, officials, deputies or other «prominent» persons were involved (Kudryavtsev, Trusov. 2004).

In the new Russia development of judicial system began with patching up and amending the old Constitution, which was supplemented with improved relevant laws. Then in accordance with the 1993 Constitution competencies of legislative and executive powers were more or less delimitated. Judicial authority was also revived: the Constitutional Court was established along with the Supreme Court. Overall, however, legal confusion, arbitrary decisions, continued to prevail, resulting in complete loss of confidence in legal system, its subjects and their activities. No one denied the need for judicial reform. Nevertheless, it failed to materialize because, paradoxical as it might sound, too many actors of the political scene were interested in rule of law: legal order, if established, would seriously threaten their interests, which were easier to preserve and defend in the face of uncertainty.

The essence of judicial reform, as defined by Chief Justice of the Supreme Court of Russia V.M. Lebedev, is «to ensure effective access of citizens to professional, fair and expeditious justice» because so far not everyone could file a complaint with the Supreme Court, and it was simply impossible to appeal against the decisions and actions of the authorities.

12.2. What stands in the way of implementing ideas of law?

Ultimately, no matter what reforms are implemented, what laws and other legal acts are adopted, societal situation is determined by practice, by actual experience, through which people daily and hourly compare and match level of expectations with possibilities of their implementation. Thus, at the beginning of the 1990's most people believed that a lawful state was being created, and many (up to 90%) expressed confidence that, finally, they would live according to the law, guided only by law. The public had spirited discussions of a possibility to create «humane» conditions for inmates (like in the West), procedures of multi-party system functioning, emergence of a new kind of officials, bound only by law.

But the reality turned out differently. Wishful thinking did not come true. Cracks started appearing in this belief in creation of a lawful state. Life itself was the main reason for that. Anxiety over their deprived conditions, threats of violence, fear of crime gradually rose from the fourth or fifth place at the beginning of 1990's to the first or second place after mid 1990's on the list of people's concerns. Not only these concerns became more important than the danger of ethnic conflicts, but they also became more significant than the depressing economic situation. People became more and more inclined to even sacrifice their own prosperity in order to avoid the threat of violence (*Sotsial'noe polozhenie i uroven' zhizni.* P. 462; Gudkov. 2000; *Rossia v poiskakh strategii*) (table 12.1).

Table 12.1.

Which of following problems of our society worry you the most?
(% of respondents)

Possible answers	VI.1997 N =2322	IX.1999 N = 2407	I.2000 N = 2407	IX.2006 N=2107
Food shortage, lack of essential goods	6,6	11,2	7,9	—
Rising prices	46,8	85,5	81,6	70
Growing unemployment	53,9	63,9	48,8	34
Crisis in economy, recession in industry and agriculture	47,2	56,3	43,9	27
Growing number of criminal offences	53,8	44,7	43,8	29
C risis of morality, culture	26,4	26,2	23,0	24
Environmental degradation	26,4	19,8	20,2	24
Aggravation of national relations	15,3	16,7	16,0	10
Sharp polarization between rich /poor, unfair distribution of income	45,0	33,8	35,9	30
Threat of fascism and extremism	2,6	4,4	2,7	10
Corruption, bribery	37,8	29,1	30,9	25
Weak, helpless government	40,0	30,4	24,3	11
Conflicts in the country's leadership	15,4	14,7	10,0	2
Armed conflicts on Russian borders of, unstable situation in the Chechen Republic (war)	12,3	7,6	43,6	4
Nonpayment and delay of wages, pensions, benefits	63,3	39,7	28,0	5
Hard to say	0,6	2,2	1,2	1

Source: Monitoring obshchestvennogo mneniya: economitseskiye i sotsialnye peremeny. 2000. No 2; Russian Public Opinion Herald. Data. Analysis. Discussions.2006. No 5. P. 81.

We should point out that the degree of confidence in all law-enforcement agencies, judicial and prosecutorial authorities remains very low (table 12.2).

Table 12.2.

To what extend are following .... credible?

(The Russian Public Opinion Monitor, in % of respondents, July 1996 N = 2404; September 2000 N = 2405; September 2007 N = 1600)

Possible answers	Deserves	Does not entirely deserve	Does not deserve at all	Hard to say
Army:				
July 1996	27,1	33,5	16,8	22,2
September 2000	34,6	34,8	15,9	14,7
September 2007	30	33	19	18
State Security				
July 1996	18,3	32,9	20,8	27,7
September 2000	20,9	36,0	22,1	21,0
September 2006	23	29	18	30
Police, court, District attorney				
July 1996	12,2	35,7	34,8	17,1
Court, District attorney				
September 2000	11,9	35,9	28,8	23,4
Court				
September 2006	14	31	29	26
District attorney				
September 2006	14	32	25	29
Police				
September 2000	13,6	38,6	36,0	11,8
September 2006	14	34	38	14
Lawyers				
September 2000	15,6	35,6	21,0	27,0

Source: Monitoring obshchestvennogo mneniya: economitseskiye i sotsialnye peremeny (Russian Public Opinion Herald. Data. Analysis. Discussions). 1996. No 5; 2000. No 6. P. 67–68; Public Opinion — 2007. Moscow. Levada-Center. 2007. P. 8.

Analysis of these data shows that confidence in legal institutions became extremely low: only 12 to 15% saw them as a force that could protect their rights. In public eyes, none of these organizations could act as a guarantor of freedom, honor and dignity. And this was the only possible way of assessing the situation, for society was drowning, swept by the wave of violence. If in 1990 recorded crime level reached 1840 thousand offences, in 1998 it was 2582, which meant that respectively 1243 and 1764 crimes were committed per 100 thousand residents, i.e. an increase of more than 1,5 times. If in 1989 only 6% of Muscovites said they were victims of violence or faced criminal behavior, in mid 1990's it was almost 25% of the capital population. This was a true reflection of their attitude toward the reality of emerging legal situation. The fact that the situation with people's safety and security has deteriorated significantly was reflected in the data of nationwide survey in February 2004 (table 12.3).

Table 12.3.

Do you fear that you and your loved ones might be victims of ....?
(% of respondents. N = 1800)

Types of threats	Very afraid	Somewhat afraid	Confident it won't happen	Hard to say
... accidents	33	52	4	9
...crime	34	52	5	8
...hooligan attacks	34	53	5	8
... despotism of political authorities	26	47	8	16

Source: Public Opinion — 2004. Moscow. Levada-Center. 2004. P. 22

The authorities themselves systematically set an example of disregarding, pr neglecting the law. Analyzing events of October 3–4, 1993 many newspapers, TV channels showed footage of Rutskoy calling to storm Ostankino and town council, Khasbulatov — to march on Kremlin, Makashov — insisting on destroying both. And almost no one wanted to mention the fact that mediated by the Patriarch of All Russia, with consent of some Federation Council members, a preliminary agreement on peaceful resolution of the conflict had already been reached. But it was never implemented since show of force was deemed appropriate. Consequently, armed violence in Ostankino and shelling of the «White house» allowed Russia's leaders to take a unique place in the history: for the first time in modern times a Parliament was shot at.

So how could spreading violence, murders for hire, deliberate bankruptcies, plundering through various funds and banks (mass consciousness was convinced that these actions were sanctioned by or carried out with approval of the state), and prevalence of bribery leave mass legal consciousness unaffected? Take, for example, popular views of corruption. In 1999 about 20 thousand (in 2004 — 35 thousand) corruption cases in public and private sectors were on record. But this was just the tip of the iceberg. Cases of robbery grew from 181000 to 306800, extortion — from 83700 to 126000, murder — from 31100 to 31800, rape — from 8300 to 8800. In 2004, there were 246 thousand economic crimes, 255 cases of terrorism (Maksimov S. V. 2000. P. 20–21). And in 2004 level of latency of bribery was estimated by experts at the rate exceeding 2000 (*Prestupnost v Rossii.* 1997. P. 3).

Yet fewer and fewer among implicated in bribery are being prosecuted. Only every fourth or fifth case results in conviction (Louneev. 1997. P. 277). More detailed analysis shows that approximately one out of 100 thousand cases of giving or accepting bribes is punished. *«Funnel effect» in relation to these violations is impressive indeed.* On the one hand, an average corrupt offender is unlikely to see such threat of exposure as a serious obstacle to commit unlawful acts. For this reason some lawyers come to conclude that inevitability of prosecution for corruption is absolute utopia both from theoretical and practical points of view (Maksimov. 2000. P. 31). Moreover, Russian authorities lack political will to fight corruption, since so far draft laws to this effect have only been discussed but not adopted. On the other hand, public consciousness cannot remain indifferent to these established practices. Outraged by obvious injustices, it loses hope of successfully overcoming these social ills, while, apparently, recognizing impossibility of seriously impacting the situation. This is reflected in opinion polls. Asked about corruption by the ROMIR agency in 2000, mere 20% replied that they never encountered this phenomenon in their life, while almost 42% faced it on several (or numerous) occasions (Argumenty i facty. 2000. No 28). According to N.I. Lapin's data, 37% of interviewed justify bribery, more than a quarter justify revenge, the same as the number of those who justify prostitution. This reflects seriousness of the potential for this illegal behavior (*Dinamika tsennostei naseleniya reformiruemoi Rossii.* 1996. P. 167–168).

Belief in the possibility of rule of law was substantially undermined by legal uncertainty reigning in the country. Almost 70% of the population is worried about growing crime; more and more people see only one option — to take matters into their own hands. This can explain (but not justify) cases of lynching of suspected rapists, use of weapons under the threat to personal safety or safety of their relatives.

In this distorted legal space, following paradox could not help ripening: an individual, on the one hand, advocates for law enforcement, for law and order, but at the same time, on the other hand, considers it possible to break the law if it is useful to him personally (and does not infringe upon his or his group's interests). Otherwise, how else can we interpret sociological data, when 36% of surveyed (all-Russian sample) do not see anything shameful in using violence for their own benefit and 56% consider it permissible to breach existing laws. Does this not resemble notorious revolutionary expediency or, better yet, the formula «the law is like a sieve...». In other words, legal nihilism is present at the household level in public consciousness, since for many people there are no deterrents when making these decisions based on their understanding of the situation, their personal perceptions, emotions and desires.

A survey among Muscovites conducted in summer of 1993 showed that 9% of them already possessed weapons for self-defense, and another 54% would have liked to have (or buy) them in order to feel relative confidence in their own safety and protection. By the end of 1990's, by expert estimates, this weapon «procurement», increased 2–3 times. As we can see, complete loss of hope in the possibility of eventual establishment of legal order in society has directly resulted in the transfer of functions that are supposed to be performed by the state and its legal structures.

Criminal deformation of many social relations is the consequence of legal chaos, which creates conditions for blossoming of large-scale organized crime. This is not just a higher level of organized crime – this is a process of involvement of general public in the «shadow economy», their participation in «black market industries» including drugs, prostitution, arms trafficking and murder for hire, which bring huge profits not only to the participants and organizers, but virtually to everyone involved, including government officials. According to some expert data, this criminalized stratum in the entire country is now no less than 10% of adult population, although only about half of them commit actual crimes (Kudryavtsev. 1998. P. 32). The danger of such a magnitude of wrongful conduct lies not just in the fact of expanding ranks of offenders, but also in the fact that Russian society quickly moves toward «Colombian model» of state, with its classical criminal-state structure. As V.V. Lapaeva noted, *one of the most striking paradoxes is that by the end of 1990's, most organized force in the reformed Russian society was organized crime.* The scale of its spread is unprecedented. According to V.S. Ovchinsky's data, of the 733 identified organized crime groups, incorporated in 150 large criminal networks, 6,4% were operating on international level, 10,4% – on interregional (inter-republican), 20% – within certain provinces, territories and republics, and 63,2% – on regional and inter-district level.

The consequence of this lawlessness of 1990's were armed conflicts that become a norm of life in some former Soviet republics and autonomous republics. This was especially clearly manifested in those regions where various unconstitutional armed groups were created. The danger was that such formations could quite easily switch from fighting the other people to fighting their own, like it happened in Georgia, Tajikistan, or Chechen republic.

Undoubtedly, while solving the issues resulting from its withdrawal from economy and other spheres of public life, the State should have understood that this withdrawal did not mean indifferent, care-free attitude to individual rights and freedoms. *For all the honest people a failed, inefficient state presents no less danger than a totalitarian, oppressive one.* The possibility of a criminal state, which in practice means legalization of criminal world and triumph of criminality, remains the most dangerous problem in the country.

At the conference on international organized crime, held in June 1993 in England, it was said, that for many years the West have feared Russian invasion, having communists in mind. The irony is that today they have indeed descended upon the Western world, but in capitalist guise. At that, they are dragging with them the worst examples from the practices of western criminal business. It is unknown, how many of them are involved in criminal activity. They all look like respectable partners for western business on the surface. However, in reality these people are the elite, the upper caste of organized crime. They don't dirty their hands, they only coordinate gang activities.

According to the Ministry of Internal Affairs of Russia, in 1999 *quasi-business* was typical for 30% of identified criminal groups. According to same data, during that period, they were also controlling over 40 thousand business units, including 2 thousand state-owned enterprises, 3 thousand joint-stock companies, 11 thousand cooperatives, 6 thousand small businesses, 160 banks, 19 exchanges, 860 markets.

There are many examples of such forms of organized crime as gangsterism, racketeering, extortion, looting, and banditry; there are also «plunderers» (operating in the area of privatization, banking, etc.), «corruption-ists» (officials, assisting Mafia) and «coordinators» (leaders of the criminal world, securing «stability» of organized crime networks).

It would appear that people are unaware of this information on interpersonal and personal levels of communication. But it is impossible to hide anything from the people. They feel, and generally assess the true atmosphere of violence and crime. Whatever statesmen may say, people know the real value of everything going on around them, including with regard to law. That is why we need to point out another factor in the analysis of legal consciousness and behavior — an assessment of nature and character of authorities. In this regard, it is very alarming that, according to the opinion of 70% of people, existing authorities represent legislatively-approved Mafia, or structures closely associated with it (Gurov. 1995). Such authorities can not guarantee the rights and freedoms of people (see table 12. 4)

Table 12.4.

Evaluation of State's duty to guarantee rights and freedoms ....
(% of respondents N=1800, 2005)

Contents of Rights and freedoms	Good	Fair	Bad	Hard to say
Right to information	28	39	21	12
Right to choose profession	25	37	28	10
Freedom of speech	19	43	27	11
Right for rest & recreation	19	32	40	9
Equality before law	6	27	56	11
Right to social security	6	28	58	8
State protection of mother and child	5	21	63	11
Right to free education	5	21	65	9
Right to housing	4	19	69	8
Right to health and health care	4	29	61	6
Right to healthy environment	3	25	57	15
Right to judicial protection	3	28	50	19

Source: Institute for Socio-Political Research, Russian Academy of Sciences

That is a true evaluation, which became wide-spread. But are those in power aware of it, especially the ones who really wish happiness and well-being for the new Russia?

Speaking of legal paradoxes, we should mention those complex challenges facing the judicial system in the country. According to the Chief Justice of the Supreme Court of Russia V.M. Lebedev, the courts are overloaded: annually they handle more than 5 million civil cases alone, 1270 thousand criminal, and 1,8 million cases related to administrative breaches. The need for judicial reform is not just timely, but urgent. Lack of mechanisms for law enforcement seriously complicates the establishment of judicial system. Particularly grave contradictions are inherent in the activities of militia, which, among all the law enforcement agencies, is the first in line to come into contact with problematic situations of interrelations between individuals and state.

12.3. Legal «thresholds» of paradoxicality

In using the word »threshold», the author proposes to conditionally accept it as a figure of speech, i.e. as a certain something, which is a «stumbling block» in the way of legal thought and legal practice. This term, despite of its conventionality, is directly related to the phenomenon of paradox, to those main characters and values, which are of interest to the real functioning social consciousness. It is these very words, terms, concepts that are the essence of everyday legal awareness and legal expertise, which, as demonstrated by their analyses, conceal a lot of paradoxes.

First of all, among them, it is necessary to take a closer look at the notion of «freedom» (Nersesyanz. 1983; Lapaeva. 2007). Analysis of existing interpretations of freedom in the Russian literature, media and statements of political figures shows that arbitrariness, confusion, deliberate and spontaneous distortions of this term are difficult to even enumerate (Shabanova. 2000; Kudryavtsev. 2006).

Typically, multiple approaches to interpretation of a concept or category enrich the process of its cognition, as well as application of its findings in human activities, allowing to take into account its new aspects and facets, which, for various reasons have not been noticed and included in prospective analysis. But in the situation with studying and especially interpreting and researching the concept of «freedom» nothing like this happens — on the contrary, interpretation of this notion tends to further obscure nature, essence, meaning and idea of freedom, thus not only contributing to existence of paradoxical situations, but inevitably generating new ones.

Present misconceptions, distortions of the essence of freedom can be summarized in following points of view.

First, freedom is interpreted as an unlimited opportunity for an individual to act as he pleases or as he thinks fit. Any attempt to restrict this freedom, to subordinate it to any common reference points is perceived as a violation of personal rights and freedoms. Paradoxically, this very interpretation was widespread in Russia in the 1990's. Strong criticism of totalitarian past, according to proponents of this point of view, increased the importance and validity of their position.

Second, a vulgarized interpretation of anarchism was developed, which employed the concepts of «will», «disorder», unrestricted, unregulated behavior, absolute negation of any role and value of the state. This position was based on rather primitive notions, misunderstanding of the essence of anarchism, on interpretation of its purpose as existence of society without any legal norms.

Third, freedom was often interpreted as existence, presence or assurance of certain rights and responsibilities, which are utilized in industrialized countries, referred to as democratic. This approach boils down to copying interpretations of the essence and functions of personal rights and freedoms based on Western concepts.

Fourthly, freedom was interpreted as predominantly political freedom, freedom to take part in various social actions, thus permitting everyone an opportunity to prove themselves, by meaningfully participating in political life.

Each of these approaches is fraught with a fair amount of contradictions, bordering paradoxes, since it is not always matched against reality or fails to take into account both objective and subjective aspects of the functioning of freedom.

It is therefore necessary to draw attention to the fact that the concept of «freedom» is inextricably linked with a number of other important principles of human life organization. *Freedom of some should not limit the freedom of others,* assuming mutual tolerance and respect, rather than seeking domination of one viewpoint over another and not supporting claims of one group to the detriment of values and orientations of the other.

At the present stage, the notion of «freedom» is inseparable from the notion of «legality» (legitimacy), which in mass consciousness is perceived as a necessary requirement for opening prospects of overcoming social and economic chaos. «Legality» represents a certain symbol of stability and sustainability of future development. A symbol is convenient and adaptive, since it is abstract, not always filled with concrete meaning. Thus, the term «rule of law» state, for the real functioning consciousness is a rather vague notion. In its literal interpretation, any concept can enter into mass consciousness only based on life experience and needs, the development of which stimulated by this experience. This largely applies to the concept of «legality» as well. Such experience is lacking in a society where legal controls were not working. Since Russia has declared itself an open society, citizens have seen for themselves (following example of Western countries), what an important role legal regulation really plays in social life. Therefore the idea of legality became justified and appealing, more and more attracting the attention of the public.

12.4. Paradoxes of mass legal consciousness

Sociological surveys show that the idea of legality is very popular in Russian society (55% support it), although its perception is rather peculiar. It is regarded only as a means of guaranteeing individual security (including protection from arbitrary government acts, corruption, etc.). At the same time, almost 18% of the people do not care about the legitimacy of authorities and public institutions themselves (*Rossia v poiskakh strategii.* 2000).

More detailed analysis of paradoxical perception of legality reveals a following paradox: in mass consciousness, the idea of primacy of the Law is combined with legal nihilism. «Law-abidance» and «voluntary submission to laws» did not gain support of even a third of respondents. For a post-Soviet person legitimacy is a requirement basically for the others (state, citizens, etc.). Due to a large number of objective and subjective reasons, people fail to recognize the significance of law-abidance and orderliness. According to a survey, conducted by the

Public Opinion Foundation in 1999, among residents of 56 cities and villages the following statement «I feel free when I obey the laws applied to all» was supported by 55% of respondents, while 26% disagreed with it. In another case it was formulated like this: «I feel free when I obey laws binding for everyone in public life, but in private I do as I please». 65% of respondents agreed with this statement, 17% — disagreed. In many respects, the second statement completes the first, but for majority of Russians, it looks fundamentally different. Most likely, this is a manifestation of the duality of consciousness that had emerged especially clearly in the last quarter century: official state sphere is one thing, private life is absolutely another. Here, possible motivational deviations from legality in private and public life take effect.

In the eyes of Russians, the fact that law does not match the voice of conscience is a strong argument for breaking it. Here we witness a traditional understanding of the law, not as an artificially created legal norm, but as natural manifestation of «the truth». In this case «law-abiding» looks rather formal, since for the sake of it one has to go against his conscience. It should be noted that a number of people willing to sacrifice law for the sake of conscience is much greater (41%) than those ready to break it for personal (or their group's) gain (20%).

Even for people with vivid imagination, many of today's laws hardly qualify as guarantee of freedom. To a certain extent, it is impossible to abide by them because of their inconsistency, lack of coordination with each other, as well as rapidly changing reality.

Legality is a sphere where consumerism oriented people, to a certain extent, feel opposed to, and set against one another. A person would explain his own difficulties and failures by the fact that the Law or its enforcers do not favor him, that in relation to the law; he is treated unequally, compared to other people. This might explain why «legal equality of all citizens» among almost all groups, except farmers, pensioners and students, is perceived as more significant (28%) than mere «equality» (23%). Because of this *economic and social inequality is perceived as legal inequality* (despite the fact that formal legal privileges in Soviet, or post-Soviet society did not and do not exist).

A desire to get rid of legal guardianship of the State, while at the same time not assuming any additional responsibility is no less paradoxical. A State that ceased to provide ideological and political guardianship and support for its citizens will be able to maintain «order», which is still expected from it, only provided that citizens themselves undergo certain changes, and the state, in turn, will successfully uphold the law, ensure its enforcement. In this regard it is very important to note the fact that in Russian society overwhelming legal illiteracy reigns supreme, when most people do not even possess minimally necessary legal knowledge. In case of conflict with society, its institutions and organizations, they are guided by certain considerations, which are often far removed from even basic legal knowledge. As a result, sociological studies show that the most comprehensive legal awareness was inherent in the persons that entered into conflict with the law, primarily present and former prison inmates.

This situation is compounded by the fact that, according to the population and representatives of law enforcement, modern Russian state has practically acknowledged its own legal powerlessness. According to sociological data, in a survey of 630 citizens and 240 police officers in September — October of 1999, in Petrozavodsk (Karelia), only 18 and 13% of respondents (population and police officers respectively) are convinced that the state is capable of handling crime, while 47 and 21% believe that the situation is out of state's control, that it lost initiative. And what do we have in exchange? 28 and 33% respectively, believe that criminal law regulates life (only 20% recognize it as a function of the official law). And we add the fact that 55% of people and 66% of policemen believe that most of life's problems are best solved with the help of «informal norms of interaction», mainly based on the principle «you give me, I give you», the extent of legal chaos becomes obvious. Under this condition the repercussions of above mentioned paradoxes become quite acceptable compared with the devastating effects of advancing *criminal subculture* (Taibakov. 2000).

Problems arising due to and in relation with private property can also be attributed to legal paradoxes. The very idea of property is perceived by many (37%) more than favorably, though it is not filled with any legal significance or meaning (only 22% regard private property inviolable). To many, the idea of property seems useful «in general»: it is linked to prospects of overall improvement of life, but most people have no idea what good it can do them personally, not in the future, but today.

A lawful State, so often debated, implies strong positions in private law, first of all — property rights. According to a survey conducted in early post-*perestroika* period by Public Opinion Foundation among residents of 56 cities and villages in 11 regions of Russia (interviewed 3483 adults in the sample, randomly chosen to represent socio-demographic, professional, age and geographical structure of adult population), over 40% were willing to accept the idea of private ownership and legal protection, while at the same time, almost over half of respondents in all mass groups (among pensioners and collective farmers over two thirds) were against any guarantees for property owners. This situation changed very little in late 1990's.

Apparently, consciousness of a post-Soviet person retains notions of legality associated with familiar functions of the former state as a guarantor of social order under the conditions of undeveloped private interests.

For society released from the state of «unfreedom» of private property, the latter often becomes an ideological symbol of what should be pursued. *Illusions, present in the consciousness, come from lack of differentiation between such concepts as ownership and property rights.* Ownership (right) — is a guaranteed right of every member of society to possess a minimum property that can provide freedom and independence. Property rights indicate that this freedom of ownership of property is guaranteed legally, without stipulating a degree of individual autonomy of the owner.

Historical negation of individual property right in this country had already been implemented. Egalitarian-redistributive practice, entrenched in the minds of Russians, has led to the fact that at the beginning of market reforms, modern capitalism was perceived in a rather peculiar way, as equal distribution of all state property. During this period, the state attempted to support the illusion of turning every person into an owner, thus automatically securing his prosperity and gaining economic independence. Real redistribution of property demonstrated that these projects have failed, since property was turned over or concentrated in the hands of a small part of the population. This, in turn, led to growing anti-proprietary sentiment among Russians.

In conclusion, we should point out that the degree of confidence in all law-enforcement agencies, judicial and prosecutorial authorities remains very low (table. 12.5).

Table 12.5.

To what extend are following .... credible?
(% of respondents, N = 2400)

Political and social institution	1999	2001	2004	2006
President	4/88	49/35	49/33	51/34
Army	38/44	39/39	27/48	15/54
Church	26/48	33/38	35/37	37/36
Press, TV	12/66	12/66	19/57	23/56
Government	18/60	23/53	17/59	18/57
Regional authorities	23/51	17/55	15/60	18/54
Parliament	14/62	12/63	6/69	10/68
Lawyers, Court, District attorney	12/70	12/70	9/72	11/76
Trade unions	15/61	17/56	16/56	15/54
Parties	7/64	12/58	5/68	8/68
Businessmen	5/78	10/68	12/62	10/59

Source: Insitute Sozialno-politicheskikh issledovanii RAN (Institute for socio-political studies. Russian Academy of Sciences).

In other words, the credibility of law-enforcement is low and continues to fall. All this suggests that the role of courts, office of Public Prosecutor, police and lawyers is negligible in the formation of legal consciousness. So, the hope that with their help legal paradoxes can be overcome is, therefore, slight. This fact, in turn, permits us to assert that major changes in relations between population and legal institutes in the foreseeable future are unlikely to occur. This means that *criminal degeneration of society is becoming a real threat,* which can escalate and spread, according to several researchers, from judicial and law enforcement spheres into political one, affecting not only the fate of the statehood but also the life of the whole Russian society (Louneev. 1996, p. 98-99; Krivosheev. 2000. P. 99). There is only one way out: to strengthen the rule of law. Especially since, according to N.I.Lapin, it occupies a leading position in the hierarchy of fourteen values (*Dinamika tsennostei...* 1996. P. 67). Therefore, in Russia, focusing on its reinforcement is a key to successful development of both — civil society and rule of law.

References

Argumenty i facty. 2000. No 28.

Dinamika tsennostei naseleniya reformiruemoi Rossii (Dynamics of Values of the Population of Russia under Reforms). Moscow, 1996.

Eltsinshchina (Yeltsin's Era) / Pod red. L.Tomash. Budapest, 1993. Under his edition also *Konets Eltsinshchiny (End of the Eltsin Era).* Budapest, 1999 was published. The above view is shared not only by many Russian researchers but also by foreign experts on problems of the USSR (Russia).

Gudkov L. *Otnosheniye k pravovym institutam v Rossii (Attitudes towards Law Institutions in Russia)* // Monitoring obshchestvennogo mneniya: ekonomitsheskiye i sotsial'niye peremeny. 2000. No 3.

Gurov A. I. *Krassnaya mafia (Red Mafia).* Moscow, 1995.

Krivosheev V.V. *Kriminalizatsiya obshchestva: sushchnost' protsessa, rossiyskaya spetsifika (Criminalization of Society: Essence of Process, Russian Specifics).* Kaliningrad, 2000.

Kudryavtsev V.N. *Genezis prestupleniya (Genesis of Crime).* Moscow, 1998.

Kudryavtsev V.N., Trusov A. I. *Polititsheskaya Iustitsia v SSSR (Political Justice in the USSR).* Moscow 2000.

Kudryavtsev V.N. *Svoboda slova (Freedom of Speech).* 2006.

Kutafin O.E. *Rossiyskoe grazhdanstvo (Russian Citizenship).* Moscow, 2004.

Lapaeva V.V. *Sotsiologhia prava (Sociology of Law).* Moscow, 2007.

Louneev V.V. *Prestupnost' v XXI veke: metodologhiya prognosa (Crime in the 21-st Century: Methodology of Forecasting)* // Sotsiologitsheskiye Issledovaniya. 1996. No 7.

Louneev V. V. *Prestupnost' XX veka (Crime of the 20th Century).* Moscow, 1997.

Maksimov S. V. *Korruptsiya, Zakon. Otvetstvennost' (Corruption. Law. Responsibility).* Moscow, 2000.

Nersesyanz V. S. *Prtavo i zakon (Right and Law).* Moscow, 1983.

Prestupnost v Rossii. Analititsheskiy obzor (Crime in Russia. Analytical Review). Moscow, 1997. P. 3.

Rossia v poiskakh strategii: obshtshestvo i vlast' Sotsialnaya i sotsial'no-polititsheskaya situatsia v Rossii v 1999 godu (Russia in Search of Strategy: Society and Authority. Social and Socio-Political Situation in Russia in 1999) / Pod red. G.V. Osipov. 2000.

Shabanova M. *Sotsiologiya svobody: transformiruiyshcheesya obshchestvo (Sociology of Freedom: Transforming Society)*. Moscow, 2000.

Sotsial'noe polozhenie I uroven' zhizni v Rossii (Social Position ana Level of Life in Russia) // Stat. sb. Vol. 2005.

Taibakov A. A. *Prestupnaya subkul'tura (Criminal Subculture)* // Sotsiologhitsheskiye issledovaniya. 2000. No 3.

Tomash L. *Eltsinizm na Vesakh Istorii (Eltsinizm on Scales of History)*. *Rossia i sovremenniy mir (Russia and the Modern World)*. 2000.

Chapter 13. **Paradoxes of national self-consciousness**

Nations, just as individuals can live in two ways:
either stealing or producing.

Claude Henri de Saint-Simon (1760–1825),
French thinker, a utopian socialist.

Now, at the beginning of the 21-th century you can hardly meet someone who still doubts that ethnic, national factor is a determinant in modern life of all mankind. Events in the world, in separate regions clearly demonstrate that many ethnicities have faced problems of national identification. But it sounds like a paradox — just *as democracy is threatened by extreme orientation toward democracy (H. Schelsky), so national identification is threatened by extreme focus on the role and importance of ethnic factor.*

Ethnic factor is increasingly manifested in growing national and state sovereignty demands, which, according to the nations' leaders, reflect aspirations and expectations of their people. At first glance, it sounds very plausible. For more than a quarter century now, based on ethno-religious factor, there have been ongoing clashes in Northern Ireland. Great Britain was unable to find a satisfactory solution to this problem for quite a time. Currently, in Great Britain, through the efforts of nationalist forces, Scotland got its own parliament, and the same issue is on the agenda in Wales. For many years in Spain, ethnic minorities — Basques, and recently Catalans have been very vocal. The first (Basques) demand an independent state on parts of Spanish and French territories, the latter (Catalans) — more autonomy from the center. Unrest in Romania, in Transylvania, where demand for autonomy comes not so much from Hungarians (their number is large enough in this region), as from local Romanians, who believe that having been part of the Habsburg Empire up until 1918 seriously distinguishes them from the population of Moldova and Walachia. For the past quarter century, a bloody conflict has been raging in Sri Lanka, where Tamils are fighting Sri Lankan government for their self-determination. Their struggle for independence (37-million people, divided among several states — Turkey, Iran, Syria and Iraq) is still an open wound for the Kurds.

In this separatist processes there are some oddities, such as nationalists (or mere adventurers) in the state of Texas (USA), the province of Quebec (in Canada), New Caledonia (French protectorate) trying to gains independence. In general, in 1998 alone, about 50 major political events that had ethnic overtones were recorded; this rather seriously affected both destinies of individual states and nations, as well as the entire world or of some of its regions.

The collapse of the USSR, Yugoslavia and Czechoslovakia attests to the fact that ethnic factor plays a leading role in solving problems of civil order, polity. There are a number of reasons for disappearance of the above mentioned states from the political map of the world. Some people speak of the inevitability of the collapse of empires, others point out errors made by political leadership of these countries, and others — about waves of nationalism, which are impossible to resist as a new phenomenon of social life.

Analyzing the surge in ethnic national tensions, more and more researchers recognize the need for serious, deep and comprehensive evaluation of not just ethnicity in general, but also of national identity. In this regard, it is appropriate to recall perhaps an exaggerated, yet rather accurate statement by L.N. Gumilev that in «human life there is nothing more fragile than social status and social relations», but at the same time, «no amount of effort or desire can change person's ethnic identity». That is why, in his opinion, there is nothing more powerful than this «ethnic element of mankind» that ultimately determines human consciousness and behavior. It has a tendency to actualize, restructure and ultimately determine the direction of human development (Gumilev, Ermolaev. 1992. P. 9–10; Guboglo. 2003).

13.1. Characteristics of national identity in post-soviet period

Modern Russia, the whole post-Soviet region is a unique arena, demonstrating epochal changes that occur after collapse of a great country. At present, on the territory of the former USSR, an objective process of materialization of national identity, national dignity and national culture is underway. Many nations and nationalities, as if anew were revived, re-awakened and reached out to their culture, language, customs and traditions of their ancestors. National forms of managing economy became more significant. But people's quest for national identity does not always correspond with a desire to live together and live in peace with the others, due to the fact that nationalistically motivated politicians joined this process in full force. In their struggle for power they came to substitute spiritual values with ambitious statements and declarations of various kinds of «sovereignty» and «independence». Manifestations of national marauding and pillaging is clearly displayed in the behavior of political leaders, whose credo is to build the well-being of their nation (and, in most cases, their own personal welfare and prosperity) at the expense of dignity and well-being of other nations. How else can we interpret declarations of Georgian President Gamsakhurdia, openly proclaiming the slogan «Georgia for Georgians» in early 1990's, or of his colleague, the first president of Azerbaijan Alchibei, implementing the same policy, during the same period, but centering on Azeri people. A popular slogan in those days was: «Russians — back to Ryazan, Tatars — back to Kazan». Something similar, but in a more implicit form, occurred in other republics and national regions. Unfortunately, nationalist ideas captivated a certain part of the population, although not as large a part as their «creators» would have liked. Sociological studies show that in everyday communications, at work or in their private lives, people of different nationalities display a high degree of tolerance and trust in spite of hysterical statements by the leaders of national political parties and movements. People regard spirituality, culture, development of their distinct national identity as basis for their coexistence instead of overt or covert political struggle that benefits only ambitious politicians, wishing to somehow «squeeze» their way into any kind of key position, presidency or leadership.

Nationalist ideas are dangerous because their proponents carefully hide their true purposes and intentions. All kinds of demagogic arguments about national language, about «ruined» national culture, which can briefly disorient parts of population, are brought to the surface. Certain para-scientific and unscientific concepts and viewpoints that became extremely widespread in the 20th century, in no small measure contributed to these nationalistic sentiments. A large variety of ideas are utilized for their «scientific» justification. For example, Carl Jung's position is interpreted as primordialist concept of ethnicity, according to which ethnic (and consequently cultural) identity is not constructed, but inherited. Such an approach serves as the basis for presuming exclusivity of national «I», for differentiating themselves from other people and creates ethnic tension and even national conflicts.

V.A. Tishkov's attempts to prove artificial and unscientific character of the concept of a «nation» and the need to recognize Western standard of «nation = state» raises serious doubts and objections as well (Tishkov. 2000). It is hard to agree with these claims, first, because any assumptions have to be based on objective realities, as well as real, and not just Western experiences. In other words, the basis for any reasoning should be life itself, not just fantasies and wishes, however attractive they may be. Therefore it is difficult to agree with this interpretation of a nation as «an imagined community». Second, no matter how efficient American, French or Spanish ways of solving national problems are, they reflect their own specificity and their own methods of influencing complex national relations. While analyzing a variety of borrowed ideas, politicians (and not just politicians) realized that mechanistically utilizing someone else's experience is a rather debatable, if not dangerous undertaking. Third, we should not be blaming political doctrines of the USSR for ethnic conflicts, since the state did a lot, as the author concedes, for national minorities. After all, other countries did not have such doctrines, but clashes (and very serious ones) of national interests were (and still remain) a reality.

But, *even those people who have succumb to shortsighted, but dangerous promises of politicians, got over this nationalistic frenzy*. The notion that the entire nations are infected with this ulcer of nationalism and chauvinism is not only wrong, but also absurd. It is necessary to «separate the seeds from the chaff» and to realize that this myth of universal national intoxication is a good cover for ambitious political goals in the struggle for power.

Of course, national consciousness of each nation requires a detailed and thorough analysis. Undoubtedly, specificity of manifestation of national identity in the Baltic States significantly differs from similar problems in Central Asia, as well as the latter — from the situation in Transcaucasia. However, adherence to national values is unquestionably the most important component of national consciousness of the majority of people living within the borders of the former USSR. Real manifestations of a nation establish themselves as essential, since individual social identity is impossible without national identity. At one time, during the Soviet years, rapid internationalization of the way of life, threat of extinction of ethnic identity has called into question the natural course of this process. It is not surprising that some ethnic groups started seeking their identity at a different level. Strong correlation between the variables of «national consciousness» and «civic consciousness» may lead to conclusion that the first is amplified by the second and that «nationalization» of self-consciousness is merely a sort of escape from national assimilation and national leveling. In our opinion, intensive process of national appeal to the past rather than the present, occurs due to the fact that the original history of people (of a nation), or, to be more specific, its content, guarantees preservation of distinctive ways of life for the new generation: to them, the past is much more attractive and unique than the new values, inherent in modernity. Emotional, affective link with the past is, perhaps, the most solid basis for «we — identity«

of the people comprising a nation. In this regard, we agree with V.A. Tishkov that «cultural complexity» of life in many countries throughout the world and in many of its regions resists globalization with its ineradicable tendency to unify everyone and everything.

Attitude of people to the «national» definitely became more positive by the end of the 1980's. *Emotionality and irrationality often became dominant in national consciousness.* «Affective components» were prevailing, while it lacked rationality and pragmatism. In a significant part of the population, this creates a likelihood of emergence of a «blind ethnic loyalty», recurrence of negative moods, including such little-known socio-psychological phenomena as ethnocentrism, ethno-egoism, ethno-phobia, and domestic chauvinism.

Analysis of national consciousness of Russian people is of particular interest (*Russkiye.* Moscow, 1992). The specificity of this problem is caused by many factors. First, by historical factor, since Rus' (Russia) that long developed within the framework of a single ethnos, gradually began to add on (here we do not dwell on reasons that influenced the expansion of the country) territories of other ethnic groups, mostly sparsely populated, and far less developed then the Russian nation. Secondly, many ethnic groups over a long period of co-existence on the basis of their own as well as Russian culture have developed such fusion of spirituality that can be described as an original synthesis of mutual enrichment. And, finally, indeterminacy of national identity of many nationalities was reflection in still unsolved issue of application of the term «Russians» (nationality) and «Russians» (citizens of the Russian Federation, regardless of their nationality).

In general, in spite of all shortcomings and nationalist splashes, Russian people have a sufficiently strong immunity from absolutization of their influence and disregard for rights and cultures of other nations. Perhaps that is why Russian nationalism never reached the heights of great political and social force, crushing interests of other nations. By the virtue of their way of life and system of values, Russians always were and still are the most internationalist-minded people, open to the whole world and, therefore, relatively indifferent to certain violations of their own opportunities and rights. In no small measure, prevailing «big brother» ideology, both in tsarist Empire and the Soviet Union, contributed to this factor.

However, everything has drastically changed with the collapse of the USSR. Following its disintegration, the *potential for Russian nationalism has grown significantly,* since in newly independent states many Russians (against their will) were turned into a national minority. And in Russia itself, in a number of national republics, there was an open assault on the rights of the Russian population that was to some extent fueled by local nationalist and anti-Moscow sentiments.

In these circumstances, national and nationalist views became ideologically more promising; promotion of national interests and, respectively, national statehood (sovereignty) became more attractive. Ethnic tolerance of the Russians began to decrease, although still remained high. According to data of the All-Russian Center for Public Opinion Studies (VTsIOM) in mid-1990's, about 70% of respondents agreed with the thesis — «Russia — for the Russians», the same as with the thesis «Russia for all who live in it». This situation leads us to conclude that the determination of which direction «the pendulum will swing», depends on the politicians (*Nuzhen li Gitler Rossii?* 1996. P. 105–110).

Table 13.1.

How do you feel about the idea of «Russia for Russians»? ....
(% of respondents. N=1800)

List of alternatives	1998	2000	2002	2004	2006
Support, its long overdue	15	15	16	16	15
Support partly, within reasonable limits	31	34	38	37	35
Do not support — it's fascism	32	27	26	25	28
I am not interested	10	12	9	12	12
Have not thought about it	5	6	8	5	8
Hard to say	7	6	3	4	4

Source: Public Opinion — 2006. Moscow. Levada-Center. 2006. P. 158.

Sociological analysis shows that the main features of nationalism such as ethno-phobia and ideas of ethnocratic state are barely manifested in Russian national identity. In a special nationwide survey carried out by the «Public Opinion» Foundation, Russians have been separated into a special group, thus permitting to reveal some distinguishing differences from the representatives of other social and national identities. There were few statistically meaningful differences. Respondents were asked to choose between «Soviet», «Russian» and «Western» values (without specifying what they were). Any combinations were allowed. It revealed general predominance of «Russian» values: 46% of «pure» Russian ones, 7% in combination with the «Western», 11% in combination with the «Soviet» and 3% combining either «Western» or «Soviet» values (*Polititsheskiye issledovaniya.* 1995. No 5. P. 70-76, 1996, No 1. P. 78-90; *Russian Public Opinion Herald.* 2006. No 6. P. 67).

Russian people's self-characterization is interesting as well. «Willingness to endure difficulties and deprivation» (opinion of 65% respondents) and «readiness to defend the Motherland at any cost» (opinion of 52%) are in the first place. However, characteristics essential for the ideology of Russian nationalism lag far behind: 23% have expressed «willingness to sacrifice personal interests for the sake of the State», 21% — «aspiration to seek the truth, the supreme meaning», 13% believe in «a special historical destiny, historical mission». With regard to their position in society relative to other ethnic groups, Russians are moderately optimistic: only 29% think their living conditions are worse than all the others, while 48% are convinced that they live no worse than other nationalities.

If primitive ethnic nationalism is not inherent in Russian people, ethnic understanding of statehood is, and to a much higher degree. In fact, 23% of respondents, «fully agree», 24% «are more likely to agree», with 21% of those «more likely to disagree» and 13% «definitely disagreeing» with the statement that «it is necessary to seek the establishment of such state, in which Russian is officially recognized as the main nation». Furthermore, 34% believed that Russia «should seek inclusion of the neighboring territories of former Soviet republics, inhabited predominantly by Russians» (44% did not support it and 21% were undecided). Almost half the Russian population is prepared to recognize the principle of ethnic structure of the state, although the percentage of apparent ethno-nationalists among Russians is low. Aggressiveness of Russian nationalism is expressed considerably weaker, probably for fear of provoking a war (only 8% considered power methods acceptable, and even among V. Zhirinovsky's supporters this percentage does not exceed 21%).

Prevailing ideas about growing national tension and ethno-centrism of Russian self-consciousness are not supported by actual sociological data. Real dynamics is much more complex. A special study «Ethno-political situation in the regions of Russian Federation» clearly demonstrates that the share of those who are «definitely» ready «to take part in the conflict in defense of their national group», «to use weapons» has remained both at the beginning as well as at the end of 1990's approximately at the same level — ranging from 13 to 15%. Sample data showed that in ethnically tense areas this figure has also changed little. Index of prejudice towards other nations has practically remained unchanged as well. Answering the question «Is there any nationality that you dislike?» in several regions (Tatarstan, Karelia, Stavropol territory), the number of those responding affirmatively ranged from 15 to 34% (*Rossiya: tsentr i reghiony.* 1999. P. 15, 221).

According to L.M. Drobizheva, statistical analysis and data of several sociological surveys show that less than half of respondents regard «nationality» as something given by God (or fate), or as ethno-historical by nature. Statistical data indicates that the appeal to national idea is much more characteristic of intellectual elite than other population groups. On the whole, only 7,7% answered the question «Are there bad nations?» affirmatively (among men this percentage was higher — 11%); 73,6% did not use ethnic factor in their definition of Russian citizenship, 69% to 79% had positive attitude toward Western countries. Therefore, we can conclude that ethnocentrism in Russia is no more developed than in European countries (Drobizheva. 2003. P. 23–32). We might agree with that, because nationalism is always directed against a specific enemy but, as surveys show, in Russian national consciousness it is manifested to a very small extent.

13.2. Main features of national self-consciousness

Contradictory and maladjusted ethnic processes in modern Russia and the entire post-Soviet expanse generate paradoxical situations where various options of achieving independence, autonomy and sovereignty, and not the process of globalization, determine the shape of ongoing events. In these conditions, national consciousness functions and develops rather inconsistently. And sometimes even paradoxically. What are its characteristics?

First, it is worth noting that lost professional, *social and cultural identity is intensely replaced by national (ethnic) component.* For many people their belonging to certain occupational groups has lost any (or at least critical) value, due to closures of industrial enterprises, mass unemployment, loss of support from their co-workers. Social status of many people also became shaky, unstable, prone to major changes and risks. Cultural values were often vague, fragile, often replaced with claims of innovation or a «new word» in literature, art, architecture, etc. This space was filled by ethnic identity. Toward the end of Gorbachev's *perestroika,* an all-Union study has revealed that people's willingness to identify with their nation, its history and culture exceed all previous identifications – with work, profession, social status, etc. In all-Russian study of historical consciousness, we conducted in 1990, the need to understand the roots of their country and people was expressed by 28% of respondents, taking the third place among social orientations after the desire to know the truth about the past (opinion of 91%) and aspiration to broaden their horizons (opinion of 30% of respondents). Approximately the same number of people (27%) said that they are interested in the history of «life, customs, household, peoples' traditions and folklore» (*Istoritsheskoye soznaniye: sostoiyaniye..... 1991).

Second, ethno-egotism became very common: people started to concentrate only on interests of their own ethno-national group, which have acquired paramount importance compared to other interests and needs. Ethno-egotism is embodied in constant attempts to secure advantages for their group by various means, including illegal. In soviet times ethno-egotism manifested itself primarily in the field of education and culture, in addressing issues related to participation in government. But, gradually, ethno-egotism spread to political and economic sphere: political power together with economic and financial influence were being consolidated in the hands of members of one ethnic group, regardless of business or other characteristics of specialists and professionals of other ethnic origins.

Third, in the depths of contemporary inter-ethnic and inter-national relations different varieties of ethno-phobia gradually come into existence, which completely or partially denied the right of other people and its representatives to not only social participation but even living in the particular territory. This was reflected in such word combinations as «uninvited guests», «migrants», «invaders» (e.g., the Baltic countries), which were used for moral and legal pressure on Russian and Russian-speaking population. In other territories ethno-phobia was expressed in creating unfavorable living environment, moral pressure, when daily life became so unbearable that people felt compelled to leave their homes, even if they had lived there for several generations (Georgia, Central Asian republics). And finally, ethno-phobia manifested itself in such reprehensible actions as forcibly evicting Russian-speaking population, turning them into refugees or internally displaced (Azerbaijan, Kazakhstan, Chechnya).

Dozens of conflicts, extremely tense situations, thousands of refugees, wounded and dead — this is the historical background of once «conflict-free Soviet society», society of «friendship of peoples». However, the perception of current state of interethnic relations on the territory of former unified state from the positions of Hobbes's universal conflict, based on assumption that «all complex social systems are unstable» *(S. Lipset)* is unacceptable, as well. Nevertheless, ignoring tendencies for change, characteristic of any society, even under stable conditions, makes it difficult to find solutions to the contradictions generated by, on the one hand, objective human desire for independence and sovereignty and, on the other hand, by subjective abilities to meet these objective requirements, without infringing on interests of other peoples or other ethnic groups. Changes, including constantly emerging conflicts of interest, require timely response from authorities, preparedness for management and regulation without destruction, since «institutions and values based on consensus provide necessary conditions for preservation of a social system» (Lipset. 1998. P. 15). Social structures, inflexible and inadequate, incapable of change, unable to adjust to new social conditions are, consequently, not always adaptable to changing circumstances. We should also add that, perhaps, contradictory development, which creates conditions for implementation of radical change are immanently inherent in hierarchically organized societies.

13.3. Forms of paradoxes of national self-consciousness

To a certain extent, national contradictions are caused by the fact that centripetal tendencies prevail over centrifugal, and paradoxically, rather than constraining, they contribute to the latter. Leaders of ethnic strata and groups are no longer satisfied with national ranking, «national hierarchy», which, in their view, was an obstacle to normal functioning of their peoples. Their position is corroborated by an appropriate set of ideological arguments, mechanisms of explaining, justifying and promoting measures to address existing inequality of nations and convincing people of the legitimacy of their national aspirations.

These national claims and aspirations often disguise themselves as nationalism, chauvinism or racism, though in modern conditions there may not be obvious signs of oppression or violence. Of course, due to distinct differences between the interests of various nations, a whole range of contradictions is inherent in national relations (Jounoussov. 1990. P. 21). And these contradictions arise not only at the level of national states, ethnic communities, ethnic groups (i.e. at macro level), but also at the interpersonal level, level of small groups (i.e. micro level). Some of them are permanent, others are situational, and some are constructive, while others — destructive. But the point is not contradictions as such, but methods of resolving them.

Analysis of ambiguous, contradictory processes in the area of ethnic and inter-ethnic relations allows to identify several forms of paradoxes of national consciousness (national identity), which, in our opinion, most completely characterize specific features of their functioning in the post-Soviet space. In one way or another, these forms of paradoxicality appear in almost all types of ethnic interaction. American researcher P. Berghe calls the first type of such interaction «*laissez-fairist*». Its essence is as follows: an ethnic group is subjected to minimal cultural influence, and solves its own problems, while only experiencing economic exploitation of some kind from another ethnic group, maintaining its ethno-cultural integrity. The second type of ethnic interaction — «*acculturalistic*» — lies in the fact that people have an opportunity of unlimited social mobility within the structure established by dominant national group, but at the cost of dissolution of culture, without preserving their ethno-cultural uniqueness. Forced «acculturation» of ethnic minorities by dominant national group has been termed *ethnocide* (Van den Berghe. 1975. P. 14).

Absence of permanent stable and proven channels for expressing national interests leads to destabilization of social relations, deepening (aggravation) of latent ethnic conflicts.

People often perceive infringement on unique ethnic characteristics or interference in their functioning as their relegation to a second-class citizens status. It encourages them to address national issues as an antagonistic dilemma. Such approach contributed to the merging together of all the efforts to achieve equality of all kinds -national, political or economic, radicalizing their struggle. Of equal significance was the extent to which nations or ethnic groups have been empowered as sovereign entities of public and state life, as well as their ways of exercising these rights. The longer and harder were economic and political rights of the people suppressed or not taken into account by the state, the greater was the likelihood of its involvement in implementation of nationalist ideas. Infringement on popular interests inevitably fueled discontent, promoted escalation of national claims, expressing a protective function — socio-cultural survival of an ethnic group.

Contradictory development of ethno-national relations is linked to changes in economic system and political order, which inevitably leads to formation of new civic values relating to interests of nations, political participation of its representatives in state affaires, in observance of human rights and freedoms. During transformation of post-Soviet society nationalist moods have intensified, internationalist components of the entire public, including cultural, life have been weakened, and started to be contrasted, set against interests of national identity, national «I» (Abdoulatipov. 1991). Attempts to combine processes of internationalization and national identity have so far failed to achieve desired effect. Moreover, fear of assimilation generates militant and radical forms of resolving this contradiction that do not correspond to objective logic of development.

A process that characterizes contrasting national interests against the interests of an individual is no less significant. Currently, the situation is such that these interests are realized not through interaction, but in the process of growing opposition to each other. Moreover, this opposition tends to increase its destructive potential, leads to emergence of new areas of tension. Let us examine this in more detail.

One of the most important indicators of maturity of national consciousness is the extent to which it has acquired features of civic consciousness, becoming an essential attribute of a democratic society. And, whether the interests of a nation or those of an individual, are deemed superior in this comparison, is a measure of this maturity. If ethnic interests begin to prevail in national consciousness to the detriment of the individual ones, we can speak of emergence of different varieties of ethno-egoism, ethnocentrism and even ethno-phobia. We have to pay special attention to this situation, since acts of disregard for individual rights in favor of national interests are rather obviously surfacing in the context of revival of national identity ideas, of growing national consciousness and national culture. It is necessary to promote all forms of establishing of national «I», but only as long as they are not implemented at the expense of well-being and normal life of representatives of other nations. This is evidenced by the data of sociological studies: in contemporary political life of many newly formed states national interests prevail over individual ones, national is opposed to personal. All actions, both social and economic, are justified by national interests. Regardless of how much some people might like it, this is a historic impasse, a dead end, basis for justification of chauvinism, racism and nationalism.

Especially paradoxical is the behavior of national political leaders, who continually act as if «sovereignty» and «independence» of their republic (country) is somehow contradictory to (at odds with) an opportunity to establish a balance of fairness in relation to other non-indigenous peoples and nations. But this obvious, as it might seem, contradiction becomes clear when one recognizes that national leaders are obsessed with only one desire, one aspiration: to stay in power at any cost, to ensure their personal well-being and welfare of their immediate entourage. This phenomenon of nationalist group egoism has become extremely widespread. Its objective is to conceal their true purposes and intentions from the public. Sociological studies show a very significant gap between political attitudes of newly emerged leaders and their peoples. They are often focused on opposite purposes and problems. If people intuitively, from their own previous experience, spontaneously realize the importance and priority of human rights and freedoms, regardless of nationality, politicians in these newly independent states exploit national issues, pursuing self-serving personal and group interests.

We should also examine characteristics of *paradox that is inherent in national consciousness of intellectuals.* Analysis of sociological data shows that representatives of ethnic intellectual stratum have increasingly become carriers of various national ideas with all their positive and negative characteristics. This fact by itself is obvious and does not reflect anything unusual. It is astonishing; however, that national intelligentsia of many of the republics, especially those in Central Asia, has been nurtured for two or three generations with the help and support of Russia and Russian culture. But then in its midst, as it turns out, there was a lot of those, who renounced this memory, trying to replace this page in their people's history with search of their roots in distant past.

In this regard, the fate of nationalist ideas of various persuasions that emerged in the Soviet Union (Russia) is quite noteworthy. First sociological attempts to analyze national relations in 1960-1970's in the republics of Volga region had shown that intellectuals, not workers and peasants, were carriers of nationalist ideas. Already during that period, representatives of intelligentsia of this region complained about their exclusion from power and authority, questioned the value of mixed marriages and considered exaggerated attention to Russian language detrimental to their national ones, etc (Toshchenko. 2003). «Grudges» against Russian «dominance» continued to exist during the 70's and 80's, until the emergence of more or less stable, mainly nationalist concepts of protecting the interests of only its own people, with obvious or latent disregard for language, culture and religion of other nationalities, especially those involved in mutual national and state associations.

During *perestroika* and post-*perestroika* period these «grievances» were aggravated, nationalist sentiment began to gain strength among intellectuals.

And since intelligentsia, represented by some of its most politically active members came to power, they did not just launch mere criticism, but various forms of expulsion and obliteration of Russian culture and Russian influence from daily social life of their peoples.

Paradox of this situation lies, firstly, in the fact that these intellectuals were opposed to the very culture, which was responsible for their emergence, or, at least, provided an opportunity to realize their full potential. As world-famous Lithuanian actor Donatas Banionis figuratively put it, «Events of universal importance are oddly superimposed on individual destinies. Had Soviet power not come to Lithuania before the German occupation, my theatre wouldn't exist. I can dislike this power, I can refuse to recognize it, but the fact remains. It was this power that made it possible to create Panevezhis Drama Theatre that I had joined» (*Nezavisimaya gazeta.* 1999, November 12). But if some people (and most gifted ones, at that) regard their involvement with Russian culture as a benefit, there is a fair amount of those who regard this interaction as a process of assimilation, infringement on national cultures; they use this as grounds for opposing Russian «imperialism». However, it is significant that in public consciousness there is little or no recorded opposition between «their own» and «someone else's» (in this case Russian) culture: majority of people continue to embrace their involvement with Russian spirituality with gratitude and appreciation.

Second, duality of consciousness and behavior among intellectuals of many ethnic groups was first recorded back in the Soviet times. Many of them advocated the development of native culture and native language. But, they also thought that it was the responsibility of the rest of the population. However, they themselves, sent their children to Russian schools, and then universities in Russia, since such young people, plugged into global culture through Russian culture, had more advantages in comparison with their peers. Similar processes occur in modern Russia, but through attempts to join American, English or Turkish culture. However, after a decade of wandering and searching for national identity many representatives of national cultures of the former Soviet Union came to realize that renouncing the culture which they had shared for many generations would be unjustified and erroneous.

Experience has shown that contrasting their own national culture with that of Russia is particularly evident in paradoxical activities of those people who have broken away, lost contact with spiritual values of their people, do not know (or barely know) its language and culture. These «representatives» often become leaders of radical nationalist organizations carrying out actions aimed at escalation of tensions between ethnic groups. Certainly, this might be regarded as an attempt to rehabilitate their previous life. But at the same time these actions may be characterized as a desire to realize their own ambitions, to obtain power or authority, or arrange their private life as prosperously as possible.

Third, in 1990th, a following paradox actively manifested itself: the difference in perception of the past and the future between intelligentsia and the rest of the population. Desire and aspiration to live together with other nations still prevails among people. Sociological data show that in many former republics up to 70% of the population hope for a possibility of eventual integration with Russia on a new basis. This might be confirmed, for example, by electoral victory of the Communist Party of Moldova in February 2001, on its way to victory openly proclaiming the policy of integration with Russia. Therefore 67% vote for this party can be interpreted as vote of support for closer relations with Russia. The majority of Belarusian population expressed approximately the same preference for alliance with Russia (*Integratsiya Belarusi i Rossii...* 1998). However, certain part of intelligentsia of many ethnic groups still continues to focus on further distancing from Russia. For this purpose, various means are utilized: Russian language studies are excluded from curriculum; training of young specialists is carried out with the help of foreign educational institutions. Nationalistically colored myths are revived and treated as historically accurate events; all sorts of possible compelling facts are embellished, highly controversial (from the standpoint of history or world culture and civilization) «significant dates» that took place in the given country are overstated.

Apotheosis of nationalist claims was the implementation of conversion of graphic representation of national language from Cyrillic to Latin alphabet based on the fact that the latter, first, «more accurately conveys the sounds of our language», and, second, to restore «historical tradition», slyly omitting the fact that Latin script was used by Eastern nations for only 10 to 15 years (in conditions of mass illiteracy), while Cyrillic — for 60 to 70 years (in conditions of universal literacy of the population). But if the decision of newly emerged states to change to Latin alphabet is to some extent understandable (after all, it was necessary to distance themselves from Russia as far and as quickly as possible), the intent of other ruling groups in regard to this subject is hardly comprehensible to the people of these nations. For example, it is hard to find a reasonable explanation for (some) Tatarstan rulers' aspiration to convert to Latin alphabet in the 21st century, regardless the fact that majority of Tartars live outside Tatarstan. Could such approach create a conflict among Tartars themselves?

Paradoxicality of national «I» is manifested in the fact that aspiration to modernize, upgrade their ethnic life, to internationalize it, to integrate into the world culture *constantly collides with ideological disputes «who is more ancient», «whose written language is older», who had what and which territory was in whose possession.* Consequently, people who had peacefully lived together for many years suddenly start to «recollect» certain historical grievances, demand restoration of historical justice or present claims for reparation of damages caused by wars, which allegedly took place in their territory. Unfortunately, certain primitive-minded politicians made a considerable «contribution« to these developments. For example, in 1992 radical democrats (Starovoitova, Shakhrai) passed the Rehabilitation Act of all peoples subjected to Stalinist repression. Falsely understanding processes of democratization, they declared not only political, economic and cultural rehabilitation, which is quite reasonable and logical, but also territorial that immediately generated a lot of ethnic conflicts, including violent clashes. Particularly graphic example being the Osset-Ingush confrontation.

In solving problems of national tension and participation of intelligentsia, it is necessary to understand contradictory and paradoxical functioning of national consciousness of those who claim to be the leaders, the guides of their people. According to I.I. Osinskiy's data, when assessing development problems of their republic, 46% of respondents among Buryat intellectuals indicated the fact that Buryats are spread across the territories of several administrative entities as a negative factor for their people. In addition, 54,8% of them mentioned disastrous repression of 1930's. With regard to events of 1990's, 23,5% of respondents gave negative assessment of policies pursued by «democrats led by Yeltsin» and 22,7% felt the same way about «*perestroika* led by Gorbachev». Yet, at the same time, they approved of events that played positive role in the life of Buryat people: 49,1% — joining Russia, 30,2% — the October revolution, 27,4% — victory in the Great Patriotic war, 24,3% — industrialization of their republic (Ossinskiy. 2001). This combination of widely different assessments is further evidence of vitality, and to a certain degree, natural character of paradoxes that reflect contradictions in the development of national consciousness of all people.

Responsibility of intellectuals is to objectively evaluate each and every page in the life and history of their people, to give balanced, rather than provoking answers to people's problems and concerns, to caution against anything that might arouse unhealthy feelings and emotions, or instigate ethnic tensions. Especially great is the responsibility of the media, which has become an instrument for exacerbating real and imaginary wounds, inflicted along the difficult path of functioning of national consciousness and identity. Unfortunately, during the transitional period some people easily adopted the position of «great I» and «lesser you». To prove these «truths» they utilized all the arguments supplied to them by narrow-, but nationalist-minded representatives of national culture.

Analysis of paradoxes of national consciousness allows for two more conclusions. First, these paradoxes are largely supported by such ideas (which, unfortunately, developed at the level of theoretical knowledge), *where interests of the nation and not individual interests become key reference points in the development of the state.* Despite its seeming attractiveness, this position is fraught with tragic consequences: it leads to nothing other than hatred, streams of blood and national mentality poisoned for decades ahead, a fact especially apparent in Nagorniy Karabagh, Tajikistan, Transnistria and other «hot spots».

Second, tragedy of this paradox is amplified when seemingly reasonable proclamation: «national interests above all else», becomes official policy. In these terms, priority of interests of one nation ultimately turns into settling «the score» with another nation, or another state, which leads not only to severed economic ties, worsening diplomatic relations, but also to spread of nationalist mentality, insulting national identity of other peoples, revival and cultivation of chauvinism and racism.

13.4. Chauvinism in everyday life — a specific form of paradox

Contradictions of national «I» are particularly apparent in such phenomenon as everyday common chauvinism. Analysis of this phenomenon suggests that mutually exclusive principles of national identity are combined in consciousness and behavior of one and the same person. The essence of this paradox lies in the fact that, on the one hand, even now, at the height of nationalist and chauvinist passions, it is unlikely you might meet a person who would consider respectful attitude towards other nations objectionable, denied them the right to their own language, their culture or identity. But, on the other hand, how can the very same people, generally professing internationalist ideas, in certain situations of exacerbated ethnic tensions, kill another person, burn down his house, humiliate him, solely on the grounds that he has a different religion, speaks a different language and has different mentality?

Real contradictions in consciousness and behavior of people generate a variety of paradoxes, among which there is such difficult to explain but worthy of attention phenomenon *as general speculative orientation of people to support socially recognized values in the area of ethnic, interethnic relations and simultaneous rejection of those values in real life.* It is this very contradiction that causes everyday common chauvinism.

Analysis of national relations issues demonstrates that common chauvinism has not yet been defined as a separate subject of scientific cognition. It is often equated to ethnocentrism, nationalism and chauvinism. However, the real problem is that everyday chauvinism is not manifested as an idea, politics or ideology, but rather as practice and psychology; it has features similar to nationalism, chauvinism and racism. When analyzing everyday chauvinism, certain difficulties are encountered in distinguishing, isolating it from the totality of phenomena, among which it arises and functions. It is due, *firstly*, to the fact that as a phenomenon of public consciousness and behavior, it does not function in isolation, closely interacting with other phenomena of social life; it is strangely intertwined with political, legal, moral, religious attitudes and orientations. *Secondly,* it is not something static or granted once and for all. New features, new elements in its content emerge, altering ties with other aspects of social reality, changing patterns of its manifestation, its place and role in peoples' lives.

Common chauvinism is an interethnic phenomenon, pertaining to interactions of different ethnic groups at the level of interpersonal communication. Such features as expansionism, hegemony, «great power» ideology, politics in general, as well as ideology are not inherent in its content, although chauvinism is capable of impacting them. In its orientation everyday chauvinism functions within an ethnos, not always outwardly pursuing aggressive goals. This can be explained by the fact that it frequently emerges and is manifested only under conditions of restriction or infringement of national, ethnic interests. Being not only a social but also a psychological phenomenon, it usually does not affect inter-state relations. Consequently, the term «everyday chauvinism» as a social phenomenon can only be applied to interpersonal and inter-group relations; therefore, its manifestations are only possible at this level. However, we should bear in mind that its components can influence state institutions and their activities (Kouvandykov. 1992; *Tsena nenavisti.* 2005).

Analysis shows that there is not a singular factor, which would inevitably cause this negative phenomenon. *The main factors leading to common chauvinism are, first, national exclusiveness; second, national egoism; third, nationalist stereotypes; fourth, nationalist psychology and, finally, nationalist character of personal beliefs.* Ethnic component, as means of communication and interdependence of these factors, certainly plays leading role in the mechanism of functioning of routine chauvinism. It defines real differences between people on the basis of national identity. These differences determine the inner workings of socio-psychological, as well as socio-political factors influencing the emergence and functioning of common chauvinism.

Basis for this type of chauvinism can originate in objective relations that develop in society, in social status or social position of ethnic groups. In addition, there are subjective causes resulting from socio-psychological factors, manifested in personal behavioral motivations, individual experiences, especially education and socialization.

Notions of Fatherland, Motherland, and nation are a source of varied emotions for individuals. Idealization of history is a form of attitude toward their past and their national roots, typical of certain groups of people. A special set of emotional reactions is inherent in carriers of routine chauvinism. Therefore, their frequent appeals to feelings of patriotism, national pride or national honor are not accidental. Common chauvinism, in many respects, is the mood and feelings of people reflecting ethnic relations from the standpoint of national exclusiveness and national egoism. Explosive power of this phenomenon lies in the fact that it does not exist in the sphere of reason, but in the realm of emotions and suggestions. We are dealing with a phenomenon, whose function is to mobilize irrational emotions, cause a surge of irritation, indignation and hatred on a signal from the outside. Carriers of routine chauvinism have no concept of «their own» fault, only a notion of «outsider».

Nationalistic prejudices and biases actually existing in the structure of common chauvinism can serve as specific incentives for committing not only immoral, but also illegal deliberate acts, including taking human life on the grounds that this person is a representative of nationality, which is at odds with «my nationality». Since environment for existence and manifestation of everyday chauvinism is multinational, and people of various nationalities make up these opposing groups, their actions appear as hostile relations between different ethnic groups.

And, in conclusion, let us take a closer look at one paradox, which was not generated by mass consciousness, but emerged only due to the efforts of ideologues of nationalism, of ethno-egoism and ethno-phobia. *This is an issue of so-called titular and non-titular nations.* In the basis of this terminology and corresponding authoritative vocabulary, including legal there is a notion, which implies that if certain people come to a specific territory first (especially if it is reflected in historical sources), such people are referred to as titular, with all the ensuing consequences. They have a right to elect or appoint leaders from representatives of their ethnic group, regard their language as the principle one, demand special attention and exclusive privileges, including political or even possessing their own statehood.

But let us put the question differently, and we discover that none of the people (I repeat, none!) can be recognized as the original owner of a territory. Hence, none of them can be the titular ones. This is first. Second, how many generations have to live on this territory, in order for their citizenship rights to be recognized? Two? Three? Five? Or more? Maybe it is better to be guided not by rule of belonging to certain nationality, but by civic rights with all ensuing consequences? But then is it even worth talking about titular peoples or their exclusive rights, their right to statehood, and not raise the issue of national-cultural autonomy, guaranteed access to culture, language, and a lifestyle of their own for every nation.

Thus, paradoxes of national identity are one of the most devastating weapons of destroying civil peace between nations, one of the most dangerous means of mobilizing internal forces of nations, nationalities and ethnicities involved in this process, since it is aimed at achieving destructive results, whose faultiness is manifested in infringement, ignoring or neglecting interests of people of another ethnicity. It is these contradictions that have arisen on this basis that resulted in bloodiest clashes of the 20th century, which sowed discord and distrust, unimaginably complicating the lives of many countries and regions of our planet. Areas of instability that emerged in the world, were largely a result of attempts to realize nationalist ambitions, which quite often did not correspond either with reality itself, nor with aspirations for effective and efficient (without bloodshed) improvement of this reality.

References

Abdoulatipov R.G. *Priroda i paradoksy natsional'nogo Ia (Nature and Paradoxes of National I)*. Moscow, 1991.

Drobizheva L.M. *Sotsial'nie problemi mezhnational'nikh otnosheniy v postsovetskoy Rossii (Social Problems of International Relations in Post-Soviet Russia)*. Moscow, 2003. P. 23–32.

Guboglo M.N. *Identifikazia identichnosti. Etnosotsiologhicheskie otcherki. (Identification of Identity. Ethno-sociological Remarks)*. Moscow, 2003.

Gumilev L.N. , Ermolaev V.Yu. *Gore ot illiuziy (Grief from Illusions)* // Alma-mater. 1992. No 79, P. 9–10.

Integratsiya Belarusi i Rossii v otsenkakh nasseleniya (Belarus' and Russia Integration in Evaluations of Population) // Sotsiologhicheskiye issledovaniya. 1998. No 9.

Istoritsheskoye soznaniye: sostoiyaniye, tendentsii razvitiya v ousloviyakh perestroiki (resul'taty sotsiologhitsheskogo analiza) (Historical Consciousness: State, Development Trends in Conditions of Perestroika — Sociological Analysis Results) / Ed. by Zh.T. Toshchenko // Informatsionniy biuleten'. 1991. No 1(10).

Jounoussov M.S. *Natsionalism v razlitshnykh izmereniakh (Nationalism in Various Dimensions)*. Alma-Ata, 1990.

Kouvandykov A.Ou. *Bytovoi shovinism kak fenomen natsional'nykh otnosheniy (Routine Chauvinism as Phenomenon of National Relations)* / Thesis, Kand. sotsiol. nauk. Moscow, 1992.

Lipset S.M. *Consensus and conflict. Essays in Political Sociology*. Brunswick. Oxford. Translation books. 1998. P. 15.

Nezavisimaya gazeta. 1999, November 12.

Nuzhen li Gitler Rossii? (Does Russia Need Hitler?). Moscow, 1996. P. 105-110.

Ossinskiy I.I. *Traditsionniye tsennosti v doukhovnoi kul'ture bouriatskoi intellighentsii (Traditional Values in Spiritual Culture of Buryat Intelligentsia)* // Sotsiologhicheskiye issledovaniya. 2001. No 3.

Polititsheskiye issledovaniya. 1995. No 5. P. 70-76, 1996. No 1. P. 78–90.

Rossiya: tsentr i reghiony (Russia: Center and Regions). Vyp. 4. / Ed. by M.S. Goutseriev, V.N. Ivanov. Moscow, 1999. P. 15, 221.

Russian Public Opinion Herald. Data. Analysis. Discussions. Moscow, 2006. No 6. P. 67.

Russkiye (Etnosotsiologhitsheskiye otsherki) (Russians (Ethnic Sociological Sketches)) / Ed. by Yu.V. Arutiunian. Moscow, 1992.

Tishkov V.A. *Natsia — eto metafora (Nation is a Metaphor)* // Druzhba narodov. 2000. No 7.

Toshchenko Zh.T. *Etnocratia: istoria I sovremennost' (Ethnocracy: History and Modernity).* Moscow, 2003.

Tsena nenavisti. Nazionalizm v Rossii I protivodeystvie rasistskim prestupleniyam. (Price of Hatred. Nationalism in Russia and Counteraction to Racial Crimes). Moscow, 2005.

Van den Berghe P. *Man in Society: A Biographical View.* New York, 1975. P. 14.

Chapter 14. Historical consciousness and historical memory: state and paradoxes

> History is the sum total of things that could have been avoided...
>
> *B. Russell* (1872–1970),
> English philosopher and historian.

Sociological studies of the second half of 1980 and 1990 have uncovered previously unknown information about a special, namely, historical facet of public consciousness and specific forms of its manifestation. Among multitude of issues, which became important to the population of our country, there has been established growing relevance of a specific form of social consciousness and behavior, encompassing knowledge, understanding and attitude of people to their historical past, its relationship with today's realities and its possible influence on future development. A more detailed study of this phenomenon enabled us to formulate sociological ideas (representation) about historical consciousness, historical memory, which proved to be rather stable characteristics of people's lifestyles, and, which largely determined their intentions and moods, indirectly exerting very powerful influence on the nature and methods of solving social problems. However, in all fairness, it should be noted that during 1980-1990's, in the years of intensive development of sociology and its analyses of various aspects of social being, data on the status and problems of historical consciousness have been recorded incidentally, in passing and have been taken into consideration only because they could not have been ignored while characterizing political and ethnic processes. Nevertheless, even given their episodic and scattered nature, they helped to clarify the essence of societal changes.

During these years sociology has faced the need for interpretation of such phenomenon of public consciousness as historical memory. Step by step examination of its various aspects and forms of manifestation, led to a more focused, more thorough and gradual evaluation of this notion, eventually gaining both theoretical grounding and empirical interpretation. On this basis, we observe the emergence of first attempts of independent sociological analysis of historical memory, its contradictory and specific essence and characteristics of functioning of historical knowledge of general population, as well as its individual social groups and communities (Levada. 1969; Ovsiannikov. 1989; Afanasiev. 2007; Ivanov. 1998; Eremenko. 2005).

14.1. What is historical consciousness and historical memory

A.I. Herzen was one of the first to utilize the notion of «historical consciousness» in domestic social sciences (Herzen. 1945. Vol.1). Later, these ideas were reflected in the works of many Russian researchers — N.G. Chernyshevsky, V.O. Kluchevsky, K.D. Kavelin, S.M. Solov'ev, V.S. Solov'ev, N.A. Danilevsky, N.A. Berdyaev, I.A. Ilyin and others (Chernyshevsky. 1950; Kluchevski. 1987; Kavelin. 1989; Soloviev. 1988; Soloviev. 1989; Danilevski. 1991; Berdiaev. 1990; Il'in. 1993).

Forms of reflection of the past in historical consciousness on its theoretical level are expressed in concepts documenting the knowledge of processes and trends of development of human society as logical connection between the past, present and future. On a trivial level, to the forms of reflection of the past we can attribute perceptions, impressions and conceptions associated with continuity relations, traditions, customs, material and spiritual experiences.

As for characteristics of the essence and contents of historical consciousness, one might say that it represents a combination of knowledge, ideas, attitudes, conceptions, feelings and moods, reflecting the perception and assessment of the past in its diversity, inherent and characteristic of both society as a whole and its various socio-demographic, socio-professional, and ethnic groups. Some researchers also include beliefs, myths, traditions, symbols and artistic images in the structure of historical consciousness. Sometimes they emphasize the ability of historical consciousness to reproduce its development in space and time (Barg. 1982; Gavrilov. 1986; Libig. 1983; Maklakov. 1987. P. 29–40; Sgibneva. 1991; Shmakov. 1990; El'tshaninov. 1984; Kamenev. 1987; Samiev. 1988; Frantsuzova. 1990. P. 6–17; Kononova. 1989; etc). The studies of particular features of historical consciousness of individual nations that rightfully emphasize its heterogeneity and specificity are especially noteworthy (Faizullin, Zaripov. 1997; Koniukhov. 1993).

As previously emphasized, sociology (unlike philosophy) does not study theoretical or everyday levels of social consciousness, but really functioning consciousness, expressed in attitudes of specific people. Either theoretical, or everyday, ordinary consciousness does not exist in 'pure' form. In daily life they are interrelated and, together, form a unity — a real, functioning historical consciousness, which is defined by its ability to directly reflect surrounding reality and to penetrate into the essence of historical process, that is, to become aware of the connection between the «past», «present» and «future», as well as their continuity. Since sociologists seek information from people themselves, they are faced with the fact, that the consciousness of every individual object of scientific study (individual, group, layer or cohort) presents a very odd combination of scientific and everyday (routine) notions of history as a whole, history of Russia, history their own people, as well as history of one's city, town, village and, sometimes, their family. Significant historical events related to the country, social strata and groups, certain problems of national historical past very often become an object of close attention.

Historical consciousness closely interacts with national self-consciousness. On the one hand, knowledge of the past is an integral part of national identity of any peoples. On the other hand, in the aspect of comprehension of the past, historical consciousness is a broader category exceeding the limits of national self-consciousness, for it accumulates knowledge of the past of humanity, of progress and essential, consistent patterns of historical process.

In a way, historical consciousness is «scattered» encompassing both, significant as well as random events; it absorbs systematic (mainly through education), as well as dispersed information (through the media, fiction, personal contacts). Here individual selection and orientation is determined by specific interests of a particular person. Random, incidental information (often mediated by group or family culture, surrounding the individual) and, to some degree, traditions and customs, which help formulate certain perceptions about the life of the people, country, and state play an important role in functioning of historical consciousness. The value of historical consciousness is significant. Without it, people cease to be a subject of social process and disappear from historical arena.

As for historical memory, this is a specifically focused consciousness, which reflects special importance and relevance of information about the past, in close connection to the present and the future. Historical memory is essentially an expression of the process aimed at organizing, preserving and reproducing past experiences of people, country and state for its eventual use in the human activities or for return of its influence into the sphere of social consciousness. Complete or partial neglect of historical experience and culture of one's country and its people leads to amnesia, which casts doubts on the possibility of the very existence of such nation in history. In this context, Chingiz Aitmatov had brilliantly described this in a legend of *mankurts* that were forced to live without knowing anything about the past, were concerned only about bare necessities, their desire to survive, to save themselves without setting nobler goals. Perhaps this loss of historical perspective is the key to explaining the mystery of disappearance of many civilizations, leaving no trace in history?

With this approach to historical memory, we should point out the fact that it is not only actualized but also selective — it often focuses on specific historical events, while ignoring others. An attempt to clarify, determine why this occurs, suggests that such actualization and selectivity are mainly related to the significance of this knowledge and these experiences for contemporaneity, for current events and processes and their potential impact on the future. In this situation, historical memory is often personified, and then through evaluation of activities of certain historical figures shapes impressions, judgments and opinions about what is of particular value to people's consciousness and behavior in a given period of time.

Historical memory (as well as historical consciousness) is often inconsistent, reflecting such specific phenomenon as zigzags in its development. This is especially clearly manifested in emergence of historical phantoms, when historical events, life and deeds of historical figures are distorted in either direction beyond recognition, until there is no sense and plausibility left to their actions, as well as causes and effects of these actions. Situational nature of these changes is usually transient, but during the period of their functioning people's ideology and activities can lead to severe consequences, significant distortions and sometimes to sufferings of a large number of individuals. There is an interesting example in A.K. Koniukhov's study. During the period of «sovereignty» in 1992, the idea of establishing an independent Komi State was supported by 57,7% of respondents. At that time, Komi ethnic group amounted to only 23% of the total population of this Republic (Koniukhov, 1993). During this particular period there were «zigzags» in perception of reality in historical consciousness of many people. On the one hand, it was a reaction to long-term neglect of domestic factors such as forgetting their native language, cutbacks in its teaching, decline of the role of national literature, intensive Russification, etc. On the other hand, there was complete disregard for the new historical situation, where the desire for preservation of historical and national past was limited to only one issue — State independence, while forgetting about other forms of solving this pressing problem.

Historical memory, in spite of some incompleteness, still has a surprising feature of retaining main historical events in people's consciousness, including transformation of historical knowledge into various forms of ideological perceptions of past experience, its depiction in legends, myths and fairy tales.

And, *finally we should note a specific feature of historical memory, when certain aspects of historical past are amplified, exaggerated in people's consciousness,* since this memory is practically unable to claim a direct and systemic reflection; it is more of an expression of indirect perception and indirect evaluation of past events.

However, the role and the importance of historical consciousness and historical memory increase, especially during the «era of upheavals and disasters», during crucial periods in societal life, when, as a rule, there are intensive processes of reassessment of existing orientations and historical events. It is during these very periods that processes of change of existing values tend to intensify. Dramatic and not always comprehensible changes encourage people to seek answers to their problems in various spheres of life, including historical past. Under these conditions, historical consciousness and historical memory become powerful factors influencing people's behavior and their way of life.

Phenomenon of historical consciousness and historical memory possesses powerful potential. Their impact might assume both positive (integrating, bringing people together) and negative character, when historical events, events of distant past serve as arguments for settling current key issues disregarding the existing situation. In conclusion, it should be noted that historical consciousness and historical memory in different social groups, communities and strata have their own special colorings. They vary among different nationalities as well, a fact that is especially pronounced in multinational countries such as Russia. One of the alarming symptoms during the period of transformation of society, was ambitions of nationalist political leaders, seeking to substantiate their claims to power by means of proof stemming from the arguments about which ethnic group is «more ancient», whose ancestors had made a greater contribution to history, etc. Reflecting on these processes a well-known historian, late M. Gefter figuratively said: «There is no grave that can say: I am closer to heaven». Such approaches to historical past often lead to growing tension and aggravation of interethnic relations.

However, current changes in Russia's social life have a considerable creative potential: popular interest in history, historical past of its people is growing, as well as in spiritual, cultural and historical heritage, which is usually compared with the life of other nations, of humanity in its entirety.

14.2. Events through the mirror of historical memory

Sociological studies show sufficient stability in assessment of historical past during the last decade; although data used for comparisons is based on a variety of empirical evidence, obtained by a number of different polling organizations, which were not using the same methods and techniques.

Thus, in a nationwide study «Historical consciousness: state, trends of development during *perestroika*» (1990, led by Zh.T.Toshenko, A.I.Afanas'eva and V.I. Merkoushin, N = 2196; 2003, led by V.E.Boikov and V.I. Merkoushin, N = 2401), the most significant events in the nation's history were identified as follows: Peter the Great era, according to 72% (61% — 2003) of respondents, Great Patriotic war of 1941–1945 — 57% (59% — 2003), Great October Socialist Revolution and Civil War — 50% (26% — 2003), *perestroika* — 38% (32%), struggle against Tartar-Mongol yoke — 28% (20% — 2003), Kievan *Rus'* period — 25% (31% — 2003). They were followed by: abolition of serfdom — 14%, NEP period — 12%, industrialization, collectivization and cultural revolution of early 1930's — 12 % (19%), reign of Ivan the Terrible — 11% (24%), Catherine the Great — 11% (36%), period of the first Russian revolution of 1905 — 11% (11%) (*Istoritsheskoye soznanie...*, P. 96). If we recall the situation of those times (survey was conducted during and after *perestroika*), a paradox becomes apparent: in spite of an overarching revision and criticism of all, without exception, events of the Soviet period, assessment of the October Revolution remained fairly high, even more significant than the years of *perestroika*. Arguably, it is as if *historical memory is fending off full-scale attacks on the past.* Peter the Great era is still seen as a historically significant reference point. For contemporary history such event is the Great Patriotic war of 1941–1945.

The order of these ratings has largely remained unchanged during subsequent years, despite certain differences. Thus, according to the data of Independent Russian Institute for Social and National Problems (1996), Peter the Great era as a matter of national pride was recognizes by 54,3% of respondents. With regard to reforms of Catherine II, they received positive assessment of only 13,1% of respondents; peasants' liberation during the reign of Alexander II — 9,25%; Brezhnev's stagnation period was positively evaluated by 17% of respondents and Khrushchev's 'thaw' — by 10,4%. 2005 sociological data also showed that recent economic developments — *perestroika* and liberal reform were rejected by 63%, and was positively evaluated by only 25% of respondents.

Consequently, despite some fluctuations and zigzags in official policy of Russian authorities during 1990's, numerous attempts to revise Russian history, popular historical memory still retains as most significant, those periods when Russia was undergoing profound and fundamental changes: period of reforms of Peter the Great and Catherine II, abolition of serfdom, Russian revolutions of the 20th century. These events represent certain points of reference for evaluating national history, despite the fact that previous experience of development underwent very critical «revision».

The situation is different when people assess events of the 20th century, since here medium- and short-term historical memory is triggered, when many real participants of the events are still alive. In this case these events represent a part of someone's life and are, therefore, not free from individual perceptions or personal understanding and comprehension. This perception is affected by official and semiofficial interpretation of events, literary, journalistic and personal judgments of state and public figures, many of which have repeatedly been revised in the context of changes in political life of the country. In other words, historical consciousness displays certain stability and consistency – it has not been much affected by severe (at times) fluctuations taking place in official propaganda. Phenomenon of rejecting of hasty conclusions about certain events is a subject of separate discussion. However, it is obvious that attempts to change or influence historical memory for political and ideological gain typically fail. Let us take a closer look.

Studies done in early 1990's determined that the Great Patriotic war was recognized as the most important event of the 20th century, taking first place (57% of respondents), compared with the second place – October Revolution of 1917 (50%). This order of assessment of these events remained unchanged in subsequent years (Table 14.1), despite the enormous social changes in political and economic system of

Table 14.1.

Most significant events of the 20th century
(% of respondents)

Event	1989 (n = 1325)	1994 (n = 2957)	1999 (n = 2000)	2005 (n=1870)
Victory in Great Patriotic War	75	73	85	86
1917 October Revolution	65	49	48	59
Collapse of the USSR	–	40	47	68
Chernobyl nuclear accident	36	34	32	12
Yu. Gagarin's space flight	33	32	54	58
War in Chechnya	–	-	24	11
War in Afghanistan	11	24	21	9
World War I	8	19	18	16
1930's repressions	31	18	11	12
Perestroika	24	16	16	15
1991 coup d'etat attempt	-	7	6	3
Collectivization	10	8	6	5
XX congress of CPSU	9	5	4	3
Fall of Berlin wall	–	6	5	4

This VTsIOM data, in a representative sample encompassing the entire population of the country, indicates that Russians assess the Great Patriotic war as the most important event of the 20th century (Levada. 2005). In others, including regional studies, the phenomenon of Great Patriotic war is also highly valued by historical memory. In our view, this opinion requires a special explanation.

Great Patriotic war is perceived by historical memory as the most significant event, first, because this memory is linked to the history of every family, affecting most fundamental and innermost aspects of personal lives. Second, this event had determined not only the future of our country, but of the entire world, and, that is why its assessment is based not only on the conscious, but also on intuitive recognition of the role this war played in the history of mankind. Third, Great Patriotic war, as Russian sociologist L. Gudkov rightfully asserts, has become «a symbol, which is...a significant element of positive collective identification, reference point and benchmark for assessing the past and, partly, understanding the present and the future» (Goudkov. 1997. P. 12).

The fact that historical significance of the Great Patriotic war was acknowledged by 70% of young men and women (under the age of 25) and by 82% of people over fifty suggests that this event has become a symbol for the entire population, all its various groups and strata. This means that evaluation of the older generation has transformed and acquired symbolic significance for future generations as well. This indication is reinforced by the fact that in today's ideological and political confusion victory in the Great Patriotic war had practically become the only positive reference point for national consciousness in modern Russian society. And although in 1990's there were numerous attempts of disavowing the outcome and various events of this war, they were rejected by historical memory. These efforts to revise the significance of Battles for Moscow and Stalingrad, attempts at de-heroisation (and sometimes simply slanderous fabrications) of Z. Kosmodemianskaya, A. Matrosov, I.V. Panfilov and others were not only rejected by scientific community, but also by mass historical consciousness. It appears as if national self-consciousness is defending itself from these attacks, refusing to validate these actions, which are demeaning for national dignity, country's history and history of its individual me. By and large, this is a refusal to support a revision of that, which unites the nation and rejection of which may result in a major spiritual, and then political disaster.

With regard to the Great October Revolution, in historical consciousness, it represents a significant milestone, a benchmark, which meant u turning point in world history. Despite all vicissitudes of fate, it consistently ranks second in importance among other events of the 20th century (Ibidem. P. 13). As a landmark event, however, its score along the scale of «positive — negative» has significantly changed during 1990's: the number of people who were critical of its consequences and results has increased considerably. Recognizing the importance of this event, people interpret it in a number of ways. In a 1990 study 41% of respondents assessed October revolution as the first successful socialist revolution in history, 15% as a popular uprising and 26% thought it as a result of spontaneous concatenation of circumstances, a coincidence that brought Bolsheviks to power. In addition, 10% assessed October revolution as coup staged by a handful of intellectuals and 7% as Bolshevik conspiracy (*Istoritsheskoye soznanie: sostoyaniye,...* 1991. P.96). Currently, this mixed and paradoxical essence of its evaluations continues to remain the same.

With regard to other significant events in the life of Soviet (Russian) society in the 20th century, at different times different events were named as most important. Under the influence of political situation and public opinion these assessments kept changing substantially, sometimes drastically. According to VTsIOM data, 36% of respondents in 1989 named 1930th mass repressions as the most important event of the 20th century, but mere 12% in 2005; beginning of *perestroika* — 23% in 1989 and 15% in 2005; war in Afghanistan — 12% in 1989 and 24% in 1994 and mere 9% in 2005. Assessment of events related to the disintegration of the USSR, its disappearance from the political map is an example of the most illustrative, representative paradox. After 1991, many people called the collapse of the Soviet Union an «alarming event» that was upsetting to them (40% in 1994, 68% in 2005). In other studies and in a different context 70 to 80% of respondents regretted what happened (Ibidem. P. 92), which is comparable with the figure of 71% of those who voted for preservation of the USSR in March 1991. But the paradox of this situation, however, lies in the fact that *regrets over the disintegration of the Soviet Union do not equate to the desire for its restoration.* More detailed analysis of opinions regarding the future of the country shows that a significantly fewer number of people want to restore the Soviet Union to its previous form: many want an updated Union, the new commonwealth, where a better balance between desires and aspirations of the USSR's former member nations could be achieved.

Thus, of all the 20th century events, basically, only the assessment of the Great Patriotic War unites and brings us together. Similar unanimity is also reflected in evaluation of scientific and technological achievements, such as Gagarin's space flight, space exploration noted by almost every third respondent in early and mid-1990's and by every second in late 1990's.

However, the ability of people to expertly judge historical past, to correctly reconstruct and evaluate historical events is highly questionable. In a 1999 study, which, along with general population, included some experts — 488 school, college and university history teachers, ability of many people to think critically and make informed conclusions was characterized rather skeptically (Table 14.2).

Table 14.2.

Evaluation of historical thinking

(% of respondents)

Abilities:	High	Average	Low	Hard to say
To reproduce historical past and feel for historical era	2	28	61	9
To navigate historic space and time	1	24	65	9
To uncover causal and resultant links in history	1	14	78	6
To freely operate with historical facts	1	21	70	7
To determine reliability, authenticity of historical facts	1	16	67	15

These limitations of historical thinking are particularly evident when we analyze historical consciousness of individual nations. When evaluating the past, events of crucial significance, those that determined the fate of these nations are actualized in their memory. Rational and emotional perception, passionate attitude to national landmark events (and their consequences) are intertwined here in most astonishing ways. Thus, public opinion studies of socio-political development of Northern Caucasus' ethnic groups noted that many of the 19th century phenomena and events are still stirring peoples' imaginations, attracting close attention of prominent figures of culture and science. Among them, 1817–1864 War of the Caucasus had left the most lasting impression in the memory of these people. As it turned out, apparently, this memory encompasses not only available and generally accessible information but also latent sources, such as family traditions and legends, stories, folk songs, official and unofficial toponymy. A special study conducted for this purpose by the Department of Philosophy and Sociology of the Adygeya State Research Institute in 1995 has shown that 84% of respondents including 95% of the Circassians possessed various information about the Caucasian War. Moreover, some 40% (55% among Caucasians) were convinced that this event was not just a memory of the past, believing that it is closely intertwined with modern socio-political reality. In this regard, in our view, it should be emphasizes that sufficiently diverse characteristics of the causes of this war are reflected in mass, real functioning consciousness. Contrary to some «scientific» and near-scientific claims that autocratic policies of Russia are to blame for this war, only 46% of respondents supported this claim, while the other 31% blamed Turkey and 8% – local feudal lords (Khunakhu, Tsvetkov. 1995). This paradoxical combination of past and present, significance of the past for current guidance and orientations demonstrates that historical memory is a powerful active phenomenon that influences people's behavior no less then their own assessment of current economic and social situation with its misfortunes and tribulations characteristic of any transition period. Moreover, we can assert that it is the historical memory that is capable of strengthening or weakening the perception of events taking place in personal and social life, exaggerating negative features, or, on the contrary, helping calm social and group opinions. Such instability, paradoxical nature of the consciousness is exacerbated, magnified by the fact that historical memory, as well as the «fruits» of certain historical research, are actively misused in current politico-ideological polemics by various political forces. Many artificial models of interpretation of the past are characterized by ethnocentrism, emotive and, being supported by mass consciousness, stimulate thinking by analogy. That is, *trying to explain current problems based on «methodology» of archaic conceptual and ideological positions*, which sometimes oddly coexists with various pseudo-scientific theories. Many of the specific but extremely important (for certain nationalities) events become rather significant factors for both public consciousness as a whole, as well as their historical memory, engaging other groups inhabiting given territory in open, or sometimes latent confrontations (past events in Tatarstan history, the fate of Tuva statehood, historical past of divided Lezghin people, etc.). Therefore, the emphasis placed in interpretation of historical events can promote (or hinder) rational comprehension of national coexistence. Otherwise, we witness emergence of suspicion, prejudices and negative clich s (Empire, chauvinistic policy, etc), which tend to persist in public consciousness, contributing to social tensions and conflicts.

14.3. Historical personalities

In assessing the ratings of historical figures, it is not so much the evaluation of an individual himself, but the totality of his deeds that had influenced the course of history, bringing about dramatic changes in lives of millions. In this sense, it is clear why evaluation of Peter the Great's reforms as one of the most outstanding events in Russian history is correlated with the assessment of Peter I himself, whose activities were positively evaluated in early 1990's by 74% of the population. The same study identifies similar attitudes, where the deeds of V.I. Lenin's (57% of respondents), G.K. Zhukov's (55%) and Alexander Nevsky's (28%) were positively assessed. Later studies demonstrated certain stability in evaluation of historical figures (Table 14.3).

Table 14.3

Ten outstanding people of all ages (in Russia)

Historical personality	1989, %	Historical Personality	1995, %	Historical Personality	1999, %	Historical Personality	2005, %
Lenin	75	Peter I	41	Peter I	46	Peter 1	48
Peter I	41	Lenin	34	Lenin	42	Lenin	44
Pushkin	27	Pushkin	23	Pushkin	42	Pushkin	41
Lomonosov	22	Stalin	20	Stalin	35	Gagarin	35
Suvorov	18	Suvorov	18	Gagarin	26	Stalin	34
Zhukov	18	Napoleon	14	Zhukov	20	Zhukov	28
Tolstoy	15	Zhukov	14	Napoleon	19	Lomonosov	21
Mendeleyev	14	Sakharov	13	Suvorov	18	Mendeleyev	19
Tsiolkovsky	14	Lomonosov	13	Lomonosov	18	Tolstoy	18
Stalin	12	Kutuzov	11	Mendeleyev	12	Suvorov	15

Source: Data of Institute of Sociology

Of course, similarly to ascertainment of people's attitudes toward historical events, evaluations of various personalities tend to be somewhat biased, since closeness to the events and participation in the social life of the 20th century makes some corrections to these judgments. Thus, when evaluating Marshal Zhukov, despite criticism of his actions and doubts expressed in various publications, his name is becoming a symbol of national pride and righteousness (holiness, as people used to say in olden days). It should also be noted that nostalgia for Soviet times increased attention to Lenin and, especially, Stalin, which can largely be explained by the fact that their names are associated with the former greatness of the state and not only political but also social orderliness in the country. It is the nostalgia for the lost that elevates the importance of success in space exploration, as well as such symbols of Russia's cultural achievements as Pushkin, Lomonosov and Mendeleyev. However, it should be noted that this list of prominent figures (compiled by respondents themselves) extremely rarely includes the names of the «culprits» responsible for the current situation in Russia – in 1999 Gorbachev was mentioned by 3% and Yeltsin by 2% of respondents.

Selectivity is a specific property of historical memory. In the consciousness of most people there is a real need for establishing basic reference points that allow us to be proud of our country and its historical figures. Human memory, influenced by information from various sources, is seeking such support, comparing personal perception with historical experience, and, in the end, retains the names of the ones that embody the glory, pride and greatness of Russia (*Istoritsheskoye soznanie: sostoyaniye,...* 1991, P. 96).

Evaluation of Russia's state leaders is mixed: it closely correlates with life experiences, personal understanding of social developments and influence of the surrounding environment (Table 14.4).

Table 14.4.

Evaluation of the positive role of Russia's leaders of the 20th century

*(Russian Centre for Pubic Opinion Research — VTsIOM,
January 2000, N = 1600, % of respondents)*

Version of answer	Total	Age				Education		
		18–24	*25–39*	*40–54*	*55 and more*	*Higher*	*Secondary*	*Below secondary*
Stalin	19	14	17	18	25	14	17	24
Lenin	16	15	12	18	20	15	13	22
Andropov	11	6	12	14	10	11	14	7
Nikolai II	9	15	13	10	3	10	12	6
Brezhnev	9	8	10	7	11	6	8	12
Gorbachev	7	9	9	6	4	14	6	4
Yeltsin	4	5	4	3	4	7	4	3
Khrushchev	3	3	2	3	4	2	3	3

In our opinion, such diversity of assessments of historical figures can be explained by personal perceptions, depending on age and education, factors directly related to short- and medium-term memory. And if evaluations of past leader are similar to memories (public opinion should not be blamed for lacking knowledge of behind-the-scenes manipulations), contemporary leaders are held responsible for all the hardships facing both the country and the people. And the fact that in January 2000, public opinion of B. Yeltsin had somewhat changed, suggests that his resignation was not perceived by the public as a change of leadership (scheduled or not — was not important), but as a sign of the end of a flawed and contradictory era. That is why people were willing to forgive his many errors, as one would forgive an irreparable loss. At the same time, as evidenced by the data of this study, 46% of respondents felt that the ex-president should not have been granted immunity from his responsibility for illegal acts and abuse of power (Levada. 2000).

In this sense, assessment of Leonid Brezhnev's character is very revealing. His name is associated with an era of tranquility, balance, stability, and clear picture of the future, guaranteed by relative prosperity, and, most importantly, confidence in one's social situation. Paradox of such assessment begs the question, why have people forgotten about constant shortage of goods, deteriorating agriculture, growing lag behind the industrialized countries. This paradox might be explained only by the fact that the balance between gains and losses in people's personal lives turned out to be rather bleak, when comparing existing and anticipated opportunities. Under these circumstances, people's social well-being, social protection, desire to be under state's guardianship, as well as guarantees of at least relatively prosperous standard of living are no less important. Increasing importance of personal and individual reflects a global trend. Unwillingness to take this into consideration led to collapse not only of *perestroika* in the second half of 1990's, but also 1990's reforms. Therefore, political leaders like Brezhnev are identified with such social atmosphere that allows people to make these, at first glance, paradoxical but very understandable conclusions (regarding this atmosphere).

As for as Putin, sociological data indicates that his activities from 2001 to 2008 were positively evaluated by 55 to 70% of respondents. Characteristically, this assessment is very stable in its nature.

And yet, these and similar evaluations of historical figures, despite their seemingly chaotic nature, are still able to identify the role and significance of outstanding events and personalities of the past at the level of mass historical consciousness. Information that circulates in public consciousness, in principle, corresponds to historical science, as well as general educational process.

Characteristic of media activities in the field of historical knowledge is somewhat of a special case. For the most part, they follow established concepts and, even if they distort certain historical facts or events in the course of their presentation, they do not radically change overall assessment of historical past. At the same time, frequent instances of blatant distortion of historical facts with all the seeming interest of viewers and readers do not go unnoticed, gradually affecting the deep layers of popular memory.

Historical preferences of Russian people in assessing public figures of the 20th century are much more clear and objective. Thus, in 1999, Russian Independent Institute for Social and National Problems conducted a survey of who were the greatest, «utmost-most» military leaders and scientists of the outgoing century. In opinion polls, among military leaders Marshal G. Zhukov was in the first place, followed by K. Rokossovsky in second and S. Budyonny in the third place. Ten outstanding military commanders of the 20th century Russia also included M. Tukhachevsky (17%), K. Voroshilov (15%), I. Konev (13%) and V. Bliukher (8%). It is noteworthy that 12% of respondents named White Admiral Alexander Kolchak and 7% — A. Brussilov, famous general of World War I. According to the same poll, the «father of Soviet space flight» Sergey Korolev was named the most outstanding scientist by 51% of respondents. In second place — great Russian theoretician of space travel — K. Tsiolkovsky (39%). The top ten outstanding scientists included: one of the creators of the atomic bomb I. Kourtshatov (28%), inventor of the legendary machine gun M. Kalashnikov (25%), biologist and plant breeder I. Michurin (17%), physiologist I. Pavlov (16%), geneticist N. Vavilov (15%), literary critic and specialist D. Likhachev (14%), aircraft designer A. Tupolev, and physicist P. Kapitsa (both 13%) (*Komsomol'skaya pravda.* 1999. December 21). Analysis of these opinions suggests that this information quite clearly reflects assessments contained in scientific and popular publications, although they do not attempt to determine the ratings of historical characters.

The fact of departure from ideological evaluations and recognition of the role and significance of a particular historical figure without necessarily correlating it with the interests of certain social or political forces has gradually become a distinctive characteristic of historical consciousness. In this regard, VTsIOM data from autumn 1999 regarding Stalin's personality is very revealing. 32% of Russian citizens believe that he was a cruel, inhuman tyrant, guilty of destroying millions of innocent lives. An equal number of people think that whatever mistakes and vices are attributed to him, most importantly, under his leadership, Soviet people had emerged victorious in the Great Patriotic War. The other 30% of respondents were convinced: «We still do not know the whole truth about Stalin and his actions» (Ibidem. December 28). In our view, this characterization reflects contradictory, ambiguous, and sometimes paradoxical evaluations of specific historical figures. Such assessments are most effective and objective, compared to some research «works», whose authors have a preset goal — to prove one or another version. For this purpose, they only select such materials that confirm their ideas and eliminate all other information, which may cast doubt on their conclusions. And so, now we are witnessing publication of materials about Lenin, Stalin and Nikolai II, as well as other historical figures, which «study» their lives from positions directly opposite to those from 20–50 years ago. But, if earlier, such «studies» were aimed at glorifying (or discrediting) a historical personality, selecting appropriate facts and ignoring everything that contradicted this positive (or negative) information, in 1990's, with the same zeal and servility, facts and information of opposite nature were being selected in order to prove completely contrary notions and positions. In this situation, public opinion data, which more completely, comprehensively and objectively describes contradictory lives and action of many historical figures, becomes rather curious.

Why is Stalin's evaluation so paradoxical and contradictory? In our view, these mutually exclusive assessments of his historical personality can be explained, first, by the extent to which one's personal (family) history is intertwined with the events occurring in the country. Second, by what in these evaluations it put at the forefront: developments in the country, its economic, military and other spheres of societal life, or priorities related to the fate of an individual in this society. Third, the assessment of Stalin's personality is affected by perceptions of various crucial measures that were implemented by him — industrialization, collectivization, repressions, participation in World War II, etc. And finally, certain «tradition» should not be discounted — looking for repercussions and costs of our development in actions of political leaders that departed from the historical arena.

14.4. Personal historical memory

A *huge layer of historical consciousness is represented by the information that relates to perception, which is associated with individual's life and his immediate environment.* Images of national heroes, geniuses, talents and their activities are stored in aggregate historical memory as in a museum of sorts. They are known from textbooks, scientific literature and fiction. But their numbers are in single digits. Yet memories of millions and millions of others are preserved in the vaults of this museum, only in the consciousness of their loved ones, relatives and friends. They are like millions of building blocks in the foundation of our historical memory, nameless workers and witnesses. Without them history itself, and, most importantly, our involvement in it is unimaginable. I am convinced that a man cannot fully enjoy himself as a citizen of his country, if not only is he ignoring landmark events and milestones of its history, but also genealogy of his own family, history of the city, town, village or region, where he was born and lives. Unfortunately, most Soviet (Russian) people have rather vague knowledge of their family tree, often no further than the third generation, i.e. their grandparents. This is evidenced by data collected by V.I. Merkoushin. Only 7% gave positive response to the question: «Does your family keep genealogical records?» When asked, «What are the reasons for poor knowledge of your family history?», 38% of respondents said that there was no one left to tell the story, while 48% claimed that their family members were not interested or indifferent to this subject. Paradox (bordering on absurdity) of this statement is astonishing because, as demonstrated by the same historical experience, knowledge of «personal» history elevates a man, ennobles his behavior and makes his life more complete and meaningful even if there was no nobility, no merchants, but only farmers, workers or clerks in his ancestry. Such attitude to the family past helped unveil amazing and surprising «discoveries», when in 1980–1990's many intellectuals (though not only them) that were far from ambitious rushed to search for their roots and origins. This desire to look into one's past, one's ancestry is quite clear and understandable. However, among so-called intelligent people, it led to emergence of a dubious ambition to discover prince, count's, or at least aristocratic roots, completely ignoring the real facts and even denying their «ignoble» origins, as if the deeds of other social classes in the past did not deserve equal pride and respect. In our view, this can be explained by an inferiority complex and aspiration to boost one's significance in current public and private life, increase social standing, which for some reasons might be lacking among this category of people. This might explain all the fuss around reviving «noblemen» assemblies, assigning princely, nobiliary and even merchant titles, like children's game of toy soldiers.

Yet, lack of personal involvement in history is prevalent in contemporary historical consciousness. This disregard for one's roots is confirmed by the fact that only 14% of respondents knew the history of the origins of their family name (20% claimed partial knowledge). Respect for family heirlooms is not fostered or encouraged enough. So far it is limited to preservation of material objects of short-term historical importance. Thus, in 1990 and 2003 73% of respondents confirmed that they had their grandparents' photographs (note that 27% did not even have those), 38% in 1990 and 53% in 2003 – that they kept regalia and other memorabilia, such as honorary diplomas, medals and other decorations as mementos. 15 and 17% of respondents respectively mentioned letters from the front and other family treasures, but only 4% in 1990 and 14% in 2003 – diaries, manuscripts, letters and correspondence (*Istoritsheskoye soznanie: sostoyaniye,...* 1991, P. 93).

How can we characterize this personal facet (slice) of historical consciousness, historical memory? In our view, it is underdeveloped, its quality is inferior and, I dare say, it undermines the foundation of higher emotions – patriotism, pride in their country and readiness to defend and protect its interests. In this regard, allow me one personal memory. In 1959, on my first trip abroad to the German Democratic Republic, according to my itinerary, I had to stay with a family of German farmers in Saxon Switzerland for two days. To my great surprise, in the evening the head of the family (a farmer!) showed me a book of records, which contained genealogical history of their family all the way from the 16th century. And, based on these records, this was a continuous chronology of the farmer's family, which successfully made it all the way up to the twentieth century and, judging by his son's and daughter's occupation, was going to continue this impressive tradition well into the future.

Unfortunately, in our country, such traditions have either been lost (for nobility and merchant families) or not cultivated (for peasant and petty-bourgeois families). Why it happened – is another story, although in sociological literature (on the basis of biographical method), we already have first attempts of thorough analysis of history of a number of families over several generations, which at first glance, produces a vivid, multi-faceted history of the country through the story of a family (Kozlova. 1994; Kozlova. 1996; Tshuikina. 2000).

Knowledge of family lineage is closely intertwined with the history of the nation, national identity, which has always played an important role in personal behavior. Its significance seems to increase, especially during transitional periods. In V.I. Merkoushin's study, among responses to the question: «Do you have personal pride for your homeland, your people, your ethnic background, your city or your colleagues?» 62% of respondents voted for ethnicity. In our view, individual's national identity is closely correlated with personal historical memory. Thus, society, as well as the media should actively promote this sense. Otherwise we will *be confronted with an amazing paradox, when people are proud of their country, their nation without recognizing the «brick», the contribution of their own personal historical memory in the destiny of their country.* Yet it is these «bricks», these building blocks that constitute the history of the country, its achievements and victories. And that is why one has to be aware of the plusses and the minuses of preservation of both collective and personal destinies. We might be moved to ponder over this problem by a reflection, an appeal to his grandson of the former senior army officer V.N. Dobrynin (Deputy Chief of Staff of the Soviet Army Logistics Administration, a former nobleman who fought bravely in the First World War, and then joined Bolshevik Red Army during the Civil war of 1918-1921). In his appeal, or rather an entry in his diary, dated 1951, he had inscribed the words depicting the importance of self-assessment in the grand history, as well as the history of his own family: «You will be the last person who remembers me and grandma. Think of us from time to time when looking at you. Remember us in the year 2000, which we wish we could have seen...»

The issue of family history is related to the information about one's town (village), where the numbers are slightly higher then the indicators of knowledge of one's ancestry: 17% of respondents said that they have some knowledge of that history. True, yet another 58% claimed to know some facts about the history of their city (village), but this is, firstly, related more to urbanites, and, secondly, it was obviously due to the 'presence' effect. However, «knowing something» does not signify the adequacy of this knowledge.

Symptomatically, there is a gap between contemplative attitude toward history and a desire, readiness to contribute to the preservation of its values, its objects and symbols. According to the available information, mere 4% of the people directly participate in restoration of historical and cultural monuments. Another 33% said that they contribute to this process, particularly by making donations for their restoration. In other words, yet another paradox emerges: people say that they know (and are proud of) their history, but civic activism in relation to national historical past is still pretty low.

In conclusion, we need to point out that *individual historical memory and historical consciousness are the basis for the renaissance of national spirit, growing interest in cultural and spiritual heritage.* Recent rehabilitation of undeservingly forgotten names has been positively received by 58% of respondents. 85–91% are actively supporting the revival of folk crafts, folk medicine, folk festivals and fairs.

14.5. An overview of historical knowledge

Once again, I would like begin with V.I. Merkoushin's data. Only 4% of respondents positively answered the question «Are you satisfied with the quality of history taught at school?» Every other teacher (48%) has acknowledged that the level of history teaching at school is low. But historical consciousness, historical memory objectively reflecting at least the most important milestones in national development can only take shape and develop if systematic historical information is available in its entirety, without predominance of emotions or attempts at tempering, when historical facts are replaced by all sorts of concoctions generated by random fantasies or arbitrary gag.

In the mean time, interest in historical knowledge is significant. It is motivated by desire to know the truth about the past (41% of respondents), while another 30% are looking to broaden their horizons, 28% need to understand the lessons of history and experiences of previous generations and 14% want to find the answers to today's burning questions in historical experiences of this past. It is apparent that these motivations are fairly convincing, sufficiently clear and, in a sense, are quite noble, since they meet people's need to be citizens of their country in a full sense of this word. This includes motives for identification (the need to feel like a part of the country and its people), as well as pursuit of objective knowledge, since that, according to 44% of respondents, helps better understand the present and, in opinion of another 20%, make the right decisions. 28% of the population sees a key to raising their children in historical knowledge, while 39% believe that one cannot be considered a truly cultured person without knowing history. Self-evaluation of people's knowledge of history is noteworthy (Table 14.5)

Table 14.5.

Evaluation of historical knowledge
(% of respondents)

Types of history	Good	Mediocre	Low	Hard to say
History of Russia	17	56	15	9
History of own people	14	50	21	10
Universal history	3	38	35	18

Note: wantage percent (in line) constitutes those abstaining from answering

Let us compare this data with experts' opinion — among history teachers and professors of historical disciplines in universities and colleges responding to similar questions in this study. 44% of them acknowledged that the level of general knowledge of history of Russia is average to low (52%); knowledge of ethnic history 25% described as average and 63% as low, and that of general history 20% and 69% respectively.

Apparently, the history of their country, their nation will always be closer to peoples' hearts, feelings, social values and moods. However their interest in different periods and stages in country's history varies (Table 14.6).

Table 14.6.

The most interesting themes of Russian history
(% of respondents)

Topic	Entire Population	Includingstudents
Lives of prominent scientists, military leaders, cultural figures	48	51
History of Ancient *Rus'*, emergence of centralized state	37	33
Life and actions of Tsars, Khans, and Princes	29	32
Customs, traditions, folklore	27	40
History of liberation and revolutionary movements	10	1
History of the Soviet society	20	6
History of religious movements and teachings	17	12
History of the peoples of our country	22	13

Everyone — education system, as well as family, media, literature and science should help meet these needs, this interest in historical issues. The demand in this sphere is great, since according to the opinion of 80% of teachers — historians, the most dangerous peril here is not so much poor, inadequate or one-sided historical knowledge, as distortion of this knowledge, dominance of outdated dogmas (*Mify novoi khronologhii....* 2000).

In other words, there is a real paradox emerging: historical scientific literature is read by a limited circle of individuals, while, at the same time, the demand for a popular presentation of the past is great among the readers. So far people's historical consciousness is resisting various fantastic theories and historical speculation, such as the works of A. Fomenko and his disciples (new chronology of history). But is it not better to resist these distortions of history by means of supporting those writers who awaken interest in history through their artistic fiction, which mainly describes personal lives of the characters, without undermining the basis of historical knowledge?

In conclusion, I would like to emphasize one significant fact: currently, in Russia, a process of creating a very interesting academic discipline — historical sociology — is underway (Afanasiev. 2007; Ivanov. 1998; Romanovsky. 2009). For a long time this discipline, to a certain degree, was covered with in the framework of historical materialism. However, it has been more of a schematic, overall trends, rather than a retrospective analysis of historical consciousness and related human activities. That is why, a number of publications in Russian magazine «Sociological Studies» are worth mentioning: B.N. Kazantsev wrote about «unknown» statistics of the Soviet working class living standards and problems of urban employment in the mid 1960's; A.A. Sheviakov published his studies of

1939 All-Union census and «secret» post-WWII repatriation, as well as Soviet food aid to the Peoples' Democracies during the same period; V.P. Popov on the demographic situation in Russia in 1940's and after the Great Patriotic War: on passport system in the USSR; V.N. Zemskov wrote a study on prisoners in 1930's and on repatriations of Soviet citizens after WWII and their fate. In 1998, the magazine had established a special section of «Historical Sociology». Since then there were many articles published, which attempted to reconstruct historical events based on the documents describing mass historical consciousness: letters to various branches of the government, career histories, 1920–1940's events, monetary reforms of 1947, 1960 and 1992, protest movements as seen through the eyes of contemporaries etc. Complex issues that lie at the crossroads of history and sociology allow us to approach characterization of historical consciousness and historical memory as part of social consciousness in all their contradictory and paradoxical development, and to discuss relative independence of this phenomenon and specific forms of its scientific analysis.

According to this analysis, it is becoming apparent that without a certain level of knowledge, understanding and respect for historical past, it is impossible to be a true citizen. Moreover, without it, we cannot build Russia's new statehood and Russia's civil society.

References

Afanasiev V.V. *Sotsiologhiya Istorii (Sociology of History)*. Moscow, 2007.

Barg M.A. *Istoritsheskoye soznaniye kak problema istoriografii (Historical Consciousness as an Issue of Historiography)* // Voprosy istorii. 1982. No.12.

Berdiaev N.A. Sud'by Rossii (Destinies of Russia). Moscow, 1990.

Chernyshevsky N.G. *Izbrannyie filosofskiye proizvedeniya (Selected Philosophical Works)*. V 3 tomakh. Moscow, 1950.

Danilevski N.Ya. *Rossia i Evropa* (Russia and Europe). Moscow, 1991.

El'tshaninov V.A. *Istoritsheskoye soznanie (Historical Consciousness)*. Barnaul, 1984.

Eremenko A.M. *Istoria kak sobitie (History as Event)*. V 2 tomach. Lugansk, 2005.

Faizullin F.S., Zaripov A.Ya. *Grani etnitsheskoy idenifikatsii (Facets of Ethnic Identification)* // Sotsiologhicheskiye issledovaniya. 1997. No.8.

Frantsuzova N.P. *Istoritsheskoye soznanie i ego struktura (Historical Consciousness and Its Structure)* // Istorizm i tvortshestvo. Part 1. Moscow, 1990. P. 6–17.

Gavrilov O.F. *Istoritsheskoye soznaniye i ego funktsii (Historical Consciousness and its Functions)*. Theses, candidate's dissertation, philos. sci. // Tomsk. 1986.

Gowdkov L. *Pobeda v voine: k sotsiologhii odnogo natsional'nogo simvola (Victory in War: on Sociology of a National Symbol)* // Monitoring obshchestvennogo mneniya. Ekonomitsheskiye i sotsialniye peremeny. 1997. No.5 . P. 12.

Herzen A.I. *Izbrannyie filosofskiye proizvedeniya (Selected Philosophical Works).* V 2 tomakh. Moscow, 1945. Vol.1.

Il'in I.A. *Put' k otshevidnosti (A Way to the Obvious).* Moscow, 1993.

Istoritsheskoye soznanie: sostoyanie, tendentsii razvitiya v ousloviyakh perestroiki (Historical Consciousness: State, Trends of Development under Conditions of Perestroika) (rezul'taty sotsiologhitsheskogo issledovaniya) // Informatsionniy biulleten' Tsentra sotsiologhitsheskikh issledovaniy AON pri TsK KPSS. Moscow, 1991. P. 96.

Ivanov V.V. *Vvedeniye v istoritsheskuyu sotsiologhiyu (An Introduction into Historical Sociology).* Kazan', 1998.

Kamenev S.V. *Voprosy metodologhii issledovaniya struktury istoritsheskogo soznania (Methodological Questions of Studying Historical Consciousness Structure)* // Sovremennaya nauka i zakonomernosti ee razvitiya. Vol. 4. Tomsk, 1987.

Kavelin K.D. *Nash umstvennyi stroy (Our Mental Order)* / Stat'iy po filosofii russkoi istorii i kultury. Moscow, 1989.

Kluchevsky V.O. *Kurs russkoi istorii (A Course of Russian History).* Chast' 1. Sobraniye sotshineniy v 9 tomakh. Vol.1. // Moscow, 1987.

Khunakhu R.A., Tsvetkov O.M. *Istoritsheskiy fenomen v sovremennom prelomlenii (A Historical Phenomenon in Contemporary Reflection)* // Sotsiologhicheskiye issledovaniya. 1995. No. 11.

Komsomol'skaya pravda. 1999. December 21.

Kononova L.I. *Istoritsheskoye soznanie i ego funktsii (Historical Consciousness and Its Functions).* Theses. Dissert. cand. philos. sci. Moscow, 1989; etc.

Koniukhov A.K. *Istoritshekoye soznaniye Komi naroda: sostoyaniye i tendentsii razvitiya (Historical Consciousness of Komi People: State and Development Trends).* Theses, cand. diss. sociol. sci. Moscow, 1993.

Kozlova N.N. *Ghorizonty povsednevnosti sovetskoi epokhi: golosa iz khora (Horizons of Studying Soviet Era: Voices from Chorus).* Moscow, 1996.

Kozlova N.N. *Krestiyanskii syn: opyt issledovaniya biografii (Peasant's Son: a Study of Biography)* // Sotsiologhicheskiye issledovaniya. 1994. No 4.

Levada Yu.A. *Istoritsheskoye soznanie i nautshnyi metod (Historical Consciousness and Scholarly Method)* // Filosofskiye problemy istoritsheskoy nauki. Moscow 1969.

Levada Yu.A. *Mneniya i nastroyeniya (Opinions and Dispositions)* // Nezavisimaya gazeta. 2000. February 9.

Levada Yu.A. *«Tshelovek sovetskiy» ('Homo Soveticus').* Moscow, 2005. P. 27.

Libig Yu. *Istoritsheskoye soznanie kak predmet filosofskogo issledovaniya (Historical Conscuiousness as Subject of Philosophical Study).* Dissert., cand. filos. sci. Moscow, 1983.

Maklakov V.T. *Istoritsheskoye soznanie: sushchnost', formy bytovaniya i yazyk (Historical Consciousness: Essence, Forms of Being and Language)* // Istoritsheskoye soznanie i sovrenmennost. Sverdlovsk, 1987. P. 29-40.

Mify novoi khronologhii akademika A.T. Fomenko (Myths of a New Chronology by academician A.T. Fomenko) (Materialy nautshnoi konferentsii v MGU) // Novaiya i noveishaiya istoriya. 2000. No 3.

Ovsiannikov A.A. *Istoritsheskoye samopoznaniye (opyt mezhdistsiplinarnogo issledovaniya) (Historical Knowledge – an Interdisciplinary Study)* // Sotsiologhicheskiye issledovaniya. 1989. No. 6.

Romanovsky N.V. *Istoritsheskaya sotsiologhiya*. Moscow, 2009.

Solov'ev S.M. *Istoriya Rossii s drevneyshikh vremen (History of Russia from Ancient Times on)* / Sotshineniya v 18 tomakh. Vol 1-4. Moscow, 1988.

Solov'ev V.S. *Natsional'niy vopros v Rossii (National Question in Russia)*. V 2 tomakh. Vol.1. Moscow, 1989.

Samiev A.Kh. *Struktura istoritsheskogo soznania (Structure of Historical Consciousness)*. Dushanbe, 1988.

Sgibneva O.I. *Istoritsheskoye soznanie: sushchnost', puti formirovaniya (Historical Consciousness: Essence and Ways of Making)*. Dissert. cand. philos. sci. Moscow, 1991.

Shmakov V.S. *Struktura istoritsheskogo znania i kartina mira (Structure of Historical Knowledge and Picture of Universe)*. Novosibirsk, 1990.

Tshuikina S.A. *Rekonstruktsia sotsial'nykh praktik (Reconstructing Social Practices)* // Sotsiologhicheskiye issledovaniya. 2000. No. 1.

Chapter 15. **Paradoxes of moral consciousness**

> «Sir, it is impossible to simultaneously
> serve you, and please you»
>
> Answer of Marshal
> *de Villars* to Louis XIV

Moral consciousness is a distinctive phenomenon of social consciousness. On the one hand, it represents a separate form, which has its own specific content and specific features distinguishing it from all other forms of social consciousness. On the other hand, it is «interwoven» into other forms of public consciousness, penetrates them forming a rather peculiar phenomenon.

Morality has always been an integral feature of humanity since the first steps of its functioning as a rational society. Although norms of morality do not remain unchanged, the majority of world's nations gradually formulated general principles that govern people's lives, their relations with one another, within a social or professional group, with other peoples and ethnic groups. These principles have most clearly been embodied in religious teachings: in the Sermon of the Mount, Koran, Buddhist beliefs, in confessional requirements of other religions. The fact of the matter is that tenets of these religions (kind of) absorbed thousand-year experience of building personal, group and public relations; reflected general features, characteristic of everyday life and social behavior of all nations, called morality. Analysis of religious beliefs leads us to the conclusion of their similarity, resemblance, shared value of this specific world of human perception. It is also interesting to note a remarkable feature of universal moral norms: they regulate people's behavior in their interactions with each other, within a group, a layer or a profession, but, in practice, do not apply to those contacts, which link people to authorities or the ones that they always react to in unique and specific ways.

15.1. What kinds of morality exist in society?

Real life constantly attests to the fact that morality presents the greatest value to mankind, demonstrating its involvement in all, without exception, processes and events of public and private life. Its norms claim to be a criterion of people's actions, serving as an assessment of their attitude toward ongoing changes, their willingness to promote spiritual, social and political renewal of the world around them. Moreover, not only common norms of morality, but also the measure of their correlation with real situations, real requirements of the time often act as such criterion. Not declared, but «practical» and functioning morality, penetrating every pore of social organism, characterizes the essence of the changes in public consciousness and behavior. Finally, it should be noted that «moral evaluation exists primarily (first and foremost) as a self-evaluation» (Guseinov, Apresyan. 2005. P. 37).

Ethical standards, in a sense, are predecessors, precursors of legal norms. As a rule, they are not enshrined in law, but are supported by traditions, customs, public opinion, unwritten requirements of everyday life. *During the periods of social conflict their functioning is paradoxical: on the one hand, they are exposed (cannot help being exposed) to changes; on the other hand, they provide stability and balance in society,* since they reflect centuries-old popular experiences that cannot be cancelled or ignored, cannot be neglected without eventual repercussions, or backlash from social environment.

During transformational societal shifts they cannot remain prone to change: complete change of economic and political orientation radically alters «the rules», thus creating various conflicts between what is needed now and what was required previously. Some moral contradictions that emerged prior to market reforms, turned out to be minor and irrelevant, while others have escalated, the third become a focus of intense public debate, the fourth turned into an independent problem requiring new approaches and solutions.

In other words, at each stage of historical development in the course of accumulating experience, moral standards have changed and were enriched; different nations emphasized different key points in relation to particular phenomena or events of personal and public life. But one thing remained constant: basic guidelines were retained, preserved, strengthened and began gaining greater moral force.

At the same time the institution of morality has always evolved in an inconsistent and contradictory way. On the one hand, *there was a regulatory, officially endorsed morality,* which prescribed relevant rules of behavior for people, groups, social organizations and social institutions. These rules of morality were largely sanctioned and supported by political authorities and were a kind of an «official» requirement for social life, especially in the part of it that relates to individual's duties and obligations before the State. On the other hand, *the sphere of morality regulating relationships between people in daily life, outside the formal, official interrelations, continued to evolve and enrich;* it was more consistent and conservative in terms of maintaining long-established moral values, from the point of view of preservation and observance of moral principles and orientations.

Of course, the boundary of interaction between official and popular morality has always been rather conditional, changeable and specific, depending on different forms of political authority, historical features of civilization and the level of general culture and education of people. But the most significant shifts in interaction of these spheres of morality have occurred during the great bourgeois revolutions, when regulatory requirements of feudal-absolutist model of society with its all-out regulation of economic, political, social and spiritual lives of people have been replaced by new requirements asserting the triumph of the rights and freedoms of every individual, his economic and especially spiritual independence, autonomy of consciousness and behavior. Under these conditions, firstly, there was a convergence of official and informal morality; secondly, significantly increased influence of real (unofficial) morality (and it constantly keeps increasing) on all of the processes of social, political and economic interactions taking place in modern society. This new phase of development of morality, in turn, has its own traits and specific characteristics applicable to each nation and every social body.

At the same time, analysis of moral consciousness and behavior would be incomplete without careful consideration of their paradoxes, which are not just diverse, but are highly relevant and crucial in determining the fate of not only individuals but also social groups, layers, communities and even of an entire society. A.A. Guseinov suggested considering these phenomena from the viewpoint of the paradoxes of moral evaluation and paradoxes of moral behavior. Regarding the *paradoxes of moral evaluation,* it is still an open question as to who has the right to administer moral judgment. The fact is that «those who should pass moral judgment will not do that; and those who wish to dispense it cannot be trusted». According to A.A. Guseinov, the way out of this situation lies in a moral requirement «Do not judge others», or «Moral judgment is a judgment a man passes on himself» (Guseinov, Apresyan. 1995, *p. 18*).

Among the paradoxes of moral consciousness (evaluation), numerous attempts to declare some people moral, others — immoral, some people — good, others — evil, should be noted. Such division, however, is possible only in a fairy tale or in abstract logical analysis of human qualities. In real life it does not exist — every human being is a combination of various qualities, of conflicting attitudes and values. We can assume that even the most moral person (from the standpoint of people around him) will always find flaws in himself, for «the more developed a person's moral sense is, the more critical he is of himself» (Guseinov, Apresyan 2005. P. 37).

No less striking is a *paradox of moral behavior, formulated by Ovidius: «I see and praise the good, but it but it's the evil that attracts me» (*Ovidius. *Metamorfozy (in Russian).* P. 170). This is a fairly common situation, which manifests itself in a contradictory relationship between ethics and professional attitudes (smoking doctor warning others against smoking), morals and legal norms (corrupt official preaching against bribery), morals and political image (hypocritical politician who believes his own promises only during election campaigns), morality and social contagion (praising religious values, with no intention of following them), morals and national traditions (resorting to them when it is profitable). It is quite logical that such people who are aware of moral demands, but are not observing them, can hardly be called moral.

Paradoxes of moral consciousness and behavior are varied and diverse. Undoubtedly, many of them have kept changing acquiring a particular form in the course of development of mankind, in their essence, however, remaining the same: «any moral posturing, when someone is speaking on behalf of morality, portraying himself as its interpreter, carrier, guardian, etc. is a false pose» (Guseinov, Apresyan. *2005.* P. 40).

15.2. Current state of moral consciousness

At the present stage of evolution of Russian society, the state of moral consciousness and behavior presents a deeply contradictory picture, where both positive and negative phenomena and processes are closely intertwined. This pattern suggests that the new situation in the country in many respects has raised eternal problems of morality in a new way, forced us to rethink accumulated experiences and see the profound contradictions of modern life realities.

What are the actual traits and characteristics of moral consciousness in Russian society? What are its inherent properties, what is typical, what tends to change and acquire new forms and new content?

If we start with most general assumptions, we can say that in today's society there is a serious concern about the state of moral and spiritual sphere as a whole. The majority of people have expressed concern over the fact that many moral norms no longer function or have lost their former significance. According to N. Popov's data, 25% of Russians surveyed in 1998 (in 1994 — 14%) agreed that morality, ethics and culture were in crisis. Some researchers emphasize the growth of individualistic attitudes, loss by Russians (and Russia's citizens in general) of a sense community and team spirit, decreased responsibility for the fate of the country, their loved ones, their profession and work. Sociological studies data suggest that it is alarming to a large extent.

People are generally concerned about a decrease in controlling function of morality, manifested in declining relevance of moral «taboos», in growing permissiveness and disregard toward restrictions that govern the process of functioning of social consciousness and behavior.

At the same time, as life experience demonstrates, attempts by certain individuals of pursuing policies of «tightening the screws», toughening the sanctions in the realm of morals produce no positive results either: the door that stays open remains most intact. Hence, indirect rather than coercive measures are required to achieve the attainment of desired moral goals. But these objectives must be openly declared, officially and informally approved, otherwise confusion, moral blindness and deafness, or triumph of questionable values begin. It is in this very situation that the life-giving force of morality, which binds the elements of social organism, disappears.

Presently, we are witnessing an *atrophy of the requirements of morality, which are superseded by requirements of rationality.* But absolutizing the latter turns a person into a robot, a mannequin, into artificial intelligence, which by virtue of single-dimensional thinking and ignoring moral aspects of any social situation is not only capable of disturbing, but also destroying a living body of either a social organization or entire society. We are witnessing this very process in Russia today when credibility and significance of moral values have either decreased considerably or are entirely absent.

In this connection it is necessary to focus on the analysis of value orientations, which are an important indicator of morality and permit to quite efficiently judge its change or stagnation. According to the data of sociological monitoring by RIISNP, in the 1990's, during the period of market reforms, mass consciousness of Russian society has undergone profound qualitative changes, influencing its rational, volitional, socio-psychological components. The study results allow us to draw conclusions about the trends and dynamics of basic value orientations of the population. In early 1990's (until about 1995) basic vital values that were characteristic of the Soviet people for a long period of time continued to be retained. Notwithstanding the severity of emerging material problems, the collapse of many former ideals and standards of living, the hierarchy of value orientations has remained virtually unchanged. Leader-values included the values associated with comfort of the inner world of a person: clear conscience, family, interesting work. Power, prestige, recognition and success were attributed to «outsider»-values. However, during this period values of material nature started to gain relative importance.

This trend began to change starting in mid-1990's reflecting qualitative shifts in previously stable and traditional (for Russia) value orientations. Values of spiritual and moral character, which always prevailed in Russian mentality, were displaced by the values of purely material and pragmatic nature. With regard to certain basic vital values, their preference sign shifted to the complete opposite one. Thus, if during the first years of reform, two thirds of Russian population gave priority to the values of freedom over the value of material well-being, since 1997 more than half of the country's population began to assess their material well-being significantly higher than values of freedom. Moreover, radical changes in preference of these two basic values affected approximately 30% of Russians (table 15.1).

Table 15.1.

The dynamics of value orientations of the Russian population
(% of respondents) in 1993–2000.

Value orientations	1993	1995	1997	1999	2000
In own life, a person should strive to ensure clear conscience and spiritual harmony	84,7	93,4	69,3	89,6	93,8
In own life a person should aspire to ensure access to authority, to ability to influence others	11,9	5,9	17,7	10,4	6,2
Equal opportunity to display abilities of everyone is more important than equality of status, income and living conditions	75,2	72,3	56,4	65,9	71,8
Equality of income, status, conditions of life is more important than equality of opportunity to display merit and abilities of everyone	18,4	23,7	38,9	34,1	28,2
Freedom is the one thing, without which human life is meaningless	55,7	70,6	39,5	59,9	66,3

End of table 15.1.

The main thing in life is material prosperity, freedom is secondary	41,1	27,1	58,3	40,1	33,7
It is possible to spend a significant part of life can only be spent on an interesting job	54,8	62,7	31,2	49,6	57,6
The main thing in a job is how much money you are paid for it	41,2	35,4	63,9	50,4	42,4
A person should live in a country, which he likes to live in	54,7	52,5	56,8	45,0	43,7
A person has only one Homeland and it is no good to leave it	41,1	46,2	41,5	55,0	56,3
Personal freedom is an opportunity to be Your own master	67,3	64,5	69,8	–	66,5
Human freedom is realized in a person's political rights and freedoms	29,1	24,4	22,7	–	33,5

Source: Data of the Russian Independent Institute for Social and National Problems (12–14 regions, N = 1800–2200).

The fall of 1998 economic and financial crisis was a turning point in the dynamics of value orientations of Russian people. *Since 1999 the tendency of prevalence of those values that have traditionally been a priority in mass consciousness has begun to recover.* Once again, the importance of clear conscience and peace of mind became not only dominant but also virtually absolute (94%). Two thirds of the population (even slightly higher than during the first years of reforms) once again began to give priority to the values of freedom, while one third of Russians still continued to stronger appreciate material well-being. Thus, these new shifts in the dynamics of basic values have arguably returned distinctive mental traits of the Russian people to their desired location. Similar trends were observed in the 1990's study led by N.I. Lapin (*Dinamika tsennostey naseleniya reformiruemoi Rossii*).

One of the distinctions of moral consciousness is that it cannot exist by itself, outside of the social context, in which it functions. It constantly feels the pressure of destructive forces, is exposed to corrosion, doubts and, frequently, to direct or indirect attacks either disguised as priority of rationality, or as updating and responding to new demands of the times. *Therefore, it would be no great exaggeration to state that morality is gaining ground in its struggle against destructive forces, in constant controversy with political conjuncture, with rabid «expediency», with rejection of compromise and attempts to establish rational uniformity.* However, requirements of morality have their own limitations; exaggerating and opposing them to requirements of rationality can lead to irresponsibility and failure to respect certain objectively determined algorithmic actions.

15.3. Moral dimension of economic paradoxes

Universal nature of morality and moral consciousness as an indicator of moral health of the people and their future is manifested primarily in the sphere of economic life, but in a peculiar way. This peculiarity lies in the fact that there is no direct correlation between the indicators of well-being and indicators of moral consciousness and behavior. Real life constantly demonstrates a lack of concurrence between economic realities and requirements of morality and its derivatives. The root of this discrepancy stems from the fact that *industrial and legal mechanisms of functioning of economic relations do not account for requirements of morality, constantly ignoring them, failing to provide for their coordination and interaction.* As a result, paradoxical situations regularly take shape and keep renewing, re-emerging, thus undermining, on the one hand, the foundations of success in economy, and, on the other — degrading moral health of society. Let us consider some of them.

If in Soviet times arguments about the role of education in improving efficiency and profitability of production were an accepted norm, in post-Soviet Russia it has become fashionable to discuss «correct» market management, entrepreneurial initiative and freedom of actions, resulting in devaluation or complete disappearance of such notions as «duty», «conscience», «honesty», «accuracy» and «decency» etc. from economic vocabulary. In other words, not only economic but also moral defects have become a key feature of both Russian society as well as the majority of its industrial organizations.

For the leaders of many economic, credit-financial and industrial organizations and associations only economic indicators: profit, revenue, profitability, costs, sales and marketing — are of paramount importance. There is no room for moral values both in their activities and in their daily chores. Moreover, they do not feel (or almost do not feel) the need for moral precepts, solving production problems without them.

Comparison of modern market practices with practices of even pre-revolutionary years calls for serious reflection. Why did a Russian merchant, as a rule, believe that if he broke his promise, he would lose customer's trust for a very long period of time, since it would undermine his personal credibility as well as credibility of his business? And why does a contemporary leader, as a rule, consider it possible to take liberties with his word or commitment, without feeling any pangs of conscience, justifying his behavior by using every excuse, except his moral obligations? And, all of this is referred to as normal management, «success in life», an «ability to live well», etc.

There can only be one explanation for this situation: moral values are not interwoven into the real economic mechanism. And why should they, if this mechanism is capable of functioning without this «verbal tinsel»? Moreover, «modern society, from the viewpoint of ethics, is characterized by the fact that the social effect and, accordingly (since common good is a moral value as well), a morally significant result less and less depend on moral incentives, measures of individual righteousness or wickedness in the traditional sense of these concepts» (Guseinov, Apresyan. 1995. P. 268). This conclusion, which was formulated by Adam Smith in reference to economics, has a very real basis to this day, since the ongoing economic reforms do not create any preconditions for taking moral demands into account in order to improve current economic mechanism. Varying modifications of market indicators resembling the era of primitive capital accumulation still remain in the foreground. The fact of the matter is, market attempts to radically change economic structure have led to the fact that victory — political and economic — over the Soviet-type management, with its practices of camouflaged deception and fraudulent results in the «name of the highest interests» has become an end in itself, while moral attitudes have turned into an obstacle in the way of prodigious enrichment of a small group of private business owners. It is impossible to create neither civil society, nor state of law without morality, since the focus on the ultimate goal — the market (as construction of socialism before, during Soviet times) is doomed to a historic defeat, if it justifies the impoverishment of a large number of «people-owners».

Moral corrosion of economic relations has generated a huge host of paradoxes. Some of them were inherited from Soviet economy and, having undergone certain modification, remained virtually unchanged. *Most clearly this first class of paradoxes is manifested in social dependence, parasitism, inaction and irresponsibility of people* who rely only on the State and blame everybody but themselves for their own as well as social faults and flaws. This social dependence (parasitism) is varied and diverse. If in Soviet times, it found its extreme expression in indifference: «We don't give a damn»; in market conditions it is: «and where was the State looking?» — even in such cases where it concerns private or group property, or one belonging to shareholders. Social dependence results in parasitism when, having lost faith that either, like during Soviet times, the State would take care of them or, like in post-Soviet period, it would completely abandon participation in their affairs, many people elect as their credo: a) trying to live as in Soviet times: as little work as possible, but as much money as possible; b) if difficulties arise in life, someone else should handle them, not me; c) renounce all claims to society and to live as a social vagabond, openly or latently. But all of them, in one way or another, appeal to the State regardless of their contribution to the common cause, demanding social justice, social protection, and help in solving personal problems. As a result, there is a paradoxical situation: regulatory requirements imply that labor behavior is differentiated depending on where people work — public or private enterprises, or joint-stock companies. In fact, it makes virtually no (or very little) difference. Actual labor behavior in general terms remains basically the same. Emergence of market relations has seriously affected labor behavior only in the shadow economy and in criminal structures (Timofeev. 2000; Aleksandrova. 2000). This confirms once again that it is impossible to reset consciousness and behavior like a machine by shifting it from one mode to another simply pressing a button.

The second class of paradoxes is generated by market relations themselves, by attempts to abandon the style and the way of life that millions of people led during the Soviet era. Thus, in the first years of market transition, a lot of people wanted to try their luck and test their abilities in the new economic conditions. According to opinion polls, in 1994 14% of Muscovites were engaged in business and another 31% would have liked to engage in this kind of activity. However, this «passion» soon died down considerably, since it turned out that it was not easy «to fit in» the new economic relations: it required much more than a desire and intention. Such qualities as «business» behavior that contradicted former vital principles: ruthlessness to competitors, insolence, impertinence, and ability «to step over corpses» were required from people. As a result, in late 1990's number of people wishing to test their skills in entrepreneurial field fell to 12–14%. And if we add that these figures are characteristic of other countries as well, it once again demonstrates that in the structure of employed population the number of businesspeople cannot exceed 7–9%. Hence, it becomes clear why this new attraction turned out to be a myth, in reality, resulting in tragedies, failures and even suicides.

This example clearly illustrates *a contradiction between economics and morality, or more precisely, the difficulty and complexity (but not impossibility) of their combining.* However, while solving economic problems, in the consciousness of active participants on market relations moral aspects are still discounted, ignored or not recognized. This is especially true of those entrepreneurs, who acquired their capital through seizure or appropriation of large chunks of state property or deception of millions of people. Some of them successfully operate (due to the gaps in legislation) to this day. Others «legally» moved abroad, having provided a «life of luxury» for their relatives for decades to come. But there is a fair amount of those who have disappeared (or are hiding from the eyes of the people), having robbed millions of people without any remorse. But all of them — the first category, the second and the third — have one thing in common: for the most part, they ignore moral requirement, or partially stick to them in exceptional cases only. Such banks as «Chara», «Vlastilina», «SBS-Agro», «MMM» (Mavrodi), etc. flourished on this very basis; for them moral rules simply did not exist or were an annoying obstacle to their «successful» business activities.

Third group of paradoxes presents a certain symbiosis of old and new gaps in the functioning of public institutions, generating or reviving contradictions in relations between economic subjects. Thus, such paradox as moral mimicry, which adapts consciousness and behavior to what you want to appear before people around you, not what you really are, is very clearly manifested in the sphere of economic life of modern Russia. In Soviet times, people like underground millionaire Koreyko (character of a popular Russian comedy) had to carefully conceal their economic capabilities, led modest lifestyle of inconspicuous employees that met all of the official moral requirements. Therefore, during the Soviet times crooks, thieves, swindlers of all sorts, in most cases did not show off their wealth, prosperity, and their claims for exclusivity. Turning-point in the behavior of these people came in late 1980's when corruption, bribery, extortion began to undermine the social organism introducing a stereotype of «the ability to lead a beautiful life» into consciousness of millions people. It is during this period, as a rule, that people stopped concealing this skill, and, on the contrary, started showing it off as a virtue. Such morality in a hypertrophied form was manifested during privatization years, when a group of people «having seized» («legally» stolen) infinite riches began to revel in their wealth. This was met with widespread rejection from society, generating hatred toward such people. Consequently, they found it necessary to once again return to mimicry but at the new level: leading a closed, inaccessible, secretive lifestyle, hidden from the world, enjoying «drinking and entertainment under the blanket», «behind tall fences», most often beyond the borders of the country. But this does not change the overall characteristics of the given *paradox: discrepancy of social status and moral claims of people in private and public life.*

Economics of Transitional Society has generated both in Russia and in all post-Soviet countries one *other paradox: the process of transformation requires a highly skilled workforce, but instead of including them in the implementation of reforms, they are ousted to the periphery of labor process and replaced by those good at deception, «blowing smoke» plundering, preferably under a nice cover story.* Analysis shows that among these newly rich, especially at the middle level, there is a lot of people, whose moral, general and professional culture causes a lot (if not a huge amount) of doubts. No wonder, public consciousness reacted with a series of jokes about the «new Russians», which have captured the absence of basic culture, combined with impudence, insolence and ability «to live a high life». In other words, these very people, who at best can be called the Pharisees, were claiming to be «the standard» of market relations. According to prognostically minded experts, the fate of Pharisees is what awaits these figures.

Massive use of highly skilled specialists in those work spheres that do not correspond to their previously received education and training became another form of plundering of national wealth. Thus, analysis of «shuttle» merchants, for example in Tatarstan, showed that 44,6% of them have higher education and 38,7% — second, vocational education, previously working mainly in scientific research institutes, universities, budgetary organizations and public enterprises. Moreover, their engaging in this kind of small business is not situational or temporary: one third of them (33,3%) have been successfully trading for more than three years, and 73,8% have officially acquired a status of individual private entrepreneur. Reflecting upon this situation researchers concluded: «Small and medium business «sucks» people in. It is increasingly clear that for many people it will be difficult to return to their former professions. Due to stagnating production it is virtually impossible to stop the processes of marginalization and de-professionalization» (Ivanov, Komlev, Tolchinski. 1998, P. 440). In other words, the process of looting of creative potential and degradation of professional personnel has crossed all boundaries of reasonable selection and has put the country on the brink of losing still remaining advantages in intellectual sphere.

Sociological data show that moral consciousness would not reach due maturity if official morality steers people toward achieving social ideals, while economic practices pushes them, if not overtly, then covertly to uphold personal and group vested interests, leading to a certain utilitarian benefit to the detriment of developmental prospects of both society and individuals. This discrepancy is especially vividly and evidently manifested in the labor sphere, in respect to its value and its values.

Value of labor has always been the highest moral characteristic of a person. Orientation toward labor had been inherent in the majority of people in pre-revolutionary Russia. In the Soviet Union this attitude had been supported ideologically, which yielded significant results. Under conditions of market reforms, however, a lesser number of people regarded labor as a value and means of achieving material prosperity: mechanism of secondary income redistribution, when individual well-being became less dependent on one's labor activity, powerfully manifested and still manifests itself in society. With the development of shadow economy, people's incomes began to not so much depend on the quality and quantity of labor, but on a variety of random factors, including questionable ones. All this had a devastating impact on labor morality: in the 1980-1990's a number of people for whom labor ceased to be the leading value increased sharply.

As a result, the ongoing process of alienation of labor has gained an enormous scale: people have ceased to be proud of their profession, of experiencing due satisfaction from the results of their labor, became less and less creatively daring. Employees were increasingly convinced that they were practically unable to influence labor process: its object and quality, as well as rewards were turning into forces unaccountable and insubordinate to them. Under these circumstances, such features as indifference, apathy, disrespect for work and its results, lack of initiative, inertia could not help emerging and becoming reality. This, in turn, has led to decline in organization, growth of theft and other obvious and latent defects.

Unfortunately, the significance of labor as a value has lost its importance in the eyes of youth. They increasingly link their future not to the desire to master a profession as such, but to acquisition of adequate social status guaranteeing access to material wealth. Under these conditions, moral aspects of career choice are replaced in most cases by utilitarian interests, low degree of civic consciousness and responsibility for the fate of society and own family.

This situation gives rise at least to two more moral paradoxes. *First*, a person, especially a young one, is more engaged in social self-determination, rather than professional one. This phenomenon was noted by a Soviet sociologist F.R. Filippov (1924–1990) in the 1970–1980's, when motivation for a better (in the sense of financial security and social prestige) life began to prevail over career choice in the future plans of young people. Under conditions of market economy this motivation has virtually become the main one. Even graduates of such prestigious universities as the Moscow State University, Moscow State University of Technology, Moscow Aviation Institute, Moscow Physics and Technology Institute do not see anything shameful in standing behind a counter, being a seller in the market, pushing various merchandise on the streets, in offices, organizations or factories if they fail to become businessmen, managers, etc. These people have a following predominant incentive: this «downgrade» in my social status is temporary but if offers a fairly substantial extra income, unlike any other job I can get, including the ones in my own specialty.

Second, change in labor morality has resulted in a situation, when in popular consciousness, not just such occupations as business, but also deviant activities like crime and prostitution, etc., began to be regarded among worthy and socially necessary jobs. Moreover, assessment of prestige and profitability of professions among younger and older generations differed only slightly, mainly in relation to public (government) service. It is also indicative that neither scientists, nor teachers or engineers, neither ordinary cultural (librarian, art historian), nor highly skilled workers made it to the list of prestigious professions (table 15.2).

Table 15.2.

Which professions do young and older generations regard as...

(% of of respondents in 1999, young — 1974,
senior citizens — 774 respondents)

Profession	Most prestigious		Most profitable	
	Young	*Older generation*	*Young*	*Older generation*
Lawyer, notary	43,1	33,9	22,5	15,8
Economist	18,6	13,2	7,9	6,7
Banker, financier	27,0	31,5	29,4	32,8
Manager	10,5	9,0	8,2	8,5
Businessman	12,7	15,2	37,4	37,0
Civil servant	9,6	15,2	9,8	11,9
Physician	9,2	11,1	2,2	5,4
Singer, actor	5,4	4,1	2,1	1,3
Journalist	2,6	1,3	—	—
Military	2,6	2,1	2,2	2,6
Crime, prostitution	—	—	5,9	7,2

Source: Rossiya na rubezhe vekov. Moscow, 2000. P. 94–95.

In an express-poll conducted by VTsIOM in February 2000, 28% of 1600 respondents in an all-Russian sample emphasized profitability of «criminal authorities», yielding to financial management/banking by mere 12%.

It is obvious that the new realities of market Russia have seriously shifted popular perception about the place nowadays occupied by one or another profession in dealing with strategic life problems. And it is clear that in this scenario, moral orientations and ethical guidelines yielded to utilitarian, pragmatic and even cynical views on prospects of both social and individual status in society.

15.4. Common and specific in paradoxes of moral and political consciousness

Politics is at its best when it is ethical and moral. Unfortunately, morality is quite a rare phenomenon in today's world of politics. One of the manifestations of this discrepancy and inconsistency between political and moral evaluations of life is the fact of electing political and public figures presidents, governors, deputies, etc. with practically simultaneous (or with some delay) lack of confidence in them. Such paradoxical contradiction has only one possible explanation: moral evaluation criteria fundamentally differ from political, State or social ones. Most regrettably, these evaluations are not mutually correlated, contradict each other and do not manifest any trend towards convergence.

This paradox — recognition of legitimacy of political power and at the same time, mistrust of it is the reality of Russia in the 1990's. Acquiescence or reconciliation with existing realities does not necessarily mean a positive evaluation of those in power, or recognition of their moral right to lead social processes.

Contradictions between politics and morality have always existed, since politicians in most cases are guided by attitudes and orientations far from requirements of morality, which gradually leads them to oppose and reject (overtly or covertly) consideration of the interests of most people, as well as to deformation, distortion or even collapse of their own goals and objectives.

In reality, in their political activities, these people prefer tactics of hypocrisy. Collapse of the USSR has clearly demonstrated the significance one of the reasons leading to disappearance of this powerful nation in the 20th century: Soviet *nomenclature* ignored moral guidelines (this was especially evident during Brezhnev's stagnation period and Gorbachev's *perestroika*). Interests of these ruling groups began to dominate over both interests of the State and society, and over popular interests as well, becoming the only reference point for their actual deeds (Cf: Panarin. 1998, P. 280–281).

The main paradox in the relationships between politics and morals in modern Russian society lies in the fact that all political actions are prepared and served in such a manner as to hide the true purpose and selfish intentions by using a whole range of political technologies to ensure manipulation of social consciousness.

It is necessary to note that this process of substitution of certain assessments with the others taking place in public consciousness, is skillfully allowing to implicitly and imperceptibly ignore moral values. And how could it be any different, when political authorities, as A.S. Panarin's aptly noted, instead of being held accountable for the results, replace them with normative expectations such as «Russia is a democratic country», it «fights for human rights», «introduces market relations», etc (Panarin. 1998, P. 280–281). Utilizing such techniques leads to the fact that human consciousness is not focused on assessing the state of affairs in society and government, but on expected positive results, which, like they say, «not yet», but will be achieved for sure. To a certain extent, it is not even a repeat or rerun but hypertrophied methods of soviet propaganda when desired results were postponed for «later» in the future, this way decreasing or reducing public pressure on state powers.

Moral consciousness is also impacted by the fact that the state keeps consistently demonstrating the techniques of unabashed utilitarianism: it tries out different ideas as improvised means of achieving certain goals and then, without any excuses or attempts of justification, rejects them if they interfere with the next idea or the next goal. *As a result political consciousness is affected with cynicism, nihilism, disbelief not only in sincerity but also in rationality of actions of authorities.*

In the 1970–1980's position of many Soviet people who constantly, daily and hourly followed a double standard became a vivid example of a political paradox: at rallies, demonstrations and official meetings they supported — «Long live the Communist Party», while at home, in private they were telling jokes about it. This contradiction in consciousness and behavior became a natural norm for the top leadership of the Soviet Union. I remember my 1995 conversation with professor Jerzy Vyatr of Warsaw University who had been a secretary of the Central Committee of the Polish United Workers Party during the 1970's. When I asked, «What do you think, Jerzy, why so many secretaries, leaders of the CPSU and the Soviet state not only rejected the past, but do not even utter the word «socialism» any more»?», he at first was evasive, saying: «It is your business and you deal with them». Next day I returned to the topic (it was at an academic conference): «Where are your former party secretaries working now and what are their political orientations?» And the reply was «all of them keep working in the ranks of socialist parties (there are several of them), and I too am working in the field of socialist ideas, although I've been criticized by your ideologists for revising them». His further arguments boiled down to the fact that Polish leaders have remained true to socialist ideals, while many Soviet leaders turned away from them. To sum things up: Polish leaders were deeply convinced of the fruitfulness of socialist ideas (though CPSU ideologists harshly criticized Polish specificities), while Soviet ones were unprincipled careerists, with boundless thirst for power. I am not sure, if he was correct in regard to Polish socialists, but as far as the Russian ones are concerned, there is no doubt.

And today we are witnessing the fact that many leaders, having risen to positions of power, are honoring only power, their darling power, while paying no attention to its color. For the sake of it they can change their convictions, roam from party to party, adapt to the strongest, just so they are not excluded from the bunch of those close to power.

15.5. Social paradoxes of morality

People in every society were always concerned about such issues as social justice, social well-being, social attitudes, social comfort, and degree of commonality of interests of society, social groups and individuals. And this in turn is reflected in moral orientation, moral compass — a social idea, which should answer the question: can this idea unite people, bring them together during years of hardship, «helping» overcome material losses and worries, come to terms and accept decline in living standards, give enough strength for hard work that society might require.

But the paradox lies precisely in the fact that decline in claims in daily life does not reduce the need for highly moral guidelines that would inspire people, make their life more meaningful and purposeful, help reconcile individuals with current hardships, failures and shortcomings. After all, it is precisely to the loss of these moral values that we can attribute a growing number of people, especially young ones, who want to leave Russia and to find refuge and solace in other countries, in foreign lands, completely abandoning what makes each citizen a patriot of his country in the highest sense of this word.

In this connection it is appropriate to mention a thesis, widely circulated in early 1990's, that «patriotism is the last refuge of scoundrels» with reference to high authority, which was propagated without considering the situation or context. At the same time, the word «ideology», the very mention of which was associated with something unacceptable and improper in a democratic society, was subjected to disparaging criticism. Proponents of this viewpoint argued that all modern societies are non-ideological, neutral to any position or any point of view. However, it soon became obvious that society cannot do without a moral national idea, i.e. without ideology that bonds social consciousness holds it together, act as its dominant notion. This is confirmed by sociological data as well: people, who are burdened with routine concerns about their daily bread, are deeply concerned about the fate of the country, state, and the absence of unifying idea in society that binds together interests of all participants in the contemporary historical process (Popova. 2000).

Under pressure from the objective circumstances, society, main political and social forces recognized and acknowledged the validity, consistency and necessity of a national idea. Under the influenced of «glorious» historical past, many remembered Count Uvarov, who, in the mid 19th century put forward his famous formula: «Autocracy, Orthodoxy, Nation». Unfortunately, persons, who took a liking to this idea did not know (or pay attention) to the fact that it had been put forward in order to solve the problems of education, not society as a whole. Furthermore, this idea failed to safeguard Russia against revolutionary upheavals and the collapse of a huge state, against demolition of the entire social structure.

Realizing the need for national ideology in Russian society, many politicians indulged in elaboration of ideas from the «top», based on their own views and ideas of what Russia needs, without paying attention and refusing to deal with popular opinion, thoughts of the majority of people that truly determine both the essence and image of the country. These «caretakers» put forward all sorts of verbal inventions — «sovereignty», «spirituality», «statehood», not to mention nationalistic orientations associated with co-called Russian idea, or suggesting authoritarian principles (such as «honor and order»), etc., etc.

Limitations of all this searches for national idea was primarily due to the fact that they essentially were invented at a level of political or para-scientific conclusions. At their best, they reflected mind games of certain politicians or intellectuals, and represented a direction of theoretical or political research, — concoctions that had little to do with real concerns of the majority of population. This myth-making did not take into account our historical past, where certain stereotypes of consciousness had formed. Therefore, these attempts to create something completely new without taking into account interests and needs of the population were doomed to failure. Furthermore, one should not flirt with the past or criticize it, but realize the values of past generations, which cannot be replaced in one quick swoop, no matter how appealing that might seem.

«Invention» of national idea is impossible without crystallization of those philosophical orientation that is «diluted» in social consciousness. «You cannot make people happy, — said a director of one of the avant-garde enterprises in Penza in 1976 (even back in Soviet times), — by deciding for them and without them what they need». Only participation and knowledge of their concerns, interests, aspirations and desires can make ideological orientations into a real social force. Thus, the collapse of Soviet system can mostly be explained by the fact that it has become increasingly reliant on certain dogmas invented by someone, and not on the real values that people truly cared for. No need to step on the same rake twice, by repeating the same mistake or putting into practice the slogan «we shall draw it and we shall live it» (that is, we shall live in the world of our imagination).

In other words, *national idea, ideology is a concentrated and crystallized version of the dominant social orientations and values.* In this regard I would like to point out the following.

First, an in-depth analysis of individual social assessments and expectations shows that there are practically no one-dimensional people in existence that would unanimously profess values of socialist or liberal, patriotic or religious consciousness. It turns out that under the conditions of crumbling social values one and the same person on certain issues adheres, for example, to neo-liberal social beliefs, on others — to nationalistic, on the third — say, socialist ones. Sociological data, however, is limited — it quite often yields information about social orientations or preferred values in relation to one group of problems, without mentioning the others, or, at best, reflecting only dominant attitudes while ignoring all else.

This approach of viewing individuals as uniform and ideologically saturated beings is fruitless, for social values of people are usually not limited to an orientation toward single goal, but are focused on realizing several objectives, expectations, preferences that form certain integrated outlook. Ongoing attempts to classify people on the basis of liberal (capitalist) or socialist orientations do not contribute to the comprehension of the real picture either. And those who are trying to determine (utilizing their own techniques) what percentage of people are still guided by the, until recently, familiar values and who rejects them, have also reinforced this divide. However, it became obvious that this Procrustean bed cannot accommodate the diversity of social orientations, social attitudes and assessments. Gradually, along with these two dominant orientations, national patriotic sentiments, religious values, monarchist and other ideas began to be recognized, which, as sociological studies show, in most cases do not exist by themselves, but in combination with other assessments and values.

The second point is of methodological order. The majority of people, when determining their social values and orientations, usually (in most cases) correlate them with their social environment, which surrounds and determines their real life. Most people are not indifferent to the country they live in. The knowledge that Russia has to be a great power to be reckoned with, respected (though not feared, as in the case with the USSR) and, which can defend its citizens, nourishes everyday beliefs of many Russians, and can help them in acquiring social and moral stability and pride in their country. It is especially important, since this notion has been inherent in the consciousness of many generations of Russian (Soviet) people and could not disappear without a trace. Especially when one takes into consideration that violation of this core attitude may turn (and for some people it did) into a tragedy. Many people are rather painfully experiencing Russia's loss of the role that was inherent in the USSR. Is it not one of the roots of nostalgia for the past? Especially since sociological surveys constantly record features of civic consciousness and behavior, which, despite certain fluctuations depending on specific political events, continue to occupy a leading position in people's social orientations and expectations, even considering serious critical assessment of what is happening in Russia today (See table 15.3.).

Table 15.3.

Are you proud...
(% of respondents. N = 1600)

Possible of answers	..that you live in Russia		...of present-day Russia	
	2006	*2007*	*2006*	*2007*
Yes	48	54	19	27
Rather, yes	35	32	29	33
Rather, no	9	8	32	23
No	4	3	16	124
Hard to say	4	3	5	6

Source: Public Opinion — 2006. Moscow. Levada-Center. 2006. P. 22–23.

As sociological studies show, for Russians, such moral value as justice, fairness is no less stable and significant. Not equality, not equalization, not common good for all, but justice. And although it is understood in different ways, for the majority of Russians, it is nevertheless an important characteristic of consciousness and behavior. In accordance with this orientation, this peculiar criterion, they assess how fairly they are treated in the industrial organization where they work, or how comfortable they are is their neighborhood, and what do local authorities do in regard to services and amenities, but, primarily, how does state government insure justice in society.

This value — social justice — like no other echoes in the hearts of millions of people. For this very reason it is necessary that its attainment as well as commitment to its maintenance and improvement become a component (and possibly the primary component) of the national idea.

And *finally, values that relate to each individual person need to be noted.* Socialist ideology proclaimed individual rights, but did little to implement them, focusing mainly on building socialist society and communism globally, where everyone would receive according to their needs. For a long time people believed it, but then got tired of waiting and hoping. The times when interests of the country, and of the state dominated public consciousness were gone. According to sociological studies, already in the 1970's certain shifts in public consciousness were recorded, which reflected the fact that people did not want to postpone their private lives «until later», that they were no longer satisfied with the stories of achievements of the entire country or certain sector of national economy — they wanted personal success. They wanted proof of positive changes, instead of listening to endless excuses for continuous «temporary difficulties».

Therefore, it is quite understandable that many people began to more and more focus on achieving personal goals. For young people this is increasingly associated with success in life, getting rich and personal comfort. For middle-aged people — with professional certainty, with family prosperity, present and future stability, especially for their children. For senior citizens — with secure old age, respect of others, and recognition of their past experiences. In other words, if we summarize the analysis of these values and orientations, we can conclude that there is a popular aspiration to achieve personal well-being in the broadest sense of this word. And achieving this well-being should become part of the national idea, ideology and morality; the state must promote realization of these goals by all means possible, reconciling various interests, not allowing anyone to build personal welfare at the expense of the well-being of other people.

Consequently, orientations toward prevailing social values, social expectations and preferences at all levels — macro, mezzo and microenvironment — can in real life fulfill the role of a unifying idea that will allow, without undue politicization, to concentrate efforts of people, society and the state on their achievement. It is very important that this idea, as a kind of a moral compass, is not oversaturated with ideological guidelines of any political forces. Such goals that take into account the interests of a person *as a citizen* (interests of the whole country**)**, *as a resident* (interests of a residential community where a person lives) and *as an employee* (interests of that local unit of society where he works and socializes with colleagues), are the crystallization of dominant preferences that can hardly be opposed even by those, who (for whatever reason) do not share them. Moreover, *this combination of personal, group and social interests produces a cumulative effect*: their organic fusion increases the role and importance of each of the elements of this unifying idea. In other words, as a concentrated accumulation of social assessments and orientations, national idea in reality expresses humanistic and moral foundations of social position of each person as an Individual, Citizen and Russian.

15.6. Moral paradoxes of spirituality

Economic, social and political conflicts are accompanied by introduction and spread of primitive spiritual values in popular consciousness. Giant invasion of mass and pop culture is reflected in the fact that shoddy publications, tabloids, newspapers, etc. are blossoming like unruly weeds. The process of yielding to poor tastes and aspirations is underway. This could be justified by a primitive range of needs of impoverished population, if it were not accompanied by propaganda of violence, human vices and even by their encouragement, on the one hand, and by falling prestige of industrial, scientific or cultural activities, on the other, which finds its expression not only in economic crisis, but also in moral decline.

As a result, Russia's moral culture is at a crossroads. Under the guise of criticism of everything Soviet or socialist, all moral values, without exception, are subject to revision, including those that evolved over centuries and that, in fact, guarantee stability of the nation in its development. In fact, *the problem is not so much in recognition of proclaimed norms, as in their implementation, safeguards and enforcement by the state.*

Generally, social consciousness evaluates the state of moral culture rather critically and impartially. Moral values have surrendered their positions under the influence of economic realities which, on the one hand, are related to rampant, flagrant and endless plunder of state property, dominated by impudent calculation indifferent to any «prejudices» and involving use of all means of profiteering — ranging from fraud to murder. On the other hand, the majority of people were facing the issue of survival, which resulted in reduction of moral claims. As a result, in public consciousness *a paradoxical image of post-soviet Russia consisting of «a field of miracles» and «a field of tears»* arose, reflecting hypertrophied forms of social inequality.

Spirituality is always based on values, which explicitly or implicitly inspire people both in public and in private life. The paradox lies in the fact that these values were being eroded, giving rise to deformed, incomplete and one-sided perception of existing spiritual contradictions. Flaws and vices of moral character are not met with public condemnation. Moreover, in Russian society, there are real conditions created for ignoring moral demands.

First of all, this is manifested in the fact that *education and upbringing are increasingly being distanced from each other.* On the one hand, a generation of people has appeared (at least their number is significant) who, as A.I. Solzhenitsyn aptly put it, are called «the educated». Availability of education, including higher one, still says nothing about morality of people, their values and outlook. Moreover, even higher education is not a guarantee against primitivism, limited intellect or professional and cultural cretinism.

Growing number of educated people is not accompanied by an increase in their morality, or their readiness to meet new moral requirements. Increasing mass of highly educated people does not lead to growth and deepening of spiritual wealth of society, instead, it is replaced with a certain breadth of coverage of those included in educational process, which does not mean expansion or strengthening of morality.

Contradiction between morality and spirituality of cultural life *is reflected in another paradoxical combination: developing polarity in culture:* on the one hand, there is flourishing and ear-splitting procession of mass-culture across the globe that has never been and will never be synonymous with true culture (in spite of attempts to prove that they are close and even identical); on the other hand, there is a growing volume of demands for an elite culture, which is progressively acquiring snobbish and pretentious character. Significance of this paradox is increased by the fact that the gap between these two cultures — mass-culture and true culture — is more and more assuming the character of deep social differences, since it is identified with a style and way of life of various social groups, layers and classes.

As a result sociologists are observing not just a growing misunderstanding, but mutual rejection of these cultures due to the differences in their philosophical grounds: one culture rejects another as being primitive, shabby, and tasteless; the second rejects the first one as useless, show-offish, wanting to stand out on the merits of the lack of normal preferences and tastes. But, in both cases, these manifestations conceal spiritual and moral poverty, squalid tastes and preferences, when the form, not the content of culture comes first.

This paradox is closely related to *showing off,* pretentiousness, and desire to stand out from the crowd at any cost. In principle, such desire to demonstrate one's knowledge, possession of special information, focus one's passions and inclinations in a certain area of culture is a normal phenomenon in a spiritual life of people. But when natural trends in consciousness and behavior become hypertrophied, when there are claims to exclusivity, desire to distinguish themselves from the rest of the world by any means possible, this suggest not only for a low level of spirituality, but also wounded pride, pretentious thinking, moral flaws in self-evaluation.

Another spiritual and moral paradox — *primitivization of culture* — is very close to the pretentiousness. This process often appeals to the roots of the past, to ethnographic characteristics of people, customs, traditions and other forms of cultural heritage. But, this quite justifiable desire to utilize spiritual achievements of previous generations of mankind in order to enrich one's life, is often reduced to a mere aspiration to preserve this past, which often represents «dead», instead of «living» knowledge. In these conditions, impossibility to distinguish between what deserves to live and continue to exist and what has already completed its natural course of development leads to flourishing primitivism, which does not only fail to enhance, but in fact denigrates the very notions of spirituality and culture. And the threat of this deformed form of conservation of cultural heritage does not consist in the fact of revitalization or artificial maintenance of these claims, but in offensive, belligerent conduct of carrier subjects of such consciousness and behavior, whose efforts are quite often characterized by aggressiveness, categorical, peremptory judgments and actions bordering on arrogance and impudence. Radicalism of these carriers of culture is further escalated when it is used to cover their interest in material benefit, profit, when all aesthetic and moral values retreat under pressure of commercial gain.

When analyzing moral paradoxes of spirituality, it is worth focusing on the following points as well. *First, moral costs and consequences are of particular importance for interaction between domestic and world cultures.* Unfortunately, «joining something» (R.V. Ryvkina) often becomes a leading motif in this interaction, when everything American, French, German, etc. is declared the best, most advanced and significant, and everything Russian — the worst, obsolete, primitive and even squalid. These attempts at belittling one's own culture, science or education, compared to achievements of Western countries became fairly widespread. It is manifested, for example, in always naming shops, banks, agencies, interest groups in accordance with foreign patterns and requirements. Such «groveling» coexists with unjustified claims of independence, self reliance and uniqueness. But they are unattainable and even ethereal, since the «umbilical cord» that connects a person with his native culture is severed. *History knows no examples of a person, who has lost ties with the culture of his own people and his country, making significant contributions to world culture.*

Second, absolutizing achievements of national culture is rather paradoxical in a moral sense, when it is compared against other (usually not Western or

U.S.) cultures of «non famous» nations; and boundless apologetics of all, without exception, «native», »own» or «homegrown». We are witnessing not simply stupidity («Georgians are ancestors of all Europeans», «Ukrainians are primogenitors of all modern nations», etc.). Such claims not only do not enhance, but they discredit these culture. But even more «tastefully» designed claims (who is more ancient: Armenians or Azeris, Tajiks or Uzbeks; did Kazakhs have their own state thousand years ago, etc.), in the final analysis, do not clarify, but only confuse the truth, distort history, filter the facts and transform the highest achievements of humanity − knowledge, culture, and information − not into a force of good, but into a source of confrontation and mistrust between peoples.

Finally, a phenomenon of «occulture» (pseudo culture) *is worth mentioning,* when spiritual life of society is being filled with things that traditionally were censored by morality: obscenity, human vices, sex exploitation, showcasing perversions and demonization of lifestyle and behavior. Carriers of this culture camouflage their pretensions by an alleged desire to get rid of «unjustified» taboos, to show human life in its «entirety». However, in reality, they do it for financial gain, − fact champions of these ideas prefer not to mention.

Thus, reference point of paradoxes of morality in spiritual sphere is a contradiction between natural human needs of spiritual enrichment and means of their satisfaction. Since latter are in the hands of various subjects of cultural life, they use different ways, forms and methods of influence − from logically justified to «substitutes», so they can cover egotistical, selfish purposes and aspirations. Society's problem lies in a fact that the number of deformed, warped methods increases, which is reflected in paradoxical nature of moral consciousness and behavior.

Sometimes, in assessing the state, trends and future of morality, paradoxical conclusion of American philosopher A. Whitehead is cited: «...a literal adherence to the moral precepts scattered throughout the Gospels would mean sudden death» (Whitehead A. N. 1990 *Russ. Ed.* P. 405). In our opinion, A.A. Guseinov's is correct, partly agreeing with this conclusion (he thinks it is applicable only to certain requirements of a number of world religions), but convinced that the author is not quite accurate in his interpretation of the moral precepts of great world religions (Guseinov, Apresyan. 1995. P. 263). Yes, these precepts are a goal, an ideal we should strive for. Reality, which never coincided and will never completely match these precepts, is another matter. But it does not mean that they should (and can) be ignored and not observed − rather, efforts should be directed at reducing a gap between existent and what should be. We cannot wait for the «new Russians», saturated with infinite riches stolen from society, to decide to «share», participate in meeting social needs, or promoting scientific and cultural development. We have no illusions about possible changes in their moral consciousness (although some rave reviews of oligarchs charitable acts have already appeared); society is called upon to strengthen social morality, utilizing economic and social levers.

Therefore another assertion is fully justified: moral assessment of people and moral evaluation of social systems are different, diverse, may not coincide and, moreover, might generate contradictions, conflicts and paradoxes. Moreover, these estimates may seriously differentiate depending on which criteria are utilized in economy, politics, and science (Guseinov, Apresyan. 1995. P. 270). In the process of societal development, however, not only moral consciousness and behavior, but also moral paradoxes become more complex, enriched and modernized.

References

Aleksandrova T. L. *Al'ternativy ekonomitsheskogo povedeniya. Tshelovek v perekhodnoy ekonomike (Alternatives of Economic Behaviour. A Person in the Transitive Economy.)* Ekaterinburg, 2000.

Dialog kul'tur v globalizipuyushchemcia mire: mirovozrencheskie aspekti (Dialog of Cultures in Global World: Ideological Aspect) / Pod red. A.A.Guseinov and V.S.Stepin. Moscow, 2005. P. 270.

Dinamika tsennostey naseleniya reformiruemoi Rossii (Dynamics of Values of the Population of Russia Being Reformed) . Moscow, 1996.

Guseinov A.A., Apresyan R.G. *Etika (Ethics)*. Moscow, 2001.

Guseinov A.A., Apresyan R.G. *Velikiye moralisty (Great Moralists)*. Moscow, 2001. P. 37.

Ivanov V.V., Komlev J.J., Tolchinski L.G. *Tshelnotshniy biznes v Kazani («Shuttle» Business in Kazan')* // Sotsiologhicheskiye issledovania. 1998. No 11.

Ovidius. *Metamorfozy (Metamorphoses)*. Moscow, 1977. P. 170. (4)

Panarin A. S. *Rossiyskaya intellighentsia v mirovykh voinakh i revoliutsiyakh XX veka (Russian Intellectuals in World Wars and Revolutions of the XXth century)*. Moscow, 1998.

Popova I. M. *Povsednevnyie ideologhii. Kak oni zhivut, meniaiutsa i istshezaiut (Daily Ideologies. How They Live, Evolve and Disappear)*. Kiev, 2000.

Timofeev L. *Tenevaya ekonomika (The Shadow Economy)*. Moscow, 2000.

Whitehead A. N. *Selected Works on Philosophy (In Russian)*. Moscow, 1990.

Chapter 16. **Paradoxes of religious consciousness**

The more perfect is God, the less perfect
is a man.

Erich Fromm (1900–1980),
German-American psychologist and
sociologist

The weather is better in paradise, but the
company is more interesting in hell.

Wojciech Jaruzelski (b. 1923),
President of Poland (1989–1990).

Religious consciousness is a rather specific kind of social consciousness.
At the dawn of human history religious consciousness was identical to social
consciousness. Influenced by unknown natural phenomena, not knowing and
being incapable of explaining these phenomena, unable to foresee the future,
people started searching for those forces that would take care of them, protect
them, give hope and support them in their confrontation with the outside world.
«Fear created gods» – this statement is not far from truth, for uncertainty,
unpredictability of events in private life and in community had always frightened
humans, forced them to seek opportunities to ensure balance, stability and
rationality of their existence. For thousands of years religion, in its different
forms, was at the core of moral-psychological experience of millions of people;
it determined their perception of the world and served as a reference point for
daily behavior.

Gradually, all-encompassing, all-pervasive influence of religious
consciousness began to weaken. However, separation of social consciousness
from religious influence was an extremely slow, inconsistent and contradictory
process. In fact, even science prior to the New Age was considered from the
standpoint of recognition of primacy of religion. «Science, – stated R. Bacon, –
which has no connection with Christian doctrine, leads to an infernal darkness».
Moreover, he argued that philosophy should prove the truth of Christian teaching
(Quoted in: *Gnoseologia v sisteme filosofskogo mirovozzrenia...*, P. 95). Impact of
religion, as V.I. Garadja rightfully asserts, affected practically everything: up
to the Renaissance period a person « had to be religious in order to be well-
educated» (Garadja. 1999). With regard to daily life, this influence remained
undisputed until $19 - 20^{th}$ centuries.

At the same time anti-clerical movements (heresy, sects) and concepts rejecting orthodoxy (deism, pantheism, agnosticism, skepticism), which paved the way for emergence of atheistic teachings, laid the first doubts in the veracity of religious doctrine (in case of Christianity). However, especially significant for the Reformation of religious consciousness has been the emergence and spread of Protestantism (16th century), which did away with ambiguity of «natural theology» of Thomas Aquinas, drawing a distinct demarcation divide between religion and other forms of culture – morality, philosophy, politics and, above all, science (Mitrokhin. 2000). The greatest significance of Protestantism manifested itself in the fact that, unlike other attempts to reform Christianity, it has become property of hundreds of millions of people, practically turning into a guide to morality of impending bourgeois era and playing a tremendous role in the development of capitalist society.

Simultaneously, during that period of time, doubts about the primacy of religion over science, about effectiveness of their interaction for cognition of the universe were growing progressively stronger. «A mathematician would argue mistakenly, – wrote M.V. Lomonosov, reflecting on impossibility of understanding diversity of the world, using only one set of instruments or means, – if he thinks he can use a compass to measure Divine Will; yet, a theologian is incorrect either, if he thinks the Book of Psalms can help him learn astrology or chemistry». Similar attempts to draw distinction between science and religion, scientific and religious outlook were undertaken by many scientists, including a significant contribution from French scholars of the 18th century Enlightenment period. This emancipation from overwhelming religious influence, triumph of criteria and standards of scientific knowledge was reflected in a proud response of P.-S. Laplace to Napoleon's question, why he did not leave a place for God in his system of knowledge: «I had no need for this hypothesis».

In 19th and 20th centuries assessment of faith and its role in human life has undergone serious changes. Criticism of religion, which most expressively and consistently sounded in writings of French Enlightenment period, was later extended, expanded and led to active opposition to various manifestations of religious consciousness. It was during this period that the process of secularization of society was clearly delineated, which found its reflection «in blossoming positivism of Comte, Mill, Spencer, so devastating for theology, in Tomas Huxley's agnosticism, Haeckel's monism and various forms of vulgar materialism, Marx's uncompromising atheism, Dewey's «naturalism» and other critics of religion, ending with Nietzsche's gloomy statement «God is dead!» (Mitrokhin. 2008).

Simultaneously, during these centuries actual atheistic (in the proper sense of the word) theories had appeared, purposefully and specifically criticizing dogmas and canons of the Church. Crisis of religious consciousness in many respects contributed to numerous sectarian and heterodox movements in all religions, without exception. But all these objections, direct or indirect criticisms of theological outlook, one way or the other originated in proclamation and then realization of the principle of freedom of conscience, which emerged under the conditions of despotism of all religions, by fire and sword imposing and defending their world outlook. The essence of freedom of conscience has deep social and historic significance, for it was not limited to an opportunity for critically minded individuals to profess «another religion», but had reflected the struggle for democratization of society, liberation from religious regulations, covering not only the way of thinking, world outlook and perception, but also all kinds of human activities – spiritual, economic, political and social (Loginov. 2005). Moreover, this was a struggle not only against absolutism and monarchy blessed (sanctioned) by religion, but also against possible manifestations of dictatorial and totalitarian regimes always aimed at strict regulation of public and private life. Proclamation of freedom of conscience meant a protest against belittling of the role and value of human beings, against the notion that «a man is a worm and a slave in front of God». This criticism in its own way expressed a new dominant of the times: each person is an active participant and creator of the historical process.

Comprehending the process of man's relationship with God continued in the 20ᵗʰ century, significantly multiplying and expanding attempts to resolve existing contradictions between science and theology. In that sense, the emergence of «dialectic theology» in the 1920's was a particularly significant development (K. Barth, R. Bultmann, R. Niebuhr, P. Tillich, etc.) (*Relighiya i politika...., 1994*).

During this period important changes were taking place in mass religious consciousness as well. Characterizing them in brief, it should be noted that this consciousness, firstly, gradually narrowed the region of its influence; secondly, it differentiated, atomized to the point of emergence of rival movements within the same faith; thirdly, it modernized, since it could neither be maintained, nor could it survive in its old form; fourthly, to a certain extent, it was secularized, saturated with elements of civil consciousness.

But in various countries and different societies these processes evolved in their own, sometimes uncharted and unbeknown ways. In the history of functioning of religious consciousness, the Soviet Union, where the relationship between religion and state acquired dramatic character is no exception. In post-soviet Russia, mutual relationship between secular and religious authorities became rather peculiar and at times paradoxical.

16.1. Religiousness in modern-day Russian society

In soviet times religion was ousted to the periphery of public life, its institutions were forbidden to pursue independent social (even charitable) activity. This rejection of church and clergy led to mass repressions, tragic fate of many religious figures and all sorts of bans and restrictions. Militant atheism was imposed as a mandatory condition in all spiritual spheres — education, literature and art. All this (along with other political and ideological actions) ultimately led to far-reaching negative consequences such as moral degradation, oblivion of many spiritual traditions, and break in continuity, growing intolerance and lawlessness.

Relationships between religion and society (state) began to change in the second half of the 1980's, during perestroika, and continued intensively in the 1990's, giving rise to the so-called religious Renaissance. Significant increase in the number of religious communities was its most obvious result. As of January 1, 2005 there were 22144 of them in Russia. According to tentative data, approximately 50 to 55 million Russians consider themselves Orthodox, 15 to 18 million — belong to various forms of Catholicism and Protestantism, 10 to 12 million — to Islam. However, sociological survey data in the second half of 1990's show that peak increase in numbers of believers' (or, rather, those who declared their faith) took place during the first half of the 1990's; then, in recent years, it stabilized and started to decrease.

Nowadays, there are ongoing debates about whether Russian society and the population of our country became more religious as a result of ongoing changes or if strong secular beliefs bordering on disbelief and atheism still remain strong. Statistical information related to the number of believers, number of parishes and their material base cannot answer this question. At the same time, however, efforts to calculate, for example, numbers of Muslims by adding all representatives of Islamic nations: Tartars, Bashkirs, Circassians, etc. — do not hold water, neither do Orthodox Church aspirations to add all those visiting churches or monasteries during religious holidays to the number of believers. That can only be estimated based on extensive and thorough research, including sociological analysis of the state of real religious consciousness. And this analysis demonstrates that people have become more open in expressing their views, and many of them have changed their attitude toward religion (*Nezavisimaya gazeta.* September 12, 1992).

Currently, we are witnessing mass participation of people in religious celebrations, in ritual processions, massive attendance of all kinds of consecrations, of each and every event. The fact that people consider themselves to be involved in religion (Christianity, Islam, Judaism or other religious persuasions) is also supported by sociological studies: 50 to 55% of interviewed answer affirmatively about their belonging to a faith (depth and degree of their faith is not analyzed here). This is also confirmed by growing number of baptisms (anointing), religious weddings and funeral services. We all had an opportunity to observe gradual establishment of correlation between what was concealed in the depths of private lives, personal preferences, orientations and their real manifestations in the form of open participation in observance of religious rites, or simply in the fact of interest in religion. This was facilitated by removal of all barriers in the way of realization of the right of freedom of conscience. Huge numbers of people are willing to join various religious communities. The state returned many religious buildings, places of worship and a portion of previously confiscated property to the church. Monasteries were revived, spiritual literature and periodicals of many religious denominations gained wide circulation.

However this very openness has generated both new contradictions and new paradoxes of religious consciousness, which quite naturally raise another relevant question: *what is going on in the country — is Russian society turning religious or atheist?*

Supporters of the opinion that clericalism is on the rise in the country, are convinced, as G. Vdovin, that: 1) there is a complete and total property transfer to its former owners. Moreover, the church is now laying claims to the property that had never belonged to it even in tsarist times, when it was administered by local parishes or the Ministry of the Court; 2) large-scale «clericalization of childhood» is implemented by means of organizing Sunday schools and patronage of children's institutions by the church; 3) there is a process underway of clericalization of governmental bodies, which is reflected not in the fact that we always see officials of different levels attending various religious ceremonies, but in the fact that every controversial issue is inevitably solved in favor of one religion or another. In doing so, decision makers are not guided by law, but by desire to create most favorable conditions for religious cults in everything, everywhere and always. And finally, introduction of new unofficial censorship, not permitting any statements against clericalism, causes alarm as well (*Nezavisimaya gazeta.* September 12, 1992).

But what is really happening in Russian society, in religious consciousness of its citizens? Both secular and clerical authorities are trying to find an answer to this question. With regard to secular authorities, they (including official representatives) display maximal goodwill (often formal) and willingness to be most helpful, to do everything possible for the church to help it express itself and find its rightful place in building of civil society in Russia. At that, present secular government can justifiably be reproached for flirting with religion, as well as for rather vulnerable position of betting on Russian Orthodox Church at the expense of other faiths. What about the intention of the Ministry of Education supported by the presidents of both Russian Academy of Sciences and Russian Academy of Education with backing from the Rector of Moscow State University to introduce a required course in theology in all universities of the country!

As far as the church authorities, in this regard a document approved by the jubilee Bishops' Council of Russian Orthodox Church in 2000, entitled «Basics of Social Concept» is of particular interest. This document made a belated, but still important attempt to harmonize positions of the church and the state, based of a full account of the real processes taking place in modern Russian society. It delineates the issues of the state and church interaction and formulates rational ideas regarding the ways of their cooperation, which permit to dissociate church canons from eventual influence of both — state totalitarianism and open clericalism. Despite the importance of this document, it is not adequate to real life. Expressed aspiration to harmonize relations between the state, society and church does not safeguard religious consciousness and behavior from paradoxes.

16.2. The new guise of the old paradoxes

Changing situation in Russia's public life has resulted in a clash of different, sometimes mutually exclusive social positions, value orientations, regulatory requirements and attitudes in social consciousness of the population. It could not have left religious consciousness unaffected. However, processes occurring in this sphere are rather peculiar, and their comprehension can be approached from various perspectives. In our opinion, contradictions and paradoxes, which have acquired new forms while preserving their old content, are of particular interest.

First paradox: despite all the statements regarding religious Renaissance, level of religiosity has changed little, signifying involvement of the majority of population in religion merely on a verbal level. To prove this point let us compare data from 1960 and 1970's with that from 1990's. Thus, in early 1970's level of religiosity (number of believers and undecided) in the republics of the Volga region, Northern Caucasus and Central Asia ranged from 40 to 60% (in some Muslim areas up to 80%) (Pivovarov. 1976). E. Kublitskaya, who studied 1988 levels of religiosity in Tadjik SSR, in Lviv *oblast'* (region) of the Ukraine, Northern Ossetian republic and Kemerovo *oblast'* of Russia cites virtually the same results. Her research has shown that this level was at 23% in the Kemerovo *oblast'*, rising to 70% in Lviv region. In other words, almost half of the population admitted their attachment to religion, which disproved the myth of the USSR as society of «mass atheism» (Kublitskaya. 1990, p.34). This information, however, was «closed» and labeled «for official use only». Official «guardians» of socialist ideology could not even entertain an idea that Soviet society was a society of mass atheism only conditionally subject to interpretation. At the same time, careful analysis of 1990's data shows that level of religiosity has remained virtually the same — only about half of respondents identified themselves as believers to a varying extent (table 16.1).

Table 16.1.

Level of religiosity (self-identification)
(% of respondents. N = 2100)

Consider themselves	1989	1991	1996	2000	2006	2007
Not religious (atheists)	53	40	43	35	26	33
Orthodox	20	34	44	52	61	56
Muslim	5	6	3	4	6	4
Believers of other faiths	9	10	1	1	2	1
Hard to say or no answer	18	10	9	8	5	6

Source: Institute Sozialno-politicheskikh issledovanii RAN (Institute for socio-political research. Russian Academy of Sciences); Public Opinion — 2007. Moscow. Levada-Center. 2007. P. 193.

Sociological surveys of specific social groups and strata yield an even more complex and ambiguous picture of religiosity. As for intelligentsia, almost every second person employed in engineering and technology, educational or cultural spheres consider themselves to be religious; 36% of young people (under 25) believe that faith is important for them (24% of 35 year olds).

Indicators of religiosity are also peculiar among students. According to an All-Russian survey conducted in 1994 (when interest in religion was on the increase) by Sociological Center of State Committee for Higher Education of Russia, 30% of the students believed in God, 20% in the supernatural, while 32% of them sympathized with religious movements of other persuasions (*Poisk.* 1995. No 12. April 22-28). 1999 survey of the students of State Humanitarian University of Russia showed that 52,4% of undergraduate and 70% of freshmen considered themselves believers (17,5 and 33% of them respectively — to be partial believers). Interestingly, the same question addressed to the faculty of this university yielded similar results — roughly the same number of believers and partial believers (60%) and the same number of non-believers and those hesitant in their attitudes toward religion (*Sotsialnyi status i imidzh...*2001). In other words, for the entire fashion and religious craze the scope of disbelief and uncertainty remains significant, and in many respects not much different from previous Soviet era. This once again demonstrates conservativeness, stability and inertia of social consciousness, which changes, reconstructs very slowly. In our opinion, objective process of its sacralization, as well as secularization or modernization should neither to be constrained, nor accelerated.

Second paradox is not less revealing: social consciousness, despite external display of religiousness, continues to remain basically secular, since popular attitudes toward the church and its guidelines have hardly changed. Thus, it is highly doubtful that there is a religious revival taking place in Russia. According to academician L.N. Mitrokhin, the main reason for the surge of interest in religion was not «positive» religious values, but «rejection of former authoritarian, coercive ideology», desire to defend spiritual and philosophical autonomy. However, rejecting dogmatic, rigid Soviet system, people did not rush into a tight embrace of another, confessional one, giving no thought to what religions they were ready to accept, preferring the term «a believer in general» (Mitrokhin. 1995). An illustrative fact: 40 to 60% of the population call themselves believers. But only 5–10% perform required rituals (prayer, regular church attendance, etc.). A curious fact was also noted by sociological studies: rising number of not only «believers in general», but also that of supporters of strange eclectic beliefs: parapsychology, UFO cult, all sorts of neo-pagan notions or astrology.

Position of intelligentsia in this situation is even more striking. »Religious boom», affecting mainly and primarily those working in cultural sphere, reflected intelligentsia's susceptibility to all kinds of religious fads. And frequently it was not a genuine conversion (intensely personal, deeply affecting the entire spiritual system of a person), but either a tribute to fashion, or decoration, a staged performance dictated by purely prosaic, for instance, political interests and ambitions, – not an inner faith, but some posture, aimed at producing an external effect. It is not genuine religious revival, but «religious thrill», when «symbolic forms of divine worship have replaced the real search for the Kingdom of God» (N.A. Berdyaev).

Data received with the help of sociological estimates of opinions obtained in an all-Russian survey may help answer the question: how deep– seated is religion in the flesh and blood of the people? Thus, respondents were asked: «Do you consider yourself Orthodox?» In 1993 50% of respondents considered themselves as such. But how accurate is this indicator? Should we assume that such declaration is synonymous with being a true Orthodox believer?

«Public opinion» foundation surveys have shown that a significant part of people regard Orthodoxy as one of the traditional elements of Russian culture and spiritual life of society, and therefore consider themselves believers, but no more that 7-10% of them participate in church life in strict accordance with the canon. Results of the VTsIOM survey (table 16.2) are even more modest.

Table 16.2.

Frequency of attendance of church services by Russians
(% of respondents, N = 1600).

Frequency of attending services	1991 (N = 3000)	1994 (N = 2957)	1999 (N = 2404)	2003 (N = 1600)	2007 (N = 1600)
Once a month or more	5	7	(5,7	7	8
One to several times a year	20	28	17,8	30	34
Less frequent	–	21	15,7	18	18
Did not attend (less than once a year)	65	44	60,8	46	40

Source: Monitoring obshchestvennogo mneniya: economitseskiye i sotsialnye peremeny (Russian Public Opinion Monitor) . 1995. No 2; 1999. No 1. P. 86–87; Public Opinion – 2007. Moscow, Levada-Center. 2007. P. 193.

In other words, more detailed analysis shows that the position of Russians that consider themselves orthodox, most likely has cultural and historical nature, rather than strictly religious one. Such self-determination (self-attribution) indicates massive demand for national-cultural identity. New historical context of social and cultural development of society puts people in situation of choice: either find a way out of the crisis in the sphere of values and models for Russian culture, or follow the path of borrowing, guided by idealized Western standards of thinking and vital attitudes. The majority of Russians see the solution to the problems of spiritual life in continuity and preservation of accumulated cultural heritage.

Logic of cultural development, in general, requires a special social mechanism (in this case, it is clearly illustrated by the example of Russian culture) aimed at preservation and reproduction of its underlying structure. Logic of traditional society, i.e. society aimed at stability, is the basis of this mechanism. Tension arising in social consciousness in a time of crisis makes individuals and specific communities replicate previously formed ideals, as well as aspiration for these ideals. But even in this case it is still necessary to clearly understand that culture in general and art in particular should be above not only purely national, but also of confessional values.

In such transitional period, religion claims to embody constancy and continuity of cultural and moral traditions. Associating themselves with

Orthodoxy or other denominations, people are trying to find a psychological «refuge» in religion and church. According to sociological data, credibility of the Orthodox Church is much higher than confidence in other official and unofficial institutions of power. However, degree of trust is not a guarantee or an indicator of deep belonging of all, without exception human beings to religious teachings, rituals and rites and, moreover, it is subject to fluctuations (see table 16.3).

Table 16.3.

Are church and religious organizations trustworthy?
(N = 1600)

Assessment	1997	2000	2005	2007
Quite trustworthy	38	38	44	41
Not quite trustworthy	22	21	23	19
Not trustworthy at all	10	13	11	13
Hard to say	30	28	22	27

Source: Public Opinion — 2007. Moscow. Levada-Center. 2007. P. 193.

According to «Public opinion» foundation (1993), 57,6% of «orthodox» never confessed or received communion, 44,1% among them never read the Gospel — the main teaching of Christianity. Our «orthodox» are convinced, that the Gospel is read as a secular book, therefore 43,1% replied they »read it long time ago» or «read and re-read it recently». They read Gospel as a novel or historical chronicles, i.e. from beginning to the end, or in several installments. The same is applicable to the knowledge of prayers, as well as praying and presence of religious literature in people's homes.

So, what is Orthodoxy to those, who consider themselves believers? Most likely, it is a symbol, associated with something traditional, stable, perhaps with «old» Russia, as a contemporary person imagines it: a country, where peasants were farming, industrialists engaged in manufacturing, merchants — in trade, intelligentsia dealt with philosophical and political issues. There were many churches, monasteries, miracle-working icons and relics of saints. People lived in «fear of God», which they later lost. So, the unifying role of Orthodoxy as a «new» ideology, «leading and guiding» force will help revive Russian people and Russia. But this desire is too vague, since it is not accompanied by a conscious decision to change one's way of thinking and way of life. Moreover, to a certain extent, it is primitive, since it simplifies complex problems of societal life. Idealizing the role of religion tends to intensify confrontations within society, rather than harmonize social relations.

No less indicative is the paradox associated with refinement of religiosity, or finding the answer to the question of validity and extent of faith. Sociological data show that it is still very difficult to sort out who really is a believer and who is not. But, at the same time, they indicate that a person, depending on the situation, might associate oneself with both, i.e. to be both a believer, and a non-believer.

This paradox is compounded by primitive division of people into atheists and believers. Such simplified gradation leaves out important differences and nuances in the interpretation of faith and atheism and allows the same people to declare themselves, depending on the situation, either involved or uninvolved with religious canons. And they do not particularly (if at all) go against the truth and their own conscience. During Soviet times, secular way of life, conformist attitude toward official anticlerical positions, episodic involvement in ethnic (and quite often religious) rites for many people served as evidence (criterion) of their atheism. Yet, under different conditions in connection with altered official position in regard to religion, these same people, with the same attitudes and ideas began to treat their incidental, episodic involvement with symbols of faith as rejection of atheism and acquisition of religious consciousness, which before had to be, allegedly, hidden or not displayed.

It is paradoxical, that in both cases people were sincere in their attitude towards religion. They were not even bending the truth, since both views could be interpreted either in favor of religion or against it depending on prevailing circumstances.

In our opinion, much more accurate are those indicators of the state of religiosity, which are expressed in more flexible terms: «I believe», «I partly believe» («go back and forth»), «I am not religious» and «I am not sure». This approach allows to identify and to more clearly represent the state of religious consciousness. Data of a VTsIOM survey, when a more flexible verification of popular involvement in religious worship was applied, confirms this assumption (table 16.4).

Table 16.4.

Which of the following statements reflects your attitude towards God now and in the past?»

(% of respondents) (November, 1997, N = 2401)

Evaluation	2002	2005	2007
Very important	8	44	41
Most important	21	27	26
Mostly not	36	39	41
Not important at all	32	21	24
Hard to say	3	2	3

Source: Public Opinion — 2007. M. Levada-Center. 2007. P. 194.

In our view, present situation with religiosity can be described as a rather specific phenomenon — *«greenhouse effect»* — characterizing the features of religious consciousness of the past quarter century: if *in 1960-1970's atheism was «clouded»*, since not only genuine non-believers, but also those who only partly shared this ideology classified themselves as atheists (following official orientations, most probably due to conformist reasons); the segment of faith remained «pure», because to declare their association with religious faith, to a certain extent, was an act of civic courage. *In the 1990's, on the contrary, faith became «clouded»*, because in this period, not only the hesitant, but also conformists, reacting to the new fashion and wishing to meet the new standards, joined true believers. But there was «purification» of atheism underway, retaining only those, who actually followed the canons of atheist worldview (Vorontsova, Filatov, Furman. 1995).

Such correlation of these specific processes suggests that atheistic and religious outlooks were not as much irreconcilable alternatives, but «transformed» forms of social consciousness reflecting deep social conflicts that existed in Soviet society. And what is presently happening in the sphere of religion reminds of a game of give-away. Characterizing these processes, academician Mitrokhin writes: «both the authorities, and «oppositional» politicians widely use religious symbols and examples to gain a more attractive public image; even many secular authors advertise religion as the only true foundation for genuine morality as indispensable means of moral and spiritual revival. Meanwhile, today these problems are being discussed at a rather superficial, moralistic level; idealizing history of the church, deleting rich materialist and anti-clerical heritage, new myth are propagated according to the principle of the «opposite». Hence, professional understanding of «the religious factor» has become an essential need for the society, a condition for its successful renewal. As a result of the collapse of former idols and ideals there was growing confusion in people's system of beliefs; accelerated spiritual and moral barbarism of society, disintegration of the social fabric of living. Resulting vacuum was filled not only by the values of developed «civilized» religions, but also with various mystical and occult notions, Neo-paganism and all sorts of devilry» (Mitrokhin. 1995).

One thing is certain: in these conditions many of the old contradictions and paradoxes have not disappeared — they have only found a new form.

16.3. Possibilities and limitations of religious paradoxes

For the majority of Russians, lacking regular personal contact with the church has resulted in a distorted view of the social role of religion and level of their own religiosity. Most often religion is not viewed as a way to salvation, but as a certain form of social structure, capable of re-establishing and maintaining moral standards and spiritual values, which are so essential to society.

In the 1990's social consciousness, having rejected atheism and doubting its own position, was drifting towards recognition of usefulness of religion and religious morality both for society as a whole, and for each person in particular. According to VTsIOM data, in July 1991, 68% of the representatives of urban and rural population were convinced of usefulness of religion for society, and 58% of respondents — of its usefulness for themselves. Realizing that what is happening around (flourishing selfishness and cruelty, alcoholism, drug addiction, etc.) poses a threat of moral decay; people are trying to find a way out of this deep moral and social crisis. And they see one of the possible means in getting closer to the ideals of faith (Christianity, Islam, Buddhism, etc.), with examples of their effectiveness being found in popular historical memory, albeit in a somewhat idealized form.

Socio-political motivation of turning to religion is very strong: a desire to belong to a large social entity — nation, country, and homeland. In the minds of Russian people, church is such a big, strong structure capable of replacing disintegrating «State». If we compare VTsIOM data, in 1994 and 2006 (2400 respondents, sample representing socio-demographic, professional and residential structures of the population of Russian Federation) respectively 51,5% and 37% trusted Orthodox Church, while 19,7 % and 51% — president of Russia, 11,2% and 18% — government, and 13,1% and 18% trusted local (regional) administration. Desire for stability, steadiness and respect for traditions in a situation of collapse of habitual way of life and structures, without which a person cannot imagine his existence — all this leads him/her to seek any social and spiritual support available.

At the same time, recognition of high authority of religion and church coexists with certain pessimism (and, perhaps, with a sober assessment of reality). Answering the question, of whether a religious idea can unite the nation, in 1994, only 4,9% of respondents answered affirmatively, while in 2005 even less than that — 2,5%. How can this paradox, this contradiction be explained? On the one hand, the authority of the Church in contemporary Russian society is substantial enough to make people declare their religiosity, but, on the other, rejection of normative atheist attitudes as such does not indicate significant changes in vital practices of individuals.

As a rule, people discuss their religious preferences when influenced by stereotypes of mass consciousness. Recognizing oneself as a believer is in many respects caused by adherence to certain valuation standards that came to replace ideological taboos. Most people still do not have inner spiritual need or true religious motivation that brings a person into a temple (or a mosque): they have no established place in today's lifestyle. But there is something else — a strong focus on achieving benevolent social-spiritual relations between people.

In this connection it is necessary to mention several problems of atheism. In our opinion, atheists can be divided into those actively spreading their beliefs among other people, fighting (debating) against religious views, and passive atheists who do not impose their disbelief in higher power on others, do not try to convince other people of the correctness of their doubts (in religious postulates, etc.) and convictions. Analyzing sociological studies data from this point of view, we find no more than 7 to 8% of militant nonbelievers (atheists), but far more of those (skeptics, agnostics — up to 30–35%), who passively adhere to atheistic beliefs or to certain intermediate models between belief and unbelief.

Sociological studies of correlation between believers and atheists have revealed another paradox — recognition of being Orthodox does not mean recognition of being a «believer». Considering himself «Orthodox», a person, first, disassociates from other religions. Second, in most cases, self-identification with religious orientation of one's nation permits him to most closely bring together his ethnic and religious orientations. Third, a person who considers himself Orthodox (but not a believer) respects and worships holy places, symbolizing the essence and contents of «their» religion. He visits these holy places, monasteries, cathedrals, churches, chapels to pay tribute to national culture that, to a certain extent, is embodied in religious teaching, in art and worldly affairs of this confession.

And, finally, we should not exclude intuition and predisposition to accepting certain dogmas of the church that symbolize common sense and moral requirements guarded and preserved by time and by the people. In our view, it is this very approach that allows to more accurately, objectively and impartially determine the degree of popular religiosity, without opposing (contra-distinguishing) faith and unbelief. It is difficult, because between the positions of true believer and atheists there is a huge layer of intermediate attitudes, which have their own justification and qualitative determination. Alas, the temptation to enlist these intermediate groups in their own ranks is too great, which leads to improper «additions», falsifications, manipulation of the facts and distortion of the truth. Many adherents of religions are now busy faking such figures nowadays. But the question is: does religion really need this kind of help?

Current state of religious consciousness has generated another surprising paradox, which involves finding an answer to the question: what is of greater threat to religion — unbelief and atheism or crisis of various faiths themselves as well as the entire religious outlook? In our opinion, if we look deeper, we would realize that religion faces serious danger, which it previously had been less fearful of: developing internal contradictions that are far more dangerous than external obstacles. World religions — Christianity, Islam and Buddhism — are in a serious crisis. They are full of secession, new emerging religious movements, many of which are aimed at thorough revision of the original teachings. Moreover, this shift manifests itself in different forms and different aspects. Carriers of dissenting actions are usually active, aggressive and militant. It should be noted that these splits are nothing new; previously, however, they were suppressed either by the State or by the church itself. *Paradox of the situation in modern Russia lies in the fact that lifting of bans, which allowed official structures of all religious persuasions to develop rigorous activity, at the same time, contributed to successful «dissenting» and blossoming of non-traditional religions* (Mitrokhin. 2000. P. 214–215).

Growing interest in religion is accompanied by increased interest in unconventional and confrontational religious movements and sects. The roots of world religions are not so much undermined by atheists, as by supporters of various quasi-religious entities (cults, non-traditional religions, «totalitarian sects»): «Unification Church of S. Moon», «Society for Krishna consciousness», «The Church of Scientology», etc. Applying sophisticated psychological techniques, they harmfully influence the psyche of people and their personal consciousness, turning their followers into virtual robots. Such groups have also emerged on the basis of orthodoxy («Great White Brotherhood», «Our Lady's Center», «Vissarion group», etc.). However, most amateurish notions of them are widespread in society, and not without help from the media. Examples include publications about events in Kiev, in connection with «White brotherhood» or activities of «Aum Shinrikyo» (Supreme Truth). Unfortunately, people responsible for regulation and legal security of relations between the state and religious associations are also displaying this amateurism. In an effort to quickly merge Russia with the «civilized» world, they frequently mechanically copy laws of Western countries, ignoring the specifics of national culture, particularly its role in the development of Orthodoxy and Islam. Thus, in early 1990's any organization could almost automatically get registered, provided it claimed to be religious – whether it was peace-loving Quakers or terrorist «Ananda Marg». The result is obvious: it is cults like these that most rapidly spread their influence. While the number of their adherents is so far relatively small, but every supporter, follower of such sects (which are usually young people) is a fanatic, who's re-incorporation, return to society and often their family is extremely difficult. Activities of certain sects had a detrimental effect not only on religious consciousness, but also social order (for example, planned mass suicide in Kiev in autumn of 1993, activity of Satanist sects like «Southern cross», «Black Mask» and other similar forces). So, where does the real threat come from?

Propaganda of rationalism and atheism, penetrating the entire system of education and upbringing in Soviet society, was replaced by broad propaganda of various religions, religious faiths and beliefs to serve as panacea against lacking spirituality and humanity. Numerous «saviors» appeared under these conditions, usually to pursue their self-serving objectives, offering their own recipes out of spiritual crisis. Moreover, they were not unsuccessful, since as result a variety of such «inventions» as «Orthodoxy without church» have emerged, sacrificing all and everything, rejecting certain doctrines of faith and exaggerating the role and importance of religious symbols.

No matter how strange it might seem, but this very confusion and ambiguity, vagueness and weak positions of officially recognized religions have contributed to emergence of extremist movements such as Wahhabism in Islam or revival of Satanism in its struggle with Christianity. Defamation of religion in no small measure contributes to the rising outbreak of «love» for it on the part of current powers that be the «new Russians», «new Ukrainians», «new Kazakhs», etc., etc.

Another paradox of religious consciousness is mass demonstration of commitment to God, especially by the category of politicians and businesspeople that graduated from Party schools and who now are stone-facedly standing in temples holding candles in their hands. True, as noted by a well-known satirist, «they hold candles like drinking glasses». According to VTsIOM data, only 7% of respondents think that the big bosses really believe in God, whereas 73% are convinced that their actions are dictated by desire for self-promotion (17% refrained from answering) (*Poisk.* 1995. No 12. April 22–28). It is all the more surprising and distressing, since many of them had assiduously displayed atheist convictions in recent past. In other words, they are typically seeking «to conform» to standard way of life and behavior, which, in their view, is officially endorsed and supported, and therefore might become a major factor in their career advancement.

But this standard of conduct undermines credibility and trust in religion far more than militant atheism. In such situation, if people do not abandon canons of faith, they quite often begin to seek support in religion, endorsing various forms of sectarianism and dissent. Such response to cynical behavior of Russia's establishment combined with an assessment of conduct of present church hierarchy cannot but raise doubts both in the truth of religious dogmas and the sincerity of the subjects promoting these cults.

Processes taking place in religious consciousness are accompanied by phenomena, which are sometimes treated as *specific forms of secularization. We are referring to individualization of religious beliefs,* when people, professing certain religious ideology and sincerely sharing its basic postulates, adapt it to their personal world outlook. As a result, some of them might attach significance to some aspects of religion, while others — to another; some are inclined to observe their favorite holidays and rituals, while others chose other dates and favor other rituals and ceremonies.

A more in-depth and thorough analysis of the state of relationship between society and religion reveals another paradoxical issue, which may clearly manifest itself in the future, namely: will the new state of religious freedom turn into a desire to get rid of everything that stands in the way of religion, by force of arms? Are there guarantees that what happened in Bosnia and Herzegovina (where people, who speak the same language, destroyed each other based on religious grounds) will not happen in Russia?

A possibility of interference of religion in a struggle for power cannot be excluded either. For example, bloody events of civil war in Tajikistan are directly linked to the Islamic «Resurrection» Party and its leaders seeking power. But as soon as the true intentions of these «champions» of popular interests became apparent, numbers of party supporters fell from 30% to 5-6%. Whatever may be said, social consciousness is very sensitive to selfish motivations of religious hierarchy. Historical memory retains abundant evidence of how, after seizing power, ecclesiastics established bloody regimes. I think, that a wise decision of the Patriarchate of the Russian Orthodox Church prohibiting its clergy from involvement in political battles was dictated exactly by their concern about the credibility of the church and its future, for, as life has shown, participation in power struggle discredited religion, reducing its influence and role, untying the hands of those preaching «holy» wars (Toshchenko. 2007).

The fact that the church ignores opinions and suggestions of its well-meaning opponents among the intelligentsia, which has its own particular notions regarding religious heritage, does not contribute to strengthening positions of the church. A number of prominent cultural figures, none of whom could ever be suspected of disregard for religion, are alarmed, writing with dismay about the violation of the bounds of relationship between church and state, generally accepted in the entire international community; about the fact that in determining the fate of cultural and religious monuments, all controversial issues are resolved in favor of the church (transfer of such national treasures as A. Rublev's icons, Vladimir Divine Mother of God icon, etc.). In fact, these treasures are not only the heritage of the church, but also of the entire nation. By stubbornly insisting on getting their own way, does not church lose its most educated and enlightened supporters?

Most importantly, however, an idea gradually starts to take shape: will all the roads be open only for believers (as previously for atheists)? For genuine or pretend ones — is another question. Public demonstration of one's commitment to religion is now very fashionable. Will this turn into a situation, when in pursuit of an office or vote, religion will be utilized as means of achieving questionable goals, which ultimately will turn against it (religion)?

Lack of a worthy choice between faith and atheism is yet another paradox of modern social consciousness. For recognition of religion, faith in God does not mean absolute freedom of conscience. Hence, exaggeration and ambiguous interpretation of the role of religion leads to intolerance towards other people's positions, resulting in inside-out atheism, and, as a consequence in reinforcing clericalism in society. The danger is that the proponents of clericalism think only in terms of antinomy within the framework of judgments «sacred — secular», «sheep and goats», «saints and sinners », etc. Whether they like it or not, such supporters of any religion are consciously or spontaneously guided by highly questionable assertions, when in order to please certain interests a live tree of culture (and religion is a part of culture) is divided into reactionary and progressive, «acceptable and unacceptable», aggressively opposing each other and fully oblivious to ideas of integrity, unity of culture and own main purpose — to set an example of peace and tolerance for the entire society.

In other words, when from the paradoxes of 1960th, when society and individuals were considered to be atheistic, while essentially maintaining a high level of religiosity, we moved on to the paradoxes of 1990's, when it is fashionable to assert that society is revived by turning to high spiritual, including religious values, while in fact having changed very little. Unless, of course, we do not confuse interest in faith, recognition of its value, fashionable trends sometimes turning into frenzy with the religious phenomenon itself. The question is not, as Mark Bloch, an eminent French historian wrote «if we establish whether Jesus was crucified and then resurrected... It is important to understand how come so many people around us believe in Crucifixion and Resurrection» (Bloch. 1986. P. 21). Modern society, it seems, should beware of indiscriminate glorification of Jesus, Mohammed, Buddha, etc., for it deprives a person of faith in own abilities, strength and capabilities. Is it not better to follow traditions of early Christianity, Buddhism, teachings of Socrates or A. Schweitzer of practicing religion of reason, faith in man's ability to independently resolve life's conflicts and problems, insisting on finding moral compass within, instead of external guidance. This phenomenon, only in its original Russian version, was noted by M. P. Mchedlov, when, based on data of a nationwide sociological survey in 1997 (sample size 2200 persons in 60 cities, towns and villages), he concluded that not those who identified themselves as Orthodox, were believers. «Many people feel a connection with Orthodoxy by tradition and their mentality, according to a pattern of being or simply on the basis of stereotype: «Russian means Orthodox». When identifying their ideological outlook, the respondents, especially young ones that deny their religiosity quite often consider themselves Orthodox. This was the case with 56,2% of those undecided between faith and disbelief» (Cf.: Mchedlov. 1998; Mchedlov, Filimonov. 1999).

Another paradox lies in the fact that «religious revival» did not result in triumph of brotherhood, love and humanity, as L.N. Mitrokhin rightly pointed out, *on the contrary, causing «rapid moral and psychological savagery, disintegration of social fabric of daily life»* (Mitrokhin. 2000. P. 215).

So far there has been *no satisfactory explanation found for reasons why growing religiosity in society and interest in religion is accompanied by rampant crime.* In fact, based on not only arguments of fierce proponents of religion, but plain common sense, it should be the exact opposite. Yet it's not. And if we add the fact, that «civilized relations» are not even observed among many clergymen, contradictions and paradoxes of religious consciousness become clear. Mutual accusations, insults, falsification of opponents' views do not escape popular attention either (no matter how much church hierarchy would like that). Thus, nearly criminal conflicts among clergymen in the Ukraine, power struggles among hierarchy of Islam, Judaism, accusations of plagiarism of Ukrainian Orthodox Church in their preparation of «Basic Social Concept» — all this does testify not to the rise or the triumph of fundamental moral ideals, but vile manifestations of human nature.

This paradoxical situation is also exacerbated by the position of the state, because the law «On freedom of religion» was drafted by «amateurs lacking sufficient professional knowledge (at least in the field of religion) or ordinary everyday experience to understand all the complexity and multi-dimensionality of the problem and, perhaps, most importantly: every step that is not carefully thought through can result in grievous irreversible consequences not only for activities of the church, but also for millions people and, moreover, for entire society» (See for details: *Putyami nesvobodi*, 2005, p. 216).

All this suggests that there is no such thing as one-dimensional and unilinear impact of religion on people's life. Hence, paradoxes of religious consciousness not only existed, exist, but also, probably, will exist for a long time, displaying this quality especially dramatically during critical periods in history.

References

Bloch M. *Apologhiya istorii, ili remeslo istorika (Apology of History or a Historian's Craft)*. Moscow, 1986.

Garadja V.I. *Rech' na kruglom stole «Filosofia, kultura I obrazovania' (Speach at the round-table conference «Philosophy, culture and education»)* // Voprosy filosofii. 1999. No 3.

Gnoseologia v sisteme filosofskogo mirovozzrenia (Gnosiology in System of Philosophical World Outlook). 1983.

Kublitskaya E. *«Obzchestvo massovogo ateizma» glazami sociologa («Society of Mass Atheism» in Sociologist' Eyes)* // Nauka i religia. 1990. No 1.

Loginov A.V. *Vlast' I vera (State Power and Faith)*. Moscow, 2005.

Mchedlov M.P. *O relighioznosti rossiyskoy molodezhi (On Religiousness of Youth in Russia)* // Sotsiologhicheskie issledovaniya. 1998. No 6; Mchedlov

M.P., Filimonov E.G. *Sotsialno-politicheskie pozitsyi veruyushchikh v Rossii (Social and Political Positions of Believers in Russia)* // Ibidem. 1999. No 3.

Mitrokhin L.N. *Filosofskiye problemi religovedeniya (Philosophical Problems of Study of Religion).* Moscow, 2008. P. 214–215.

Mitrokhin L.N. Relighia i kultura (Religion and Culture), Moscow, 2000.

Mitrokhin L.N. *Relighioznaya situatsia v sovremennoy Rossii (Religious Situation in Contemporary Russia)* // Sotsiologhicheskiye issledovania. 1995. No 11.

Pivovarov V.G. *Nauchnye osnovy issledovaniya relighioznosti (Scientific Bases for Studying Religiousness).* 1976.

Poisk. 1995. No 12. April 22-28.

Putyami nesvobodi (By Ways of Non-freedom), Moscow, 2005.

Relighiya i politika v postkommunistisheskoi Rossii (Religion and Politics in Post-Communist Russia), Moscow, 1994.

Sotsialnyi status i imidzh gumanitarnoy intelligentsii (Social Status and Image of Humanitarian Intelligentsia) / Pod red. Toshchenko Zh.T., Kozlova O.N., Levicheva V.F. Moscow, 2001.

Toshchenko Zh.T. *Teokratiya: mif ili realnost' (Theocracy: Myth or Reality),* Moscow, 2007.

Vorontsova L.M., Filatov S.B. Furman D.E. *Relighia v sovremennom massovom soznanii (Religion in Contemporary Mass Consciousness)* // Sotsiologhicheskiye issledovania. 1995. No 11.

Part IV. Forms of paradoxes

Chapter 17. Elite: cliques, clans or castes?

He who sows privileges, reaps revolution

Claude Tillier (1801–1844)
French writer

In late 1990's the word «elite» and its various combinations such as «economic elite», «political elite», «military elite», «trade union elite», etc. was more and more frequently being used in Russian political vocabulary, in scientific and quasi-scientific literature. To a large extent, this was due to numerous discussions of who was now running Russia. These discussions were intentionally supported by those, who badly desired to be classified and regarded as elite, wanted people to talk about current problems of this elite. It was made-to-order, deliberate propaganda of groups and individuals, who had power or capital (or both), and were wishing to be more significant in the eyes of public opinion than just «mere» politicians or businessmen. But it is the journalists that made and keep making the biggest contribution to polishing, improving the image of those in power. Today it is hard to find any adequate analysis of political and economic life in a newspaper, social, political or economic magazine, radio or TV show, which does not persistently and sometimes importunately hammer in the message: those in power should be called elite.

Scholars, who started using this term without even giving it a second thought, are no less guilty. Perhaps, they bear even larger degree of responsibility than the journalists for incidental and intentional attempts to mislead social consciousness. So, let us focus on these notions (born in academic circles).

I would like to state my position: there is absolutely no such thing as modern or yesterday's elite in Russia. It is long gone and does not presently exist either. Using this term applicable to the present day situation in Russia means to consciously (or subconsciously) engage in falsification of existing reality, indulging low-down passions, and ultimately distorting the entire picture of contemporary life.

We all remember some of the biggest names in political corridors of power. Once popular, they vanished, disappeared into the oblivion. In their «glory» days, many of them managed to snatch their pieces of «privatization», «stock», «banking» pies, thereby paving their way to becoming «economic elite».

What is happening in this case? Yesterday they were elite, but today they are not? If you have money and power, are you elite? And if you lose them, even if you are a genius, you no longer belong to this select group, since there are only two criteria — financial and political leverage? Isn't that paradoxical? Let us examine it in more detail.

17.1. What is elite?

The word «elite», from French «elite», means the best, selected. In S.I. Ozhegov's «Dictionary of Russian Language» the term «elite» in relation to society is explained as «the best representatives of any part of society, or a group» (Ozhegov. 1991, P. 907). In the dictionary of Russian language published under the auspices of USSR Academy of Sciences elite is defined as «the best representatives of society or any of its segments» (*Slovar russkogo yazika.* 1981, Vol 4, P. 758). So why doesn't journalistic and scientific literature adhere to this widely accepted interpretation of the word?

Currently, among most analysts of social life (and political sphere in particular), status and functional approach in defining elite is especially widespread. For example, the famous American sociologist C.W. Mills (1916–1962) in his acclaimed «Power Elite» (translated into Russian in 1960s) claimed that elite are the figures occupying such socio-political positions, which give them the opportunity to rise above the ordinary environment and make decisions that have major consequences. This view emphasized the fact that those who occupy key positions in economy, politics and other spheres of public life are the elite. This, of course, is important. But status or position, as well as the fact that people in positions of power make decisions that determine destinies of nations and entire countries, should not be absolute. If we follow this logic, any tyrant (e.g. Pol Pot who destroyed a third of his country's population) should be attributed to elite: he made decisions that had «major implications» (!?). This position was specified by T. Dye, who believes that the term «elite» means: senior officials, who have formal authority in organizations and institutions, and dictate the rules of governance of life in the society. Such definitions of higher echelons of bureaucracy, in advance justifies all the actions undertaken by this group «in the interest of society».

To a certain extent many representatives of contemporary domestic thought share the status-functional approach. In their attempts to persuade society that the ruling class is this elite *per se,* they substitute and even misrepresent these notions, intentionally attributing conclusions and ideas to scholars who never used this term, for instance, Aristotle, Holbach, Montesquieu, More and others.

Scientific literature contains another, as a matter of fact, historically first interpretation — based on norms and values. This interpretation is derived from the original essence of the concept, rejecting or seriously questioning the fact that someone who holds a senior position in the power structure, or has financial resources is the «best», «select», «quality» person. Therefore, we should consider the opinion of V. Pareto (1848–1923), Italian sociologist and economist, who was among the first to introduce this term (he first used it in 1902). He wrote that in addition to having power and wealth, people claiming to belong to elite should possess certain qualities — valor, noble origin, personal dignity and art of governing. Unlike V. Pareto, Max Weber (1864–1920) did not focuse on particular traits and social status of elite but on the functioning of government institutions and political organizations, and on characteristics of those individuals who serve them, on professionalism — functional quality, which is inherent to all of them. Weber made an important conclusion that in various institutional orders we distinguish specific types of elites: political, economic, scientific, etc., and that the process of differentiation (autonomy) of elite is becoming a part of modern civilization. Later these ideas were particularly clearly expressed and further developed in the work of Spanish philosopher and social thinker J. Ortega y Gasset (1883–1955). He thought that people, who have intellectual or moral superiority and the highest sense of responsibility, should be attributed to elite. A. Toynbee (1889–1975), a well-known English philosopher and historian, repeatedly emphasized that creativity should be inherent in elite. In other words, formation of elite, in the opinion of this group of scholars, is a result of natural selection of the most capable, deserving persons of high moral character.

There is one more approach to the notion of elite — Machiavellian, named after a famous Italian politician and thinker, Niccolo Machiavelli (1469–1527). The essence of his approach lies in the recognition of elitism of any power, in rejection of the ideas of popular sovereignty and absolutization of domination and subordination. The underlying notion of his theory is the concept of eternal, original inequality and aspiration of the ruling groups to retain power by all possible means.

Summarizing the above, we may conclude that elite is comprised from representatives of society that possess not only economic, political or military power, but primarily certain social and moral qualities. Initial assumptions of modern domestic social thought, alas, in sharp contrast to the opinions of many Western thinkers hastily classifies those who have power and capital as elite, without, however, specifying the necessary level or amount of power and capital in order to be «selected».

These differing interpretations of elite became particularly noticeable in the assessments of Russian scholars when they began to rethink the new economic and political realities of the 1980–1990's Russia.

First of all I would like to note the works of G.K. Ashin (Russian philosopher), who was the first to describe the phenomenon of elite in Soviet social science (Ashin. 1985). However, in his works, especially in 1960-1970's, he studied elite only applicable to bourgeois society (he later started exploring this phenomenon in Russian society). He was analyzing one of the numerous theories of power — «theory of elites», which comprehended such phenomenon as political and moral domination of ruling strata in Western society. It should be emphasized that during this period Western European and American thought was developing other theories, which studied in detail problems of political democracy, pressure groups, establishment, bureaucracy, plutocracy, oligarchy and a number of other social phenomena related to the division of power and capital.

In domestic social and political sciences, when comprehending the new realities of post-reform Russia, the problem of elite did not immediately flood political science and sociological writings. Studies dedicated to analysis of political and economic power widely used such concept as «leadership» (E. B. Shestopal, V.D. Vinogradov, G.G. Sillaste and others). A leader is a person who is ahead, who rises above all others, who determines political guidelines. This term is neutral in relation to the evaluation of its carrier: it can be both positive and negative. Or contradictory, if a leader, in some of his activities, follows certain social values, while in others — contrasting guidelines, often opposite to the first. Different social groups may have different attitudes to such leader. Some of them might support him and become his allies in the implementation of certain actions, others might be in opposition. In this situation, a leader, carrying out governing functions, is supposed to insure maximum coordination, reconciliation of all, including opposite interests. In any event, a leader in politics and economics is a certain legitimate necessity. Institution of leadership is characteristic of the more stable society where people that set the tone in politics and economy reconcile the interests of the main social groups in a balanced and consistent manner, ensuring an orderly progress of development that meets the demands of the majority. Incidentally, people in these societies are not particularly keen on the word «elite», they believe it should be used with caution when applied to those in power. This notion should be used all the more carefully in societies that are at a crossroads. This is why this term can be applied in Russia only with certain stipulations.

Along with the notion of «leadership», many authors utilize the term «bureaucracy» to characterize relations of power (E.V. Okhotski, P.D. Pavlenok, V.G. Smol'kov, R.I. Khasbulatov and others). These author's theories are based on existing definitions of bureaucracy, thereby continuing and developing sociological traditions (notably Max Weber). They characterize bureaucracy as a social phenomenon, having both positive and negative features, constantly at serious risk of distancing of executive power from the real interests and needs of the people. Thus, those in power appear in front of us in controversial unity: on the one hand, bureaucracy as a social layer implements the instrumental, control functions of management, which are essential for the normal functioning of society, on the other hand, it is becoming a self-contained force, not accountable to the people and imposing on them its own understanding of political and economic realities.

Sometimes when characterizing the government the notion of «ruling class» is used (Yu.E. Volkov, N.A. Golovin, N.V. Romanovsky, V.T. Lipinsky and others). This balanced notion free from emotional coloration allows to impartially assessing the power, to formulate an objective attitude towards it, and to identify both positive and negative aspects of its activities. This is one of the more accurate options for the description of a functioning government in modern societies.

The term «nomenclature» — a synonym of the top Soviet ruling elite, was widely used in scientific and journalistic literature. This term is usually associated with the name of M. Djilas and later of M.S. Voslensky. Use of the term «nomenclature», on the one hand, more accurately reflects the essence, the intrinsic characteristics of top positions in the party and state of Soviet society and, on the other — indicates their (authorities) certain moderation, perhaps reservations in using the term «elite» and attributing certain exceptional qualities to themselves. But the value and the meaning of this term is great. Bulgarian sociologist, Yu. Kristeva, studying the phenomenon of power in post-socialistic countries, states that besides such concepts as «objective data», «system» and others, the notion of nomenclature concealed the mechanism of control over society, and therefore suited the top ruling groups (Kristeva. 1996).

Meanwhile we witnessed absolutization of the concept of «elite» starting in 1990's and its application in and out of context in the analysis of the ruling class. Gradually this concept started to be applied to all without exceptions individuals close to power or capital (O.V. Kryshtanovskaya, K.I. Mikulsky, L.V. Babayeva, I.E. Diskin, A.V. Ponedelkov and others).

Desire to find elite while analyzing any political and economic process led to the emergence of multiple new terms: *«regional elite»* (I. Kukolev, T. Ryskova), *«business elite»* (L.V. Babayeva, A.E. Chirikova), *«national elite»* etc, let alone exotic terms like *«criminal elite».* Aspiration to analyze political power as elite contributed to its broader interpretation. M.N. Afanasiev, for example, began to interpret elite not only as a group of people who possess considerable political power, but as a whole system of political, economic and spiritual parameters of functioning of social sphere of power (Afanasiev. 1996).

Absolutization and exaggeration of the importance of this phenomenon led to the fact that even historical aspects of functioning of the ruling circles in Russia were often viewed through the prism of elite. Thus, in her interesting work, O.V. Gaman-Golutvina analyzed the history of the ruling class of Russia, beginning with «boyars» and gentry and ending with bureaucracy of Russian Empire and Soviet nomenclature as a process of «elite-making». The author clearly articulated her understanding of elite as «a category of people, who have power, regardless of the factors leading to acquiring this power – background (origin), fortune, or accomplishments» (Gaman-Golutvina. 1998. P. 5).

Other authors define their positions in more restrained manner. Thus, E.V. Okhotski reveals a variety of approaches to the interpretation of elite phenomenon. He analyzes elite in both narrow and broad senses, together with other notions associated with this concept, such as «counter-elite», «near-elite environment», etc. (Okhotski, 1998. P. 166–167). V.N. Titov is even more cautious in his use of this notion: he believes that it is better to use the expression «ruling class», for it more accurately and objectively defines the essence of those in power (Titov. 1998). S.T. Minakov uses the notion of «Soviet military elite» applicable to those chosen by the time and circumstances to lead the troops (Minakov).

An all increasing stream of works on the subject of elite together with disappearance of other approaches to the analysis of ruling class indicates: sociology and political science are in the middle of the latest craze, similar to those, which in the past have already more that once afflicted scientific research (e.g. problems of lifestyle, social administration, economic reforms, etc.). However, excesses led to rejection, and sometimes discrediting of the very objects of these studies.

In addition, making one approach an absolute denies the right to existence of the other forms and types of analysis, not to mention the fact that they might provide significant, sound and compelling evidence of their applicability. Many of these types of analysis have the advantage of not embellishing reality, providing a more objective characteristic of those ruling our society (Tancher.1999).

Supporters of a broader, one-dimensional and formal approach to the notion of elite are also guilty of adhering (in their argumentation) to only one position of social philosophy that creates ideal models (why not assume that those in power are the wisest, most dignified, most intelligent, etc., etc.), and not to reality, reality, which is always very different from the idealized picture of the normative notion of elite. This reality most likely contains only a few details, some strokes at best, which cumulatively are far from abstract, hypothetical hopes for exclusivity of «the chosen» stratum.

In our opinion, there is one more very convincing argument, which is ignored by many of the researchers – taking into account the impact of macro- and micro factors (conditions) of the formation of elite. As V.V. Tancher, a Ukrainian scholar, rightly pointed out, «elitism blooms where poorly developed civil society is trying to compensate for the absence of its institutions. Theories of elite have been most prevalent in «catch-up» countries of Western civilization, at the outskirts of Europe, where the rule of clan communities hindered the development of civil society» (Tancher. 1999).

Finally, the vulnerability of the positions of those, who consider the entire top ruling political and economic group to be an elite, lies in the fact that the very essence of elitism contradicts the processes of democratization of society. It objectively leads to the emergence of various new forms of authoritarianism and totalitarianism, as well as to other restrictions on social life, as repeatedly noted by V. Pareto, G. Mosca and R. Michels. Proponents of the theory of elites do not notice this paradox, they ignore this contradiction, attempting to justify and combine the uncombinable, giving rise (with this logic) to a centaur-problem of attempting to reconcile conflicting values – democracy with elitism – a paradox concealing not just popular, but clan and caste interests as well.

This paradoxical reasoning is particularly clearly manifested when the composition of elite, its criteria, characteristics and functions are being defined. There are several approaches. The first one (V.F. Anurin, 1996) is based on self-identification, i.e. depending on who considers himself as part of this social group, this upper stratum of society (Anurin. 1999). The second approach (E.V. Okhotski, 1999) is based on calculating how many and what types of officials at the federal or regional levels, in ministries and agencies should be attributable to elite (Ashin, Okhotski. *Kurs elitologii*). Those supporting the third approach (L.V. Babayeva, 1995, 1997), without further ado, apply a loose but simple indicator: if you are rich, a businessman, a banker, a merchant, it means you belong to elite (*Rossiiskaya elita*). The same «criterion» is applied to political figures: if you are a party (movement) leader, a deputy or a senior official – you belong to elite. In our view, all these approaches are very vulnerable from the standpoint of qualitative definitiveness, from scientific point of view. None of them answer the question: do those individuals who allegedly belong to elite possess any of the essential characteristics that would actually elevate them above the rest, regardless of the thickness of their wallet or their political office, but based on the fact that they represent the values and intellectual orientations of Russian society.

Comparison of various perspectives (including foreign), allows us to make significant adjustments to characterization of essential features of elite, revive some forgotten or half-forgotten interpretations, comparing them with existing reality. *Summarizing all of the above* we can conclude that if elite is indeed the best, quality, select group of people, *first of all this means that it (elite) should serve higher interests of society*, without allowances or reservations, without any doubts that it first and foremost should defend national interests in the highest sense of this word, geopolitically and in solving domestic problems.

Second, elite demonstrates loyal, patriotic service to the entire society in major and minor, in visible and hidden, in work and on the battlefield, in a creative or everyday routine situation. In other words, it implies a constant display of citizenship, civic loyalty to the society in which we live and work.

Third, elite is characterized by adherence to the moral requirements, without lecturing or moralizing, by permanent manifestation of responsibility in all, without exception, life situations, by demonstration of personal dignity, particularly sovereignty of the individual, or, as M. Weber used to say, by possessing «ethics of beliefs», «ethics of society», qualities of being «politician by calling» (*Beruf*).

Fourth, elite is characterized by high level of intelligence, which helps rise above the ordinary and momentary and contributes to skillful, effective and rational solutions of life problems.

And finally, continuity in the formation of elite should be taken into consideration, since many of the skills have to be mastered for decades and over successive generations, whether it is British aristocracy or Russian nobility, dynasties of physicians, teachers, scientists or farmers.

Therefore, not just those who have power or capital belong to elite, but those who are characterized by a necessary set of civic and moral qualities, which allow to call such people, without exaggeration or deception, representatives of the best that mankind has accumulated in the course of its development, integral part of world civilization, rather than its distorted modification.

17.2. The realities of Russian «elite»

Judging the true features and qualities of modern ruling group, first we have to point out three major characteristics: two obvious — possession of power and capital, and one latent — a desire to rise above common people, deep down considering the other members of society — losers, or (which is even easier) — «cattle», incapable of anything worthwhile and only worthy of a whip and contempt (V. Novodvorskaya) (*Slovo ne vorobei...* P. 69). Based on this logic, some people believe that having a post in a power structure or being in possession of substantial financial (or other) resources is sufficient to be considered elite. This is taken for granted. And, unfortunately, hardly anyone questions this assumption. But, following the logic of this argumentation, let us see what do those people who are called, or who enthusiastically call themselves the elite really represent.

Usually the press and scientific literature describes *several groups of people that represent the high and mighty. Firstly, these are former Party, Soviet, Komsomol and economic leaders,* those who got «second wind» in market economy. Secondly, these are former players of Soviet shadow economy, experienced in underground, semi-legal businesses, whose chances to realize their aspirations before market economy were rather limited. Finally, a motley group of individuals seeking wealth, glory and fame — ranging from entrepreneurial risk seekers to adventurers, predators, all sorts of robbers and demagogues (the latter being active mainly in politics). But, can we call them elite?

Regarding the first group, undoubtedly, many former members of nomenclature started to depart from former orthodox positions of the official ideology even during early perestroika years, and began to lay the groundwork for future business or political activities. The key to their economic «success» was participation in the division of state property and their ability to snatch the best, tastiest piece of this pie, regardless of the rules of the game. Analyzing this situation, S. Magaril recalled the words of L.D.Trotsky's, who, from his Mexican exile, predicted that eventually the Soviet bureaucracy would seek opportunities to return to the institution of private property, which essentially has become the core of so called 1990's reforms (Magaril. 1999). And the more brazen one or another of these characters was in his aspirations, the more «benefits» he was able to «grab» for himself. In addition, this group (or at least its substantial part) was not burdened by moral principles. Moreover, it skillfully camouflaged personal and group interests as public ones. These people had no desire to serve public interests, although this desire was very well simulated and demonstrated, however, mainly on formal occasions, since their career depended on it. Intellectual potential of its representatives (knowledge, professional training and organizational skills) has often manifested in a rather peculiar way, obeying the laws of shadow accounting, double and triple bookkeeping. Similar processes took place in politics: the more people were criticizing socialist legacy the more opportunities they had to move up in the ruling elite. These people were characterized by mimicry, chameleon-like ability. Their main goal was to remain in power no matter what color it was: white, red or striped. The most important thing in life was to seize power or to be close to it, in order to have the right to attain the largest possible number of benefits and privileges.

Based on history tested traditions of selecting the best to the ranks of elite, these characters could not have remained in this group, since it recruited people from all walks of life, primarily based on political and ideological criteria. Yet, these criteria in their original essence could not (and can not) be true indicators of intellectual and moral development. So, is it possible to talk about «decency», «honor», «valor» and «the art of managing society» in reference to this group? Moreover, to use the word «elite»?

Second group — representatives of shadow economy, who during Soviet times gained a lot of experience in latent and camouflaged, essentially illegal business activities. With limited opportunities in the Soviet economy, they managed to acquire vast experience of deception, mimicry and chameleon-like behavior and fully transfer this «baggage» into the market economy. Moreover, many of the members of this group learned first hand that they cannot survive and stay afloat without improving these methods and techniques. Like many «underground» politicians former shadow men could not and cannot be considered elite. Many years of trying to combine desirable and appropriate, personal and official, adjusting and maneuvering engendered such type of consciousness and behavior, which in itself, in its original logic could not have brought out anything «good» or «selected» in these people. In this case, the term «elite» is hardly applicable, when the entire style of thinking and acting is intended to deceive, mislead and lie about their true goals and intentions. It became their second nature, which they could not escape, even when market economy transition was officially proclaimed and there were no more obstacles in the way of displaying, manifesting one's true self.

Another interesting phenomenon deserves closer attention, a specific type of paradox — shadow men and criminal elements are not satisfied with just material well-being any longer (what more could they want?); according to the results of election campaigns at all levels, they are heading for power structures. Members of various criminal organizations actively participated in parliamentary, gubernatorial, regional and local elections of 1999–2000. Many of them have actually been elected. By that logic, will we have to call a crime boss, not only deputy (senator), but also a representative of elite?

Regarding the third group, despite its diversity, its representatives are obsessed with one desire — to grab a bigger and fatter «piece», to win their place under the market economy sun, deceiving all people, near and far. What kind of moral qualities, ethics, and honesty are we talking about? There is a cruel and unscrupulous struggle for property and its redistribution. And only the most brazen, immoral, desperate risk takers survive, those ready to spare no one standing in the way of achieving their goals. Yes, they certainly displayed (and display) wonders of resourcefulness, efficiency, and ability to combine and calculate. But what does this have to do with elite?

Did not the gap between proper and existent, between reality and claims prompt the appearance of anecdotes about the «new Russians», whose intellectual «wealth» is reduced to a jargon, akin to criminal slang? And wasn't it them, who came up with the notion of «criminal elite» (??!) in an attempt to at least partially rehabilitate themselves? You would probably agree that it is better than gangster, robber, or mafia. These people behave similarly in politics. However, with one notable difference. If in economic sphere, they somehow demonstrated their practical skills, their ability to operate in market conditions, in politics; in their majority they displayed a complete inability to do anything specific, to organize any kind of activity. Few of them succeeded in implementing anything of significance. And how can such people be called elite, when yesterday they had absolutely nothing, but after a year (or even less) in power, say, a minister, a deputy minister or a senior official, now became owners of banks, foundations and companies with sky-high incomes?

Thus, the reality of Russian elite is very, very controversial, where the form truly does not match its content. The main objective pursued by those who have power or capital, is to retain (and multiply if possible) what they have, under any circumstances; to protect themselves from society, to do everything possible to keep people silent, patient and non-resistant to manipulation, particularly during elections. They do not necessarily seek support of the vast majority, which is essentially necessary to reach a consensus in the traditional sense; merely positive attitude to their claims and demands is quite sufficient. And of course, in any case, under any circumstances, their most important task is to retain power, preserve and increase their wealth, whatever the cost.

17.3. What should we call those who govern us?

If the above analysis leads us to reject the notion of ruling elite, then what should we call those who control our destinies, the present and the future of Russians?

Recognizing the problematic and paradoxical use of this term with regard to Russian realities, many researchers call this stratum other names, use other terms and notions. Most of the scientific and journalistic literature uses the word *«leaders»* or *«political leaders»*. In our opinion there are several reasons for using these terms. A *«leader»* is a person who actually performs administrative functions in one or another sphere of public life and has sufficient authority or reputation. *«Leaders»* are those people who are heads of certain organizations, enterprises, movements or social initiatives that have real influence on the processes, in which they participate. As a rule, these individuals tend to set the tone in politics and economics, make responsible decisions affecting the fate of other people or implement certain fundamental acts. But what kind of leadership can we be talking about in the country where all existing types of leaders of all levels and ranks are replaced with a kaleidoscopic speed: how can this mess embody the leadership phenomenon?

Sometimes when analyzing political and socio-economic life, people who run the country are called the *ruling group (class)*. This is a relatively balanced definition, free of emotional overtones. It permits to impartially evaluate their actions, to neutrally formulate an attitude towards them, to identify both positive and negative aspects of their activities. Finally, we should mention the term *«establishment»*, which is used in a lot of research, meaning the very top part of the ruling class in a given society. It too is emotion-free, just stating the fact of the existence or presence of a group of people ruling the country that hold all the main and decisive levers of power in their hands.

We should also mention such concepts «*political figures*», «*heads of...*» that are used when analyzing political and economic power. However, these notions have a very vague meaning; they are applicable to a wide range of politicians — from regional or municipal to the officials of country-wide scale, from those belonging to the ruling stratum to the opposition, from politicians addressing local problems to those of international level.

Paradoxically, those people and groups of people who are running economic and political affairs in Russia today have no right to be called elite. Such concepts as «cliques», «clans», and «castes» are most applicable to them, fitting their spirit, goals and methods of work. They describe specific social formations, cohesion of which is based on corporate consciousness and group, not public interests. To illustrate my thoughts let me remind you of the original meaning of these concepts.

A *clique*, in S.A.Efirov's opinion, is a group of associates, united to achieve unseemly and selfish purposes by any means possible (as an example, he considers financial, governing and courtier cliques). Sometimes a clique is associated with a fraction, whose main criterion is not the interests of society but the interests of local associations. Sometimes the term «clique» is used as a synonym of the word «gang». «Clique» is also a term for describing ruling groups illegally seizing power or possessing it without any legal and/ or moral grounds (*Sovremennaja zapadnaja sotsiologia.* P. 130). And in fact, how can we in good conscience say that any of the political or financial-economic groups in modern Russia represent vital public interests and needs? They certainly talk about it, claiming that they do. In fact, they do not really believe it themselves. Their constant assurances that if something is beneficial and useful to them, it is also beneficial and useful for society are a real measure of their cynicism. The spread of corporatism, group egoism is reaching such unbelievable proportions that it completely negates possibility of making reasonable decisions in the interests of society. Interests of cliques and interests of society never coincide.

As for the word «*clan*», one of its meanings is — «a closed group of people, who consider themselves «chosen», the best in a certain area» (Ozhegov, P. 276). Clans are formed on the principles of kinship, common origin, protectionism, or a closed inner circle, sometimes they could be based on occupational preferences. And in response to these claims, we witness emergence and functioning of other clans, also competing for power, but not based on a political concept or national idea, but on the principles of narrow tribal, group and selfish ambitions. It is these clan interests that are tearing apart the living body of many former Soviet states — both in Russia, in the Ukraine, and especially the Caucasus and Central Asian states.

Often clans are modified and transformed into *castes.* According to S.I. Ozhegov, caste is «a narrow social group that protects its privileges and interests, and to which access to outsiders is either difficult or impossible» (Ozhegov, p. 270). In fact many Russian closed joint-stock companies and open joint-stock companies (as stipulated by recent Russian legislation) are essentially castes, consisting of a narrow circle of people with links to criminal groups or shadow economy. Many of the so-called political groups, which proudly call themselves political parties or movements are also nothing but closed communities unwilling to cooperate, collaborate or interact, often enjoying notoriety. Their conduct as well as the behavior of many political and economic decision-makers responsible for the fate of millions of Russians reminds me of a recent joke: «Program of Reforms in Russia: 1. Make people rich and happy (the list of people is attached below)».

These (above mentioned) concepts are rather similar and most fully depict the essence of consciousness and behavior of those who embody the current regime in Russia. Economic expanse has long been divided among various clans, castes and cliques. They were formed rapidly, based on previously existing (back in Soviet times) family ties, personal loyalty, friendly relations, which helped them divide the most profitable segments of economy. However, some cliques, clans and castes consider this division of property unjust, a fact fuelling criminal and semi-criminal forms of struggle, redistribution of spheres of influence, open or covert «liquidation» of the «elite» rivals.

In politics, the struggle among castes, clans and cliques is somewhat different. Here, there is a constant rotation, when one group replaces another, or when two or three clans or cliques join forces, with all of them claiming to represent public interests, when in fact pursuing their own ambitious and selfish goals. The main danger of these groups lies in their attempt to persuade the public that their goals are the goals of society (the people). Turned upside-down, this notion «allows» political clans to feel «offended» by the people, who do not understand and do not support them in their «noble» aspirations, refusing to trust them, especially in during the elections. Their essence, however, remains the same — rejecting economic and moral obligations to the people. Breaking the law has become a basic principle of their enrichment.

Analysis of current situation demonstrates that Russian economy and politics are dominated by specific groups of ruling stratum, who seek to attain group, corporate, selfish and often ignoble purposes, completely unrelated to the interests of society. Moreover, members of these networks often join forces with criminal groups that pursue anti-social goals. Even the authorities, in spite of their tolerance of this kind of alliances, sometimes still launch criminal proceedings against them (although, how many of them are being concealed?). How can we explain the actions of economic castes, clans or cliques, when they hide capital abroad, evading taxes, create all sorts of «pyramids» or simply steal? It is difficult to understand the behavior of politicians that emerged from the people, but are only «returned back to the people» upon conviction. This, however, happens mostly after they, as a rule, had managed (thanks to their time in office) to secure a prosperous and independent living, not only in their own country but also abroad. So, what should we call those, whose life, in essence, consists of money laundering, financial speculations, embezzlement and merging with criminal groups?

Social consciousness is sensitive to hypocrisy, ambition and exorbitant claims of people in power, who have difficulty comprehending that they first are assessed based on their intentions, but ultimately — on the results. No matter how hard one or another group tries to prove their honorable and sincere intentions to rebuild the country, people have already returned their final verdict, which is impossible to escape: these latter-day saviors initiated unprecedented plundering of the people, giant embezzlement of socialist property and theft of national wealth.

Arbitrary use of the word «elite» is not as innocuous as it may seem at the first glance. The very fact of its use by the people in power elevates their status, justifies their existence, creates certain illusions or stimulates positive emotions. Besides, following idea is being implicitly introduced: the elite or some of its individual representatives may have some flaws or shortcoming, which is completely natural. However, the public has a right to know the truth about the stratum, which, without any justification, claims this title. Scientists and journalists should not contribute to this deception and camouflage, succumb to the tricks and to silently approve self-glorification of those, who consider themselves «chosen», or even conduct made-to-order studies or portrayals of «elite».

Thus, our society has what it has. And what it has is yet another colossal paradox, when we are told to call something dubious, very questionable and suspicious in every respect the « elite».

Russian «elite strata» cultivate these definitions and attitudes, since they do not want people's attention focused on their bad deeds, based on fraud, corruption, embezzlement and boundless shamelessness. For example: the price of annual corruption in Russia amounts to 40 billion dollars, while bribes alone are estimated at 6 billion dollars (*Figuri i litsa.* P. 3). Feeling like temporary favorites, those in possession of power and capital want to be called elite, since it brings them satisfaction, while distracting people from trying to control their actions and demand accountability for their policies.

References

Afanasiev M.N. *Praviashie elity i gosudarstvennost' posttotalitarnoi Rossii (Ruling Elite and Statehood of Post-Totalitarian Russia)*. Voronezh, 1996.

Anurin V.F. *Postindustrialnoe i/ili communisticheskoe obchestvo (Postindustrial and/or Communist Society)* // Sotsiologhicheskiye issledovania. 1999. No 7.

Ashin G.C., Okhotski E.V. *Kurs elitologii (A Course of Elitology)*. Moscow, 1999.

Ashin G.C. *Sovremennie teorii eliti. Kritichecki analiz (Current Elite Theories: A Critical Analysis)*. Moscow, 1985.

Kristeva Yu. *Vlast i elita v obshestve bez grazhdanskogo obshestva (Power and Elite in Society without Civil Society)* // Sociologhicheskiye issledovania. 1996. No 6.

Figuri i litsa. Interview s I. Hakamada (Figures and Persons. An Interview with I. Hakamada) // Nezavisimaya gazeta. 1999. No. 7.

Gaman-Golutvina O.V. *Politicheskie eliti Rossii (Political Elites of Russia)*. Moscow, 1998. P. 5.

Magaril S. *Intelligencia i budushchee Rossii (Intellectuals and Russia's Future)* // Almanakh Centra obchestvennikh nauk i economitsheskogo fakul'teta MGU. Moscow, 1999. No 6.

Minakov C.T. *Sovetskaya voennaya elita 20-kh godov (Soviet Military Elite of the 1920th)*, Orel, 2000.

Okhotski E.V. *Politicheskaya elita (Political Elite)* // Osnovi politicheskoi sotsiologii: Utshebnik (Textbook) / Pod red. Zh. T.Toshchenko. M., N. Novgorod, 1998. P. 166–167.

Ozhegov S.I. *Slovar russkogo yazika: 70 000 slov (Dictionary of Russian Language: 70 thous. words)*, Moscow, 1991.

Slovar russkogo yazika: V 4 t. (Dictionary of Russian Language, in 4 vols) / Ed by A.P. Evgeneva. Moscow, 1981.

Rossiiskaya elita (Russian Elite). Moscow, 1996.

Slovo ne vorobei...(A Word is no Sparrow). Moscow, 2001.

Sovremennaja zapadnaja sociologia. Slovar' (Contemporary Western Sociology. Dictionary). Moscow, 1990.

Tancher V.V. *Teorii neoelitizma v svete democraticheskoi transformatsii i ukrainskie realii (Theories of Neo-elitism in the Light of Democratic Transformation and Ukrainian Realities)* // Sotsiologhicheskiye issledovania. 1999. No 10.

Titov V.N. *Politicheckaya elita i problemy politiki (Political Elite and Problems of Politics)* // Sociologhicheskiye issledovania. 1998. No 7.

Chapter 18. **Centrists in Russia: all or none**

> The best and most lasting changes
> are those that are based on improving
> morality, without any violent upheavals.
>
> *A.S. Pushkin* (1799–1837)
> Russian poet

In late 1990's, Russia witnessed a clearly manifested paradoxical phenomenon. Centrism has become the most «fashionable attire,» worn by almost every politician, political party and social movement. The desire to declare oneself a centrist was boundless and irrepressible; left and right politicians, nationalists and patriots, anarchists and federalists, white and pink, etc., etc. all crammed under this banner. Even LDPR (Liberal Democratic Party of Russia) leader V. Zhirinovsky constantly declares that he and his party are the only true centrists. Basically, everyone around wants to be called a centrist. In such situation, almost everything that is spoken, written and debated across the whole spectrum of economic, social and political issues is crammed or squeezed into centrism. And now it turns out that those who are for private property, and those against private property, for the monarchy and against it, as well as those who are opposed to unemployment all call themselves centrists. Even those who do not have any definite opinion, taking a «rubber» stand — borrowing bits and pieces from the most varied points of views, also frequently call themselves centrists. This situation gives rise to an interesting phenomenon, where those who are pushing and shoving under the banner of centrism continue to implement the old Soviet saying «yours does not stand here» (you were not standing in this line), which later caused a lot of controversy — so who is most «central centrist» in Russia?

Intuitive understanding of the fact that not all was clear cut in the interpretation of the essence of centrism, moreover, even doubtful, has led to a variety of new derivations — «right center», «left center», a little «left from right (left) center», «left» («right») leaning toward centrism. Even such definition as «political centrism» has emerged, as though it could be achieved by ignoring demands of economic, social and spiritual spheres of society. A.I. Soloviev even proposed a surprising idea that «among both, right and left they can have their own centrist parties» (*Nezavisimaia gazeta.* June 17, 1999). Many scientists are (regrettably) to blame for all the confusion in the interpretation of centrism. This commotion is persistently supported by a considerable number of politicians and journalists, who on TV and in newspapers contribute to growing disarray in people's notions about the essence and purpose of centrism.

Unlike the 1995–1996 elections, when the word «centrism» was in vogue among some political forces, currently not just individuals and political groups, but virtually everyone is sticking to the «center». People borrow (steal!) each other's ideas, slogans, appeals and programs, claiming that only they represent these public sentiments. But (they also claim), people are ignorant — they do not notice noble aspirations of «centrist» souls and for some reason have no desire to «benefit» from these charitable parties, associations or politicians.

18.1. Realities of Russian centrism

In our opinion, centrism mainly exists in verbal or virtual imagination, for it never really existed and does not presently exist in Russia, nor is it expected to become a dominant force in the near future. Yet, *there are a large number of explanations of the essence of centrism, including some simply unique ones.* In most cases, each such interpretation expresses its own understanding of centrism based on thoughts and ideas that are only clear to its authors. Let us get acquainted with the existing points of views.

According to the first, perhaps the most common and primitive interpretation, centrism is declared a middle ground between two extreme points of view — radical right and left concepts. Supposedly, if you do not share the positions and political views of extremists and adhere to something intermediate, this is centrism. Thus, according to former deputy Prime Minister Victor Khristenko, only those forces that are able to break away from radical left and right, creating a specific synthesis of various social forces should ultimately win in Russian political arena (*Nezavisimaia gazeta.* July 9, 1999). This position is reminiscent of an old eastern fairy-tale about neutrality, which is fully applicable to this situation. When asked what neutrality (centrism) is, the answer is: «It is when Ahmed is pulling the blanket over to his side and Mahmoud — over to his side, while I am lying in the middle, keeping neutrality (centrism)». It is in this confrontation between various conflicting viewpoints, such centrists envision their positions, their intentions and aspirations. By the way, if there is no «blanket» to be pulled over by these extreme political forces, does it mean that centrism would simply disappear?

The second interpretation of centrism is based on the notion that people are stupid, uneducated and unprepared to accept «true» political culture. Therefore, we must seek consensus at the level of political forces, government leaders, policymakers and top officials — all those in power or those, assertively seeking it. Allegedly, this coordination of positions and points of views constitutes centrism, since it is capable of avoiding extremes, reaching concessions and, on this basis, lead people to a happy future, since they (people) should not be burdened by unnecessary concerns, for they still do not fully understand the entire depth of the projected positive changes; furthermore, they might even hurt their chances for happiness. In other words, in this case centrism is understood as a kind of conspiracy of top politicians, which are the only ones who know how to put Russia back on the right track. Clearly, in this case, centrism becomes an agreement (conspiracy), mutual coordination of interests of political castes (cliques), rather than a mechanism of satisfying popular needs and demands (Sulakshin. 1998).

Third viewpoint, circulating among certain part of intelligentsia, is based on the opinion that centrism should be able to please everyone and suit everybody, be convenient to all, should promise something to every person and even keep a few of these promises. According to this position, centrism is a tactic «to proclaim both left and right slogans and orientations» depending on the audience (Tregubova. 1999). As far as the essence of this position is concerned, centrism is a complete lack of principles, pursuit of momentary selfish interests, profit, and chameleon-like behavior under the guise of best intentions. In this case, we should not even be discussing centrism, we just need to point out its time-serving nature, indecency and disregard for those whom it is supposed to benefit.

Fourth interpretation sees the meaning of centrism in its ability to express the will and hopes of so-called middle class. It is based on the fact that, as experience of foreign countries shows, centrism focuses on demands and concerns of this particular class, which allows it to regulate socio-economic processes in the interests of the majority of population (Blazhenkova, Gurova. 2000). However, supporters of this position for some reason fail to notice that there is no real middle class in Russia, or its numbers are so insignificant that focusing on it means defending interests of something that practically does not exist in real life.

It is worth mentioning an interpretation of centrism, which is based on the fact that we must find practical, real successes and pursue their achievement by all possible means. These real, tangible results would supposedly ultimately benefit not only its architects, but also the entire society and the whole country, though perhaps not immediately. Such interpretation of centrism means protecting the interests of business-minded and enrichment-oriented individuals. This position is shared by many regional leaders, who base their policies on creating an image of a strong manager, whose sole purpose is to build homes, clean up streets, and keep their towns and villages neat and tidy. This position, however, ignores or fails to mention by what means this all will be implemented. They claim that the most important issue is the welfare of the population.

There is another approach (and fairly common one), which idealizes politics and ideology of centrism turning it into a kind of an icon. This idealization has its distinctions: some (e.g. M. Sokolov) believe that centrism is a doctrine of harmony (Sokolov, 1998), others (S. Modestov) turn to examples of historical past, attributing centrist policy to all those who were more or less lucky and consistent in carrying out their economic policies (Modestov, 1999). But this, in our opinion, does not mean that their success or their intentions in politics should be called centrism.

Finally, eclecticism — a set of opinions and ideas, which strangely combine everything that exists in today's political and ideological trends, *is also sometimes called centrism.* Take some ideas from the left, some from the right, and you get «a complex fusion of ideas» (L. Andreev). There are capitalist ideas mixed in with socialist hopes, nationalist claims and religious overtures. All of these (and God knows what else) are presented as genuine aspirations of the people. In this context, many refer to the convergence theory (convergence of capitalism and socialism), its interpretation by academician and Soviet dissident A.D. Sakharov, attempting to pass this conglomerate for a very useful thing (Ofitova, 1999). Supporters of this view forget that merely combining different viewpoints and positions can hardly be interpreted as centrism. There are also very peculiar versions of eclecticism, when extremely common slogans are declared centrism (e.g. social security, protection of national interests, guaranteed decent standard of living), objectives that all political forces claim to pursue.

Analysis of diversity of these approaches suggests that there are so many opinions and positions that it makes centrism a vague, unintelligible and inexplicable phenomenon. In reality, however, «supporters» of centrism do not just argue, but squabble, labeling their opponents quasi and pseudo-centrists (Il'in, 1997).

18.2. On essence of centrism

Real analysis of social development shows that you cannot declare yourself centrism supporter in advance, based on pure speculation. Centrism is shaped by the very logic of life, not by the intentions or wishes of individual leaders, parties or political alliances, no matter how good they appear at first glance.

Centrism is not defined by those who consider themselves part of this political trend, but by whether it (centrism) reflects prevailing attitudes and orientations of major population groups. That is why only those who take into account these interests and needs, preferences and values and are guided by them in their policies earn their right to claim this definition worthy of civil harmony. In other words, true affiliation with centrism is determined by the people. And, following people's wishes and expectations (regardless of personal likes and dislikes) is the law of centrist policies. Even if these orientations do not coincide with political attitudes and preferences of social forces, it should not become grounds for their rejection under spurious slogans — people «are mistaken», «do not understand», or «we have to explain», etc. Basic rule and principle of centrism is to promptly respond to these concerns by establishing specific measures without ignoring people's opinions, no matter how wrong they might seem.

Currently, according to sociological surveys, people are concerned about a number of issues, not just one, contrary to what the media and some politicians claim. Namely: declining standards of living, impoverishment (in 1999 — 76%, and in 2007 -51% of respondents), violence, lawlessness and criminalization of society (respectively 61% and 38%), official corruption (54% and 26%) and genetic degeneration of the nation (46% and 31%) (*Monitoring obshchestvennogo mneniya.* 1999. No 3. P. 32; *Public Opinion 2007.* P. 45). Resolving these issues should determine the essence of centrist positions.

People are largely guided by real life experiences. And that is fine. We should not condemn them for incorrect thinking or misunderstanding certain issues, as many politicians do. Instead, we have to draw conclusions. According to VTsIOM survey in 1999 and 2007, true intention of a majority of Russians, 40% and 27% respectively, is to see Russia a democracy, market economy and a legal state (similar to the Western countries). Some 22% and 35% respectively preferred returning to Soviet-style socialism, and another 22% and 19% thought that Russia needs a «completely exclusive polity with its own particular path of development» (*Monitoring obshchestvennogo mneniya.* 1999. No 4. P. 21; *Public Opinion — 2007.* P. 20). The number of people pessimistic about future development of Russia in the 21st century remains high: 34,3% of respondents think that there is a growing probability that «Russian economy will continue to deteriorate»; 27,1% believe that Russia, both economically and politically will fully depend on the West; 26,9% fear establishment of authoritarian regime, and 17,5% — that «Russia will disintegrate into a number of independent states (*Rossia na rubezhe vekov,* P. 416).

In this regard, we can only state that people keenly feel the tensions in the country, they are aware of shortcomings in Russia's development, and sincerely advocate for ensuring future prosperity of the country. However, in order to achieve this, it is necessary to resolve earthly matters that are of great concern to the majority. In other words, many people, critically assessing their present situation, as well as the situation in the country, support reasonable and rational ideas, are focused on a balanced, thoughtful, comprehensive approach (to the problems) based on common sense. The only criterion that defines a political force as centrist is its focus on the aspirations of the people, not their arbitrary self-proclamations, regardless of popular wishes.

The fact that the majority of the people adhere to centrist positions is supported by following data: only 2 to 6–7% of respondents supported the views and ideas of extreme left or right-wing politicians. The population rather clearly understands existing problems and their impact on people's lives, as well as the ways of addressing them. Entire logic of social development demonstrates that people can not be deceived, even if it happens, it is not for long. *People always were and still are a centrist force, and therefore those, who focus on people's interests and needs have a right to call themselves centrists.* It is, however, necessary to, first, let people, not the party in question, and determine that centrist definition, i.e. the degree of support of party's position. And if this party is capable of taking preferences of the majority into account, it can then be considered a centrist force. Secondly, it is important not to confuse the requirements of «demos» — the people (democracy) with the demands of «ochlos» (the crowd or mob). Disappearance of ultra-radical left and right-wing leaders from the political scene in early 1990's gives us hope that ochlocratic methods and their intrusion on political life have no future, for they are not shared by the population.

Centrism criteria are not merely limited to following the position of majority, since, by and large, our nation is not uniform: it comprises various social, socio-demographic and socio-professional groups. Therefore, one of the greatest challenges of centrism is not only to respond to the needs of the majority, but also to coordinate and attempt achieving balance of interests of main, leading social groups. Accordingly, centrist policy is not simply limited to registration and general response to basic orientations of the people, *as the next step, the interests of major social groups* that define the base of society have to be identified and evaluated, in order to provide a social *niche* for each of them, where their main claims could be satisfied, and, most importantly, where their interests could be coordinated with the interests of contiguous groups. Moreover, history constantly teaches us that neglecting or disregarding these interests can create tensions, which in the 1990's in Russia manifested in a conflict with the miners, the army, military-industrial complex, farmers and retirees.

Emergence of these hotbeds of conflict became possible due to the fact that particular social groups felt that their interests were at a disadvantage compared to the interests of other social groups. In other words, from the centrist viewpoint, each social group should be offered an opportunity (based on the analysis of its place and role in society) to have a special program of actions backed by appropriate economic mechanism and legislative acts. Disregarding positions and interests of these groups is fraught with social tensions and even a social explosion, which we are occasionally reminded of by the actions of these groups (e.g. miners' movement, retirees blocking the roads because of rents monetization policy), aimed at drawing public attention to their plight.

Significantly, in many such actions, occasionally, a situation emerges, where satisfaction of the claims of one social group can lead to infringement on interests of the other groups, resulting in painful reaction to the changing situation, which can, in turn, give rise to another hotbed of social unrest. Civic harmony is not possible without a sense of fellowship, mutual responsibility and understanding. This is why the recognition of its social *niche* by every social group is an important indicator of the stability of centrism. In the opposite case, it presents a threat of disruption of social life, settling of scores, endless insults and claims, and as a consequence, growing social tension and conflicts.

18.3. Mechanism and methods of centrism

Centrism implies skills and art of compromise. This cannot to be interpreted as conciliatory tactics, unprincipled collusion or even as a concession. It should not be treated as a betrayal of previously proclaimed principles that «can not be renounced» either. A possibility of balanced, adequate (alternate) response to the popular needs is a true measure of a genuine sound compromise. In these conditions, it is not just possible, but also necessary to adopt guidelines and orientations of the major population groups in such a way that all of the groups would recognize the opportunity to consider the claims of the other groups and be willing to make concessions. The genius of French President Charles de Gaulle, lies in the fact that in late 1960s', when the country was threatened by disorder and anarchy, he was able to reconcile the interests of major population groups — small landowners, farmers, youth and students, workers, intellectuals and big bourgeoisie. Moreover, he was able to persuade many of them to either make mutual concessions in this confrontation or to wait for their just demands to be satisfied for the sake of universal peace in the country.

Underlying centrist compromise demands rejecting rigid confrontation based on the principle «either — or». Life shows that there are many half-tones, transitional stages, where seemingly contradictory attitudes and orientations of political and social forces can be combined in most fantastic ways. In these circumstances, coordinating, adjusting ones' actions to a previously proclaimed goal, would mean deliberately provoking the emergence of an unstable situation or making interests of some groups of people clash with interests of the others. It is much more difficult to understand why mutually exclusive guidelines appear in political preferences of the population and what measures of their mutual reconciliation would be effective in this situation.

Compromise does not preclude clarity and accuracy in defining centrist political position. Not every response, reaction, or simply hope that the danger (or problem) will «miraculously dissolve» defines the value of the position of centrism, its consistency and distinctness. It is obvious that some government actions (including in a number of republics) bordered on policy of open nationalism with chauvinistic overtones, rather than a desire to find mutually acceptable compromise. This, however, does not exclude, but rather involves both a dialogue, as well as finding common points of view, even with the forces that reject compromise and attempts to reach an agreement, or to ease the tension. Although, in this case, an opponent should know how the other party qualifies his deeds.

Common sense, which is usually treated with skepticism both in theory and in practice, should be attributed to *the mechanisms of functioning of centrism*. At one time, philosophy of common sense was strongly criticized as obviously flawed, not corresponding with perspective aspirations and strategic changes in social development. Critics often accused supporters of common sense of not seeing an inch beyond their own noses.

In Soviet times, common sense was often rejected under the guise of fighting retrograde views, since satisfying people's everyday needs and concerns was considered harmful and short-sighted: a politician, political activist was supposed to inspire people to implement «progressive ideas», to get rid of petty bourgeois attitudes and tastes, to demonstrate inferiority of the intentions arising from routine, everyday concerns. But even in Soviet times there were many people that disagreed with this approach, refusing to accept the thesis that following people's wishes is something reprehensible and not a true duty of a politician. After all, more or less viable concepts and political ideas (including Marxism) arose from realization, validation and formalization of popular wishes and aspirations. We are firmly convinced that as soon as a political party or social movement stops taking popular needs and aspirations into account, it results in its political death and historical oblivion. Collapse of the CPSU, as well, was caused, in no small measure, by the fact that vital concerns of the people had become secondary or tertiary matter.

Common sense rejects extremes in thinking and actions. Russian population in the first half of the 1990's disagreed with radical democrats' demands, who insisted on «wiping out», eliminating «everything red». At the same time, the majority of population does not support appeals of leftist radicals either, calling for a «total return», «restoration of all things Soviet». In both cases, most people were rational, rather than dogmatic, they were guided by their own concerns and search for possible effective solutions to their problems, i.e. common sense.

Common sense presumes adjusting to fluctuations, changes and even zigzags in popular attitudes, not ideological framing of political intentions. Consideration of the state and trends of development of social consciousness is the real, actual embodiment of centrist ideas. Consistency of centrism is derived from objective logic of development, logic of functioning of social forces, rather than goals (even rational ones, at a first glance), devised by someone in advance. But, if these concepts fail to resonate with the majority, political oblivion for these ideas is practically guaranteed.

With regard to the methods of centrism, it is worth noting that it is often perceived as a policy of trying to please everyone, to tell each audience what they would like to hear, to come to an agreement, reconcile everyone, and conform to everything. Meanwhile, centrism as a coherent, consistent and balanced policy has its own scientifically grounded and life-tested methods. *Centrism is characterized by specific methods of work,* which closely link, relate it to well-proven experience, similar to or matched against the past.

First, it rejects quarrels and arguments, preferring debates — to establish the truth by comparing different points of views, i.e. it follows the principles of a dialogue instead of insults, suspicions, accusations that are so prevalent in contemporary political life. Centrist methods of work, its strategy and tactics are incompatible with aspirations to infringe upon opponent's interests, to humiliate or «expose» anyone — they involve a thorough and careful analysis of each and every argument.

Second, in supporters of different points of view, centrism does not see antagonist, and certainly not enemies that must be destroyed, but an opponent, with whom it is necessary to coordinate common approaches and proposals in order to find mutually acceptable solutions to the problems affecting society. This certainly does not mean that centrism should be transformed into a kind of a «swamp». Centrism presumes consistency and perseverance, adherence to the principles, rather than short-term interests. In addition, centrism is incompatible with ideology of revenge, with modified forms of implementing an ancient principle: «An eye for an eye, a tooth for a tooth».

Third, centrism rejects the tactic of partial truth, when, for whatever reason (sometimes even plausible) truth is partly hidden or withheld. Unfortunately, we are witnessing constant tricks and evasions on the part of those who consider themselves centrists, who regularly withhold information or underscore (over-emphasize) the facts, which at the moment seem advantageous. The fact of active participation of the so-called centrists in manipulating social consciousness is particularly troubling. Such practices are not only far from optimal politics, but simply from normal ones as well.

Fourth, centrism is focused on decisive rejection of dogma by consistent renewal and support of everything rational, emerging and promising. In this regard, it should be noted that centrism presumes getting rid of certain stereotypes of political rhetoric, such as «nation above all», «our (liberal, socialist, monarchist, etc.) point of view is the only correct one». It is also highly doubtful that such terms as «titular nation», «persons of Caucasian nationality», «immunity of deputies», «political elite» etc. are acceptable in centrist policies.

Fifth, centrism rejects conjuncture — it is based on long-term policies that ultimately result in success.

18.4. Prospects of centrism

History teaches us that centrism is a policy that became reality in the lives of many countries, especially in the 20th century and, in particular, after World War II. In this context, General de Gaulle's policies, as well as the actions of ruling parties of Sweden, Switzerland and Finland are frequently analyzed.

In Russia, however, the fate of centrism turned out to be rather turbulent and complex. Everywhere and at all times, political leaders in Russia, which called for the middle ground — the centrist views, had been beaten in literal and figurative sense. They were booed, driven off the podium, denied the right to speak, made a mockery of, accused of all mortal sins — clericalism, revisionism, idealism and being out of touch with reality. Unfortunately, our history is full of the opposite examples, when people with extremist and radical views regularly came to power, which resulted in new ordeals for our society.

Neither before, nor after the 1917 revolution, had Russia's ruling strata been guided by politically or economically tested and verified programs. All attempts to develop and implement such programs resulted in serious failures, even when people who disliked and even rejected the extremes, like N.S. Khrushchev (Soviet political leader, 1894-1971) came to rule the country. He too, had a tendency to slide either to the left, or right in his policies. Having implemented many principles of centrism, Khrushchev, at the end of his career, did his best to leave no trace of this policy. This is characteristic of many leaders of modern Russia, who, realizing the negative attitude of social consciousness towards the radical liberal wing began to look for a *niche* that would satisfy or reconcile many people and would help restore popular confidence in today and tomorrow. Centrism became such a *niche*, which was also used to conceal their true motives and intentions.

But most importantly, the majority of our politicians advocating centrism ignores and forgets the main thing: the people, their mood and their feelings are the key to the success of centrism (Primakov. 2006). Moreover, some of the so-called centrists, in an outburst of candor, often in one form or the other follow this reasoning: people's political consciousness (according to some irresponsible statements — crowd), they say, is not mature enough to understand their own historical responsibility. Thus, tens and hundreds of years would be required in order for them to learn modern Western standards of political culture. And history takes revenge on them for neglecting popular opinion: they lose people's trust, suffer defeats, since they consider themselves to be smarter and more far-sighted than the people of the country of their birth (See table 18.1)

Table 18.1.

Evaluation of the quality of Soviet and contemporary Russian government
(% of respondents, N = 1600)

	Soviet Government			Contemporary Russian Government		
Qualities	1998	2001	2005	1998	2001	2005
Legitimate	32	22	28	12	10	9
Honest, open	14	11	13	3	3	3

End of table 18.1

Criminal, corrupt	14	13	12	63	50	62
Close to the people	36	30	34	2	3	5
Stable, powerful	27	25	30	2	4	7
Effective	5	10	11	3	3	6
Short-sighted	23	14	21	28	17	25
Fair	16	16	11	3	3	3
Weak, helpless	8	6	8	31	21	20
Our own, familiar	32	24	26	3	2	4
Inconsistent	8	6	9	32	25	29
Closed, «secretive»	17	4	13	8	7	8
Pragmatic	2	2	5	4	5	6
Parasitic	8	6	5	18	12	15
Limited, dimwitted	9	7	8	12	4	8
Authoritative, respected	21	21	24	2	4	7
Competent	6	5	7	3	6	9
Illegitimate	1	3	3	13	10	16
Unprofessional	6	6	8	13	7	12
Distant from the people, «alien»	8	8	10	41	34	42
Intelligent, educated	8	12	13	6	12	13
Bureaucratic	30	26	30	22	24	39
Hard to say	11	12	13	9	11	8

Source: Public Opinion — 2005. Moscow, Levada-Center. 2005. P. 58.

Analysis of sociological information shows that popular consciousness is alive and well, and capable of rational actions. People are more actively rejecting various ideological fairy tales of all, without exception, extremist political forces. This suggests that there is no other way other then to listen to the people. And no matter how different their viewpoints are, let the one that people share become victorious. This guarantees stability and trust in authorities, as well as hopes for a civilized future.

Thus, we are not talking about self-titled «Centrism», but centrist policy based on very real and visible trends of objectively evolving social consciousness and social activity of people. It is this objective truth and not obsolete political dogmas, no matter how attractive they may be, that is the basis of centrism, a measure of reconciling interests, a form of interaction between various social forces without accusations of usurpation of power, or exaggeration of only one approach of resolving urgent problems over others. There can be only one basis for the policy of centrism, while resolving all, without exemption, social problems — the people, their consciousness and behavior. And all those who aspire to participate in developing centrist policies should define and defend only those measures that are effective for that particular situation from the point of view of the entire population.

In conclusion — two remarks. First. Today, centrism is fashionable. Various political forces use its image to more profitably sell themselves in upcoming battles for votes. And, there is a real danger of making a wrong choice — after the elections, once these forces gain power, they tend to gravitate to one of the flanks.

And the second. There is a real risk of devaluation of the term «centrism», when it is beslobbered and disgraced to such an extent that it will cause the same hostility in Russian people as the word «democracy». And the main conclusion is disappointing and paradoxical: the reality is that in Russia, virtually all political forces, without exception, which are trying to cling to centrism, are not centrist neither in essence, nor in content.

References

Blazhenkova O., Gurova T. *Sredniy class (Middle Class)* // Expert. No 34. September 18, 2000.

Il'in M.V. *Slova I smisli: opit rekonstruktsii politicheskikh ponyatiy (Words and Meaning: Expierence of Reconstruction of Poltical Concepts)*. Moscow, 2003.

Modestov S. *Politicheskiy centrizm v Rossii (Political Centrism in Russia)* // Nezavisimaia gazeta. July 29, 1999.

Monitoring obshchestvennogo mneniya. Ekonomitsheskiye i sotsialniye peremeny. 1999. No 3. P. 32; *Public Opinion 2007*. Moscow. Levada-Center. 2007.

Monitoring obshchestvennogo mneniya. Ekonomitsheskiye i sotsialniye peremeny. 1999. No 4; *Public Opinion — 2007*. Moscow. Levada-Center. 2007.

Ofitova S. *Politicheskiy centrizm v deistvii (Political Centrism in Action)* // Nezavisimaia gazeta. June 17, 1999.

Primakov E.M. *Minnoe pole politiki (Mine Field of Politics)*. Moscow, 2006. *Rossia na rubezhe vekov (Russian at the Close of the Century)*. Moscow, 2000.

Sokolov M. *Centrizm kreptchal (Centrism Was Getting Stronger)* // Izvestia. November 21, 1998.

Sulakshin S.S. *Izmena (Betrayal)*. Moscow, 1998.

Tregubova E. *Tsentristskaya terapia (Centrist Therapy)* // Izvestia. January 20, 1999.

Chapter 19. **Intelligentsia or intellectuals?**

Wise is the one whose knowledge is
useful not the one whose knowledge is
plentiful

Aeschylus (525–456 BC)
Greek Poet and playwright

A one-sided specialist is either a rude
empiricist or a street charlatan.

N.I. Pirogov (1810–1881),
Russian surgeon, anatomist

19.1. History of the problem

These days, a lot is being said about Old Russian intelligentsia becoming part
of history, part of the past and just a stage in the development of Russian society.
Is this true?

Let us recall some historical facts. Intelligentsia began playing a leading role
in Russia's public life from the moment, when *Zemstvo* teachers, doctors, land
surveyors etc. entered the historical arena, i.e. social stratum called upon to
spiritually enrich everyone thirsting for knowledge, and not just those belonging
to the privileged social groups. It was in the 19ᵗʰ century Russia that this unique
phenomenon has emerged under the name of «Russian intelligentsia», unknown,
uncharacteristic for any other country in the world. This phenomenon survived
all the vicissitudes of nearly two centuries, retaining a number of unique features.
*What does belonging to intelligentsia mean? Firstly, it is not simply a possession of
knowledge, but active participation in sharing this knowledge with the people.* The
idea of serving people, the responsibility to the people was the glue, bonding the
behavior of those who called themselves intelligentsia. *Secondly, it was the idea
of morality, of serving the good, the idea of sacrifice. Thirdly, an aspiration to be an
example, a mentor and even an ideal to others not only in major, significant aspects,
but also in minor, everyday routine ones.* Such perception of their responsibility
has often produced Quixotical relapses and even foolishness, but, no matter how
strange it may seem, it enriched the worldview and philosophical outlook of
Russian society. *And finally, it is genuine willingness to serve not only their own
people, but also the entire humanity.* Russian intelligentsia has always been
concerned with what was happening in other countries, about the changes in
the fate of other nations. Several studies have also noted such features of the

behavior of intelligentsia (that goes back to characteristics of Russian ethnos) as a combination of sacrifice and messianism (Panarin, 1998), of the energy of asceticism and moral authority (Goudkov, Dubin. 1994).

During the Soviet period these traditions of serving the people were supported and developed, although they were subject to fairly rigid ideological regimentations.

And now Russia has entered a new stage in its development. At this new stage, social thought again turned its attention to the eternal question: whether intelligentsia still exists in the same sense, in which this concept was used for the past two centuries? Or, if the age of Western-style intellectuals is approaching? Will the youth inherit what was accumulated by previous generations? These are not idle questions.

Currently, the country is facing fundamentally new issues. An intensive transformation of economic relations is underway. Political landscape of Russian society is changing. New guidelines and values are emerging in social consciousness. Amongst these fundamental changes, a question arose: Will the phenomenon of Russian intelligentsia be preserved or destroyed? (*Intelligentsia.* 1994; Kara-Murza S.G. 1997; *Na pereputie.* 1999; etc.). Presently, we are witnessing the deeds and actions, which by far do not enhance the prestige of this social group. Many of its representatives acted as destroyers of previously established values. Promoting individualism became quite popular. Part of intelligentsia is infected with chauvinism and rabid clericalism. Certain individuals among them openly refer to people as cattle, or are affected by the cult of money and cynicism. Statements in the spirit of hatred toward nonconformity and dissent and appeals to destroy those, who think differently, are not so rare either. And, the numbers of those who pillage the spiritual needs of people and society are not that insignificant.

Against the backdrop of economic, political and spiritual changes in Russian society, we shall try to trace the fate of intelligentsia, to understand the tremendous upheavals that took place in the minds and hearts of these people, to sort out their confusion and hesitations, often paradoxical, but also very instructive from the historical perspective. Particular attention should be paid to the reasons why intelligentsia, with such kaleidoscopic speed, has changed their convictions and preferences, why so many political and social movements fractured, impoverished in spirit, and how yesterday's friends today become embittered rivals. And, most importantly, whether 19th century values of Russian intelligentsia are dying off, or if they are being replaces by the new values of modern intellectuals.

It should be emphasized that even in the 1970th, the majority of Soviet (Russian) intelligentsia realized the need for profound, radical changes. Already at that time intelligentsia lived in anticipation of significant political and economic changes in the life of the country. This was evidenced by sporadic and recurrent outbursts of debate in the pages of such official periodicals as «Pravda» (The Truth), not to mention the 'free-thinking' «Literaturnaya Gazeta» (Literary Gazette) and «Sovetskaya Rossiya» (Soviet Russia), which, during those years, were the «flagships» of radical proposals and rather sharp criticism of the authorities. During those years, dissident movement became an independent force. Hopes for the coming changes that emerged with Yu.V. Andropov's and later M.S. Gorbachev's rise to power were also the reflection of those expectations. Sociological research of the problems of social consciousness rather clearly indicated growing changes in social mood of intelligentsia. It was also evidenced by numerous proposals (according to official data, the main Government agencies, mainly the Communist Party Central Committee received thousands of letters, analytical programs and recommendations), justifying the need to urgently address the problems facing the country.

Activism of intelligentsia has increased dramatically during the perestroika years, when an opportunity to openly express one's ideas and suggestions for improving the existing system became widely available.

Culmination came in August, 1991. In an instant, all of the old foundations were swept away. To many people it seemed that there were no more obstacles in the way of implementation of the desired objectives, concepts and plans. Quite a few people wanted to make others happier, to show them how they should live. Popularity of Western standards of living has reached unprecedented heights.

Over two decades have passed since the beginning of perestroika. So, what happened with the social group that calls itself intelligentsia during this rather lengthy period of time?

19.2. On typology of contemporary Russian intelligentsia

The events of the 1990's have questioned the existence of such phenomenon as Russian intelligentsia. And this statement is not an exaggeration. Huge differentiation, fragmentation and «paradoxicalization» of the consciousness and behavior have split previously united Soviet (Russian) intelligentsia. More than ever, it became apparent that talking about intelligentsia as a single, unified social community is impossible and even absurd. There is virtually not a single common component (except the formal one — higher education), which is inherent if not to all, then at least the majority of intelligentsia (Pokrovskiy, 1999). Another paradoxical fact deserves our attention: «the rate of decay and degradation of Russian intelligentsia as a distinct community increases proportionately to the country's successful development along the path of democracy and market economy» (Kiva. 2000) Several researchers do not share these concerns raised in regard to «the end of intelligentsia» (Panarin, 1998).

A viewpoint that Russian intelligentsia is an embodiment of a special kind of paradoxical, mutually exclusive traits is no less prevalent: «... Intelligentsia cannot be considered national, for their entire attitude to Russian traditions and historical life is hostile. It cannot be considered a carrier of Western culture either. For intelligentsia, the West is always a myth, a legend or an ideal, either positive – in which case one has to emulate it, strive for it; or negative – thus turning it into an enemy, which has to be feared and destroyed» (Cherkasov, Chernyshevskiy. 1994). However, in order to obtain valid conclusions, it is necessary to identify the actual types (and not make speculative judgments), analysis of which will allow to describe the current state of Russian intelligentsia. We should also point out some of the more vivid manifestations of its creative and social activities, without a detailed examination of everything that is happening in its midst.

Publications of early 1990's contain a number of fair objections against portraying intelligentsia as a monolithic, economically and socially homogeneous group. And, if we were to characterize the largest groups within intelligentsia in generalized social and political terms, we would conclude that they are represented by: *first*, a relatively small layer of active participants in the ongoing transformation processes; *second*, the majority of engineering and humanitarian intelligentsia, who largely stayed away from all attempts to reform Russia, or restore the old foundations of Soviet society. Third, this stratum is represented by people who are lost, doubters, trapped between past and present, between reason and emotion, hope and disillusionment, between understanding the need for change and refusal to accept this change in its present form. However, idealism, eternal magnanimity, political naivet and legal illiteracy remain common features of the entire intelligentsia. Moreover, Russian intelligentsia bears historical responsibility for the fact that it condoned plundering of the national wealth of the country, looting its treasures, and to certain extend, for the rise of comprador bureaucracy to power. Intelligentsia has failed to comprehend what was happening in post-Soviet Russia, to organize opposition against those, attempting to ruin the country, to become a unifying national force. Therefore, analysis of the state and trends of evolution of contemporary intelligentsia primarily pertains to its more advanced groups, which, whether someone likes it or not, most completely embody its essential characteristics. These very groups of dynamic, active intellectuals continue to participate in the ongoing reforms in the country, attempting to influence social consciousness, make others listen to them, or, at least, draw public's attention to their civic positions.

And if we analyze the group of intelligentsia, which advocated and even participated in these transformation from that point of view, it appears rather unattractive, contradictory, paradoxical, if not worse. The image of this particular group, however, calls into question the very existence of intelligentsia, for along with creative, selfless and innovative forces, there were people, who burst in, determining its face, ambitious, looting, and reckless and at the same time irresponsible, absolutely convinced of their own exclusiveness, embodying ideology of the «big score» in all its unsightly combinations and variations. Gradually, creative and extraordinarily thinking representatives of intelligentsia were forced out of the decision-making process, or voluntarily left politics. And, those groups of intellectuals, essentially reflecting principles of organization of social life, characteristic of the period of initial accumulation of capital (adjusted to the realities of the late twentieth century) began to dictate their will.

A group of intelligentsia, which can be called *«predators»*, most vividly represents ideology of radical change. It is they who symbolized the beginning of a new era by demonstrating their ability to plunder national wealth, their open, boundless thirst for profit and willingness to step over corpses for the sake of unprecedented wealth. This category of people is also characterized by lack of basic morals, which they are trying to pass for rationality, ability to efficiently organize business and arrange their lives. For the members of this group, there is nothing more prestigious then the cult of money. For the sake of profit some of them, using numerous loopholes in the legislation and a lack of clear political strategy, seized huge chunks of state property; others bought up most profitable state-run enterprises for next to nothing; the third became founders of financial pyramid schemes, or banks, accumulating vast resources by robbing a lot of people, who have entrusted them their money; the fourth grew rich through dizzying speculations and manipulations based on principle of deception and building their success on discarding even those devoted to them. We can mention other forms of appropriation and plunder of national wealth, they are, however, truly countless. But this does not change the essence the matter: a small group, having seized power, managed to not only lay their hands on enormous wealth but also started to dictate their conditions to the entire society. Moreover, these conditions are only beneficial to them, allowing further increase of their economic power and political influence.

In their essential, intrinsic characteristics, *«marauders»* or «looters» are very close to «predators». This is a category of people, completely devoid of any moral principles, guided solely by one motivation — to snatch, grab another piece, to profit from what is not under protection of law, what promises a dividend, even if their own wealth is built at the expense of others. This pertains not only to material wealth. The situation after the collapse of the Soviet Union was reminiscent of a battlefield, where it was not quite clear who won and what was in store for the participants of this battle tomorrow. Under such conditions, these people developed an urge to grab as much of the neglected property as possible, being fully convinced of their own impunity. They were looting everywhere — in economic field, in political jungle, in the midst of ethnic conflicts and even in the cultural sphere. And this illegally (or semi-legally) accumulated wealth was justified under the pretext of public benefit: this is, ultimately, the wealth of the entire society, since someday it might once again become public property. «Marauders» often argued that in America, the first generation of the rich was a generation of robbers, but their children and grandchildren (next generations) became honorable members of democratic society.

In 1990's, a group of intelligentsia, which can be termed «*mutants*» loudly announced its entry into the social arena. Its numbers were considerable. It was characterized by the following algorithm of behavior. During a considerable – Soviet (!) – part of their lives they shared one ideology and were active participants in its implementation. Then, during the period of upheaval, they declared themselves supporters of diametrically opposite ideas and aspirations, and not just in the form of denial, but severe criticism.

The emergence of a fairly large group of the so called «*wandering players*» or «*prowlers*» attests to an unsightly nature of this part of Soviet (Russian) intelligentsia. Moving across the entire spectrum of the political scene, they alternately become democrats, then monarchists, reformists, socialists, or radicals but most often the supporters of that political force, which is closest to the authorities, to governing political centers. They continue to «migrate» from one party (social movement) to another and then the third, the fourth, etc. There are already side-switching and party-hopping champions emerging among the members of this intelligentsia group, which once again confirms their complete lack of principles. And all this is justified by the assertions that their newly acquired political orientations are the embodiment of the «voice of the people», reflecting popular aspirations and desires. In essence it is a hypertrophied craving for political authority, real or simulated participation in its division, lust for money and desire to satisfy their thirst for power ambitions.

A *part of intelligentsia that mercilessly exploits national ideas,* bordering ethnic intolerance, political and domestic chauvinism is also very actively asserting itself. Usually, these people, on the one hand, declare their commitment to common cultural values, but on the other, they (in specific circumstances) resort to discrediting people of other nationalities, only because they adhere to different beliefs and «interfere» with well-being and lifestyle of «my» people. This very part of «intelligentsia» often advocates mental abuse. Its envoys and representatives revive social myths, «reshuffle» history, and prove the legitimacy of the claims against other peoples and nations on «scientific» basis.

But if the above mentioned groups occupy leading positions in economy and politics, and are able to impose their will and narrow group interests on society and the State, a number of marginalized communities (generated by the turmoil of the transition period) that exist side by side with them also demonstrate qualities that hardly enhance the image of intelligentsia.

First of all, there is a group, which can be called *«chameleons»*. As a rule, its representatives are always loyal to the government: imperial, Soviet, neo-liberal, as well every successive leader — be it Khrushchev, or Brezhnev, Yeltsin, or Putin. As soon as the situation changes, they light-heartedly switch sides in favor of the strong one, and abandon the sinking ship. Proximity to power, the desire to bask in its «sun», hoping to somehow benefit from it — these features are characteristic of a large group of people who consider themselves intelligentsia.

Behavior of the part of intelligentsia that may be called *«infantiles»* is no less striking and revealing. These people are usually inspired by some kind of an idea — no matter, important or unimportant, great or small, advanced or obsolete — but, in most cases completely out of touch (or, on rare occasions, loosely connected) with objective reality. They exist in an outer and inner world of their own design, and are ready and willing to devote their lives, actions and thoughts to organizing and arranging this world. Characteristically, they are not merely creators or supporters of their own controversial ideas, they are also actively promoting and imposing them on society, and are unwilling to accept the fact that their fantasies are defeated or rejected, resorting to various measures, including staging public scandals. Such people, like Novodvorskaya (an eccentric social figure), Zhirinovskiy (leader of pseudo-liberal party), Shandybin (former member of parliament from Communist party), might have ideas and goals worthy of public attention. But, the limitation of these ideas lies in the fact that they have very little in common with the real life. Their authors, however, tend to blame the fact that their ideas are either rejected, or that the legitimacy of their existence is being questioned, and not the ideas themselves.

Another type of «intelligentsia» that can be called *«lackeys»* or flunkies was brought to light by market reforms. These people are under the influence of the powerful, ready for humiliating subservience of any kind, characterized by loss of personal dignity and willingness to fulfill any assignment, including dirty ones. Their essence is rather loathsome and disgusting. And no high rank or affiliation to artistic unions can improve their image, since the basic postulate of their behavior can be expressed in a single phrase: «What is your pleasure, Sir?» We should point out that some people join the ranks of these lackeys not only on their own free will, but also due to certain socio-psychological characteristics — suggestibility, weak will, and lack of independence in making responsible decisions.

The times of transformation processes have created another type of behavior among people who call themselves «intelligentsia»— *demagogues.* Due to its blatancy, intolerance and bad manners, initially this group «showcased» its qualities during demonstrations, rallies and meetings, and then in «free» media, mixing lies with the truth, fiction with reality, imaginary with hypothetical. However, the demagogues who reached the top of the power structure proved to be particularly dangerous. In fact, they constantly, regularly, intentionally and willingly distort the facts to influence feelings, instincts and consciousness of the people, inflame passions in order to achieve their own selfish (mainly political) interests. This process is accompanied by arrogant reasoning; it encourages plebeian servility and desire to please the crowd. Cheap populism is also inherent in this category of people, for it enables them to achieve political victories. Some of them managed to reach top political positions, both in the capital and the regions, even presidency and leadership of political parties or movements. True, life tends to quickly restore political balance: usually their attempts end up in scandal and resignation. Another type of demagoguery is also worth noting. It is demagoguery of the media, which is very hard to fight, for under the guise of plausibility, they conceal self-promotion and self-advertising, or resort to tabloid journalism in pursuit of readers.

Those among intelligentsia, who (with certain allowances) can be called *«new dissidents»*, stand apart. This is a conditional name for a group that once enthusiastically welcomed the dismantling of Soviet system and wholeheartedly contributed to the establishment of declared principles for building a new social order. Then, many of them directly or indirectly repudiated the new regime created with their help and support. New realities have transformed them into staunch fighters against their own materialized dreams of first «rosy» years of the new Russia. A few returned to their previous professional activities, focusing their attention on the strategy of «small deeds». Some of them, professing commitment to the ideals of democracy, are trying to determine feasibility of combining these ideals with patriotic or social orientations.

Analysis of these major groups of intelligentsia does not exclude consideration and evaluation of other social communities, reflecting specificity of their consciousness and behavior. However, with all the diversity of intelligentsia, we still have to answer the question — does it have a future? After all, like other segments of the population, it is trying to survive in a rapidly deteriorating situation. Consequently, orientation toward material goals reduces their interest in such motif as content of labor (Cherkasov, Chernyshevskiy. 1994).

Analysis of real state of consciousness and behavior of Russian intelligentsia attests to its historical defeat. Although «it made an enormous contribution to cultural advancement of the people» (N.E. Pokrovskiy), this was insufficient for democratic modernization of political and economic system in Russia. Russian intelligentsia could not withstand advancing anti-intellectualism. It was defeated by bureaucracy in its struggle for people's minds, unable to consolidate and organize, defend its own interests (it is impossible to take seriously an attempt to convene a Congress of the Intelligentsia by a single fairly biased group). Therefore, we fully agree with the statement that «moral and historical duty of Russian intelligentsia to its own people was poorly conceived and even worse executed» (Magaril. 1999).

19.3. Intellectuals: who are they?

In recent years, in Russian social sciences, the term «intellectuals» has been used increasingly more often. We should point out that Western scientific literature refers to the broadest range of specialists and experts as 'intellectuals' (in the West, the notion of 'intelligentsia' is virtually absent).

Elaboration of *the concept of «intellectuals»* is developing in several directions:

First, it is believed that intelligentsia has fulfilled its historic mission of educating and enlightening people. Education has become available to all segments of the population, thus enabling them to fairly effectively take care of educating their children, as well as their own professional development. In this situation, they say, intermediaries are not needed. Let people with specialized education attend to their professional duties, rather than general civic concerns – this is what the State is for, as well as its social institutions that are designed and ready to meet a variety of educational needs. Moreover, the state is hardly neutral in this process, and unlike 19th and even early 20th centuries, it made teaching young people, their general and vocational education, regular training and re-training a subject of its close attention.

Second, in an age of rapid scientific and technological transformations, *there is a particularly important issue of training professionals, capable of acquiring vast array of information, constantly working with and updating it,* which requires tremendous amounts of time, energy and intellectual effort. And every distraction from these efforts leads to weakening of national intellectual potential, loss of opportunities for further breakthroughs into the unknown, substituting addressing strategic problems with short-term, transient worries and anxiety.

Third, as many believe (e.g. Yu. A. Levada), *«the number of dirty tricks» played by Russian intelligentsia is incalculable* (Levada. 2000). Its constant zigzagging, fluctuations – from loyalty to betrayal, rapid changes in sympathies and antipathies are beyond rational comprehension and understanding. Its constant flirting with the government or the game of opposition to an equal extent characterizes instability of its civic consciousness and behavior. Going from one extreme to another, participating in stirring up tensions, bringing itself to hysteria, these, too, are real traits of a group of persons who continue to regard themselves as intelligentsia. These traits are often reinforced by absurd behavior, tainted with paranoia and psychosis, with inability to assess new realities and with appetite for intrigue.

Some researchers draw attention to the fact that *intelligentsia's many complaints* (that people refuse to support it, lack of demand in their participation in issues of governance, increasing conformity in its ranks, inconsistency of assessments of Soviet and modern times) *resemble «lamentations»* (S. Magaril).

Intellectuals, however, reject wavering, uncertainty and complaints, believing that their role and significance are determined by the results of their activities. In other analytical materials and publications their authors point out the fact that younger generation of professionals is increasingly moving toward individualism, professionalism and strong focus on successful careers. They are sometimes called «yuppie» (young urban professional). According to «Kommersant» newspaper, they are the exact opposite of «intellectual outsiders», incapable of making money, achieving success in life, and therefore, in this «new life», doomed to stagnation and extinction (!).

Often times, discussions of the fate of intelligentsia are reduced to attempts at belittling or humiliating it, or to dismissive remarks. They resemble mockery and disrespect on the verge of contempt. According to these assertions, a member of intelligentsia is an «educated social drifter, alienated from his caste or class, unfamiliar with his social roots, yet having an opportunity and taste for lengthy discussions about the meaning of life and own personal role in world history (or world revolution)» (Mau. 2000). From this point of view, Vladimir May, while criticizing Lenin's attitude to intelligentsia in most disparaging way, practically expresses solidarity with his scathing assessments of thoughts, intentions and deeds of this layer of Russian society. Regrettably, these statements also reflect (in a latent form) his contempt not only for intelligentsia, but also for the people, who, he claims, supposedly resemble a herd of cattle, incapable of comprehending their own «luck» in market society.

And finally, this confusion in social consciousness not only characterizes the entire intellectual community, but also every modern-day member of intelligentsia, whose conduct is literary woven of paradoxes and contradictions. As popular journalist E. Sagalaev, once said of himself, «sad, but true: this era made a monstrous conglomerate out of me: *Sovok* (homo soveticus), Romantic, Cynic, Businessman, Conformist, follower of Gorbachev, Yeltsin, Berezovsky, Primakov. I dissolve in von Trier, Almadovar and Dostoevsky. I suffer for the people. I feel sorry the elderly, for our boys in Chechnya and for Chechen children. And hope for something» (Sagalaev. 2000). However, the author of this otherwise rather accurate statement blames the era. It is often used to justify one's conduct, hopes, and wavering. But, why is this intelligent man, like so many others, is reluctant to accept any personal responsibility, in contrast to his 19th century predecessors?

But, even more regrettable is a recurrent historical paradox, where part of politically active intelligentsia is once again gripped by the idea of «making people happy», opening their eyes, demonstrating luminous future prospects to «these silly creatures» who for some reason refuse to believe and follow them, against sincere intentions of those intellectuals. How else can we explain the words of Yuri Karyakin, a bright and ardent representative of democratic intelligentsia, who in 1993, after the announcement of election results to the first State Duma exclaimed: «Russia, you are nuts!», believing that the majority of those who voted in opposition to what he wanted, were acting improperly, were misguided and mistakenly supporting the wrong side. This self-conceit, this absolute confidence in one's oracle-like infallibility, as well as absolute cretinism of those who disagree, is not just surprising and alarming, it once again raises the issue of exorbitant claims and ambitions of individuals seeking power, or at least being close to it.

Based on these unfavorable characteristics of modern Russia's intelligentsia, some believe that *another group of creatively thinking people should be referred to as intellectuals, in contrast to intelligentsia.* And this is not just a term; it is a reflection of new features and new characters of people's consciousness and behavior. These are primarily *high-class professionals,* who constantly and relentlessly improve their professional skills, since they are confident (and actually demonstrate that confidence) that contemporary society can be efficiently developed and improved only if they are responsibly fulfilling their duties. This technocratic approach is gaining increased popularity that resonates in the mind-set of modern (and not only scientific and technical) intelligentsia. Standards of education, high qualifications and employment in vanguard industries are of extreme importance to intellectuals.

Its ability to adjust to new realities, refusal to follow such moral postulates like «poor, but honest», «broke, but independent» , etc., etc. is no less significant for this group of people. They can guarantee relatively high living standards for themselves; they are cable of applying their talents to resolving production problems, as well as coordinating their own personal interests with group, corporate and public ones.

Furthermore, intellectuals claim that their approach to resolving problems is more balanced and free of personal and ideological issues, even if it goes against the interests of those, unable to «make it» and adapt to changing situation. «Don't feel sorry for inept» — this motto is characteristic of many professionals who would rather pay to support misfits then waste their energy turning them into independently functioning full-fledged members of civil society.

Their aspiration to live according to legal norms and the law, legislation and not moral criteria, which often interfere with adequate performance of their professional duties, can be attributed to specific features of consciousness and behavior of intellectuals. Protest against intelligentsia-like soft approach is expressed in hard, rigid (sometimes cruel) course of action, where there is no place for feelings («sentimentality»), there are only business or production interests, fulfillment of their obligations. A number of scientific studies also point out such qualities of intellectuals as their exceptional mobility, lack of ideological preferences and self-realization of their usefulness and significance as holders of unique and important information, awareness of their equality in relations with owners of means of production, and qualitatively different motivation for activity (Inozemtsev. 2000).

We disagree with some of these statements. Despite apparent neutrality, many intellectuals often exhibit pathological desire to impose their attitude and worldview on society, which is often based on inconsequent ideas, self-importance or egotism. This group of intellectuals tends to speak not only on behalf of intelligentsia, but the entire nation. This attitude is based on high self-assessment and on philosophy of *«homo homini lupus est»*, on limitless selfishness. It is easy to imagine that these people might want to impose a technocratic regime on the country, if they ever come to power.

In other words, in market economy, ideology of a new generation of professionals is gaining momentum, mobilizing new supporters and replacing ideas, concepts and views of those who call themselves intelligentsia. Does this mean that intelligentsia as a subject of historical reality is now a thing of the past? Sociological data show that among value orientations of the population, including those who have college education and are engaged in highly intellectual jobs, a high percentage of people are guided by such virtues as compassion, mutual assistance, understanding and support of public interests, ability to subordinate personal to public and more.

Among intelligentsia, like the entire population, there still remains a high percentage of so called workaholics, who, despite all the vicissitudes of Soviet and post-Soviet period, continue to work selflessly, above all appreciating the content of their work and it focus on benefitting society as a whole. According to VTsIOM data, they account for 14–16%, i.e. over one in sixth people, who believe that working for a common cause is a value worth living for. We should also point out the fact that there is still a strong conviction that «today, the true calling of our intelligentsia is to help society find an Alternative — a new historical perspective» (Kruglyakov. 2005).

However, the future of intelligentsia in many respects depends on whether the next generation, today's students, would be able to not simply preserve the ideals of Russian intelligentsia, but also follow them. Some, though unrepresentative surveys suggest that these ideas continue to live in the hearts of young students. For example, a survey of students of Russian State Humanitarian University in 1999 and 2005 showed that 46–48% of them fully or partly share the opinion that intelligentsia should serve popular interests. This means that the ideals of Russian intelligentsia, although subject to corrosion, continue to exist (*Tsennostnaya i sotsialnaya identitshnost'...* 2000). So, the discussion of «member of intelligentsia or an intellectual» is far from over. It might take some time to dot the i's and cross the t's in this debate. At the same time, we can not exclude a possibility that it will remain an eternal question, eternal paradox, at least for Russian culture and Russia's mentality.

References

Cherkassov P.P., Chernyshevskiy D.V.*Istoria imperatorskoi Rossii ot Petra Velikogo do Nikolaya II (A History of Imperial Russia from Peter the Great to Nikolas II).* Moscow, 1994. P. 324.

Goudkov L., Dubin B. *Russian Public Opinion Monitor.* 1994. No 4.

Inozemtsev V. L. «*Class intellectualov*» *v postindustrial'nom obshchestve ('Intellectual Class' in Postindustrial Society)* // Sotsiologhicheskiye issledovania. 2000. No 6.

Intelligentsia. Moscow 1994; Kara-Murza S.G. *Intelligentsia na pepelische Rossii (Intelligentsia at the Ruins of Russia).* Moscow, 1997; *Na pereputie (Novyie vekhi) (At crossroads (New 'Signposts')).* Moscow, 1999; etc.

Kiva A.V. *Budushchee intelligentsii (Future of Intellegentsia)* // Nezavisimaya gazeta. September 18, 2000.

Kruglyakov E.P. *Ucheniye s bol'shoy doroghi («Scientists»—Gansters).* Moscow, 2005.

Levada Yu. *Interviu ob intelligencii (Interview on Intelligentsia)* // Izvestia. July 14, 2000.

Magaril S. *Grazhdanskaya otvetstvennost' intelligentsii (Civic Responsibility of Intelligentsia)* // Sotsiologhicheskiye issledovania. 2001. No 2.

Mau V. *Neskol'ko slov ob intelligentsia (A Few Words about Intelligentsia)* // Izvestiya. September 12, 2000.

Panarin A.S. *Rossiyskaya intelligentsia v mirovikh voinakh I revolutsiakh XX veka (Russian Intelligentsia in World Wars and Revolutions of the 20th Century).* Moscow, 1998. P. 3.

Panarin A.S. *Rossiyskaya intelligentsia v mirovikh voinakh I revolutsiakh XX veka (Russian Intelligentsia in World Wars and Revolutions of the 20th Century).* Moscow, 1998. P. 12.

Pokrovskiy N.E. *Proshchai, intelligentsia (Farewell, Intelligentsia)* // Na pereputie. Moscow, 1999. P. 49.

Sagalaev E. *Chto est' intelligentsia (What is Intellegentsia?)* // Izvestia. August 8, 2000.

Tsennostnaya i sotsialnaya identitshnost' rossiskoi gumanitarnoi intellighentsii (Value and Social Identity of Russian Humanitarian Intelligentsia). Moscow, 2000.

Chapter 20. **Education and quasi-educated**

...Rushing human beings
Are overwhelmed by approximations,
They study some things, they know a few things
When it looks like they sow, in fact they cut
Explain approximately,
Cherish relatively

R.I. Rozhdestvenskiy (1932–1994)
Soviet Russian poet

Vivid and imaginative words of the epigraph expresses the pain, the worry and a warning — a poorly understood approaching threat of potential loss of viability of our society and future prospects of withstanding challenges of our times. And this threat is — unprofessionalism, ignorance or half-knowledge, knowledge without morality, knowledge without general culture.

We can use statistical and sociological data to prove this thesis, as well as numerous examples, quotations of the best minds of the country and the rest of the world, and recall historical experience. However, in this case poetic image is more illustrative, convincing and persuasive. In the words of the poet there is a warning against indifference, and passionate conviction that all our action, all our failures and shortcomings have nothing to do with evil or mythical forces. They primarily depend on us, on our position, our principles, our skills (no wonder the poem was entitled «About the Masters». Master here means a master-hand, craftsman, expert or artisan) and our orientations, our attitude to good and evil, or perhaps our choice to treat them with indifference and detachment.

In 1974, prominent Russian writer A.I. Solzhenitsyn came out with a document «Quasi-educated» (smatterers), which angrily denounced an increasingly widespread lifestyle, mainly oriented towards satisfying utilitarian, rather than spiritual needs. In this aspect, the writer raised a very important and pressing issue, focusing on the topic that worried and alarmed him. After all, the reason for all these trials and tribulations lies not just in those immense transformations that take place during educational process, but in those shifts that led people to change their attitudes towards education and its social functions, as well as the emergence of a new class of contradictions, questioning the achievements of modern society. *Essentially, society faced a huge paradox in the era of information revolution: growing number of those receiving education and professional training is simultaneously accompanied by a process of growth of (a special type of) illiteracy and professional incompetence (as failure to meet the requirements of scientific and technological revolution).*

20.1. New facets of illiteracy

Modern society has made remarkable progress: breakthrough in space exploration, uncovering secrets of micro world, invention and application of new (avant-garde or high) technologies, creation of materials unknown in nature, mass computerization, etc.

Along with these successes, science has greatly contributed to the development of education, its improvement, involvement of large number of people in its sphere of influence. The role of not only elite, but also mass education has become prominent in the second half of the 20th century. The US Congressional Committee, established by President Eisenhower in 1957 to ascertain the reasons for Soviet space victory (launching first Sputnik on October 4, 1957), concluded that it was the Soviet educational system that was responsible for this achievement. Based on this conclusion, United States included education into the number of their top priorities, and did a tremendous job in their struggle for leadership in the modern world.

The USSR, however, not only failed to exploit their achieved successes, but also was not paying attention to the necessity for continuous improvement and updating of educational strategy and tactics. Gradually, little by little a *paradox emerged in this sphere — along with increasing numbers of educated people, new illiteracy, its present-day forms came into existence* due to rapid increase in a number of people, lacking literacy in modern sense of this word.

We should recall that in 19th century literacy and education was interpreted as a combination of the writing and reading skills (Soloviev. 1834, 551). Anyone who did not meet this requirement was considered illiterate. This interpretation of illiteracy has lasted almost throughout the entire 20th century. Even back in 1958 UNESCO defined an illiterate person as «an individual unable to read and write sufficiently to understand simple and brief information concerning his daily life». But gradually the interpretation of literacy (illiteracy) was expanded to include the degree of assimilation of spoken and audio-visual culture. This is why in late 1970's, early 1980's a *new concept* was introduced in everyday life — *«functional illiteracy» as «inability to apply acts of reading, writing and counting necessary for relevant life activities, as well as personal and social development».* In L.N. Lesokhina view, *literacy means not only the traditional ability to read* (perceive information), *write* (convey one's thoughts, broaden the range of communicative interaction), *speak* (capacity for verbal communication and verbal expression), but, more importantly, *ensuring the ability of social orientation and social self-regulation.* This rises a necessity to discuss not just (il)literacy, but also functional illiteracy. What is it?

In all fairness, it should be noted that regular illiteracy is not yet a thing of the past. Hundreds of thousands, millions of people in many countries of Asia,

Africa and Latin America are not covered by initial basic educational training. According to expert estimates, millions of people can neither read nor write even in the United States. Having inherited a developed educational system from the USSR, Russia failed to preserve it. As a result it lost its leadership positions in such an index as intellectual potential. Without proper control, numbers of elementary illiterate people continue to grow, becoming a sort of silent reproach for irresponsibility of the state and its inability to see future prospects.

However, at the present stage of development, *many countries, including Russia are facing the threat of functional illiteracy, including half-knowledge, ersatz-knowledge, false knowledge and phantom knowledge.* More detailed analysis of this phenomenon shows that a degree of inclusion of the majority of world population in the educational environment leaves much to be desired. Even in those countries, which guarantee universal right to education, approximately 25-40% of people experience difficulty with reading, writing and math, as well as routine social activities, such as voting, filling in application forms, understanding instructions, reading schedules, not to mention skills of verbal or written self-expression (Kliucharev. 2000). Lack of education and professional skills does not allow this category of people to raise their social status and social position, as well as demand social prestige in accordance with requirements of industrial and information society.

Functional illiteracy is not so much a matter of absence of general education, as inability to use writing and reading skills. Sociological surveys show that in Russia, the number of functionally illiterate people is fairly high. Among older individuals it ranges between 15 to 33%, depending on occupation, place of residence and other life circumstances. But the country is facing a new wave of complete functional illiteracy in the first quarter of 21st century: experts estimate that some 2 million children are not attending school, not studying. Illiteracy is a symptom of social crisis, a sign of impending disaster, comparable to ecological calamity, with human beings in its epicenter. Finally, illiteracy is an indicator of human bondage in man's interaction with the world around him. Here we are faced with one of the most amazing paradoxes: the desire to know, meaning willingness to accept freedom «with eyes wide open», resulting in abandonment of internal harmony. Modern world is questioning N.G. Chernyshevsky's (1828–1889, the Russian writer and revolutionary) motto: «Let's study — and knowledge will set us free» from his novel «What Is To Be Done?»

Another paradoxical phenomenon is related to educational process: an educated person is increasingly dissatisfied with the world around him, while an illiterate individual is «unassuming,» lives in harmony with his/her environment and easily accepts all its shortcomings, problems and vices. Illiterate people often refer to insufficient general and professional (vocational) training to justify their social status, their limited claims, as well as quality and quantity of work performed. This is very close to developing protective stereotypes, like contemptuous attitude to the work of intellectuals, especially when this process is accompanied by declining prestige of teachers, doctors, or engineers. Functional illiteracy can also be regarded as the result of contradiction between education and practical activities, resulting in lacking demand for knowledge and cessation («winding down») of educational activities. Finally, functional illiteracy is manifested in opposition between scientific and practical activities. Some researchers call this subjective condition a phenomenon of «pathos» (Karmadonov. 2000).

Functional illiteracy among people with higher education is of particular concern, although, naturally, this phenomenon has its own peculiarities, its particular forms of manifestation. In this category of people, illiteracy is manifested in an inability to communicate with the outside world in written (and sometimes oral) form, express one's thoughts and ideas on paper: in an article, scientific report or survey, review or business document. Unfortunately, even in the teaching profession there are a lot of people, who for years have not written anything, did not participate in scientific discussions, or have avoided stating their positions on various issues.

Functional illiteracy among university graduates is also manifested in the fact that they pay little attention to the problems of understanding (not just knowledge and learning), which promotes the development of creative, practical attitude to comprehended, digested or digestible information. Therefore, people with higher education are supposed to know all of the different approaches within the scope of their professional activity, focus on the available patterns in sciences and practice, they should understand their specific characteristics and peculiarities, their quality and be able to assess their credibility and validity. This approach to knowledge represents a developing type of training. But working based on the best examples does not mean copying them (copies are always vulnerable, flawed, limited for other people). It means grasping their essence, their spirit, and their research, approach and comparison principles. Creativity in labor, training and learning processes allows for flexibility, as well as avoiding stereotypical solutions and behavior.

Functional illiteracy of people with higher education sometimes manifests itself in rather unusual ways. It is often disguised by specific terminology, pretentious language, misuse or simple copying of terminology adopted in other science or other language. This kind of «bird» talk quite successfully conceals real knowledge (or lack thereof), inability and failure to reach the audience. Incomprehensible phraseology covers often poverty of thought, claiming, however, the significance of the findings. In our opinion, there is only one criterion for such situations:

inability to reach other people, establish contact with the audience, and convey the meaning and clearly express one's thoughts or position is the result of specific functional illiteracy of so-called specialist.

Functionally illiterate people tend to adapt to the situation without changing their own essence: they are unable to express knowledge or information distinctly and clearly, either in written or in oral form. Functional illiteracy is both evidence and consequence of educational crisis, or, more precisely, its inability to realize one of its main functions: to teach people to actively interact with their environment. Moreover, in this process, significance of humanities is very high, since the original requirement can only be implemented with their help — ability to write, read and speak, which prepares an individual for action and professional work in all spheres of social life.

Unfortunately, our life is such that it is not shameful to be functionally illiterate, and it is not hard to pass for an educated person. This is facilitated by, on the one hand, nihilistic attitude to intellectual professions (mental work), practices of attitude and behavior toward the process and organization of education, on the other, i.e. undeserved high grades, getting quasi-education, buying university diplomas, etc. Distorted personal ambitions (primarily motivated by latent condescending attitude to education) are the basis for functional illiteracy.

Among the causes of functional illiteracy we should point out the following:

First of all, *the quality of education.* It is obvious that educational demand is not always satisfied by means relevant to the needs of information society. Diminishing professional skill requirements of the specialists who are supposed to transmit knowledge contribute to this factor. To add is that *modern educational environment*, taking into account the need to transfer increasing volume of information, requires finding and utilizing new teaching methods, which in turn, requires retraining teachers themselves. Due to low social prestige, meager supply of teaching staff, these requirements are rarely implemented, which certainly affects *quality of training* of future specialists.

A *number of social causes and circumstances also contribute to functional illiteracy.* Thus, mastering latest skills and information depends not only on people's wishes and aspirations, but also on the government policies manifested in varying degree of real public accessibility to educational institutions. For a significant number of people, access to higher education is increasingly becoming a nominal paper declaration. Moreover, it is reasonable to assert that inequality in educational access shows a steady growth trend. Single-dimensionality (linearity) as well as, to a certain degree, primitivism of general and professional training, contributes to this inequality. The process of social stratification and, as a consequence, divergent opportunities of access to education cause inferiority of professional training.

20.2. Professional incompetence as a precursor of professional cretinism

Several approaches are typically used to assess the level of professional qualification and training. First, the most traditional and frequently used method: add up the number of people with vocational training (higher, specialized secondary, primary), the number of all types of vocational schools plus the number of students in all forms of education. Sometimes these figures are supplemented by the analysis of temporal intervals and analysis of increase in the number of professions taught in the already existing or newly opened education institutions. The growth numbers are always positive, since the overall trend is undeniable: our times require specialists, so, even in the most underdeveloped countries numbers of students are steadily increasing.

Secondly, no less common approach, which focuses on achievements, responsibilities of a specialist and his/her professional qualities. This concept is based on identifying what is this specialist required to be like (including future specialists); what are his future goals and guidelines; what he should emulate and what qualities he should develop. This normative-value approach focuses on future characteristics of a specialist, wittingly or unwittingly ignoring the real situation, neglecting the fact that the analysis of what a specialist should not be, is no less (if not more) important for assessing a specialist.

It is the identification of professional incompetence indicators that discloses the limitations, imperfection and deficiencies and of a specialist, which constitutes the essence of the third approach.

Why should we discuss *professional incompetence?*

First, in the new Russia, too many faulty, hasty and uninformed decisions have been made whether during economic reforms, restructuring of political institutions, war in Chechnya, relations with other countries, etc. Although, we cannot say that these decisions were all made with malicious intent, or the desire to harm society. Furthermore, initiators of many of them were genuinely trying to contribute to well-being of the country. But good intentions do not equate to competent resolution of existing problems. It is incompetence, inaccuracy, superficiality that became the basis of the protracted crisis that hit Russia in economic, political, social and spiritual life. Moreover, the cause of many industrial accidents, technological disasters lies in professional incompetence and irresponsibility of specialists. This also applies to higher education. Certainly, this sphere of spiritual life should respond to the demands of our time. However, this reaction often turns into a primitive imitation or simply bowing down to foreign experience. Thus, the system of bachelors and masters' degrees is alien to Russian educational traditions and, as practice shows, is rejected by many universities after first few years of its attempted implementation. In this regard, we should note just accusations by German scholars and educators, who often point out many similarities between Russian and German education systems (indeed, historically, education in Russia was developed under the influence of German concepts, starting with Peter I and Catherine II). They are perplexed by excessive haste in transplanting American experience onto the Russian soil.

Secondly, starting from early 1990's, there has been an ongoing devaluation of intellectual labor affecting hundreds of thousands of teachers, doctors, engineers and other professionals, which was manifested, on the one hand, in the fact that intelligentsia itself was lowering the standards its members held themselves to; on the other hand, in changing attitudes of society towards people involved in intellectual labor accompanied by negative assessments of its value and lacking social protection. Sociological surveys show that after graduation very few students want to work as educators, researchers, or be employed in public sector. Unattractiveness of the status of scientist, teacher, professor or engineer in our society from all angles (including material) certainly does not contribute to influx of young specialists into these professions.

Thirdly, incompetence is not an obstacle to the so-called enterprising people. In Russian society, one can have an easy life both without knowledge and without qualification, often much better than with them. Education is no longer a structure-forming component. «Ability to live well» is becoming perhaps most important, while education at best is playing a supporting role in dealing with personal and production matters. When incompetence becomes a way of life due to lawlessness and political shortcomings in society, professional qualification becomes an unnecessary or redundant component of human activities. Thus, a survey of people engaged in «shuttle» business (1998, Tatarstan), showed that 45% of them had higher education and 38% — secondary special one. Obviously, for this kind of work they did not require such level of education. But what prompted people to go into «shuttle» business? Main reasons — situation in society, attitudes towards people with higher education, inadequate economic and social relations. The same study showed that only 5% of respondents felt that this type of business activity is attractive (Cf.: *Sotsiologhicheskiye issledovania.* 1998. No. 11. P. 41-42). Such situation with specialists is a consequence of opposing academic work to practical activities, of absolute neglect of sciences on the part of the state, as well as appeals to abandon former orientations and expectations, and adopt new values.

Fourth, a period of upheaval is not only the time of necessary change, but it is also a time of ambitions, time of emergence of incompetent people at different levels of power hierarchy, with no knowledge of general scientific principles, without the slightest practical experience, without conscience, trying to use their position to seize their chance, to achieve their own selfish goals, even up to decorating themselves with academic regalia. For example, in mid-1990 the Higher

Qualification Committee had to address the question of conferring a degree of Doctor of Science, which was filed by an author of three monographs and 57 articles published within one year (!?!). And as a result we have a physician whom we would never entrust with our health; we are not sure that a certain engineer is capable of making a balanced and correct technical or technological decision, including those for high-risk environment; we are not convinced that creatively-minded people are involved in scientific sphere; we doubt the ability of a teacher, who is often just a lesson-giver, not a wise guide in the world of knowledge. And, as a result, we all do not trust the authorities, their integrity, decency, honesty, and ability to organize work and be zealous representatives of common interests.

Thus, professional incompetence is a peculiar paradox of the times. It is both a cause and a consequence of material and spiritual poverty of society, the source of deviant behavior and tragedies of life and a social risk factor. The danger is increasing in proportion to how incompetence turns from local into a nation-wide phenomenon: before, we used to talk about professional incompetence in certain organizations, some sectors of economy and culture, in some regions — now this feature has become a national scourge.

Incompetence is characterized not only by functional illiteracy, but also by professional limitations, lack of general culture and common moral guidelines. Let us examine it in more detail.

Professional limitations (narrow-mindedness) have their own specifics and manifestations. The number of people engaged in occupations, other than the ones they have been trained for and studied, has increased significantly. On one hand, meeting an engineer or a teacher employed as a loader, seller or just doing any job available has become a norm. On the other hand, producers turned bankers, philosophers — entrepreneurs, historians turned managers of missile or excavator factories, biologists consulting on governance issues, etc. are not uncommon either. In principle, it is possible, but then we should not complain that things are not working out, that the decisions are ineffective, that Russian experts are not valued or respected by their foreign colleagues, or that they are not trusted, their abilities to solve problems are questioned, as required by of modern science and practice. All this suggests that it defeats the purpose of professional training, since, in the first case, training is a waist of money, and in the second, such people's actions are amateurish, superficial or even irresponsible, which — put together — leads to huge economic and social costs for society.

Professional narrow-mindedness manifests itself in large-scale change of professional occupations, when increasing number of people undertake fulfilling the duties, which do not correspond to the essence of their professional training. True, they get involved in this process practically regardless of their will and desires, under pressure of life circumstances, often involuntarily. But this does not change the fact that in this case we also dealing with incompetence. Such situation has a direct relevance to the implementation of functions of higher education. However paradoxical it may seem, but the very system of higher education contributes to professional limitations by responding to immediate needs. Obviously, training practices of specialists, in particular — economists and lawyers, which took amazing scale during the 1990's, according to expert estimates, has reached a saturation point, whereas traditional specialties due to emerging circumstances can confirm their relevance, their necessity only in the future, claiming their niche in the social division of labor. Second education or vocational training might be an option, a compromise to help people meet the requirements of the time.

One of the reasons for professional incompetence is lack of general culture, absence of that humanitarian base, which forms a foundation for successful professional activity. The decline of overall culture, unfortunately, contributes to weakening of attention to literary sphere, arts and information, the kind of knowledge that makes a person real member of society, an engaging communicator and an interesting partner, co-worker.

Sociological surveys carried out at industrial enterprises in 1980's and 1990's revealed an interesting and somewhat paradoxical feature. Based on previous information, it has long been thought that in order to succeed in business, organizational skills and professionalism of the leaders, their professional training were of paramount importance. However, surprisingly, many employees and production workers, among primary qualities required of a modern leader, named high level of general culture, ability and desire to demonstrate it in conjunction with professional and organizational skills (Boikov, Ivanov, Toshchenko. 1990; Sokolova. 1999). In our view, changing perceptions of managerial qualities reflect new requirements of the time, which increasingly demand a well-educated specialist, a personality. In other words, in order to meet the requirements of the information revolution, it is not enough to be a narrow professional. Surveys, conducted at modern production enterprises clearly reflect high ratings of the leaders constantly exploring, searching for alternatives, not confined to the narrow professional framework, and who are of great value to the people around them as experts on the broader culture.

The problem of general culture is more than relevant. Many experts still resemble a «gumboil» (ironic expression of Koz'ma Prutkov), like a swollen cheek, they are one-sided. This is becoming a social disease. Sociological research of theatrical issues shows that up to 80% of Muscovites have not been to a theater in years and many — in decades, yet, they are living with self justification, confident that if they want, they can even get into Bolshoi Theater.

No matter how odd or funny this may seem, this realization that «I can, if I want to» elevates many Muscovites above people from the provinces. By the way, specialists trained during the 1990's were not much different with regard to their devotion to arts, either. In a survey of students of Moscow State University for Humanities (1999), in response to the question: «If you could spend two days off at your own discretion, what would you do?» only 3% of respondents said that they would visit a Conservatory or Philharmonic, 8% — Theater (Opera or Ballet), 12% — Drama Theater, 10% — pop concert, while 47% would prefer to party with friends, 19% — disco or club, 7% — restaurant (*Tsennostnaya i sotsialnaya identichnost...* 2000). Similar results were obtained in surveys of students in other universities as well, and the data from some of them can be described as plain depressing.

Unfortunately, at a time when personal survival becomes a real challenge, there is a noticeable reduction in people's claims and demands, and primarily cultural ones. In sociology, there is a concept of hierarchy of demands, expressed in a well-known formula of A. Maslow's (1908–1970), American psychologist and sociologist. He believed that after satisfying physiological needs and safety and security requirements, spiritual needs are met next, than we have to satisfy respect and creativity requirements. However, when life becomes too difficult, too severe, individuals start abandoning certain «elevating» needs and are content with more limited opportunities. Perhaps that is where the secret of this Russian tragedy lies, when many people, under pressure, are forced to simplify or abandon their spiritual life, give up what elevates an individual as a person in the process of sharing cultural achievements of mankind.

Computer literacy as part of general human culture deserves special mention. Unfortunately, it rarely comes up in discussions of general culture, although it is becoming a vital necessity for people's lives and activities. Many specialists either hope to do without it or assume that computer literacy is unrelated to general culture. This is a wide-spread misconception. It is the lack of this literacy that turns many of them into hostages of their own narrow-mindedness, making their inclusion into modern informational space extremely difficult. Mankind is entering the age in which computer illiteracy is equivalent and tantamount to general illiteracy.

And finally, the most important component of professional incompetence is (lack of) morality. Whatever may be said, in case of society without morals we are not dealing with people, but with businessmen i.e., persons for whom nothing is sacred, or, at best, with so-called intellectuals, who only recognize their right to benefit, right to succeed, often at the expense of other people's interests, interests of those around them. We are more and more often encountering irresponsible people, who do not acknowledge any other right except the right for themselves to act in their own best interest, in a way that seems advantageous to them, without any obligations to other people. However, regardless of what may be said, whatever business or other essential qualities a person might possess, one cannot serve the public (an enterprise, or an organization) without certain ideals and moral norms.

In this regard, attitude of young people to such moral value as willingness to serve people and the nation is quite significant. One of the main priorities of Russian intelligentsia (we should remind you), was to bring knowledge to people, remain committed to such moral guidelines as willingness to make sacrifices, recognition of the priority of public over private and, most importantly, not letting personal sympathies and preferences interfere with the implementation of one's duties. In 2005, students of Russian State University for Humanities were asked: «In your opinion, is the statement «Intelligentsia should serve the people» outdated?» The answers require serious consideration. Merely 13% thought that this orientation was not outdated. Another 33% only partially shared this assessment of mental activities of intellectuals, i.e. their own future activities. But many students were convinced that people with higher education should be «just an intellectual, a professional» and nothing more (*Tsennostnaya i sotsialnaya identichnost'...* 2000, P. 145). Perhaps we are really witnessing the decline of Russian intelligentsia and sharing the fate of intellectuals of the Western world?

Loss of moral principles, in our view, stems from the fact that contemporary Russian intellectuals do not accept any restrictions, limitations in their activities, and are severely infected with imitation «bacilli», a mix of feelings of envy and inferiority towards their Western colleagues. This also affects their professional integrity, self-confidence in their abilities, both professional and civic.

20.3. Paradoxes of social enlightenment

Along with growing functional illiteracy and professional incompetence, we are also facing an important issue of *social enlightenment*. What is it? *It is information and knowledge, their comprehension, as well as desire to be guided by them in life, when in comes to health, lifestyle, nutrition, daily habits and predilections.* In analyzing this issue, we can only marvel at how incurious we are, how passive and irresponsible toward the essence of what constitutes value of life itself, of what makes life more meaningful and free from vices, from anything that restricts the joy and pleasure of one's work and recreation; acculturation, an opportunity to interact with others in the name of elevation of spiritual demands.

Birthrate, mortality, life expectancy, as well as such human costs as industrial and household accidents, human safety in various life situations do not only depend on people themselves, but also on society, on socio-economic, political and socio-cultural relations that prevail in that society. As far as Russia is concerned, the situation is bleak. Russia's population has decreased by almost 12 million people during 1990's — 2000's. And it would have been even greater if this decline had not been partially offset by migration of Russian-speaking population from the neighboring states. In addition, Russia is ahead of civilized countries in terms of birthrate, while its mortality rate equals most undeveloped. Demographic situation continues to deteriorate. Mortality exceeded birthrate 1,87 times (in 1998 the «gap» was 1,6 times). The situation with male life expectancy is very alarming as well: an average male does not reach retirement age of 60, since average life expectancy (in 1990–2000) ranges between 57–58 years. If this current trend continues, in 20 to 25 years the population of the country will be only 100 million people, and approximately 50 to 55 million in 2075 (*Sotsial'noye polozheniye i uroven' zhizni...* 2005, P. 53).

The concept of healthy lifestyle takes shape in early childhood. However, in reality we witness incomplete, distorted socialization of a significant part of younger generation. There are at least 2 million homeless children in the country, 3 million raised in families leading a-social way of life, one in five children is raised in an orphanage, and after leaving these orphanages almost 90% of their «graduates» become 'persons without a definite place of residence' (Kovaleva, Stepanova. P. 58; Slutskiy. P. 120).

What kind of social health of future generations can we be talking about? *Health of a society depends on how widespread physical and social ills and vices are:* cardiovascular disease, cancer, infectious diseases, as well as prostitution, alcoholism, drug addiction, tuberculosis. Thus, in Russia, 69% of those involved in prostitution are under 25 years of age. There is a rapidly growing problem with drug addiction and drug trafficking: between 1992 and 1996, poppy straw seizures went up 2,4 times, opium — 16,3 times, heroin — 180 times, cocaine — 740 times. In expert opinion, these figures represent a mere 10% of total offences related to illicit drug trafficking. According to the Health Ministry of Russian Federation, in 2000 there were between 3,5 — 4 million drug users in the country. With regard to alcohol, in 1990's its average consumption ranged between 14 — 18 liters per year (8 liters, according to World Health Organization, is considered the critical point, beyond which a threat of physical degradation of the population dramatically increases) (Cf.: Shcherbakova. P. 70). There are objective reasons for that. Health care system is funded, or rather under-funded by the State, amounting to mere 2 to 3% of GDP. State officials often blame economic crisis, but in this regard, we can bring up an example of certain countries that do not neglect the health of their people even during hard times. In Finland, for example, during economic crisis, 9% of GDP, instead of usual 7%, was allocated to healthcare, to prevent further deterioration to people's well-being.

In addition to objective reasons affecting the lifestyle and health of the people *there is also a number of subjective factors.* One of them (not insignificant) is social enlightenment that cannot be characterized otherwise than paradoxical. On the one hand, official and public media provide a variety of materials regarding benefits of sports, staying in shape, maintaining healthy appearance and attractiveness. On the other — there is an entire industry promoting alcohol, tobacco, questionable beverages, etc. i.e. all the things that shorten human life. However, attempts, and even decisions to ban advertising of these products generate new tricks to circumvent these bans and prohibitions, in order to continue profiting at the expense of nation's health.

It is necessary to, first of all, have all the media (including electronic) continuously, daily explain and expound, clearly, colorfully and convincingly what we need to know about our health and what we have to do to improve it. And, participation in social enlightenment should be made mandatory for some (like public channels), and recommended for others, with a system of benefits and financial penalties (for refusing to participate) in place.

Struggle against drug addiction is no less paradoxical. The emphasis here is not on prevention or prophylaxis, but on the treatment of already acquired vice, since this type of information allows to make money by preying on grief and distress of millions of people. In this case it is a struggle with effect, not with the cause of these vices.

The public had repeatedly raised the issue of quality and importance of family and sex education. This is undoubtedly a necessary and important task of social enlightenment. However, it is often reduced to sexual information, discussing problems, methods and techniques of sexual intercourse, while not adequately addressing serious dangers associated with the intimate sphere of human life. As a result, the rate of syphilis infection increased more than 30 times, with HIV/AIDS infection rates growing rapidly.

In fact, both secondary as well as specialized secondary and graduate schools do not participate in matters of social enlightenment, ignoring forms and methods of properly educating young people in terms of leading a healthy lifestyle. According to various sociological studies, up to 70% of young people smoke, up to one third of them have at least once used narcotics, and up to 60% are regularly consuming alcohol.

Medical efforts are extremely important for social enlightenment as well; however, their participation cannot resolve all of the problems of improving nation's health. Experts suggest that money should be invested not only in fighting disease, but also in prevention, in promoting healthy lifestyles.

* * *

So what are the prospects for overcoming functional illiteracy and professional incompetence?

At the moment they are still vague, unclear, and most importantly, there is no assurance that the steps taken today will rid society of these evils, or reduce their impact tomorrow. So far, we are facing circumstances and conditions that support, maintain and do not limit or restrict functional illiteracy and professional incompetence.

This paradoxical situation is not facing Russia alone. Is not the situation, where, on the one hand, the United States is promoting the achievements of its educational system, while, on the other, «buying up brains» all over the world and attracting professionals by providing them with better conditions for personal and business activities, paradoxical as well?

As for Russia, during the 1990's, mono-functional model of education was virtually eliminated, although it remains largely predominant. Many alternative forms of personnel training that came to replace the pre-existing ones are still far from perfect, and some of them are generally busy imitating serious work. Often pioneering and innovation coexist with both traditional system and with imitations of creativity as well. Innovative models of education stimulate creativity, helping overcome retrograde, rusty, outdated, backward traditions in youth education. Their implementation, however, is not trouble-free, for sometimes they turn into outright gag of little interest to students and have nothing in common with advanced professional training.

Sociological studies show that today's students require not only knowledge related to their future professional activities. They increasingly need knowledge linked to specific features of their future work (and not just to the needs of society). This, at first glance, is a contradiction: extensive broad general training combined with specifically targeted distinct kind of activities. In fact, that is the embodiment of modern features of vocational training of professional, mature and competent specialists that would be able to cope with corresponding demands of the times.

Besides, more then ever there is a growing demand for such leader-professional, who could serve as a fair and demanding mentor, a wise guide in the world of knowledge and realities of life, especially when it concerns young specialists. A fairly common situation, however, prevents this from happening, since traditional public schools rely on the form, where these potential mentors often have multiple (at times unnecessary) duties, while new commercial schools in one form or another implement the principle of «you give us money, we give you diplomas».

Thus, functional illiteracy and professional incompetence are the greatest, if not the main vices of our spiritual culture and, therefore viability of our society. The words of R. Rozhdestvenskiy's poem related to «masters» are more relevant than ever:

The world is aging in past hopes, but today, as yesterday
They are holding our world on their shoulders
They stretch their hands to reach the crossroads of celestial worlds.
The time moves them and the time believes in them.

References

Boikov V.E., Ivanov V.N., Toshchenko Zh.T. *Sotsialnye grani truda* (*Social Facets of Labor*). Moscow, 1990; Sokolova G.N. *Ekonomicheskaya sotsiologhia* (*Economic Sociology*).. Minsk, 1999.

KarmadonovO.A.*Prestizhipafoskakzhiznennyestrateghiisotsioeconomicheskoi gruppy (analiz SMI)* (*Prestige and Pathos as Life Strategies of Social Economic Group (media analysis))* // Sotsiologhicheskiye issledovania. 2000. No 1.

Kliucharev G. *Obutchayushchyi mir (Teaching World)* // Nezavisimaya gazeta. April 18, 2000.

Kovaleva T. V., Stepanova O. C. *Podrostki smutnogo vremeni (K probleme socializacii starsheklassnikov)* (*Adolescents of the Times of Turmoil (Highschool students socialization problems))* // Sociologhicheskiye issledovania. 1988. No 8. P. 58; Slutskiy E.G. *Besprizornost' v Rossii: vnov' groznaia realnost (Homeless Children in Russia: a Dreadful Danger Again)* // Sociologhicheskiye issledovania. 1998. No 3. P. 120.

Shcherbakova E.M. *Narkonashestvie v Rossii.O tchem govorit statistika (Drugs Invasion in Russia. What Does Statistics Say.)* // Sociologhicheskiye issledovania. 2004. No 1. P. 70.

Soloviev P. *Obshchiy Tserkovno-Slavianskiy Russki Slovar'* (Slavonic Church Russian Dictionary). St.Petersburg, 1834, P. 551.

Sotsial'noye polozheniye i uroven' zhizni naselenia Rossii. 2005: stat. sbornik (Social Situation and Level of Living of Russia's Population, 2005: Statistic Collection). Moscow, 2005, P. 53.

Sotsiologhicheskiye issledovania. 1998. No. 11. P. 41–42.

Tsennostnaya i sotsialnaya identichnost' rossiyskoy gumanitarnoy intellighentsii (Value and Social Identity of Russian Humanitarian Intelligentsia) // Tezisy Vserossiyskoy teoretiko-metodologhitcheskoy konferentsii. April 26–27, 2000. / E. by Zh.T. Toshchenko. Moscow, 2000.

Part V. **The situation of paradox**

Chapter 21. **Must and cannot**

> If you shouldn't, but really want to − you can
>
> *Popular saying*

A person's life is always accompanied by contradictory guidelines − propriety («must do the right thing», «have to do it the right way», «and have to behave a certain way») and restriction («cannot do that», «cannot demand that», «cannot live like that/spend time like that», «support someone or somebody»).

As a result an individual is surrounded by «musts» and «don'ts», like a wolf by red flags that represent a warning against certain deeds and actions, like a scarecrow, or a whip coercing a person into acting differently. Although, just like wolves, persons can jump over the flags, but first they have to overcome a barrier within. A feeling of being stuck, encircled by these flags does not lead to internal harmony, since many of the «have to» and «don'ts» − are something society came up with, not realizing the contradictory and paradoxical nature of these taboos. But when an individual is faced with the necessity to resolve this contradiction within his own consciousness and behavior, he finds himself in a difficult, often paradoxical situation (Sogomonov. 2005).

21.1. Must

Since early childhood and the first steps a person keeps hearing: «you must», «you must do this as well», «you have to − you are an adult now», etc. Becoming a citizen, an individual is placed within even stricter confines, when he has to live by multiple legal and moral requirements: he has to work hard, he must abide by morality and law. If these regulations are handed down from generation to generation, these «must» and «don'ts» become an integral part of one's lifestyle and mentality.

During the years of turmoil in the history of a country, they acquire a different overtone: it becomes necessary to discard certain things outdated, obsolete or questionable and get used to the new, unexplored, or not yet generally accepted. For example, «we must switch to private property». This «must» is understood by all; it is accepted, according to the sociological surveys, by up to 80% of the population. The popular majority, however, still can not understand that most people will never become private owners, especially when it comes to private ownership of means of production. Even in the United States of America 75–80% of the population do not own land, factories or companies. They make their living by selling their labor or intellectual abilities. This affords them comfortable living, existence, allows being competitive in the job market. In Russia, talking about private property, we often forget that not everyone will actually own it, and that this «must», applicable to this particular situation has an extremely limited and specific meaning.

An individual is often summoned under various «banners» appealing to one's civic consciousness. This has certain merits. But *the key to proper understanding of «must» — is answering the question, one asks him/her-self: «What happens if I don't comply with this «have to» or «must»?* If there is no clear answer, these «have to» and «musts» can be discarded without any remorse. If a refusal to fulfill this «have to» does not violate the interests of another person (other people, other social groups, etc.) — this is the real criterion of truth, justification and legality of one's actions.

«Must» can reach a level of absurdity. The novel of A. Beck «New Appointment», about a People's Commissar (based on a real life story of Minister of Metallurgy of Stalin's times — I.V. Tevosyan), who implemented daily accounting for all metallurgical plants. This had serious merits during the early period of establishment of this branch of industry, and then during the Great Patriotic War (1941–1945); yet a quarter century later it became completely pointless and absurd. But, instead of lifting this almighty «have to», the bureaucratic mechanism kept on spinning, despite of the fact that uselessness and futility of this information was apparent. Nevertheless the rule was never discarded, since it turned into a decade old dogma, creating an illusion that managers are closely monitoring the pulse of the industry and are aware of everything that is going on.

Passion for detailed, comprehensive and total control is in the flesh and blood of millions of people. Many of them cannot imagine themselves without petty bookkeeping, loosing sight of what is most important, promising and necessary. If we take a look around, we need to ask if the State is abusing daily and humiliating control over how people should behave what they should say or do. And that concerns not only the big bosses, leaders of certain branches of management. Do we attempt petty control at home, at work and in regard to the affairs of our loved ones and colleagues?

For decades, the majority of Soviet people followed the voice of inner censorship, Controller, placed inside each and every person, sternly asking: do your actions and deeds follow the generally accepted and approved values, desirable to the official structures' line? Under these conditions most people became collaborators and conformists, despite the fact that they did not believe in what they were doing. This explains the collapse of confidence in the Communist Party and socialist ideas — for many people they became just a nominal, formal indicator of loyalty to the existing system.

21.2. «*Must not*»

At the dawn of my sociological career, when I was conducting a survey at the factories of Krasnoyarsk region in late 1960's, I was astonished by the multitude of instructions related to production and manufacturing. Essentially all of them (over 90%) were taboos, «must nots». This situation was created due to the fact that the ministry of Finance, State Committee for Labor and other departments saw a potential thief, who wants to cheat the state, in every director of a factory. So they created a multitude of various warnings, restrictions against possible violations. All this legislation, all departmental acts and directives were aimed at ensuring that, God forbid, there is not even a potential possibility of independent actions. In order to do that, they created a narrow space, surrounded by warnings and threats (like red flags), violation of which was severely punished.

Although individuals with most outspoken initiative attempted to overcome this officially declared mistrust (reasoning: 'my actions are not detrimental to society or manufacturing process'), very few were ever able to pull it off.

This «must not» was manifested at the level of behavior of common citizens in far more serious and destructive ways. Individual's consciousness was constantly hammered (during 1950-1980's): «must work», «must not steal», «can not listen to the BBC», «can not dance to jazz», etc., etc. So, individual consciousness had simply split, since it was not always able to distinguish: a) which of these «must nots» were centuries-old traditions, taboos, dictated by customs, centuries or millennia old («must not hurt small and weak», «thou shall not kill», «must not commit adultery»); b) which «must nots» were undermined by life's circumstances (how can you not steal, if 70–80% of the people are convinced that theft in all shapes and forms — from petty to public deception became a norm); c) which of the «must nots» are just the arbitrariness of the bureaucrats, unwarranted, but still quite powerful and efficient (during the years of stagnation: «you can not build a country house larger that 4 by 5 meters», «cannot work abroad», «can not have two jobs», etc). During the years of market reforms: «cannot start a business (without complying with 127 regulations)», «cannot reside in Moscow without a permit», and so on, and so forth.

At the same time, *in early 1990's, in conditions of developing market relations, all of the multiple 'can nots» were supposedly lifted.* People were granted the right to behave the way they wanted, the way they saw fit and necessary. External prohibitions were the thing of the past. But other restrictions, which in their essence and consequences were not much different from the times when everything was forbidden, appeared instead. And this democracy of freedom turned out to be no less, if not more rigid (and degrading) that the Soviet restrictions. You can now vacation anywhere you want, including abroad. In reality, statistically, an average citizen can not, and will not in any foreseeable future be able to afford it, since, even according to the official statistics in years 2000 and 2006 respectively 32% and 21% of the entire population of the country were living below official poverty line, and 35% and 41% could barely make ends meet (*Rossiya reformiruyushchayasya.* 2007. P. 3–4).

Paradoxes of the new situation are all around us. You can buy or build a house, send your children to any college, anywhere in the world. But 95% of the population simply cannot afford such luxury. You can start your own business, become an entrepreneur, owner of a hair salon, shop, and factory. But where can you find startup capital, since, obviously, you cannot depend on anyone's help, especially not predatory and guaranteed?

You can have land in private ownership and become a farmer. But in order to plow and sow, feed cattle, work the field, you need equipment. The state aid is minimal and involves multitudes of bureaucratic obstacles. It turns out that there is no more formal «cannot», no direct warning not to do something. But *there is an influential mechanism in place that revives this powerful «must not» in a new capacity.* The result is clear — everybody is all for farming, but the number of farmers is insignificant — only a few percent of the total number of people involved in agriculture; their output — just 2% of the total market revenue. Thus, human consciousness is still split, but now on a new basis: in absence of any restrictions, it is still in the grip of strict «must not» and «cannot».

How can we find that precise point where «cannot» is obligatory, and when it is not? The real essence is not in the directives, orders, permissions and bans. The principle is the same: just as in the case of «must», we need to ask ourselves a question in each separate case: «What would happen, if, despite the «must not», we would still do it?» If there are no reprehensible consequences for society or other people, we can safely discard this «must not».

21.3. Is everything that is not prohibited, permissible?

In the heat of *perestroika* many approved of this idea, voiced by Gorbachev following lengthy discussions in the press and scientific forums. Worn-out by the long years of endless bans and restrictions almost all welcomed this slogan, since in Soviet practice a single method was utilized: if the situation was not being brought up, and there was no answer to the question «what to do?»

everything was approached from the standpoint of prohibition rather than permission.

However, many quickly realized that Gorbachev's truth was not absolute. *First they discovered that it could be partially applied in law, legal regulations, and did not (or poorly) fit into the social and spiritual spheres* that utilize other criteria than the law. If prostitution is not prohibited as such — does it mean that it is permitted? It is not forbidden to have all sorts of private orientations; does it mean that they are allowed to be used as propaganda?

Second, this rule can work only in extremely stable conditions. When a person is unclear about what is in fact prohibited, or indeed allowed, some chaos is inevitable, and, as a result, all kinds of activities, including illegal ones, get all mixed up. For example, in the opinion of employees of the Nizhni Novgorod «Teplokhod» Factory (survey of 520 people in 1996), only 1,5% were convinced that the new methods of management at the factory were successful (it became a joint-stock company), and, as a result, only 2% of them felt that they were ready to work under these new conditions (*Stanovlenie trudovikh otnosheniy...*, 2004).

Third, following this formula creates a type of relations that function according to the rule of exceptions: «If you mustn't, but really want to — you can». This creates dual morality, double standard. One must not steal from society, from his colleagues? But my circumstances are exceptional! I need nails (chairs, car, and money, building materials or an «extra» phone, a bank account or, perhaps, a profitable enterprise). Especially when theft is thriving in cases when not just millions, but billions of rubles are at stake.

Individuals should not own arms? But the threat of violence is so great that one has to obtain all possible means of protection, including prohibited ones. Sample surveys show that depending on the region from 7 to 18% of the population own weapons. According to the statistics of the Ministry of Internal Affairs of Russia, in 1998, citizens of the country were in possession of 5.269 million fire arms. In addition, private security companies and security services own over 90 thousand registered weapons, on top of countless unregistered ones. Thus, even according to official data, nearly one in six adults in the country is armed (*Author's archive*).

Fourth, in reality, in living history of mankind, there are certain norms that cannot be fully defined by the dichotomy of «must» and «cannot». Thousand-year-old guidelines of human behavior barely correlate with these terms, since they accumulate everything that makes up natural order of things, but unwritten rules of behavior still exist and will continue existing. And approving, or refuting them is utterly ridiculous. They are absorbed with mother's milk, emerge in the midst of real life, and are supported by the people. Moreover, they often morph into each other and can be applies with a plus or a minus sign, depending on the specific situation. Abiding only by «bipolar» thinking in this situation — means accepting the fact that people's consciousness has only two choices — «red or white», «a person from the Caucuses or not», «patriot or nationalist», «for the market economy, or against it». As B. Kagarlitski pointed out, not only outside-the-market, but also anti-market regulations are applicable to the laws of free market (*Nesavisimaya gazeta.* October 14, 2001). Such approach not only violates scientific, but fundamental logic of life as well, since society constantly operates with a large spectrum of shifting, making opinions that in fact correspond with day-to-day realities, not artificial theories and views.

21.4. Paradoxes of reconciling «must» and «must not»

An individual is always faced with choices. *Life experience constantly demonstrates that actions based on the principles of «must» and «must not» are strictly limited.* They do not have and never had an absolute meaning. In real and normal life they are very flexible and change their emphasis not only in time, but also in relation to various aspects of human life. This, of course, does not mean that such flexibility should to be interpreted as eternal permissiveness, instability, relativity and constant limitation in absence of a reference point.

In this regard, as an example, I would like to bring up the plot of V. Bykov's novel «The Bridge». During the war, two resistance fighters were ordered to blow up a bridge (there was a major Nazi offensive expected in the area, with grave consequences for the resistance, as well as the population of this area). Along the way they meet a boy, lost in the forest. It turns out that he lost his parents, so they have no choice but take him along with them. In order to fulfill the task, under extremely difficult conditions, one of them had sacrificed the boy's life, since he felt he had no other choice. His partner, convinced that he should not have used a child even in accomplishing his vitally important mission, shoots him. He would not listen to the reasoning that his comrade did not want the boy's death, but had to carry out his orders, thereby saving hundreds and thousands of people.

Where is the truth in «must» and «must not» in this example? The author does not answer this question, leaving the conclusion up to his readers. We can draw multiple conclusions, and there will be as many opinions. But it is quite clear, that we cannot completely oppose or match them to each other. Otherwise we will end up with a robot that acts strictly according to instructions.

In addition, *a person lives by motivations. They vary during different periods of one's life.* But at all times, during various periods we discuss — stagnation, in the midst of and following *perestroika* — personal motivations have always been a strong factor: yearning for higher wages, aspiration for a prestigious job, providing for the family, caring for children. Against this general background there were some splashes of patriotic and altruistic motives: duty to the country, commitment to the company, professional ethics, and desire to help society, or colleagues and disadvantaged groups in solving various problems.

But can we presently, for the sake of our families, friends, society and personal «I» reconcile this «have to» with contradictions and possibilities of implementation, *when the government is no longer saying «you cannot», but is doing everything to make that «cannot» happen anyway?*

That is why reconciliation of «must» and «must not», to some extent depends on the society and the state. And, mostly on them. But neither the state nor society is in any rush to create these favorable conditions. And the response did not take long: up to 70% of the people (according to a nation-wide survey) do not trust anybody and depend only on themselves or close relatives and friends. Widespread mistrust, among other things, also makes it impossible to observe these requirements of «must» and «must nots» (or the desire to follow them) (*Sotsiologhiya vlasti.* 2006. P. 33–34).

When people see that the state does not promote talent, skill, ability and creative urge (in any sphere — from writing a book to operating a lathe), such reconciliation between «must» and «must not» is extremely difficult.

People these days do not have a firm foothold. Which means that not only people's lives, but the state itself is unstable, since it cannot offer the wisdom of reconciling the age-old «have to-s» and «must nots».

As a result *a paradoxical perception* of the current period of fundamental changes in economic and political life in Russia is emerging: *on the one hand, proclamation of democracy, freedom, constitutional guaranties of human rights and freedoms in accordance with the UN «Human Rights» resolution; on the other — a huge increase in theft, embezzlement, deceit, tax evasion, which brings harm to society, as well as the state and the majority of population,* which is forced to cope with miserable level of existence. This contradiction does not go unnoticed for social consciousness: the response to this phenomenon is anger, or apathy, which takes a heavy toll on the creative potential of society (*Public Opinion.* 2005. P. 26).

References

Public Opinion — 2005. Moscow. Levada-Center. 2005.

Rossiya reformiruyushchayasya (Russia during Reforms) / Pod red. M.K.Gorshkova. Vol. 6. 2007.

Sogomonov A.Yu. *Geneologhiya uspekha I neudach (Geneology of Success and Failures).* Moscow, 2005.

Sotsiologhiya vlasti (Sociology of Political Power). 2006. No 6.

Stanovlenie trudovikh otnosheniy v postsovetskoy Rossii (Labour Relation Making in Post-soviet Russia), Moscow, 2004.

Chapter 22. **Enemy or opponent**

To the right of them is the wall

Randolph Churchill (1849–1895)
British politician

Visible and latent processes of democratization deserve a specifical mention: universal declaration of commitment to renewal and no less aggressive search for the enemy. In Russia, it became an all-encompassing, all-consuming passion. This symptom of intransigence, intolerance infected and still infects virtually all political forces that were never willing to yield to each other. Modern Russia is no exception. The paradox is that everyone swears that they strive for civil harmony, and, at the same time, do everything in their power to prevent it. This reminds me of a joke: «Will there be a Third World War? — No, there will be no war, but the struggle for peace will leave no one standing».

22.1. *Polarity of thinking*

Genetically in Russia, since ancient times, people were always searching for obstacles — «transverses», standing in the way of progress. Oprichniks (guardsmen) of Ivan the Terrible, repressions of Peter the Great, pulling Russia away from barbarism using barbaric methods, «cleansings» of Catherine the Second, constant palace and near-palace intrigues of the 19th and 20th centuries — all of those, one way or the other, were connected with the fact, which can only be attributed to a two-tone perception of reality — black and white. Other shades have practically eluded people's perception. So, it is not surprising that during the Soviet period the general rule: «those, who are not with us — are against us» was quickly adopted. Especially since, starting in early 1920's, we persistently and thoughtlessly tried to achieve the unity of the party, or class, as well as the unity of the whole soviet people.

Consciousness of the majority of people has been programmed to believe that someone who is not with the majority, and primarily with those in power, has no right to his own perception of reality.

The tragedy of this situation lies the fact that the desire to force, to impose the idea of exclusivity and importance of their opinions on other people and to make them think in a certain way, turn the tide in their favor, is characteristic not only of those who seized power (or aspires to), but almost for all inhabitants of our strange, non-standard country.

These rules of the game dictate certain logic of behavior. The entire Soviet history is filled with constant struggle against somebody — mysterious saboteurs, «enemies of the people», «talentless slanderers», or «rootless cosmopolitans». *Our history is an endless chain of searching for enemies that have to be removed at all cost.* Even during *perestroika*, especially toward its end, Democrats were identified as the enemy, along with the Popular Fronts, — emerging new parties that were guilty of different way of thinking. After 1991 the winners did not have to wait long for payback: a new enemy was chosen — red-browns, communists-fascists, which now had to be removed from political scene. In turn, the winners were labeled as the ones who «sold out Russia», chose «an anti-people policy», *compradors*, occupants, etc., etc.

Here, the danger is not in different outlooks — it is frightening and insidious, when everybody insists that their way is the only right way and is ready to eradicate any opposition, any resistance. *Paradox emerges: everybody is all for tolerance and respect of different opinions and judgments, at the same time doing everything to get rid of the civil tolerance.* Such fierce opposition often spills out onto the streets, followed by journalists, political scientists and public figures of different political shadings arguing fiercely over the numbers of their supporters, overestimating, inflating the number of those with whom they associate their vision of the future, underreporting the numbers of opponents, whose political views they do not share. This was especially apparent during the State Duma election campaigns of 1990's, when numerous sociologists, political scientists and think tanks were overestimating the numbers of Yavlinski's party, since the holders (and owners) of these organizations, as well as the media sympathized with this political movement, and saw nothing wrong with trying to present their own opinion as the opinion of the people. When this «equilibrism» slams ordinary citizens from the pages of newspapers and TV screens, they have no other choice but stop believing anything hey see and hear, develop their own understanding, own perception, measure the events with their own yardstick (*Obraz vraga*, 2003).

Apparently, people wise up faster than those who claim to lead them. People are becoming increasingly indifferent to the variety of colorful political assurances. In the eyes of ordinary citizens the enemy is the one who stands in the way of them living peaceful lives, or threatens their safety. *That is why the threat of violence concerns people no less than their chances of surviving economic crisis.* Is this not what makes people want protection? And this is really so: surveys show that almost every third person in the country has encountered violence or threat of violence, and another 40% do not rule out such possibility. People are extremely prejudiced against the elements that without being open and known members of the mob, or criminal groups, force them into a degrading position of a beggar, being responsible for the poverty-stricken lifestyle. This can explain sharp criticism of all the people in power, which, according to popular opinion, interact with criminals and criminal groups, as well as those who unlawfully acquired their wealth. More and more people realize that the state not only fails to guarantee protection for its citizens against crime, but it (represented by state officials, bureaucrats, etc.) merges with criminals and criminal groups. And if so, in the eyes of the majority, these people become enemies rather than opponents. Thus, this dramatic change in popular sentiment at the turn of the millennium is not surprising: fear of the unknown turns into thirst for order, and the stick — into a vertical of power (a kind of power pyramid — from Moscow to regional management) — people who do not hesitate to use all of their administrative powers to achieve their goals (Petukhov. 2006).

22.2. What are the differences between an enemy and an opponent?

An individual is constantly comparing his «I» to the others' «Is» throughout his/her entire existence. It is normal. Since all of us are beautiful just by being ourselves.

When a person is convinced that everybody must be just like him, have similar virtues and behave the same way — that is far more dangerous and scary. As a result, other person, other 'I», differing opinions, differing way of life are entirely negated.

In this regard, we have to point out the criteria that differentiate enemies from opponents.

First, evaluating an opponent, we try to understand his logic, his arguments, to grasp not only his weaknesses, but also strong points of his position, willing to consider his suggestions and utilize them in one form or another. *There is only one method known of dealing with an enemy — he has to be defeated at all cost.*

Unfortunately, there is a lack of understanding, as well as unwillingness to understand the other person. According to sociological data, the majority — up to 70% of the people — feel that currently they can only trust their closest friends and family, and rely only on themselves (*Kollektivniy strakh i stereotypy...*, 1995. P. 17). During the Soviet period the concept of prestige of the collective groups of workers and various other organizations, as defenders and protectors of human dignity, was embedded in people's consciousness (and found confirmation in life). Presently, this stereotype is destroyed, and an individual is left to face his troubles and problems on his own, at least in the opinion of the majority of people.

Second, generally, the opponent is respected as a person with different opinion; as far as the enemy is concerned, respect, as well as the right to have an opinion is out of the question. At best, information at hand is packaged as own perception of reality and dissected emphasizing the points that are needed for an uncompromising struggle. Public clashes of political parties during the election campaigns are especially vicious, when opponents demonstrate utter contempt for other candidates and strong desire to insult people (groups, parties) defending differing interests or orientations. But people had a lot of experience with political games. Many intuitively detect false notes, despite of the fact that they themselves suffer from this fatal flaw. And how can they make any other conclusions, when they see dirty political tricks, such as using people with the same last name as prominent politicians, publishing slanderous materials, making it impossible to separate truth from fiction. And, as a rule, during these political battles, the public discovers that every candidate has his own truth, contradicting the «truths» of his opponents (*Public Opinion.* 2006. P. 154–155, 192).

Third, usually opponents debate the issues — academic, business or production — by comparing the facts and information. *As far as enemies are concerned, it turns into a violent, armed ideological battle that does not even remotely resemble the search for the truth, rather a pursuit of selfish group, corporate goals.* The methods widely utilized are: demagogy, attempts to humiliate, smear and discredit the opponent's views and actions. When seeking to implement their principles and orientations, these extremes pop up left and right. While the percentage of such people is low — a few percent in any social group — they are noisy, loud and not shy with the insults and harsh epithets. Paradoxically, even within the social group that regards itself as intelligentsia, the number of «irreconcilables» is growing rapidly. Among the very people that consider themselves intelligent beings — the conscience of the nation, the number of individuals that respect other people's opinions and viewpoints is insignificant at best.

Fourth, debating an opponent, the language of dialogue, discussion or negotiation is used; ultimatums are the way of dealing with an enemy. We mastered that skill quite well. Sadly, this is inherent in those in power, as well as aspiring rulers. This ultimatum, categorical mindset is widespread in the consciousness of the majority of population. Under these circumstances, many people have chosen the only «true» path they consider to be correct. Every fifth or sixth person — 16-19% (according to VTsIOM survey), still feel that in order to resolve the problems (inflation, national-ethnic, decreasing standards of life) they are ready to resort to violent actions and armed forms of protecting interests of their people.

Finally, and the most dangerous, when hatred is artificially supported and promoted, in absence of a real enemy, one is invented and held responsible for all the troubles, even results of one's own mistakes. Our nation's entire history, including the post-*perestroika* period is a continuous attempt to find a scapegoat.

With enviable consistence, the authorities invented and still invent the forces of opposition. The rest of the population follows suit. The main enemies these days are: mafia (in the opinion of 70%), corrupt part of the state apparatus (56%) and new economic structures (35%). The only consolation is that people's consciousness does not invent mythical enemies; they look out for them and find them in real life (Levashov. 2007. P. 476).

We have to point out that depending on the nature of the confrontation — an enemy or opponent — every minor flaw in an enemy is noticed, exaggerated, hypertrophied, and completely blown out of proportion. This means cutting off any informational exchange, coordination of viewpoints in search of a mutually acceptable solution. Methods of distorting all available information, originating from the opposite side, or imposing one's own perception of reality are also widely utilized. Using labels, language of ultimatums, and rejection of all forms of dialogue is also common practice. Finality of statements and opinions, which are presented as something unquestionable, harms the chances of establishing a constructive dialogue. Thus, first, a certain perception, vision of the goals, means and methods of solving the problem is formulated, than other participants are invited to adopt it as the only correct, true and utterly indisputable.

Thus, a certain idea is formulated about an aim, means and methods to achieve it, and then other participants are suggested to accept it as the only correct, indisputable, and true one. In other words, under these circumstances, social consciousness is always afflicted with a syndrome of an enemy, it does not matter which enemy, but an enemy nevertheless, supposedly standing in the way of prosperity, well-being of society and every common citizen.

22.3. Is there a cure for this 'ailment'?

The paradox of the situation lies in the fact that on the one hand, society and many individuals declare their right to an alternative point of view. On the other, they often characterize such viewpoint as contrary to common sense and normal development, and therefore, having no right to exist. In reality, most people still don't realize that alternative viewpoints have just as much right to exist, as the ones supported by them, or the ones officially proclaimed. So, once again we come across an ineradicable, incurable: «I know what people need» or «I am always right». The root of this unwavering stereotype lies in socio-political features and characteristics inherent to most people. The notion of the enemy that is so hard for society to get rid of, is so deeply embedded — perhaps at the subconscious level, and lodged in the public mind. Escaping it may be possible for the next generation, or even beyond.

All of us, without exception, will have to build a conviction that alternative viewpoints not only have the right to existence, but to equality, equivalence to our own, so that every side has an opportunity to express its position and be heard, to compare its opinions with others and act accordingly.

And yet everyone without exception has to nurture conviction that not only an existence of other point of view is possible, but its equal right to exist, its equal value to one's olwn4 that others have an equal level of claims to represent it and be heard and be compared to other opinion in order to act correspondingly.

We should point out that finding answers to the question: *how to build relations between majority and minority*, can cure intolerance. Experience shows that by rejecting opinions of the minority, predominant viewpoint upsets the balance of power, bankrupts, weakens itself, and stands in the way of preserving and defending positions that may turn out to be correct. In this situation special efforts are necessary in order to insure that a minority becomes an opponent (in politics − civilized official opposition) and not turned into an enemy, whose ideas and opinions are rejected right away. However this approach is not an absolute (Frankl. 2006. P. 60).

The other method, which is equally effective − is to make all viewpoints a subject of discussion. This method though is associated with some difficulties. Many people would rather die than let their version, their interpretation be questioned. And if it becomes a subject of discussion (another paradox), they are just waiting for approval, support and confirmation of their correctness.

We have to overcome underclass-like mentality of many people that is characterized by fairly primitive, «cannibalistic» thinking impulses to «remove», «prohibit», «not allow», «and not permit». These positions are not far from such dehumanizing demands as «annihilate», «destroy», «wipe out», and if not physically, then mentally. This radicalism is flirting with disaster. And humanity, including our own history is replete with such examples.

That is why it is extremely important to realize that an opponent is the expression of constructive opposition (especially in formal structures), imperative for normal development of the state and society. Different points of view cannot exist without opponents and opposition, developing and correcting one's orientations. But, most importantly, we have to accept and be prepared that opposition may come to power and continue (with dignity) perusing the common goals. And this, to no small degree can be learned from of the experience of the Soviet Union, when all and every oppositional thought was outlawed, first inside the Party (Resolution of the X congress of Russia's Communist Party (Bolsheviks) «On the Unity of the Party»), and later in the entire country. As a result, Party and the state leadership from top to bottom was overgrown with «political» fat, lost their ability to argue, prove their point and validity of their methods of solving social problems. The conviction that if a person is in position of power, he is automatically correct became dominant. As a result every district Party secretary spoke not only on behalf of the Central Committee of the CPSU Program, but identified his words and actions with Marx and Lenin, based solely on the fact that he was in charge of his particular district.

This black-and-white perception of reality became the basis for political collapse of the CPSU that had forgotten or ignored the most important principle of development: the truth (and relative at best) can only be discovered in the process of discussing, comparing ideas, which in turn, demands constant, continuous search for desired effective solutions.

Statements and actions of certain representatives of radical liberals, who identify their personal position with democracy, freedom, «top achievements of the West» are no less ambitious and intolerant. The degree of intolerance — on the one hand, and absolute infallible confidence, that only their ideas are the embodiment of truth — on the other, is astounding. But, how much progress have they made, compared to their predecessors, who, foaming at the mouth, passionately argued almost holiness (at least — implicit obedience) of the resolutions of the next session of the Central Committee, attempting to pass them off as indisputable and unquestionable wisdom?

Overcoming this polarity of thinking when deciding «either-or» can be accomplished not only as a result of acquiescence to the existence of opponents (opposition), but also active participation in discussing and aiding the emergence of alternate viewpoints. Orientation and support, focusing on finding a single, singular (absolutely optimal) model leads to emergence of the «the warm blanket effect», which for a certain period of time creates comfortable conditions; but eventually you are forced to leave this comfort for chilly reality.

References

Frankl V. *Chelovek v poiskakh smysla (Man's Search for Meaning).* Moscow, 1990.

Kollektivniy strakh i stereotipy nenavisty (Collictive Fears and Stereotypes of Hatred). Moscow, 1995.

Levashov V.K. *Sotsiopoliticheskaya dynamica rossiyskogo obshchestva (Sociopolitical Dynamics of Russian Society).* Moscow, 2007.

Obraz vraga v obshchestvennom soznanii i v sredstvakh massovoy informatsiy (Emeny Image in Social Consciousness and Mass-Media). Moscow, 2005.

Petukhov V.V. *Byurocratiya i vlast' (Bureaucracy and Political Power)* // Sotsiologhicheskiye issledovaniya. 2006. No 3.

Public Opinion — 2006. Moscow. Levada-Center. 2006.

Chapter 23. **Freedom or boundlessness**

> Only fools equate freedom to willfulness
>
> *Tacitus* (circa 58–117 AC),
> Roman historian

What is happening to freedom these days?

In late 1980's — early 1990's there was no word sweeter and more desirable. It soothed, comforted, offered hope; it seemed to help people breeze deeper and enjoy all conceivable and inconceivable blessings of democracy. This word, «freedom», received the most ecstatic, enthusiastic epithets among the ones pertaining to modern political life.

So, why do some people look away, or are annoyed, while others are angered, when the word «freedom» is uttered today? What happened to people's perceptions, the same people, in whose name all of these changes were accomplished? Why is the long-awaited freedom fraught with serious flaws, why did our expectations turn into apathy, disillusionment and even hatred?

23.1. Freedom as a short-lived exaltation over the impossible

Many people experienced their first life-giving breath of freedom with the arrival of *glasnost'*. Step by step opportunities of obtaining information (that people were interested in) were expanded; data that was previously banned or marked «for internal use only» was now available. After the lifting of all restrictions, the right to criticize any leader, all the way to the top, became very real. *Glasnost*, its conditions and possibilities were positively evaluated by almost all of the Russian citizens. Sociological surveys of late 1980 are consistently confirmed: people praised the right to information and the opportunity to use it. Few doubted its positive influence on our lives.

But granted freedom to openly access and examine the information, to criticize anyone you want did not bring complete satisfaction. Just like ill-fitting clothes, freedom in Soviet society became constricting, limited, and therefore a subject to even greater expectations for future changes.

At the same time, people intuitively felt that freedom was not meant just for self-expression, that it signified something better, something that they seek in their daily lives.

A new stage for expansion of concepts and realization of freedom began in August 1991, after collapse of the CPSU. All pre-existing restrictions were finally lifted. It was now possible not to associate socialism with freedom, to criticize totalitarian past without fear and calculate how much damage it has caused people and their way of life.

There were unlimited opportunities for freedom. Jubilation caused a new surge of hopes and illusions. Reality, however, was far more sobering. *Interpretation of freedom in public consciousness was extremely colorful and scattered. Some people equated it to full irrevocable rejection of socialism, its ideas, methods, its past and present.* For some, the word «socialism» became a curse word. Rejection, different kinds of disassociation, not to mention direct and categorical criticism of socialism (and mostly communism), became a norm and a rule of good taste.

Others, without further ado, started promoting forms and methods of expression of freedom *borrowed from our former ideological opponents, mindlessly praising all of them without exception — from the principles of the electoral system to brothels.* Everything «over there» was good; and when we did not follow «their» traditions and habits, it was undoubtedly bad.

The third group was interpreting freedom as the freedom of national self, as freedom to express the potential of their nation and people, even if it was to the detriment of other people, other nations and nationalities.

The fourth group interpreted freedom as an opportunity to express themselves in the political arena, concentrating on organizing rallies and demonstrations, forming new political parties and movements, thinking that this very diversity of interests will ensure benefits of the civilized world for our society.

Finally, freedom was interpreted as economic freedom, freedom to take charge of own assets, to mobilize resources, accumulate wealth, and, instead of getting a small allowance from the government, reap benefits of their business and searching activities, despite N.A. Berdyaev's warning back at the beginning of the 20th century, that «freedom is not a guarantee from economic slavery».

M.A. Shabanova in her brilliant book «Sociology of Freedom: Transforming Society» (2000) examined various perceptions and interpretations of freedom, demonstrating how many different goals, directives and orientations hide behind this broad concept. Real value of this book lies in the fact that the author presents classification of notions of freedom based on empirical data, not on multiple scientific or journalistic opinions. In a survey of 602 individuals among the working population of the city of Novosibirsk, 551 residents of Altaiski *krai* (province) and Novosibirski *oblast'* (region) (1997–1998), 28% of respondents interpreted freedom as an opportunity to behave in accordance with their own principles, their own will, without any restrictions. The same number of people basically shared their opinion with one major difference — they recognized such freedom within the bounds of moral and legal norms. Another 26% interpreted freedom as independence from arbitrary rule, while the equal number of surveyed identified it with the presence of something extremely meaningful and important, without fear of losing it (work, confidence in the future, independence from vicissitudes of fate). 6% described freedom as a subjective feeling; slightly higher percentage (10–12%) understood it as an absence of any kind of dependence — physical, moral, etc. Some people linked their perception of freedom to guarantee against severe restrictions in the structure of their daily lives (prison, army, captivity). But the most common perception of freedom — more than half of the respondents pointed it out — was material independence, financial freedom and stability (Shabanova. 2000).

We can conclude that this bouquet of freedoms, its various interpretations blossoms with millions of colors that exist in the universe and were accumulated by humanity over the entire history of our civilization. On this very basis, in post-Soviet Russia people were proclaiming slogans, making various statements and declarations, discovering real and concocting fictitious enemies of freedom. It was now possible to express one's opinions about everything, even when they were completely baseless; promote the issues that were desirable, and insist on certain things that just yesterday seemed like nonsense. *But violations of reasonable bounds led to limitless, endless interpretation and implementation of different notions of freedom, leading to social tensions, conflicts, and, in some cases, to tragedy.*

23.2. Freedom or the heavy burden of doubts

The paradox of the current situation lies in the fact that people do not want to give up freedom, but, at the same time, they are very concerned about what they gained from this freedom (See sociological data: table 23.1.)

Table 23.1.

Do you feel like a free man in our society?
(% of respondents. N=1600)

Possible answers	1997	2000	2006
Yes	16	21	20
More likely, yes	24	32	33
More likely, no	28	22	26
No	19	18	18
Hard to say	10	6	3

Source: Public Opinion — 2006. Moscow. Levada-Center. 2006. P. 25.

Analysis of these data shows that nearly half of the population seriously doubts that long-awaited freedom arrived with the market. So, it is not surprising that previously declared rejection of socialism and its ideas has started gradually turning around. People are beginning to recognize its certain values. The idea of academician Andrei Sakharov, who urged the convergence of the best features of capitalism and socialism in the new Russian State, is recalled more and more often. Opinion polls show that up to 30% of the population now prefer socialist path of development and approximately the same percentage think that certain ideas and policies of socialist system, especially the ones related to social protection of the people were meaningful and useful (*Public Opinion*. 2006. P. 20).

In our opinion, the idea of convergence began to penetrate the minds of our fellow citizens: many of them are already accepting a possibility of effective combination of socialist and liberal (capitalist) principles of development. This notion, however, is full of contradictions: wanting to lead «western» lifestyle, people don't realize that western-style work ethics are required as well. In other words, the minds of our countrymen are filled with versions of different ideas and options for future development, like a salad, which sometimes, in certain combinations becomes simply inedible.

Ones, who began to realize that political and social freedom has its limits — have encountered some difficulties as well. Turns out, it is extremely hard to admit.

In early 1990's, many hopes were centered on the incipient process of formation of multi-party system as a guarantee and a stronghold of political freedom. But instead of real political parties, society got small, pathetic groups of vain and pompous individuals, torn but not by true political struggle, but a rat race for leadership, where getting a larger piece of a pie and satisfying their own ambitions was a priority, instead of the fate of the nation. People watched in amazement as these «parties», these defenders of national interests, turned into schemers that did not care about the interests of a common man. Naturally, the question arose: «Is this the freedom we fought for, advocated for and hoped for in our expectations?» As a result, 88% of respondents in all-Russia study did not identify themselves with any political party or socio-political movement. A mere 1,5–2% admitted that they were members of a political party. For many, membership in any of the existing political parties is not an index of freedom, but rather its limiter, or, at least, a waste of time and effort (Levashov. 2007. P. 446).

The ones that equate freedom with the right to national self-determination were deeply disappointed: wishful thinking and attempts to create national parties and movements turned into nationalism and chauvinism, since nationalistic policies led to the situation where representatives of other nations were downgraded to the status of second class citizens, whose interests could easily be ignored and whose freedoms could easily be brushed aside. Such ethnic interpretation of freedom led, first, to ethnic conflicts (Nagorno-Karabagh, Pridneprovye — Transnistria) and then to civil wars (Georgia, Tajikistan). *The banners of freedom of a nation increasingly became stained with blood.*

Even in those cases where struggle for freedom of the nation has not reached an extreme degree of aggravation, less tense situations did not mean the problem was completely resolved. Russian-speaking population of Latvia and Estonia is still in shock: after they fought for independence of these republics, they were the ones left without the right to vote, without citizenship, any hope for equality with those whom they once supported through tough times. Is this a paradox or a tragedy? It is hard to determine. This is yet another lesson of history we need to learn from.

And finally, the thirst for freedom led many people to support private initiative, and, most significantly, private property. 30% of the population in 1988 (when the first public opinion polls were conducted) voiced their support for private property, which went up to 70–80% at the beginning of 2000's (*Russian Public Opinion Herald.* 2006, P. 68). But initial elation over the first successful Russian entrepreneurs, first Russian millionaires turned into dismay and confusion, and later — hostility. It could not have happened any other way, since the income of the majority of population is below official standard of living, and a third — below official poverty level. Moreover, the process of reforms demonstrates that existence of poverty is not a situational coincidence, but a steady trend. According to the UN Theme Group on Poverty Reduction in Russia, there were three peaks of poverty increase registered in the country. The first peak (1992) was associated with price liberalization and transition to the new model of economy and social structure. At that time the number of people with income below the subsistence level increased by more than 8 times reaching 49,7 million people, or 33,5% of the entire population. The second peak (1995) was, to a large degree, a consequence of the financial crisis of October 1995 (so called «Black Tuesday»). Finally, the third peak occurred in 1999, following August 1998 default, when the number of the poor reached 43,8 million, 29,9% of the population (*Sotsial'noe neravenstvo,* 2008). So, under these circumstances, how can we discuss the virtues of freedom with a straight face?

All this led to a paradoxical interpretations of freedom: the desire for the new oddly combined with the aspiration to preserve the old; outrage over the results, which were the consequences of many acts of «free» will; disagreement over what was gained compared to what was promised and seemed so perfect in theory, declarations and political statements.

23.3. Freedom with no duty?

Recently I once again was standing over an unmarked grave in the woods outside Moscow, not far from the village Kriukovo, where «the last platoon» (popular Russian song) was slain. No last names, no gravestones. Only a brief inscription: «Three Red Army soldiers are buried here; they died after a short struggle, slowing down a company of advancing Nazis for several hours.» How many of these graves are scattered throughout Russia, where the ones that met death without any witnesses, without hope for glory, obeying the soldiers' duty — «must» — were laid to rest? Indeed, this «must» was a must for our country. May 9 celebrations are recognition of the greatness of the soldiers' duty, our gratitude to those who stopped the avalanche of fascism and took the glory of their last moments to their grave.

So, were these people truly free? Is duty reconcilable with the person's right to life, future, hope?

These are still relevant questions for us, living today. But from the standpoint of correlation between duty and freedom, the answers to these questions have changed. The opinion that is predominant, perhaps, boils down to one thing: who need this duty?

Duty to the country? How can there be a duty, when the country itself has disappeared?

Duty to society? Can this society guarantee minimal opportunities for survival?

Duty to colleagues? Can they provide work and support under new economic conditions?

Duty to friends and family? What if each and every one of them is saving his own skin, as best he can?

Duty to one's own conscience? How does that help in this particular difficult situation?

So, it turns out, we are all for freedom, but freedom without duty — this onerous attribute of freedom. People are usually quite sincere when advocating for freedom, but, in their understanding, it is the freedom to do as they please and when it is advantageous. And there is more and more people who do not care if this brand of freedom makes someone's life harder, that their interests are not met and desires are not satisfied.

This boundlessness is manifested in individual actions, following one's personal, selfish plan, not according to the sense of duty, or acceptable norms of behavior. Whether we like it or not, new egotism in all of its manifestations: from petty (I don't want to limit my desires), to significant (whoever is standing in my way has to be removed) is flourishing in our society.

That is why there is a mass alienation of everything even remotely reminding people of their duties. How can there be responsibility to the state? Some argue that the state does not care for them, so they are free and clear of any obligations to the state. Others (with no less zeal) object: why should the state take care of the people? People should be able to take care of themselves, and the state should stay out of their business. In other words, different initial premise, but the result is the same — total renunciation of any sort of obligations to anyone, or anything whatsoever.

Duty coexists with freedom when, and only when freedom is perceived as an internal state of being, when it was chosen freely. That is why there is no responsibility graver, than a freely accepted duty, responsibility to the people that are close to us, since this responsibility cannot be shared with the others — people have to answer to themselves. There is no greater violence than that, which man inflicts upon him. This violence can be in the name of ideas, God or welfare of the others. Our actions have to be free and natural, it is imperative that they are not forced, and, if they are voluntary, they cannot be anything else, but free. There is no freedom in fulfilling one's duty, if we are waiting for reward or recognition for our «good, wise» deeds — this means that you fulfill your duty because of this recognition and not on your own free will.

23.4. Freedom or necessity?

This phrase was perhaps, one of the most popular in Marxist philosophy. The right to think and act the way people saw fit was recognized, but only so long as it did not contradict the interests of the society and their colleagues. But, who determines the extent, the measure of this concordance? The judge of that was usually the state. For a long time, the CPSU proclaimed that the interests of the State came first, society — second, people — third. In other words: individual interests have to be secondary to the interests of the state. Just like in a popular song — «Think first about the Motherland, and than — about yourself».

But even Hegel, trying to comprehend the relationship between man and the state, for the first time in history, declared that *the rights and interests of an individual are equivalent to those of the state.* I emphasize, equal, meaning no less important and no less influential or significant. This interpretation has nothing to do with turning a person into some derivative of the state, or triumphant egoism that considers human interests above the interests of the state and society.

Generations of Soviet people until the 1970's believed that their labor, even their hardships were necessary for the Sate, and that their lives will be better in the next five-year period. Well, if not their lives, their children's for sure. But their faith in such necessity was destroyed. The new generation links this necessity firmly with the present: 1) We do not need the promise of a beautiful distant future — give it to us today; 2) do not talk about achievements of the whole country or all the people — this should apply to my family, or me personally; 3) if it is impossible to improve overall quality of life, at least make some meaningful changes.

In other words, necessity works for freedom when, and only when there are real benefits both from freedom as well as necessity, and from their interaction with each other. Necessity should not humble or humiliate people. But freedom means little without necessity as well. What does the fact that only 20% of the drafted recognize that they are serving, most and foremost, for their country, and, only very indirectly — for themselves, really means? Is this necessity really necessary? No one (or few) doubts — it is not necessary. But only until it concerns them personally. Than a paradoxical flip occurs: this necessity is declared necessary and mandatory for others, with the exception (for very valid reasons, of course!) of themselves and their loved ones.

But should individual citizens be solely held accountable? What about the powerful source of influence on social consciousness — the MEDIA, especially television, that cleverly absolve themselves from any responsibility, but campaign for unlimited freedom for themselves, equating their own freedom with freedom of the entire society? *But freedom of expression does not equate to the freedom of the media* (contrary to what they are trying to tell us). Whatever may be said about freedom in Russian society, we have to realize that the media is a parallel world reflecting reality in a very specific way; and this reflection cannot be considered a manifestation of the realization of freedom of speech, as much as some «knights of the pen» would like to convince us (Tret'yakov. 2001).

23.5. Freedom or responsibility?

Analysis of the situation shows that growing human freedom is not accompanied by a similar increase in responsibility. In this situation, many understand freedom as rights without any restrictions.

Nevertheless, this responsibility still penetrates people's consciousness, if not directly, then indirectly. Having realized that the long awaited freedom came at a price, resulting in certain consequences for their social and private lives, people have chosen not to accept responsibility and confront the negative phenomena, but to shift this responsibility onto others. Paradoxically, more and more people are willing to sacrifice their freedoms in favor of yet another «strong hand», so that they do not have to fight the forces of evil and destruction themselves and accept responsibility for its existence. That is why up to 40% of respondents said they are ready for a strong and strict authority in the country, without realizing that it will undermine their freedoms (Kudryavtsev. 2006).

Responsibility is always associated with duty, but only to the extent to which people are guilty of not fulfilling it. There is, however, another side to responsibility. Indian president J. Nehru (1889–1964) once said: *«Freedom must be judged by the degree of freedom of the lower classes».* So far in Russia, freedom is still measured primarily by those, who have real opportunities to realize their rights and freedoms. In other words the degree of freedom should be measured by those who live below the subsistence level. We should measure their degree of responsibility to society, but, to an even greater extent, we should be aware of society's responsibility to them.

Throughout our lives, each and every one of us has to answer these questions: am I capable of fulfilling the necessary requirements; did I understand and interpret them correctly; to what extent should I be held responsible for the consequences of my actions?

Attempts to absolve ourselves of any responsibility, and place it, for example, on the previous generation (sins of the fathers) ultimately lead to the same thing — justification of own conduct under present circumstances.

23.6. Freedom or conscience

Despite of everything, the spark of conscience was not extinguished in Russian people. Sociologists in 1986, under the conditions of early *perestroika*, began asking people: «Can you work harder and better than you do now?» Over 90% of respondents answered affirmatively. It was not always the people's fault that their willingness to work harder, produce more higher quality goods was not in demand. In later surveys of 1980's and early 1990's sociologists noted a decline in the number of those who expressed self-criticism and listened to the voice of conscience.

In 2001–2004 we repeated this question. First, we were not sure whether to include it in the questionnaire or not. How could we appeal to people's conscience amidst crisis and devastation, especially considering that this chaos was not their fault? The results were truly impressive. Over 60% of the people said they would still like to work better, more productively (Boykov. 2006. P. 153–156).

Are individuals capable of formulating moral, civil responsibilities and requirements of their implementation, fulfilling them and evaluating their own actions? Positive answer to these questions is the essence of understanding of conscience. How does this work in reality? Tragically, the requirements of morality in Russia have been eroded. And the problem is not that the old ones were rejected, rather that the new ones were not formulated. As a result lack of moral bounds sweeps away everything in its path that is associated with true freedom and fulfillment of civil duties (*Istoriya eticheskikh...*, 2003).

Conscience is an ongoing critical analysis of, primarily, oneself and one's own actions. But, among people, a strong desire to critically evaluate actions of others always prevails. Overconfidence in own infallibility is another flaw that stands in the way of conscience, and consequently freedom.

23.7. Freedom is not a given

In the song of the French Resistance «Poppies» there are these words: «Freedom will not be granted, we have to take it... Others will greet the sun, will sing and drink, and, perhaps, will not remember, how much we wanted to live«. Sacrifices made in the name of freedom were always an important motive in human behavior. Freedom must be fought for. It is an axiom. But what methods should we use? Guns, violence, trampling people's honor and dignity? Yes, freedom is worth fighting for, it has to be defended, but not through violence. And the paradox here lies in the fact that in modern society freedom is gained primarily through use (or demonstration) of force. That is why countless enemies are invented, forgetting that the most effective way of establishing freedom is granting it to other people. «There is no better protection, than an open door», — says an old proverb.

Typically, the fight for freedom is perceived as a choice between good and evil, between morality and immorality. In reality it is much more complicated. Concepts of «good» and «evil» can shift into the dimension of violence against people, based a certain «higher» understanding of freedom. The words of Elbert Hubbard, an American writer and publisher (1856–1916) are very wise: «Every tyrant who has lived has believed in freedom — for himself.»

23.8. Freedom? Is this what we wanted?

Reality is a cruel thing. But, at the same time it is most definite, descriptive and quite revealing. Social consciousness willy-nilly is forced to consider this reality. Is this truly the freedom people wanted?

How can we not question it, if there is virtually nothing left from promised freedoms? First news reposts were flooded with stories about inadmissibility of violating prisoner's rights, than inhumane behavior of law-enforcement, obsolescence of Russian criminal law and superiority of the Western one. Then the spiral of rejecting the old and supporting the new untwisted further, leading people to doubt the authority of the courts, legality of death sentence; there were discussions of liberalizing criminal punishment and harsh criticism of the police.

As a result, violence is now the number one concern of many people, along with economic hardships and turmoil. Most of them are now willing to sacrifice a lot in order to stop the crime wave that literally engulfed our cities. Voices of supporters of humane treatment of criminals grew silent. Moreover, anxiety and outrage of ordinary citizens, defenseless against violence — physical or mental (associated with humiliation of their honor and dignity), is growing rapidly.

Recent enthusiasm over private property is no less paradoxical. The nature of its support is fraught with a lot of mysteries. It is especially strikingly evident when an individual is faced with a particular dilemma. More and more people began pondering over the consequences of the actions of the state, which just recently seemed so necessary and desirable.

Paradoxically, the more often the word «freedom» is uttered, the more worried all those wishing to enjoy its real benefits become. At the end of the 1980's, only a small percentage of people said that they were victims of violence, were faced with threats or have encountered violations of their rights in daily life. At the beginning of this century, it was every fourth person. Why? On the one hand — the opportunity to try one's luck in some sort of business became wide open. You could say what you want, openly criticize without looking over your shoulder, think and behave any way you want. On the other — many people began to feel disempowered, overwhelmed by daily necessities, under constant strain from fact that someone is prospering while they have been cast aside, not based on their talent, knowledge or education, but on the basis of access to money or power.

But, according to an eastern wisdom, no matter how much you yell «halva, halva», your mouth won't taste any sweeter. As time went by, people started having doubts — do we need this freedom? Is it for everybody? And under what conditions? Does it mean a certain kind of lawlessness in accordance to the principle: »I do what I want»? The result of such freedom is beyond paradoxical: freedom for people turns into violations of their rights, absence of civil guarantees. Furthermore, it becomes not just a rejection of everything that preserves human dignity and honor, but an incentive to indulge in basest passions, releasing a person from any responsibility for the state of his own environment.

Lawlessness that increased to unprecedented dimensions was the result of the realities of such freedom in Russia. The desire to stop this lawlessness, even at the cost of losing a number of recently coveted freedoms, is quite understandable.

But does this mean that we are ready to return to totalitarian, albeit modernized past, in the name of restoring peace and social order? Highly doubtful, though social consciousness is indeed at a crossroads.

Anther aspect is no less dangerous. In the consciousness of every individual, «their own» understanding of freedom often prevails, which inevitably leads to comparing it with other interpretations. Everybody is fighting for freedom, but in such a way, that some would have more freedom, some — less; some will have to be subordinate, listen and follow the instructions of those who granted themselves the right to be superior (*Putyami nesvobodi*, 2005). But *the real, true freedom is not defined by actions without restraint, but, in the words of B. Spinoza, by constant comparison with a degree of wisdom.*

Personal freedom is a part of the freedom of society; it cannot be build at the expense of its other members. Furthermore, it is a continuous process of choosing between good and evil, between rights and obligations.

References

Boykov V.E. *Narod I vlast' (People and Political Powers).* Moscow, 2006.

Istoriya eticheskikh ucheniy (History of Ethics Theories) / Pod red. A.A.Guseinova. Vol. 2003.

Kudryavtsev V.N. *Svoboda slova* (Freedom of Speech). Moscow, 2006.

Levashov V.K. *Sotsiopoliticheskaya dynamika rossiyskogo obshchestva (Sociopolitical Dynamics of Russian Society).* 2000–2006. Moscow, 2007.

Public Opinion — 2006. Moscow. Levada-Center. 2006.

Putyami nesvobodi (Ways of Unfreedom) // Sb. statey / Sostavitel' A.Verkhovskiy. Vol. 2005.

Russian Public Opinion Herald. Data. Analysis. Discussions. 2006. No 6.

Shabanova M.A. *Sotsiologiya svobody: transformiruyushcheesya obshchestvo (Sociology of Freedom: Transforming Society).* Moscow, 2000.

Sotsial'noe neravenstvo I sotsial'naya politika v sovremennoy Rossii (Social Inequality and Social

Tret'yakov V.T. *Russkaya politika i politiki 1990-2000. (The Russian Policy and Politicians 1990–2000).* Moscow, 2001.

Chapter 24. **Between the past and the future**

> Knowing the past is unpleasant enough;
> Knowing the future would be simply intolerable
>
> *Somerset Maugham* (1874–1965)
> British writer

> Market fundamentalism is today a greater threat to open society than any totalitarian ideology
>
> *George Soros* (circa 1930)
> American millionaire
> and philanthropist

Social consciousness has never been indifferent to the evaluations of both past and future. But these assessments always bore the imprint of the present. It was under the influence of the present the pictures and shadows of the past are drawn and conceptualized, while the future prognosis is not devoid of likes and dislikes of the real functioning social consciousness as well.

If we attempt to classify different types of attitudes towards the past and the future through the prism of the present, *we will most frequently encounter following combinations: denying the past, approving and welcoming the future; approving the past and rejecting the future; equally negative assessment of both — past and future; optimistic, although often critical attitude towards past and future.*

There is another classification of the problem of relation between ends and means: First, *rational type of behavior* when goals and means are equally justified and approved; successful attempts of their coordinated use and implementation are carried out. Second, *an innovative type of behavior*, which implies positive attitude towards the goals and rejection of restrictions in choosing the means used in real life. Third, *ritual type* (according to R. Merton), focusing on the means of achieving the goal despite negative attitude towards them. Fourth, *retreatism as a type of behavior*, which implies denial of ends and means leading to withdrawal from realities of daily life (it is especially evident in the behavior of alcoholics, drug addicts and suicidal individuals). And finally, *another type of possible behavior, which signifies rejection of the «old» ends and means, and simultaneous replacement with the new ones* — rebellion, revolt, uprising, coup, revolutionary changes. Various combinations of these types of behavior are possible, but, in essence, these main options remain basic and fundamental.

All of them, with the exception of the first type of behavior create paradoxical situations. Evaluations of these situations demonstrate limitations, one-sided and often flawed nature of each one of these attitudes.

24.1. Primitivism of the nihilism

A relatively small, but energetic and ambitious, feisty group of intellectuals, that consider Soviet past to be a failure in Russian history, fateful twist in the country's development, a break in continuity, disruption of the normal progress of socio-economic changes, operates under the motto «to reject the past and build a radiant, free market future». In their view, the Soviet period consists mainly of GULAGs, forced collectivization, economy of shortages, organized starvation, destruction of Orthodoxy and Islam, ridiculous economic projects, etc., etc. Reaction of the members of this group to everything they disagree with is usually outrageous, deliberate demonstration of their «intransigence» (Gaydar. 2006).

At the same time, the proponents of these ideas are convinced that the only key to achieving their goals is not just through liberal market economy, but market society, which they see as yet another «bright» future. Russian «ultra-market» supporters even disregard moderate opinions of their Western colleagues, such as the former Prime Minister of France (1990's) L. Jospin, whose policy was to implement the requirements of *«Yes — to market economy, no — to market society*». Like many of his colleagues, he rejected market fundamentalism, «attempting to extend its (market) regulators in the spheres beyond the scope of market impact — the environment, fundamental sciences, culture in its highest manifestations, national nature preserves, as well as human rights and morality» (Abalkin. 2000, P. 33).

Just as the past maximalism of the Bolsheviks — «the entire world of violence we shall destroy down to its foundation, and then, we shall build our own, new world», the new right-wing radicalism is directed only at such revolutionary approach to solving pressing social problems, namely through destruction, through uncompromising rejection of everything old.

In principle, in real life of society, as well as social groups and communities, certain phenomena and occurrences, characteristic of the passing epoch, are withering away, disappearing, replaced by new emerging and consolidating trends, new processes; while certain latent occurrences are transformed into significant changes and events. However, the contrast between these tendencies or making one of them absolute leads to the formation of contradictory, or mutually exclusive versions of development in people's consciousness and behavior.

A common characteristic of this paradoxical consciousness is, on the one hand, nihilism in relation to the past, and beaming, «puppy-like» enthusiasm for the anticipated «market future», on the other. But the opposition of these trends does not lead to the creation of the new, but to the destruction of existing social space, which, devoid of any factual basis, is left hanging in the air.

Contradictory and paradoxical nature of this approach to the past and the future leads to the disruption of historically proven logic of thinking and development. This is manifested, *first of all, in the way its supporters reject common sense, as well as pragmatism, and switch to the positions of abstract opportunities*, which their market concept, presumably, promises to secure. In other words, from the means, necessary for addressing economic and social problems, this concept is turned into a goal, automatically making it into an instrument of increasing social inequity and social tension.

Second, individuals advocating this approach virtually ignore scientific data, or use scientific information as a «fig leaf». Meaning, if certain scientific data suits their proclaimed goal, it is approved, welcomed; if not — it is simply rejected. However, when scientists are too persistent, they are accused of being isolated from reality, utilizing erroneous initial methodological principles or incomplete and inferior techniques, in order to ensure that they do not interfere with manipulation of social consciousness and demagoguery in politics (Gaydar. 1999).

Third, proponents of nihilism de facto and de jure abandon traditions do not see any positive points in the past (especially Soviet past). Naturally, such approach turns into a fairly primitive form of imitation of other people's experience and lifestyle. This rejection of one's routes and legacy is never without consequences. And, conversely, when new realities are closely interwoven with consideration for nation-specific traditions of the past, the progress is much more impressive. This is evidenced by the experience of such economies (quite different in their political orientations) as China and Japan, whose success is largely due to skillful combination of emerging social demands with specific national characteristics and mentalities. «Taking into account national features and peculiarities of the country, — said the Roman Club Executive Committee member, Jordanian Prince Al Hassan Bin Talal, at the meeting of the Club in Moscow State University in May 2000, — is a traditional approach; and it will remain a scientific instrument, while these differences still exist not only for the entire world, but also for every individual» (*Conference of the Roman Club.* 2000).

Fourth, the attitude to the methods of achieving these goals is no less paradoxical. Gradual approach is completely rejected; shock (not even shock as therapy) is promoted as means of bestowing happiness on the entire population of the country. In this connection, we should recall a quote of Nobel Laureate, German writer Guenter Grass, who insisted that «democracy must move at a snail's pace». Meanwhile, rapid pace of creation of private ownership led to the demise of national economic organism, to widespread theft and embezzlement in gigantic proportions, deception and impoverishment of the majority of the people. The results of market reforms in other countries have repeatedly demonstrated that gains cannot be attained by a head-on attack, but rather by persistent, slow, long-term effort, just like in the People's Republic of China and in Japan, where modernization process was not rushed, but carried out gradually and carefully.

Fifth, with this approach, we witness a profanation of such ideas as freedom, market and nation that are vital for the future of the country. Russian Liberal Democrats' idea of free market is no different from the era of primitive accumulation of capital, when «freedom» to use any available means of seizing material, financial and other resources was flourishing. People, however, treat this as means of achieving selfish goals, under the guise of yet another promise of happiness, which they (the people), «somehow», do not understand or accept.

Sixth, those, who reject the past, or treat it nihilistically, in most cases, act as a cold, calculating mechanism, completely ignoring socio-psychological positions of the people. Everything related to people's suffering and experiences, they treat as a chimera not worthy of attention. They tend to forget that the protestant ethics made famous by Max Weber was necessary for capitalism not because it promoted enrichment at any cost (one does not need ethics to do that), but rather because it harnessed the greed in accordance with strict moral standards famous (Kagarlitski. 1999).

24.2. Misery and poverty of dogmatism

In the 1990, against the backdrop of prevailing trends and preserving positive assessment of the processes and phenomena of the Soviet past, dogmatism has fully flourished in people's consciousness. It advocated that «bright» Soviet past and rejected the future. Its influence and pressure were widespread — no less than rabid nihilism in the example analyzed above.

Dogmatism that presently exists is also paradoxical. But its paradoxes are manifested differently than characteristics of nihilism, since the latter denies the all and everything, while dogmatism stubbornly and persistently opposes the new, the emerging. In the consciousness of dogmatically-minded individuals, all the changes that took place in the past are perceived as absolutely positive. Figuratively speaking, this style of philosophy is similar to walking facing backwards into the past. Representatives of this group justify the past, recognize only the accomplishments, rejecting everything that casts doubt, completely lacking critical analysis (and when they do criticize it, it is only for the petty, insignificant flaws).

Dogmatic way of thinking lacks vision, perspective, sense of novelty, need for constant change, requirement to find other, non-standard solutions. The future seems the same as the past, with minor corrections in accordance with the new realities.

Dogmatists suffer from primitive life orientations, oversimplification in explaining various processes, as well as implementation of their own actions. In such situation, the entire world appears black-and-white, not allowing halftones, transitional models, and therefore, compromises, concessions, agreements or contractual process.

Such understanding of the future, combined with non-acceptance of the present is perceived either as a return to the past, or as continuation of the already established that, in their opinion, defies logic and interests of social development.

As a result this approach gives rise to paradoxes of its own.

These include *simultaneous coexistence of «internationalization of interests» ideas with notions of exclusivity of the Soviet (Russian) path in **hi**story*, which ultimately, gives rise to rabid chauvinism. This logic of reasoning and respective behavior leads to emergence of peculiar socio-political cretinism, since only primitive thinking allows reconciling the process of globalization with glorification of national interests.

Paradox that arises from glorifying the past and rejecting the future is also embodied in attempts to adapt the criteria of class division, which was formed in 19th century, *to the new, emerging realities.* The concepts of the «working class» and «peasantry» are presently blurred, primarily due to the fact that professional, as well as property ownership attributes have lost their former significance. In this situation, the «new poor» are represented by a wide variety of social groups: intelligentsia, office workers, fairly large portion of retirees, multi-child families, and groups of people unable to compete in the job market due to poor health or certain other limitations.

Among the paradoxes of this type of mentality, we should also point out exaggeration of significance of social deviation, which, on the one hand, is interpreted as a product of modern stage of capitalist (imperialist) development, on the other, as a reserve for revolutionary transformation of the world, force capable of opposing «destructive» tendencies of the market economy. Constantly switching plusses and minuses and visa-versa, individuals that possess this type of consciousness and behavior constantly juggle facts, numbers, personal impressions and opinions, randomly chosen examples, in order to prove one thing — impossibility to interpret the future by using present realities: in their opinion, it would be much better, if the present is nullified, and the future is build on the postulates of the past.

24.3. Social anomie

Social anomie (from the Greek a— denial, *nomos* — law, order) essentially symbolizes negative attitude in relation not only to the present, but also the past and the future. Let us reiterate that anomy refers to a moral-psychological state of social and individual consciousness, which is characterized by disintegration of the system of values, contradiction between declared values and impossibility of their realization. This condition creates value-normative «vacuum», low degree of influence of social norms, their ineffectiveness as means of social regulation of behavior. However, an important role is also played by instability, vagueness and inconsistency of newly proposed or prescribed norms.

This condition has affected large segments of the population, whose consciousness was awakened by expected positive changes resulting from *perestroika* of the second half of 1980's and early 1990's, when most people thought that a new paradigm of development, proposed by liberal radicals would lead to desired results, which Soviet rule failed to deliver. But the reality was quite different. So, people's hopes were dashed once again engendering not just simple frustration, but — disruption of the social consciousness, namely — anomie, i.e., complete atrophy, stable indifference and utter apathy to any social impulse, regardless of its positive or negative orientation.

Paradox of this situation lies in the fact that even under the conditions of certain positive changes, the majority of people are still deeply pessimistic. Even many of those, who seemingly successfully fit into market economy, are deeply dissatisfied with the current changes in society, with the overall developments that affect them as citizens of our country (*Public Opinion. 2006. P. 12).

Under these circumstances, if radical-liberals are favoring individualism, radical patriots — community and teamwork; social anomie is indifferent to both. People feel lost, helpless and confused; this indifference penetrates their daily lives; their behavior becomes insular, characterized by withdrawal, transforming into detachment from the problems and worries of surrounding reality. Indifference to any political and socio-economic innovations is manifested in refusal to participate in election campaigns or in voting against all candidates, without exception; in rejecting all social actions and membership in social movement and political parties.

This type of mentality is characterized by refusal to comprehend, ascertain the relationship with the past, thereby demonstrating irresponsibility, indifference and atrophy of historical consciousness. At the same time, people are indifferent to what happens to them and their country at the present moment and in the foreseeable future, since they realize that they have no influence over anything that is going on around them.

Social anomie is manifested in lack of acceptance, in rejection of the ideas of collectivism, communitarism (sobornost'), communality, as well as ideas of individualism: people are increasingly leaning toward privacy, seclusion and isolation in the narrow circle of personal, family and group interests. According to many sociological studies, 70% of Russians, i.e. absolute majority favor interests of friends and family over personal, as well as social goals. In our view, this analysis reveals an interesting phenomenon: departure from social orientation of one's interests does not mean switching to protection and preservation of personal interests, which would indicate dominance of individualism in social consciousness. There is orientation toward focusing of the interests of a small group, contact community or family, where the ties, the connections are built based on principles of trust, socio-psychological acceptability, recognition of virtues and confidence in mutual protection.

The destruction of mass, as well «high» culture, that bonded the lives of tens of millions of Russians contributed to the emergence and spread of social anomie as well. The destruction of official culture has led to their decline and decay, since the new government, as usual, did not see any sense in supporting this complex and unprofitable «branch of industry».

Incidentally, similar problems of social anomie ware clearly manifested after the reunification of East and West Germanys, GDR and FRG. In GDR, just like in Russia, after the collapse of socialist system, the future was painted according to alluring Western patterns, showcasing delights of a free society. The gap between these illusions and the reality of the situation was shocking. It quickly becomes clear, how under these conditions, the need for a strong state and a «strong hand», in turn, among other things, creates a breeding ground for nationalist, ultra-patriotic and even chauvinistic sentiments and expressions, which are increasingly becoming a reality of contemporary life in Russia (*Izvestiya*. 2001. September 14).

In conclusion, I would like to point out one other very important fact arising from social anomie: it can, and does act as a basis for deviant and delinquent behavior, which is caused by inability of achieving individual goals «in a lawful way». In order to overcome this contradiction all available means are utilized, even the ones that are officially not supported by society; the goals, attained by these means, however, are welcomed and approved. This very principle is a basis for shadow economy, the cult of wealth at any cost, the principle of «living well», since, in the final analysis, our society might not justify these phenomena, but treats them with indifference (*Perestroyka glazami rossian.* 2005. P. 25).

References

Abalkin L.I. *Smena tysiacheletiy i sotsial'nye al'ternativi (Shift of Millennium and Social Alternatives)* // Voprosy Economiki. 2000. No 12.

Conference of the Roman club. Moscow University. Moscow, 2000.

Gaydar E.T. *Gibel' imperii. Uroki dlya sovremennoy Rossii (Destruction of Empire. Lessons for Contemporary Russia).* Moscow, 2006.

Gaydar E.T. *Gosudarstvo i evolutsia (State and Evolution).* Moscow, 1999.

Kagarlitski B. *Nuzhna li etika rossiyskomu kapitalizmu? (Is Ethics Necessary for Russian Capitalism?)* // Nezavisimaya gazeta. 1999. May 15.

Perestroyka glazami rossian: 20 let poszhe (Perestoyka : Russian Public Opinion: 20 years later), Moscow, 2005.

Public Opinion − 2006. Moscow. Levada-Center. 2006.

Chapter 25. **Europeans? Asians? Eurasians?**

> Yes, we are Scythians,
> We are Asians with hungry, slanted eyes
>
> *A.Blok* (1880–1921)
> Russian Poet

Attempts to find, to grasp our own place, as well as the place of our country in the world, in the family of other nations are reflected in several orientations prevalent in social consciousness of modern Russia.

First, there is a clearly expressed desire to merge with European culture, civilization, join in political, economic, cultural and social space created by developed

Western European and North American countries. However, this desire is often manifested (and still manifests) in hypertrophied way, just like it happened during the period when radical-reformists (Atlantists) came to power in early 1990, when multiple attempts were made to indiscriminately borrow from other countries without any thought or critical analysis of their achievements and accomplishments. That resulted in failures in economy and politics, attempts to «wear someone else's clothes» in the cultural sphere, loosing «face» in literal and figurative sense. In principle, in social consciousness, there are no serious trends detected, which could offer an alternative to the European civilization. It is rather a question of a degree and the nature of its influence on the development of Russian reality.

Second, more modest, but still fairly weighty presence of «Asian» direction has an important place in social consciousness as well. Accomplishments of Asian countries: Japan, the «young tigers» — Singapore, Malaysia, South Korea and Taiwan, as well as Communist China, which all have achieved impressive results in socio-economic development, represent examples of harmony, prosperity and success to the proponents of this direction. Supporters of Eastern orientation are trying to persuade the public, that Russia is not a European, but rather an Asian country; that Russian mentality is much closer to the mentality of eastern nations, and, therefore, the route of the prosperous countries of the East is the most appropriate way out of the economic and social crisis.

Third, orientation toward the original, distinctly Russian route of development, based on the uniqueness of Russian history, Russian culture and national mentality, is gaining definite and rapidly growing influence. This position rejects both western and eastern orientations, rightly noting that every country has its own unique, specific way of development, its own place and role in human history. But, since proponents of this viewpoint often consider the specifics of Russian history and Russian reality absolute, they, whether they like it or not, are pushing Russia toward isolationism, insularity, complete and unquestioning disregard of others' experiences. Supporters of this idea tend to forget that, historically, such orientation has never lead to success in any given country in the world.

Finally, so-called «Eurasian» orientation is gaining momentum. It reflects dissatisfaction with apologia of both western and eastern development, at the same time disagreeing with the views of the devotees of the notions of Russian exclusivity. In its essence (by the way, interpreted in different ways) it is the concept of a unique path of future development of the country, combining intertwined European and Asian cultures with the culture of numerous peoples of Russia, creating an entirely new entity on the border between Christianity, Islam and Buddhism.

But, since these logical constructs in their pure form affect and characterize the consciousness of certain groups of people, embodied primarily in the outlook of the intelligentsia, *in real life we encounter a mixture of these ideas, which create very bizarre combinations — centaur-problems.* Spiced up with various conflicting political and economic views, these combinations of Eurasian, western, eastern and exclusively Russian ways of development give rise to paradoxes that have a major impact on social life in Russia. Moreover, these paradoxes of social consciousness can be considered in two main aspects — assessment of Russia and its palace in the world, and evaluation of ourselves, Russians in general and Russians in particular, in comparison with other nations — our neighbors, as well as other countries that play significant role in modern historical process.

25.1. Paradoxical image of russia in the modern world

After the collapse of the Soviet Union, social consciousness was excited, electrified by discussions, doubts and deliberations: what is the new Russia, what is its true place in history, and what kind of future lies ahead? All of the concepts and views mentioned above were involved in these discussions. All of them had different answers to these questions. For example, the survey of 1250 people in 1989 and 1600 in 2000 showed that, on the one hand, the number of people that thought Russia is lagging behind most developed countries has declined (from 75 to 50%), but, on the other — the number of people, convinced that Russia should chose its own, unique way of development increased from 10 to 34% (VTsIOM data, 2000) (*Public Opinion. 2006. P. 158*). Comparing these data with existing socio-economic and political realities helps explain the existence (and emergence) of the multiple paradoxes. Among them we have to point out following:

First, the interpretation of the role of Russia is rather paradoxical: on the one hand, the conviction that Russia always was, is, and will be a great country; that the progress of the rest of the world is hard to imagine without it — is always present (and is instilled by the propaganda) in social consciousness. On the other hand, no less aggressive propaganda (which is also reflected in mass consciousness) claims that Russia has entered a period of decline, changing from the world power to a regional power. Within this approach, there is a point of view that Imperial Russia is the thing of the past, and that its very existence is in question; that its demise is eminent, just like it happened with the Soviet Union, and all of the empires of the past — Roman, Byzantine, Austro-Hungarian, British.

However, social consciousness cannot be reconciled with the fact that Russia has lost its former position as a Great Nation. For example, VTsIOM data (survey of 1600 people in October 2000) illustrates this point: 39% of Russian citizens called it (Russia) «Great», while in 2006 — 76% of respondents. So, from acknowledgement of modest role of Russia, thee-quarters of the population switched to chauvinistic orientations (or ambitions?). When compared with evaluation of the role of other countries, these data are even more impressive, since 70% of this group of respondents called the United States a great country, and 44% — Japan (*Public Opinion. 2006. P. 190*). In addition, these data also suggest that even during the period of severe crisis that hit Russia, there were still quite a few people that did not lose faith in the greatness of their country (in reality, this was more faith than fact). This contradictory evaluation leads to an amazing phenomenon, when people, at the same time, are both proud and ashamed of what is happening in their country. Judging by the results of surveys of Russian people, including the younger generation, over 77% consider themselves patriots, 16% — do not.

The second paradox is derived from the one analyzed above. Its essence lies in the fact that *social consciousness is simultaneously accepting and rejecting the future of Russia, as well as prospects of its development.* Specificity and particularity of this position lies in the fact that these mutually exclusive characteristics contain contradictory assessments and opinions regarding actual and prospective development of Russian society. If Russia's future is conceived based on daily occurrences, its evaluation is based on its contemporary socio-economic and political situation, level and quality of life. This approach leads to very pessimistic conclusions — that the level of development of western countries will not be achieved in Russia in any foreseeable future. If prospects of future development of Russia are evaluated through the prism of geopolitics, availability of natural resources, military-strategic capabilities, it allows a more optimistic assessment.

Third, assessments of Russia's future potential are influenced by the paradoxical perception of historical journey of the country, when, on the one hand, the main (primary) milestones in its history, as well as the actions of its most influential characters, who embody the strength of the country are being glorified, on the other — this very journey is characterized in the most derogatory manner. In the latter case, history of Russia is presented as a history of turmoil, uprisings, misfortunes, hostility toward any progressive changes, or simply failures that increasingly alienate it from achievements of world civilization. Moreover, if positive assessment of Russia's role is associated with Eurasian outlook and with concepts of its original development, negative evaluation of Russia's historical development reflects the approach of «Atlantic», Western-oriented forces, which, based on various assumptions, arrive at the same conclusion — worthlessness, unpredictability and inferiority, or, at least, inadequacy of Russia's historical journey.

Fourth, comparison of original, «Eurasian» and Asian approaches lead to contradictory and sometimes paradoxical assessment of Russia's culture in general and its cultural heritage in particular. Two viewpoints coexist in social consciousness:

1) Russian culture is a beneficial fusion of not only the achievements of Russian, but all the nationalities of the former Soviet Union; 2) Russian culture is an eclectic mix of all, including international cultures. The presence of great names in Russian culture is an exception to the rule, rather than a logical pattern of development. A lot of people recognize that Russian culture never was, and never will be represented in cultures of both western, as well as eastern countries, and, therefore, there is no need to adapt to them. We need to nurture our own unique benefits of Russian or Eurasian culture (Shendrik. *Teoriya kul'turi.* 2004).

Finally, another paradox has to be noted. New Russia is accepted (or formally recognized) as a democracy, but it is still viewed as a threat. The first viewpoint, reflecting democratic character of Russia, was prevalent during late 1980's, early 1990's. It was actively promoted by «Atlantists» (proponents of Westernization of Russia). This orientation was supported by the people of many developed countries of Europe and America. The «Young Reformers» who came to power tried to conform to this orientation, largely sacrificing Russia's interests, in an attempt to «meet» certain Western standards. Moreover, supporters of Western democratic values were so zealous in their efforts that they shocked even most sensible people in the West. As a well-known publicist M. Sokolov aptly noted, the Atlantists that claim to be the most vehement advocates and fans of progressive Western values, would rather shock and perplex even progressive westerners themselves, since such dedication and devotion violates all the rules of decency, distorts the essence of Western democracy, upsets the measure of balance between independence and imitation (Sokolov. 2000).

25.2. Paradoxes of national identity

Paradoxical, contradictory nature of national identity begins with the question what should people of Russia call themselves: «Russki» or «Rossiyanin» (Russian in ethnic sense *or Russians* in the sense of citizenship*).* A lot of debates and conjectures surround this issue. Western-oriented polemicists, based on the experience of European countries and the United States, are trying to convince the public that affiliation with the State should at the same time mean belonging to the Nation (Tishkov. 2001). Yes, many Western countries managed to achieve that quite successfully, since the constituent nation, first, was significantly (quantitatively) prevalent (and still is) over the representatives of the other peoples, and secondly, the majority of representatives of other nations (merging with the existent one) are for the most part migrants that have no historical (or any other) roots in that country.

Russia is a very different story, since dozens of different nationalities (even numerically small ones) have their own, centuries-old history, and are indigenous. And although they are intermingled with the Russian culture, they are entitled to claim and preserve their national identity, self-worth, their own language and culture. Furthermore, pursuit of preservation of these peoples, to some extent, became a tradition: at no point in Russian history, the country became a melting pot. On the contrary, assimilation processes evolved quite naturally. During the long history of co-existence, various ethnic groups, small nations assimilated not only with the Russians, but other larger nationalities as well.

Eurasian idea implies a compromise: inevitable convergence of the peoples should be regarded as a natural historical process that cannot be rushed or held back, and on this basis, we should help reinforce the already established uniqueness and originality of this special brand of Eurasian culture. This particular approach, according to supporters of Eurasian concept, will put an end to uncertainty that exists in the interpretation of interaction between the cultures of all peoples living in Russia.

It is not only the Russians that experience this uncertainty (in this situation, the interests of Russian people are neglected), but other nationalities as well, since focusing exclusively on their interests is detrimental not only to the interests of the Russian, but other neighboring nations as well, thus creating unexpected complications in interpretation and implementation of rights and freedoms of every nation.

The collapse of the Soviet Union caused serious damage to national identity. There are still a high percentage of people that consider themselves Soviet people. According to an all-Russia survey (headed by V.A. Mansurov), in 1999 — 47,8% of respondents still regarded themselves as Soviet people, 51,1% — citizens of CIS (CIS citizenship can also be regarded as a variation of the soviet). However, this study revealed the fact that 72,7% considered themselves Russians as well, which does not constitute refutation of belonging to the Soviet people, rather an acknowledgment of the ongoing changes in the life of the country (*Sovremennoe obshchestvo*, 1998).

Opposition between ethnicity and democracy became a very significant paradox of national identity. Again, based on the standards of Western democracy and certain universally accepted humanitarian considerations for the protection of human rights, it was proposed that the mention of national belonging of a person should be removed from official documents (passports etc.), i.e. eliminate famous and infamous clause 5 in standard CV, as part of the legacy of Soviet totalitarianism, as provision «demeaning to human dignity». What really happened? It was not only representatives of Russia's ultra-nationalist circles (by the way, their reaction was predictable, but not as strong as expected) that met this action with loud protests, as much as representatives of other nations, which interpreted it as an attempt to downplay the significance of their national identity and ignore their national interests. Contrasting ideas of democracy and ethnicity resulted in denial of the introduction of Russian passports in

Tatarstan and Bashkortostan. Representatives of other minorities, and even tiny ethnic entities expressed their disagreement in one form or another. Contrary to the pseudo-guardians of democracy, Russian population chose a very intelligent approach: according to the M.K. Gorshkov's data, only about 20% of respondents agreed that nationality should not be registered in the passport, one third believed that it should be, while 38% felt that it has be optional, left for the individual to decide (*Izmenyayushchyasya Rossiya.* 2004, P. 116). Although the way out of this situation (including notations in passports) was found through compromise, this incident once again demonstrates that following the blueprint of Western standards does not necessarily improve relations between the peoples of Russia, that all of the postulates tried and true for other countries cannot be mechanically transplanted onto the real soil of Russian society.

Assessment of civil and personal qualities of Russian people in comparison with similar qualities of other nations is paradoxical as well. This contradiction is reflected in virtually everything, including self-evaluation. On the one hand, Russians are the best, most reliable, most resourceful; on the other — embodiment of laziness, inertia, unpredictability, unreliability and even treachery. Such characterization, to a certain extend, is supported by socio-psychological studies, where these contradictory traits of Russian character are manifested quite clearly. According to the I.V. Groshev's data, an average Russian is, on the one hand, kind (in the opinion of 38,4%), patient (24,4%), hospitable (21,2%), diligent (18,9%), courageous (15,5%) and has other positive characteristics (patriotism, openness, friendliness, responsiveness, etc.), on the other — he is lazy (less that 12,1%), an alcoholic (8,4%), careless and negligent (4,7%) (Groshev. 2000).

Russian worldview and ideology simultaneously encompasses such traits as heightened loyalty to other countries and peoples, as well as certain mistrust of them, which is usually aggravated and actualized in connection with extraordinary political events. «We are peaceful, yet combative» — this stereotype is very typical for many Russians. A question: «What do you think about representatives of other nationalities?» was periodically posed to 2400 respondents between 1992 and 2000. According to VTsIOM data, during this period, characterizing their attitude towards representatives of foreign nations, generally positive evaluation of American people ranged between 74 and 90%, Germans — 86 to 93%, Arabs — 84%, African nations— 91%, Japanese — 95%. As far as different peoples of the former USSR were concerned, there were far greater fluctuations in their evaluation. Interestingly, by the end of the 1990's, the level of hostility toward Azerbaijanis, Georgians, Armenians and even Chechens has declined (*Public Opinion. 2006.* P. 154–155). According to the data of the Russian Institute of Social and National Problems, Russians had most favorable attitude to the Ukrainians, Belarusians, Bulgarians, Serbs, Tatars (both younger and older generations); among foreign nations — French, Finns, Italians,

Japanese, Germans and Americans. At the same time, it should be noted that outbursts of confrontational attitude often occurred due to deterioration in bilateral relations. This, for example, was clearly manifested in 2005–2008 in assessments of Georgian people, during the conflict between Georgia and Russia. Sometimes this hostility extends to other countries, when, for instance, in spring of 1999, animosity toward the United States of America has greatly increased, as a reaction to the bombing of Serbia by NATO forces, for which Russians blamed US authorities.

Among paradoxes of national identity, contradictory assessment of relations between Russia and the West deserves special attention. According to our surveys, positive evaluations of the West are higher among Russians than positive evaluations of Russia among Europeans. According to VTsIOM data, in a survey, conducted in August 2000, 34% of the population felt that they respect Western countries, but only 8% thought that people in the West had similar feelings about Russia. At the same time, 21% of respondents thought that Westerners treat Russia with contempt, 12% — with anxiety, 24% — with sympathy (*Russian Centre for Pubic Opinion Research.* 2007. No 1. P. 61). So, it turns out — in Russians views — to be sure — that we «respect» them more, than they «respect» us, while they «despise» or treat us with suspicion.

Under these circumstances, Eurasian orientation is gaining even more support, since, according to the 1999-2000 studies, Western countries have lost their status of a model (pattern) of development even among those groups that in late 1980's to early 1990's felt it necessary to focus on utilizing their experience. Russian socio-economic realities, their evaluations by Western countries caused increased negativity among Russian people towards the West. There was a significant shift in social consciousness: what once was considered as a model, an example, now began to acquire traits of hostility and antagonism.

Examining paradoxes of national identity, we have to conclude that, despite the presence of ideas of Euro-centrism, and, to a lesser degree, an orientation towards Asian countries, in Russia, ideas of original, uniquely Russian and Eurasian routes of development are gaining increasing popularity.

References

Groshev I.V. *Gendernoe predstavlenie o vlasti (Gendered Ideas about Political Power)* // Sociologhicheskiye issledovaniya. 2000. No 12.

Izmenyayushchyasya Rossiya v zerkale sociologhii (Changing Russia in the Mirror of Sociology) / Pod red. M.K.Gorshkova i N.E.Tikhonova. Moscow, 2004.

Public Opinion — 2006. Moscow. Levada-Center. 2006.

Russian Centre for Pubic Opinion Research. 2007. No 1.

Shendrik A.I. *Teoriya kul'turi (Theory of Culture)*. 2004. **(3)**

Sokolov M. *Newspaper Satire* // Izvestiya. 2000. May 15.

Sovremennoe obshchestvo: perekhodniy period (Modern Society: Transition Period) / Pod red. Mansurova V. A. Moscow, 1998.

Tishkov V.A. *Obschestvo v vooruzhennom conflicte: etnografiya chechenskoy voyni (Society in Armed Conflict: Ethnography of Chechen War)*. Moscow, 2001.

Chapter 26. **Private versus public**

> Whenever you find yourself
> on the side of the majority -
> it is time to pause and reflect...
>
> *Mark Twain* (1835–1910)
> American writer

For a long time in scientific and journalistic literature, private (personal) was interpreted as individual, which in turn, was identified with individualism, with western lifestyle. Public was often equated with collective, communal, which was a characteristic of eastern, including Russian lifestyle and way of thinking. In reality, there are no clear-cut manifestations of either one. We can only estimate the degree of presence of personal or public in various processes. So, heightened attention to dialectics of private and public is not only caused by eternal problems of their interaction, but also traumatic character of transformation processed taking place in Russian society. In these circumstances, *social consciousness generates not only different, but also inadequate reactions to the ongoing processes, and, consequently, various forms of paradoxical combinations of personal and public.* This paradox is manifested as an imbalance between them and is expressed in such phenomena as group selfishness, aggression, (non-) conformity, anomie, absolutizing interests of a certain social group or community, inadequacy of the relationship between minority and majority. It is important to stress that in the interrelation between individual and social interests, the former more often and more consistently demonstrates its activity, its own self, persistence, aggressiveness, which allows us to focus primarily on its role, relevance and consistency of its implementation.

26.1. Irrationality of paradoxes of private and public

Every person, without exception, possesses character traits, which inherent exclusively to him, yet have public significance, play a certain social role and determine effectiveness and impact of one's behavior, the degree of its consistency with behavior of other people. The paradox here lies in the fact that individuals often embody conflicting traits of consciousness and behavior.

Among the most frequently mentioned characteristics of Russian people are: heroism, dedication, and readiness to participate in resolving extraordinary events. And, at the same time, passivity, dislike of routine and hard work, rejection of dullness, everyday life, repetitiveness, which is common for most daily activities. Both Russian, as well as foreign researchers note this character trait of Russian people. Life itself often attests to these contradictory characteristics. At one time, Bismarck, pondering over peculiarities of Russian character noted: «Russians harness slowly, but ride fast». Temporizing, infamous slowness, even lethargy accompanies many undertakings. At the same time, Russian history is full of examples, where many, not only major, but minor problems were resolved as a result of active intervention, which required enormous, superhuman effort. This was equally manifested (and still is) during the war, natural disasters, technological failures and catastrophes. It is then, when Russian nature is clearly demonstrated, ready to make sacrifices to save others, in the name of achieving important public purposes or ending difficult and complex situations that carry great risks for our country. Unfortunately, these qualities of the Russian people are often exploited, misused, even when there is no need to sacrifice people's health, let alone people's lives. Utilizing these qualities was to a great extent justified in the time of wars (including the Great Patriotic War), during completion of important industrial projects, in the time of making decisions, which were necessary, but carried a lot of risks (during natural disasters, catastrophes, etc.). The State and authorities of various levels often used these character traits in order to cover up their own incompetence, lack of daily planning and timely initiative. Furthermore, they often cultivated contempt for the ordinary, everyday and routine, in order to (under certain conditions) be able to create an emergency situation, to fully exploit the potential of sacrifice.

We can add such opposing characteristics as egoism and altruism that have enormous social importance to the list of paradoxical combinations of the traits of Russian people. As for altruism, even A. Comte, whose name is linked to the introduction of this term into philosophy and sociology, thought that such qualities as selflessness, desire to please others, satisfaction from a certain act or action that helped other people are inherent in individuals. These traits border on self-sacrifice, readiness and desire to contribute to the accomplishment of important social goals, minimizing or even neglecting the importance of personal interests.

At the same time, selfish traits that are embodied in a wide range of different shapes and forms — from self-absorption to greed, are present in the Russian character as well. Selfishness takes shape of theft, fraud, larceny, all in the name of personal or group gain. Moreover, these forms of egoism become more and more open, shameless. And if in Soviet times, such manifestations of selfishness as enrichment by fraud, embezzlement and deception were not only condemned by law, but public morality as well, and criminal element tried to be discreet and invisible, assuming «Koreiko»-like (a popular character of an underground millionaire) appearance, during the 1990's, and the *perestroika* years, possession of stolen property, illegally obtained capital was flaunted, paraded as «know-how» of the «good life».

We are witnessing amazing transformations (metamorphoses) of people belonging to different social strata. On the one hand, Russian people whose income is below the subsistence level can hardly afford to express their altruism, since in the present situation their own survival is at stake. However, even retirees participate in charitable event, when they are convinced that their pennies will benefit the cause. Furthermore, without significant financial means, these people selflessly donate their time, labor, their own pair of hands to help with cultural, educational or religious projects — in building, reconstruction and restoration of spiritual values and cultural heritage. Finally, there is solid expert data, which suggests that lower and middle class are the part of the population who do pay their taxes and supplement state budget. On top of that they are regularly contributing to a number of charities (*Sotsial'naya otvetstvennost'*, 2006). At the same time, among the other part of the population, which can be attributed to the upper class, a very small percentage exhibit elements of altruism (since they are consumed by thirst for financial gains) in the form of some handouts to the elderly, sports clubs or individual schools. Many of them do not even do that.

We have to point out another paradox — simultaneous existence of trust and suspicion in consciousness and behavior of Russian people. Trustfulness (approaching daydreaming) demonstrates age-old habit of believing in miracles and superstitions — from witches and prophets to hidden meaning of words and clairvoyance. At the same time, people tend to be very suspicious. However, their faith in promises of the authorities (especially Tsar, Secretary General or President) is constantly renewed.

Simultaneous coexistence of endorsement (support, recognition) and nihilism is another paradoxical combination that exists in people's consciousness and behavior. Analysis of actual functioning consciousness and behavior shows that the level of approval and support of rational ideas, opportunities to inspire people to take specific actions are fairly significant, and, in most cases, do not require much effort. Especially if the goals are reflecting people's needs and interests. This equally applies to both national and local level objectives.

So, why does nihilism, which gradually turns not only into a silent, but active resistance and opposition to these goals, emerge in people's consciousness?

This becomes possible, first, when people realize (based on practical experiences) that the declared goals have nothing (or very little) in common with the real goals, perused by their initiators and instigators; second, when social consciousness cannot approve and support the means of achieving the goals, if they violate honor and dignity of the other participants of ongoing social changes; third, (this in particularly important) when social consciousness does not condone or forgive violations of norms of morality, decency and the rule of «unity of word and deed» (*Russian Centre for Pubic Opinion Research.* 2005. No. 5. P. 61). In people's consciousness there is a tenacious belief that injustice, unrighteousness never succeeds; when all is said and done, it is ultimately rejected by the people and real life practice.

Failure to meet these requirements often led not only to nihilism, but to cynicism, which, in turn, was an unjust response to what, in real life, was deliberately distorted and falsified by those called upon to improve, modernize and advance it.

26.2. Phenomenon of conformism and non-conformism

Contradiction of private and public, as reflected in conformism and non-conformism, is of particular interest.

Nonconformists represent the part of humanity, whose consciousness embodies the exact opposite reactions to those inherent to social conformism that personifies compromise, uncritical acceptance and adherence to prevailing standards and opinions, stereotypes of mass consciousness, traditions, authority, official principles, predominant attitudes and propaganda clichés (Efirov. 1990). If conformists are characterized by such traits as lack of individuality, personality that is stereotypical, easy to manipulate, conservative, etc., nonconformists constantly demonstrate individuality (at times sharply and irreconcilably), uniqueness, distinct and paradoxical nature of their relationship to their own environment. Nonconformists constantly display the features and functions of opposition to official (ruling) propaganda, have fanatical belief in supreme truth, and reject the imperatives of intra-group solidarity, unthinking adherence to commonly accepted standards. With regard to *conformists,* they perceive alienation, slavish dependence on authorities, social stereotypes and prejudices as natural and necessary, proper and, sometimes, the only possible state of being. Therefore, *conformism* is an essential socio-psychological foundation of authoritarianism and totalitarianism, which attempt to create »monolithic unity» of citizens. Nonconformists greatly contribute to the emergence and functioning of society, based on pluralist principles. They are a direct opposite to an impersonal average man, whose mentality is shaped by social and group pressure, submission to stereotypes of mass consciousness.

Paradox of current situation lies in the fact that many Russians are presently exhibiting features of both conformism and non-conformism. On the one hand, a citizen of modern Russia represents a combination of such features of consciousness and behavior, as a desire to submit (non-resistance), be protected from violence, to identify with prevailing sentiment, as well as fear of loneliness and social isolation. It is from these positions, that an individual becomes a «one-dimensional man», «organization (company) man», «mass man», foothold for «strong authority».

On the other hand, nonconformist behavior appears as a reaction to the manifestations of conformism in the same people that, first of all, resist the attempts of leveling and uniformity, second, represent the desire to defend their right to individuality in their interactions with oppressive social forces, despite the fact that these features of non-conformism are not just rejected, but persecuted by the official ruling structures.

Participation of the carriers of this type of consciousness in activities of various dissent and resistance groups, opposition to prevailing opinions, including open forms of its manifestation are typical features of non-conformist behavior. However, this does not mean that non-conformism can only manifest itself in the form of active protest; it can be passive as well. There is a well-known historical phenomenon of the Young Hegelian Max Stirner (1806–1856), who overthrew all the authority of his, as well as preceding generations. Acting as an uncompromising defender of the freedom of individual «I», he became a theoretician of individualist anarchism (Stirner. Russ. Ed.1994). But, at the same time, he personally led a very mundane, quiet life, without any thunderous, or original events, expressing defiance only in the sphere of consciousness. How many of these quiet and rebellious max stirners are there in every society?! Therefore, even non-conformism can be expressed in a variety of forms.

True non-conformists are usually persistent, stubborn and determined, but despite their «transverse» attitude, they do not necessarily support violent acts, revolutions and coups (if they move to this category, they fall under different definition). Nevertheless, in any society, especially during the times of major changes there is always a certain amount of supporters of radical actions. Thus, according to the data of Russian Independent Institute of National and Social Problems, 5–6% of the population are ready to defend their interests by force of arms.

Another notable feature of non-conformism is provocative judgments, based on their paradoxical nature, especially regarding the eternal problems of life: man's destiny, meaning of existence, relationship with powers that be, attitude towards moral values, etc. In this regard B. Russell noted that sometimes he thought it would be better if people were unable to read and write. Since the majority of them become exposed to propaganda, and in every country, propaganda is controlled by the state and represents whatever the state wants. And, what the state wants, is our readiness to commit murder, when ordered (Russell. Russ. Ed. 1958, p. 26).

Sociological data suggests that the most damning critics of the ongoing reforms are not the poor, but the representatives of the advanced groups — entrepreneurs, people with higher education and youth. While supporting and accepting the strategy of development of market economy, they openly reject the methods of achieving this goal, an attitude which, in our opinion, can beneficially affect the entire course of socio-economic development of the country.

26.3. Paradoxes of group egoism

Even during the years of Soviet rule, during the period of so-called stagnation, *sociologists have discovered phenomenon of group egotism,* which in most cases was a form of mimicry, individualism, or interests of a small group, packaged as a collective interest. This was a very convenient form of the demagogic consciousness, since the interests of the majority (the team) were interpreted as a specific, but very important expression of social (state) aspirations, which took priority over personal, individual interests. Such policies and attitudes toward individual interests could not have gone unnoticed. So, pseudo-collectivist phraseology was developed and effectively applied in dealing with the state. In reality, this often turned into confrontation, and at times was detrimental to other social and professional groups.

In modern day Russia, new forms of group egoism have emerged: interests of entrepreneurs, bankers and other subjects of market economy are now camouflaged as the interests of community, various groups and organizations. But, unlike the Soviet era, in the new environment, enormous profits are at stake, which (due to flawed legal system) the «new Russians» and Russia's new bureaucracy stand to gain or lose. And, since it was clear from the very beginning that these subjects of market economy were aiming at maximizing their personal and group gains, acts of manipulation, with a poorly camouflaged goal — «not to share», were not surprising (including manipulating the interests of firms, banks and joint stock companies). As former Finance Minister of Russia used to say, «do not share, under any circumstances with state or society». A whole bag of tricks was utilized for that purpose, starting from tax relief and receiving benefits, to moving capital into offshore accounts, maintaining double (triple) accounting, creating «one-day companies», etc. In other words, group egoism took a dangerous turn, directly threatening Russia's strategic interests, rather than simply slowing down, impeding or causing difficulties for successful functioning of state and social mechanisms.

Forms of the group egoism are diverse and multidimensional. One of the specific forms of group egoism is the cult of position (post or appointment), which, despite all the changes in Russian society, continues to exist. Its essence lies in the fact that actual practice of management, where the person that occupies top position is all-powerful, indisputable, always right in relation to subordinates, not only exists but is strengthening its positions. It is paradoxical that all the talk about democracy, responsibility of leadership, individual rights cannot prevent growing authoritarianism at all levels of management of social processes. Furthermore, power is increasingly usurped, not just by the leaders, but by the surrounding «close-to-power» clans, interested in having their protégés «rule», trying to pursue their own agenda, but under the guise of statements about legitimacy, legality and expediency of administering affairs on behalf of the people.

This phenomenon completely ignores the precept of Aristotle: «He, who wants to rule well, must first learn to obey. And any power...can be used, in the interests of the master on the one hand, in the interests of the slave — on the other» (Aristotle. Russ. Ed. 1985, P. 616).

Group egoism constantly produces bizarre combinations of personal and public. Attempts to revive social structures of the days gone by, which had their own place, but primarily fulfilled certain social functions, is just one of such amazing phenomena. It is clearly manifested in attempts to bring back such controversial (if not dubious) re-emerging social structures as Cossacks and nobility.

These «atavisms» of traditional society are historically limited. Their revival without any regard to actual needs may temporarily preserve the old, outdated and also limit the emergence and development of the new social phenomena. Such manifestations of group egoism are acceptable in the life of Russia's society, but only as independent, amateur organizations, whose existence will possibly enrich cultural and social life of the country, without infringing upon the interests of other social groups, and, most importantly, will help or will contribute to solving pressing social problems (Kozlova. 2005).

References

Aristotle. *Works* (Russ.). Vol. 4. Moscow, 1985.

Efirov S.A. *Prinzip uchastiya. Sotsial'no-politicheskiy context (Principle of Participation. Social-Political Context)* // Sociologhicheskiye issledovaniya. 1990. No 9.

Kozlova N.N. *Sovetskie lyudi. Stzeni iz istorii (Soviet People. Scene from History)*. Moscow, 2005.

Russian Centre for Pubic Opinion Research. 2005. No.5.

Russell B. *Pochemu Ya ne khristianin? (Why am I not Christian?)*. Moscow, 1958.
Sotsial'naya otvetstvennost' biznesa (Social Responsibility of Business). Moscow, 2006.
Stirner M. *Edinstvenniy i ego sobstvennost' (The Only and his Property)*. Khar'kov, 1994.

Chapter 27. **Good and evil**

Surely oppression maketh a wise man mad...

Ecclesiastes. 7:7

Good and evil constantly accompany the lives of people in everyday, personal matters, as well as matters relating to society. Notions of good and evil are relative, conditional, and dependent on ever-changing social life, prevailing circumstances and certain social situations. Changing perceptions of good and evil, related to the various philosophical and sociological postulates play a very important role as well: do good and evil have equal significance; do they represent two sides of the same coin; do they mutually negate each other; are they comparable in their axiological status? Problems of good and evil have always been a matter of particular concern for humanity at all stages of its development. Therefore, good and evil, on the one hand, are eternal categories, but, on the other, their borders are very fluid and changeable and reflect their specific ratio depending on existing reality, dominant interest and morality (Likhachev. 2006. P. 36).

Obviously, under the conditions that are traumatic for people's consciousness and behavior, their perceptions of good and evil are seriously deformed and largely represent different combinations, different correlation than in recent past. Let us take a closer look at the present specific, paradoxical relation between good and evil on the verge of XX and XXI centuries, when the boundaries between them became arbitrary, transient and vague. Let us also compare these notions with not so distant, to be precise — Soviet past, in order to clearly understand and compare the changes taking place in social perception of good and evil.

27.1. Aggressiveness as a paradoxical combination of good and evil

Analysis of aggression in people's consciousness and behavior shows, that it is an acute reaction to the disruption of balance between good and evil, realization of impossibility of changing this unfavorable ratio by «peaceful» means, which in turn leads to a conclusion about the necessity of violence, even if it qualifies as evil.

The first cause of aggressiveness is the realization of the fact that the basic values of human coexistence that are associated with the notion of goodness are grossly violated. In most cases, in social terms «the good» means social justice, which is supposed to defend and fulfill (within reasonable bounds) needs and interests of the people, their desires and aspirations, ensure rational proportions between pleasure and suffering, happiness and sorrow. This means that in social consciousness, in consciousness of certain groups the ideas of retribution are being formed, notions of adequately rewarding each member according to what they deserve. Moreover, this assessment (and mutual assessment) of the relations between society and individuals is based on the determination of the share of responsibility for their actions, as well as amount of compensation, reward, incentive and even protection, which, according to a person, should be provided by society. Despite existing distortions in the perception of fairness, in the assessment of its condition, we can still determine a certain common component (denominator) that clearly reflects the focus of social consciousness. According to the data of Russian Institute of Social and National Problems, 96% of Russian people are convinced that fairness has to be a fundamental characteristic of human behavior, as well as the entire moral and ethical sphere of social life. At the same time, up to 80% of respondents (with 15% that abstained from answering) believe that current Russian society and its power structures are far from the demands of justice in comparison with Soviet times. Moreover, such an assessment is shared not only by underprivileged but also those who are fairly successful in the new socio-economic situation (*Russian Centre for Pubic Opinion Research.* 2005. P. 72).

The second cause of aggressiveness lies in the offensive nature of the forces that are identified with evil and must be confronted in order to ensure relatively stable social situation, to avoid sacrificing guiding principles of normal human behavior. In this regard, data that shows what spheres of public life people regard as flawed or evil, and which ones affect the creation of favorable living environment, are quite remarkable. According to VTsIOM data, among the negative results of reforms initiated in 1985, 51% of respondents named the growing chaos and confusion in the government, 49% — increase in uncertainty over the future, 38% — deepening economic crisis, 33% — weakening of the county's defense capabilities and 32% — crisis of national relations (*Russian Public Opinion Herald.* 2004. P. 47).

The third cause of aggressiveness lies in the negative assessment of importance, relevance and effectiveness of the means available to an individual (or a group), which can be used against the decline of quality of life. The majority recognizes that they cannot depend on the participation of official organizations in providing an acceptable standard of living. According to sociological research data the assessment of the authority of the State and its official structures (federal, regional and local authorities, judicial system, and police) is fairly negative. People are not convinced that multiple political parties or trade unions can fulfill this role either. Even the authority of the church, after initial surge of confidence in early 1990's has declined by the year 2000. Not surprisingly, under these circumstances people mobilize their own resources in order to actively resist ongoing, as well as anticipated changes. And while throughout the 1990's the number of people, willing to participate in active forms of protest has decreased, in the beginning of 2000, their number is still quite substantial (up to 30% in certain regions) which suggests a possibility of emergence and manifestation of significant aggression (*Public Opinion. 2006. P. 15*).

We should especially highlight such phenomenon, when a situation is over dramatized, and in accordance with that, based on group interests, the enemy (or a symbol of evil) is identified (selected, appointed). This enemy must be destroyed, removed, eliminated. For example, persons of Caucasian nationality became such «appointees to the position of evil». In other words, aggression is «channeled», i.e. consciously guided into a certain channel, which, as history shows, allows achieving results, but for a relatively short time. At the same time, public opinion, although susceptive to these emotions for a certain period of time, has a tendency to bounce back. For example, during the Kosovo crisis in spring of 1999, distrust and condemnation of the United States (but not the American people) has sharply increased, but then the ratio of positive-negative attitude toward that country returned to the previous level (*Public Opinion. 2007*).

Finally, we have to point out that the attitude towards protest actions in Russian society is neither simple nor one-sided. Moreover, the distinction here lies along the lines of the relation of official structures to the existing or emerging forces of opposition to their economic policies and political changes, not in the positions of various social groups. Citizens' opposition to evil, as a rule, meets with official condemnation, since it does not only call into question the existing political and legal order, but also questions State's efforts to overcome injustice.

In this confrontation between good and evil we commonly hear voices claiming that the individuals, unwilling to let go of the Soviet values, are the source of all-evil. *But the paradox lies in the fact that they were replaced by the new temptations and no new values to fill (or attempt filling) the void.* Most people, based on their experience of living in a market economy, recognize that to them these values— temptations are unavailable (and unattainable), and that they do not speak the same language as the authorities. Under these circumstances, they do not exclude a possibility of using various forms of aggression, including rather outrageous ones, harsh criticism turning into name-calling, insults, open refusal to follow official instructions, and similar actions that do not help the establishment of civil accord. In general, according to the opinion of 91,1% of Russians, aggression, as an indicator of the relations between people, along with cynicism (83,9%) has increased over the past 10-15 years, and became predominant characteristic of human behavior, while sincerity (in the opinion of 84%), kindness and goodwill (85,7%) decreased, lost their significance and influence compared with the Soviet period (according to the data of Russian Independent Institute of Social and National Problems) (*Perestroika. 2006. P. 17*).

27.2. Utopia as means of achieving the unachievable

In this case we are examining Utopia as a type of consciousness and the way of relating to reality, leaving aside its analysis as a literary genre or artistic method, as well as a form of predicting the future.

General characteristics of Utopian consciousness belong to K. Mannheim, who in his «Diagnosis of Our Time» described it as consciousness that does not correspond with the reality (Mannheim. Russ. Ed. 1994. P. 164). In our view such a generalized description is insufficient: it needs clarification and more profound, detailed explanation.

We have to point out the fact that the goal of almost every Utopia — is to achieve well-being, tranquility, satisfaction with one's existence, which is personified in the concept of «good». Allegorically, it (Utopia) reflects the aspiration to avoid evil, overcome it, and find a way out of unsatisfactory circumstances. People resort to it as means of resolving not only social, but also personal problems. At the same time historical experience clearly demonstrates that Utopia has never been implemented — along the way, it always encountered forces of evil, which overturned utopian expectations, aspirations and dashed people's hopes.

Utopia is akin to the ideal, and is sometimes identified with it. They have a lot in common, and, as I. Kant aptly remarked, they can be expressed as maximum perfection, unattainable in real life, but serving as a guiding light (Kant. Russ. Ed. 1989. P. 87). This very focus on achieving the unachievable is the main problem with Utopia. Differences between Utopia and Ideal are expressed only in the fact that ideal can be established once and for all eternity, while Utopia characterizes a particular stage in the development of civilization, as well as the development of individuals, which is reflected in their consciousness and behavior. Another one of Kant's ideas is connected with this: he was convinced that we need to evaluate an ideal not by the criteria of its attainability, but, rather, by its role in the life of society and individuals. In this respect, we should point out that both Utopia and Ideal regard the idea of freedom and equality as an absolute value. This value, preserved by humanity throughout its history, plays a role of social relay, which is modified, depending on changing socio-economic, socio-political and cultural situation. This very «eternity» of the ideal, helps resist evil, supports people's aspirations even after defeats, constantly inspires and brings forth new forces that are seeking perfection in the continuous development of humanity and individual.

Utopian consciousness, in turn, gives rise to «selfless devotion», recognition and acceptance of necessity, duty and self-sacrifice, which conservatism and traditionalism has always opposed and rejected. In this regard, we have to point out following peculiarity of utopian consciousness: if it is focused on achieving an absolute perfection, uncontested or indisputable benefit, it is rejected by the historical process. If utopian consciousness helps identify the conditions and incentives to improve the present, to reduce the influence of forces of evil, than it is fulfilling a great creative function (Novgorodtsev. 1991). And, despite its social limitations, contributes to the search for rational and efficient ways of the development of society, even if its ideas are rejected. Attractiveness and, at the same time, limitations of utopian consciousness are manifested in the fact that «the future is not formulated as an extension of the present, but as its alternative» (Chertkova. 1996).

Ideas that embody the good are vulnerable, can not stand the test of time, but can long withstand official, regulatory guidelines and requirements, while the forces of «evil» are more practical, pragmatic and are better aligned, coordinated with the interests of mass consciousness.

Contradictory nature of Utopia, which does not always reflect true ratio of good and evil, leads to the fact, that the good always looks abstract, all-encompassing and comprehensive, whereas in reality the forces of evil are always characterized by certainty and focus on solving specific problems, which ultimately rejects orientations of supporters of Utopia. In this regard, I would like to recall the word of F. Nietzsche, for whom the good was only good because of the weakness of its carriers, while evil was energetic, persistent and purposeful (Nietzsche. Russ.ed.1990).

The fact that Utopian consciousness often turns its back on everything that threatens to shake its faith and interfere with its desire to change the order of things (Mannheim. Russ. Ed. 1994. P. 131) often stands in the way of implementation of good deeds and intentions. In reality this «ostrich-like» behavior, i.e. desire to avoid the need to address pressing issues is very common, spread throughout the activities and lifestyles of many social groups, often stubbornly «not noticing» the obstacles to realizing their aspirations. Similar reactions are inherent in the consciousness of certain individuals who are constantly tormented encountering contradictions and discrepancies. And as their way of dealing with unacceptable and undesirable situation, they ignore various unpleasant and unexpected events and processes.

Utopian (as well as religious) consciousness has great merit: it stimulates creative forces, although it is often content with insignificant result, and sometimes abandons implementation of its ideas, postponing their achievement for «later», for the future. In contrast to religious consciousness, utopian consciousness possesses surrogate properties, usually has a shorter lifespan and is exposed to fast-moving socio-economic, socio-political processes. Within spiritual culture, utopian consciousness is associated with positive expectations, intentions, which embody the possibility of the coming, the arrival of «the Good». Paradoxical combination of good and evil in Utopia is brilliantly reflected in a statement that «Utopia is a non-existence (non-being), permeated, pervaded by existence» (Davidov. 2004. P. 689).

* * *

In general the correlation, the ratio of good and evil in modern Russian society is rather contradictory and paradoxical. On the one hand, we are witnessing a weakening and a decrease of the influence of norms of morality, and on this basis, an increase in aggressiveness or escape from reality into the realm of dreams and utopias. On the other — deep down in their consciousness, people feel that things should be different, and are looking for a way out of this situation: in positive assessment of values, traditionally considered moral (consciousness, compassion, loyalty, etc.), or in strengthening of forces, capable of «restoring order». Under these circumstances, an appeal for a strong State is considered justified, in hopes that it will find the way out of this all-encompassing crisis (including moral crisis).

In conclusion I would like to quote a reflection of a famous Russian philosopher, N.A. Berdyaev on good and evil: «The main provision of ethics, which comprehends the paradox of good and evil, can be formulated this way: do as if you hear God's call, and, in a free and creative act, have been called to participate in God's work; discover a pure and original sole within; learn to discipline yourself, fight evil within and all around, but not to drive evil ones and evil into hell and create the kingdom of hell, but in order to truly defeat evil and promote enlightenment and creative transformation of the evil ones» (Berdyaev. 1994. P. 49.).

References

Berdyaev N.A. *Filosofiya svobodnogo dukha (Philosophy of Free Spirit)*. Moscow, 1994.

Chertkova E.L. *Utopiya kak vid soznaniya (Utopia as a Form of Consciousness)* // Obshchestvennie nauki i sovremennost. 1996. No. 3.

Davidov Yu. N. *Postmodernism: vyzov stabilizatsionnomu soznaniyu v sotsiologhii (Postmodernism: Challenge for Stabilizing Consciousness in Sociology)* // Istoriya teoreticheskoy mysli. Vol. 4. Moscow, 2004.

Kant I. *Kritika chistogo razuma (Critique of Pure Reason)*. Moscow, 1989.

Likhachev D.S. *Pis'ma o dobrom (Letters about the Good)*. Moscow-Saint-Petersburg, 2006.

Mannheim K. *Diagnoz nashego vremeni (Diagnosis of OurTtime)*. Moscow, 1994. P. 131.

Nietzsche F. *Volya k vlasti (Will to Power)*. Works. Vol. 1. Moscow, 1990.

Novgorodtsev P.I. *O obshchestvennom ideale (About Social Ideal)*. Moscow, 1991.

Perestroyka: 20 let spustya (Perestroika: 20 years later). Moscow. 2006.

Public Opinion – 2006. Moscow. Levada-Center. 2006. P. 15.

Public Opinion – 2007. Moscow. Levada-Center. 2007.

Russian Centre for Pubic Opinion Research. Moscow 2005. No. 6.

Russian Public Opinion Herald. Data. Analysis. Discussions. 2004. No. 4.

Instead of conclusion

Comments

This is an important contribution to the general theory of social consciousness, as well as to the understanding of post-communist Russia. The author combines philosophical, sociological and socio-psychological considerations with the empirical analysis of attitudes, mental frames and values of Russian people in the period of transition. The multiple paradoxes internal to human mind are treated as a reflex of contradictions, tensions and conflicts in the social structure and culture. The original and fruitful concept of 'paradoxical man' opens up many secrets and puzzles of Russian 'soul' and unravels deep, mental reasons for the traumas and obstacles on the road to democracy.

Piotr Sztompka
President of International
Sociological Association (2002–2006).

What sort of creatures human beings are? Rebellious or conservative? Creative or conformist? Sociable or individualistic? Altruistic or egoist? Guided by reason or misguided by passions? Peaceful or aggressive? Good or evil? Philosophers tried hard to answer — they broke heads, but not the mystery. Toshchenko looked at human conduct at a time when the forces that make such choices for them but disallow them to make choices of their own fell apart or were dismantled — and found human beings just paradoxical — anything but logical and consistent, full of possibilities, fulfilled or lost. An opportunity for insight seldom available, and even less frequently put to such an excellent, and illuminating, use.

ZYGMUNT BAUMAN, *Professor, Leeds University, UK*

This work is a deeply grounded, yet unexpected discovery of actual and latent causes of real consciousness and behavior. It highlights societal and everyday life contradictions in a completely new way.

Sociologists are always faced with the need to comprehend the processes and phenomena that are generated by a new stage in the development of society, as well as the ones that have long remained unnoticed, undiscovered.

Pioneering approach, implemented in this study seriously enriches our understanding of a man. Along with one-dimensional man of Herbert Marcuse, A. Camus rebellious man, F. Kafka's lonely man and internalized «self-restraint» man of Norbert Elias, we now have a paradoxical man.

This approach is nontrivial and has an impressive depth of generalization.

I would particularly like to note that the analysis of paradoxes is closely linked with current and relevant processes that occur in modern Russia.

G.V. Osipov, Academician,
Member of the Russian Academy of Sciences,
Director of the Institute of Socio-Political Research,
President of the Soviet Sociological Association (1961–1972)

An appealing theoretical treatment of the dynamics of paradoxes emanating from revolutionary changes in social consciousness. The pervasive explanatory power of paradoxes is cast onto a comprehensive analysis of the recent transformation of Russia. The book is leavened with insights, sensitive to the human dimensions of everyday life, and supported by the best of public opinion research.

Henry Teune, Professor of Political Science
University of Pensylvania, USA

It is my pleasure to introduce to English-language readers this interesting and problem-rich book. The author demonstrates in his analysis of social consciousness and behavior that deep dislocations in economy and politics had generated a new interesting phenomenon to emerge – the 'paradoxical' man. As a matter of fact, here we are facing emergence and protracted co-existence of mutually excluding, incompatible, mutually opposing values, views and orientations in the consciousness of many individuals and personalities. The feature of «paradoxical» individuals is their position of confronting, combating themselves, a position that cannot but affect their social activities. The scope of this phenomenon is an important peculiarity of contemporary Russia.

A thorough analysis of paradoxical consciousness and behavior of the Russians permitted the author to bring to light a number of phenomena that cannot be explained by any statistics or sociological data. What are after all the causes for unexplainable, at the first sight, paradoxes within the generally rational and stable public consciousness of Russians?

Paradoxical people cannot be either ignored, or got rid of: they are to be lived and interacted with. That is why they have to be thoroughly studied. Results of these studies, including those presented in this book help to answer burning issues facing the development of many countries on the globe.

Tatiana I. Zaslavskaya, Academician,
Member of the Russian Academy of Sciences;
Member of the Academy of Europe;
President of the Soviet Sociological Association (1987–1991);
Doctor Emeritus, Georgetown, Pennsylvania,
and Helsinki Universities.

New interpretations of the issues of consciousness and behavior

The title of the new book of the Correspondent Member of the Russian Academy of Sciences Zh.T. Toshchenko immediately invokes many associations. In the history of XX century philosophy definitions of a modern man as «rebellious» (Albert Camus) and «one-dimensional» (Herbert Marcuse) are firmly established. And now — «paradoxical» man. Opening the book one would expect a nontrivial depth of generalizations. Happily, the book meets these expectations.

As the actual epigraph for his publication the author deliberately chose one of the most vivid quotations of B. Pascal: »What sort of a chimera is this man? What innovation, what monster, what chaos, what a tangled knot of contradictions, what wonder is he! The judge of all things, a feeble-minded worm; bearer of truth, cesspool of incredibility and mistakes, glory and scum of the Universe... Discover, oh proud one, what a paradox you are to yourself!» These words express the critical essence of entire philosophical anthropology, astonishment in the face of incomprehensible and fierce inner contradiction and intellectual and ethical ambivalence of a human being. Nevertheless, this book is not so much about Eternal in a person; rather it is about the paradoxical nature of a modern Russian man. This is where the specific nature of this book lies: it has been written by one of the most prominent sociologists in the country, and is based on many years of research and observations. This work combines two, seemingly different perspectives: philosophical-anthropological and specifically sociological, in such a way that not only they are not contradictory, but they seem to compliment, complete and enrich each other.

Zh.T. Toshchenko's research represents analysis of interaction of a person with society that is filled with paradoxes as well. In the author's opinion, paradoxical mentality and behavior are characteristic not only of the subject — as a certain deviation from what is expected and required from him by surrounding reality. On the contrary: «Sociological approach to paradoxes, he writes, reveals their manifestations in real life, in the process of implementation of various types of activity, for paradox is inherent not only in the process of cognition, but also in reality itself». This methodology allows the author to establish a correlation between the emergence of paradoxical mentality/behavior and paradoxical social organization. Later in the book he states: «Analysis of the real situation in Russia shows that paradoxicality became an integral part of modern life». And indeed, the current situation that Russians find themselves in keeps causing profound changes in their consciousness. If during the decades preceding the reforms, the population was constantly bombarded by targeted ideological propaganda, cultivating a number of myths that became quite familiar to many generations, as well as a number of simplified explanations, devised in an attempt to effectively and without much effort interpret the past, the present and the future, presently mass consciousness is trapped in the crossfire of conflicting streams of information, falling victim to attempted manipulation by various political forces. Naturally an «average man» in Russia is no longer the same. His/her consciousness is not so much «de-mythologized», as it is complicated, polarized and fragmented. Paradoxical mentality has «settled» there. Zh. T. Toshchenko correctly points out that: »Our disoriented contemporary, frequently, unwittingly professes opposing truths, and surprisingly, tends to trust mutually exclusive opinions and judgments, sincerely relying on them, quite often unaware of this blatant discrepancy« (p. 64).

The exploratory interest of the author concentrates on detangling this knot, on the detailed analysis of the causes and mechanisms of the changes, occurring in the social and individual consciousness. Since this book is at the same time both sociological, as well as philosophical, the first part covers the essential examination of the nature of metamorphosis and paradoxes of social consciousness. Utilizing extensive scientific data, the author explores the essence of paradox in general and paradoxical behavior in particular. Following the history of the social consciousness of Russians, he sets out to analyze the gradual process of its mutation. The nature of the search for the roots of this process alone is quite interesting and complicated. But the author steps up to the challenge. In his opinion, the mutation of the consciousness started during the pre-*Perestroika* decades, when general population, to a certain extent, developed resentment toward the «primitive forms of ideological coercion», imposed by the standards of thought and behavior that were essentially «double standards». Further deterioration has been occurring during the past fifteen years, when the concepts of liberal ideology, previously harshly criticized by the Soviet media, entered the lives of millions of people. This caused a true intellectual revolution, turning the value system upside-down, deeply embedded not only into the consciousness, but also the subconsciousness of the masses.

Zh.T. Toshchenko categorizes the modern state of social consciousness with the help of a number of definitions. First, as a catastrophic consciousness, characterized by heightened anxiety and lack of strategic personal future outlook, or perspectives for the country in general. «Catastrophism» can be manifested as a feeling of loss of stability, self-confidence and civic self-respect. This characteristic is integrally linked to the other one: social consciousness of modern Russian society, which is defined as «twilight», signifying the loss of guidelines in both social and personal lives, crisis of values and motivations, rejection of social circumstances, multiple new values and ideological orientations.

The author classifies the development of its protest forms, linked to passive or active disagreement over occurring social changes, governmental policies, evaluation of various events; formation of utopian consciousness, fixating on idealizing various moments in history or certain future concepts (such as the famous show «500 days») — as metamorphoses of social consciousness.

At the same time in the Russian society, in Zh. T. Toshchenko's opinion, a demagogic and easily manipulated consciousness, characterized by duality, double standard, hypocritical use of morally accepted social values as means of ideological assurance for preservation of certain egoistic group interests, etc., has emerged. The author sums up the results of his analysis of the distortion of social consciousness by concluding: «All these metamorphoses have laid a foundation, created a framework, which has led to the emergence of one of the most striking phenomena of the transition period — paradoxicality of social consciousness. It is the result and direct expression of instability and inconsistency of changes occurring in Russia, the consequence of disrupted rhythm and specificity of the life style, which has clearly registered in popular consciousness» (p. 52).

Thus, according to the author's logic, the «paradoxical man» is as much a product of society built on social paradoxes, just as Herbert Marcuse's «one-dimensional man» was a creation of «one-dimensional society» that has been the subject of his research. The obvious parallel is clear: both types of social consciousness are the result of a certain focused, altering influence (since one-dimensional and paradoxical men are not so much philosophical-anthropological models, as designations of certain common and constant types of social consciousness). Soft manipulation of the consciousness, achieved by ways of promoting false material demands, with the help of advertising and mass media; emergence of «one-dimensional» culture, that displaces the «high» culture, according to H. Marcuse's concept, it is deliberately implemented in order to create a society of carriers of «one-dimensional consciousness» — like-minded, indifferent, lacking any values more substantial than consumerism. Why are such people needed? Because these people, whose consciousness has «short-circuited» in a single dimension, are incapable of critical comprehension of modern society.

«Paradox man» is a result of altering «deforming» influences. The key difference, according to Zh.T. Toshchenko's model, is that the transformation is not conducted in a purposeful manner, at least not in a *completely* purposeful manner. To a larger extend it represents a creation resulting from an overlap of deliberate demagogic manipulation on one hand, and spontaneous internal changes that occur in response to the alterations in social reality, on the other. This is why the paradoxical man is immeasurably more complex than the one-dimensional. If the second one is more complacent and convenient since he is completely predictable in his reactions and behavior, the first one is considerably more unpredictable and uncontrollable, capable of protest and civic actions in general. But, this protest in usually based on motivations that are utopian and catastrophic in their nature.

The one-dimensional and the paradoxical men can be qualified as diametrically opposed from the viewpoint of the analysis of personal needs and their satisfaction. While the one-dimensional man is busy discovering more and more necessities and ways of their satisfaction, the paradoxical man, according to the author, on the contrary, is experiencing growing frustration due to the blocking of many of his pressing social needs. One-dimensional man is happy in his narrow-mindedness, while the paradoxical one is keenly unhappy, and his paradoxical nature lies in the fact that he relies on values and reference points largely discredited by society.

In my opinion, the comprehensiveness of the scope of the problems against the background of the continuity of logical story line is the unquestionable virtue of the book by Zh.T. Toshchenko. The unified logic of discovery of the paradox as a concealed, hidden essence, allows the author a deep comprehension of the mechanism of the inner workings of certain aspects of social consciousness, revealing new facets of its paradoxical nature. This logical, consistent portrayal of the paradoxes of economic, political, historical, legal, moral and religious consciousness is aimed at an accurate depiction of the image of a specific social «universe» of modern day Russia that possesses peculiar traits and characteristics of paradoxical universe, which combines, seemingly, mutually excluding qualities. This «universe» is highlighted in the portrayal of paradoxical man — the bearer of an indelible imprint, birthmark of the society he belongs to.

This book, in my opinion, is an extraordinary phenomenon in Russian cultural life. And not just because of the importance of the challenges the author is addressing or the answers he offers, it is due to the specific character of his approach, the degree of objectivity, unbiased political neutrality, which can probably be characterized as wisdom in our complex times. Regardless of that, there is an undertone (the author makes no attempt of concealing it) of firm negative attitude towards the «market» ideologists. However, it seems unbiased. It is more of a sad statement of the fact that all the best intentions produced no results, and grand idea of democracy in Russia was ruined by people, selfishly and unprofessionally attempting to undertake the reforms. The author offers no universal solution to the situation, which he evaluates with a large degree of pessimism. Nevertheless, the final chapter of the book — «Good and Evil», the name alone implying ethical and philosophical generalizations, contains a powerful implicit charge of optimism, which we could qualify as ontological. Since, under the circumstances when social practice offers no basis for optimism, people seek and find these foundations in the realm of extreme hopes and aspirations. This is no coincidence that at the end of the book the author steps out of the spotlight to surmise his work with a memorable quotation from N.A.Berdyaev: «The main tenet of ethics, addressing the paradox of good and evil, can be summed up in these words: act like you are following the Lord's calling to participate in God's work freely and creatively. Discover a clear and original conscience within yourself, instill discipline in your character, fight evil inside, as well as around you, however, not in order to push the wicked ones and evil toward hell, creating the kingdom and reign of hell, but to truly conquer evil and contribute to enlightenment and creative transformation of evil people».

And indeed — isn't this not a way out of a paradoxical situation for a paradoxical man?

Yu.G. Volkov,
Professor, Doctor of Philosophy

Is the modern Russian paradoxical?

They say that no discoveries have been made in social sciences, especially in recent years. But reality is beginning to contradict this common notion. Following the complete revision of the Soviet Marxism, a number of sociologists were busy denying and refuting the very notions that they worshiped during the previous years, the rest were passionately attempting to transplant some «interesting» and «outstanding» western concepts onto the Russian soil. This resulted in a lot of primitive imitations, generally very far removed from our reality.

In my opinion, after many years of *Perestroika* and post-*Perestroika* we are finally approaching the path toward significant creative discoveries, attaining the ability to raise toward important scientific generalizations, offer new perspectives on the ongoing life processes. Like anything creative or innovative, it is not indisputable. I would like to share my thoughts on one such achievement in our social intellection.

Paradox man. This is the title of a new book by the Correspondent Member of the Russian Academy of Sciences Zh.T. Toshchenko. The very title of the book raises eyebrows. It intrigues and puzzles even prior to opening the book. Perhaps, this is the way it should be, if the publication contains really fresh and original material and examines the issues no one has ever addressed before.

These days a lot of theoretical books are being published. Some books are smart but boring, interesting but hardly insightful, sincere but superficial, and enticing but sly. The book in question is a deep, serious, probative, and, which is very important, undoubtedly honest. The author is not being cunning or evasive. He offers an objective, realistic picture of modern Russian consciousness. It is quite captivating, since it offers the reader a completely fresh perspective on the well-known issues. Its riveting content calls for contemplation over the most deep-seated problems of our modern domestic existence. The work is very informative, based on an enormous layer of diverse sociological data. Thankfully, the author has wide access to this information.

In the book, the notion of «paradox» as a specific class of contradictions of consciousness is used to analyze spiritual life and real human behavior of the Russian people at the turn of the centuries. The definition of paradoxical is interpreted as a characteristic of consciousness and behavior of people, using sociological, versus philosophical or psychological approach. In the genre of pondering over the concept, I am focusing my attention on ideas and findings, made by the author, drawing on a wealth factual data.

So, what is this book about? The author introduces a concept of «real consciousness» as a combination of theoretical and the common, rational and emotional, the interweaving of philosophically and practically functioning elements. It is this very consciousness that embraces rational thinking and does not exclude an in-depth, penetrating insight into the underlying processes. It is worth mentioning that real consciousness, practical behavior and conditions of their functioning — are what we refer to as basic components of sociological research.

From these methodological viewpoints, he is analyzing the metamorphosis of modern social consciousness. The very application of this notion allows us to gauge the ratio between the changes and the constants, to comprehend and interpret the on-going social processes of the past decade. Examination of global metamorphoses of social consciousness allows the author to characterize it as broken and split, and, at times, to define it as marginal, appearing as a false consciousness. Such alarming definitions as «catastrophic», «sick», «pathological», «demagogic», «twilight», «non-conformist», «protesting», «utopian», «manipulated», etc. are applicable to this consciousness. Reading this gives you the chill. But alas, this is not an exaggeration, or empty dramatization of this consciousness; it is a harsh, but truthful assertion.

It is against this background that the author moves on to examining the essence of paradoxes. It is a well-known fact that paradoxes reveal connections in unconnected, coincidences in non-coincidental. This is the reason why they are called «paradoxes». Based on their understanding in semantics, in logical constructs, Zh. Toshchenko finds it possible and necessary to depict life's paradoxes, paradoxes of life circumstances, people's consciousness and behavior. In his opinion, paradoxes of life emerge when the bizarre combination of good and evil, honor and malice, loyalty and betrayal, reckless innovation and stubborn traditionalism is present in consciousness and behavior. As sad as it is, this paradoxical consciousness became an integral part of modern life. It is as though people at the same time, are looking in different directions and trying to run the opposite ways. Transitive, transitory nature of our social life generates frustrations, anomalies, a crisis of consciousness, creates prerequisites for increasing the paradoxical at all levels.

These days, many ideological concepts are more mythological, rather than theoretical. Myths about the sacredness of the state power, leaderism and exclusivity of Russia, etc. are widespread. The book outlines a number of areas of paradoxical manifestation. Primarily — stereotypes that simplify reality. It is precisely these stereotypes of thinking that breed such paradoxes as: halo effect, attributing wisdom and significance to any persons in charge, effect of «rejection and lost souls», self-belittling, marginalization, effect of group egoism, the emergence of changelings, etc. This typology alone is quite impressive. It helps create a dimensional picture of the state of consciousness.

The author successfully uses certain neologisms. He introduces the so-called «centaur-problem» that refers to the people that adhere to mutually exclusive socio-political orientations. Strangely enough, such person, for example, can be a socialist, and a liberal internationalist, and a chauvinist, a monarchist, and a republican. This is completely true. If we look around, in a significant number of people, in their consciousness (and, perhaps, in our own), we discover a distinctive peculiarity, a miracle — combining the incompatible. Perhaps, this trend is a sign of our times, the result of various factors converging, something typical, and representative of the transitional period we are facing. These days, monolithic consciousness is more of an exception than a rule. The author offers a number of examples of «centaur-problems» as a specific form of manifestation of paradoxes in consciousness and behavior, analyzing manipulation as a mechanism of their (paradoxes) creation.

Classification of paradoxes, described in the book, introduction of their types and categories — from economic to religious, is of considerable interest. This classification is not arbitrary; it is based on a large number of balanced and fairly effective sociological findings. The world of imaginary and objective, desired and real, intricately interwoven, interpenetrating, creates a paradoxical vision of reality.

Historical memory is deeply paradoxical as well. The characters of the Soviet history are demonized, while the figures of the Tsarist era and the White movement are idealized. It happens according to a certain formula: «I burnt what I used to worship, and worship what I used to burn». However, elegiac memories of the Soviet times are ever-present, and the attempts to unceremoniously bash, arrogantly reject and criticize everyone and everything were rejected.

A wave of ethnic nationalism that swept over the entire territory of the former Soviet Union has created a paradox of the national «I». The search for ethno-cultural identity revealed its paradoxical nature. Zh. Toshchenko calls these paradoxes of ethnical interaction — «acculturation, ethnocide, duality and split of consciousness and behavior» and «preservation of your own, without breaking away from the values of another». The ethno-cultural myths, such as: who used to own what and who predates whom, emerged and flourished lavishly.

The legal consciousness is also paradoxical through and through. Verbally, it seems everyone is for the Constitution and the rule of the law. However, such forces as «vorovskoi business (business of thieves)», «blood crimes » and «corrupt officials» have grown monstrously. Everyone is talking lawfulness, but the law is being broken every step of the way. And, many experts, researchers and politicians are questioning the existing legal system, starting with Constitution and thousands of bylaws. Their legitimacy is highly doubtful. As the author points out, Russian society is swiftly moving toward the «Columbian model» of government with its classical criminal-state structure.

Ethical standards have become unstable and the morals are shaky at best. The book points out that in modern-day Russia, standards of morality are fading away, replaced with the criterion of rationality. The credibility and importance of moral requirements has decreased substantially or is non-existent. There is no longer a place for them within the current economic mechanism. The group of moral paradoxes includes: flourishing social dependency, openly predatory business conduct, marginalization of the significance of labor, etc. Morality is quite a rarity in political life. Proclamation of high principles is combined with tactics of hypocrisy while the true goals and selfish intentions are concealed.

Paradoxes of religious consciousness are striking — galvanization of religion after many year of atheism. But the so-called religious renaissance spawned many conflicts. Under pressure from clergymen, flirtation of the authorities with religion has to face the fact that the real, rather than verbal level of religiosity has not changed much at all. Spiritual leaders themselves are admitting that their congregations consist of mostly visitors, not regular parishioners. Orthodoxy is perceived by many as more of a historical-cultural phenomenon, rather than a religious one. The lines between the so-to-speak true believers and the ones that *consider* their own selves to be believers are blurred. Crisis phenomena in the world's religions (Christianity, Islam, Buddhism, etc.) are sharply refracted in our existing reality. There has been a strong increase of interest in non-traditional, confrontational religious fractions and sects. There is an occasional formal declaration of religiosity, manifested in such characters as «candlesticks», i.e. the politicians and businessmen that hold their candles in church, as if they hold drinking glasses. The individualization of religious beliefs, religion of self-permission and adaptations of various tenets to fit personal outlook have emerged.

In the conception of the author, there are many original ideas that are rooted in the notion of paradoxical. For example, let's look at the interpretation of such a widespread notion as the elite. According to the author, those who rule over us, i.e. the persons in charge of government and finances could hardly be characterized as elite. Of course, political and economic leaders are inclined to define themselves not as a clan or caste, but as elite. They fancy themselves as «cream of the crop», crème de la crème (and the rest of sour cream) of society. This makes the situation paradoxical.

There is a similar situation with the contradictory and obviously paradoxical fate of centrism in modern day Russia. Apparently, it is a fair statement that centrism here never existed; and if it is ever mentioned, it is purely as a virtual apparition. This is a paradoxical situation: the truth of the matter is that practically all of the political parties are trying to join centrism in Russia. But, in essence (or content) not a single one of them is a centrist party.

Paradoxical phenomena occur among intelligencia as well — these days the very existence of such a phenomenon as Russian intelligentsia is called into question. Today, there is no doubt that it is socially divided. It is split and fragmented. In essence, it is represented by a number of groups: predators, mutants, chameleons, infants, lackeys (servants), wanderers, demagogues, the new dissidents, etc. Very expressive characteristic, I must say. And, quite unsightly. Many are convinced that the number of dirty deeds, attributed to intelligentsia, is hard to measure. Some of the characteristics of its behavior are: zigzagging and switching sides, leapfrogging of opinions and changing of sympathies and antipathies. Moreover, these negative features ARE not unique to only the totality of those who can be counted among the intelligentsia, but, to a certain degree, to almost every one of them. Although a portrait of intelligentsia is painted in pretty grim colors, the author believes that the ideals of the Russian Intelligentsia, while corroded, are still alive. So, the debate regarding «an intellectual or an intelligent?» is not over yet.

The subject of intelligentsia is closely related to the paradoxical situations in education. The author is once again harsh and merciless in his definitions. Its threat, its essence, its semi-professionalism, ignorance, half-knowledge and knowledge without morals, knowledge without general culture, are quite apparent.

New faces of illiteracy, — from elementary to the functional, — incompetence, leading to the professional cretinism, the emergence of a social stratum of «the educated ignoramuses» with college diplomas, focusing on satisfying utilitarian, rather than spiritual needs, sharp decline in the overall culture — all these phenomena can be described as a paradox of the sphere of education. In broad strokes, the author not only offers an assessment of forms of paradoxes, but also highlights their typical situations. He graphically demonstrates how such motivations as «must» and «can not» correlate in the behavior of our people, to what extent the «enemy images» are wandering through people's minds, and why the «opponent» figures are so poorly perceived.

The book vividly covers the subject of freedom, the issue as eternally present in philosophy, as love is in poetry. Following all the turmoil in our recent history, the interpretation of freedom in public opinion turned out to be quite colorful, extremely fragile and vulnerable. Ranging from elation, heavy burden of doubt, attempting to comprehend the relationship between freedom and duty, to reflection on various perspectives of Freedom. The spectrum of various approaches is broad and paradoxical. Unfortunately, the understanding of freedom has drifted away from the traditional Russian interpretation of free will, and toward the lawlessness, or «no-limits» (*bespredel*) using the term of criminal jargon. The problems of defining our place between the past and the future, fluctuations of the consciousness between political nihilism and misery of dogmatism are vividly examined. With apparent sadness Zh. Toshchenko notes the state of vacuum of values, also known in sociology as anomie. Apathy, indifference, confusion and pessimism are spreading throughout the country. Society is concerned with a problem of national identity, awareness of their own and their country's place in history. The image of Russia is truly paradoxical. Is it still a great world power, or are we descending to the regional level? Are we gravitating toward Europe, or are we assuming Eurasian appearance? We have to pause and think, whether we should still be proud of our country, or should we be ashamed? These are all paradoxes of national identity, the rifts in the unified consciousness.

The relationship between the personal and societal is equally strained. Many generations of people in our country were raised with an unconditional belief in superiority of communal interests over purely personal ones, and then, suddenly, a variety of egotistic traits ranging from selfishness to thievery have surfaced. Contradictions between personal and communal were clearly manifested in the phenomenon of conformity and non-conformity, in paradoxes of group egoism. And, finally, the book ends on the coverage of a greatest problem — the relationship between good and evil. The secret of the origin of evil, its existence in the world, has always been and still remains one of the deepest mysteries. It does not have a clear comprehensive solution. Every era, every civilization has created own cultural-historical models of evil. An endless amount of essays, opinions, religious and folk images exist on the subject of universal, social and moral evil. The author suggests that a paradoxical relationship between good and evil, when the boundaries between them become arbitrary, blurred, transient and uncertain, is characteristic of our society. The heightened level of aggression cannot be considered accidental. Clearly, this is an exacerbated response to the disruption of the correlation between good and evil. The meteoric rise of wandering utopian consciousness is one of the consequences of this situation as well.

This is a brief overview of the main issues of Toshchenko's conception. This, to be precise, is my personal perception of his book. In general, I would like to once again emphasize that it makes us very seriously reflect on the root problems of our existence. The harsh, powerful wording is puzzling. And there lies the book's value, and oddly, its charm. But... I would like to share a few thoughts that came to mind when I finished the last page of the book.

They say that there are four stages in medical practice. First comes analysis, than diagnosis, followed by prognosis and prescription. Undoubtedly, a sociologist is not a doctor and his thought process is very different. But, I should point out that the first two are present in the book. There is a thorough, well-grounded, evidentiary analysis of the situation at hand. There is a truthful and harsh but realistic diagnosis of the state of public consciousness of the Russian people. It is truly paradoxical. But what are the prospects? What is the prognosis? And what do we do to get out of the state, so vividly described by the author?

Unfortunately the author ended the book there. This, of course, is his right. The future forecast and the means of salvation (precisely salvation) have to be thought through and carefully considered. Considered by all of us, with no exception — theorists and politicians. We cannot afford to wait too long. We cannot live in a pervasive paradoxical state indefinitely. Harmony does exist. But how do we achieve it? This is a question of questions. Let us not be too hard on the author. He accomplished a lot. Our bookshelves are flooded with numerous books on the pressing issues of the modern day life, however, this one, the one I am writing about, clearly stands out. It firmly merges scientific accuracy and juicy journalism. It makes for an interesting reading.

One final note to wrap things up, so to speak. I would not want to leave the impression that the book is pessimistic or even hopeless. At first glance you can get this impression. However, in my opinion, Zh. Toshchenko, regardless of the severity of his analysis, remains soundly optimistic. I am sincerely convinced that this book is destined to a good future, it will be read, and it is a very necessary book. As a long time professional, and just as a reader, I found it very enjoyable and greatly beneficial. I highly recommend it to the future readers.

V.E. Davidovich, Professor, Doctor of Philosophy,
Scientist Emeritus of the Russian Federation

Index

Contents

UDK 316
BBK 60.5
T77

Toshchenko Zh.
T77　Paradox Man in Contemporary Russia / Zh. Toshchenko. — St. Petersburg: Aletheia, 2010. — 428 p.

ISBN 978-5-91419-412-0

The purpose of this manuscript is to raise an unusual social problem — paradoxes of social consciousness and behavior. It is a result of a longer work dealing with paradoxes of consciousness and behavior as they have been massively displayed in USSR/Russia transition. Paradoxes always exist in the life of humankind. For the first time attention to them had been paid in the Ancient Greece, than in the Middle Ages and New History. Hence paradoxes of social consciousness are inherent not only to previous stages of historical development — science and social practice have been facing them in modern time. Paradoxes tend to increase and to affect most spheres of social life.

Sociological approach to paradoxes permits to reveal their manifestations in real life, in process of realizing these or other kinds of activity, for paradoxicality is inherent not only to process of cognition, but also to reality itself. But especially evident, sharp and outspoken this paradoxicality becomes for societies with an unstable development, those in a state of instability, amorphy, uncertainty with regard to vector of historical process. In these conditions paradoxes of consciousness and behavior become massive, universal, give rise to freakish combinations of good and evil, honor and intent, fidelity and treachery, reckless innovation and obstinate traditionalism.

For the researchers of social and political life, social consciousness and behavior, for the students and for all people, studying contemporary Russia

UDK 316
BBK 60.5

Zhan Toshchenko

PARADOX MAN

Translated by prof. Romanovskiy N.V.
and Southwell (Romanovskiy) I.N.

Saint-Petersburg   ALETHEIA   2010